43. Does International Law Still Hist. By Sir H. Erle Richards.

44. Germany the Economic Problem. by Charles Grant Robertson

45 The Deeper causes of the War. By Dr Sanday.

46 Through German Eyes By E. A. Sonnenschein.

47. German Sea Power. By Charles Sanford Terry.

48. The Navy and the War, By J. R. Thursfield.

49. Greek Policy since 1882 By Arnold. J. Toynbee.

50 India and the War, By Sir Ernest J. Trevelyan

51. Turkey in Europe & Asia. By

52. Russia the Psychology
    of a Nation. By
    Paul Vinogradoff.

53. Great Britain and
    Germany. By
    Spencer Wilkinson.

" 54. Concerning True War. By
    Wilhelm Dimdt.

1914–1915

THE ACTION OFF HELIGOLAND

AUGUST 1914

BY

L. CECIL JANE

WITH TWO MAPS

Price Threepence net

OXFORD UNIVERSITY PRESS
HUMPHREY MILFORD
LONDON   EDINBURGH   GLASGOW
NEW YORK   TORONTO   MELBOURNE   BOMBAY

MAPS

Between pages 20 and 21

HELIGOLAND AND THE COAST
CHART OF HELIGOLAND

(On a larger scale)

OXFORD PAMPHLETS
1914–1915

Crown 8vo. Separately, in paper covers. Also in series as numbered (I–X), stiff covers, One Shilling net each series. 49 Pamphlets have now (Jan. 1, 1915) been issued, and others are in preparation. The historical pieces are illustrated by sketch-maps.

Saturday Review:—'These little books are easily the best books of the war—accurate, quietly written, full of knowledge, and quite unspoiled by vainglory or bitterness.'

OXFORD UNIVERSITY PRESS
HUMPHREY MILFORD
LONDON   EDINBURGH   GLASGOW
NEW YORK   TORONTO   MELBOURNE   BOMBAY

OXFORD PAMPHLETS
1914–1915

I

1. The Deeper Causes of the War.

By W. SANDAY. 3d. net. *Sixth Impression.*

The psychology of Prussian militarism ; German public opinion and Germany's aggressive ambitions.

2. To the Christian Scholars of Europe and America: A Reply from Oxford to the German 'Address to Evangelical Christians'.

2d. net. *Fifth Impression.*

The answer of Oxford theologians to a recent manifesto of the German evangelical theologians. This manifesto, which is reproduced in the present pamphlet, argues that Germany is in no sense responsible for the present war. The Oxford reply states that the German theologians cannot have studied either the events which led up to the war or the political utterances of their own countrymen.

3. The Responsibility for the War.

By W. G. S. ADAMS. 2d. net. *Second Impression.*

A brief discussion of the question of responsibility : 1. Austria and Serbia ; 2. The responsibility of Russia ; 3. The intervention of England.

4. Great Britain and Germany.

By SPENSER WILKINSON. 2d. net. *Third Impression.*

Three letters to the *Springfield Republican*: 1. By Prof. Spenser Wilkinson, stating Great Britain's case ; 2. By Prof. John W. Burgess of the University of Columbia, stating Germany's case ; 3. By Prof. Wilkinson, in reply to Prof. Burgess.

5. 'Just for a Scrap of Paper.'

By ARTHUR HASSALL. 1d. net. *Fifth Impression.*

Explains why England stands for the sanctity of European treaty-law.

[d]

II

6. The Germans, their Empire, and how they have made it.
By C. R. L. FLETCHER. 2d. net. *Fourth Impression.*
A historical account of Prussian policy from the seventeenth century.

7. The Germans, their Empire, and what they covet.
By C. R. L. FLETCHER. 2d. net. *Fourth Impression.*
An account of the ambitions avowed by the Pan-German school.

8. Might is Right.
By Sir WALTER RALEIGH. 2d. net. *Third Impression.*
Why Germany may win; what will happen if she wins; why we believe she will not win.

9. Austrian Policy since 1867.
By MURRAY BEAVEN. 3d. net. *Second Impression.*
Austrian policy in the Balkans has been of the 'offensive-defensive' order. The Archduke Francis Ferdinand might have saved Austria from rushing to destruction; but 1912 was the beginning of the end.

10. Italian Policy since 1870.
By KEITH FEILING. 2d. net. *Second Impression.*
Italian policy has been and must be guided by her own interests. The results of her colonial policy have not yet been satisfactory enough to tempt her into adventures.

III

11. French Policy since 1871.
By F. MORGAN and H. W. C. DAVIS. 2d. net. *Fourth Impression.*
A historical sketch, discussing the question whether French policy has been aggressive.

12. Russia: The Psychology of a Nation.
By PAUL VINOGRADOFF. 1d. net. *Fifth Impression.*
A reply to the German taunt that Russia is still in a state of barbarism, and is the enemy of European civilization.

13. Serbia and the Serbs.
By Sir VALENTINE CHIROL. 2d. net. *Fourth Impression.*
A sketch of Serbian history, which is incidentally an indictment of the policy pursued by Austria-Hungary towards the Serbian kingdom.

14. Germany and 'The Fear of Russia'.
By Sir VALENTINE CHIROL. 2d. net. *Fourth Impression.*
Shows that before 1879 Germany preferred Russia as an ally to Austria. The ambition of Germany to establish a protectorate over Turkey has led her to assist Austria in the Balkans and so to challenge Russia.

15. The Eastern Question.
By F. F. URQUHART. 3d. net. *Third Impression.*
The history of the Balkan nations; their future.

[4]

IV

16. War against War.
By A. D. LINDSAY. 2d. net. *Fourth Impression.*

Denies that war is good in itself, or a necessary evil. National greatness, if founded on brute force, cannot endure. International law represents an ideal, but an ideal that may be realized.

17. The Value of Small States.
By H. A. L. FISHER. 2d. net. *Fourth Impression.*

The author argues that the debt of civilization to small states is incalculable.

18. How can War ever be Right?
By GILBERT MURRAY. 2d. net. *Fifth Impression.*

A well-known lover of peace and advocate of pacific policies argues against the Tolstoyan position. Right and honour compelled Britain to make war; and war—like tragedy—is not pure evil.

19. The National Principle and the War.
By RAMSAY MUIR. 3d. net. *Third Impression.*

Considers the principle of nationality and its application to the settlement of Europe—particularly of S.E. Europe—after the War.

20. Nietzsche and Treitschke. The Worship of Power in Modern Germany.
By E. BARKER. 2d. net. *Fifth Impression.*

An explanation of the main points of interest in the ethical and political doctrines of the German ruling classes.

V

21. The British Dominions and the War.
By H. E. EGERTON. 2d net. *Fourth Impression.*

Explains the ideas for which the British Empire stands, and the political and moral issues of the war affecting the Dominions.

22. India and the War.
By Sir ERNEST TREVELYAN. 1d. net. *Fifth Impression.*

Discusses the reasons for the striking manifestations of Indian loyalty.

23. Is the British Empire the Result of Wholesale Robbery?
By H. E. EGERTON. 2d. net. *Second Impression.*

A historical sketch in answer to a common taunt.

24. The Law of Nations and the War.
By A. PEARCE HIGGINS. 2d. net. *Second Impression.*

The violation of Belgian neutrality and the conduct of England to Denmark in 1807; the doctrine of German lawyers that military necessity overrides the laws of war; the balance of power and the sanctity of treaties.

25. England's Mission.
By W. BENETT. 2d. net. *Second Impression.*

Answers the question, In what cause are we fighting?

VI

26. August, 1914: The Coming of the War.
By SPENSER WILKINSON. Stiff covers. 1s. net.

VII

27. The Retreat from Mons.
By H. W. C. DAVIS. 3d. net. *Third Impression.*

28. The Battles of the Marne and Aisne.
By H. W. C. DAVIS. 4d. net.
The Dispatches, with commentary, maps, &c.

29. The Navy and the War.
By J. R. THURSFIELD. 3d. net. *Fourth Impression.*
Estimates the military and economic value of the silent pressure exercised by our fleet, and warns the faint-hearted and the captious of the perils of lack of faith.

30. Bacilli and Bullets.
By Sir WILLIAM OSLER. 1d. net. *Fourth Impression.*
Calls attention to the fact that disease kills more men than the bullet. The most dangerous diseases are preventable by inoculation.

VIII

31. The Double Alliance *versus* The Triple Entente.
By JAMES M. BECK. 3d. net. *Second Impression.*
The judgement of a well-known American lawyer.

32. The Germans in Africa.
By EVANS LEWIN. 3d. net.
A historical account of the German colonies.

33. All for Germany, or the World's Respect Well Lost. 2d. net.
'The conversation here imagined, between a new (and perhaps less naïf) Candide and a new (and perhaps less benevolent) Dr. Pangloss, is concerned with the political thoughts and ambitions entertained by the Germans of these latter days.'

34. Germany, the Economic Problem.
By C. GRANT ROBERTSON. 2d. net.
Estimates the strength and weakness of Germany's economic position and inquires how long she can stand the strain of the war.

35. German Sea-Power.
By C. S. TERRY. 3d. net.
Traces the growth of Germany's navy. With a map of the North Sea.

IX

36. What Europe owes to Belgium.

By H. W. C. DAVIS. 2d. net.

Reminds us of the past achievements of the Belgian people in war and in peace.

37. Poland, Prussia, and Culture.

By LUDWIK EHRLICH. 3d. net.

The author is a Doctor of the University of Lwòw (Lemberg) in Galicia.

38. Turkey in Europe and Asia. 2d. net.

The strength and weakness of the Ottoman Empire considered. The secular prestige of Constantinople, the religious prestige of the Caliphate, and the racial and economic weaknesses which may cause their downfall. A map shows the unfinished railways.

39. Greek Policy since 1882.

By A. J. TOYNBEE. 4d. net. *Second Impression.*

A historical account of the policy of Greece ; the economic future of Greece ; the problem of *Graecia Irredenta.* With a map.

40. North Sleswick under Prussian Rule, 1864–1914.

By W. R. PRIOR. 2d. net.

The policy of Prussianization and the resistance of Danish Nationalism. 'If the children do not understand German, they must be treated and taught like deaf-mutes' is quoted from a Prussian educational authority. A map shows the distribution of languages.

X

41. Thoughts on the War.

By GILBERT MURRAY. 2d. net. *Second Impression.*

Reprinted from the *Hibbert Journal* for October.

42. The Leadership of the World.

By F. S. MARVIN. 2d. net.

A discussion of German aspirations.

43. The Leading Ideas of British Policy.

By the Hon. GERARD COLLIER. 2d. net.

Places the principles of our policy in the perspective of history.

44. The War and its Economic Aspects.

By W. J. ASHLEY. 2d. net.

A comparison of Germany's and Great Britain's powers to stand the strain of a prolonged war. Probable effects of defeat or victory.

45. Food Supplies in War Time.

By R. H. REW, C.B. 2d. net.

An authoritative discussion by an expert who has been 'for over thirty years engaged in the service of British Agriculture'.

Published separately and will also appear shortly in series.

Non-Combatants and the War.

By A. Pearce Higgins. 2d. net.

States the rights and duties of the non-combatant population of territory under hostile occupation.

Troyon : an Engagement in the Battle of the Aisne.

By A. N. Hilditch. 2d. net.

Scandinavia and the War.

By E. Bjorkman. 2d. net.

Considers the policy and sympathies of the three Northern Kingdoms.

Asia and the War.

By A. E. Duchesne. 2d. net.

Describes German intrigue, and its failure, in Turkey, India, and Egypt.

INTRODUCTION

HELIGOLAND was originally a Danish possession ; its population is mainly of Frisian extraction. From 1807 to 1890 it was held by Great Britain, having been seized for naval reasons, and was used as a naval station during the last stages of the Napoleonic War. In July 1890, by the Anglo-German agreement, concluded between Lord Salisbury and General von Caprivi, it was transferred to the German Empire.

The island lies in the North Sea, about 35 nautical miles NW. of Cuxhaven, 43 nautical miles N. of Wilhelmshaven, and 260 nautical miles E. by N. from Yarmouth. It consists of a rocky plateau, with an approximate area of 130 acres ; a stretch of excellent sand to the south-eastward made it a favourite summer bathing resort for the people of Hamburg and north-eastern Germany. The island is peculiar in the fact that there is an entire absence of wheeled traffic.

HARBOURS OF HELIGOLAND

The original, or inner, harbour of the island is some 400 yards long by 200 yards wide. A new, or outer, harbour is in process of completion ; it is intended to be about 900 yards long by 600 yards wide. The harbour is entered from the east,

There are also two havens. The North Haven lies to the NE. of the island, between it and the sand-bank, known as Olde Hoven Brunnen ; it is impossible to proceed from this haven to the harbour. The South Haven is ESE. of the island, between it and the rock of Düne. To the north of this haven, between it and the North Haven, there is an anchorage for torpedo craft, prohibited to all other vessels than those of the German Navy. This anchorage is about five cables by two cables in area, and has an average depth of $2\frac{1}{2}$ fathoms.

Naval Value of the Island

Since its cession, considerable attention has been devoted to the island by the German Admiralty. One of the most serious difficulties with which the German naval administration has had to contend is the fact that on the North Sea coast of the empire there is no really satisfactory port. Hamburg and Bremen lie far up the rivers Elbe and Weser. The original naval base on the North Sea, Wilhelms-haven, where is an imperial dockyard, suffers from the fact that Jade Bay is extremely sandy ; the harbour can only be kept open by means of constant dredging. The new base, Cuxhaven, opposite the junction of the Kaiser Wilhelm Canal with the Elbe, suffers, in a slightly lesser degree, from the same drawback. Hence every effort has been made to utilize Heligoland. It has been converted into a base for torpedo craft and submarines, and two Zeppelin sheds, said to be of the ' disappearing ' variety, have been constructed on the island. But the value of Heligoland is much reduced by the fact that it suffers in a peculiar degree from erosion, and can, indeed, only be preserved from destruction by artificial means and at a considerable annual cost. The shores of the island are carefully protected by deposits of cement, which are constantly washed away in westerly gales and require frequent renewal.

FORTIFICATIONS

Heligoland, as well as the whole North Sea coast of Germany, has been very carefully fortified. The forts are of the cupola type, built of concrete, and are defended by 11-inch guns ; the statement that the guns are 12-inch seems to be unfounded. Theoretically, both the island and the whole coast should be impregnable ; it is supposed that a single shot from one of these guns would suffice to sink any ship. It must, however, be remembered that the value of cupola forts has been somewhat discounted by the experiences of Namur and other places.

ANCHORAGE OF HELIGOLAND

To the east of the island, immediately beyond the ' prohibited ' anchorage, is the rock of Düne. It is protected by groynes, but both its area and shape are subject to frequent changes ; it is in reality little more than a sandbank, serving as the site for three beacons. Beyond it, eastward, there is an anchorage for large vessels, which is satisfactory in westerly winds. It is probable that this is the anchorage which is mentioned in the dispatches as having been ' examined ' on September 14, and that it has been utilized as a station for light cruisers. It is commanded by the guns of Heligoland.

Bight of Heligoland

The Bight of Heligoland, the scene of the operations described in the dispatches, is to the NE. of the island, from which it is distant some seven miles. It forms a channel, with an approximate width of eighteen miles and an average depth of nine fathoms, between the shallows near Heligoland and the shoals off the Holstein coast. Through it lies the regular course for ships proceeding northwards from the Elbe ports.

British Ships Engaged

The following are brief details of the British vessels, mentioned as having taken part in the operations.

The date signifies date of completion ; D. displacement ; C. complement ; G. guns. The speed given is the best recent speed, unless otherwise stated.

(i) Battle Cruisers

Lion (1912 : Devonport). D. 26,350. C. 1,000. Sp. 31·7 kts. Guns : eight 13·5-inch ; sixteen 4-inch.

Queen Mary (1913 : Clydebank). D. 27,000. C. 1,000. Sp. 33. Guns : (as *Lion*).

New Zealand (1912 : Fairfield). D. 18,750. C. 800. Sp. 25 (designed : her sister's best recent speed is 29·13). Guns : eight 12-inch ; sixteen 4-inch.

Invincible (1908 : Elswick). D. 17,250. C. 750. Sp. 28·6. Guns : (as *New Zealand*).

All these vessels possess three submerged tubes. Their armour is Krupp.

(ii) CRUISERS

The cruisers mentioned are the *Bacchante, Cressy, Euryalus,* and *Hogue.* They were sisters. Displacement, 12,000 tons : complement, 700 (*Euryalus,* as flagship, 745). Guns : two 9·2-inch ; twelve 6-inch ; thirteen 12-pounders. Two submerged tubes. Armour, Krupp.

The *Bacchante* (1902) was built at Clydebank ; *Cressy* (1901), Fairfield ; *Euryalus* (1903) and *Hogue* (1902), Vickers.

Best recent speeds were : *Bacchante,* 19·5 kts. ; *Cressy,* 19·2 ; *Euryalus,* 20·3 ; *Hogue,* 17.

The *Hogue* and *Cressy,* with their sister, the *Aboukir,* were sunk by a German submarine on September 22.

(iii) LIGHT CRUISERS

Arethusa (1913). D. 3,520. C. ——. Sp. (designed) 30 kts. Guns : two 6-inch ; six 4-inch. Four tubes, above water. (Chatham.)

Lowestoft (1914). D. 5,400. C. ——. Sp. (designed) 24·75. Guns : nine 6-inch ; four 3-pounders. Two submerged tubes. (Chatham.)

Liverpool (1910). D. 4,800. C. 376. Sp. (designed) 25. Guns: two 6-inch ; ten 4-inch ; four

3-pounders. Two submerged tubes. Armour, Krupp. (Vickers.)

Fearless (1913). D. 3,440. C. 320. Sp. (designed) 25. Guns : ten 4-inch ; four 3-pounders. Two tubes above water. Unarmoured. (Pembroke.)

Amethyst (1904). D. 3,000. C. 296. Sp. 20. Guns : twelve 4-inch ; eight 3-pounders. Two tubes above water. (Elswick.)

(iv) Destroyers

The destroyers mentioned were :

(*a*) Four of the L Class : D. 807 tons. Sp. 35. Armament : three 4-inch ; four tubes. (1912–13.) The *Laurel* and *Liberty* are White boats ; *Laertes*, Swan, Hunter & Richardson ; *Laforey*, Fairfield.

(*b*) Two special boats of I Class, *Lurcher* and *Firedrake*. D. 790. C. 72. Sp. (designed) 32. Armament : two 4-inch ; two 12-pounders ; two tubes. (1911.) (Yarrow.)

(*c*) Three boats, Admiralty design, I Class : *Defender*, *Goshawk*, and *Ferret*. D. (nominal) 750. C. 72. Armament, as *Lurcher*. Sp. (designed) 27. (1911.) *Defender* is a Denny boat ; *Ferret*, White ; *Goshawk*, Beardmore. The actual displacement varies slightly from the nominal ; speed in some cases rather above designed speed.

(v) Special Service

Maidstone (1911 : Scott's S. and E. Co.). Submarine dépôt ship. D. 3,600 tons. Sp. 14 kts.

(vi) SUBMARINES

(*a*) D Class. Nos. 1, 2 and 8. D 1 (1907). D. 550–600. Maximum speed, 16·9. Tubes, 3. D 2 and D 8 (1910–11). D. 550–600. Maximum speed, 16·10. Tubes, 3.

(*b*) E Class. Nos. 4 to 9. (1912.) D. 725–810. Sp. 16–10. Tubes, 4.

GERMAN SHIPS MENTIONED

Of the German vessels mentioned :

(i) *Mainz* (1909) (Vulkan Co.). D. 4,350. C. 362. Sp. (designed) 25·5. Guns : twelve 4-inch ; four 5-pounders ; four machine. Two submerged tubes. One of *Kolberg* class.

(ii) *Hela* (1896 : refitted, 1910), (Weser, Bremen). D. 2,040. C. 178. Guns : four $15\frac{1}{2}$-pounders; six 6-pounders ; two machine. One submerged tube ; two above water. Sp. 18. Was to be replaced.

(iii) V 187 (1909–11) (Vulkan). C. 82. Sp. 32·5. D. *circa* 650 tons. Armament : two 24-pounders ; three tubes.

(iv) S 126 (1906). D. 487. Sp. 28. C. 68. Armament : three 4-pounders ; two machine. Three tubes.

The four-funnelled cruiser mentioned must have been either one of the *Breslau* and *Karlsrühe* class, or one of the *Roon* class. The former class comprises twelve vessels, four of the *Breslau* type, and eight of the *Karlsrühe* type (of which two were completed in 1913, two were due to be completed

in the present year, two in 1915, and two later).
Details of the *Breslau* class are as follows : D. 4,550.
C. 370. Sp. (designed) 25½ kts. Guns : twelve
4·1-inch. Two submerged tubes. (The actual
speed of these ships is above the designed speed.)
Details of the *Karlsrühe* class are as follows : D.
4,900. C. 373. Sp. (designed) 28 kts. Guns :
twelve 4·1-inch. Two submerged tubes. (1912–13.)
The *Roon* class, containing two vessels, the *Roon*
and *Yorck* (the latter since sunk), have : D. 9,050.
C. 557. Sp. (designed) 21 kts. Guns: four 8·2-inch;
ten 6-inch ; eleven 24-pounders ; four machine.
Four submerged tubes. (1905–6.)

PAST SERVICES OF BRITISH OFFICERS

Some of the British officers concerned had already
seen active service and gained distinctions.

Vice-Admiral (Acting) Sir David Beatty served
as a lieutenant on the river Nile, during the operations of 1898, and conducted the bombardment of
the Dongola forts. He also served as commander
of the *Barfleur* at Tientsin in 1900.

Rear-Admiral Arthur H. Christian served on the
expedition against King Kobo of Nimby, 1895, and
captured M'weli, the stronghold of the Arab chief
Mburuk in the same year.

Commodore Reginald Y. Tyrwhitt commanded
the landing party during the disturbances at Blue-
fields, 1894, and was thanked by the inhabitants.

Commodore Roger J. B. Keyes served against the
Sultan of Vitu, 1890. In the *Fame*, he cut out four

Chinese destroyers, 1900, and was promoted for this service.

Captain William F. Blunt was present at the blockade of Zanzibar, 1888–9, and also served in Crete, 1897–8, and in China, 1900.

Commander Charles R. Samson served in Somaliland, 1902–4. He made the first flight from the deck of a British warship in 1912.

NAVAL ENGAGEMENT OFF HELIGOLAND

Admiralty, 21st October, 1914.

The following despatches have been received from Vice-Admiral (Acting) Sir David Beatty, K.C.B., M.V.O., D.S.O., H.M.S. 'Lion', Rear-Admiral Arthur H. Christian, M.V.O., H.M.S. 'Euryalus', Commodore Reginald Y. Tyrwhitt, Commodore (T.), H.M.S. 'Arethusa', and Commodore Roger J. B. Keyes, C.B., M.V.O., Commodore (S.), reporting the engagement off Heligoland on Friday, the 28th August.

A memorandum by the Director of the Air Department, Admiralty, is annexed.

H.M.S. 'Lion',
1st September, 1914.

Sir,—I have the honour to report that on Thursday, 27th August, at 5 a.m., I proceeded with the First Battle Cruiser Squadron and First Light Cruiser Squadron in company, to rendezvous with the Rear-Admiral, 'Invincible'.

At 4 a.m., 28th August, the movements of the Flotillas commenced as previously arranged, the Battle Cruiser Squadron and Light Cruiser Squadron supporting. The Rear-Admiral, 'Invincible', with 'New Zealand' and four Destroyers having joined my flag, the Squadron passed through the pre-arranged rendezvous.

At 8.10 a.m. I received a signal from the Commodore (T), informing me that the Flotilla was in action with the enemy. This was- presumably in the vicinity of their prearranged rendezvous. From this time until 11 a.m. I remained about the vicinity ready to support as necessary, intercepting various signals, which contained no information on which I could act.

SUBMARINE ATTACK

At 11 a.m. the Squadron was attacked by three Submarines. The attack was frustrated by rapid manœuvring and the four Destroyers were ordered to attack them. Shortly after 11 a.m., various signals having been received indicating that the Commodore (T) and Commodore (S) were both in need of assistance, I ordered the Light Cruiser Squadron to support the Torpedo Flotillas.

Later I received a signal from the Commodore (T), stating that he was being attacked by a large Cruiser, and a further signal informing me that he was being hard pressed and asking for assistance. The Captain (D), First Flotilla, also signalled that he was in need of help.

INTERVENTION OF THE BATTLE CRUISERS

From the foregoing the situation appeared to me critical. The Flotillas had advanced only ten miles since 8 a.m., and were only about twenty-five miles from two enemy bases on their flank and rear respectively. Commodore Goodenough had detached two of his Light Cruisers to assist some Destroyers earlier in the day, and these had not yet rejoined. (They rejoined at 2.30 p.m.) As the reports indicated the presence of many enemy ships —one a large Cruiser—I considered that his force might not be strong enough to deal with the situation sufficiently rapidly, so at 11.30 a.m. the Battle Cruisers turned to E.S.E., and worked up to full speed. It was evident that to be of any value the support must be overwhelming and carried out at the highest speed possible.

I had not lost sight of the risk of Submarines, and possible sortie in force from the enemy's base, especially in view of the mist to the South-East.

Our high speed, however, made submarine attack difficult, and the smoothness of the sea made their detection comparatively easy. I considered that we were powerful enough to deal with any sortie except by a Battle Squadron, which was unlikely to come out in time, provided our stroke was sufficiently rapid.

THE ' MAINZ ' ATTACKED

At 12.15 p.m. ' Fearless ' and First Flotilla were sighted retiring West. At the same time the Light Cruiser Squadron was observed to be engaging an enemy ship ahead. They appeared to have her beat.

ENEMY CRUISER ENGAGED WITH THIRD FLOTILLA

I then steered N.E. to sounds of firing ahead, and at 12.30 p.m. sighted ' Arethusa ' and Third Flotilla retiring to the Westward engaging a Cruiser of the

'Kolberg' class on our Port Bow. I steered to cut her off from Heligoland, and at 12.37 p.m. opened fire. At 12.42 the enemy turned to N.E., and we chased at 27 knots.

'Lion' Engaged with an Enemy Cruiser

At 12.56 p.m. sighted and engaged a two-funnelled Cruiser ahead. 'Lion' fired two salvoes at her, which took effect, and she disappeared into the mist, burning furiously and in a sinking condition. In view of the mist and that she was steering at high speed at right angles to 'Lion', who was herself stéaming at 28 knots, the 'Lion's' firing was very creditable.

Our Destroyers had reported the presence of floating mines to the Eastward and I considered it inadvisable to pursue her. It was also essential that the Squadrons should remain concentrated, and I accordingly ordered a withdrawal. The Battle Cruisers turned North and circled to port to complete the destruction of the vessel first engaged.

Sinking of the 'Mainz'

She was sighted again at 1.25 p.m. steaming S.E. with colours still flying. 'Lion' opened fire with two turrets, and at 1.35 p.m., after receiving two salvoes, she sank.

The four attached Destroyers were sent to pick up survivors, but I deeply regret that they subsequently reported that they searched the area but found none.

Submarine Attack on ' Queen Mary '

At 1.40 p.m. the Battle Cruisers turned to the Northward, and ' Queen Mary ' was again attacked by a Submarine. The attack was avoided by the use of the helm. ' Lowestoft ' was also unsuccessfully attacked. The Battle Cruisers covered the retirement until nightfall. By 6 p.m., the retirement having been well executed and all Destroyers accounted for, I altered course, spread the Light Cruisers, and swept northwards in accordance with the Commander-in-Chief's orders. At 7.45 p.m. I detached ' Liverpool ' to Rosyth with German prisoners, 7 officers and 79 men, survivors from ' Mainz '. No further incident occurred.—I have the honour to be, Sir, your obedient Servant,

(Signed) DAVID BEATTY,
Vice-Admiral.

The Secretary of the Admiralty.

Work of the Cruiser Force

' Euryalus ',
28th September, 1914.

Sir,—I have the honour to report that in accordance with your orders a reconnaissance in force was carried out in the Heligoland Bight on the 28th August, with the object of attacking the enemy's Light Cruisers and Destroyers.

The forces under my orders (viz., the Cruiser Force, under Rear-Admiral H. H. Campbell, C.V.O., ' Euryalus ', ' Amethyst ', First and Third Destroyer

Flotillas and the Submarines) took up the positions assigned to them on the evening of the 27th August, and, in accordance with directions given, proceeded during the night to approach the Heligoland Bight.

Assistance Rendered to Injured Vessels

The Cruiser Force under Rear-Admiral Campbell, with ' Euryalus ' (my Flagship) and ' Amethyst ', was stationed to intercept any enemy vessels chased to the westward.   At 4.30 p.m. on the 28th August these Cruisers, having proceeded to the eastward, fell in with ' Lurcher ' and three other Destroyers, and the wounded and prisoners in these vessels were transferred in boats to ' Bacchante ' and ' Cressy ', which left for the Nore.   ' Amethyst ' took ' Laurel ' in tow, and at 9.30 p.m. ' Hogue ' was detached to take ' Arethusa ' in tow.   This latter is referred to in Commodore R. Y. Tyrwhitt's report, and I quite concur in his remarks as to the skill and rapidity with which this was done in the dark with no lights permissible.

Individual Services Mentioned

Commodore Reginald Y. Tyrwhitt was in command of the Destroyer Flotillas, and his report is enclosed herewith. His attack was delivered with great skill and gallantry, and he was most ably seconded by Captain William F. Blunt, in ' Fearless ', and the Officers in command of the Destroyers, who handled their vessels in a manner worthy of the best traditions of the British Navy.

Commodore Roger J. B. Keyes, in 'Lurcher', had, on the 27th August, escorted some Submarines into positions allotted to them in the immediate vicinity of the enemy's coast. On the morning of the 28th August, in company with 'Firedrake', he searched the area to the southward of the Battle Cruisers for the enemy's Submarines, and subsequently, having been detached, was present at the sinking of the German Cruiser 'Mainz', when he gallantly proceeded alongside her and rescued 220 of her crew, many of whom were wounded. Subsequently he escorted 'Laurel' and 'Liberty' out of action, and kept them company till Rear-Admiral Campbell's Cruisers were sighted.

As regards the Submarine Officers, I would specially mention the names of :—

(a) Lieutenant-Commander Ernest W. Leir. His coolness and resource in rescuing the crews of the 'Goshawk's' and 'Defender's' boats at a critical time of the action were admirable.

(b) Lieutenant-Commander Cecil P. Talbot. In my opinion, the bravery and resource of the Officers in command of Submarines since the war commenced are worthy of the highest commendation.

I have the honour to be, Sir,
Your obedient Servant,
A. H. CHRISTIAN,
Rear-Admiral.

The Secretary, Admiralty.

Work of Destroyer Flotilla

H.M.S. ' Lowestoft ',
26th *September,* 1914.

Sir,—I have the honour to report that at 5 a.m. on Thursday, 27th August, in accordance with orders received from Their Lordships, I sailed in ' Arethusa', in company with the First and Third Flotillas, except ' Hornet ', ' Tigress ', ' Hydra ', and ' Loyal ', to carry out the prearranged operations. H.M.S. ' Fearless ' joined the Flotillas at sea that afternoon.

At 6.53 a.m. on Friday, 28th August, an enemy's Destroyer was sighted, and was chased by the 4th Division of the Third Flotilla.

From 7.20 to 7.57 a.m. ' Arethusa ' and the Third Flotilla were engaged with numerous Destroyers and Torpedo Boats which were making for Heligoland ; course was altered to port to cut them off.

Enemy Cruisers Engaged

Two Cruisers, with 4 and 2 funnels respectively, were sighted on the port bow at 7.57 a.m., the nearest of which was engaged. ' Arethusa ' received a heavy fire from both Cruisers and several Destroyers until 8.15 a.m., when the four-funnelled Cruiser transferred her fire to ' Fearless '.

Close action was continued with the two-funnelled Cruiser on converging courses until 8.25 a.m., when a 6-inch projectile from ' Arethusa ' wrecked the fore bridge of the enemy, who at once turned away in the direction of Heligoland, which was sighted slightly on the starboard bow at about the same time.

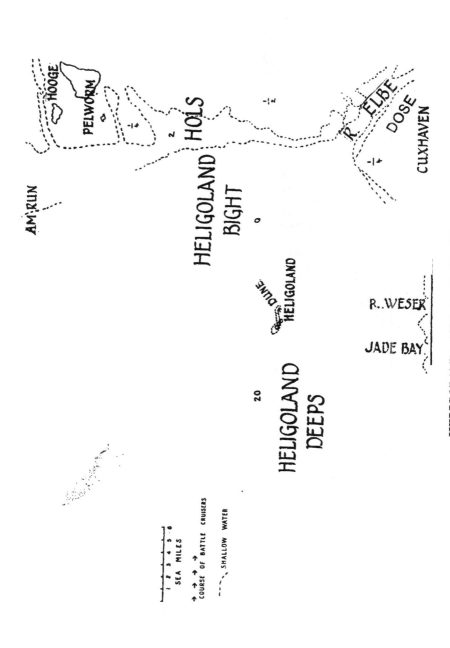

HOOGE

PELWORM

AMRUN

HELIGOLAND
BIGHT

HOLS

R. ELBE

DOSE

CUXHAVEN

DUNE

HELIGOLAND

R. WESER

JADE BAY

HELIGOLAND
DEEPS

1 2 3 4 5 6
SEA MILES

↑ ↑ ↑ ↑ ↑
COURSE OF BATTLE CRUISERS

SHALLOW WATER

HELIGOLAND AND THE COAST

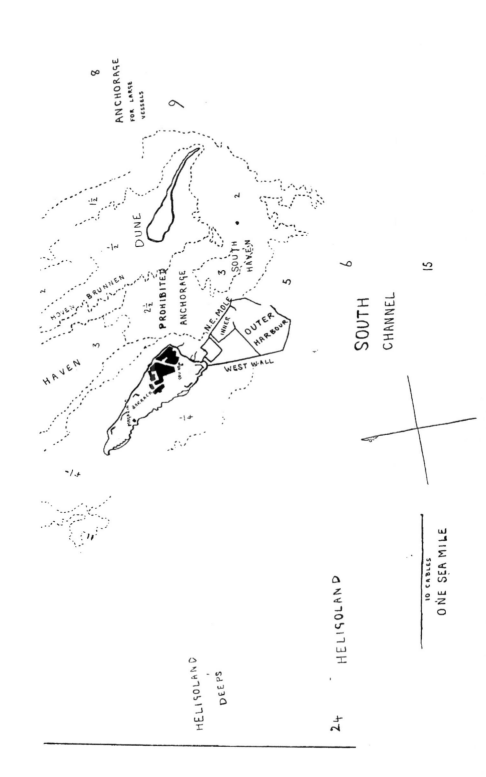

All ships were at once ordered to turn to the westward, and shortly afterwards speed was reduced to 20 knots.

DAMAGE DONE TO THE 'ARETHUSA'

During this action ' Arethusa ' had been hit many times, and was considerably damaged ; only one 6-inch gun remained in action, all other guns and torpedo tubes having been temporarily disabled.

Lieutenant Eric W. P. Westmacott (Signal Officer) was killed at my side during this action. I cannot refrain from adding that he carried out his duties calmly and collectedly, and was of the greatest assistance to me.

A fire occurred opposite No. 2 gun port side caused by a shell exploding some ammunition, resulting in a terrific blaze for a short period and leaving the deck burning. This was very promptly dealt with and extinguished by Chief Petty Officer Frederick W. Wrench, O.N. 158630.

The Flotillas were re-formed in Divisions and proceeded at 20 knots. It was now noticed that ' Arethusa's ' speed had been reduced.

SINKING OF AN ENEMY DESTROYER

' Fearless ' reported that the 3rd and 5th Divisions of the First Flotilla had sunk the German Commodore's Destroyer and that two boats' crews belonging to ' Defender ' had been left behind as our Destroyers had been fired upon by a German Cruiser during their act of mercy in saving the survivors of the German Destroyer.

ENGAGEMENT WITH ENEMY CRUISERS

At 10 a.m., hearing that Commodore (S) in 'Lurcher' and 'Firedrake' were being chased by Light Cruisers, I proceeded to his assistance with 'Fearless' and the First Flotilla until 10.37 a.m., when, having received no news and being in the vicinity of Heligoland, I ordered the ships in company to turn to the westward.

All guns except two 4-inch were again in working order, and the upper deck supply of ammunition was replenished.

At 10.55 a.m. a four-funnelled German Cruiser was sighted, and opened a very heavy fire at about 11 o'clock.

Our position being somewhat critical, I ordered 'Fearless' to attack, and the First Flotilla to attack with torpedoes, which they proceeded to do with great spirit. The Cruiser at once turned away, disappeared in the haze and evaded the attack.

About 10 minutes later the same Cruiser appeared on our starboard quarter. Opened fire on her with both 6-inch guns; 'Fearless' also engaged her, and one Division of Destroyers attacked her with torpedoes without success.

The state of affairs and our position was then reported to the Admiral Commanding Battle Cruiser Squadron.

We received a very severe and almost accurate fire from this Cruiser; salvo after salvo was falling between 10 and 30 yards short, but not a single shell struck ; two torpedoes were also fired at us, being well directed, but short.

The Cruiser was badly damaged by ' Arethusa's ' 6-inch guns and a splendidly directed fire from ' Fearless,' and she shortly afterwards turned away in the direction of Heligoland.

SINKING OF THE ' MAINZ '

Proceeded, and four minutes later sighted the three-funnelled Cruiser ' Mainz '. She endured a heavy fire from ' Arethusa ' and ' Fearless ' and many Destroyers. After an action of approximately 25 minutes she was seen to be sinking by the head, her engines stopped, besides being on fire.

At this moment the Light Cruiser Squadron appeared, and they very speedily reduced the ' Mainz ' to a condition which must have been indescribable.

I then recalled ' Fearless ' and the Destroyers, and ordered cease fire.

We then exchanged broadsides with a large, four-funnelled Cruiser on the starboard quarter at long range, without visible effect.

The Battle Cruiser Squadron now arrived, and I pointed out this Cruiser to the Admiral Commanding, and was shortly afterwards informed by him that the Cruiser in question had been sunk and another set on fire.

STATE OF THE WEATHER

The weather during the day was fine, sea calm, but visibility poor, not more than 3 miles at any time when the various actions were taking place, and was such that ranging and spotting were rendered difficult.

Withdrawal of the Flotilla

I then proceeded with 14 Destroyers of the Third Flotilla and 9 of the First Flotilla.

' Arethusa's ' speed was about 6 knots until 7 p.m., when it was impossible to proceed any further, and fires were drawn in all boilers except two, and assistance called for.

At 9.30 p.m. Captain Wilmot S. Nicholson, of the ' Hogue ', took my ship in tow in a most seamanlike manner, and, observing that the night was pitch dark and the only lights showing were two small hand lanterns, I consider his action was one which deserves special notice from Their Lordships.

I would also specially recommend Lieutenant-Commander Arthur P. N. Thorowgood, of 'Arethusa', for the able manner he prepared the ship for being towed in the dark.

H.M. Ship under my command was then towed to the Nore, arriving at 5 p.m. on the 29th August. Steam was then available for slow speed, and the ship was able to proceed to Chatham under her own steam.

Individual Services

I beg again to call attention to the services rendered by Captain W. F. Blunt, of H.M.S. ' Fearless ', and the Commanding Officers of the Destroyers of the First and Third Flotillas, whose gallant attacks on the German Cruisers at critical moments undoubtedly saved 'Arethusa' from more severe punishment and possible capture.

I cannot adequately express my satisfaction and pride at the spirit and ardour of my Officers and Ship's Company, who carried out their orders with the greatest alacrity under the most trying conditions, especially in view of the fact that the ship, newly built, had not been 48 hours out of the Dockyard before she was in action.

It is difficult to specially pick out individuals, but the following came under my special observation :—

H.M.S. 'Arethusa'.

Lieutenant-Commander Arthur P. N. Thorowgood, First Lieutenant, and in charge of the After Control.

Lieutenant-Commander Ernest K. Arbuthnot (G.), in charge of the Fore Control.

Sub-Lieutenant Clive A. Robinson, who worked the range-finder throughout the entire action with extraordinary coolness.

Assistant Paymaster Kenneth E. Badcock, my Secretary, who attended me on the bridge throughout the entire action.

Mr. James D. Godfrey, Gunner (T), who was in charge of the torpedo tubes.

The following men were specially noted :—

Armourer Arthur F. Hayes, O.N. 342026 (Ch.).

Second Sick Berth Steward George Trolley, O.N. M.296 (Ch.).

Chief Yeoman of Signals Albert Fox, O.N. 194656 (Po.), on fore bridge during entire action.

Chief Petty Officer Frederick W. Wrench, O.N. 158630 (Ch.) (for ready resource in extinguishing fire aused by explosion of cordite).

c

Private Thomas Millington, R.M.L.I., No. Ch. 17417.

Private William J. Beirne, R.M.L.I., No. Ch. 13540.

First Writer Albert W. Stone, O.N. 346080 (Po.).

I also beg to record the services rendered by the following Officers and Men of H.M. Ships under my orders :—

H.M.S. ' Fearless '.

Mr. Robert M. Taylor, Gunner, for coolness in action under heavy fire.

The following Officers also displayed great resource and energy in effecting repairs to ' Fearless ' after her return to harbour, and they were ably seconded by the whole of their staffs :—

Engineer Lieutenant-Commander Charles de F. Messervy.

Mr. William Morrissey, Carpenter.

H.M.S. ' Goshawk '.

Commander The Hon. Herbert Meade, who took his Division into action with great coolness and nerve, and was instrumental in sinking the German Destroyer ' V.187 ', and, with the boats of his Division, saved the survivors in a most chivalrous manner.

H.M.S. ' Ferret '.

Commander Geoffrey Mackworth, who, with his Division, most gallantly seconded Commander Meade of ' Goshawk '.

H.M.S. ' Laertes '.

Lieutenant-Commander Malcolm L. Goldsmith, whose ship was seriously damaged, taken in tow, and towed out of action by ' Fearless '.

Engineer Lieutenant-Commander Alexander Hill, for repairing steering gear and engines under fire.

Sub-Lieutenant George H. Faulkner, who continued to fight his gun after being wounded.

Mr. Charles Powell, Acting Boatswain, O.N. 209388, who was gunlayer of the centre gun, which made many hits. He behaved very coolly, and set a good example when getting in tow and clearing away the wreckage after the action.

Edward Naylor, Petty Officer, Torpedo Gunner's Mate, O.N. 189136, who fired a torpedo which the Commanding Officer of ' Laertes ' reports undoubtedly hit the ' Mainz ', and so helped materially to put her out of action.

Stephen Pritchard, Stoker Petty Officer, O.N. 285152, who very gallantly dived into the cabin flat immediately after a shell had exploded there, and worked a fire hose.

Frederick Pierce, Stoker Petty Officer, O.N. 307943, who was on watch in the engine room and behaved with conspicuous coolness and resource when a shell exploded in No. 2 boiler.

H.M.S. ' Laurel '.

Commander Frank F. Rose, who most ably commanded his vessel throughout the early part of the action, and after having been wounded in both legs, remained on the bridge until 6 p.m., displaying great devotion to duty.

Lieutenant Charles R. Peploe, First Lieutenant, who took command after Commander Rose was wounded, and continued the action till its close, bringing his Destroyer out in an able and gallant manner under most trying conditions.

Engineer Lieutenant-Commander Edward H. T. Meeson, who behaved with great coolness during the action, and steamed the ship out of action, although she had been very severely damaged by explosion of her own lyddite, by which the after funnel was nearly demolished. He subsequently assisted to carry out repairs to the vessel.

Sam Palmer, Leading Seaman (G.L. 2) O.N. 179529, who continued to fight his gun until the end of the action, although severely wounded in the leg.

Albert Edmund Sellens, Able Seaman (L.T.O.), O.N. 217245, who was stationed at the fore torpedo tubes ; he remained at his post throughout the entire action, although wounded in the arm, and then rendered first aid in a very able manner before being attended to himself.

George H. Sturdy, Chief Stoker, O.N. 285547, and Alfred Britton, Stoker Petty Officer, O.N. 289893, who both showed great coolness in putting out a fire near the centre gun after an explosion had occurred there ; several lyddite shells were lying in the immediate vicinity.

William R. Boiston, Engine Room Artificer, 3rd class, O.N. M.1369, who showed great ability and coolness in taking charge of the after boiler room during the action, when an explosion blew in the after funnel and a shell carried away pipes and seriously damaged the main steam pipe.

William H. Gorst, Stoker Petty Officer, O.N.305616.

Edward Crane, Stoker Petty Officer, O.N. 307275.

Harry Wilfred Hawkes, Stoker 1st class, O.N. K.12086.

John W. Bateman, Stoker 1st class, O.N. K.12100.

These men were stationed in the after boiler room and conducted themselves with great coolness during the action, when an explosion blew in the after funnel, and shell carried away pipes and seriously damaged the main steam pipe.

H.M.S. ' Liberty '.

The late Lieutenant-Commander Nigel K. W. Barttelot commanded the ' Liberty ' with great skill and gallantry throughout the action. He was a

most promising and able Officer, and I consider his
death is a great loss to the Navy.

Engineer Lieutenant-Commander Frank A. Butler,
who showed much resource in effecting repairs during
the action.

Lieutenant Henry E. Horan, First Lieutenant,
who took command after the death of Lieutenant-
Commander Barttelot, and brought his ship out of
action in an extremely able and gallant manner under
most trying conditions.

Mr. Harry Morgan, Gunner (T), who carried out
his duties with exceptional coolness under fire.

Chief Petty Officer James Samuel Beadle, O.N.
171735, who remained at his post at the wheel for
over an hour after being wounded in the kidneys.

John Galvin, Stoker Petty Officer, O.N. 279946,
who took entire charge, under the Engineer Officer,
of the party who stopped leaks, and accomplished
his task although working up to his chest in water.

H.M.S. ' Laforey '.

Mr. Ernest Roper, Chief Gunner, who carried out
his duties with exceptional coolness under fire.

I have the honour to be, Sir,
Your obedient Servant,
R. Y. TYRWHITT,
Commodore (T).

WORK OF SUBMARINES SINCE THE OUTBREAK OF WAR

H.M.S. ' Maidstone ',
17th October, 1914.

Sir,—In compliance with Their Lordships' directions, I have the honour to report as follows upon

the services performed by Submarines since the commencement of hostilities :—

RECONNAISSANCE IN HELIGOLAND BIGHT

Three hours after the outbreak of war, Submarines ' E.6 ' (Lieutenant-Commander Cecil P. Talbot), and ' E.8 ' (Lieutenant-Commander Francis H. H. Goodhart), proceeded unaccompanied to carry out a reconnaissance in the Heligoland Bight. These two vessels returned with useful information, and had the privilege of being the pioneers on a service which is attended by some risk.

PROTECTION OF TRANSPORTS

During the transportation of the Expeditionary Force the ' Lurcher ' and ' Firedrake ' and all the Submarines of the Eighth Submarine Flotilla occupied positions from which they could have attacked the High Sea Fleet, had it emerged to dispute the passage of our transports. This patrol was maintained day and night without relief, until the personnel of our Army had been transported and all chance of effective interference had disappeared.

OPERATIONS ON THE GERMAN COAST

These Submarines have since been incessantly employed on the Enemy's Coast in the Heligoland Bight and elsewhere, and have obtained much valuable information regarding the composition and movement of his patrols. They have occupied his waters and reconnoitred his anchorages, and, while so engaged, have been subjected to skilful and well-executed anti-submarine tactics ; hunted for hours at a time by Torpedo Craft and attacked by gunfire and torpedoes.

ENGAGEMENT OFF HELIGOLAND

At midnight on the 26th August, I embarked in the ' Lurcher ', and, in company with ' Firedrake ' and Submarines ' D.2 ', ' D.8 ', ' E.4 ', ' E.5 ', ' E.6 ', ' E.7 ', ' E.8 ', and ' E.9 ' of the Eighth Submarine Flotilla, proceeded to take part in the operations in the Heligoland Bight arranged for the 28th August. The Destroyers scouted for the Submarines until nightfall on the 27th, when the latter. proceeded independently to take up various positions from which they could co-operate with the Destroyer Flotillas on the following morning.

At daylight on the 28th August the ' Lurcher ' and ' Firedrake ' searched the area, through which the Battle Cruisers were to advance, for hostile Submarines, and then proceeded towards Heligoland in the wake of Submarines ' E.6 ', ' E.7 ', and ' E.8 ', which were exposing themselves with the object of inducing the enemy to chase them to the westward.

STATE OF THE WEATHER

On approaching Heligoland, the visibility, which had been very good to seaward, reduced to 5,000 to 6,000 yards, and this added considerably to the anxieties and responsibilities of the Commanding Officers of Submarines, who handled their vessels with coolness and judgment in an area which was necessarily occupied by friends as well as foes.

Low visibility and calm sea are the most unfavourable conditions under which Submarines can operate, and no opportunity occurred of closing with the Enemy's Cruisers to within torpedo range.

Sinking of ' V.187 '

Lieutenant-Commander Ernest W. Leir, Commanding Submarine 'E.4', witnessed the sinking of the German Torpedo Boat Destroyer 'V.187' through his periscope, and, observing a Cruiser of the 'Stettin' class close, and open fire on the British Destroyers which had lowered their boats to pick up the survivors, he proceeded to attack the Cruiser, but she altered course before he could get within range. After covering the retirement of our Destroyers, which had had to abandon their boats, he returned to the latter, and embarked a Lieutenant and nine men of 'Defender', who had been left behind. The boats also contained two Officers and eight men of 'V.187', who were unwounded, and eighteen men who were badly wounded. As he could not embark the latter, Lieutenant-Commander Leir left one of the Officers and six unwounded men to navigate the British boats to Heligoland. Before leaving he saw that they were provided with water, biscuit, and a compass. One German Officer and two men were made prisoners of war.

Individual Services

Lieutenant-Commander Leir's action in remaining on the surface in the vicinity of the enemy and in a visibility which would have placed his vessel within easy gun range of an enemy appearing out of the mist, was altogether admirable.

This enterprising and gallant Officer took part in the reconnaissance which supplied the information on which these operations were based, and I beg to submit his name, and that of Lieutenant-Commander Talbot, the Commanding Officer of ' E.6 ', who exercised patience, judgment and skill in a dangerous position, for the favourable consideration of Their Lordships.

Sinking of the ' Hela '

On the 13th September, ' E.9 ' (Lieutenant-Commander Max K. Horton) torpedoed and sank the German Light Cruiser ' Hela ' six miles South of Heligoland.

A number of Destroyers were evidently called to the scene after ' E.9 ' had delivered her attack, and these hunted her for several hours.

Examination of the Heligoland Anchorage

On the 14th September, in accordance with his orders, Lieutenant-Commander Horton examined the outer anchorage of Heligoland, a service attended by considerable risk.

On the 25th September, Submarine ' E.6 ' (Lieutenant-Commander C. P. Talbot), while diving, fouled the moorings of a mine laid by the enemy. On rising to the surface she weighed the mine and sinker ; the former was securely fixed between the hydroplane and its guard ; fortunately, however, the horns of the mine were pointed outboard. The weight of the sinker made it a difficult and dangerous matter to lift the mine clear without exploding it. After half an hour's patient work this was effected by Lieutenant Frederick A. P. Williams-Freeman and Able Seaman Ernest Randall Cremer, Official Number 214235, and the released mine descended to its original depth.

Sinking of ' S.126 '

On the 6th October, ' E.9 ' (Lieutenant-Commander Max K. Horton), when patrolling off the Ems, torpedoed and sank the enemy's destroyer, ' S.126.'

The enemy's Torpedo Craft pursue tactics which, in connection with their shallow draft, make them exceedingly difficult to attack with torpedo, and Lieutenant-Commander Horton's success was the result of much patient and skilful zeal. He is a most enterprising submarine officer, and I beg to submit his name for favourable consideration.

Lieutenant Charles M. S. Chapman, the Second in Command of ' E.9 ', is also deserving of credit.

Difficulties of the Submarine Work

Against an enemy whose capital vessels have never, and Light Cruisers have seldom, emerged from their fortified harbours, opportunities of delivering Submarine attacks have necessarily been few, and on one occasion only, prior to the 13th September, has one of our Submarines been within torpedo range of a Cruiser during daylight hours.

During the exceptionally heavy westerly gales

which prevailed between the 14th and 21st September, the position of the Submarines on a lee shore, within a few miles of the Enemy's coast, was an unpleasant one.

The short steep seas which accompany westerly gales in the Heligoland Bight made it difficult to keep the conning tower hatches open. There was no rest to be obtained, and even when cruising at a depth of 60 feet, the Submarines were rolling considerably, and pumping—*i.e.*, vertically moving about twenty feet.

I submit that it was creditable to the Commanding Officers that they should have maintained their stations under such conditions.

EAGERNESS TO SERVE IN THE BIGHT

Service in the Heligoland Bight is keenly sought after by the Commanding Officers of the Eighth Submarine Flotilla, and they have all shown daring and enterprise in the execution of their duties. These Officers have unanimously expressed to me their admiration of the cool and gallant behaviour of the Officers and men under their command. They are, however, of the opinion that it is impossible to single out individuals when all have performed their duties so admirably, and in this I concur.

SUBMARINES ENGAGED

The following Submarines have been in contact with the enemy during these operations :—

'D.1' (Lieutenant-Commander Archibald D. Cochrane).

' D.2 ' (Lieutenant-Commander Arthur G. Jameson).

' D.3 ' (Lieutenant-Commander Edward C. Boyle).

' D.5 ' (Lieutenant-Commander Godfrey Herbert).

' E.4 ' (Lieutenant-Commander Ernest W. Leir).

' E.5 ' (Lieutenant-Commander Charles S. Benning).

' E.6 ' (Lieutenant-Commander Cecil P. Talbot).

' E.7 ' (Lieutenant-Commander Ferdinand E. B. Feilmann).

' E.9 ' (Lieutenant-Commander Max K. Horton).

I have the honour to be, Sir,
Your obedient Servant,
(Signed) ROGER KEYES,
Commodore (S).

MEMORANDUM BY THE DIRECTOR OF THE AIR DEPARTMENT, ADMIRALTY

Commander Charles R. Samson, R.N., was in command of the Aeroplane and Armoured Motor Support of the Royal Naval Air Service (Naval Wing) at Dunkerque, between the dates 1st September to 5th October.

Aeroplane Skirmishes in September

During this period several notable air reconnaissances were made, and skirmishes took place. Of these particular mention may be made of the

Aeroplane attack on 4th September on 4 enemy cars and 40 men, on which occasion several bombs were dropped ; and of the successful skirmishes at Cassel on 4th September, Savy on 12th September, Aniche on 22nd September, Orchies on 23rd September.

ATTACK ON DÜSSELDORF (SEPT. 22)

On the 22nd September, Flight Lieutenant C. H. Collet, of the Royal Naval Air Service (Naval Wing of the Royal Flying Corps), flying a Sopwith tractor biplane, made a long flight and a successful attack on the German Zeppelin Airship Shed at Düsseldorf.

Lieutenant Collet's feat is notable—gliding down from 6,000 feet, the last 1,500 feet in mist, he finally came in sight of the Airship Shed at a height of 400 feet, only a quarter of a mile away from it.

ATTACK ON DÜSSELDORF (OCT. 8)

Flight Lieutenant Marix, acting under the orders of Squadron Commander Spenser Grey, carried out a successful attack on the Düsseldorf airship shed during the afternoon of the 8th October. From a height of 600 feet he dropped two bombs on the shed, and flames 500 feet high were seen within thirty seconds. The roof of the shed was also observed to collapse.

Lieutenant Marix's machine was under heavy fire from rifles and mitrailleuse and was five times hit whilst making the attack.

FLIGHT TO COLOGNE

Squadron Commander Spenser Grey, whilst in charge of a flight of naval aeroplanes at Antwerp, penetrated during a 3¾ hours' flight into the enemy's country as far as Cologne on the 8th October. He circled the city under fire at 600 feet and discharged his bombs on the military railway station. Considerable damage was done.

11th October, 1914.

Oxford: Horace Hart Printer to the University

WHY WE ARE AT WAR

GREAT BRITAIN'S CASE

BY MEMBERS OF THE OXFORD FACULTY
OF MODERN HISTORY

E. BARKER.	H. W. C. DAVIS.
C. R. L. FLETCHER.	ARTHUR HASSALL.
L. G. WICKHAM LEGG.	F. MORGAN.

With an Appendix of Original Documents
including the Authorized English Translation
of the White Book issued by the
German Government

THIRD EDITION REVISED (TENTH IMPRESSION)
CONTAINING THE RUSSIAN ORANGE BOOK AND
EXTRACTS FROM THE BELGIAN GREY BOOK

TRANSLATIONS INTO FRENCH ITALIAN SPANISH
GERMAN DANISH AND SWEDISH
ARE NOW READY

Paper Covers Two Shillings net (70 cents)
Cloth Two Shillings and Sixpence net (85 cents)

OXFORD: AT THE CLARENDON PRESS
LONDON: HUMPHREY MILFORD
EDINBURGH   GLASGOW   NEW YORK   TORONTO
MELBOURNE   BOMBAY

(*a*)

28

OXFORD PAMPHLETS
1914

THE GERMANS IN
AFRICA

BY

EVANS LEWIN

LIBRARIAN OF THE ROYAL COLONIAL INSTITUTE

Price Threepence net

OXFORD UNIVERSITY PRESS
HUMPHREY MILFORD
LONDON   EDINBURGH   GLASGOW
NEW YORK   TORONTO   MELBOURNE   BOMBAY

MAP OF AFRICA

Between pages 16 and 17.

THE GERMANS IN AFRICA

I.—The Colonial Movement in Germany

In an article which appeared in the *Kölnische Zeitung* on April 22, 1884, three days before it was announced officially that Germany's first colony in Africa had been placed under the protection of the Imperial Government, Africa was compared with a large pie which the English had prepared for themselves at other people's expense. ' Let us hope ', said the writer, ' that our blue-jackets will put a few peppercorns into it on the Guinea coast, so that our friends on the Thames may not digest it too rapidly.' It is the purpose of this pamphlet to show how Germany, after some years of careful preparation and in spite of much opposition, finally succeeded in peppering the African pie by establishing four important colonies upon the African continent.

The growth of the colonial movement in Germany coincided with the remarkable outburst of patriotic feeling which heralded and followed the wars in which the Germanic States achieved their political unity. It was essentially a modern development of the growing national spirit, for although in the seventeenth century a German trading colony under the patronage of the Great Elector of Brandenburg had been attempted on the Guinea coast, the experiment had been unsuccessful, and after a short and chequered career the Brandenburg settlements had been abandoned. Germany was not then ready for any form of colonization. The country was divided into a number of States having little political cohesion, in which the ruling classes were animated by the narrow spirit of provincialism and were unwilling and unable to unite for any national object. The little State of Brandenburg, afterwards to develop into the Kingdom of Prussia and to form the nucleus of the future German Empire, was alone capable of pursuing an active policy. But at the outset the efforts of its sovereign were frustrated owing to the lack of sea-power and the fact that other and stronger countries had already acquired large interests in the then profitable Guinea trade. France, England, Denmark, and Holland regarded the intrusion of a new and petty State upon their African domain with jealous interest. The Dutch in particular, upon whom the Elector had mainly to rely for the supply of seamen and officials, proved irreconcilable, and owing to mismanagement and peculation the settlements at Gross-Friedrichsburg, near Axim, and at other places, were abandoned and passed into the limbo of almost forgotten adventures, only to be fetched therefrom to serve the needs of patriotic exponents of the colonial theory.

For one and a half centuries there was no German settlement upon the African coasts. Britain, the great colonizing nation, in spite of the fact that Germany was rapidly becoming the foremost military Power in Europe whilst her commerce was extending to every quarter of the globe, refused to read the signs of the times and paid no attention to the growth of a movement which was ultimately destined to lead to such tremendous results. Even when the colonial party in Germany had secured a strong and influential following and Bismarck had practically made up his mind to enter upon the colonial scramble, the British Ambassador in Berlin, Odo

Russell, afterwards Lord Ampthill, wrote that 'the German Government feel more the want of soldiers than of colonies' (Sept. 18, 1880), believing that when Bismarck had stated that 'this colonial business would be for us in Germany like the wearing of sables in the noble families of Poland by men who have no shirts to their backs', he meant exactly what he had said. When Bismarck was convinced that the time for action had arrived he was as eager for expansion as the most advanced exponents of colonialism.

Four main causes drove Germany to seek for overseas territorial expansion : (a) the steady and increasing economic pressure at home which compelled Germans to search for new markets for their surplus manufactures and for new sources of supply of the tropical products needed for their growing industries ; (b) the need to establish colonies which might absorb the large number of Germans who annually left the Fatherland to find economic salvation in new countries, and who by settling in the United States or South America were lost to the nation ; [1] (c) the belief of patriotic Germans that their country, by becoming a maritime Power, might share in the benefits to be acquired from sea-power and might in her turn dominate the ocean ; (d) the attention that was then being focused upon Africa owing to the discoveries of Livingstone, Stanley, and other explorers, English, French, German, and Italian. In Germany the movement was cleverly engineered by a number of brilliant thinkers

---

[1] ' A German who can put off his Fatherland, like an old coat, is no longer a German for me,' said Bismarck. The Chancellor was quite right. Most of the emigrating Germans, of whom over three and a half millions left Germany during the nineteenth century, became Americans first and foremost, and only retained a sentimental interest in their Fatherland.

and writers. The creation of colonies was considered by the leaders of the movement as indispensable if the prosperity of the nation were finally to be achieved and its dignity and prestige to be upheld.

Friedrich List, a disciple of Adam Smith, was one of the earliest exponents of the movement. He taught that a nation is united by material interests rather than through any feeling of unity arising from a common origin or a common language ; and he formulated an economic programme which included the creation of a customs union for Germany, the establishment of a net-work of railways and the building of a mercantile marine, the appointment of consular representatives common to the whole of Germany, and the acquisition of colonies and the concentration therein of the surplus German population. Nearly all his ideals found realization save the last. The ideas of List were further elaborated by Ernst Friedel in 1867, who in a work advocating the establishment of ' Prussian-German colonies ' in the Far East and the Pacific Ocean, stated that ' maritime commerce, ships of war, colonies, are three complementary terms. The value of each is diminished if one of the three be wanting ', and suggested that the rich island of Formosa, since acquired by Japan, should be taken in order that Germany might rival the commercial enterprise displayed by Great Britain at Hong Kong. The ideas put forward by List and Friedel represented the views of a considerable section of the thinking populace which was soon to acquire great influence throughout the country. In particular they met with the approval of Heinrich von Treitschke, the great apostle of force, whose ideas were subsequently to be taught in every university and school in the country. Treitschke, whose doctrines prepared the way for the brutal frankness of writers like Bernhardi, Bülow, and von der Goltz, took a wide view of German destinies and stood for the Pan-Germanic doctrine in its widest extent. 'Whatever one may think of British liberty,' he wrote, 'her power is clearly an anachronism. . . . England is to-day the shameless representative of barbarism in international law.' Like others who have written of our national perfidy, Treitschke believed that Germany ought to take advantage of British weakness. 'In the south of Africa,' he wrote, 'if our Empire has the courage to follow an independent colonial policy with determination, a collision of our interests with those of England is unavoidable.'

Treitschke was by far the most serious advocate of German colonial expansion because he was the most dangerous. The doctrines he taught were not unknown to other writers, who believed that Germany was justified in appropriating whatever other nations were unable to hold. But most of the German writers believed that Germany should acquire her colonies in a legitimate way. Dr. Fabri, for example, who exercised so great an influence upon the movement that when he died in 1891 he was referred to in the German press as the Father of German colonization, uttered a sane and vigorous plea for the entry of Germany upon the colonial sphere in his now celebrated pamphlet published in 1879.[1] Whilst recapitulating the favourite arguments of the colonial party, he deplored the error committed by Bismarck in following a continental to the exclusion of an overseas policy, and stated that Germany lacked an important element in her greatness, because colonies were necessary for the economic development of the Empire and the growth of her commerce.

[1] *Bedarf Deutschland der Kolonien ?* Gotha, 1879.

In the period from 1870 to 1884 many other writers insisted upon the necessity for colonies. A wave of enthusiasm was sweeping over Germany. Merchants and political thinkers, economists and theological professors, missionaries and travellers, in fact all sections of the population who cared to think of the future, with the exception of the purely official classes who were fearful to foster a movement the fruition of which might lead to international complications, gave it their support. Emigration societies engaged in the work of forwarding Germany's surplus population to America—a migration which reached its maximum in 1882, when over 250,000 Germans left the Fatherland, and which has since become almost a negligible quantity—turned their attention to the possibility of finding regions where Germans might settle under their own flag. Chambers of Commerce, and particularly those of Hamburg and Bremen, took up the movement ; the former forwarding a lengthy report to the German Foreign Office in 1883, in which special attention was directed to the continual growth of German interests in Africa and to the number of German trading firms which had established relations with the natives. Societies were formed specially to direct and foster the movement, such as the *Deutsche Kolonialgesellschaft*, founded in 1881 under the Presidency of Prince von Hohenlohe-Langenburg, which organized meetings that were addressed by the foremost travellers and merchants. All this activity, carefully directed and fostered, not positively discouraged by the Chancellor and at a later period secretly and afterwards openly supported by him, and representing a perfectly legitimate and natural desire to achieve a triumph where other nations had succeeded, led naturally and inevitably to the events of 1884 which plunged Germany into the stormy waters of colonialism.

II.—German Exploration and the Germans in South Africa

Germans have never taken an active part in maritime exploration. Whilst Spanish and Portuguese navigators were crossing the Atlantic or exploring the coasts of Africa ; and British, French, and Dutch explorers were traversing the unknown seas, founding new settlements in America, the East, and Australasia ; Germans remained in the Fatherland, unable to organize maritime expeditions because they lacked the mercantile marine necessary for the prosecution of overseas adventures and possessed few seaports from whence to fit out expeditions. The activities of the Hanseatic League had been mainly confined to commercial enterprises of a lucrative rather than of an experimental nature, and by the time the maritime nations of Western Europe had firmly established themselves in the New World, on the coasts of Africa, or in India, the Hansa had practically ceased its commercial activities owing to the disastrous series of European wars during the sixteenth and seventeenth centuries, which had brought about the downfall of the mediaeval German commercial system. Thus there has been no German Columbus, Cabot, or Magellan in the Atlantic and no German Vancouver, Cook, or Bougainville in the Pacific.

But in Africa, Germans seized and utilized the opportunity that occurred during the nineteenth century to organize exploring expeditions, and their explorers and travellers performed a notable service in opening many portions of the Dark Continent to European enterprise. In the work of scientific exploration they were perhaps unequalled, and German agents travelling in every part of the Continent laid the foundations of the German colonial empire, whilst British and French explorers were engaged upon a similar work. Germans realized with pride that their countrymen had been instrumental in solving many geographical problems, and that their explorers were active agents in the establishment of German influence in countries that were as yet unoccupied by any European Power and where there was ample opportunity for the foundation of German plantation-colonies.

So long ago as the beginning of the eighteenth century individual Germans, generally in the employment of other countries, had been fired with the desire to acquire fame in the Dark Continent. In South Africa the talented but mendacious Peter Kolbe, a German pastor in the service of the Dutch, had won renown through his excellent account of the Hottentots, whilst at a later period Heinrich Lichtenstein, Professor of Natural History in the University of Berlin, travelled in the Sub-Continent where he wrote one of the best and most scholarly works on the country. But neither of these writers was in any sense an explorer, and it was not until the nineteenth century was well advanced that Germans began to take an active part in the penetration of Africa. The first German to win imperishable renown in Africa was Friedrich Hornemann, who entered the service of the African Association in 1796 and made a remarkable journey from Tripoli to the Niger, dying in the country of Nupe which had not hitherto been visited by Europeans. He was followed by Heinrich Barth, a citizen of Hamburg, whose great expedition in North Africa marched under British auspices. Starting from Tripoli, Barth crossed the Sahara by a new route, reached Lake Chad, visited the mysterious city of Timbuctoo, and helped to fill up gaps in our knowledge of the central Niger regions.

Following in his tracks, Vogel arrived in 1856 in the Sudan State of Wadai, whilst Carl Moritz von Beurmann also reached Wadai a few years later. Other Germans performed notable work in Northern Africa, especially Alexander Ziegler and Georg Schweinfurth, a German born in Russia, who revealed to the world the extensive Bahr-el-Ghazal and other upper waters of the Nile.

But it was in Eastern Africa that the Germans made their most profitable discoveries. In 1860 Baron Karl von der Decken made a remarkable survey of Mount Kilimanjaro, which had been seen twelve years previously by the missionaries Krapf and Rebmann, and continued his exploration of the coastal regions between Cape Delgado and the River Jub. Von der Decken was one of the first to conceive the idea of a German colony in East Africa. ' I am persuaded ', he wrote, ' that in a short time a colony established here would be most successful, and after two or three years would be self-supporting. . . . It would become of great importance after the opening of the Suez Canal. It is unfortunate that we Germans allow such opportunities of acquiring colonies to slip, especially at a time when it would be of importance to the navy.' But although von der Decken had stated that he would not hesitate to buy Mombasa from the Sultan of Zanzibar, it was left for others to carry out the enterprise he had suggested, and the final establishment of German East Africa was due to the unceasing labour of Dr. Karl Peters, Count Joachim Pfeil, and the gallant Hermann von Wissmann.

In South Africa also, German explorers were extremely active. In 1869 Eduard Mohr undertook his journey to the Victoria Falls, and at the same time Karl Mauch travelled in the Zambesi regions, visited the Mashonaland goldfields, and discovered the Zimbabwe ruins, those wonderful architectural remains of a long-past civilization. Mauch was one of the most active exponents of German enterprise in South Africa. 'Would to God', he said on his return from the Transvaal, 'that this fine country might soon become a German colony.' Two names, however, stand prominently as evidence of German activity in Africa—those of Gerhard Rohlfs and Gustav Nachtigal. Both were active in all parts of the Continent. The former first attracted attention by his daring and perilous journey from Morocco to Tripoli by Tafilet, Tuat, and Ghadames, and at a later period, as will be seen, was active in the Kameruns and Western Africa generally. Like von der Decken and Mauch, Rohlfs dreamed of the time when Germany would be ready to take her place in the African sun. 'Is it not deplorable', he asked in a lecture delivered after his return from the Kameruns, 'that we are obliged to assist, inactive and without the power to intervene, in the extension of England in Central Africa?'—a sentiment which accurately represented the feelings of the then powerful colonial party in Germany. Nachtigal, who had been sent in 1870 with presents from the King of Prussia to the Sultan of Bornu, continued his explorations in the Sudan and connected his discoveries with those of the explorers of the valley of the Nile.

The activities of these and of other German explorers who in the sixties and seventies of the last century were traversing the unknown wilds of Africa found full and ready recognition in the Fatherland, and the movement for geographical exploration received a national impetus in Germany and formed an important factor in solidifying public opinion in favour of the cherished schemes of the colonial party. Quite apart from the political motives which animated many of its supporters, it was associated with economic interests ; and German citizens, with a keen eye to the commercial possibilities of Africa, recognized exploration as one of the methods of fostering the economic interests of their country. Under the influence of von der Decken, Otto Kersten in 1868 founded one of the most important of the societies for the promption of German interests abroad —the *Centralverein für Handelsgeographie und Förderung deutscher Interessen im Auslande*, the main objects of which were the study of those countries in which organized German settlements already existed, the promotion of emigration to districts where the conditions were favourable to German settlement, and the establishment of trade and navigation and the *acquisition of colonies*.

But in 1876, through the initiative of Leopold, King of the Belgians, the movement received its greatest impetus. Posing as the friend of the oppressed, the Belgian King summoned an international conference at Brussels for the purpose of discussing the problems connected with the future of Africa. After lengthy discussions, in which Nachtigal, Rohlfs, and Schweinfurth took part, a scheme was drawn up for concerted and co-ordinated action with respect to the exploration of the immense districts covered by the term Central Africa ; and the immediate outcome was the foundation of the International Congo Association, which afterwards developed into the Congo Free State and degenerated into one of the most awful instruments for the degradation of mankind and destruction of personal liberty that the world has ever seen.

It would have been thought that, with the opening

of Africa, opportunities would have been presented for cordial co-operation between the chief European Powers in the great work of civilizing the Continent. Unfortunately, however, the Germans, instead of pursuing an open and straightforward policy, descended to methods of intrigue unworthy of a great nation, whilst Great Britain, and more particularly the mercantile community, were unwilling to welcome the presence of an intruder in regions where British interests were already well established. The result was an unfortunate and undignified scramble for territory, marked with considerable ill-feeling on both sides, which led to a series of misunderstandings and incidents that might have been avoided if the initial steps had been less open to misconstruction. In the founding of colonies there must inevitably be clashing of interests, especially when other nations have acquired or are seeking to acquire territories in the neighbourhood. True statesmanship consists in the reconciliation of these divergent interests and in the conciliation of conflicting claims and apparently irreconcilable desires. At the period in question, there was scarcely any part of the African littoral in which the substantial interests of one or other of the Great Powers were not involved, whilst those of Great Britain, who had been first in the field, were paramount in most of the coastal districts that were worth appropriating. Although there were then many portions of the coast that had not been officially annexed, it was a matter of great difficulty for any Power to acquire fresh territory without paying the most careful attention to the national susceptibilities of some other country. Portugal, resting upon her historic past, sprawled lazily along the African coasts, claiming to exercise control over the most valuable portions of South Central Africa. From the north of the Congo River to the southernmost limit of Angola on the western littoral, and from the River Rovuma to Delagoa Bay on the east coast, she claimed sovereignty on the strength of past discoveries and present occupations, and attempted to secure the vast interior districts separating the two coasts. The basins of two of the largest waterways—the Congo and Zambesi—were within the regions claimed by Portugal. To the north the Sultan of Zanzibar held a precarious and often disputed tenure of land stretching from the limits of Portuguese territory to the coasts of Somaliland, and claimed that his territories, which were in reality only effectively controlled at the ports on the eastern coasts, reached inland as far as Lake Tanganyika. On the western coasts British, French, and German traders were struggling to oust each other from points of vantage, whilst the basin of the Niger and the upper waters of the Nile had fallen under the influence of both France and Britain.

Prior to the acquisition of German South-West Africa, Germans, acting with or without the secret support of the German Government, were intriguing to obtain territory in the neighbourhood of the British colonies in South Africa. Ernst von Weber, writing in 1879, had called attention to the opportunities which existed for obtaining a footing on the Sub-Continent, owing to the supposed affinity of the Boers to the German population of the Fatherland. He uttered in writing the opinion held by a not inconsiderable section of German residents in South Africa, and from the practical standpoint elaborated the theories which were held by Treitschke. Ignoring the possibility of German intervention in Damaraland, he concentrated his attention upon the opportunity which existed for acquiring a German settlement on the south-east coast of South Africa and of obtaining from Portugal the invaluable harbour at Delagoa Bay—the maritime key to the Transvaal. It has always been a favourite theory with the Germans—a theory which has lately been put into active practice—that the Boer population, smarting under the injustice of British rule, would be prepared to welcome German intervention and to foster, apparently blinded to the real objects of the movement, the establishment of a powerful German colony in their immediate neighbourhood. To put the matter frankly, von Weber and his associates advocated the flooding of South Africa, and especially the Transvaal, with German immigrants, so that eventually the country might become a German province and, when fully ripe, fall into the German net.

In an article in the *Geographische Nachrichten*, von Weber stated that ' a new empire, possibly more valuable and more brilliant than even the Indian Empire, awaits, in the newly discovered Central Africa, that Power which shall possess sufficient courage, strength, and intelligence to acquire it '; and he continued that, ' in South-East Africa we Germans have a peculiar interest, for here dwell a splendid race of people nearly allied to us by speech and habits . . . pious folk, with their energetic, strongly marked, and expressive heads, they recall the portraits of Rubens, Teniers, Ostade, and Vaneyck . . . and one may speak of a nation of Africanders or Low-German Africans which forms one sympathetic race from Table Mountain to the Limpopo. What could not such a country ', he exclaimed, ' become if in the course of time it were filled with German immigrants ? The constant mass immigration of Germans

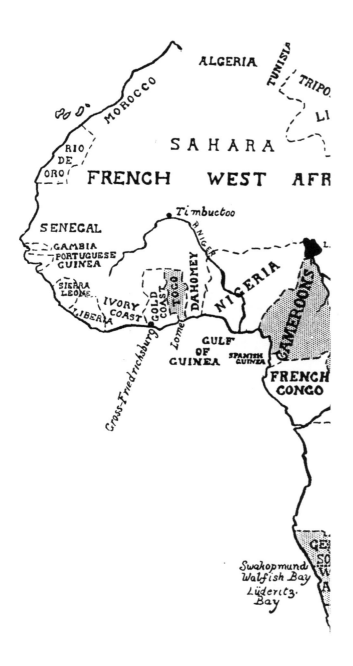

would gradually bring about a decided numerical preponderance of Germans, and of itself would by degrees affect the Germanization of the country in a peaceful manner.'

At the time of the first British annexation of the Transvaal, Kruger, afterwards President of the South African Republic, and Dr. Jorissen, had made a pilgrimage to Berlin with the object of obtaining German intervention; and at a later period, after the Boer War of 1881, another deputation, consisting of Kruger and Dr. Du Toit, again visited Berlin (1884), where they were most cordially received by Bismarck and the Emperor. At the time of the Jameson Raid similar efforts were made to secure German support. But these intrigues, as is well known, were fruitless. In South Africa itself, however, three determined efforts were made to establish a footing—at Delagoa Bay, St. Lucia Bay, and Pondoland. At St. Lucia Bay, a shallow harbour on the coast of Zululand, Herr Lüderitz, who successfully established himself at Angra Pequena on the opposite coast, endeavoured to found a trading settlement. Through his agent, Herr Einwald, he obtained from Dinuzulu a grant of a considerable tract of territory; but the British Government, forewarned, hoisted the British flag before Lüderitz could bring his intrigues to a successful conclusion. Sir Donald Currie, speaking before the Royal Colonial Institute on April 10, 1888, stated that ' the German Government would have secured St. Lucia Bay and the coast-line between Natal and the possessions of Portugal, had not the British Government telegraphed instructions to dispatch a gunboat from Capetown with orders to hoist the British flag at St. Lucia Bay. It would be easy for me to give particulars ', he continued, ' of the pressure which had to be put on the late Government to secure this result.'

In Pondoland an attempt was made by a Dresden merchant to establish one of the trading settlements favoured by Bismarck ; but here again the British Government fortunately successfully intervened. ' You can easily imagine ', said Sir Donald Currie, ' what issues would be raised by the introduction of foreign authority in Pondoland, separating as it would the Cape from Natal.'

These attempts and the long series of German intrigues in South Africa were indicative of the determination of Germans to acquire territory in a country which they believed would shortly pass from British control. They led to an embittered feeling between British and Germans in South Africa, and indirectly contributed to the unfortunate relations which were the outcome of the successful attempts of Germany to found colonies in other parts of the Continent.

III.—How Germany obtained her African Colonies

' If Germany is to become a colonizing Power,' said Gladstone in the House of Commons, ' all I say is, God speed her. She becomes our ally and partner in the execution of the great purposes of Providence for the advantage of mankind.' This pious aspiration typified the conciliatory attitude adopted by the Gladstone-Granville-Derby administration after—but not before—Germany had definitely committed herself to a policy of colonial expansion in Africa. Yet it was apparently wrung unwillingly from the British premier ; for Granville during the time he had acted as Foreign Secretary had done nothing to facilitate German plans for acquiring territory in Africa, unless his policy of vacillation and his unwillingness to depart from the dilatory methods of the Foreign Office or to decide upon a forward move in South Africa may be considered as a calculated aid to the German colonial movement. In South Africa, where Germany obtained her first colony, the British Government only advanced the frontiers of British territory when strong and continuous pressure was exerted upon them. Residents well acquainted with the needs of the country were fully persuaded that, if British interests were to be maintained, a strong and vigorous policy of expansion was necessary.

But the British Government were unwilling to sanction an advance, believing that no other Power was likely to seek territory in the neighbourhood and fearing that any forward movement would lead to fresh troubles with the Boers and might bring about a further series of native wars. They had already been called upon to expend large sums of money in the suppression of the Kafir War of 1877, the Basuto War of 1879, and the contemporary war in Zululand. Sir Bartle Frere had indeed written in 1878 to Lord Carnarvon, then Colonial Secretary, that ' you must be master, as representative of the sole sovereign Power, up to the Portuguese frontier, on both the east and west coasts. There is no escaping from the responsibility which has been already incurred ever since the English flag was planted on the castle here. All our difficulties have arisen, and still arise, from attempting to evade or shift this responsibility.' But his warnings were unheeded and no attention was paid to his representations as to German designs upon Damaraland and Namaqualand. The Imperial Government wished to place the responsibility upon the Cape Ministry, who were unwilling to undertake the expense of administering the territory which was subsequently to pass into other hands.

The attitude of Lord Granville gave Bismarck the opportunity he sought. For some years German missionaries and traders had been operating in Damaraland ; and although they, in common with the natives, had at first petitioned for an extension of British authority over the country, they subsequently and naturally turned to Berlin, where it was felt that their representations would be more sympathetically received. All the British Government had done to meet their wishes had been to sanction the sending of Mr. Coates Palgrave as Special Commissioner to the tribes north of the Orange River. He on his return to Cape Town reported in favour of an immediate annexation. In the meantime, whilst the Cape Government hesitated and whilst the Foreign Office definitely stated in reply to the German Government that British responsibility in Damaraland and Namaqualand was strictly limited to Walfish Bay, the weapon was being forged at Berlin with which the South African oyster was to be forced open. It cannot be doubted that Herr Lüderitz, before establishing his trading settlement at Angra Pequena, now known as Lüderitz Bay, had carefully sounded the German authorities ; whilst it is quite certain that he had the enthusiastic support of a large section of the German colonial party.

It is not possible to describe here the negotiations which led to the hoisting of the German flag in Damaraland.[1] It is sufficient to state that they were unduly prolonged and reflected little credit upon the diplomatic ability of the British Foreign Office. They at once revealed to the world the ability with which Bismarck

[1] A full account is contained in my article ' The First German Colony ', in the *Nineteenth Century* for November, 1914.

had turned to German advantage a situation which, but for British procrastination, might have ended very differently. They also demonstrated the strength and intensity of the German colonial movement, and showed that Germany had at length determined to play an important part in the opening of Africa to European civilization. The official announcement that Germany had definitely entered upon the colonial scramble was made at Cape Town on April 25, 1884. Two months later Prince Bismarck defined his policy in connexion with the founding of colonies. Acting on the principle that ' the flag follows the merchant ', he stated that, whilst it was not his intention to found provinces, he would extend the protection of the Empire to German trading establishments in territories not already in the occupation of any European Power. ' The whole question of German colonization ', he said, ' has necessitated a thorough examination of the subject. He was entirely opposed to the creation of colonies on what he considered the bad system of acquiring a piece of ground, appointing officials and a garrison, and then seeking to entice persons to come and live there.' His policy was to found ' mercantile settlements which would be placed under the protection of the Empire '. Moreover, he complained that he had not been treated fairly by Britain, a feeling which ' was strengthened by the explanations which several English statesmen have given, with the purport that England has a legitimate right to prevent settlements by other nations in the vicinity of English possessions and that England establishes a sort of Monroe Doctrine for Africa against the vicinage of other nations '.[1]

The foundation of German South-West Africa was the

---

[1] German White Book, June 10, 1884.

signal for an immediate scramble for territory. Even before the official announcement had been made, Dr. Nachtigal, charged with a special mission, owing to ' the evident need felt that the interests of German commerce should not be left to the protection of trading consuls ',[1] left Kiel in the gunboat *Möwe*, accompanied by the African traveller Dr. Buchner, in order to hoist the German flag in West Africa. He arrived at the settlement of Little Popo, and after making arrangements with the paramount chief of Togoland declared the country a German Protectorate on July 5, 1884. He then proceeded to the Kamerun country, a district in which British interests were firmly established, and where the two chieftains King Bell and King Acqua had frequently petitioned for British protection, and succeeded in persuading the natives, by means of substantial payments of money, to agree that their country should be placed under German control. When the British consul arrived on July 19, it was to find that he had been forestalled, for the German flag had been flying for five days and the Kamerun colony had been definitely acquired by Germany.

This action, in a country which British traders had long regarded as their own peculiar sphere, aroused keen resentment amongst the mercantile community. British Chambers of Commerce, and particularly those at London, Glasgow, Bristol, and Liverpool, as well as the African Association, passed vigorously worded protests ; but Lord Granville was obliged to accept the situation, and on October 23 he wrote that the Government ' being solely actuated by the desire to secure freedom of trade for all countries in the Cameroon district, are far from

---

[1] *Nord-Deutsche Zeitung*, April 21, 1884.

viewing with distrust the recent movements of German agents ', and suggested that ' the Protectorate already acquired by Germany in the neighbourhood of the Cameroons should be extended over the adjoining rivers in a southerly direction '. Lord Granville was aware that continued opposition to German designs would only lead to a close colonial understanding between Germany and France to the ultimate detriment of British interests. At the same time he was unable to pursue a vigorous policy owing to the threatening position of affairs in Egypt.

Britain and Germany were about to advance upon converging lines, and it was apparent that questions of the greatest moment would arise when and if these lines of advance should cross each other. Britain was then establishing herself in Egypt, and the ideal of a great British territory stretching from north to south—an object which Cecil Rhodes had at heart when he worked for the acquisition of the countries to the north of the Transvaal—was incompatible with the secret desire of Germany to establish a Central African empire, with harbours on the western and eastern coasts and occupying the territory that was then being explored in the Congo regions. The idea underlying the prophecy of Gladstone (in 1877) that ' our first site in Egypt, be it by larceny or be it by emption, will be the almost certain egg of a North African empire that will grow and grow . . . till we finally join hands across the Equator with Natal and Cape Colony ' appealed with peculiar force to patriotic Britons, but its accomplishment was naturally fraught with grave dangers.

A question of this magnitude could not be settled by founding coastal establishments without eventually leading to international complications. Lord Granville attempted to checkmate German plans by negotiating a treaty with Portugal and recognizing the claims of that country to the mouth of the Congo ; but Bismarck successfully intervened, and acting on a hint from Lisbon, and in concert with France, he issued invitations to an international conference to consider the whole question involved in the partition of Africa. The British Government, smarting under their initial diplomatic defeat and fearful lest Germany and France should already have come to some arrangement prejudicial to British interests, did not immediately accept the invitation but afterwards agreed to discuss the question with other interested Powers. The celebrated Berlin Conference met under the presidency of Prince Bismarck on November 15, 1884, and after lengthy discussions agreed to a General Act, approved by the representatives of Germany, Belgium, Denmark, Spain, the United States, France, Great Britain, Italy, Holland, Portugal, Russia, Sweden and Norway, and Turkey. The Conference laid down certain rules that should be followed when new territory was acquired in Africa ; recognized the important principle that all occupations on the coast in order to be valid should be effective ; and established the doctrine of ' spheres of influence '—a convenient term that came into use at this period to designate territory which, whilst not precisely under the control of any European Power, was yet of importance as an area of communication with other regions, or whose inhabitants were more or less under European influence, commercial or missionary as the case might be. The decisions of the Berlin Conference at once relieved the diplomatic tension.

Whilst the Conference was sitting, three of the most active workers on behalf of German oversea expansion, Dr. Karl Peters, Dr. Jühlke, and Count Pfeil, were journeying under false names and as third-class passengers from Trieste to Zanzibar, with the secret object of founding a colony in East Africa. They acted on their own responsibility and with little active encouragement from the ˌ German Government. Peters, the leader of the expedition, had at first suggested to Bismarck that they should acquire the Comoros, a group of islands to the north of Madagascar; and when the Chancellor, desirous of maintaining the most friendly relations with France, had warned him that he could not permit any interference with the French ' sphere of influence ', Peters had suggested that, as the French had not thought it worth while to fight for the recovery of Metz and Strassburg, they were not likely to do so for the Comoros and Sakalavaland. The three associates, however, were determined to secure a new territory for the Empire. Within a few weeks after their arrival at Zanzibar, they had obtained cessions of territory from several native chieftains on the mainland (who were generally quite unaware of the consequences of their acts and in any case preferred unlimited spirits to legal documents), and by means of duly attested papers they acquired a considerable block of country with full rights of sovereignty.[1] The society of which they were the representatives received an Imperial Charter of Protection on February 17, 1885. In the meantime the British Government had become alive to the dangers of the situation, especially when Gerhard Rohlfs was sent to Zanzibar early in 1885, charged with a special mission as Consul-General. During the year British and German expeditions were

---

[1] The Society for German Colonization (*Gesellschaft für deutsche Kolonisation*) was formed by Dr. Peters, Count Pfeil, and Count Behr-Banddin early in 1884, and afterwards developed into the German East Africa Association (*Ostafrikanische Gesellschaft*).

active in every part of East Africa. No less than eleven
German expeditions left Zanzibar for the mainland, and
in spite of the opposition of the Sultan secured enormous
tracts of territory. After negotiations at Zanzibar,
during which Colonel, now Viscount, Kitchener represented the British Government, the territories of the
Sultan were defined ; and by the important agreement of
1890 [1] the boundaries of German and British East Africa
were settled so as to include in German territory the
fertile district around Mount Kilimanjaro, a country
which was also claimed by Britain, whilst Witu,[2] a
country to the north of the Tana River, which had been
acquired by two Germans named Denhardt, was recognized as within the British sphere. The rights of the
Sultan of Zanzibar over the coast lands were also recog-

---

[1] Under this important agreement the respective British and
German spheres of influence in Africa were clearly defined, and the
island of Zanzibar was recognized as a British protectorate. It was
in recognition of this ' friendly' action of the German Chancellor
(Caprivi) that Lord Salisbury made the fatal mistake of ceding
Heligoland to Germany, behind the shelter of which her navy is able
to remain in comparative safety. Germany had been anxious to
secure Heligoland as early as 1884, when certain ' clever people '
had suggested to Bismarck that Britain might be willing to exchange
it for Damaraland. A suggestion for the cession of Heligoland was
actually made by Count Munster, then German Ambassador, to
Lord Granville on May 17, 1884. Under this agreement Germany
also secured what is known as the ' Caprivi strip', a block of territory
stretching inland from the north of German South-West Africa,
ostensibly obtained to give the Germans access to the upper waters
of the Zambesi, but in reality intended to form a wedge dividing
the Bechuanaland Protectorate from Angola and North-Western
Rhodesia.

[2] In a memorandum from Count Münster to Lord Granville it was
asserted that in the year 1867, Sultan Simba of Witu had requested
the Prussian Government, through the African traveller Richard
Brenner, to take him under its protection.

nized, although under pressure he was compelled to lease the littoral to the contending parties.

Thus, within less than a year, Germany had obtained four important footholds on the African continent, which by the process of accretion were developed into the enormous territories over which she held undisputed sway until the outbreak of the present war. Her empire in Africa, acquired through the foresight and energy of her merchants and explorers and held owing to the vigorous and spirited action of Bismarck, had an area of 1,028,000 square miles, as large as Germany, Austria-Hungary, France, England, Spain, Portugal, and Italy combined, but nevertheless far smaller in extent than the African possessions of either Britain or France.

IV.—The Value of the German African Colonies.

It has frequently been assumed that Germany in acquiring her colonial possessions in Africa only secured territories which other countries had considered more or less worthless. This may be true with regard to German South-West Africa, where the long stretch of desert coast-line—an absolutely sterile belt varying in width between thirty and fifty miles, with only one good harbour at Walfish Bay [1]—had supported the erroneous impression that most of the interior was useless for agricultural purposes ; but it is certainly incorrect so far as Togoland, Kamerun, and German East Africa are concerned. By obtaining these three territories Germany secured most valuable tropical storehouses, where the products needed for her growing

---

[1] Walfish Bay and a small surrounding strip of territory were proclaimed a British possession in 1878 and annexed to Cape Colony in 1884.

industries could be successfully cultivated. It would be idle to suppose that Germany was actuated by philanthropic motives in extending her sway over the native races of Africa. Nor was the idea of some of the leaders of the colonial party, that German colonies would form an outlet for her surplus population, destined to be realized, partly because the colonies in Africa were not suited for any extensive schemes of European settlement, with the exception of South-West Africa, and partly because, owing to the great increase of prosperity in the Fatherland, emigration practically ceased. As a matter of fact the demand for labour increased to such an extent that, instead of sending forth emigrants to settle in her colonies, Germany has actually imported labour from Galicia and other provinces to serve her own industrial needs. For some years immigration into the Fatherland has largely exceeded any loss of population occasioned by emigration. In all the German colonies there were only about 24,000 European inhabitants in the year 1913; and of these over 15,000, including the military garrison, were settled in German South-West Africa. Germany's African possessions, therefore, may be almost exclusively regarded as plantations.

Taking them in their order round the African coasts, the first, Togoland, in spite of its small area of some 33,700 square miles, has long been regarded as a model colony, not only because it produces large quantities of palm-oil and kernels, cotton, rubber, and cocoa, but also because the natives, unlike those of other German colonies, have given little trouble and have been contented and prosperous. The colonial Government has always laid great stress upon the cultivation of indigenous and other products; and the country contains a network of roads which for cheapness and

excellence of construction are unrivalled anywhere in
West Africa. Situated between the British colony of
the Gold Coast and the French colony of Dahomey, it
forms a valuable wedge of territory capable of great
economic expansion ; for less than one-tenth of the
palm-oil that might be obtained is annually collected,
whilst not one - quarter of the country has yet been
geologically surveyed.

The great territory of Kamerun which stretches from
Lake Chad in the north to the Ubangi and Congo rivers
in the south, and a large portion of which is contained
in the geographical basin of the latter river, is also of
great importance as a plantation-colony, being capable
of producing vast quantities of rubber, cocoa, palm-oil,
bananas, and coffee. The entry of the Germans into
this territory was marked by trouble with the natives, and
the policy of the Government has not been altogether
successful in overcoming this initial set-back. Further
along the coast German South-West Africa, stretching
from the confines of Portuguese territory to the Orange
River, is more suitable for agricultural and pastoral
settlement. Here the Germans have built important
railways—not without an eye to their strategic importance in the event of an invasion of Cape Colony—but
their economic progress has been hampered owing to
the fact that the native labour-supply was almost
entirely destroyed during the long war with the Hereros,
or Damaras, when German methods of warfare were
revealed in their most unfavourable aspect. As Professor Bonn, of Munich, has said :—' In South-West
Africa we solved the native problem by smashing tribal
life and by creating a scarcity of labour.' The most
conclusive evidence of Germany's failure to administer
this territory for the benefit of its native inhabitants is

furnished by the fact that, prior to the year 1898, the native population was estimated by the then Governor, Colonel Leutwein, to be about three hundred thousand, whereas in 1912. it was estimated at a little over one hundred thousand, of whom the Ovambo, a warlike tribe in the north who have not yet come into active conflict with the Germans, furnished about two-thirds. Prince Bismarck foresaw the possibility of the introduction of too much ' iron ' into Germany's dealings with the dependent peoples of her new colonies. In other words, being well aware of the peculiarities of the Prussian bureaucratic mind, he feared that Prussian methods were not quite suited to the sunnier clime of Africa. So far as South-West Africa is concerned, his forebodings have been abundantly justified, for the Damaras and Namaquas were practically destroyed, whilst a pitiful remnant was driven into the fastnesses of the Kalahari Desert, there to die of slow starvation. Nevertheless, German South-West Africa is the only German colony where agricultural settlers, as distinct from owners of large plantations such as are settled in German East Africa and especially in the Kilimanjaro districts, have secured any measure of success. Entirely apart from its agricultural possibilities, the country is rich in minerals, and the discovery of diamonds in 1906 at once gave a decided value to the sterile districts around Lüderitz Bay.

It is in German East Africa, however, that Germany possesses her most valuable African colony. This great country, almost twice as large as the Fatherland, possesses a number of excellent harbours, such as those at Tanga, Dar-es-Salam, Kilwa, and Lindi, and stretches inland to the four great lakes of Victoria Nyanza, Kiwu, Tanganyika, and Nyasa—an incomparable waterway for the products of the interior. By constructing a railway from Dar-es-Salam, through Tabora, to Kigoma (near Ujiji) on Lake Tanganyika—a railway built at remarkable speed and only recently completed—Germany hoped to tap the rich interior districts and to divert to the eastern coasts much of the agricultural and mineral produce from Katanga, the southern portion of the Belgian Congo. Another railway from Tanga to Moschi is opening out, the great agricultural country around the slopes of Mount Kilimanjaro. The mineral wealth of the country is as yet almost entirely undeveloped, although gold, mica, and soda have been found in considerable quantities ; whilst the forest and agricultural products are capable of enormous development.

These four colonies, whatever may be their ultimate destiny, are a rich prize of ever-increasing value, and will ultimately form vast economic reserves for the production of the materials needed to feed the European industrial machine. When they and some of our African possessions were acquired, it needed the eye of faith to foresee their economic importance ; but no one acquainted with the industrial system of to-day, and able to realize the vast extension of commerce that must occur as the world advances in material civilization, can now fail to understand the importance of Central Africa to the future of mankind. Central Africa, with the western and eastern coasts, will be the prize of the strongest and most fully equipped European nations.

Oxford : Horáce Hart Printer to the University

WHY WE ARE AT WAR
GREAT BRITAIN'S CASE

BY MEMBERS OF THE OXFORD FACULTY
OF MODERN HISTORY

E. BARKER.   H. W. C. DAVIS.

C. R. L. FLETCHER.   ARTHUR HASSALL.

L. G. WICKHAM LEGG.   F. MORGAN.

With an Appendix of Original Documents
including the Authorized English Translation
of the White Book issued by the
German Government

THIRD EDITION REVISED (EIGHTH IMPRESSION)
CONTAINING THE RUSSIAN ORANGE BOOK AND
EXTRACTS FROM THE BELGIAN GREY BOOK

TRANSLATIONS INTO FRENCH ITALIAN SPANISH
GERMAN AND SWEDISH ARE
NOW READY

Paper Covers Two Shillings net (70 cents)
Cloth Two Shillings and Sixpence net (85 cents)

OXFORD: AT THE CLARENDON PRESS
LONDON: HUMPHREY MILFORD
EDINBURGH   GLASGOW   NEW YORK   TORONTO
MELBOURNE   BOMBAY

(*a*)

OXFORD PAMPHLETS
1914–1915

THE CHURCH AND
THE WAR

BY THE

BISHOP OF LINCOLN

Price Twopence net

OXFORD UNIVERSITY PRESS

HUMPHREY MILFORD

LONDON   EDINBURGH   GLASGOW

NEW YORK   TORONTO   MELBOURNE   BOMBAY

THE CHURCH AND THE WAR[1]

THE outbreak of a tremendous European war is a challenge to the nation in every department of its common life : it becomes a touchstone of our patriotism, our unity, our physical strength, of the intelligence and energy of our people, of our resources in every kind of wealth. But it is more : it is a challenge to our ideals. Our moral and religious convictions find here a searching and inevitable test.

To many of us who had hoped and laboured for international peace, and especially for friendship with Germany, the war comes as a terrible shock, upsetting all our plans, and setting back the European clock ; destroying in a moment all the efforts of two generations. Gradually but surely there had grown up among us an ideal of international brotherhood, of mutual understanding, through which the European nations might cease from being like crouching panthers waiting to spring upon their prey, and might begin to live in amity. The stupidity of war, its cruelties, its social and other mischiefs, its essential futility—all this seemed so obvious that we wondered men were so slow to learn it. In the life of individual citizens private vengeance, and even private self-defence, have given place to the law of the community, whose decisions are enforced by a common sanction. Was it unreasonable to hope that by degrees the principle of law and the voice of collective humanity (or some organized portion of humanity

[1] Reprinted, by permission, from the *Political Quarterly* of December 1914.

like the European nations) should be capable of enthron-
ing public law so strongly in the midst as to make
appeal to warfare needless, absurd, and impossible ?

Such were our hopes. They have been rudely stricken
down. Violence has broken out and is being repulsed
by violence. Nearly all the European nations are
embroiled in the conflict. Christendom perhaps never
before exhibited so hideous and shameful a spectacle.
What has the Church to say to it ? Is Christianity
helpless ? Is the Gospel bankrupt ? I want to answer
this question as one who has passed through the gloom
of the first days of the war, as if stunned, but having
been stunned is recovering from the shock, and begins
to open his eyes to the light of day and the living facts
of life.

We may derive consolation first of all from the
attitude of our statesmen. The Prime Minister in his
speech at Dublin laid it down with emphasis that this
war·has, and must have, for its object the dethrone-
ment of violence, the exaltation of law and justice, by
means of arbitration, as the appeal of nations. His
noble utterance has received confirmation from the
language of his colleagues. We are at war not only to
defend the neutrality of Belgium, not only to defend
the existence and independence of small nationalities.
We stand not only for the defence of France from
wanton attack, and thereby defend our own freedom
as a people ; but we avow it as our resolve, should
God grant victory to the Allies and permit us a ·pre-
vailing voice in the settlement of terms of Peace, to
make a war like the present impossible in the future,
and this not by merely crushing one or two peoples,
but by securing international good understanding and
a very large measure of general disarmament.

It is because we have entered upon the war in this spirit, and with these aims, that we feel able to invoke upon our effort the benediction of God, of a God who is the God of all the nations of the earth, and the Father of all our brother men. For we did not want to go to war. It accords with none of our aims and ambitions. We sought no territory, we looked for no reward in gold or in glory. The only hope we have as we bid good-bye to our sons on their way to the front, is the hope of ridding Europe, and ourselves and the German people also, from the curse of Prussian militarism. This is why the nation has entered upon the war in so calm, grave, and resolute a spirit. The issue means life or death to all the ideals we hold dear. Our people in general have displayed a wonderful spirit of quiet courage, without noise or bluster. If we may speak on behalf of the Christian public, we seem to have found and exhibited an austere faith in God, such as speaks well for the character of our people. The churches and chapels are filling, and are frequented at unusual times ; the clergy are more than busy with praying, preaching, and leading their people in all kinds of charitable activity. If pleasures and amusements have become impossible through lack of means, or distasteful through a sense of nearing danger, their place has become more than filled by the sense of service, the joy of doing kindnesses. The Christian spirit is spreading wide and deep.

But also, as the war opened, and the invaders supplied us with the evidence of their national temper and aim, as with Bernhardi in our hands, or Professor Cramb to guide us, we studied the doings of the German armies in Belgium, we began to interpret these hideous phenomena, and to understand what the war really meant. It is avowedly the outcome of a theory of history, and of a conception of ethics in violent contrast with anything like the moral ideas hitherto preached and to some extent followed in Christian Europe. That Christian ideals are impossible, that the Gospel has nothing to do with international conduct, that Germany made an initial mistake in adopting the decadent creed of her decadent Roman conquerors, that Thor and Odin are or should be the national deities and not the Christ of the Gospels, that war is the outcome of all noble nationalism, its flower and fruit, that the virility and splendour of the German race surpass all else of the kind in the world, that Germany takes the lead in all the things of the mind, that German culture is called upon, by its superiority to all other types of civilization, to impress itself forcibly upon all mankind —this was and is the Prussian creed to be thundered from the cannon's mouth and enforced by universal conquest. It was high time, therefore, that Britain, tired of Eimpre, weary with long wars of conquest and perpetual annexations, rent by internal dissensions, incapable of strong government, already enfeebled by luxury, decrepit with age, should be shaken and shattered by the German legions and her Empire pass to abler and better hands. For this purpose Belgium was to be the avenue to the conquest of Paris and France, and from France the way would be open for the real objective, the humiliation of England. All this we soon grasped, not as a hideous dream, but as the deliberate programme of a Christian and civilized neighbour. Of course these ideas were not new to us : they existed in German literature. In reviews and in translations, at the least, these horrible notions had been brought to our knowledge. But one thing we had not grasped, for it was incredible : we had no idea that these hideous views had been adopted by the German Government, that they were approved by the German intellectuals, that they were shaping German policy at home and abroad. But as soon as we knew it, we felt that this war, awful as it is in its extent, and its sacrifices, and momentous as will be its results, is yet a war forced upon us by a nation gone mad, a nation possessed by a horrible idea, a nation that should be our friend but had become our bitterest foe. And therefore we have entered upon the war not only in self-defence but in defence of the old moralities, and to vindicate conceptions of national duty that, so far from being obsolete, were growing in public importance and were fast developing into a wider and deeper sense of international obligation. The Hague tribunal was one, and only one, embodiment of the further hope of Christianizing and moralizing international relationship. But the waves of war have swept over all these hopes. History has received a strange set-back.

We British people are not wholly innocent in this matter. We have had our militarists, and we have them with us still. There is one important section of the press which never fails to deride the friends of peace and proclaim the splendours of war, and seldom can forget the doctrines and language which were once named jingoistic. And the source of this tendency goes back rather far. Thomas Carlyle constantly proclaimed the importance of the great man, the great man with the ' big stick ', and as constantly he derided democracy and parliamentary government. His greatest consecutive work was the *Life of Frederick the Great*, whom he always hails as the one great ruler of his age.

That Carlyle would approve of the heathenish and barbarous doctrine of present-day Germany I by no means imagine or assert. But it is clear enough that his exaltation of one-man government and his contempt for the people served as a prelude to the harsher doctrines of modern Prussia. And therefore there is the highest need for us all to clear our minds of the cant of militarism and to fortify our faith in freedom, and in constitutionalism, and in the people. For it is important to observe that our strength in this hour of danger, in this deadly conflict with the foe, is derived precisely from our prevailing Imperial policy, which was the reverse of military or jingoist and proceeded on lines of freedom, of democracy, and of popular government. Why do Canada, Australia, New Zealand send us their sons to help us ? Precisely because they are free ; they are tied to us less by constitutional bonds than by their own will ; their loyalty is the loyalty of free choice, of personal affection. Why is Ireland eager to be at the front with us ? Because England is committed to an emancipated Ireland. Why is South Africa making a splendid response, leaders and people ? Because a democratic England wiped out the memories of a miserable war by a grant of constitutional liberty. Why is India giving us such powerful and magnificent aid ? Because there also, in spite of manifold difficulties and many mistakes, India's peoples prefer the Raj of Britain to any other nation ; if India must be subject, she would prefer England, not Prussia because she desires more freedom and not less.[1]

[1] A missionary in Calcutta writes thus : ' The student community is a very good political thermometer ; it indicates the popular temperature. Indeed, it is more than a thermometer, for it helps

We dare not say we have no international crimes to confess, no useless wars, and even wars of aggression to be laid at our door. But nations, like individuals, grow not only in strength and in experience but also in moral ideals. We have been led by a Gladstone, at the very time when Germany was being led by a Bismarck. The creed of the latter was the creed of blood and iron ; the other believed in human nature, in freedom, in justice, and in international brotherhood. There were many in that day who laughed at Gladstone's idealism, or called it hypocrisy ; there were many even on this side of the North Sea who professed their faith in brute force, in a strong policy, in efficiency, in ' Empire ', and so forth. But the war of to-day—if by God's mercy it ends as we pray and hope—will be the *reductio ad absurdum* of the Prussian policy of Frederick the Great, of Bismarck, and of William II. Our safety as a nation, and as an Empire, will have

to create the atmosphere which it indicates. All over India great meetings have been held ; there is no doubt of their spontaneity or of their enthusiasm. One student was speaking to me very candidly. "If we must have any foreign Power over us," said he, "and we know that we must, we want England." And then he added, "Suppose that there had been any other power ruling India when that bomb was thrown at the Viceroy and he was nearly killed, we know that the troops would have been let loose on the people to cut them down ; but all that Lord Hardinge said, when his body was torn and bleeding, was, 'I have not lost my faith in the Indian people.' " I have never heard anything like that said by an Indian before. I did not know that they secretly regarded it as an act of great forbearance that the troops had not been let loose to punish the city where the outrage had taken place ; but it is certain that the Viceroy's love of India and faith in India, manifested at a moment when his pain might have concentrated his thoughts on his own suffering and disappointment, have contributed something to the loyalty of India to Great Britain in this hour of her great trial.'

been secured just because in our dealings with other people we have followed in a large degree a policy the very reverse of the Prussian, and have been devotees of democracy, of freedom, and of the popular vote. The loyalty of South Africa, despite the seditious machinations of German agents, is the most wonderful and convincing justification of the policy pursued by us after the deplorable Boer War, the policy which undid at start the political mischief of the war and gave freedom to the provinces we had conquered. Germany could not have done this, neither was it supported in Parliament by our British militarists. It was carried by a democratic vote in a very democratic House of Commons. But it has saved the Empire.

But while we plead the justice and necessity of our action in this war, and declare our hands to be clean and our motives generous, let us be well assured that a nation engaged in a bloody war can seldom escape the Nemesis of spiritual deterioration. To become accustomed to acts of bloodshed, to read daily of scenes of carnage, to be obliged to rejoice in the news of sinking ships, of the blowing up of troop-trains, and the intercepting of communications—all this must tend to blunt the moral sense and to make callous the spirit of compassion. We begin to hate our enemies and all that pertains to them. The sense of human brotherhood is dulled and extinguished. There is a common fallacy that war ennobles, exalts, purifies the sentiment of a nation. The fact is quite the reverse. The energies of unselfish charity, the labours of wise benevolence, the efforts of the teacher and the educational organizer, the self-sacrificing career of the social and moral reformer—usually derided as a crank or disliked as a fanatic until, too late for him, he is hailed as a benefactor—these are the elements in a community which make for progress, for enlightenment, for moral elevation. Nor is personal courage more developed by war than by the example of our thousands of colliers, quarrymen, sailors, and others who constantly carry their life in their hands in pursuing their daily vocations, and who when a mate is knocked over by an accident exhibit extraordinary courage in endeavouring to rescue him. And to these we may add unrecorded examples occurring like them in the ranks of peaceful duty. What of our doctors and nurses, engaged every hour, night and day, in fever hospitals and amid all forms of infection, whose heroism is called forth by no circumstance of publicity or excitement, and who are upborne by sheer pity for their fellow men, or by professional duty alone ? We do an immense wrong to humanity when we point to war as the great school of courage or self-sacrifice, of devotion to the good of others. We forget the hourly conflict of industrial armies with all the force of the elements, with all the terrific powers of nature. Nor again must we forget that love of fighting is an instinct deeply planted in the British nation : the blood of Vikings, of Danish invaders, of a long ancestry of barbarous warriors runs in our veins. And this instinct has been encouraged since we became a nation by centuries of war. It is the common assertion of German publicists that Britain has ever been a combative Power, and has won her world-wide Empire by the sword. That she pretends now to be tired of fighting is a confession that her day is done. In the sixteenth century she fought and conquered Spain ; in the seventeenth she wrestled with the Dutch ; in the eighteenth she wrested half a world from France. If she is now weary and longs for peace, it is a proof

that she is effete and deserves only herself to be subdued by a younger and stronger people and superseded
in the empire of the world.   Such is the German plea.
Let us frankly confess our barbarous antecedents, our
turbulent career.   But that confession does not bind
us to perpetual militarism.   The Empire which was so
strangely won by force can only be retained by wise
government, by generous extension of liberty, by
home rule, i.e. by consent of the governed.   There
is a dry saying of Tacitus : *nemo flagitiis occupatum
imperium bonis artibus exercuit.* ,Is it not possible
that Great Britain has learned in time rather that
Empire, even if won by force, can only be retained
by freedom, and strengthened by peace ?   In speaking
of the Church in relation to the war, it is essential for
Christian people to be on their guard against a glorifica-
tion of War, and an unconscious depreciation of Peace
—whose victories are far greater than of war though
(in spite of that fact) far less renowned.

If we want to appraise the loss incurred by our country
through the war, we cannot arrive at our conclusion
merely by calculating the numbers of dead and wounded,
the misery and impoverishment of families, the destruction of property, the magnitude of the pecuniary cost
and the vastness of the ultimate scale of debt and taxation.   All these lines of calculation will lead us to
appalling sums of loss.   But even more serious is the
diversion of the thought of the whole people from the
study of social problems to the exclusive reading of
the war news.   We were steadily enlisting the sympathy
of all good people, the interest of scientific students,
the oratory of politicians and the energies of statesmen, on the side of a mighty battle with social and

moral evils. To quote the words of an eminent peace-
lover : ' Far from wishing to destroy the energy or
even the combativeness which has made us such fit
instruments for the battle-field, we [shall] require these
qualities for abating the spirit of war and correcting
the numberless moral evils from which society is suffering.   Are not our people uneducated ?   Juvenile
delinquents uncared for ?   Does not drunkenness still
reel in our streets ?   Have we not to battle with vice,
crime, and their parent ignorance, in every form ?
And may not even Charity display as great energy
and courage in saving life, as was ever put forth in
its destruction ? '   These words were uttered in 1853.

Much still remains to be done to fulfil that noble
prophecy ; but so deeply have the principles of social
reform been impressed upon the modern mind, and so
strongly has it come to be felt that national greatness
is based upon social justice and moral virtue, that our
great military commanders find themselves forced to
be preachers of ethics and reformers of social evils.
The Tsar of Russia, aware of the injury wrought upon
his army by intoxicants in the war with Japan; forbade
all sale of spirit and of beer during the period of mobilization.   The Government of Russia is still so far autocratic
that such a decree could be issued and made effective
in the interests of the army.   And the Government
having years ago assumed the perilous monopoly of
the liquor traffic, such a sweeping law could only be
made by Imperial order.   No doubt it caused individual
hardships and gave a shock to many prejudices and
social customs.   But the drinking habits of Russia
were horrible and bade fair to demoralize the peasantry.
Accordingly this decree issued in the interests of the
army was found immediately to bring a great blessing

to the whole country. Crime suddenly diminished, order reigned, the land was better cultivated, people felt themselves improved in health as well as in pocket, and also labour had increased in productivity by 25 per cent. Such an inflow of moral and economic advantage convinced the nation of the soundness of the decree, and the Tsar has yielded to advice, and made prohibition perpetual. Certainly the onward sweep of the Russian army, so vital to our success, is a powerful argument for Prohibition which is not likely to be lost upon English ears. In France the Government, for similar reasons, has prohibited the sale of absinthe, and in Great Britain an Emergency Act (which would have conferred larger powers had not Mr. McKenna surrendered to the Trade) enables magistrates in any licensing area to close liquor shops as early as 9 P.M. or even earlier by permission of the Home Secretary. Lord Kitchener also, as Minister of War, has issued repeated appeals to the nation requesting that no one will treat recruits or put difficulties in the way of those who wish to keep our soldiers chaste and temperate. None of these facts are likely to be lost on temperance reformers. Social reformers of another type, who desire to see the State take stronger steps in the direction of collectivism, have been startled by the freedom with which the Government has dealt with economic difficulties. Paper currency has been extended, the banks have received all kinds of assistance, our railways have been in a sense taken over by the State, the supply of sugar and foodstuffs has been secured by large Government purchases, and the prices of commodities have been regulated by law. In a word, before we knew where we were we found ourselves living under a condition of State Socialism. And nobody complains :

rather everybody praises the Government for its courage and skill in meeting all emergencies. It seems unlikely that we shall ever be willing to go back again to a situation in which grave social evils were allowed to thrive because we were too timid or too dull to employ State interference for their redress. We have had a taste of Socialism, and we like it. In all these developments the Christian reformer may find reason to thank God and take courage. It is too early to forecast the duration or the precise issue of this vast and momentous conflict. While these words are being written the tide of battle in the East is going against our enemy, and in the West, though the balance trembles from day to day, yet we have reason to hope that it will settle definitely on our side. But be the campaign long or short, we have a right to hope and pray for a victory for our arms, and for all the great human issues committed to our keeping. If so, it is by no means too soon for us to be asking ourselves what are the terms and conditions we should desire to secure, if Providence grant us a powerful voice in the settlement of Peace. Let us answer this question as Christian people with the Sermon on the Mount in our minds.

1. While we dislike and disclaim any motive of revenge, we must insist on the complete overthrow of Prussian militarism ; we must combine to exorcise this spirit of evil from Germany and from all Europe.

2. We must not attempt again to secure peace by any balance of power or new grouping of European States. This method has been found disastrous again and again. To safeguard peace by exalting certain other Powers in place of the Power defeated, would be to prepare the way for the repetition of this awful

war. We must effect some serious disarmament, and secure that no State shall go to war before its grievance has been laid before a European tribunal. All this is difficult, but not impossible if we really wish to have a lasting peace.

3. We must encourage the independence and neutrality of small States. Perhaps Europe may have the advantage of several new Republics and a number of new and lesser States. Small States, though they cannot be conspicuous for great wars or make extensive conquests, have probably rendered greater services to humankind in the achievements of painting, poetry, architecture, and sculpture, not to speak of religion and philosophy, than great Empires. Above all, no population must be handed over to any State without the declared consent of that population. Government must be by the consent of the governed.

4. We must have no secret treaties any more. Our Foreign Policy needs to be democratized. Parliament and the people should know far more about negotiations concerning war and peace. These colossal issues should not depend upon the secret bargainings of a dozen European statesmen. Ours at least is a country of free government and of free speech.

5. If we have learned anything from the conduct of business by firms like Krupp and others, then we shall insist that all manufacture of arms and weapons of war shall be nationalized. It is not consistent with the welfare of any nation that a certain large and wealthy section of its citizens should be able to commercialize war and amass enormous fortunes by fomenting war-scares, thus drawing their profit from the misery of their countrymen. This is the business of a ' Wrecker ' only on a European scale.

These are a few suggestions, written down in hot haste.   Others with larger experience of affairs and more leisured pens will restate our argument with greater skill.   Enough if it has been suggested how a Churchman as a reformer and lover of peace may hold fast to his principles and yet take sides with the Allies in this hideous war.

Oxford : Horace Hart Printer to the University

WHY WE ARE AT WAR

GREAT BRITAIN'S CASE

BY MEMBERS OF THE OXFORD FACULTY OF MODERN HISTORY

E. BARKER. H. W. C. DAVIS.

C. R. L. FLETCHER. ARTHUR HASSALL.

L. G. WICKHAM LEGG. F. MORGAN.

With an Appendix of Original Documents including the Authorized English Translation of the White Book issued by the German Government

THIRD EDITION REVISED (TENTH IMPRESSION) CONTAINING THE RUSSIAN ORANGE BOOK AND EXTRACTS FROM THE BELGIAN GREY BOOK

TRANSLATIONS INTO FRENCH ITALIAN SPANISH GERMAN DANISH AND SWEDISH ARE NOW READY

Paper Covers Two Shillings net (70 cents)
Cloth Two Shillings and Sixpence net (85 cents)

OXFORD: AT THE CLARENDON PRESS
LONDON: HUMPHREY MILFORD
EDINBURGH GLASGOW NEW YORK TORONTO
MELBOURNE BOMBAY

(*a*)

4 30

OXFORD PAMPHLETS
1914

WAR AGAINST WAR

BY

A. D. LINDSAY

THIRD IMPRESSION

Price Twopence net

OXFORD UNIVERSITY PRESS
HUMPHREY MILFORD
LONDON EDINBURGH GLASGOW
NEW YORK TORONTO MELBOURNE BOMBAY

I

The Deeper Causes of the War.

By W. Sanday. 3d. net. *Third Impression.*

The psychology of Prussian militarism ; German public opinion and Germany's aggressive ambitions.

To the Christian Scholars of Europe and America: A Reply from Oxford to the German 'Address to Evangelical Christians'. 2d. net. *Second Impression.*

The answer of Oxford theologians to a recent manifesto of the German evangelical theologians. This manifesto, which is reproduced in the present pamphlet, argues that Germany is in no sense responsible for the present war. The Oxford reply states that the German theologians cannot have studied either the events which led up to the war, or the political utterances of their own countrymen.

The Responsibility for the War. By W. G. S. Adams. 2d. net.

A brief discussion of the question of responsibility : 1. Austria and Serbia ; 2. The responsibility of Russia ; 3. The intervention of England.

Great Britain and Germany.

By Spenser Wilkinson. 2d. net. *Second Impression.*

Three letters to the *Springfield Republican* : 1. By Prof. Spenser Wilkinson, stating Great Britain's case ; 2. By Prof. John W. Burgess of the University of Columbia, stating Germany's case ; 3. By Prof. Wilkinson, in reply to Prof. Burgess.

'Just for a Scrap of Paper.'

By Arthur Hassall. 1d. net. *Third Impression.*

Explains why England stands for the sanctity of European treaty-law.

II

The Germans, their Empire, and how they have made it. By C. R. L. Fletcher. 2d. net. *Third Impression.*

A historical account of Prussian policy from the seventeenth century.

The Germans, their Empire, and what they covet.

By C. R. L. Fletcher. 2d. net. *Third Impression.*

An account of the ambitions avowed by the Pan-German school.

Might is Right. By Sir Walter Raleigh. 2d. net.

Why Germany may win; what will happen if she wins ; why we believe she will not win.

Austrian Policy since 1867. By Murray Beaven. 3d. net.

Austrian policy in the Balkans has been of the 'offensive-defensive' order. The Archduke Francis Ferdinand might have saved Austria from rushing to destruction; but 1912 was the beginning of the end.

Italian Policy since 1870. By Keith Feiling. 2d. net

Italian policy has been and must be guided by her own interests. The results of her colonial policy have not yet been satisfactory enough to tempt her into adventures.

WAR AGAINST WAR

THE war in which we are now engaged has been called 'a war against war'. It is certain that most people in this country have not wished this war but have looked on it as a hateful necessity, and combine with a determination to see the war through a resolve to do all that can be done to prevent such a war recurring. We feel it an intolerable disgrace to Christendom that this thing should have happened. We recognize that for the general condition of Europe which made such a war possible we may, along with other nations, have been partly to blame, yet we hold that in the immediate situation we were guiltless and that it made most for the eventual peace of Europe that we should fight. In that sense we are making war against war, and we can endure all the suffering and horror which war involves if we can sustain ourselves with the hope that we shall make a recurrence of such things impossible for our children, that we shall once for all do away not only with actual wars like the present, but with the restless peace which preceded it, with the wasteful rivalry in armaments, with the uneasy searching after alliances and the balance of power.

It is well therefore that we should ask ourselves what ground we have for our hope, and how we can best realize it. For there are some who say that such a hope is an illusion ; that if we cherish the comfortable belief that we are making war against war we are only refusing to face the facts; that our belief is based on hypocrisy and blindness. Let us therefore examine the arguments of those who hold that war against war is a delusive ideal.

Our critics are of two very different schools. There are those who hold that it is of no use trying to abolish war, for war between nations must always exist; there are others who believe that war is unnecessary and futile but that it cannot be abolished by war (that were to cast out Satan by Satan), but only by our all recognizing the horror and futility of war and refusing to fight. The first would probably approve the present war but laugh at our description of our ideal. The second would approve our ideal but condemn unsparingly the method we have taken to attain it. We must therefore ask ourselves whether or no there need necessarily be war between nations, and if there need not, whether war itself can ever be a weapon against war, can ever help to make war impossible, or at least improbable—if impossible it can never be made. These questions clearly concern the elementary principles which govern the relations of states to one another or the elements of international policy.

We need not deal with our two classes of critics separately. For if we examine the arguments of the first class, we shall probably find that we shall be compelled by the way to answer those of the second.

The supporters of the doctrine that wars are inevitable may be divided into those who hold that war is an evil, though one that cannot be avoided, and those who like General von Bernhardi and some writers and preachers in this country do not want to abolish war. Such persons as the latter must not be confused with those who hold that in certain circumstances war is desirable. Most of us might agree to that but deplore the circumstances which called for war. General von Bernhardi thinks that it would be a catastrophe to mankind if war were abolished; he believes that the natural relations of nations to one another are enmity and competition, which, unlike the envy and competition of individuals, have no higher power to control them, and thinks that such enmity and competition are good in themselves.

The question whether war is in itself a good thing need hardly be discussed. It has plausibility only when war is identified with any kind of competition or struggle and justified on biological grounds. A moment's consideration will show that the growth of civilization and peace has not eliminated struggle and competition, but changed their nature. Progress consists largely in raising the terms on which competition is carried on, and the qualities in which men compete; and in the higher forms of competition co-operation plays a greater and greater part, and the success of one competitor means less and less the death or ruin of the other. We think it a good thing that there should be rivalry between German and French and English culture, and that the best should prevail, but we think that it ought to prevail because it is the best culture, not because those who have made it happen to be more ruthless in war or less scrupulous about treaties than are others.

Now though there may be much that is ignoble as well as much that is noble in the rivalry and competition of peace, no one would deny that the life of a modern nation at peace is better than it would be in a state of internecine strife. No one can disagree with Hobbes's famous description of a time of war where every man's hand is against his neighbour's:

'In such condition there is no place for industry, because the fruit thereof is uncertain ; and consequently no culture of the earth ; no navigation nor use of the commodities that may be imported by sea ; no commodious building ; no instruments of moving and removing such things as require much force ; no knowledge of the face of the earth ; no account of time ; no arts ; no letters ; no society ; and which is worst of all, continual fear and danger of violent death ; and the life of man, solitary, poor, nasty, brutish and short.'

The most inspiriting facts in modern war, the common devotion and patriotism of a whole nation, are possible only because that nation has been at peace with itself. If it fights to defend its culture, that culture is possible only through peace ; for in war, as Thucydides said, we lose that 'margin of everyday life' in which culture can flourish. There is no sense in defending war as a good thing in itself. Even General von Bernhardi does not desire war between the component parts of Germany. All Germans would agree that the united Germany of the end of the nineteenth century is preferable to Germany of the Thirty Years' War.

Further, there can be no sense in saying that men *must* make war on each other, as though that were a fundamental element in their nature. For as we look back in history we can see how within the area now occupied by any of the great nations continual internecine strife has given place to settled and orderly government. It is true that we have not made civil war absolutely impossible. Orderly and constitutional government demands of a people a certain mutual forbearance and respect for mutual rights in which under stress of circumstances they may fail. Nevertheless no one would say that if we determined so to act that our children should never suffer the horrors of civil war, we were following an illusory ideal. Rather we feel that, thanks to the political good sense of our ancestors, that ideal is already practically realized and we are the children who are benefiting by it.

If towns and districts which once lived in a state of war with one another can without giving up their local individuality, unite to form one nation under orderly and peaceable government, why cannot nations in turn give up war among themselves? Why should the relations between men of different nations be different from those between the men who now form one nation? These are the questions which those who disbelieve in the possibility of putting an end to war, have got to answer.

There are two kinds of answers given to such questions, based on very different considerations and very different conceptions of the state.

It is said sometimes that war is a relation between states and not between individuals, and that the relations between states are and must necessarily be different in kind from those existing between individuals; that the sole aim and duty of the state is and must be the acquisition of power. Within the state, the upholders of this doctrine would say, there ought to be justice and respect for law and indeed all the virtues. For only so are common life and culture possible. But the state is the supreme bond of social life. Beyond it there can be nothing. Security and culture having been given to the individual inside the state, each state is self-sufficing and has no need of law in its relations with its neighbours. The world is thus thought of as a collection of independent sovereign states, who acknowledge no common law and who are engaged in a constant struggle for power amongst themselves. The choice before every

nation is, in Bernhardi's words, ' world power or downfall'. Every nation must strive after power in order
that it may impose its civilization and ideas upon the
world. This ideal, when stated with Bernhardi's down-
rightness, is so repellent that it is difficult to have
patience to answer it. It is an obvious abomination.
Many of us have been familiar with it in the writings
of German professors but have never imagined that
any one could really believe that sort of stuff. The
apparent obsession of the German mind with this
astounding doctrine is a portent which we can only
wonder at and deplore.

For look at the doctrine a little more closely. In
the first place, this attempt to distinguish entirely
between the relations between individuals and between
states is obvious nonsense. The power of Germany
over Alsace Lorraine or over Belgium means, if it
means anything at all, that a certain number of human
beings, Belgians or Alsatians, are forced to act in
various ways against their inclinations at the commands of other individuals, not because they admire
or respect these individuals but from fear of the consequences of disobedience. The will of Germany is
decided by the wills of individual Germans. It is being
exercised at this moment upon individual Belgians,
with what results of suffering and anguish to the
victims and of brutalization to the oppressors we
are every day learning. The power of one nation over
another which can be gained by war means this and
nothing else than this, in whatever various forms it may
be exercised. If we believe that it is not good for one
man to have arbitrary power over others, if we believe
that slavery is bad for the master as well as for the
slave, we must believe it to be equally bad for one

nation to rule over another against its will. To adapt Lincoln's words : No nation is good enough to rule over another nation without that other's consent.

Further, the strength of a nation to exercise dominion over other nations is very limited. We sometimes think of a nation becoming a world-power by steady increase of the territory it possesses, and there seems no reason at first why such a process should not go on indefinitely. But a nation's strength depends upon the individuals who compose the nation, and their readiness to make all those efforts and sacrifices which the exercise of power demands. The number and readiness of such individuals is not increased simply by changes in the map. A nation cannot grow stronger by conquest if it has to hold down those it conquers. Conquest makes it stronger only if it puts those it conquers on some kind of level with itself and manages to inspire them with its ideals. The Prussian domination of Germany has apparently meant that most Germans have been inspired with Prussian ideals and united Germany is stronger than was Prussia alone. But then Prussia did not conquer Germany. The Prussian possession of Poland and of Alsace Lorraine has not had the same effect, and the efforts of Germany to hold down those provinces have not strengthened but weakened her. The self-governing dominions and India are a source of strength to the British Empire just because or in so far as they share and approve of England's political aims. If they did not so share, if we had tried to treat them merely as possessions which gave us strength to exercise our will on other nations as we pleased, the Empire would have been the source of fatal weakness that the Germans, arguing logically from profoundly mistaken premises, imagined that it would be. The ideal of world-power is thus an impossible as well as an evil ideal. That does not mean, as some writers imply, that there is therefore no need to resist it. It is impossible just because it must drive so many men to resist it; and an evil ideal may be unattainable in its completeness and yet may lead to endless suffering, misery, and wrong in its partial fulfilment.

So much for the doctrine that the sole aim of nations is power. But if we have disposed of that doctrine, we have not thereby shown that states are or ought to be governed in their relations to one another by the same principles of conduct as are individuals. Many persons who would not subscribe to Bernhardi's views still hold that ordinary moral obligations do not apply to nations. They hold either that the behaviour of nations is governed by mysterious forces, sometimes described as fate or destiny, or that it is the duty of nations to look after their own interests, and that when the interests of nations conflict there is bound to be war. Such persons would describe the conflict between Germany and England either as the result of both countries following their destiny, or as due to the fact that both Germany and England had to pursue their own interests; it was Germany's interest to expand, it was England's to stop that expansion, and hence war had to come.

Talk about national destiny is usually nonsense. It implies that nations have no intelligent control over their actions. It is commonly only a hypocritical way of excusing actions for which there is no decent excuse. It is true that the outcome of national actions depends upon the joint effect of a large number of factors, which cannot all be known to the statesman who commits the nation to action, and that therefore a statesman has much less power of anticipating accurately the outcome of actions than has a man who is acting for himself in ordinary life. That, however, does not acquit him or the nation which follows him of responsibility for his deliberate actions: rather it increases that responsibility. Even Bismarck has borne witness to that. In a famous passage in his Reminiscences he dissents from what is known as the policy of a 'preventive war', the policy that a nation ought to make war at a time that is favourable to itself if it thinks that otherwise war will be made on it in the future. He opposed that policy 'in the conviction that even victorious wars cannot be justified unless they are forced upon one, and that we cannot see the cards of Providence far enough ahead to anticipate historical development according to one's own calculation'. If his successors had remained faithful to his teaching, we should not have had this war.

The second view that nations must follow their own interests is more plausible because it is the duty of *statesmen* to think primarily of the interests of their country, and it is from studying the actions of statesmen in international relations that we tend to form our opinion of the real nature of such relations. The truth is that the statesman, having power to commit the nation to action, is acting on behalf of or as a trustee of the nation. His line of action is therefore restricted. He has no right of himself to sacrifice his country's interests because he thinks it right to be generous. As a trustee his first duty is to his country. But statesmen are not the only persons in such a position. We are all familiar with the position of a trustee. We admire the man who sacrifices his own interests to others, we do not so admire the man who sacrifices to others the interests of his family or of those for whom he is trustee. That does not mean that a trustee has no moral obligations to other men. He has no right to assume that those for

whom he is acting are prepared to be generous : he must
assume that they are prepared to be just. Further, the
fact that we have some one acting in our name does
not absolve us from the responsibility of seeing that
his actions are right. On the contrary, it throws the
responsibility on us.

The fallacy arises from the fact that we constantly
think of men who are not acting collectively as nations,
as though they were acting as isolated individuals. But
men are very seldom in a position when they can so act.
A nation is not a collection of isolated units. We are
limited by all manner of ties, family, kinship, religion,
nationality, citizenship ; and our duties to our fellow men
are affected by the existence of these ties. Men have
special duties to their family, to their fellow trade
unionists, to their coreligionists, and inasmuch as the
interests of these several associations may conflict, it is
often hard for a man to know how to reconcile conflicting claims. Family loyalty, church loyalty, trade
union loyalty seem often to set at enmity men who as
individuals are really good friends. No one, however,
really thinks that these different loyalties cannot be
reconciled, or that because we can see no reconciliation
between conflicting groups, therefore to one of the
groups we have no duties. No one thinks that the best
citizen is the man who has no loyalty to his family,
his church, or his trade union. The possibility of conflict between these various claims is a problem for the
statesman, but we do not think it an insurmountable
problem. The relation of nations to one another is
analogous to the relation of families to one another.
Family loyalty may become a danger to the state if it
means entire disregard of all other obligations, but it
may and ought to be the bulwark of the state. And

state loyalty must be added to it, not substituted for it. Loyalty to our country may endanger international peace if it means disregard of all other nations. It need not do that, and we become 'Good Europeans' if we think of Europe not instead of but as well as our own country.

We may claim now to have answered the doctrine that states are quite different from individuals and are therefore not governed by moral obligations in their relations to one another, and that war is therefore a necessity. Let us now turn to a second line of argument.

This second argument is that peace, the decent observance of law and respect for mutual rights are possible within a state only because they are preserved by the force of the state. Law, according to this argument, can only exist when there is force to protect it. There can therefore be no such thing as international law, because there is no power supreme over the separate states which could compel observance of law. So long, then, as separate states exist, there can be nothing but enmity between them, and the only hope of universal peace is that one state should be powerful enough to compel all the others to obedience. We have lately been given two very good instances of this argument by German professors. *The Times* of September 11th contained a brief report of a lecture on the war delivered at Charlottenburg by Professor von Wilamowitz-Moellendorff. He is reported to have said that the present war showed how useless international law was without a superior power to enforce it, and that the only hope for the world was that Germany and Austria should win and *dictate peace and the observance of law to Europe.* Professor Ostwald, a famous German scientist, has written to a friend in America a letter on the war in which he says :

'According to the course of the war up to the present time' (he was writing very early in September) 'European peace seems to me nearer than ever before. We pacificists must only understand that unhappily the time was not yet sufficiently developed to establish peace by the peaceful way. If Germany, as everything now seems to make probable, is victorious in the struggle, not only with Russia and France, but attains the further end of destroying the source from which for two or three centuries all European strife has been nourished and intensified, namely the English policy of World Dominion, then will Germany, fortified on the one side by its military superiority, on the other side by the eminently peaceful sentiment of the greatest part of its people and especially of the German Emperor, dictate peace to the rest of Europe. I hope especially that the future treaty of peace will in the first place provide effectually that a European war such as the present can never again break out.'

These utterances are worth noting, for they are the views of two very eminent and fine Germans on how to make ' war against war '. We on our side may perhaps have a dream similar save in our choice of the country which shall play the principal rôle. Such an ideal seems at first sight feasible. Did not Rome by force dictate peace to Europe ? has not England dictated it to India ? Why should not Germany or Great Britain dictate peace to Europe ? All such dreams are vitiated by the most fruitful source of fallacy in international politics, the refusal to look at the situation from the point of view of other nations. Professor Ostwald at one and the same time thinks that England's world dominion has been the source of all war, and that Germany's world dominion would produce peace. The

elementary fact about the European situation is that
there are a number of European nations who are more
or less equal and, what is just as important, who think
that they are.

If Europe can only be given peace by force, it can
never be given peace, because no one state in Europe
is strong enough to hold down the rest. Professor
Wilamowitz-Moellendorff talks of Germany *and Austria*
enforcing peace ; we, if we are honest, talk of the *Allies*.
That means that we assume that two or more independent nations can act together without being themselves held down by force. And if two or three are
able to observe mutual obligations, why not a dozen ?
Even two nations can only hold together if they observe
law and justice in their mutual relations. In the Roman
Empire and in India one strong homogeneous state
enforced peace on a number of smaller disunited states.
That is possible. The conditions are entirely different
when, as in modern Europe, the great nations are more
or less equal.

And as we had occasion to notice before, no nation
can ever permanently hold down another nation or
nations by *force*. If its empire is to last, it must rest on
the consent of those it governs. The British Empire is
united now, and is able to use united force in this war,
just because the nations which make it up have not
been kept down by force. We are rejoicing in the
support of the Empire in the very year that we learned,
somewhat to our disappointment, that we had no power
to enforce in South Africa our views of the proper treatment of labour leaders.

These obvious facts show that there is something
wrong with the theory that law rests upon force. It
may perhaps be worth while looking more closely at

the part played by force in the state. For if we understand what binds men together in a law-abiding society, we may see how states may be bound together to a common observance of law.

At first sight it looks as though law did obviously depend upon force. All states use force to compel the obedience to law, and the use of force is often looked upon as the peculiar characteristic of the state. No one, unless he be a theoretical anarchist, imagines that states and the ordered life they make possible could exist if they entirely refused to use force to compel obedience to law. This seems but a short step from saying that the state depends upon force, and that the setting up of an irresistible force is the necessary step to the making of a state. The opinion is widely held that force is at least the ultimate basis of the state. But whose is the force on which the state depends? It is not the Government's, for they are in a minority; nor even the force of what are called the forces of the administration, for their force depends on their having been organized and supported by the action and authority of other people. We all know that no government can enforce a law which its whole people is determined to break. If we then say that the force at the basis of the state is the force of the majority of its inhabitants, we must see that the majority has force to use only because it is prepared for concerted action. Force does not organize men who would otherwise be at enmity with one another. It is itself brought into being by organization, by the power and readiness of the people to act together to respect certain principles and to enforce certain laws. Force does not make government possible. On the contrary it is the mutual trust and sense of a common interest which makes possible the force which government uses. At the same time it is important to notice that the use of force is necessary to a government. For although it is in the general interest that men should keep the law and respect their obligations to one another, occasions continually occur when an individual might profit by disregarding his obligations, and profit more just because other men kept their obligations to him. It is this conflict between the private interests of individuals and the general interests of the community which makes force necessary. Force seems to be the basis of the state because the state must be prepared to enforce the law on any member of the state who may violate it, but the state can only use its force because most of its citizens support its action and do not wish to violate its law : in other words, because most of them do not need to be controlled by force.

The argument then that international law can have no validity because there is no power above the different states to enforce it is invalid. For law does not depend upon force but upon respect for law. International law is of much narrower scope than state law and less effective, because there is yet little mutual trust and little power of common action between members of different states. Common political action is possible only between men who to some extent understand, respect, and trust one another. Such mutual trust and respect is of slow growth, especially between men who are organized in different groups, with different history and traditions and to some extent different ways of life. That is the real difference between the problem of political union in a nation and in Europe. The elements which go to make up a nation have behind them a long tradition of common understanding and of a sense of belonging together. The nations of Europe have behind them a long tradition of enmity and jealousy. Some modern writers have thought that the enormous increase in economic relations between different nations which has marked the last two generations is of itself creating that mutual trust which will make war impossible. That is, I think, a vain hope. Economic relations give us an opportunity to understand and know each other better, but they also produce new sources of rivalry. For it is of the nature of economic relations that they can be entered into by men who are in spirit more rivals than co-operators, and who have no real purpose in common.

Are we then to wait for peace till in course of time we come fully to understand and respect all men? That were to wait for the millennium. If the state had waited for mutual understanding amongst all its members, it would have waited till law and the state itself was unnecessary. The sense of common interest and the respect of mutual rights at the basis of many states is weak enough, but an orderly society is secured in so far as that respect for rights is formulated in law and enforced by the organized force of the community. The common principles of action on which modern Europe has been able to agree are not very elaborate or far-reaching. They are none the less precious for that. The only way to make war impossible is at one and the same time to do all we can to increase common understanding between different nations, and to keep safe the position we have reached by the strengthening and enforcing of the public law of Europe, such as it is.

Modern Europe, with its distrustful rival nations, might not unjustly be compared to the Iceland of the Sagas. Iceland in the tenth century was a land of independent vikings, living each on his farm, owning no political superior. They are proud, distrustful of one another, and intensely warlike. Yet they are kept from utter barbarism by their respect for law. The Iceland of the Sagas has an elaborate law with no State to enforce it. It depends entirely on public opinion, on a bad man's knowledge that if he breaks the law, not only his enemies but men with whom he had no quarrel will be against him. They will not let him marry into their families if he wants to, they will not help him if he gets into a difficulty, and if he shows more than usual disregard of the law they will combine to make an end of him, though they themselves may get no immediate profit from so doing. There is a famous passage in *Burnt Njal Saga* describing the coming of Christianity to Iceland and the dissensions that arose from the conflict of Christian and Pagan law. All Iceland came together to the Hill of Laws, and the speaker of the laws was asked his opinion. 'Thorgeir' (that was his name) 'lay all that day on the ground, and spread a cloak over his head, so that no man spoke with him; but the day after men went to the Hill of Laws and then Thorgeir bade them be silent and spoke thus : "It seems to me as though our matters were come to a deadlock, if we are not all to have one and the same law; for if there be a sundering of the laws, then there will be a sundering of the peace and we shall never be able to live in the land." '

If it was possible for the vikings of Iceland to submit to a common law though there was no power outside themselves to force them to do it, it should not be impossible for the nations of Europe. In no other way can we hope for lasting peace. For in this way alone we claim for ourselves nothing more than we allow to other nations. We have been told in the past that peace was best preserved by our being so strongly armed

that no one dare attack us.   But because every nation
acted on such advice, Europe became an armed camp
where peace was almost as burdensome as war, and where
the militarism was encouraged and fostered by which
this war has been produced.   We have also been told
that we must preserve the balance of power in Europe.
The doctrine of the balance of power implies that
nations are natural rivals and enemies and make treaties
with one another only for their own advantage.   It is
natural for a diplomacy which aims at the balance of
power to regard treaties as having no real binding
force.   They are made purely in the self-interest of
the nations who enter into them ; when circumstances
change and they no longer serve the interests of one
of these nations, their whole basis and reason is gone.
The balance of power too, when the powers balanced
are ponderous and unwieldy and the equilibrium
unstable, has a way of being upset by circumstances
over which we have no control.   This war has largely
been brought about by Germany's efforts to correct the
balance of power which the Balkan wars had disturbed to
her disadvantage.   Further, while all nations think they
are trying to create a balance of power, they are really
seeking an over-balance in their own favour.   That they
cannot possibly all get, and hence must arise rivalry
and eventually war.   Common respect for public law
alone calls not for rivalry but for common action.
The neutrality of the small states of Europe like Belgium
was agreed to by the joint act of the Great Powers of
Europe, not in the interests of this or that Power but
in the interests of European peace.   In fighting to
defend that agreement, in fighting for the public law
of Europe, we are fighting to give peace its only sure
foundation.   To this doctrine Mr. Asquith has recently

in his speech at Dublin given expression. I cannot end
this paper better than by quoting his words :

'I should like if I might for a moment, beyond this
inquiry into causes and motives, to ask your attention
and that of my fellow-countrymen to the end which in
this war we ought to keep in view. Forty-four years
ago, at the time of the war of 1870, Mr. Gladstone used
these words. He said : "The greatest triumph of our
time will be the enthrônement of the idea of public
right as the governing idea of European politics."
Nearly fifty years have passed. Little progress, it
seems, has yet been made towards that good and bene-
ficent change, but it seems to me to be now at this
moment as good a definition as we can have of our
European policy.

'The idea of public right, what does it mean when
translated into concrete terms? It means, first and
foremost, the clearing of the ground by the definite
repudiation of militarism as the governing factor in the
relation of States and of the future moulding of the
European world. It means, next, that room must be
found and kept for the independent existence and the
free development of the smaller nationalities, each for
the life of history a corporate consciousness of its own.
Belgium, Holland, and Switzerland, and Scandinavian
countries, Greece and the Balkan States—they must be
recognized as having exactly as good a title as their
more powerful neighbours, more powerful in strength
and in wealth—exactly as good a title to a place in the
sun. And it means finally, or it ought to mean, perhaps
by a slow and gradual process, the substitution for force,
for the clashing of competing ambition, for groupings
and alliances and a precarious equipoise, the substitution
for all these things of a real European partnership based

on the recognition of equal right and established and
enforced by a common will. A year ago that would
have sounded like a Utopian idea. It is probably one
that may not or will not be realized either to-day or
to-morrow. If and when this war is decided in favour
of the Allies it will at once come within the range, and
before long within the grasp, of European statesmanship.'

Oxford : Horace Hart Printer to the University

French Policy since 1871.

By F. Morgan and H. W. C. Davis. 2d. net. *Third Impression.*

A historical sketch, discussing the question whether French policy has been aggressive.

Russia : The Psychology of a Nation.

By Paul Vinogradoff. 1d. net. *Third Impression.*

A reply to the German taunt that Russia is still in a state of barbarism, and is the enemy of European civilization

Serbia and the Serbs.

By Sir Valentine Chirol. 2d. net. *Third Impression.*

A sketch of Serbian history, which is incidentally an indictment of the policy pursued by Austria-Hungary towards the Serbian kingdom.

Germany and ' The Fear of Russia '.

By Sir Valentine Chirol. 2d. net. *Third Impression.*

Shows that before 1879 Germany preferred Russia as an ally to Austria. The ambition of Germany to establish a protectorate over Turkey has led her to assist Austria in the Balkans and so to challenge Russia.

The Eastern Question.

By F. F. Urquhart. 3d. net. *Second Impression.*

The history of the Balkan nations ; their future.

IV

War against War.

By A. D. Lindsay. 2d. net. *Second Impression.*

Denies that war is good in itself, or a necessary evil. Power is not the sole or chief end for which the State exists. National greatness, if founded on brute force, cannot endure. International law represents an ideal, but an ideal that may be realized.

The Value of Small States.

By H. A. L. Fisher. 2d. net. *Third Impression.*

The author argues that the debt of civilization to small states is incalculable. They are useful, at the present time, as laboratories of political experiments and as buffer-states between the greater powers.

How can War ever be Right ?

By Gilbert Murray. 2d. net. *Second Impression.*

A well-known lover of peace and advocate of pacific policies argues against the Tolstoyan position. Right and honour compelled Britain to make war ; and war—like tragedy—is not pure evil.

The National Principle and the War.

By Ramsay Muir. 3d. net.

Considers the principle of nationality and its application to the settlement of Europe—particularly of S.E. Europe—after the War.

Nietzsche and Treitschke : The Worship of Power in Modern Germany.

By E. Barker. 2d. net. *Third Impression.*

An explanation of the main points of interest in the ethical and political doctrines of the German ruling classes.

[a]

The British Dominions and the War.

By H. E. EGERTON.   2d. net.   *Second Impression.*

Explains the ideas for which the British Empire stands, and the political and moral issues of the war affecting the Dominions.

Is the British Empire the Result of Wholesale Robbery?

By H. E. EGERTON.   2d. net.

A historical sketch in answer to a common taunt.

India and the War.

By Sir ERNEST TREVELYAN.   1d. net.   *Second Impression.*

Discusses the reasons which account for the striking manifestations of Indian loyalty.

Bacilli and Bullets.

By Sir WILLIAM OSLER.   1d. net.   *Third Impression.*

Calls attention to the fact that disease kills more men than the bullet. The most dangerous diseases are preventible by inoculation.

The Navy and the War.

By J. R. THURSFIELD.   3d. net.   *Second Impression.*

Estimates the military and economic value of the silent pressure exercised by our fleet, and warns the faint-hearted and the captious of the perils of lack of faith.

The Retreat from Mons.

By H. W. C. DAVIS.   3d. net.   *Second Impression.*

Introduction; the Dispatch of Sept. 9; the Statement by the War Office, published Aug. 31.   Appendixes (soldiers' narratives); two maps.

The Law of Nations and the War.

By A. PEARCE HIGGINS.   2d. net.

The violation of Belgian neutrality and the conduct of England to Denmark in 1807; the doctrine of German lawyers that military necessity overrides the laws of war; the balance of power and the sanctity of treaties.

Others in preparation.

OXFORD PAMPHLETS

1914

THE LEADERSHIP

OF THE WORLD

BY

F. S. MARVIN

Price Twopence net

OXFORD UNIVERSITY PRESS
HUMPHREY MILFORD
LONDON EDINBURGH GLASGOW
NEW YORK TORONTO MELBOURNE BOMBAY

OXFORD : HORACE HART
PRINTER TO THE UNIVERSITY

THE LEADERSHIP OF THE WORLD

THE war goes on, with all its heroism and devastation, with no realization of •German hopes, with a growing certainty that the Allied Powers will be able sooner or later to impose on a defeated foe the conditions which his criminal breach of international duty and the security of Europe appear to them to demand. It may not be amiss at such a point to examine one of the great fundamental questions in dispute, a question which has for many years tormented the mind of German publicists, and led them to many dangerous and perverted conclusions. What is meant by the hegemony of the civilized world ? Where are we to look for it ? By what organs and to what end can it and ought it to express its will ?

It is not surprising that so great a question should have issued in the greatest armed conflict which history records. Many of us in all the leading countries of the world hoped that the latent danger might have been averted and a peaceful solution reached by reason and conciliation. Theoretically it was possible. In practice the problem has proved to surpass our powers.

It is significant that the greatest war since the Roman Empire should lead us back to the Roman Empire for its full explanation. The question of the leadership of the civilized world dates from then. For more than six hundred years, from the time when Rome defeated her greatest rival in the second Punic War to the final dissolution of the Empire before the barbarians, there was one undisputed leader. Rome combined in her own hands during that period the intellectual primacy which had been won by the Greeks, with moral and military forces drawn from herself. It was a moment of inestimable benefit to mankind, a consolidation which seems to us in the retrospect indispensable to the progress of the world ; but it has floated ever since as a mirage to misguide and lead to destruction the headstrong ambitions of nations who have found themselves in possession of a temporary superiority over their neighbours. The mediaeval Empire fought and broke in a vain endeavour to regain it, for the Holy Roman Emperor was always struggling in vain to secure the dominion of Italy. Spain was ruined in the same pursuit for Empire. France has had more than one fatal paroxysm. We ourselves have not been exempt. Germany, as we shall see, has had many motives driving her to compete for the same now unattainable goal.

Now no conclusion from history can be more certain than this : what Rome did, she did once for all, and it cannot and should not ever be repeated.

The change of conditions which has made such an hegemony as that of ancient Rome for ever impossible again in the world, is so obvious that only a few of the maddest claimants, an occasional Napoleon, have openly aspired to it. The area of civilization which Rome had incorporated round the Mediterranean was extended by the Catholic Church, and the discovery of the New World made it far larger. The growth of trade, of science, of communication, produced a complex so vast and varied that no one centre could possibly control or keep in contact with the whole. In our own days it is less clear than it was that Europe as a whole can retain the leadership of the world. But meanwhile the growth, the grouping, the inter-relations of the heirs of the Roman Empire have provided incessant problems for the two thousand years since. It is an acute crisis in this movement which is now upon us.

For though the hegemony of one State in the world has passed for ever, there is still somewhere a leading force in the world's progress, a nucleus of stronger and more civilized nations who contain among them the fruits of man's evolution in far greater abundance and better diffused than among the remaining less-advanced peoples of the globe. There is a vanguard, which may lead if it will.

· A concert of leading nations, bound one to another by links of high achievement in science and the arts of life, in political organization and outlook on the world, pressing on in friendly rivalry to greater strength and prosperity for themselves, while guiding and helping the more backward races,—this has been the generous ideal of multitudes of thinkers in all ages ever since the break-up of the Roman Empire destroyed the temporary hope of a world-wide civilization, diffused from one centre. It has taken various colours in successive epochs. The Catholic thinkers of the Middle Ages saw it in the light of a religious unity binding the most distant and diverse nations in a common hope under a common head. The better minds of the Renaissance, such as those who inspired the testament of Henri IV, saw it as a political alliance of independent States under enlightened rulers. The eighteenth century conceived the notion of free national democracies handing on the light to peoples sitting in the darkness and the twilight. But again and again the vision has been broken and hopes dashed to the ground by disasters which sometimes seemed comparable to the fall of the Roman Empire itself. The wars of religion which followed Henri IV were one such overthrow. The Napoleonic wars were another. The present struggle bears some ominous marks of likeness. We need to see through it, to discern the recuperative forces, to reconstruct at least ideally and for ourselves this comity of nations which history and reason compel us to accept as the guiding human force in the affairs of the world.

How then can we explain, before we come to healing, this last great breach among the leading nations of the West ? The diplomatic case has been so clearly and so unanswerably stated in papers and in speeches that it would be idle, even if relevant, to review it here. But it is necessary also to appreciate the popular German view which is quite unaffected by the course of diplomacy, carefully concealed from the popular mind. They are faced, they think, by a danger of expansive barbarism on their Eastern frontier. This foe has, by the fatal accident of their central position, become allied with the Western foe they had to fight for their national unity in 1870, and we have taken the opportunity of dealing a felon's blow at our most serious naval and commercial rival.

The picture is a hideous nightmare of fear, hostility, and distrust. But so far as it is really present to the minds of multitudes of otherwise rational and moral people—and of this there is no doubt—it behoves us to understand its genesis, and, if possible, its cure. It is true that Germany is faced on the East by masses of men less civilized, according to ordinary Western standards, than herself. It is true that she has on the West a neighbour alienated from her by centuries of conflict pressed to a ruthless issue forty years ago. It is true that owing to a long series of historical causes she achieved such national unity as she possesses, much later and by more violent and artificial methods than her great Western neighbours. All this is to say that in spite of the strength of her central position in the continent, she has had exceptional difficulties to face in reaching the degree of cohesion and of international weight which her numbers and her mental force deserve. It explains, without wholly justifying, the fact, which Comte pointed out more than fifty years ago, that she remains the most military of the Western Powers. But precisely in these facts lies also the menace to European peace and security of which we have now the disastrous evidence before us. The strong and exceptional methods and organization which Germany needed as medicine for her own ailments, she has used as poison for her neighbours and the world.

This is the explanation of the strange paradox, noticed by more than one writer on the crisis, that German action was prompted both by fear and by overweening strength.

One gets the impression, in reading the modern German political writers, people like Treitschke and his school, of men peering at the world through the loopholes of a mighty fortress, constructed with the utmost skill, but giving the least possible inlet to light or life from without. They are afraid, and yet they have built themselves a stronghold in which they might, if they would, rest in security from any probable assault, and from which they may, if they will, commit the most damaging excursions upon their neighbours with the minimum of loss to themselves. We know the story of scores of such fortresses in earlier and wilder days. Built for defence, they became the home and instrument of lawless tyranny and wide-spread devastation. Treitschke himself is the type of the bluff, genial, not unattractive chieftain, a builder and a man of insight, not without moments of tolerance and even sympathy for his neighbours. The Germans themselves have compared him with some justice to our own Carlyle. But his followers—the Pan-German League and the like, whom he repudiated himself—received from his hands tools that they have used to deadly purpose, without the glimpses of humanity and progress which one may trace in his own work. In his own sphere much to the same purpose might be said of Bismarck. Take some of the pithy sayings in Treit-schke's *Lectures on Politics* :

> The map of our part of the globe has been much more natural since [i.e. since 1870]; the centre is strengthened ; *the inspired idea that the centre of gravity of Europe must lie in the middle, has become reality.* Through the founding of the German Empire a tran-quillity has entered spontaneously into the system of States, inasmuch as ambition in Prussia can now be silent ; Prussia has essentially attained the power she required.

This has a ring of sincerity. The man who said it did not desire an aggressive, world-conquering empire. But the ' inspired idea ' is just the heady stuff which sets on other people to do the mischief. Why, because Germany happens to be the central land-mass of Western Europe, should she become the ' centre of gravity of Europe ' in a political or moral sense, still less of the world, which has tended more and more towards the West ?

> The North Sea has the worst coast imaginable in Germany because of the sandflats. . . . But even here can be seen how man is able to overcome natural

obstacles. This Germany, with its forbidding coast-line, was yet once on a time the leading sea-power and, please God, it shall become so again.

This is more dangerous, though one cannot help admiring the confident challenge to Nature. So far as it is aimed at England, it ignores the fact that an island has a natural claim to a stronger navy and that we have never aspired to a commanding army.

But there is a further and more serious point in Treitschke's teaching which needs closer attention. We rejoice that any neighbouring nation is consolidated and gains security and strength : we may even admire the energy and determination that make of the most un-promising sea-board in the world the home of a rising sea-power. But what of the place which this aspiring and strengthened nation is to play in the comity of leading States in whose hands the future civilization of the world mainly rests ? It is on this side that the recent political philosophy of Germany leads to such an abyss. We find, it is true, one or two perfunctory statements in Treitschke that ' every nation exhibits a different picture and a different conception of the divinity ' and that ' all civilization aims at making human life more harmonious ' ; but no guidance whatever is offered as to the way in which the leading Powers generally and Germany in particular are to co-operate in what must be the greatest and crowning achievement of mankind. On the contrary, words, ideas, arguments crowd on one another, which directly oppose the combination of human efforts to further the common interests of the race.

We all know the theory of the divine State and the divine monarch. It has played a part in our own political history, but has an even greater importance with the Germans. Treitschke is a late inheritor of the doctrine, and has given one aspect of it a particularly dangerous turn. It assumes that the basis of the State is power—the collective power of all the members used primarily for the common good of all. What are these common interests ? 'It is very obvious,' says Treitschke, ' that the first task of the State is a twofold one ; it is, as we have seen, power in an external direction and the regulation of justice internally ; its fundamental functions must therefore be the organization of the army and the administration of the law. . . . The second essential function of the State is to make war.' Thus not only is the first part of its primary function to organize the army, but the whole of the second essential function is to set this organization in motion. Whatever function in civilization the State may also possess, this stands in the forefront and proclaims the militarist régime. It is interesting to compare the conclusions on the same point of the greatest of early theorists on the nature of the State. Aristotle, living himself in a time far less suited to rational and peaceful contemplation than our own, declared that the primary function of any community was ' Life ', and the next to that ' A good life '.[1]

The whole point in these questions, as in those of private morals, is where we lay the stress. We may pay perfunctory lip-homage to the duty of kindness at home and educating our children, but if we spend our main energies on personal display and arranging pleasure-trips for ourselves, we are worse than a sounding brass or a tinkling cymbal. But in some of these Treitschkean writings we hardly get lip-homage to the duty of the State towards other members of the human family. The old Kantian ideal of a condition of universal and per-

[1] Aristotle's *Politics*.

petual peace—not of course to be immediately realized
but to be worked for steadily through years of compromise and agreement, broken by occasional and inevitable conflict—this is openly flouted as nonsense.
' Self-sacrifice for a foreign nation is not only not moral
but it contradicts the idea of self-preservation, which
is the highest thing for the state.' From such a State,
it is clear, whatever may be the private virtues of its
citizens, no help could be expected for the victims of
the Turk, no stay of execution for the Chinese, no pity
for the Belgians.

The bias which such a theory of the State must give
in dealing with colonies and weaker races is obvious.
Every great nation must have its colonies as a fair share
in the ' domination of the transatlantic world by the
aristocracy of the whites '. If it has not a share pro-
portioned to its strength and its ambition, it will fight
for it, and it will ' anticipate the obvious dangers of
over-population by colonization, on a large scale '. The
' scramble for Africa ' is thus elevated into a principle
of State, without any real concern for the millions of
men of other races and colours who form at least the
rear-guard of the human army on the march. Have we
not advanced in four hundred years beyond the position
of the ' conquistadores ' of the New World ?

One knows of course that there are thousands of good
Germans who would not subscribe to the doctrine and
are working for the betterment of mankind in every
quarter of the globe. But unfortunately the doctrine,
which again is not confined to them, finds expression
in its most naked and brutal form in their public writers
and their public actions. It is the worst devil which
has to be cast out, before the leadership of the world,
in the common interest of all its inhabitants, can be

established with any hope of large success, and without the imminent risk of the recurring cataclysms which have hitherto interrupted all great efforts at concert.

The group of great nations which emerged from the dissolution of the Roman Empire were England, France, Spain, Italy, and Germany. It was in this order that they gained their national unity, which is one very important factor, among others, in the problem before us. From this point of view it seems fair to give the preference to England and date her final consolidation from Chaucer and the end of the fourteenth century, whereas France had to wait for the end of the Hundred Years' War and Louis XI's absorption of the feudal States. In Spain the Moorish occupation postponed the process still further, and the intellectual and material ravages due to religious persecution exhausted the nation and have till the present prevented her taking a place in the concert of people correspondent with her size, position, and population. Both Italy and Germany come much later in the race for political unity and strength, and both were affected by that conflict between the Pope and the mediaeval Emperor which was the leading political issue in the Middle Ages. Both nations, however, counted for far more in Europe at the revival of learning and intellectual life in the fifteenth and sixteenth centuries, than their political and military power would have warranted, and Italy, when her union was achieved in the 'sixties of the last century, became a compact, well-defined country, needing only small rectifications of her northern boundary, to be coincident with her nationality and easily defended from external attack.

Germany, however, unfortunately for herself and for the rest of the world, was beset by political difficulties both within and without. With a large, vigorous, and intensely patriotic population she was, and to a large extent still is, divided into a number of politically independent States. The incorporation which France achieved four hundred years before, through the personal activity and political genius of Louis XI, Germany only secured, and to a smaller degree, by a great war carried out at the expense of France. The stamp of blood and iron was thus set, for long if not for ever, on her national life. Nor is this all. The problems on her western and eastern frontiers were bound to call forth either self-restraint or ambition on the part of any people. On the west, kindred people holding the mouths of great rivers draining her own land : on the east, people of lower civilization, often turbulent, always expansive. In these circumstances the success of a strong and ambitious Power, such as Prussia, able and willing to lead and unify the nation, was a foregone conclusion. Prussia herself was served by a series of able and devoted men. From the time of Frederic the Great to her fight against Napoleon, and again in the crowning victory of 1871, she won the allegiance of all patriotic Germans by her supreme power of organization, her bold strokes of foreign policy, her persistence, and her national enthusiasm. But the triumph of the centralizing State, with that tragic discord which has so often marked the evolution of German life, involved the decay of the generous instincts of the older, less organized German, and a set-back to ideals, except of force and material success.

Of the five great nations, three preserve their intellectual eminence. France, Germany, and England, judged by their contributions to science, literature, and the arts of life, stand in a group apart. But in the volume of its learning, its detailed scientific work, its music, Germany is easily first. The industry and docility of her population are beyond compare. Whether socialist or bourgeois, they have been led to the barracks, the class-room, and the polling-booth, with the same marvellous precision and discipline as we have witnessed in a hundred rushes upon our trenches on the Aisne and the Yser. How to combine this order and teachableness with some understanding and regard for the rights and feelings of others, to harness these incomparable forces not in servitude, but in willing co-operation with the progressive nations throughout the world,— this is the true problem, secondary in time to the immediate necessity of inflicting a decisive blow on an aggressive and ruthless enemy, but supreme in importance for the well-being of Europe and mankind. For humanity must be justified of all her children.

The group of five nations which took up the work of Rome has varied much. Spain, since the seventeenth century, has no longer a seat at their council-board. The United States, Russia, and Japan have within the same period established their place in the first rank. The present grouping is the result of long historical evolution, working within the limits of the land masses of our planet. You have a central group— France, England, and Germany—with a nucleus of Belgium and Holland offering a neutral meeting-place for international associations in their capitals. A fringe of small and highly cultivated States to the north, with two large and two small States to the south, complete the great *massif* of European culture. East and west are the colossal powers of Russia and the United States, standing the one for Eastern Europe and Northern Asia, the other for the New World. On the east come

the Japanese, now clearly marked out as the guardians
and tutors of the undeveloped giant of the Yellow race.
Further south the offshoots of the British race in
Africa and Australasia and of the Latin States in South
America complete the picture.

The German people have thus a strong position in the
central group, and to them would naturally fall the
primacy and guardianship of the northern States of
Europe. No one would grudge it, did not the guardian
show so strong an inclination to devour his wards.
But this question of the right relation of the strong
Power to the weak is at the root of the present
conflict. It is a hopeful feature both for the issue of
the war and the future happiness of mankind that the
cause of the Allies is bound up, both on the east and
west, with the fortunes of a small State struggling for
its independence, while their opponents, Germany and
Turkey, are detested by all their subject races. In this
matter the United States, in Cuba, in Porto Rico, as in
China, have set a high example to the world. France has
done well in Tunis, and latterly in Algeria and the East.
England, whatever her errors in the past, has now
a practically unanimous Empire to support her cause.
Russia, we hope and believe, will crown her career of
heroic efforts for freedom abroad with larger grants of
freedom at home. But Germany, full of national self-
consciousness and with the thoroughness which marks
all her actions, does nothing for her subject peoples,
except impress upon them with relentless vigour the
stamp of German ideas, German institutions, and
German language.[1]

[1] A characteristic story has just reached us of the treatment
of the prisoners of war in the fortress of Königstein. There was
an Englishman there with a number of Frenchmen. He reported

Happily the war finds us serving with zeal the general commonwealth. It is in the mid stream of our best tradition to clinch the opposition of Europe to any Power which threatens the security and independence of others. And this time, happily also, we are side by side with the Power which has, more often than any, illuminated Europe with the light of a new principle or a' burning watchword. France led the Crusades for religion in the eleventh and twelfth centuries, and for freedom in the eighteenth. But since the latter, heroic and externally disastrous like the first, so great a change has come over the texture of human society, especially in the West, that we must expect the results of the present war to differ, as widely as the tactics and dispositions of the armies on the field differ from anything on record. The growth of two human factors in the century since Waterloo is really its most notable feature ; these two are science and sympathy. Both are indispensable, and her triumphs in the former will not save Germany from the consequences of her deficiency in the latter.

It may seem a strange and unseasonable hour to be looking for traces of a growing sympathy and amity among the nations of the globe. Yet it is obviously true that the world has become one in the last century in ways and to a degree which had not been dreamt of before steam and electricity were turned to the purposes of man. Larger aggregates of men are now collected in cities and in political conmuties than at any previous period in history. They are in hourly receipt of news from the ends of the earth, except when Govern-

that they had no complaint to make of their food or general condition. The govemor was fortunately a gentleman. But they were all compelled to receive lessons in German every evening !

ments for their own ends obstruct or suppress the passage of the truth. Lines of commerce, exploring travellers, have knit up the most remote regions with the centres of intensest life. By intercourse, small and eccentric languages and cults are being blotted out, and common ways of thought and life more and more diffused. So many different societies for international purposes have been formed, that two special centres for transacting their business have been opened, one at Brussels and the other at The Hague. At the root of all lies the extension of scientific methods and results, greater in the nineteenth century than in all earlier centuries put together. For science is the great unifier of the world, as language is the unifier of nations.

Now, throughout this process, especially on its mechanical side, the Germanic people have played a distinguished part. The Humboldts at the beginning of the century were the pioneers in international co-operation for scientific expeditions and recording observations. In the hundred years which have elapsed since their time the mass of German work has steadily grown. There are at the present moment as many German members of foreign learned societies as of any other two nations put together. Their mass of printed books far exceeds any other country's. They have organized their national life and social service with a thoroughness with which no one can compete. This contribution to the world's work and progress would remain, even if they were blotted out by an overwhelming defeat from the front rank of nations.

But such an issue to the war is by no means to be expected, even if we desired it. The break up of a mighty nation which has achieved its unity by years of costly and deliberate effort, is not promoted by external attack. With them, as with us, the loud blast which tears the skies will serve but to root more firm the native oak. Any changes in the direction either of constitutional government or of decentralization must and should come from within, and they do not directly concern our present argument. What we are trying to see in focus is Germany, or the Germanic Powers, as an essential part of the leading human forces of the globe, Germany and Humanity, a hard collocation for us at the moment, but one that must be faced if the war is to leave us with a balance of hope in the world.

The results of this growth of science and sympathy, both on the present situation and the future, are of the highest moment. We are absorbed just now in tracing the effects of the scientific evolution on the fighting both by sea and land. But far more profound and decisive ultimately will be the influence of science on the restitution of prosperity and the future organization of the world. So great is the increase of productive power due to science, that the huge expense and the ravages of war will be repaired—so far as they can be materially—within less time than any previous great war has required. This is, on the one hand, an assurance to those who fear that a decisive victory may leave Europe lopped of one of her vital members. On the other hand, the community of the world created by science must persist and deepen. It is idle for German men of science to turn their back on the world and divest themselves of foreign degrees. They must for many purposes still use the common scientific nomenclature and still enjoy the fruits of scientific discoveries made by the university of mankind. Thus

it is to science that we may look for the great recuperative forces which will be needed to fill up the chasms
and rebuild the ruins of the war. It can do much,—
except restore the young lives and the old beauty that
have gone.

But for the future unity and guidance of the world
it has a deeper meaning. The world has been made
one by science in a new, intimate, and permanent
sense. But it is not only or mainly the material links
which count—the railways and steamers, the telegraphy,
the international finance. These may be, and often
are, destroyed or disturbed by external causes, by war
and rumours of war. But the achievements of science,
especially as applied to ameliorating human life, are
a common possession of which no national jealousy
can prevent the diffusion or hinder the use. Can any
one suppose or conceive that a Pasteur or a Koch,
a Lister or a Virchow, will be less universally acclaimed
after than before the war ? And deeper still are those
currents of thought which are bringing men of all
nations closer together on questions affecting the
validity of their knowledge and the purpose of their
life. We are coming gradually to recognize that it is
these things, far more than armed strength or political
hegemony, which give a title to the leadership of the
world, and the claim is open to members of all States,
irrespective of size.

Our argument has brought us to the point from
which we may appreciate the need and the appropriate-
ness of the Latin-French word ' Humanity ', in its twofold sense of feeling, and of the concrete whole of human
beings considered as one. It would be exceedingly
interesting and instructive to trace its history ; but
one point is clear. The equivalent German word

'Menschheit' or 'Menschlichkeit' has never had the
vogue which 'Humanité', 'Umanità', 'Humanidad'
have enjoyed among the Latin races, and, through one
of our happy borrowings, among ourselves. The leading
French Socialist journal is *L'Humanité*, the German is
Voruärts.

It is a commonplace among a certain school of somewhat cynical criticism to treat 'humanitarianism' in
politics as a passing phase of pure sentiment, which
was swept away by the inroads of what the Germans
call 'Realpolitik'. Nothing could be further from the
truth. With certain ebbs and flows due to transient
causes there has been, ever since Europe recovered
from the shock of Napoleon, a steady growth of the
belief among the masses of the population in the West
and all intelligent statesmen, that the activities of the
State should be concentrated upon securing the best
conditions of life for all, and that this is only possible
by peaceful and active co-operation with other nations.
The 'sentiment' of the early nineteenth century has
only given place to a more deliberate and reasoned
prosecution of the same end. Nor has the sentiment
itself suffered any abatement. In England, France,
and Germany there have never been so many multitudes as at the present day who would respond to any
appeal to human brotherhood, and one may safely say
the same of Italy, the United States, and Russia. The
passion is there, and within each State steps have been
taken in various degrees to secure the desired welfare
for its own citizens. The failure has been in co-operation between States to avoid conflicts and reduce
armaments and to unite the forces of the leading
Powers in helping and guiding the weaker. China,
Persia, the Congo, the Balkans, the Indians of South

America, the Arabs of Tripoli have cried aloud in recent years for more collective wisdom and humanity from those who are able to coerce them in the name of science and Western policy. Their needs will not be satisfied until each Great Power recognizes larger interests beyond its own, and, without endangering itself, prepares to treat others as a good man tries to treat his neighbours.

The special causes at stake in this war are therefore bound up with the widest issues which can appeal to mankind. They embrace the maintenance of treaties, but go beyond them. We are dealing with the terms on which the nations of the world, especially those in a commanding position, are to associate with one another, and the objects of their common action. On the threshold of this question it will occur to the plain man that any useful co-operation must be to the last degree difficult and often impossible in the atmosphere of deceit, lying, jealousy, and suspicion, which is now revealed and hangs like a stifling miasma over the field of battle. It is a sensible relief that the main source of this is not with us, and we are marching in full force and determination against its most responsible authors. But after all a sword is a poor instrument for dispersing a fog ; and until the general tone between nations is one of security and goodwill, little will be effected by specific proposals for arbitration and disarmament, open diplomacy, or insurance against war. Definite reforms can, of course, be secured by force of arms, e. g. in resettling the uneasy provinces to the west and east of Germany. But, given our success in this—a restored Belgium, a liberated Alsace and Lorraine, an autonomous Poland, and a Slav Switzerland in the Balkans—the work of the future, the active co-operation of the leading Powers for the prosperity and advancement of the whole world would still remain to be begun.

The hindrances in the past have been as manifold as the weaknesses of human nature. The actual occurrence of occasional wars is not the most serious of them. Much worse than this is the generally ineffective and negative character of the concerted action of the Great Powers when they come together. They are usually quite satisfied and happy if they prevent anything worse occurring than they have actually before them. The Balkan problem which is the immediate cause of the present war is a conspicuous instance. It was difficult, but clearly not beyond the wit of man, to devise a settlement better than anything realized in those regions. The Powers met and discussed it in the fullest detail. Their positive constructions have in each case already broken down, and their preventive measures, which it was hoped had averted a general war, only succeeded in postponing that event for less than two years. It will be said that in this case the local conflict only veiled an irreconcilable opposition between some of the Great Powers themselves, which nothing but the sword could settle. This may be so ; at any rate after the event we are unable to deny it. The most certain point is that in public as in private differences, the essential preliminary of any agreement is a determination to settle and a frank exposition of rival points of view. These were wanting, and though they are found not unattainable in private disputes, they still appear Utopian in international matters.

There is, however, a large range of questions on which exchange of views and effective decisions are taken even between countries which are sharply divided on *la haute politique*. It would enhance the goodwill of nations and increase the chances of harmonious joint action in other matters, if the settlements in these more obscure though vital questions received more public recognition.

Two recent instances may serve to illustrate many others. For several years an international committee has been meeting under the authority of various Governments to decide on joint action affecting the conditions of labour. On this committee, France, Germany, and England were always able, when they agreed, to impose their will on the rest. Even in the throes of the Moroccan crisis the three Powers were working to limit still further the hours of women and children, and to give a universal half-holiday to factory workers. Another instance, a few years earlier, was the adoption, at the instance of France, of a universal nomenclature of diseases by all the Powers now engaged in destroying life.

The special significance. of such agreements lies in the fact that they are a new development, due to the industrial revolution and the spread of science. There is nothing comparable before the nineteenth century, and the movement grows apace.

It is important to note that many, perhaps the most binding, of international links are not connected with State action at all. This is the case with religious and with most scientific work, which is constantly bringing men's minds closer together without any apparent approximation to a confederation of Europe. Some of the organs of the new spirit will be political—arbitration courts, international labour committees, possibly some day an international police. Others, the most far-reaching, will and should remain non-political.

For this lies at the heart of our criticism of the modern German theory and tyranny of the State, that the greatest and deepest things which bind mankind together and create what we call ' humanity ', are independent of State control, and would grow even without State support. Religion, science, sympathy, these are the strongest bonds, and the changing groups of nations which hold for a time the leadership of the world, will attain the common end of human good only so far as their policy is inspired by these moving forces greater than themselves. We believe that in this crisis our cause and that of France is in the true line of human progress, and that a defeated and regenerated Germany will bring priceless contributions to unite with ours. We believe, too, that the war has brought for ever into the inner circle of leading Powers the half-Asiatic Russian, whose simple life has long concealed a power of affection and devotion, an enthusiasm and strength of character, which more highly organized and materialist civilizations often blunt.

Some changes in the grouping of Powers and the sympathy of nations, the greatest of wars was bound to bring. It will not go deeper, or destroy the immemorial links of European culture, based on a common inheritance of science, language, and history. When the storm has passed, we shall see again, enthroned in its ancient seat, the spirit which inspired the greatest of modern poets, the Spirit of Union, without which man's activity would revolve in a barren circle to sheer destruction.

Strange contradiction, that we turn to the leading poet of Germany both for the strongest condemnation of Germany's recent and present spirit and for the strongest hopes of healing hereafter.

> Alle menschlichen Gebrechen
> Sühnet reine Menschlichkeit.[1]

---

[1] Goethe to Krüger (1827): 'All the sins of human nature pure humanity redeems.'

1914

Crown 8vo. Separately, in paper covers. Also in series as numbered (I–VII), stiff covers, One Shilling net each series. 35 Pamphlets have now (25 November) been issued and others are in preparation. The historical pieces are illustrated by sketch-maps

I

1. The Deeper Causes of the War.
By W. SANDAY. 3d. net. *Fifth Impression.*
The psychology of Prussian militarism ; German public opinion and Germany's aggressive ambitions.

2. To the Christian Scholars of Europe and America: A Reply from Oxford to the German ' Address to Evangelical Christians '. 2d. net. *Fourth Impression.*
The answer of Oxford theologians to a recent manifesto of the German evangelical theologians. This manifesto, which is reproduced in the present pamphlet, argues that Germany is in no sense responsible for the present war. The Oxford reply states that the German theologians cannot have studied either the events which led up to the war or the political utterances of their own countrymen.

3. The Responsibility for the War.
By W. G. S. ADAMS. 2d. net. *Second Impression.*
A brief discussion of the question of responsibility : 1. Austria and Serbia ; 2. The responsibility of Russia ; 3. The intervention of England.

4. Great Britain and Germany.
By SPENSER WILKINSON. 2d. net. *Third Impression.*
Three letters to the *Springfield Republican*: 1. By Prof. Spenser Wilkinson, stating Great Britain's case ; 2. By Prof. John W. Burgess of the University of Columbia, stating Germany's case ; 3. By Prof. Wilkinson, in reply to Prof. Burgess.

5. ' Just for a Scrap of Paper.'
By ARTHUR HASSALL. 1d. net. *Fourth Impression.*
Explains why England stands for the sanctity of European treaty-law.

[d]

II

6. The Germans, their Empire, and how they have made it.
By C. R. L. FLETCHER. 2d. net. *Fourth Impression.*
A historical account of Prussian policy from the seventeenth century.

7. The Germans, their Empire, and what they covet.
By C. R. L. FLETCHER. 2d. net. *Fourth Impression.*
An account of the ambitions avowed by the Pan-German school.

8. Might is Right.
By Sir WALTER RALEIGH. 2d. net. *Second Impression.*
Why Germany may win; what will happen if she wins; why we believe she will not win.

9. Austrian Policy since 1867.
By MURRAY BEAVEN. 3d. net. *Second Impression.*
Austrian policy in the Balkans has been of the 'offensive-defensive' order. The Archduke Francis Ferdinand might have saved Austria from rushing to destruction; but 1912 was the beginning of the end.

10. Italian Policy since 1870.
By KEITH FEILING. 2d. net. *Second Impression.*
Italian policy has been and must be guided by her own interests. The results of her colonial policy have not yet been satisfactory enough to tempt her into adventures.

III

11. French Policy since 1871.
By F. MORGAN and H. W. C. DAVIS. 2d. net. *Fourth Impression.*
A historical sketch, discussing the question whether French policy has been aggressive.

12. Russia: The Psychology of a Nation.
By PAUL VINOGRADOFF. 1d. net. *Fourth Impression.*
A reply to the German taunt that Russia is still in a state of barbarism, and is the enemy of European civilization.

13. Serbia and the Serbs.
By Sir VALENTINE CHIROL. 2d. net. *Third Impression.*
A sketch of Serbian history, which is incidentally an indictment of the policy pursued by Austria-Hungary towards the Serbian kingdom.

14. Germany and 'The Fear of Russia'.
By Sir VALENTINE CHIROL. 2d. net. *Third Impression.*
Shows that before 1879 Germany preferred Russia as an ally to Austria. The ambition of Germany to establish a protectorate over Turkey has led her to assist Austria in the Balkans and so to challenge Russia.

15. The Eastern Question.
By F. F. URQUHART. 3d. net. *Third Impression.*
The history of the Balkan nations; their future.

16. War against War.

By A. D. LINDSAY. 2d. net. *Third Impression.*

Denies that war is good in itself, or a necessary evil. Power is not the sole or chief end for which the State exists. National greatness, if founded on brute force, cannot endure. International law represents an ideal, but an ideal that may be realized.

17. The Value of Small States.

By H. A. L. FISHER. 2d. net. *Third Impression.*

The author argues that the debt of civilization to small states is incalculable. They are useful, at the present time, as laboratories of political experiments and as buffer-states between the greater powers.

18. How can War ever be Right?

By GILBERT MURRAY. 2d. net. *Fourth Impression.*

A well-known lover of peace and advocate of pacific policies argues against the Tolstoyan position. Right and honour compelled Britain to make war; and war—like tragedy—is not pure evil.

19. The National Principle and the War.

By RAMSAY MUIR. 3d. net. *Second Impression.*

Considers the principle of nationality and its application to the settlement of Europe—particularly of S. E. Europe—after the War.

20. Nietzsche and Treitschke: The Worship of Power in Modern Germany.

By E. BARKER. 2d. net. *Fourth Impression.*

An explanation of the main points of interest in the ethical and political doctrines of the German ruling classes.

21. The British Dominions and the War.

By H. E. EGERTON. 2d. net. *Second Impression.*

Explains the ideas for which the British Empire stands, and the political and moral issues of the war affecting the Dominions.

22. India and the War.

By Sir ERNEST TREVELYAN. 1d. net. *Third Impression.*

Discusses the reasons which account for the striking manifestations of Indian loyalty.

23. Is the British Empire the Result of Wholesale Robbery? By H. E. EGERTON. 2d. net.

A historical sketch in answer to a common taunt.

24. The Law of Nations and the War.

By A. PEARCE HIGGINS. 2d. net. *Second Impression.*

The violation of Belgian neutrality and the conduct of England to Denmark in 1807; the doctrine of German lawyers that military necessity overrides the laws of war; the balance of power and the sanctity of treaties.

25. England's Mission. By W. BENETT. 2d. net.

Answers the question, In what cause are we fighting?

[d]

26. August, 1914: The Coming of the War.
By Spenser Wilkinson. Stiff covers. 1s. net.

VII

27. The Retreat from Mons.
By H. W. C. Davis. 3d. net. *Third Impression.*

28. The Battles of the Marne and Aisne.
By H. W. C. Davis. 4d. net.
The Dispatches, with commentary, maps, &c.

29. The Navy and the War.
By J. R. Thursfield. 3d. net. *Second Impression.*
Estimates the military and economic value of the silent pressure exercised by our fleet, and warns the faint-hearted and the captious of the perils of lack of faith.

30. Bacilli and Bullets.
By Sir William Osler. 1d. net. *Fourth Impression.*
Calls attention to the fact that disease kills more men than the bullet. The most dangerous diseases are preventable by inoculation.

Published separately and will also appear shortly in series.

The Double Alliance *versus* The Triple Entente.
By James M. Beck. 3d. net.
The judgement of a well-known American lawyer.

Thoughts on the War. By Gilbert Murray. 2d. net.
An article written in August and now reprinted.

The Leading Ideas of British Policy.
By Gerard Collier. 2d. net.
Examines the political genius of England.

Greek Policy since 1882. By A. J. Toynbee. 4d. net.

Poland, Prussia, and Culture.
By Ludwik Ehrlich. 3d. net.
The author is a Doctor of the University of Lwow (Lemberg) in Galicia.

The Germans in Africa. By Evans Lewin. 3d. net.

What Europe owes to Belgium.
By H. W. C. Davis. *In the press.*

Spectator :—'These little books are easily the best books of the war—accurate, quietly written, full of knowledge, and quite unspoiled by vainglory or bitterness.'

Others in preparation.

HUMPHREY MILFORD

OXFORD UNIVERSITY PRESS, AMEN CORNER, LONDON, E.C.
[d]

OXFORD PAMPHLETS
1914

FRENCH POLICY
SINCE 1871

BY

F. MORGAN

AND

H. W. C. DAVIS

THIRD IMPRESSION

Price Twopence net

OXFORD UNIVERSITY PRESS
HUMPHREY MILFORD
LONDON   EDINBURGH   GLASGOW
NEW YORK   TORONTO   MELBOURNE   BOMBAY

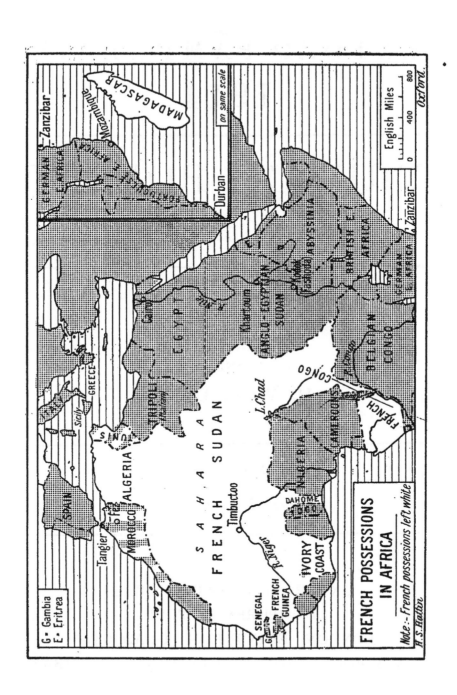

FRENCH POSSESSIONS
IN AFRICA

Note:– French possessions left white

H.S.Halton.

G = Gambia
E = Eritrea

English Miles

0   400   800

Oxford.

FRENCH POLICY SINCE 1871

THE foreign policy of France, since 1871, is a fascinating subject. The history of France has always been the history of her foreign policy; for it is in their dealings with foreign friends and enemies that the French people have expressed most clearly their ambitions and ideals. Not that the thoughtful Frenchman has ever been indifferent to problems of domestic government and social organization. It was the French statesman Colbert who, as long ago as the seventeenth century, first reduced to a system the protection by the State of native industries. The wave of enthusiasm for democratic government, which swept over Europe in the early nineteenth century, spread outwards from France. More recently French thinkers have taken a foremost place among the pioneers of industrial co-operation and of socialism. But it would be difficult, if not impossible, to convince the French people as a whole that the supreme duty of the State is merely to secure good and just government for all its subjects, or an equitable distribution of material wealth. From the French point of view, a state which pursued no other objects would be as contemptible as a private individual who cherished no ambitions beyond those of earning an assured income and of leading a comfortable existence.

The Frenchman holds that the State, no less than the individual, should seek renown (*la gloire*) in performing

' deeds of noble note'. The French conception of glory
has been modified from one age to another, sometimes
for the worse, sometimes for the better.   But, until
comparatively recent times, the noble deeds expected of
a powerful French Government were always deeds of
war, to be accomplished in the name of some cherished
national idea.   Under Louis XIV the nation fought for
natural frontiers, under Louis XV for colonies and
commerce.   The statesmen of the French Revolution
roused their fellow countrymen to the most astounding
military efforts by announcing that France would
compel all other nations to be free in the same sense
as herself.   Under Napoleon I, and more obscurely
under his nephew, Napoleon III, France aspired to
impose her suzerainty by force of arms upon the whole
of Western Europe.   Since 1871 times have changed,
and with them the temper of France.   In the last forty-
three years she has produced some visionary soldiers
who dreamed of a new French ascendancy in Europe; but
their vapourings have been nowhere more mercilessly
satirized than in their own country.   The French people
are wise enough to know that they can no longer hope
to overrun Europe, imposing their authority or their
ideas of government at the point of the bayonet.   They
do not hope for this, and they have even ceased to wish
that it were possible.

Still it is not to be expected that old traditions should
be entirely extirpated in a moment, even by such a
catastrophe as the Franco-Prussian war of 1870.   That
disaster made it imperative for France to maintain a
huge military establishment, as a safeguard against future
attacks; therefore, since 1871, the majority of Frenchmen have still been trained as soldiers, and still the
influence of French military leaders upon national policy

is sometimes greater than the wisdom of their counsels.
The French nation, as might be expected of a military
nation, are keenly sensitive to any slight; they have
not always avoided the mistake of supposing that any
opposition to their cherished schemes must be the
outcome of malevolence. They have ceased to think
of war as the obvious means of furthering national
interests; but they are by no means so pacific as the
Anglo-Saxon peoples, who have hitherto dispensed
with conscription. The foreign policy of France still
strikes the average Englishman as too audacious and
too restless. The French are less cautious than ourselves in counting the cost of foreign enterprises; what
we call common prudence they would call want of spirit.
And they are the more disposed to run great risks for
relatively slight advantages, because they still believe
that their national credit depends upon their foreign
policy. The Minister of Foreign Affairs in a French
Government is expected to pursue a policy which is not
only safe and dignified, but something more. He must
have a clear-cut programme, which holds out the promise
of tangible results (for the French mind is attached to
the concrete), and which at the same time is based upon
some broad principle of right, or some far-reaching
theory of the proper course of national development.
Frenchmen do not demand that their foreign policy
should be aggressive, in the sense of constituting a
menace to other civilized states. But they are imbued
with the idea that great states always are, and always
must be engaged in competition, in a race for the
acquisition of allies, of markets, of spheres of influence.
They would feel humiliated if they thought that France
was dropping out of the race from want of foresight,
from timidity, or from lack of interest. It is not the

prize of victory which they value so much as the consciousness that their country is honourably distinguished in the competition.

Once we have grasped the French point of view, we have surmounted the chief difficulty under which an Englishman labours when he tries to understand French policy. There are other difficulties, and they are not to be underrated. The materials upon which to found a thorough judgement are not yet available. It is probable that France is bound by secret treaties, the nature of which we can only guess. The published treaties to which she is a party will not be fully intelligible until we know much more about her aims in subscribing to them, and her share in framing their provisions. These, however, are difficulties which beset us equally when we turn from France to the consideration of the foreign policy of any other modern state. The peculiar difficulty, in studying French diplomacy, is to apprehend and to keep in mind the French point of view; it is so different from that of the Englishman, whose insular position leads him to think of foreign relations as a regrettable necessity, and to demand of his statesmen that they shall only intervene in foreign complications when some very obvious and very pressing interest is at stake. For England, perhaps, this is the wiser rule of action. But the course which is safest for an island power may be highly dangerous for a continental power; and a theory of the mission of the State which suits the Anglo-Saxon temperament may be altogether unsuitable to Latin peoples. We should not only endeavour to understand how a Frenchman thinks about foreign policy; we should also do our best to appreciate the reasons which make him differ so widely from ourselves. upon this topic.

Remembering then that, in a Frenchman's eyes, there is a world of difference between activity and aggression, between stealing a march upon a rival and aiming a blow at his existence, between winning a race and inflicting an injury, let us attempt to form some judgement of French foreign policy in the last forty years or so. Has it been aggressive? Has it carried competition to the point of wanton and unforgivable provocation? Has the mainspring of it been the desire to revenge upon the German Empire the disgraces and the losses of 1870? Or has it aimed at restoring French prestige, in a less dangerous way, by discovering and developing new fields for French influence? These are questions which cannot be answered with dogmatic confidence until the archives of all the Great Powers have been thrown open. But they are questions on which it is important that we should form a provisional judgement from such material as is available. For they concern the honour and the trustworthiness of a cherished ally.

These questions can best be answered in a brief historical survey. It is a complicated story that we have to tell; but it becomes simpler if one observes that there are three well-marked phases through which French policy has passed since 1871; and that in each successive stage there is one national interest which exercises a predominating influence upon the minds of French statesmen and determines their attitude towards other powers.

(1) From 1871 to 1880 the key-note of French statesmanship was expressed in the words, Recuperation and Reorganization. In these years the Republic, as it exists to-day, was founded and endowed with a fixed constitution. The Republic rapidly paid off the enor-

mous indemnity (£240,000,000) which the victorious German Empire had exacted. The army and the defences of the eastern frontier were put upon a satisfactory footing; and these were only the more striking manifestations of the new spirit of reform which was in the air. The nation, no less than the Government, set to work with amazing energy and success to build up national prosperity on new foundations. The French put away their old illusions and vaingloriousness; they cultivated the clearness of thought and thoroughness in action which had given victory to the Germans. It was for France a time of melancholy, of regrets, of stern self-examination, but any patriotic Frenchman, as he looks back upon the work of those ten years, must feel that there never was a more creditable period in the history of his people.

In foreign policy France did little during the years 1871–80. She stood in constant dread, perhaps exaggerated dread, of a new attack from Germany. The French people would never formally acknowledge the title of the German Empire to Alsace and Lorraine; it was hardly to be expected that they should, while the population of the ceded provinces remained obstinately French in sympathies—as it does to this day in Alsace at least, if not also in Lorraine. But on the whole the French people were wise enough to obey the warning of Gambetta, their most popular statesman in those days, who said: 'Think of it (*Revanche*) always and never speak of it.' A German historian complains that the German Empire, from the day of its birth, has always been 'burdened with a French mortgage', that is, with the danger implied in the latent hostility of France; and Bismarck taught his countrymen, only too well, the lesson that, for their own safety, France must be kept

in a state of weakness.   France, however, did not allow
herself the dangerous luxury of translating her natural
resentment into action.   There was, it is true, a prospect
of a new Franco-German war in 1875 ; but it arose from
a feeling, which prevailed in German military circles,
that France had been let off too lightly in 1871, and
that it was advisable to ' bleed her white '.   War was
averted by the intervention of Russia and of England ;
and Bismarck's apologists now allege that he never
intended to do more than scare the French out of any
thoughts of revenge which she might still be harbouring.
Whatever his intentions, he had certainly acted in such
a way as to give France every reason for strengthening
her defences and for watching the slightest move of
Germany with deep suspicion.

(2) In 1881 the French showed the world that they
had at last recovered confidence and strength.   That
year saw the French occupation of Tunis and the beginning of the new colonial policy which, from that date
to 1904, was the main interest of French statesmen.   For
twenty-three years France was engaged in acquiring and
developing tropical or sub-tropical territories, partly in
Africa and partly in the Far East.   These new possessions
were, and are, as Bismarck once sardonically remarked,
' colonies without colonists '.   Since she lost Canada in
the eighteenth century France has never aspired to
become, like Great Britain, a mother of new nations.
Indeed, if she had the aspiration, she would find it
difficult to provide the emigrants, or to secure a land in
the temperate zones where they could settle.   But both
in Africa and in Asia she has copied with remarkable
success the model afforded by the Indian Empire.

At the fall of Napoleon there remained to France, of all
the colonies which she had established in the seventeenth

and eighteenth centuries, only a few trading posts in India, a few of the West Indian Islands, the islets of St. Pierre and Miquelon off the coast of Newfoundland, and Cayenne (French Guiana) on the east coast of South America. When France began to think once more of colonial enterprises, it was to the Mediterranean that she first turned her gaze. Between 1830 and 1847 Algeria was completely subdued ; and it was no mere accident that the Suez Canal was originally planned in France and was finally constructed (1859-69) by De Lesseps, a retired French diplomat. Napoleon III probably dreamed, as his uncle Napoleon I had dreamed, of a French protectorate in Egypt ; he and his advisers certainly hoped that the Suez Canal would make the Mediterranean a highway for French trade with the Far East. Under Napoleon III France acquired Cochin-China, thus staking out for herself a considerable sphere of influence in Asia. But Napoleon III was distracted between many and conflicting schemes ; there was no consistent plan in his colonial enterprises.

The Republic, in and after 1881, pursued a more energetic colonial policy than Napoleon III, because it was not distracted by any hopes of aggrandizement on the European mainland. Tunis was the first considerable prize to be gained (1881) ; and Tunis was occupied with the goodwill of England. At the European Congress of Berlin (1878) Lord Salisbury said to the French representative : ' Do what you think fit in Tunis ; England will offer no opposition.' Neither did Germany oppose the occupation. In fact Bismarck had prompted Lord Salisbury's offer, in the hope of diverting France from the pre-occupation of *Revanche*. It seemed a remarkable piece of good fortune, an omen of returning prosperity, that such a prize could be obtained without exciting the jealousy of the two powers whom Frenchmen regarded as most jealous of their nation.

The occupation of Tunis has indeed proved a landmark in the history of French colonial enterprise; though, like many other notable events, it has not produced the consequences which were predicted at the time. Tunis did not become a stepping-stone to Egypt, for reasons which we shall narrate hereafter; and, now that Italy has occupied Tripoli, to the east of Tunis, it is improbable that France will ever succeed in drawing nearer to the Nile delta. On the other hand, the possession of Tunis gave France a stronger claim to the Sahara and the Western Sudan, when the powers interested in the partition of Africa agreed to recognize the 'doctrine of the hinterland', the principle that any power which possesses the sea-coast is entitled to the inland districts of which that coast is the natural outlet. Further, it was in Tunis that the French first proved the value of a remarkably flexible and inexpensive system of colonization—the method of establishing a protectorate which allows the native forms of government to continue, under careful supervision, but gives the fullest opportunities for 'peaceful penetration' by the explorer and the merchant. It is a method which France has applied on an extensive scale since 1881. In 1885 she applied it to Madagascar in the Indian Ocean, and to the states of Tonkin and Annam in the Indo-Chinese peninsula. Quite recently (1912) she has applied it to the larger half of Morocco.

It is easier to pass a sweeping condemnation on such a method than to recognize the fact that, under certain circumstances, it affords the only way out of an intolerable position. Protectorates of this kind have too often been created to protect imaginary interests, to exploit unoffending populations, or to gain a monopoly of commerce. But they are often as beneficial to the country which is annexed as to the power which annexes; with one or two glaring exceptions, they have always meant the establishment of better justice, better police, and greater security of person and of property. Every one must admit that Egypt, for example, is infinitely better governed under the British supremacy than she had been at any time since the Mohammedan conquest; and the history of independent Morocco between 1904 and 1912 is the best apology for the protectorate which France has now established in that country. Nor is it true to say that these protectorates, however justly exercised, are always founded upon an unjust usurpation. No one objects when the subjects of a civilized power begin to settle and to trade in a country like Tunis or Morocco. Every one agrees that, if these settlers are ill-used by the native government, their mother-country has the right to demand redress, and, if necessary, a reform of the laws and institutions which have produced oppression or have failed to prevent it. Why then should it be called unjust if, in the last resort, when protests have proved ineffectual, the offended power undertakes to reform and to supervise the offending government? No doubt the colonizing powers of Europe have sometimes alleged a grievance which did not exist, or have made a mountain of a molehill, in order to justify the establishment of a protectorate. But each case must be judged upon its merits; and we have no right to denounce France as a robber simply because she has become the protector of numerous uncivilized or half-civilized communities.

This, however, is a digression. If the French policy of protectorates has created difficulties between France and other powers, this is not because those powers disapprove

of the system, which they are equally ready to apply
when opportunities occur, but because they complain
that France has usurped a right of intervention which
properly belonged to themselves, or that she has protected her own interests by destroying those of her
rivals. The occupation of Tunis led at once to a complaint
of this kind from Italy, who regarded Tunis as lying
within her lawful sphere of interest, both on the score
of geographical position and also because Italians were
heavily interested in the foreign trade with Tunis. It
was natural too that a country which had been a Roman
province, and was now politically derelict, should be
claimed as a suitable outlet for the trade and the colonial
ambitions of the young Italian kingdom. Since France
turned a deaf ear to these complaints, Italy proceeded to form the Triple Alliance with Austria and
Germany (1882) ; and she was encouraged by her powerful allies to prosecute the feud. Until 1898 there was
constant friction between Italy and France. Mutual
ill will found expression in a war of tariffs, and in 1888
the two powers were on the brink of war.

Happily that crisis was averted, the feud has
been healed ; and Italy is now indemnified with Tripoli
for her disappointment in Tunis. Still we must call it
an ominous feud. It showed how inevitably the race for
new markets and new spheres of influence was leading
the European powers into quarrels which reacted on the
European situation. Of such disputes France has had more
than her full share—not because she has been more lawless
than her rivals, but because she has been more energetic
and adventurous. In the last thirty years no country
has produced so many pioneers who have worked heart
and soul to extend the influence of their native country
by systematic exploration. There is something romantic,

indeed we might almost say fantastic, in the rapid
extension of French power over the hinterlands of
North-West Africa. Sometimes France has appropriated
with surprising avidity a desert diversified by small and
rare oases. Sometimes she has based a claim to more
fertile districts upon the possession of a tiny outpost,
hundreds of miles beyond the effective jurisdiction of
any of her colonial governors. But she has not been
singular in her methods. Her fault, if it be a fault,
has consisted in the adroit circumvention of slower-
witted rivals. Germany has never forgiven France for the
skill with which France enveloped and hemmed in the
German colony of the Cameroons, although the French
success was ratified in 1894 by a convention between
the two governments.

But until 1904 the most serious colonial rivalry of
France was that with England. It was stimulated no
doubt by memories of older quarrels in the eighteenth
century. Frenchmen felt that, both in Canada and in
India, the English had reaped where they had not sown.
France entertained profound suspicions of English
colonial policy, imagining that England was restlessly
and insatiably ambitious of new conquests. These suspicions were strengthened by the English occupation of
Egypt (1882), which was begun as a temporary measure
of precaution, to protect the great European interests in
that country when they were threatened by a native
revolution, and which has continued ever since. As
a matter of fact the suspicions were unfounded.
Mr. Gladstone, the Prime Minister of that day, was
sincerely anxious to keep England clear of the complications which were bound to follow if we interfered in
Egypt. He desired the joint intervention of all the
interested powers; and England only undertook the

task single-handed when every power, France among the rest, had declined to share in it. England remained in Egypt with the intention of restoring the native system of government to tolerable efficiency; but, before she had completed the work of reorganization, the new and formidable problem of the Sudan was thrust upon her; and though the solution of this problem was brought nearer by the capture of Khartoum (1898), the evacuation of Egypt has been indefinitely postponed.

It was long before France could bring herself to accept the English occupation as something more than a temporary expedient. As late as 1898 a singularly bold attempt was made by a French explorer, Major Marchand, to occupy the basin of the White Nile. The French flag was hoisted at Fashoda just when the English forces were entering Khartoum, three hundred miles lower down the river. The English refused to recognize the legitimacy of the French occupation, and the dispute was at length settled in England's favour; but not before it had threatened to produce a war in Europe. Happily this episode, which both countries have agreed to forget, was the last rumble of a storm-cloud which for sixteen years had overhung every frontier, from Western Africa to Eastern Asia, where French and English interests came into close contact. As Italy had become reconciled to France, so France entered by degrees upon friendlier relations with England.

The causes of the Anglo-French reconciliation were manifold. Undoubtedly one cause was the respect which each nation felt for the characteristic virtues of the other. One is tempted to say that the English and the French were predestined to be allies. No nations could be more unlike; but the very unlikeness made for mutual respect. Englishmen have always admired the elasticity of the French temperament and the idealism of French policy. Frenchmen, on their side, have not been slow to recognize the pacific and reasonable character of the English, their readiness to accept a compromise and to abide loyally by an agreement. In the colonial sphere it has often happened that English interests have clashed with those of France. But a way of settlement, honourable to both parties, has always been discovered; and France has never had occasion to complain that England regards the prosperity of a competitor as an insult or a menace.

(3) The third period, from 1904 to 1914, has been remarkable for the steady and deliberate preparations of France to face the German peril. For at least ten years her statesmen have not only feared invasion, but have been pretty well informed of the plan of campaign which the German General Staff would pursue. Indeed the more militant of German newspapers, and the leading exponents of German strategy, have not troubled to disguise the intentions of the German governing class. The only doubts in French minds have been as to the date at which the German plan would be put in execution, and the exact nature of the pretext which would be alleged. It was, however, reasonable to expect that the blow would be struck when German military and naval expenditure had reached the maximum permitted by the state of the public revenue; and that the occasion would be found in the Franco-Russian alliance which the Pan-German party have affected to treat as a crime against European civilization.

The Russian alliance was in fact projected and concluded during the years 1891-7, when France asked for nothing more than freedom from continental embarrassments and the fullest opportunity of developing French interests in Africa and Asia.   Russia stood in need of loans from French financiers. France on her side felt that a Russian alliance would protect her against Germany, and might be a valuable support in her colonial rivalries with England.   Some such measure of insurance was necessary to France; her population was becoming stationary, her colonial policy required the maintenance of a strong navy, and her military resources, relatively to those of Germany, were rapidly declining.   But even in Bismarck's time the German Empire had watched with apprehension the growth of the Russian power on its eastern flank; and this apprehension was intensified as German statesmen, after Bismarck's fall, committed themselves more and more deeply to the support of Austrian designs in the Balkans.   It was impossible for Russia to tolerate the prosecution of those designs, which involved the destruction or the mutilation of small Slavonic states.   Germany and Austria-Hungary were steering a straight course towards a racial war of Teuton against Slav. They counted themselves superior to Russia in military organization, and were not afraid so long as Russia stood alone. But they feared that the Dual Alliance of France and Russia would be too strong for them; and they vented their irritation upon France.

From 1897 it was apparent that an armed conflict, of the Triple Alliance or its two Teutonic partners against the Dual Alliance, was well within the range of possibility.   Neither Russia nor France desired a continental war; but their union was the most dangerous obstacle which German and Austrian projects of expansion had hitherto encountered.   The one redeeming feature of the situation, from the German point of view, was that England also viewed the Dual Alliance with some apprehension—as was shown by the fact that the English standard of naval construction was fixed, for some time after 1897, with reference to the combined strength of the French and Russian navies. It was fortunate for France that Germany was encouraged, by the outbreak of the South African War, to develop a new naval policy which could only be explained on the assumption that she intended, sooner or later, to strike directly or indirectly at British interests. The events of the present year, and especially the terms of the now notorious German bid for British neutrality, suggest that the immediate object of the German fleet-laws was to prepare for an attack upon French colonies. But undoubtedly the remoter object was the ruin of the British Empire; and the consciousness of a common danger brought England to the side of France just at the moment when Russia, owing to her war in the Far East with Japan (1904), was incapacitated from helping her ally. In the year 1904 England and France publicly made up their differences on the chief points which had hitherto kept them apart—the question of French fishing rights off Newfoundland, the question of the English occupation of Egypt, the question of French intervention in Morocco.[1] The most important features of the settlement were that the French withdrew their old demand for the evacuation of Egypt by some fixed date;

---

[1] Two of these disputes were old, the last was of comparatively recent date. France had now become mistress of the hinterlands behind Morocco, and her trade interests in that country had developed. She felt that the time was at hand when she could no longer tolerate the state of anarchy which seemed normal in Morocco. England was the other power largely interested in Moroccan trade, and feared at first that France would find means of excluding all merchants but her own, when Morocco had been made French.

and that the English agreed to leave the French a free hand in Morocco, so long as all nations were permitted to trade there on equal terms, and the Straits of Gibraltar were left open. But these written terms of agreement were of less importance than the silent understanding that it might be desirable, in the near future, for France and England to form a closer alliance.

Since 1904 the Anglo-French Entente has been twice robustly, not to say rudely, tested by the statesmen of the German Empire, who have spared no pains to sow mistrust between the two great colonizing powers. In 1905 and 1911 Morocco served as the pretext. In the first of these years the German Emperor announced that he would not recognize any arrangement concerning Morocco which prevented him from treating directly with the Sultan ; in 1911 a German warship was sent to seize the Moroccan port of Agadir, on the pretext that the safety of German commercial interests was imperilled by the disorders of Morocco. It is probable that Germany coveted Morocco ; a German minister is said to have declared that Agadir, once occupied, would never be evacuated. The country was the most promising of those which still remained to be occupied by some European state. But it is certain that Germany expected England to desert France on each of these occasions, and that such a desertion would have ended the Entente. On each occasion England stood firm, and Germany experienced a diplomatic rebuff which was keenly resented by all German parties except the Socialists. Under cover of the Entente, France was enabled to establish the Protectorate over Morocco, which she had so long desired. Italy and Spain, who next to England were the powers most concerned, have accepted this arrangement ; some arrangement of the kind was imperative if any Europeans were to continue trading in Morocco.

On the whole Germany had no cause to complain of the terms upon which she was twice allowed to escape from a false position. The dispute of 1905 was adjusted, amicably enough to outward appearance, by the international conference of Algeciras. In 1911 German honour was salved by some French concessions concerning the boundary-line between the French Congo and the Cameroons. Germany, it is true, had demanded much more than she obtained; she had asked for the coast-line of the French Congo, and the territory behind it as far as the river Sangha. But enough was conceded by the French ministry of the day to arouse feelings of lively dissatisfaction in the French legislature. In 1912 the French Government continued the work of conciliation by coming to an arrangement with Germany about the boundaries of Togoland and the French Sudan. But it is clear that, after 1911, if not earlier, the German colonial party came to the conclusion that France was their superior in the art of 'peaceful penetration', and that the short way of establishing a German colonial power was to strip France of her African territories.

France has not been blind to this danger. Like England, she has often, in the past few years, given foreigners the impression of being wholly absorbed in party politics and of wilfully turning her back upon the European situation. But in France, as in England, though party differences are clamorously expressed, there is a broad basis of agreement on which all parties take their stand when the national existence is in question. Whatever have been the quarrels of French politicians in domestic questions, they have worked harmoniously and unobtrusively against the common foe. They have not done so in any spirit of *Revanche*. They have not boasted, and they have not threatened; and they have shown their conviction that France was unequal to the task of an aggressive war. It was not until the eleventh hour, in 1913, that they agreed to increase the strength of the army, and to demand three years of military training (instead of two) from every conscript; and this step was only taken in answer to the sensational German Army Bill of the same year— a Bill, it may be mentioned, which frightened Belgium into adopting universal military service.

Until 1913 the preparations of France were mainly diplomatic. Her Foreign Ministers have been eminently pacific since 1905, when M. Delcassé was relegated to the background as being a statesman too brilliant and original for the national safety. This was no ordinary concession to German susceptibilities; for M. Delcassé is the most distinguished Foreign Minister whom the Republic has produced. His successors have occupied themselves in clearing up old differences with foreign powers, more particularly with Italy and Spain. In 1906 France and Italy agreed that each would respect and would defend the interests of the other in Ethiopia; and, significantly enough, both agreed to defend the interests of England in Egypt and in the basin of the Nile. In 1912 France and Italy made a further agreement concerning their interests in Morocco and in Libya; and in the same year Spain, by the Treaty of Madrid, acquired a protectorate over definite zones in Morocco in exchange for a recognition of the French protectorate over the remainder of the country. The effect of these transactions has been to establish friendly relations between

the three Latin powers of the Western Mediterranean.
They have made it clear that they neither invite nor
desire the intervention of Germany in their disputes ;
Spain and Italy will not allow themselves to be used, as
the cats'-paws of German colonial policy, to molest a sister
nation.   Italy and France will not tolerate a German
or an Austrian descent upon the Nile valley.   It is to
agreements of this kind that German publicists refer
when they complain that the German people is being
strangled in a network of diplomacy.   The complaint
will only become justifiable when the right to steal is
recognized by European public law.

But these agreements of the Latin peoples among
themselves, instructive as they are, only helped France
negatively, by releasing her from embarrassments which
might have hampered her in a war of life and death.
It is to the Entente with Russia and with England that
she has looked, and not in vain, for actual support.
Until 1909 the weak spot in her armour of alliances was
the absence of any direct understanding between her
two chief supporters.   She had one set of agreements
with Russia, another set of agreements with England.
She felt that she could certainly depend on Russian
help, and that England, though not definitely committed in the same way as Russia, could not afford to
stand neutral while French territory or French colonies
were being appropriated by another power.   But there
was no guarantee that England and Russia would work
harmoniously together when both were ranged upon the
side of France.   From 1904 to 1909 it was a leading object
of French foreign policy to secure this guarantee.   There
can be no doubt that French influence was largely
responsible for the gradual reconciliation of England
and Russia in those years, for the growth of a feeling in

both countries that their Asiatic interests, hitherto the main cause of disputes, were by no means irreconcilable. In 1905 England acted as a mediator between Russia and Japan ; in 1907 England and Russia came to an agreement respecting their claims in Persia, Afghanistan, and Tibet.   Finally, in 1909, the Tsar paid a ceremonious visit to England ; and from that moment the Triple Entente became a new and vital factor in the European situation.   The* immediate effect was that France found herself able to concentrate practically the whole of her fleet in the Mediterranean, where it would be ready to defend her North African colonies.   For it was understood that, if the three powers found themselves jointly engaged in a war against a common enemy, Russia would guard the interests of her allies in the Baltic, and England would be responsible for holding the North Sea and the English Channel.

There can be no doubt that the Triple Entente has operated as a bar against some cherished hopes of Germany and Austria-Hungary.   Since 1909 it has been the fixed intention of Germany, if not also of Austria-Hungary, that France should be made to pay heavily for her presumption in building up this coalition. Apparently Germans think that the Triple Entente exists largely, if not entirely, to thwart German colonial ambitions, and to promote those of France.

To such suspicions we can only answer that no proof of them is offered, and that they are not confirmed by any facts which are generally known.   There is evidence that French statesmen have feared a war with Germany as one of the greatest evils that could befall their nation.   There is evidence that France has been relatively less prepared than Germany for the present war.   We do not contend that France has pursued

a policy of peace at any price; but the events of 1905
and 1911 are in themselves a proof that she has been
prepared to pay a high price to avert the ill will of
Germany. In the colonial sphere, as we have shown,
France has pursued an active and sometimes an audacious
policy. She has quarrelled over colonial questions with
other powers besides Germany. But her differences with
England, with Italy, with Spain, have been amicably
settled by compromises not invariably too favourable
to France. Her colonial policy has been one of competition, but not of war to the knife; and she owes
her most brilliant successes not so much to her
diplomacy as to the industry of her traders and the
self-devotion of her explorers. Her rivals, with one
exception, have not found it necessary to remain her
enemies, to treat her prosperity and the prosperity of
her colonies as an insult and a wrong. Germany is the
exception; and Germany has no reason to complain if
France has woven a network of alliances to protect
herself against the overt and covert threats to which
she has been exposed in the last generation.

Oxford : Horace Hart Printer to the University

No. 19

OXFORD PAMPHLETS

1914

THE NATIONAL PRINCIPLE AND THE WAR

BY

RAMSAY MUIR

SECOND IMPRESSION

Price Threepence net

OXFORD UNIVERSITY PRESS

HUMPHREY MILFORD

LONDON   EDINBURGH   GLASGOW

NEW YORK   TORONTO   MELBOURNE   BOMBAY

SWEDEN
openhagen

BALT

HUNGARIAN

nna

oBudapest

TRIA - HUN

Agram

R

BOSNIA

THE NATIONALITIES
OF
CENTRAL & EASTERN EUROPE

0   50   100 Miles   *Frontiers*

mans; also Rumanians   Serbs & Creats   Russians & Ruthenians   Bulgarians, also

Bohemians & Slovaks also Albanians   *Hungarians, also Danes, also Greeks*   Poles

The solid black lines show the present political frontiers; the broken
lines, the racial frontiers.

THE NATIONAL PRINCIPLE
AND THE WAR

I

THE issues raised by a great war are always wider and deeper than the immediate causes which bring it about ; because war, by sweeping away the timidities of diplomacy and its unwillingness to endanger the existing state of things, seems to bring within reach of realization hopes or theories which in time of peace appear remote and unpractical.

One of the great issues which this war is likely to bring within the realm of practical politics is the fuller realization of what may be called the national principle—the idea, that is, that states ought, so far as possible, to be organized upon a national basis. Those who believe in this principle believe that wherever there exist divided nations which long for unity, or subject nations which aspire to be freed from alien control, it is not only just, and not only desirable in the interests of these nations themselves, but it is also in the long run to the advantage of civilization and humanity at large that these aspirations should be satisfied.

Perhaps it may appear to many people that the nationalist dreams of the Poles, or the Serbians, or the Rumanians, or the Greeks, or the Italians, however warmly we may sympathize with them in theory, are after all no direct concern of the Englishman, but concern only the Poles, Serbians, Rumanians, Greeks, and Italians themselves. But that is a narrow view, for two reasons.

In the first place the civilization of Europe has in a large degree derived its progressive character from the fact that, while there is a basis of unity common to all the peoples of the west, there has always been a great variety within this unity, caused by the different temperaments, traditions, and modes of life of the various peoples who compose Europe. Each people has its own excellences, and its own contributions to make to the common stock ; and the freer all the peoples are left to develop their own civilization in their own way, in rivalry with one another, the better it must be for the world. Each people naturally tends to think its own ways of life and thought the best ; and whenever one people gets power over another it inevitably tries to force its own character and ideas upon the subject people. In so far as it succeeds, it impoverishes the common life of civilization by suppressing one of the elements of variety. Of course it is true that there are some peoples even in Europe which have been kept in a backward condition by the accidents of history ; and it may perhaps be argued that a backward people will profit from being brought under the tutelage of a more advanced people. That is sometimes true ; but it is very dangerous to assume too readily that it is true, especially in the case of European peoples, whose natural abilities, though different, are singularly equal if they have anything like equal opportunities. The Russians, for example, have long been in many ways backward as compared with the French or the Germans. But if they had been forced into a French or a German mould, it is doubtful if Europe would have been enriched by the peculiarly Russian vein of genius shown by a Tolstoy or a Turgenev, or if Northern Asia would have achieved the degree of civilization which Russia has brought to it. Again, no doubt the Romans were politically superior to the other peoples of the ancient world; but one of the reasons for the gradual decay of civilization in the period of the Roman Empire was just that the Romans had succeeded (in spite of their tolerance) in impressing too high a degree of uniformity upon the world, and in fusing too completely the life-giving variety and contrast of different peoples. In the same way, even though it were true that the 'culture' of the Germans is, as they proclaim, higher than that of any other nation, still if they succeeded in imposing that culture upon the whole civilized world, the result would be stagnation and decay. The greatest security for the progress and vitality of civilization is that there should be the greatest possible variety among civilized states; and this can be best secured by giving to every nation which can establish its title to the name a free chance of developing its own modes of life and its own ideas in its own way. That is the first reason for believing that the extension of the principle of nationality is an issue of great importance for the whole world, and not only for the nations which have yet to establish their unity and freedom.

But there is another, and much more important or practical, reason for believing that the national aspirations of Italians or Serbs directly affect the interests of Englishmen : and that is, that the satisfaction of national aspirations is essential as a safeguard against war. Glance over the history of the nineteenth century, and you will see that almost every revolutionary outbreak, and almost every war or alarm of war which has disturbed Europe, has been due directly or indirectly to unsatisfied aspirations for national unity or freedom. The revolutionary movements of 1820,

1830, and 1848, the Greek war of the twenties, the Italian *Risorgimento*, the three wars which were engineered by Bismarck—all these were the direct outcome of movements for national unity or freedom. Even the Franco-Prussian war of 1870 was deliberately arranged by Bismarck as a means of securing the unity of Germany. Even the Crimean war, though it seemed to turn on other issues, really arose out of the position of the suppressed nationalities of the Turkish Empire, and the same is true of all the Russo-Turkish wars of the nineteenth century. If Western Europe has enjoyed peace since 1871, it is because the nationalist cause had everywhere triumphed in Western Europe by that date, and because with small exceptions there was no survival of the rankling bitterness of unsatisfied national aspirations. And since 1871 the one danger-spot, whose complications have from time to time threatened to plunge Europe into war, has been that region where national aspirations were unsatisfied, or incompletely satisfied—the south-east. It is no mere coincidence that the disastrous war of to-day has arisen directly out of the aspiration of the Serbians for union with their brother Serbs within the Austrian Empire. In view of these facts it is certainly not too much to say that, if the national principle could be carried out in those parts of Europe where it has as yet been incompletely established, the danger of future European wars would be, if not completely removed—that may be too much to hope—at any rate enormously diminished. For that reason the nationalist aspirations of Serbs, Poles, and Rumanians have a very real and practical importance for every Englishman.

II

But although it is true that the extension of the national principle enriches civilization and is a safeguard against war, these benefits can only be realized if the peoples who claim nationhood are in a real sense nations. A nation is more than the inhabitants of a given area of land across which a particular name is printed on the map. It is a body of people so strongly bound together by natural ties of affinity that they readily sympathize with and understand one another, and can live happily together. The bonds which create this affinity vary in character from one case to another, so that it is impossible to give an exact definition of them. But a nation at its highest is united by some community of race, by a common language and the distinctive ideas which that language expresses, by the common possession of fundamental religious and moral ideas, and by a common tradition, or memory of achievements and sufferings shared in the past. It is easy to name real nations which lack one or other of these features. But no people which lacks them all, or most of them, can be called a nation ; nor can the claim to national unity be regarded as a sound one unless, in all the divided sections of the nation, there is a real sense of affinity, and a real desire for unity. Where these things are lacking, the unification, if it is established on merely theoretic grounds, is likely to do more harm than good ; to create, rather than to heal, dissatisfaction.

It is important to keep these considerations in mind when we deal with claims that are put forward on grounds of nationality. For example, the Germans (a nation very prone to be captivated by theories) asserted in 1871 their right to the provinces of Alsace and Lorraine on the grounds that these provinces had been part of Germany up to the•seventeenth and eighteenth centuries respectively, and that their inhabitants were of German race. But the vital fact was that the Lorrainers and (still more) the Alsatians had become thoroughly French in sentiment; it was with France, not with Germany, that they were bound by conscious ties of affinity. Accordingly they have always resented their severance from France, and the annexation of these provinces has been a standing source of unrest for forty-four years, has prevented the establishment of any permanently friendly relations between France and Germany, and has contributed to the causes which have produced the war.

There is a powerful and noisy party in Germany called the Pan-Germans, who, basing their policy upon the theory of nationality, claim that German unity is incomplete so long as Holland, Belgium, and German Switzerland remain outside the limits of the empire. They claim Holland and Switzerland because their peoples are of Teutonic blood, and because they were in the Middle Ages part of the kingdom of Germany. They try to put forward similar arguments in the case of Belgium. Of course the real reason for these claims is the desire to control, for trade and military purposes, the harbours of the North Sea coast and the Alpine passes, and to get possession of the rich Dutch and Belgian colonies. But these claims are absolutely inconsistent with the national principle, when honestly interpreted. By all the tests of nationality the Dutch are a nation, proudly conscious of their nationhood, and of their glorious history: though originally of German

blood, their history has turned them into a distinct
people, and their language has developed along different
lines. This is still more clear in the case of Belgium.
Holland certainly has no sense of affinity with Germany,
and would desperately resist any attempt to incorporate
her in that country. Belgium has heroically shown that
she is prepared to undergo the uttermost suffering rather
than submit to such a fate. The claims of the Pan-
Germans are really an insult to the principle of nationality, which they use as a pretext to cover schemes of
naked aggression.

Again, we must remember that there are some regions
where nationalities are so intermixed that the national
principle gives no clear guidance as to the proper lines
of division between states. Such regions are to be found
in several parts of South-eastern Europe, notably in
Macedonia, and their existence constitutes the chief
difficulty in the settlement of that region. But the
existence of such regions ought not to stand in the way
of the establishment of full nationhood in cases where
all the marks of nationhood are present; nor should
the fact that the national principle is sometimes used
as a cloak for projects of greedy aggression weaken our
belief that nationality is the strongest and most natural
basis for the organization of states.

The organization of states on the basis of nationhood
has spread gradually over Europe, from the west
eastwards. It began in England and France in the
Middle Ages. Spain and Holland and the Scandinavian
countries achieved their nationhood in the sixteenth
and seventeenth centuries. In Central Europe the
national unity of Germany and Italy was only worked
out, with labour and travail, in the nineteenth century;
and the same period saw the beginning of the rise of

the little long-suppressed nations of the south-east, a process still uncompleted. But there still remains a large area of Europe which is as yet (if we may coin a word) ' unnationalized ', or very incompletely nationalized. This area is represented in our map. It includes part of the Russian Empire, a small piece of Germany, practically the whole of the Austro-Hungarian Empire, and the Balkan peninsula. The map has been drawn so as to show how, in this region, political boundaries disregard the lines of division between nationalities. But it is worth while to analyse this region more closely.

III

The first large region occupied by a distinct nationality is the country of the Poles, which lies mainly in Russia, but includes also part of Eastern Germany, and much of the province of Galicia in the Austrian Empire. The kingdom of Poland was once one of the greatest states of Europe. In the fifteenth century it seemed to overshadow Germany, and was vastly more important than Russia ; in the sixteenth and seventeenth centuries it played a very gallant part in resisting the Turks. But the kingdom fell into decay, owing to a faulty social and political system, and in the last quarter of the eighteenth century, by one of the most cynical crimes of history, its whole territory was unscrupulously divided out, in three partitions, by its three neighbours, Russia, Prussia, and Austria. The prime mover in the first partition was Frederick the Great of Prussia, but Russia got the lion's share of the plunder, including a good deal of really Russian territory which had earlier been acquired by the Poles. From the time of these iniquitous partitions the Poles, among whom patriotism is a passion, never ceased to pray, to conspire, and on favourable occasions to rebel, in the hope of regaining the unity of their realm. Their national tragedy has turned the Poles into a nation of conspirators and anarchists, and they have had a hand in every revolutionary disturbance of the nineteenth century, in other countries as well as their own. Napoleon tried to make use of Polish patriotism, taking most of the Prussian and Austrian sections of the old kingdom to form a Grand Duchy of Warsaw, and for a few years Poland lived again. But when Napoleon fell, free Poland fell with him. The Grand Duchy was taken over by Russia, whose Tsar promised that it should remain a distinct state, with a constitution of its own ; but the promise was kept only for fifteen years. Galicia was kept by Austria, and the Poles of Posen and West Prussia fell once again under the rule of Prussia. On the whole, of recent years, the Poles of Galicia have been better treated than the other sections of the divided nation : they have been allowed a substantial amount of Home Rule, as a means of securing their support for the Austrian Government against the other restless national elements in the Austrian Empire, and on the whole they have been reasonably contented, though they have never forgotten the days of their ancient unity and greatness. But the Poles of Russia have been, spasmodically, very bitterly persecuted, and a vain attempt has been made to turn them into Russians. And the Poles of Prussia, especially during the last thirty years, have had to endure a more scientific and systematic, but not less intolerable, oppression, the German Government having entered upon a regular programme of Germanizing these regions by banning the Polish language, and buying up Polish land for German settlers from the west. This policy has been a complete failure. It has only intensified the passionate yearning of the Poles for the unity and freedom of their ancient realm —a yearning which seemed hopeless until the outbreak of this war. The deliberate brutality of the German policy in Prussian Poland has been defended, for example by Prince Bülow, on the ground that the history of the Poles shows that they are incapable of ruling themselves. It is an ironic commentary on this view that only a hundred years ago exactly the same thing used to be said about the Germans.

Now a new prospect of hope has opened for the Polish nation, by the issue of the Tsar's proclamation promising that if the Allies are victorious in this war Poland shall be reunited, granted a measure of Home Rule, and linked with its sister Russian nation under the Russian Imperial crown. No doubt that proclamation is prompted by Russian interest, and the promise may not seem altogether reliable in face of the fate of the previous promise of 1814, just a hundred years ago. But certainly unity under the Russian crown is the only practicable unity for Poland under existing conditions. If the Germans and Austrians were successful in the war, all hope of Polish unity would be killed : the Poles know what to expect from the Germans. And the situation has been greatly changed in Russia during the last few years, since the institution of the Duma, in which Polish representatives have sat side by side with Russians, and since the rise of a school of Russian politicians who look forward to the transformation of the Russian Empire into a federation of autonomous states on national lines. The Poles themselves have accepted the promise in all good faith, despite their unhappy experiences in the past ; and such extreme Radicals as Prince Kropotkin, and such moderate Russian Liberals as Professor Vinogradoff, unite in believing that a new era is about to dawn in Russia, and that in this era the satisfaction of the long disappointed Polish dream of unity and freedom will be inevitable. Thus there seems ground for hoping that at the end of this war the most cruelly suppressed nationality of Europe will obtain not indeed complete independence, but unity and a real measure of freedom. If that happens, one of the most dangerous centres of revolutionary agitation will have been calmed down, and all Europe will gain.

IV

South of the divided realm of Poland lies the Austro-Hungarian Empire. It is the only great state of Europe which has no national basis, and that is why its condition has long been held to be precarious. This Empire is a bundle of nations, and fragments of nations, originally brought together by the lucky marriages and conquests of members of the Habsburg family, and in more recent days held together mainly by fear of what would happen if they broke asunder. The Empire is divided into two distinct halves, with distinct governments, and each of these halves is dominated by a ruling race, the Germans of Austria proper in the Austrian half, and the Magyars or Hungarians in the Hungarian half. Austrians and Hungarians have fought bitterly in the past, and do not love one another even now. But since the Hungarians were given Home Rule, in 1867, the two ruling races have managed to work together, and the reason for this is that they are both largely outnumbered by subject races, who dislike them both, and desire either independence, or union with their free brethren on the other side of the imperial boundary. Both the German-Austrians and the Hungarians occupy clearly-defined areas—the Austrians in the territory immediately south and south-east of their brothers in Germany proper, the Hungarians in the central part of the Danube and Theiss valleys ; but all the outlying parts of the Empire are mainly occupied by other races, quite distinct from both the Austrians and the Hungarians, and in most cases closely related to other free races over the border, as in the case of the Poles, already discussed.

First among these subject races may be named the Bohemians or Czechs, who occupy a large area in the north, a sort of island among the German-speaking peoples, walled in by mountains. The Bohemians look back to a proud national history, the greatest days of which were in the fifteenth century, when the enthusiasm raised by the doctrines of John Hus, and the military genius of a group of great Bohemian soldiers, enabled them triumphantly to defy the might of Germany, and indeed of Europe. The kingdom of Bohemia passed by marriage to the German Dukes of Austria, but the Bohemians proudly maintained their separate national existence, until it was for the time crushed out by a fierce Austrian persecution in the seventeenth century. During the nineteenth century there has been a great revival of national feeling among the Bohemians. They have eagerly studied their own history ; they have made their ancient language, long confined to the peasantry, once more respectable by making it the vehicle of a literature of some value. They unsuccessfully revolted against the Austrian rule in 1848 ; but the failure of that year has not stopped the national movement, and the government of Bohemia has been a constant difficulty to the Austrians during the last two generations. Unquestionably the Bohemians would like to regain some sort of national independence. They might naturally become a small independent state with guaranteed neutrality : for, if the Allies win in this war, it is not unlikely that powerful monarchies will in future hesitate to disregard such guarantees, and little states will be much safer than they have been in the past.

The whole of the south-eastern part of Hungary, a hilly region known as Transylvania and lying between the Carpathian Mountains and the Danube, is mainly inhabited by Rumanians, of the same race and language as the people of the independent kingdom of Rumania, on the other side of the Carpathians. The Rumanians are a very interesting people. They claim to be descended from Latin soldiers and colonists settled in this region in the second century of the Christian era ; and although they must be a very mixed race—for during many centuries they were lost to sight, submerged beneath wave after wave of invading tribes who passed over this region into Europe—yet they have with a singular tenacity preserved a language which is a corruption of ancient Latin, and are thus clearly marked off from all their neighbours. They occupy not only the modern kingdom of Rumania and the Hungarian province of Transylvania, but also the province of Bessarabia, which was rather unfairly taken by Russia in 1878. These regions are fertile and rich in minerals, and the prosperity of the kingdom has shown that the people have real capacity for civilization ; and if the kingdom of Rumania could be extended to correspond with the limits of the Rumanian people, it would certainly become a solid and powerful state, with a very distinctive character of its own. The Rumanians have, of course, long desired this expansion, and their agitation for this development has for many years been one of the vexing questions of Austro-Hungarian politics. That is why they are watching the course of the war with such tense interest.

In the opposite, or south-western, corner of the Austro-Hungarian Empire there is a considerable population of Italians. If you look at the map of Italy you will see a triangular piece of Alpine land jutting into the north Italian plain. This is the ' Tridentine ', or district of Trent. It is purely Italian in character, though politically it is part of the Austrian Tyrol. Again, the peninsula of Trieste, which projects into the northern waters of the Adriatic, has a population which is mainly Italian, and, practically until the nineteenth century, it has always been historically as well as geographically a part of Italy. The same is the case with many of the islands and part of the Dalmatian coast of the Adriatic. These lands were part of the old free republic of Venice, which was suppressed by Napoleon, and after his fall was seized by Austria. The Italian inhabitants of these historic Italian lands naturally long to be united with their Italian brothers, and they have given a great deal of trouble to the Austrian Government, which has not treated them well. These lands form what is called *Italia irredenta*, or unredeemed Italy ; and the acquisition of them is an object of longing to all good Italians, who hope thus to complete the great work of nation-building on which their fathers spent so much blood.

Lastly, the southern and south-western provinces of the Austrian Empire—Slavonia, Bosnia, Herzegovina, and part of Dalmatia—are mainly inhabited by Serbians, of the same race, language, and traditions as their brothers in the little free kingdom of Serbia. Indeed these regions were all part of the historic Serbia of the great days before the coming of the Turks, when Serbia seemed likely to become one of the great nations of Europe. The longing of all good Serbians to see these great old days revived has led to an agitation for a Greater Serbia which could only be satisfied at the expense of the Austrian Empire, and which has formed the immediate cause of the present war. But of that we shall presently have more to say.

V

The Austrian Empire thus consists of two small nations —the Hungarians and the Bohemians, and of divided fragments of five other nations, the Germans, the Poles, the Rumanians,. the Italians, and the Serbs, the bulk of which in each case lie outside the limits of the Empire. There are also other races, or fragments of races : Ruthenians (in South Galicia), who are closely related to the Russians ; Slovaks in the north, cousins of their Bohemian neighbours ; Slovenes or Croats in the south- west, who are near relatives of their Serbian neighbours. Among all these races there is a constant state of friction and misunderstanding, due to their forced union, and for a long time the supreme problem of Austrian states- manship has been the problem of driving this motley and discordant team in single harness. The task is, indeed, impossibly difficult, and cannot be ultimately successful. There is no great state to which the triumph of the national principle would be so ruinous as to the Austrian Empire, for all the other great states of Europe are organized upon a national basis, and derive their strength from that fact.

Just because the national principle is so dangerous

to Austria, she has always been its most resolute foe ;
and the history of Austrian policy in the nineteenth
century may almost be summed up in the formula,
' resistance to the national principle wherever it shows
itself.' This is strikingly illustrated if we recall the
great struggles for national unity which have been the
chief features of European history during the last
hundred years. When the Greeks rose against the
Turks in the '20's, their most steadfast enemy, next to
the Turks themselves, was the Austrian Government :
the Powers whose intervention made the establishment
of Greek independence possible were the Allies of to-day,
Russia, France, and England. When the Belgians, in
the '30's, revolted against the supremacy of Holland,
Austria and Prussia would have been ready to reduce
them by force ; the Powers whose intervention saved
the freedom of Belgium were Belgium's allies of to-day,
France and England. The heroic story of the freeing
and unification of Italy is essentially the story of a fight
against Austria; and so far as Italy did not owe her
freedom to the valour of her own sons, she owed it to
the armed intervention of France and the steady sympathy and diplomatic support of England. Most remarkable of all, Austria formed the supreme obstacle to the
unification of Germany, and it was not until Austria
had been crushed by Prussia, in 1866, that the establishment of a united Germany under Prussian control
became possible.

VI

But the most remarkable illustration of the anti-national policy which is forced upon Austria by the condition of her own empire is to be found in her attitude towards the nationalities of the Balkan peninsula, which have been for so many centuries suppressed, and in a large degree barbarized, by the stupid and oppressive dominion of the Turks.

There are five distinct nationalities in this region, not including the Turks, who have never been more than a thinly sprinkled caste of warrior-rulers. We have already said something about the Rumanians, whose independent kingdom as yet occupies less than half of the area peopled by the Rumanian race. The Greeks are the second race, and their history has attracted far more attention in Western Europe than that of the other races. The Greeks have nearly attained their natural limits, though there are still some essentially Greek islands which ought to be added to the kingdom of Greece ; one of these is Cyprus, which is at present under English administration. Once the disorder which has for generations been chronic in South-eastern Europe has been brought to an end, there is every hope that we shall see a vigorous revival of Greek civilization, to the enrichment of the world.

The third of the Balkan nations is the Bulgarians, an honest and solid race of peasants, who in the thirteenth century set up a very formidable power, but whose very existence was forgotten by Europe during the long centuries of subjection to the Turkish yoke. Most people had never heard of them when, in the '70's, the stories of the Bulgarian atrocities aroused the horror of Europe and formed the theme of Gladstone's

Midlothian speeches. Bulgaria was almost the last of the Balkan nations to achieve the beginnings of freedom ; her existence as a free nation only began after the Russo-Turkish war, in 1878. How great is the effect of freedom upon the spirit of a nation is shown by the subsequent development of this little state. The chroniclers of the war of 1878 repeatedly emphasize the servile and spiritless character of the Bulgarian peasantry ; that was the result of five hundred years of alien rule. But after only a single generation the sons of these servile and spiritless peasants showed on the field of Lule Burgas and elsewhere that, fighting in a national cause, they yielded in valour to no soldiery of the world. Bulgaria has now almost reached its natural national limits ; almost, but not quite, for the circumstances of the settlement after the Balkan wars (circumstances indirectly due in a large measure to Austria) robbed her of some regions which ought to belong to her.

The fourth of the Balkan peoples is the most ancient of all, the Albanians, who have dwelt since the dawn of history among the inaccessible rocks in the middle-western part of the peninsula. Never really subjugated or assimilated by any conqueror, they have never escaped from a crude state of unending tribal warfare. Yet they have produced not only fine soldiers, but many able administrators, without whose aid the Turkish power would scarcely have lasted so long as it has. Whether or no the Albanians, if left to themselves, could evolve a stable and orderly system, is hard to say. But it is clear that the Albanian problem is not to be solved by the loan of a German ruler to these wild and proud people.

The last, and in many ways the most interesting, of the Balkan peoples is the Serbian nation. It is spread

over not only Serbia proper, but also the kingdom of
Montenegro and (as has been already noted) the
Austrian provinces of Bosnia, Herzegovina, Dalmatia, and
Slavonia, while the province of Croatia is occupied by
a closely kindred people. If the Serbian kingdom were
enlarged to its natural limits it would thus reach the
Adriatic Sea, and form a realm of substantial size,
approximately equal to the enlarged Rumania. In
the fourteenth century, when we were fighting the
French at Cressy and Poitiers, the Serbian Empire
included almost the whole of this area, and more ;
indeed, under the greatest of their kings, Stephen
Dushan, who died in 1355, the Serbians bade fair to
extend their power over the whole of the Balkan
peninsula. But, before their power was consolidated,
they had to meet the brunt of the Turkish invasion ; and
after a hard struggle the freedom of Serbia was broken
for four hundred years in the disastrous battle of Kossova,
and Europe forgot the existence of this suppressed
nationality. But the memory of ancient greatness and
of its sudden and tragic downfall is very real to every
Serbian peasant. Stephen Dushan is still a national
hero ; and when in the Balkan war a Serbian army
defeated the hated Turks at Kumanovo, almost on the
site of the fatal battle of Kossova, the effect upon
patriotic emotion was electric. The Serbs were the
first of the Balkan peoples to revolt against Turkish
rule ; indeed, one branch of them, the inhabitants of the
little mountain nook of Montenegro, were never really
conquered by the Turks at all. The first rising began
in Serbia proper in 1804, long before the Greek rebellion ;
and although the Serbs got little help from Europe, in
a long-drawn-out struggle under their gallant leader
the swineherd Kara George, they held their own, and

in the end compelled the grant to them of self-government under Turkish suzerainty, in 1826. From that date onwards their dream has been the union of the whole Serbian people, and the revival of some shadow of their ancient greatness. They achieved full independence with the help of Russia in 1878. But both before and since that date it has been made plain to them that their inevitable foe, and the great obstacle to their dream of Serbian unity, was to be found in Austria. Hence the agitations which led to the unhappy murder of last June, and thence to the great war. But to understand this, and its bearing upon the national principle in this region, it is necessary to consider the policy of Austria in regard to the little Balkan nations.

VII

The Turks, who had crushed the rising nations of Serbs, Bulgarians, and Rumanians, afterwards overthrew the Hungarians also, and pressed on to the very gates of Vienna, which they twice besieged, in the sixteenth, and again in the seventeenth century. Accordingly the business of driving back the Turkish power fell in the first instance to the Austrians. In a series of remarkable campaigns at the end of the seventeenth century they drove back the Turks beyond the Danube, and won from them the territory occupied by the Hungarians, by the Rumanians of Transylvania, and by the Serbs of Slavonia. For a short time they even crossed the Danube and occupied a part of Serbia proper (1718–39). But it did not occur to the Austrian conquerors to give independence or self-government to these peoples whom they had released from Turkish rule. They merely added them to their own empire. From this time the Austrian Government made it a principal object of policy to expand south-eastwards at the expense of the Turk, in the hope of ultimately reaching Salonika and the Aegean Sea. That ambition the Austrians have steadily pursued ever since, though with singularly little success. And as the rise of free states in the Balkans would be inconsistent with this ambition, as well as a source of disturbance to the composite Austrian Empire itself, Austria has never welcomed the creation of these states.

The reason for the non-success of Austria's policy of expansion at the expense of the Turk was that during the eighteenth and nineteenth centuries she found a serious rival in this field in Russia, who possessed this great advantage, that she was of the same race and religion as most of the Balkan peoples, and could therefore appeal for their loyalty in a way that Austria could not, and did not desire to, imitate. There has always been this marked distinction between the policy of the two rival empires in the Balkans, that while Austria has consistently opposed the rise of free states, Russia has as steadily encouraged and supported this idea. Since the time of her first serious intervention in Balkan affairs, in 1772–4, she has (unlike Austria) scarcely attempted to annex territory directly ; but every victory which she has won over the Turks (and there have been many Russo-Turkish wars between 1772 and 1878) has been marked by an increase in the number of free states or in the degree of self-government allowed to them. It would, of course, be absurd to suggest that this has been due to any exalted magnanimity on Russia's part : she has hoped to increase her influence by appearing as the patron of the little nations ; her policy has no doubt been quite as much dictated by self-interest as that of Austria. But this at least is true, that Russia's view of her own interest has led to the freedom of the suppressed nationalities in this region, and that Austria's view of her own interest has made her the steady foe of all such developments. The success of the Russian policy was largely due to the fact that she was able to make use of the powerful force of national feeling. But her success was regarded, throughout the nineteenth century, with great anxiety, not only by Austria, but by England, which, elsewhere the friend of the national people, was here turned into its enemy by jealous fear of Russia. Neither England, nor Russia herself, realized until a very late date that, once these states were really free and began to prosper, they would refuse to be the mere puppets even of the Power to which they owed their liberty.

The last and most important military intervention of Russia in Balkan affairs was the war of 1877-8, which followed on the revolt of the Bosnian Serbs and the Bulgarian atrocities. Having beaten the Turks to their knees, Russia compelled them to grant complete independence to Rumania and Serbia, and to establish the new State of Bulgaria as a practically independent State, within limits nearly corresponding to those which Bulgaria gained in the last Balkan war (Treaty of San Stefano, 1878). But this did not at all suit Austria. The setting up of these states, under Russian influence, put an end to all hope of her realizing her ambition of controlling the territory between the Danube and the Aegean Sea. Backed by Germany, with whom she was about to make that intimate alliance which has lasted ever since, and also by England, still governed by her old fears of Russia, she got the Treaty of San Stefano revised by the Powers ; the territory of Bulgaria was cut down ; and the Serbian regions·of Bosnia and Herzegovina were placed under Austrian administration. The Bosnians resisted their new masters, but in vain ; and their defeat seemed to put an end to all hope of Serbian unity, and made Austria appear—what indeed she was—the inevitable foe of the Serbian national cause. Nevertheless there was for a long time a pro-Austrian party in Serbia ; and the fact that the king and court were largely identified with this party, which seemed to most Serbians anti-national and unpatriotic, helps to explain the most discreditable episode in the recent history of Serbia —the murder of the last Serbian king of the Obrenovitch line, and his replacement by a member of the rival and exiled family of Karageorgevitch, the descendants of the hero of the Serbian rising at the beginning of the nineteenth century.

The fact that Austria was the inevitable foe of the cause of Serbian national unity has been made clearer than ever during the last twenty years—when Austria and Germany, now closely united, began to work out the old programme of expansion towards the south-east on new and more ambitious lines. This bold scheme, which looked far beyond the Balkan peninsula, and aimed at the establishment of Austro-German influence through Asia Minor and Mesopotamia to the Persian Gulf, and perhaps ultimately to India, has been, together with the equally bold naval and colonial ambitions of Germany in the west, the main cause of the new grouping of European States, and of the present war. Its successful accomplishment depended upon several things. First of all, there was to be a close alliance with Turkey —the ancient and hated oppressor of the Balkan nations. Turkey was practically to become a member of the

Triple Alliance, and to leave the exploitation of her commercial resources in German hands. General Bernhardi has told us that Turkey is the 'natural ally' of Germany, and Prince von Bülow says that Turkey 'serves German interests from the industrial, military, and political points of view', and has been 'a useful and important link in the chain of our political relations'. So the Kaiser began to cultivate friendly relations with Abdul Hamid, and, after his disconcerting fall, with the Young Turks, and German officers took in hand the reconstruction of the Turkish army. But the bolstering up of the Turkish power was a direct challenge to the Balkan nationalities, which could only achieve their unity at the expense of the Turks. Secondly, the great scheme involved that the Balkan States should be kept apart, and as weak as possible. This particularly applied to Serbia, which lay right in the path of Austrian advance towards the Aegean Sea, and intervened between the German powers and their 'natural ally'. So Serbia must be somehow reduced to dependence on Austria; and this was at first attempted by commercial methods, through a tariff war, which was ruinous to Serbian trade, and reduced the Serbians to the highest pitch of exasperation. Lastly, the direct power of Austria in the Balkans was to be increased as far as possible. A splendid opportunity of doing this presented itself in 1908, when Austria, backed by Germany, suddenly announced the annexation of Bosnia and Herzegovina, hitherto administered under the nominal suzerainty of Turkey. The Serbians were, of course, wild with indignation, but they were powerless to resist. Russia, scarcely recovered from the Japanese war, was unready to fight; and Germany announced, in the grandiloquent phrase of the Kaiser, that she 'stood in shining armour beside her ally', like a knight of romance succouring the weak and the oppressed. From that moment the feeling of the Serbians for Austria became one of inextinguishable hatred, and, both in Serbia itself and in the annexed provinces, secret societies and conspiracies began to spring up, as was indeed inevitable.

It was a grave blow to the Austro-German plans when three of the Balkan States—largely under the influence of the fears which these plans had aroused—forgot their jealousies and formed a league against the Turks. It was a greater blow still when this league proved its superiority in the field, and the German-trained Turkish army was defeated, and the Turk almost driven out of Europe. The threads of the great scheme had to be painfully gathered up again. In the London conferences, when the Powers intervened to regulate the terms of peace, the influence of Austria and Germany could not prevent the weakening of the 'natural ally' and the strengthening of the little conquering nations ; but they devoted all their efforts to preventing Serbia from getting a foothold on the Adriatic, because that would have made her commercially independent of Austria. And as Serbia could not win the natural price of her victories in the addition to her realm of territory occupied by Serbs, since most of this territory was in the hands of Austria, she had to be compensated elsewhere, in a region which should naturally have fallen to Bulgaria. This had, from the Austro-German point of view, the happy effect of bringing about a quarrel between the victorious allies, which led to the wretched second Balkan war ; and if it had not been for the intervention of Rumania, it is quite likely that the result would have been the downfall of Serbia and the revival of ' our natural ally '. Thus Austrian and German policy succeeded in ruining an unequalled opportunity for the satisfaction of national aspirations in the Balkans, and for the making of a permanent friendly alliance between the reinvigorated Balkan powers. These things would have been a blessing for the peace of Europe ; the Balkans would have ceased to be the running sore in the polity of Europe which they have been for so long. But the peace of Europe, and the satisfaction of national aspirations, were not to the interests of Austria or of Germany.

Is it wonderful that this truncated settlement, which left Serbia, after her heroic efforts, apparently as far as ever from her dream of national unity, should have been followed by a new activity of agitation in the Serbian provinces of Austria ? The murder of the Archduke last June was the sort of result that might be expected from a proud and baffled people who have but recently escaped from four centuries of training in lawlessness under the Turkish yoke. Deeds as horrible, done under no greater provocation, are to be found in the history of every nation ; and although that is no defence for an indefensible crime, it is at any rate an explanation. Although no proof has yet been afforded that the Serbian Government had any previous knowledge of the deed, or that the Serbian people sympathized with it, the murder obviously presented a splendid excuse to Austria and Germany for dealing once and for all with Serbia, which had proved so inconvenient an obstacle to the great scheme, and for reducing her to complete dependence. The opportunity came at a moment when the German military machine was in a state of perfect readiness, with everything prepared for war, the Kiel Canal just deepened, the secret of the great Krupp guns not yet out, the Zeppelins equipped in their sheds, the quarries and cement-beds all prepared in France, the coal-ships ready to set out from distant ports to supply commerce-raiders, and all the army of spies at their posts. A moment so admirable might never recur ; and so the war began.

VIII

It had arisen immediately out of a great stroke against the natural aspirations of a little and divided nation in the south-east ; it was driven home promptly by a villainous and cowardly blow against another small nation in the north-west, whose sole offence was that it trusted to the plighted honour of a nation that had once itself known the miseries of weakness and disunion ; and it had for its immediate aim the permanent ruin of a great nation which has through centuries been in the van of civilization in Europe, and which, if it was once led astray by the dream of dominion over other peoples, has long since learnt to be satisfied with its own freedom and prosperity. If ever the cause of nationality were at stake in any war, it is at stake in this war. And if the ultimate victory falls where it must fall if honour and freedom are to survive in the world, then one outcome of the victory must be the final triumph of the national principle, the final adjustment of the political geography of Europe on the sound and just basis of nationality. Belgium, the martyr, must be recompensed and assured for ever of the sanctity of her territory. The brutal injustices which Prussia has inflicted upon other nations in the pursuit of German unity and greatness must be redeemed, and the Alsatian allowed to regain citizen-

ship in his beloved France if he wishes it; the Dane
of Schleswig must be no more severed from his brother
to the north; the Poles of Posen and of Cracow must
be reunited, after so long a severance, in the fatherland
which they once shared with the Pole of Warsaw. The
little nations of the south-east must at last be allowed
to achieve national unity, and to work out their
destinies and develop their distinctive civilization in
peace. Greater Serbia and greater Rumania must
make their appearance as solidly organized states on the
map of Europe. Bulgaria must regain the Bulgarian
lands of which she has been stripped, largely because
of the selfish ambitions of greater states. The last of
the Isles of Greece under foreign rule must be added
to the Hellenic realm. Unredeemed Italy must be
rejoined to her mother-state. The Bohemians must
regain their long-lost freedom, either in full independence or in a federal autonomy. The proud Magyar
must be content with a Hungary which is truly Hungarian, and cease to lord it over peoples of another
race. And finally, the Germans themselves, though
they have been in these latter years the villains of the
nationalist drama, must be content with the rich and
wide lands which their sons have peopled; but they
must not, any more than any other free nationality,
be made to suffer the indignity of partition and
disunion which they have been ready to force upon
others. If they think fit, the Austrian Germans must
be allowed to join the great confederacy of their fellow
countrymen; or, if that seems better, to join with
their fellow Catholics, the Bavarians, with whom they
have more sympathy than either feels for the Prussian,
in a new confederacy. There are many difficulties in
these readjustments. But only if the statesmen who

will have the task of constructing the new Europe keep constantly in mind the principle of nationality will they be able to build permanently and well. Only then shall we have a Europe from which the bitterness of disappointed national aspirations, the fruitful source of discord, will have been banished—a Europe in which each member of the great European family will be free to develop its distinctive character and civilization as it best can, unthreatened by the arrogant claim of any single member of the family to force its own *Kultur*, its own ideas, its own modes of organization, upon the rest, and protected by a universal respect for mutual rights, guaranteed by treaties that none will dare to dishonour.

Oxford: Horace Hart Printer to the University

WHY WE ARE AT WAR

GREAT BRITAIN'S CASE

BY MEMBERS OF THE OXFORD FACULTY
OF MODERN HISTORY

E. BARKER.   H. W. C. DAVIS.

C. R. L. FLETCHER. ARTHUR HASSALL.

L. G. WICKHAM LEGG. F. MORGAN.

With an Appendix of Original Documents
including the Authorized English Translation
of the White Book issued by the
German Government

THIRD EDITION REVISED (EIGHTH IMPRESSION)
CONTAINING THE RUSSIAN ORANGE BOOK AND
EXTRACTS FROM THE BELGIAN GREY BOOK

TRANSLATIONS INTO FRENCH ITALIAN SPANISH
GERMAN AND SWEDISH ARE
NOW READY

Paper Covers Two Shillings net (70 cents)
Cloth Two Shillings and Sixpence net (85 cents)

OXFORD: AT THE CLARENDON PRESS
LONDON: HUMPHREY MILFORD
EDINBURGH GLASGOW NEW YORK TORONTO
MELBOURNE BOMBAY

(a)

8 94

OXFORD PAMPHLETS

1914–1915

ERMAN PHILOSOPHY
AND THE WAR

BY

J. H. MUIRHEAD

Price Twopence net

OXFORD UNIVERSITY PRESS
HUMPHREY MILFORD
LONDON EDINBURGH GLASGOW
NEW YORK TORONTO MELBOURNE BOMBAY

OXFORD PAMPHLETS
1914-1915

Crown 8vo. Separately, in paper covers. Also in series as numbered (I–X), stiff covers, One Shilling net each series. 49 Pamphlets have now (Jan. 1, 1915) been issued, and others are in preparation. The historical pieces are illustrated by sketch-maps.

Saturday Review :—'These little books are easily the best books of the war—accurate, quietly written, full of knowledge, and quite unspoiled by vainglory or bitterness.'

OXFORD UNIVERSITY PRESS
HUMPHREY MILFORD

LONDON   EDINBURGH   GLASGOW
NEW YORK   TORONTO   MELBOURNE   BOMBAY

OXFORD PAMPHLETS
1914–1915

I

1. The Deeper Causes of the War.

By W. SANDAY. 3d. net. *Sixth Impression.*

The psychology of Prussian militarism ; German public opinion and Germany's aggressive ambitions.

2. To the Christian Scholars of Europe and America: A Reply from Oxford to the German 'Address to Evangelical Christians'.

2d. net. *Fifth Impression.*

The answer of Oxford theologians to a recent manifesto of the German evangelical theologians. This manifesto, which is reproduced in the present pamphlet, argues that Germany is in no sense responsible for the present war. The Oxford reply states that the German theologians cannot have studied either the events which led up to the war or the political utterances of their own countrymen.

3. The Responsibility for the War.

By W. G. S. ADAMS. 2d. net. *Second Impression.*

A brief discussion of the question of responsibility : 1. Austria and Serbia ; 2. The responsibility of Russia ; 3. The intervention of England.

4. Great Britain and Germany.

By SPENSER WILKINSON. 2d. net. *Third Impression.*

Three letters to the *Springfield Republican*: 1. By Prof. Spenser Wilkinson, stating Great Britain's case ; 2. By Prof. John W. Burgess of the University of Columbia, stating Germany's case ; 3. By Prof. Wilkinson, in reply to Prof. Burgess.

5. 'Just for a Scrap of Paper.'

By ARTHUR HASSALL. 1d. net. *Fifth Impression.*

Explains why England stands for the sanctity of European treaty-law.

[d]

II

6. The Germans, their Empire, and how they have made it.
By C. R. L. FLETCHER. 2d. net. *Fourth Impression.*
A historical account of Prussian policy from the seventeenth century.

7. The Germans, their Empire, and what they covet.
By C. R. L. FLETCHER. 2d. net. *Fourth Impression.*
An account of the ambitions avowed by the Pan-German school.

8. Might is Right. .
By Sir WALTER RALEIGH. 2d. net. *Third Impression.*
Why Germany may win; what will happen if she wins; why we believe she will not win.

9. Austrian Policy since 1867.
By MURRAY BEAVEN. 3d. net. *Second Impression.*
Austrian policy in the Balkans has been of the 'offensive-defensive' order. The Archduke Francis Ferdinand might have saved Austria from rushing to destruction; but 1912 was the beginning of the end.

10. Italian Policy since 1870.
By KEITH FEILING. 2d. net. *Second Impression.*
Italian policy has been and must be guided by her own interests. The results of her colonial policy have not yet been satisfactory enough to tempt her into adventures.

III

11. French Policy since 1871.
By F. MORGAN and H. W. C. DAVIS. 2d. net. *Fourth Impression.*
A historical sketch, discussing the question whether French policy has been aggressive.

12. Russia: The Psychology of a Nation.
By PAUL VINOGRADOFF. 1d. net. *Fifth Impression.*
A reply to the German taunt that Russia is still in a state of barbarism, and is the enemy of European civilization.

13. Serbia and the Serbs.
By Sir VALENTINE CHIROL. 2d. net. *Fourth Impression.*
A sketch of Serbian history, which is incidentally an indictment of the policy pursued by Austria-Hungary towards the Serbian kingdom.

14. Germany and 'The Fear of Russia'.
By Sir VALENTINE CHIROL. 2d. net. *Fourth Impression.*
Shows that before 1879 Germany preferred Russia as an ally to Austria. The ambition of Germany to establish a protectorate over Turkey has led her to assist Austria in the Balkans and so to challenge Russia.

15. The Eastern Question.
By F. F. URQUHART. 3d. net. *Third Impression.*
The history of the Balkan nations; their future.

[d]

IV

16. War against War.

By A. D. LINDSAY. 2d. net. *Fourth Impression.*
Denies that war is good in itself, or a necessary evil. National greatness, if founded on brute force, cannot endure. International law represents an ideal, but an ideal that may be realized.

17. The Value of Small States.

By H. A. L. FISHER. 2d. net. *Fourth Impression.*
The author argues that the debt of civilization to small states is incalculable.

18. How can War ever be Right?

By GILBERT MURRAY. 2d. net. *Fifth Impression.*
A well-known lover of peace and advocate of pacific policies argues against the Tolstoyan position. Right and honour compelled Britain to make war; and war—like tragedy—is not pure evil.

19. The National Principle and the War.

By RAMSAY MUIR. 3d. net. *Third Impression.*
Considers the principle of nationality and its application to the settlement of Europe—particularly of S.E. Europe—after the War.

20. Nietzsche and Treitschke: The Worship of Power in Modern Germany.

By E. BARKER. 2d. net. *Fifth Impression.*
An explanation of the main points of interest in the ethical and political doctrines of the German ruling classes.

V

21. The British Dominions and the War.

By H. E. EGERTON. 2d. net. *Fourth Impression.*
Explains the ideas for which the British Empire stands, and the political and moral issues of the war affecting the Dominions.

22. India and the War.

By Sir ERNEST TREVELYAN. 1d. net. *Fifth Impression.*
Discusses the reasons for the striking manifestations of Indian loyalty.

23. Is the British Empire the Result of Wholesale Robbery?

By H. E. EGERTON. 2d. net. *Second Impression.*
A historical sketch in answer to a common taunt.

24. The Law of Nations and the War.

By A. PEARCE HIGGINS. 2d. net. *Second Impression.*
The violation of Belgian neutrality and the conduct of England to Denmark in 1807; the doctrine of German lawyers that military necessity overrides the laws of war; the balance of power and the sanctity of treaties.

25. England's Mission.

By W. BENETT. 2d. net. *Second Impression.*
Answers the question, In what cause are we fighting?

[d]

VI

26. August, 1914: The Coming of the War.
By SPENSER WILKINSON. Stiff covers. 1s. net.

VII

27. The Retreat from Mons.
By H. W. C. DAVIS. 3d. net. *Third Impression.*

28. The Battles of the Marne and Aisne.
By H. W. C. DAVIS. 4d. net.
The Dispatches, with commentary, maps, &c.

29. The Navy and the War.
By J. R. THURSFIELD. 3d. net. *Fourth Impression.*
Estimates the military and economic value of the silent pressure exercised by our fleet, and warns the faint-hearted and the captious of the perils of lack of faith.

30. Bacilli and Bullets.
By Sir WILLIAM OSLER. 1d. net. *Fourth Impression.*
Calls attention to the fact that disease kills more men than the bullet. The most dangerous diseases are preventable by inoculation.

VIII

31. The Double Alliance *versus* The Triple Entente.
By JAMES M. BECK. 3d. net. *Second Impression.*
The judgement of a well-known American lawyer.

32. The Germans in Africa.
By EVANS LEWIN. 3d. net.
A historical account of the German colonies.

33. All for Germany, or the World's Respect Well Lost. 2d. net.
'The conversation here imagined, between a new (and perhaps less naïf) Candide and a new (and perhaps less benevolent) Dr. Pangloss, is concerned with the political thoughts and ambitions entertained by the Germans of these latter days.'

34. Germany, the Economic Problem.
By C. GRANT ROBERTSON. 2d. net.
Estimates the strength and weakness of Germany's economic position, and inquires how long she can stand the strain of the war.

35. German Sea-Power.
By C. S. TERRY. 3d. net.

IX

36. What Europe owes to Belgium.

By H. W. C. DAVIS.   2d. net.

Reminds us of the past achievements of the Belgian people in war and in peace.

37. Poland, Prussia, and Culture.

By LUDWIK EHRLICH.   3d. net.

The author is a Doctor of the University of Lwòw (Lemberg) in Galicia.

38. Turkey in Europe and Asia.   2d. net.

The strength and weakness of the Ottoman Empire considered. The secular prestige of Constantinople, the religious prestige of the Caliphate, and the racial and economic weaknesses which may cause their downfall.   A map shows the unfinished railways.

39. Greek Policy since 1882.

By A. J. TOYNBEE.   4d. net.   *Second Impression.*

A historical account of the policy of Greece; the economic future of Greece; the problem of *Graecia Irredenta.*   With a map.

40. North Sleswick under Prussian Rule, 1864–1914.

By W. R. PRIOR.   2d. net.

The policy of Prussianization and the resistance of Danish Nationalism. 'If the children do not understand German, they must be treated and taught like deaf-mutes' is quoted from a Prussian educational authority. A map shows the distribution of languages.

X

41. Thoughts on the War.

By GILBERT MURRAY. 2d. net. *Second Impression.*

Reprinted from the *Hibbert Journal* for October.

42. The Leadership of the World.

By F. S. MARVIN. 2d. net.

A discussion of German aspirations.

43. The Leading Ideas of British Policy.

By the Hon. GERARD COLLIER. 2d. net.

Places the principles of our policy in the perspective of history.

44. The War and its Economic Aspects.

By W. J. ASHLEY. 2d. net.

A comparison of Germany's and Great Britain's powers to stand the strain of a prolonged war. Probable effects of defeat or victory.

45. Food Supplies in War Time.

By R. H. REW, C.B. 2d. net.

An authoritative discussion by an expert who has been 'for over thirty years engaged in the service of British Agriculture'.

OXFORD PAMPHLETS

Published separately and will also appear shortly in series.

Non-Combatants and the War.

By A. PEARCE HIGGINS.   2d. net.

States the rights and duties of the non-combatant population of a territory under hostile occupation.

Troyon: an Engagement in the Battle of the Aisne.

By A. N. HILDITCH.   2d. net.

Scandinavia and the War.

By E. BJORKMAN.   2d. net.

Considers the policy and sympathies of the three Northern Kingdoms.

Asia and the War.

By A. E. DUCHESNE.   2d. net.

Describes German intrigue, and its failure, in Turkey, India, and Egypt.

GERMAN PHILOSOPHY AND THE WAR

PROFESSOR CRAMB has said that it would be possible to treat the wars of 1866 and 1870 as the work of professors and historians. With the addition of philosophers this might be said *a fortiori* of the war of 1914. It is at least true that no account of the events which led up to the present crisis can be complete which does not include the course of philosophical ideas. There is the more need to recall this inner history at the present moment as attempts have not been wanting to fix a large part of the responsibility indiscriminately on what is popularly known as German Philosophy which has dated from Kant.[1] What I believe on the contrary can be shown is that, so far as philosophy is responsible, it is one that represents a violent break with the ideas for which Kant and the whole early idealist movement stood. It is a story of a great rebellion, I believe on the whole a great apostasy.

I

GERMAN IDEALISM

If we would understand the significance for modern thought and life of the work of Immanuel Kant (1724–1804), we must recall the spirit that dominated the leading thinkers in England and France in the eighteenth century. It was an age of steady advance in physical science, the method of which is the resolution of objects

[1] See *Times*, Sept. 21, 1914. Letter by 'Continuity' on 'The New Barbarism'.

and entities into their constituent parts, with a view to understanding their nature and operation. Its motto might be said to be 'Nothing can be more than the aggregate of its parts'. We are not here concerned with the value of this method as applied to the special sciences, but with the consequences it brought with it when it came, as it did,[1] to be applied to the problems of organic and particularly of human life. In the life of intelligence it meant the attempt to explain experience as the mechanical connexion through the laws of 'association' of ideas which were the fading remnants of isolated impressions. In the life of the will it meant that actions were the result of impulses, appetites, instincts and passions that own no lord but that one amongst themselves which chanced to be the strongest. 'The Will', Hobbes had said, 'is the last appetite in deliberating'. Applied finally to society and the State it meant individualism. Society is the aggregate of individual wills, and as water cannot rise above its own level neither can the State rise above the self-seeking of its members. Itself resting ultimately on force for the cohesion of its parts, it owns no other law in its relations with other States. These ideas might be developed, as they had been by Hobbes, into a complete system of State politics and a morality based on fear, or they might be played with in a sort of *jeu d'esprit*, as they were in Mandeville's *Bees*, as the basis of a doctrine that 'private vices were public benefits', but in one form or another they constituted the philosophical enlightenment of the whole period.

Against all this the German spirit may be said to have

---

[1] Descartes had already suggested that animals were only machines. It remained to show that man, too, was a machine. Lamettries' *L'homme machine* appeared in 1748.

been in continual revolt. 'Search for the ideal runs through the whole century,' [1] and Goethe may be said to have summed up the mind of his time when, speaking of Holbach's *System of Nature*, the Bible of Materialism, he wrote, 'We could not understand how such a book could be dangerous. It appeared to us so dark, so Cimmerian, so death-like, that we could scarcely find patience to endure its presence.' All the same the deeper mind of the nation felt that it was dangerous so long as it went unanswered, and may be said to have been continuously occupied with the problem of a philosophical substitute for it. The most notable attempt to find such a substitute was that of the mathematician Leibniz. Unfortunately Leibniz's philosophy was vitiated by the acceptance of the very individualism that was the stronghold of materialism. After splitting up the universe into monads which were without windows, far less doors opening on the world without, he had no principle to reunite them and was fain to have recourse to the miracle of an external creator and regulator of their actions.

From the alternative that was thus forced upon the thought of the century of materialism, or unreason and incoherence, and the moral chaos to which it inevitably led, it was the merit of Kant to have offered a way of escape. The metaphysical basis of his system is too long a story to enter on here. It amounted to the demonstration that no experience of any kind, even that on which materialism itself relied, was possible except on the assumption of a constructive or, as he called it, a synthetic principle which was supplied, or at least first revealed itself consciously in mind, and was the source of our judgements of value, whether of truth, of beauty,

[1] Lange, *History of Materialism*, vol. ii, p. 143.

or of good. It is with the last and its application to
morals and politics that we are here concerned.

As against the naturalism of his time, Kant maintained that in all judgements of moral good and bad it
was implied that while man is undoubtedly part of a
mechanically determined system, so far as his body and
senses were concerned, yet in virtue of the law of his mind
he was able to rise above his merely natural relations,
and maintain himself in a spiritual, or as he called it
an intelligible, world as a person among persons. The
deepest thing in man was not therefore the instinct of
self-assertion that separated him from others, but the
self-imposed law which united him with them — the
touch of reason that made all the world kin. While
just in virtue of the possession of freedom it was possible
to take natural impulse as his guide, and so to fall from
human fellowship, it was possible also for man by accept-
ing the rule of reason to raise himself into membership
of what Kant liked to call the Kingdom of Ends. Whereas the law of nature was to treat everything only as
a means to the ends of the self, the law of reason was to
'treat humanity in their own person and the person of
others always as an end and never as a means only '.

These ideas are sometimes spoken of as transcendental,
as though they had no ground in experience. In reality,
as William Wallace has shown,[1] they were suggested to
Kant by a profound reading of history as a continuous
effort to substitute the rule of law for the rule of force, and
thus vindicate man's true freedom. It is for this fact that
the civilized State stands. *Might* the State must possess,
but it is only the might of the *State,* when it is employed
in the service of law and freedom. Kant was profoundly
influenced by the French Revolution. He was a repub-

[1] Kant, c. xiv.

lican ; but a republic meant to him, as it ought to mean, the reign of a law which embodies the public good and from which all individual or class egoism has been purged away. So long as the State meant the obedience of the citizens to a self-imposed law, the actual form was comparatively unimportant, and Kant was content in his own day to be the subject of a monarch who thought of himself as the ' first servant of the State '.

But the reign of law was not confined to the relations of individuals within the State. States, too, were units—in a sense persons—and over their relations with one another there reigned the same law as bound the citizens together within them. Here, too, the appeal was to history, which showed that just as the reign of force was gradually being superseded within States, so it was being superseded by law between them. In this way there dawned upon Kant, not as a mere poetic dream, but as at once a consequence of his philosophy and a promise of actual fact, the idea of a federation of States, a republic of the world, consisting of members small and great, owning allegiance to a common law as much in the interest of the strong as of the weak. This is the idea he works out in his essay *On Perpetual Peace*, which was published in 1795. It is in the form of a treaty, of which it lays down the articles. Some of these have a special interest at the present time. The first two enjoin that the States shall themselves be free, and that the civil constitution of each shall be republican. Only thus, Kant thought, could not only the causes of discontent be removed, but the seeds of international hatred be destroyed. Kant saw in all forms of absolutism one of the most potent causes of war. Other articles refer to standing armies, in which he sees a continual menace to peace ; secret reservations in treaties which are merely a means of

blinding an enemy to the real designs of a nation and
' material for a future war ' ; the actual conduct of war
which must be such as to avoid ' all modes of hostility
which would make mutual confidence impossible in a
subsequent state of peace '. As to war itself Kant was no
pacificist. He was ready to recognize in it ' a deep-hidden
and designed enterprise of supreme wisdom for preparing,
if not for establishing, conformity to law amid the freedom of States, and with this a unity of a morally grounded
system of those States '. He was further ready to
recognize its purifying and exalting effect upon a nation.
But he was under no delusion as to its true nature.   It
was the outcome of the bad principle in human nature,
and however we may be tempted to find compensation for
it in the evil that it uproots and in its superiority to the
deadness of a universal monarchy, ' yet, as an ancient
observed, it makes more bad men than it takes away '.[1]

There can be no doubt that Kant's ideas had a profound
influence on the politics of the time.   In spite of Carlyle,
Frederick the Great is not a hero in England.   Yet, on
the whole, the spirit of his reign may be said to have been
the spirit of Kant.   ' The Categorical Imperative of
Kant ', says Seeley,[2] ' was appropriately first named and
described in the age and country of Frederick the Great.'
His claim was to be the first servant of the State, and the
saying is reported of his extreme old age, ' Did the whole
Gospel contain only this precept : " What ye would that
men should do to you, do ye even so to them ", it must
be owned that these few words contain the summary
of all morality.' [3]

[1] See *Critique of Judgement*, App. § 83, and *Philosophical Theory of
Religion*, I. iii.
[2] *Life of Stein*, vol. i, p. 44. Cf. Carlyle's account of the celebrated
Miller-Arnold case in his *Frederick the Great*.
[3] Wallace, ibid., 152.

of humanity, trust in you. If ye sink, Humanity sinks with you without hope of future restoration.[1]

When the time came, in 1813, to strike for the freedom which the spirit claims, Fichte was again to the fore announcing in his *Political Fragment for 1813* that 'A nation becomes a nation through war and through a common struggle. Who shares not in the present war can by no decree be incorporated in the nation.'

Hegel, the third in this great succession, was elected to Fichte's chair in Berlin in 1818 and became the spokesman of the re-established constitution. 'Let us greet the dawn of a better time,' he had already said in his inaugural address at Heidelberg, 'when the spirit that has hitherto been driven out of itself may return to itself again and win room and space wherein to found a kingdom of its own.'

But it was in his theory of the State,[2] which he developed in the Berlin period, that we have to look for the chief source of his political influence. The State he conceived of after Kant as 'the actualization of freedom'. It is 'the world which the spirit has made for itself'. It is sometimes thought that the State has weakened in modern times. Not so, says Hegel: 'The modern State has enormous strength and depth.' It is just this that enables it without detriment to itself to do full justice to individual and sectional interests. The political disposition, in other words patriotism (Hegel will not separate them as Fichte does),

---

[1] Some courage was needed for this plain speaking. A luckless printer of Nürnberg in the previous year had been shot for publishing a pamphlet on *Germany in its Deep Humiliation*. See Adamson's *Fichte*, p. 81.

[2] *Philosophy of Law*, English translation by Dyde.

is just ' the confident consciousness that my particular interest is contained and preserved in the interest and end of the State '.

It is on the ground of his exaltation of the State and his manifest leaning to the Prussian form of mon-. archy that Hegel has been accused of having cast a slight on international law and organization and of being the philosopher of the Prussian military tradition.[1] This view can only be maintained if to have vindicated one factor in the moral order of the world must be taken to mean the denial of others. Hegel had lived through the enthusiasm of the French Revolution and, like Burke in England, had come to realize the element of individualism and anarchy which it contained. He felt that the time had come to vindicate the reality of the State as of the very substance of individual, family, and national life. Further than this there is no ground to ally his political teaching with military tradition. He expressly rejects the militarist doctrine that the State rests upon force. ' The binding cord is not force, but the deep-seated feeling of order that is possessed by us all.' He has no words strong enough for von Haller, the von Treitschke of his time, who had written :

> It is the eternal unchangeable decree of God that the most powerful rules, must rule, and will for ever rule,

and who had poured contempt on the national liberties of Germany and our own Magna Charta and the Bill of Rights as mere ' documentary liberties '.[2]

With equal decisiveness he would have rejected the doctrine that war is the ' continuation of politics '.

---

[1] See Mr. Barker's *Nietzsche and Treitschke* in this series, p. 4, and Dr. Michael Sadler's *Modern Germany and the Modern World*, p. 10.
[2] op. cit. p. 243, n.

He would have agreed with Aristotle that the State
' comes into being for the sake of life, but continues in
being for the good life '. War is not the continuation
but the failure of politics. Its true continuation is the
life of art, science, religion, for the full development
of which it is the essential condition. Nor would he
have tolerated the doctrine that the State is the ultimate
appeal in matters of right. Above and beyond the
State there is the Spirit of the World or the Spirit of
God : ' the history of the world is the judgement of
the world '. It was he who said of Napoleon that he
had brought the highest genius to victory only to show
how little victory alone could achieve against the moral
forces of the world. It is true that his political theory
was approved by contemporary statesmen, but before
his death they had come to suspect that there was
' perilous stuff ' in it for all reactionary and repressive
policies.[1] It is not in Hegel but in the violent reaction
that set in shortly after his death, in 1831, against the
whole Idealist philosophy that we have to look for the
philosophical foundations of Prussian militarism.

II

THE REACTION AGAINST IDEALISM

The story of this reaction is a complicated one.
That it was due in part to a certain high-handedness in
method and obscurity in result of the older philosophy
cannot, I think, be denied. But the main causes lay
elsewhere. I select two of the chief factors in it.

1. Germany has been accused of culpable absent-
mindedness in occupying herself with mystical specula-
tions while other countries, by commerce, colonization,
mining, and manufacture, were laying the foundations

[1] See E. Caird's *Hegel*, p. 94.

of material power. I believe that, on the contrary, never was Germany truer to herself than when, in the instinctive conviction that no civilization could be secure in which the things of most value in life rested on no surer foundation than tradition or unverified instinct, she devoted herself to the task of verifying them to the reason. But this only made the reaction more violent when the time for material expansion came, and coal and iron took the place of reason and freedom as the watchwords of the time. The 'forties and the 'fifties were years of rapid development in all parts of Germany. With the needs of industry went the need of concentrating the intellectual resources of the nation on the physical sciences. This is what had taken place in other countries. What was peculiar to Germany was that the old metaphysical habit reasserted itself in the changed circumstances, and chemists and physiologists seized the trowel which the metaphysicians had dropped.[1] The result was that, going along with the material expansion and the devotion to the special sciences it evoked, we have a philosophy which sought to invert the old order and to read matter and body where it had read mind and spirit. ' The old philosophy ', said Feuerbach, who first raised the standard of revolt, ' started from the principle : I am a thinking being, the body is no part of my being. The new philosophy, on the other hand, begins with the principle : I am a real and sensible being ; the body is part of my being ; nay, the body is its totality, is my ego, is itself my essence.' To the same period belong Karl Marx's materialistic interpretation of history and his exaltation of the economic interests to the place of the ruling factor in human development. But not in vain

---

[1] See Lange, loc. cit.

had Feuerbach and Marx sat at the feet of Hegel. In both the humanitarian note was more pronounced than the materialistic, and the development of the implications of their starting-point was left to younger writers.

The way was prepared by two events in the field of science which roughly divide the period, the experimental demonstration by Robert Mayer of the Conservation of Energy (1842), and the publication of Darwin's *Origin of Species* in 1859. Belonging to the first period we must reckon a group of writers of whom probably Büchner was the most widely known, his book, *Matter and Force*, published in 1855, going through sixteen editions in as many years. They may be said to have expressed the reigning spirit in the great period of industrial development that marked the middle of the century and made possible the victories of 1866 and 1870. It is, of course, a mistake to hold that either of these movements—the practical or the theoretical—by itself is necessarily hostile to a comprehensive view of life. Materialism has been the creed of some of the noblest of the human race. It is the combination of them that is dangerous—when the commercial, money-making spirit is tempted to seek in a materialistic philosophy for the justification of what it would like to believe as to the chief ends of life. That something like this happened in Germany at this time is borne out by the judgement of the greatest of German historians. 'Everything', wrote Ranke of it, 'is falling. No one thinks of anything but commerce and money.' [1]

. The social and political implications of Darwinism have from the first been a subject of controversy. There

---

[1] Quoted by Professor Hicks in his article on ' German Philosophy and the Present Crisis ', *Hibbert Journal*, Oct., 1914.

are two ways in which Natural Selection may be interpreted. The struggle for existence may be taken to be one among other agencies in development. In the lower orders of creation it may be said to be of dominant importance, as in fishes, where thousands of the spawn are sacrificed that one may survive. But as we advance in the scale of intelligence, it is gradually superseded by the power of organizing the environment and securing the survival of the species with growing economy. In civilized communities it may be said, in its crude form, to have been altogether superseded. The struggle is no longer for bare existence, but for a particular form of existence involving the opportunity of becoming a parent—'selection for parentage', as it has been called. What is true, moreover, within societies, may, in the course of time, without detriment to the race, come to be true of societies in their external relations with one another. According to another interpretation, struggle is the supreme law of life, and rages, in however disguised a form, in the higher as in the lower orders of creation, between societies as between individuals. While, according to the first of these two views, there is no limit to the extent to which the rule of force may be eliminated consistently with a high level of physical and mental fitness, according to the latter, struggle is the sole effective instrument, and all attempts to eliminate it are doomed to failure.

If we turn to Darwin himself there is nothing to connect him with the second of these views. On the contrary, he more than once distinctly repudiates it.

> With highly civilized nations continued progress depends, in a subordinate degree, on natural selection, for such nations do not supplant and exterminate each other as do savage tribes

And again :

Important as the struggle for existence has been, and
still is, yet as far as the highest part of man's nature is
concerned, there are other agencies more important.
For the moral qualities are advanced either directly or
indirectly much more through the effects of habit, the
reasoning powers, instruction, religion, &c., than
through natural selection.[1]

This has, on the whole, been the view taken in England.
In Germany the seed fell on ground prepared by a quarter
of a century of materialistic thought.   Whether it is the
one generally accepted by biologists it would be difficult
to say.   At any rate it was the one adopted by the most
distinguished in this field of his time in Germany.

' The theory of selection teaches us ', writes Haeckel,
' that in human life, exactly as in animal and plant life,
at each place and time, only a privileged minority can
continue to exist and flourish.   The cruel and relentless struggle for existence which rages throughout all
living nature, and in accordance with nature must
rage, this ceaseless and pitiless competition of all living
things is an undeniable fact ;   only the select minority,
the privileged fit, is in a position to successfully survive
this competition, the great majority of competitors
must meanwhile of necessity perish miserably.   We
may mourn this tragic fact, but we cannot deny or alter
it.   Obviously the principle of selection is anything
but democratic ;   it is aristocratic in the precise sense
of the word.'[2]

Had this been an academic opinion as to the social
tendencies of Darwinism without specific application to
ethics and external politics, it would have had little significance in the present connexion.   But it was the view

[1] These passages are quoted from the *Descent of Man* by Karl
Pearson, in his *Chances of Death*, vol. i, pp. 127-8.
[2] *Freie Wissenschaft u. freie Lehre,* quoted ib.

underlying the writer's *Riddle of the Universe*, which was
published in the last year of the nineteenth century and
probably had a wider circulation in Germany than any
work of the kind has ever had. It ran through several
editions in two years, was subsequently issued in popular
form, and by 1906 was being sold in tens of thousands.
It contains a remarkable chapter on ' Our Monistic
Ethics ', in which the external policy of England is
attacked for its direct contradiction of every precept of
Christianity, while at the same time the principles which
are attributed to her are claimed as those which rightly
govern international relations.

> ' The glaring contradiction ', so the passage ends,
> ' between the theoretical *ideal* and altruistic morality
> of the human individual and the *real* purely selfish
> morality of the human community, and especially the
> civilized Christian State, is a familiar fact. It would be
> interesting to determine mathematically in what pro-
> portion among organized men the altruistic ethical ideal
> of the individual changes into its contrary the purely
> egoistic " real politics " of one State and the nation.'

2. This is ominous doctrine. But it was along the
second line of development mentioned above that it
received its most sinister expression.

Side by side with the development of the materialistic
element in Feuerbach's philosophy, there rose out of the
disturbed times that preceded the revolutions of 1848 a
violent reaction against the humanitarian ideas with which
Feuerbach had sought to combine it. 'My first thought',
Feuerbach had announced 'was God, my second was
Reason, my last was Man.' But if, as he held, God and
Reason were mere abstractions, why not also Man ?
This was the question raised by a remarkable book
which appeared under the *nom de plume* of Max Stirner,

with the title of *The Sole One and his Own*,[1] in 1844.
'God and man', so runs its claim, 'have concerned them-.
selves for nothing but themselves. Let me likewise
concern myself for myself who am equally with God,
the nothing of all others ; who am my all, who am the
only one.' After showing that the life of the individual
and the course of civilization is a progress towards emancipation, first from things, then from ideas (' the child
is realistic, the youth is idealistic, man is egoistic '), the
writer boldly applies his doctrine to current ethics and
politics, demanding a transvaluation of all values, which
anticipates in a remarkable way the teaching of Nietzsche.
'What's good? what's bad?' he asks. 'I myself am my
own concern and I am neither good nor bad. Neither
has any meaning for me.' From this it follows that my
' rights ' have no foundation except in my power, and
that whatever opposes this in the name of family, society,
nation, or State, is my enemy.

My rights are what I can master. Whatever inter-
feres with this is my enemy. As enemy of myself
count I therefore every form of community.

'To neither man nor the State do I owe anything at all.
I offer it nothing. I use it only. That is, I annihilate it
and put in its place the society of egoists.' ' Sacred,' say
you. 'Take courage while there is time. To be rid of the
sacred you have only to devour it.' The note of revolt
against all the recognized standards of present-day
civilization was struck by Stirner in what has been
called ' the most radical, unsocial, and subversive book
which last century produced '. It was taken up, combined with the other factors in the revolt above mentioned, and carried through a hundred variations by
Nietzsche (1844–1900).

[1] Eng. tr. *The Ego and his Own* (Fifield), 1913

III

THE NEW NATURALISM

The chief ideas for which Nietzsche stands have already been indicated in this series; [1] it is with their connexion with a general philosophical movement that we are here concerned. (a) In his own view Nietzsche stood with Schopenhauer in open rebellion against the whole philosophy which sought in the organizing work of mind for the type of reality. 'The mind', he declares, ' counts for us only as a symptom of relative imperfection and weakening of the organism as a stage of experimenting and feeling about and missing our aim.' Our true life is to be looked for not in experiences that (in his own phrase) have been 'sifted through with reason ', but in the dark, unconscious, and instinctive elements of our nature. (b) He goes beyond Schopenhauer and allies himself with Stirner in interpreting these instincts in terms of the ego :

> I submit that egoism belongs to the essence of a noble soul. Aggressive and defensive egoism are not questions of choice or of free will, but they are fatalities of life itself.

But again he goes beyond the author of *The Ego and his Own* in declaring that the central impulse of the ego is neither life nor enjoyment, but Power :

> A living being seeks above all to discharge his strength. Life itself is the will to power. It is this that every man in his inmost heart desires—to assert himself against the world without, to appropriate, injure, suppress, exploit. . . . Exploitation belongs to the nature of the living being as a primary organic function. It is a consequence of the intrinsic will to power.

---

[1] See Mr. Barker's finely balanced appreciation in *Nietzsche and Treitschke.*

The mortal sickness of our age, the sign of its decadence, is that we have been willing to exchange this unchartered freedom for the slave's portion of security, and low-scale gregarious well-being represented by Christianity and the democratic State. But it was not always so. Primitive natural morality recognized a wholly different standard of values, and in the history of civilization these were at least once embodied in a worthy form in the Roman Empire—only to fall a victim to the vampire of Christianity. But ' Vengeance only lingers. False values and fatuous words bear a fate with them. Long it slumbers and waits, but at last it comes, and awakes and devours and engulfs.'

The call of the age is for a deliverer who can stamp it, as Napoleon stamped his, with the image of power, the image of a new ethics, ' under the pressure and hammer of which a conscience shall be steeled and a heart transformed into brass to bear the weight of the new responsibility.' The danger is that when he appears he should be captured by the old false philosophy and sublimated, as Kant tried to sublimate Frederick the Great, into a servant of the people. It is for this reason that there runs as a recurrent strain through Nietzsche's writings the necessity of stamping out the last remnants of the Tartuffian philosophy of Königsberg—the Will to Good— and substituting for it the true gospel of the Will to Power.

It would be easy to find in Nietzsche another note and even to show, as William Wallace does,[1] that in the later phases of the development of his thought on the Superman, he was forced into the recognition of something approaching the old Greek doctrine of a divinity that shapes our ends. But these remained only hints,

[1] *Lectures and Essays*, p. 540

and it is the less necessary to follow them here as this higher note was not likely to be caught by a generation whose ear had been trained in a different music, and as Nietzsche himself did his best to drown it in the blare of his paradoxical naturalism.

Yet even on this level it would be difficult to find in his teaching anything that could be taken as an incentive to a policy of national violence. On the contrary it would be easy to find much that condemns it. It has been pointed out by the writer of ' The New German Theory of the State ' in *Why we are at War*, that 'in his later years Nietzsche revolted against the Prussian military system '. But he was never enamoured of it. So early as 1871 we find him deeply disturbed by the spirit that was being fostered in the nation by its military successes. Developing the theme in *Unseasonable Contemplations*, in 1873, he warns Germany against the error of supposing that the success of 1870 was due to anything that could be called German Culture. ' A great victory ', he writes, ' is a great danger. The greatest error at the present is the belief that this fortunate war has been won by German Culture. At present both the public and the private life of Germany shows every sign of the utmost want of culture.' The same note is struck in 1889 when he complains that ' There are no longer German philosophers. German seriousness, profundity, and *passion* in intellectual matters are more and more on the decline. The State and civilization are antagonistic. Germany has gained as to the former, but lost in regard to the latter. Education has been vulgarized to utilitarianism and has lost its high aim.' [1] It would scarcely be too much to say that his ideal approximated nearer to

[1] *The Twilight of the Idols.*

Kant's, of a new non-national or supernational type of
civilization, than to that of the idolizers of any particular
nation. 'Nations', he tells us, 'are something artificial
at present and unstable', wisely adding : ' such nations
should most carefully avoid all hot-headed rivalry and
hostility '. ' In Europe at least ', he hoped, ' the barriers
between different nations will disappear more and more
and a new type of man will arise—the European.' But
these were reservations which, along with the whole philosophical atmosphere that accompanied them, it was only
too easy to overlook, and not the least of the tragedies
of my story is that there had risen up historians and
military writers prepared to accept and give currency
to the philosophy of power in its barest and crudest
form.

Of these Treitschke has rightly been taken as the
typical. Born at Dresden in 1834 and professor of
history successively at Freiburg and Heidelberg, he
placed himself in violent antagonism to South German
particularism and liberalism :

> ' I am longing ', he wrote, ' for the North, to which
> I belong with all my heart, and where also our fate
> will be decided. If I am to choose between the two
> parties I select that of Bismarck, since he struggles
> for Prussian power, for our legitimate position on the
> North and the Eastern Sea.' [1]

He was, as he tells us himself, more patriot than professor, and when at last, in 1874, he was called to the
Chair of History in Berlin he felt that the time and
opportunity had come to rouse his country to a sense
of the great destiny which awaited it. After describing
the crowded audiences of princes, statesmen, soldiers,

[1] *Treitschke : His Life and Works* (Allen & Unwin), p. 18.

diplomats, and leaders of society which he addressed with a natural eloquence which made them feel there was nothing he was not ready to dare for his opinions, Professor Cramb asks what they came together to hear ? and he answers :

> They came together to hear the story of the manner in which God or the World-spirit, through shifting and devious paths, had led Germany and the Germans to their present exalted station under Prussia and the Hohenzollern—those great princes who in German worth and German uprightness are unexampled in the dynasties of Europe and of the world. Treitschke showed them German unity and therefore German freedom lying like the fragments of a broken.sword, like that of Roland or of Sigurd or the Grey-Steel of the Sagas ; and these fragments Prussia alone could weld again into dazzling wholeness and might.' [1]

But this was only one side of his teaching. He supported it with lectures on politics, in which the changed spirit that had come to pervade the philosophy of Germany since Hegel occupied a similar place stood out with startling clearness. In one thing he was in agreement with Hegel's teaching. The lesson, we might say, of the State and the Nation had in the meantime been learned, some would say over-learned. ' The State ', says Treitschke, ' dates from the very beginning and is necessary. It has existed as long as history, and is as essential to humanity as language.' [2] But here agreement ceases. For the rest we have a vehement reassertion of doctrines of which the whole Idealist movement had been the denial. Hegel, as we have seen, repudiated the doctrine that the State was founded upon force. It rested on the disposition and the will

---

[1] *Germany and England*, p. 89.
[2] *Lectures on Politics*, i, § 1 (English translation by Gowans).

of the governed. With Aristotle he held that it came into existence for the sake of life, its abiding purpose was the good life—the life of science, art, religion.

In opposition to all this Treitschke fiercely announces :

> The State is in the first instance power. It is not the totality of the people itself, as Hegel assumed. On principle it does not ask how the people is disposed ; it demands obedience.
> The State is no academy of arts ; if it neglects its power in favour of the ideal strivings of mankind it renounces its nature and goes to ruin. The renunciation of its own power is for the State in the most real sense the sin against the Holy Ghost.

If art is incompatible with politics, religion is its sworn enemy. It starts from an opposite principle : ' Religion wishes to know only what it believes ; the State to believe only what it knows.' [1] So of the form of union required by each. ' The ideal of a religious fellowship is there public. But as the State is in the first instance power, its ideal is undoubtedly the monarchy, because in it the power of the State expresses itself in an especially decided and consistent way.' True—real monarchs are becoming scarce, even in Germany. ' Prussia alone has still a real monarch who is entirely independent of any higher power,' [2] and who is prepared to say with Gustavus Adolphus, ' I recognize no one above me but God and the sword of the victor.' [3] But that can be remedied by extending the benefits of the Prussian

---

[1] This I take to be a parody of Hegel's statement ' The State is that which knows ', op. cit., § 270, n. Hegel's own view is condensed in the sentence : ' Since ethical and political principles pass over into the realm of religion and not only *are* established but *must be* established in reference to religion, the State is thus furnished with religious confirmation.'

[2] op. cit., iii, § 17.   [3] Ibid., i, § 1.

monarchy and the Culture it represents, as Treitschke generously desires to do to other less favoured lands.

The instrument of this idealistic extension is war. 'It is precisely political idealism that demands wars, while it is materialism that condemns them.' [1] International law certainly has to be taken into account as an historical development. But it succeeds best in time of peace in adjusting the forms of intercourse between nations. It has a more limited application to the manner of conducting war after it has broken out. But to apply it to the limitation of the right to declare war is a vain and degenerate dream. Here ' no State in the wide world can venture to relinquish the *ego* of its sovereignty'. 'It has always been the tired, unintelligent, and enervated periods that have played with the dream of perpetual peace.' [2]

It is not surprising that these doctrines should have found favour among military writers in Germany, descending in them to even a lower grade of crudity. A great deal has been said by the apologists of Germany as to the obscurity in his own country of von Bernhardi. But that is not the point. His books are written for the military class, and you would no more expect to find them on the bookshelves or drawing-room tables of the ordinary educated man than you would expect Hegel's *Logic* or *Philosophy of Right*. The point is that these ideas have been taken up by able specialists and made by them the philosophical background of military instruction.

It is not my business here to discuss the truth of *Realpolitik* as thus interpreted. My task has been to show

---

[1] op. cit., § 2.

[2] op. cit., v, § 28. It follows naturally from these principles with regard to neutrals that ' If a State is not in a condition to maintain its neutrality, all talk about the same is mere claptrap.'

that it comes to us not as a continuous and legitimate development of which we are accustomed to think as ' German Philosophy ', but as a reaction against it. I may, however, be permitted to remind the reader that as these ideas are not new in theory neither do they appeal for the first time to ' the judgement of the world '. They have been judged in a hundred decisive battle-fields from Marathon to Waterloo. If they are now judged once more and if there is truth in this story, we shall be able to appeal for confirmation of the judgement of history not to any philosophy of ours but to the better mind of Germany itself, the mind that found its highest and most condensed expression in Kant and Hegel and the doctrine of the Will to Good.

Oxford : Horace Hart Printer to the University

WHY WE ARE AT WAR

GREAT BRITAIN'S CASE

BY MEMBERS OF THE OXFORD FACULTY OF MODERN HISTORY

E. BARKER.	H. W. C. DAVIS.
C. R. L. FLETCHER.	ARTHUR HASSALL.
L. G. WICKHAM LEGG.	F. MORGAN.

With an Appendix of Original Documents
including the Authorized English Translation
of the White Book issued by the
German Government

THIRD EDITION REVISED (TENTH IMPRESSION)
CONTAINING THE RUSSIAN ORANGE BOOK AND
EXTRACTS FROM THE BELGIAN GREY BOOK

TRANSLATIONS INTO FRENCH ITALIAN SPANISH
GERMAN DANISH AND SWEDISH
ARE NOW READY

Paper Covers Two Shillings net (70 cents)
Cloth Two Shillings and Sixpence net (85 cents)

OXFORD: AT THE CLARENDON PRESS
LONDON: HUMPHREY MILFORD
EDINBURGH GLASGOW NEW YORK TORONTO
MELBOURNE BOMBAY

(*a*)

935

OXFORD PAMPHLETS
1914

THOUGHTS ON THE
WAR

BY

GILBERT MURRAY

Price Twopence net

OXFORD UNIVERSITY PRESS
HUMPHREY MILFORD
LONDON   EDINBURGH   GLASGOW
NEW YORK   TORONTO   MELBOURNE   BOMBAY

THOUGHTS ON THE WAR [1]

I. 'Not much news : Great Britain has declared war on Austria.' The words fell quite simply, and with no intention of irony, from the lips of a friend of mine who picked up the newspaper on the day when I began to write down these thoughts, August 13. So amazingly had the world changed since the 4th. And it has changed even more by the time when I revise the proofs.

During the month of July and earlier, English politics were by no means dull. For my own part, my mind was profoundly occupied with a number of public questions and causes : the whole maintenance of law and democratic government seemed to be threatened, not to speak of social reform and the great self-redeeming movements of the working class. In the forefront came anxiety for Home Rule and the Parliament Act, and a growing indignation against various classes of 'wreckers' ; those reactionaries who seemed to be playing with rebellion, playing with militarism, recklessly inflaming the party spirit of minorities so as to make parliamentary government impossible ; those revolutionaries who were openly preaching the Class

[1] Reprinted, by kind permission of the editor, from *The Hibbert Journal* for October, 1914.

War and urging the working man to mistrust his own leaders and representatives and believe in nothing but some helpless gospel of hate.

And now that is all swept away. We think no more of our great causes, and we think no more of our mutual hatreds. Good and evil come together. Our higher ideals are forgotten, but we are a band of brothers standing side by side.

This is a great thing. The fine instinctive generosity with which the House of Commons, from Mr. Bonar Law to Mr. Redmond, rose to the crisis has spread an impulse over the country. There is a bond of fellow-ship between Englishmen who before had no meeting-ground. In time past I have sometimes envied the working men who can simply hail a stranger as 'mate': we dons and men of letters seem in ordinary times to have no 'mates' and no gift for getting them. But the ice between man and man is broken now.

I think, too, that the feeling between different classes must have softened. Rich business men, whom I can remember a short time ago tediously eloquent on the vices of trades unionists and of the working classes in general, are now instantly and without hesitation making large sacrifices and facing heavy risks to see that as few men as possible shall be thrown out of work, and that no women and children shall starve. And working men who have not money to give are giving more than money, and giving it without question or grudge. Thank God, we did not hate each other as much as we imagined ; or else, while the hatred was real enough on the surface, at the back of our minds we loved each other more.

And the band of brothers is greater and wider than any of us dared to believe. Many English hearts must have swelled with almost incredulous gratitude to hear of the messages and the gifts which come flooding in from all the dominions overseas : the gold, the grain, the sugar, the tobacco ; its special produce coming from each State, and from all of them throngs of young men offering their strength and their life-blood. And India above all ! One who has cared much about India and has friends among Indian Nationalists cannot read with dry eyes the messages that come from all races and creeds of India, from Hindu and Moslem societies, from princes and holy men and even political exiles. . . . We have not always been sympathetic in our government of India ; we have not always been wise. But we have tried to be just ; and we have given to India the best work of our best men. It would have been hard on us if India had shown no loyalty at all ; but she has given us more than we deserved, more than we should have dared to claim. Neither Indian nor Englishman can forget it.

II. And there is something else. Travellers who have returned from France or Belgium—or Germany for that matter—tell us of the unhesitating heroism with which the ordinary men and women are giving themselves to the cause of their nation. A friend of mine heard the words of one Frenchwoman to another who was seeing her husband's train off to the front : ' Ne pleurez pas, il vous voit encore.' When he was out of sight the tears might come ! . . . Not thousands but millions of women are saying words like that to themselves, and millions of men going out to face death.

We in England have not yet been put to the same test as France and Belgium. We are in the flush of our first emotion ; we have not yet had our nerves shaken by advancing armies, or our endurance ground down by financial distress. But, as far as I can judge of the feelings of people whom I meet, they seem to me to be ready to answer any call that comes. We ask for 200,000 recruits and receive 300,000, for half a million and we receive three-quarters. We ask for more still, and the recruiting offices are overflowing. They cannot cope with the crowds of young men who cheerfully wait their turn at the office doors or on the pavement, while fierce old gentlemen continue to scold them in the newspapers. Certainly we are a quaint people.

And in the field ! A non-combatant stands humbled before the wonderful story of the retreat from Mons— the gallantry, the splendid skill, the mutual confidence of all ranks, the absolute faithfulness. One hardly dares praise such deeds ; one admires them in silence. And it is not the worshippers of war who have done this ; it is we, the good-natured, un-militarist, ultra-liberal people, the nation of humanitarians and shopkeepers.

Our army, indeed, is a professional army. What the French and the Belgians have done is an even more significant fact for civilization. It shows that the cultured, progressive, easy-living, peace-loving nations of Western Europe are not corrupted, at least as far as courage goes. The world has just seen them, bourgeois and working men, clerks, schoolmasters, musicians, grocers, ready in a moment when the call came ; able to march and fight for long days of scorching sun or icy rain ; willing, if need be, to die for their homes and countries, with no panic, no softening of the fibre . . . resolute to face death and to kill.

III. For there is that side of it too. We have now not only to strain every nerve to help our friend—we must strain every nerve also to injure our enemy.

This is horrible, but we must try to face the truth. For my own part, I find that I do desperately desire to hear of German dreadnoughts sunk in the North Sea. Mines are treacherous engines of death; but I should be only too glad to help in laying a mine for them. When I see one day that 20,000 Germans have been killed in such-and-such an engagement, and next day that it was only 2,000, I am sorry.

That is where we are. We are fighting for that which we love, whatever we call it. It is the Right, but it is something even more than the Right. For our lives, for England, for the liberty of Western Europe, for the possibility of peace and friendship between nations; for something which we should rather die than lose. And lose it we shall unless we can beat the Germans.

IV. Yet I have scarcely met a single person who seems to hate the Germans. We abominate their dishonest Government, their unscrupulous and arrogant diplomacy, the whole spirit of ' blood-and-iron ' ambition which seems to have spread from Prussia through a great part of the nation. But not the people in general. They too, by whatever criminal folly they were led into war, are fighting now for what they call ' the Right '. For their lives and homes and their national pride, for that strange ' Culture ', that idol of blood and clay and true gold, which they have built up with so many tears. They have been trebly deceived: deceived by their Government, deceived by their own idolatry, deceived by their sheer terror. They are ringed about by enemies; their one ally is broken; they hear the thunder of Cossack hoofs in the east coming ever closer; and hordes of stupid moujiks behind them, innumerable, clumsy, barbarous, as they imagine in their shuddering dread, treading down the beloved Fatherland as they come. . . . What do Germans care for punctilios and neutrality treaties in the face of such a horror as that ?

No : we cannot hate or blame the people in general. And certainly not the individual Germans whom we know. I have just by me a letter from young Fritz Hackmann, who was in Oxford last term and brought me an introduction from a Greek scholar in Berlin : a charming letter, full of gratitude for the very small friendlinesses I had been able to show him. I remember his sunny smile and his bow with a click of the heels. He is now fighting us. . . . And there is Paul Maass, too, a young Doctor of Philosophy, recently married. He sent me a short time back the photograph of his baby, Ulf, and we exchanged small jokes about Ulf's look of wisdom and his knowledge of Greek and his imperious habits. And now of course Maass is with his regiment, and we shall do our best to kill him, and after that to starve Ulf and Ulf's mother.

It is well for us to remember what war means when reduced to terms of private human life. Doubtless we have most of us met disagreeable Germans and been angry with them ; but I doubt if we ever wanted to cut their throats or blow them to pieces with lyddite. And many thousands of us have German friends, or have come across good straight Germans in business, or have carried on smiling and incompetent conversations with kindly German peasants on walking tours. We must remember such things as these, and not hate the Germans.

' A little later it may be different. In a few weeks English and Germans will have done each other cruel and irreparable wrongs. The blood of those we love will lie between us. We shall hear stories of horrible

suffering. Atrocities will be committed by a few bad
or stupid people on both sides, and will be published
and distorted and magnified. It will be hard to avoid
hatred then ; so it is well to try to think things out
while our minds are still clear, while we still hate the
war and not the enemy.'

So I wrote three weeks ago. By the time I revise
these lines the prophecy has been more than fulfilled.
No one had anticipated then that the nightmare doctrines of Bismarck and Nietzsche and Bernhardi would
be actually enforced by official orders. ' Cause to non-
combatants the maximum of suffering : leave the
women and children nothing but their eyes to weep
with. . . .' We thought they said these things just to
startle and shock us ; and it now appears that some
of them meant what they said. . . . Still we must not
hate the German people. Who knows how many
secret acts of mercy, mercy at risk of life and against
orders, were done at Louvain and Dinant ? Germans
are not demons ; they are naturally fine and good
people. And they will wake from their evil dream.

V. ' Never again ! ' I see that a well-known imperialist writes to the papers saying that these words
should be embroidered on the kit-bags of the Royal
Navy and painted on the knapsacks of all our soldiers.
The aspiration is perhaps too bold, for ' Never ' is
a very large word ; but I believe it is the real aspiration of most civilized men, certainly of most Englishmen. We are fighting for our national life, for our
ideals of freedom and honest government and fair
dealing between nations : but most men, if asked what
they would like to attain at the end of this war, if it
is successful, would probably agree in their answer.
We seek no territory, no aggrandizement, no revenge ;

we only want to be safe from the recurrence of this present horror. We want permanent peace for Europe and freedom for each nation.

What is the way to attain it ? The writer whom I have quoted goes on : ' The war must not end until German warships are sunk, her fortresses razed to the ground, her army disbanded, her munitions destroyed, and the military and civil bureaucrats responsible for opening hell gates are shot or exiled.' As if that would bring us any nearer to a permanent peace ! Crushing Germany would do no good. It would point straight towards a war of revenge. It is not Germany, it is a system, that needs crushing. Other nations before Germany have menaced the peace of Europe, and other nations will do so again after Germany, if the system remains the same.

VI. It is interesting to look back at the records of the Congress of Vienna in 1815, at the end of the last great war of allied Europe against a military despotism.

It was hoped then, a standard historian tells us, ' that so great an opportunity would not be lost, but that the statesmen would initiate such measures of international disarmament as would perpetuate the blessings of that peace which Europe was enjoying after twenty years of warfare '. Certain Powers wished to use the occasion for crushing and humiliating France ; but fortunately they did not carry the Congress with them. Talleyrand persuaded the Congress to accept the view that the recent wars had not been wars of nations, but of principles. It had not been Austria, Russia, Prussia, England, against France ; it had been the principle of legitimacy against all that was illegitimate, treaty-breaking, revolution, usurpation. Bona-

partism was to be destroyed ; France was not to be
injured.

Castlereagh, the English representative, concentrated
his efforts upon two great objects. ¦ The first, which he
just failed to obtain, owing chiefly to difficulties about
Turkey, was a really effective and fully armed Concert
of Europe. He wished for a united guarantee from all
the Powers that they, would accept the settlement
made by the Congress and would, in future, wage
collective war against the first breaker of the peace.
The second object, which he succeeded in gaining, was,
curiously enough, an international declaration of the
abolition of the slave trade.

The principle of legitimacy—of ordinary law and
right and custom—as against lawless ambition : a concert
of Powers pledged by collective treaty to maintain and
enforce peace ; and the abolition of the slave trade !
It sounds like the scheme of some new Utopia, and it
was really a main part of the political programme of
the leaders of the Congress of Vienna—of Castlereagh,
Metternich, Talleyrand, Alexander of Russia, and
Frederick William of Prussia. . . . They are not names
to rouse enthusiasm nowadays. All except Talleyrand
were confessed enemies of freedom and enlightenment
and almost everything that we regard as progressive ;
and Talleyrand, though occasionally on the right side
in such matters, was not a person to inspire confidence.
Yet, after all, they were more or less reasonable human
beings, and a bitter experience had educated them.
Doubtless they blundered ; they went on all kinds of
wrong principles ; they based their partition of Europe
on what they called ' legitimacy ', a perfectly artificial
and false legitimacy, rather than nationality ; they
loathed and dreaded popular movements ; they could

not quite keep their hands from a certain amount of picking and stealing. Yet, on the whole, we find these men at the end of the Great War fixing their minds not on glory and prestige and revenge, not on conventions and shams, but on ideals so great and true and humane and simple that most Englishmen in ordinary life are ashamed of mentioning them ; trying hard to make peace permanent on the basis of what was recognized as ' legitimate ' or fair ; and, amid many differences, agreeing at least in the universal abolition of the slave trade.

VII. Our next conference of Europe ought to do far better if only we can be sure that it will meet in the same high spirit. Instead of Castlereagh, we shall send from England some one like Mr. Asquith or Sir Edward Grey, with ten times more progressive and liberal feeling and ten times more insight and understanding. Even suppose we send a Conservative, Mr. Balfour or Lord Lansdowne, the advance upon Castlereagh will be almost as great. Instead of Talleyrand, France will send one of her many able republican leaders, from Clémenceau to Delcassé, certainly more honest and humane than Talleyrand. And Germany, who can say ? Except that it may be some one very different from these militarist schemers who have brought their country to ruin. In any case it is likely to be a wiser man than Frederick William, just as Russia is bound to send a wiser man than Alexander.

And behind these representatives there will be a deeper and far more intelligent feeling in the various peoples. In 1815 the nations were sick of war after long fighting. I doubt if there was any widespread conviction that war was in itself an abomination and an outrage on humanity. Philosophers felt it, some

inarticulate women and peasants and workmen felt
it. But now such a feeling is almost universal. It
commands a majority in any third-class railway carriage ; it is expressed almost as a matter of course in
the average newspaper.

Between Waterloo and the present day there has
passed one of the greatest and most swiftly progressive
centuries of all human history, and the heart of Europe
is really changed. I do not say we shall not have
Jingo crowds or that our own hearts will not thrill
with the various emotions of war, whether base or
noble. But there is a change. Ideas that once belonged
to a few philosophers have sunk into common men's
minds ; Tolstoy has taught us, the intimate records
of modern wars have taught us, free intercourse with
foreigners has educated us, even the illustrated papers
have made us realize things. In 1914 it is not that
we happen to be sick of war ; it is that we mean to
extirpate war out of the normal possibilities of civilized
life, as we have extirpated leprosy and typhus.

VIII. What kind of settlement can we hope to
attain at the end of it all ?

The question is still far off, and may have assumed
astonishingly different shapes by the time we reach it,
but it is perhaps well to try, now while we are calm and
unhurt, to think out what we would most desire.

First of all, no revenge, no deliberate humiliation of
any enemy, no picking and stealing.

Next, a drastic resettlement of all those burning
problems which carry in them the seeds of European
war, especially the problems of territory. Many of the
details will be very difficult ; some may prove insoluble.
But in general we must try to arrange, even at considerable cost, that territory goes with nationality. The

annexation of Alsace-Lorraine has disturbed the west
of Europe for forty years ; the wrong distributions of
territory in the Balkan peninsula have kept the spark
of war constantly alive in the East, and have not been
fully corrected by the last Balkan settlement. Every
nation which sees a slice of itself cut off and held under
foreign rule is a danger to peace, and so is every nation
that holds by force or fraud an alien province. At this
moment, if Austria had not annexed some millions of
Servians in Bosnia and Herzegovina she would have no
mortal quarrel with Servia. Any drastic rearrangement
of this sort will probably involve the break-up of Austria,
a larger Italy, a larger Servia, a larger Germany—for
the loss of Alsace-Lorraine, of Danish Schleswig, and
the Polish provinces would be more than compensated
by the accession of the Germanic parts of Austria—
and a larger Russia. But it is not big nations that are
a menace to peace ; it is nations with a grievance or
nations who know that others have a grievance against
them.

And shall we try again to achieve Castlereagh's and
Alexander's ideal of a permanent Concert, pledged to
make collective war upon the peace-breaker ? Surely
we must. We must at all costs and in spite of all
difficulties, because the alternative means such un-
speakable failure. We must learn to agree, we civilized
nations of Europe, or else we must perish. I believe
that the chief counsel of wisdom here is to be sure to
go far enough. We need a permanent Concert, perhaps
a permanent Common Council, in which every awkward
problem can be dealt with before it has time to grow
dangerous, and in which outvoted minorities must
accustom themselves to giving way. If we examine
the failures of the European Concert in recent years

we shall find them generally due to two large causes.
Either some Powers came into the council with unclean
hands, determined to grab alien territory or fatally
compromised because they had grabbed it in the past ;
or else they met too late, when the air was full of mistrust, and not to yield had become a point of honour.
Once make certain of good faith and a clean start, and
surely there is in the great Powers of Europe sufficient
unity of view and feeling about fundamental matters
to make it possible for them to work honestly together
—at any rate, when the alternative is stark ruin. . . .
It is well to remember that in this matter, from
Alexander I onward, Russia has steadily done her best
to lead the way.

And the abolition of the slave trade ! It is wonderful
to think that that was not only talked about but really
achieved ; the greatest abomination in the world
definitely killed, finished and buried, never to return,
as a result of the meeting of the Powers at the end of
the Great War. What can we hope for to equal that ?
The limitation of armaments seems almost small in
comparison.

We saw in the first week of the war what a nation
and a government can do when the need or the opportunity comes. Armies and fleets mobilized, war risks
assured, railways taken over, prices fixed . . . things
that seemed almost impossible accomplished successfully in a few days. One sentence in Mr. Lloyd George's
speech on the financial situation ran thus, if I remember
the words : 'This part of the subject presents some
peculiar difficulties, but I have no doubt they will be
surmounted with the utmost ease.' That is the spirit
in which our Government has risen to its crisis, a spirit
not of shallow optimism but of that active and hard

thinking confidence which creates its own fulfilment.
The power of man over circumstance is now—even
now in the midst of this one terrific failure—immeasur-
ably greater than it has ever yet been in history. Every
year that passes has shown its increase. When the next
settling day comes the real will of reasonable man
should be able to assert itself and achieve its end with
a completeness not conceivable in 1815.

IX. This is not the time to make any definite proposals. Civilization has still many slave trades to
abolish. The trade in armaments is perhaps the most
oppressive of all, but there are others also, slave trades
social and intimate and international; no one can tell
yet which ones and how many it may be possible to
overthrow. But there is one thing that we must see.
This war and the national aspiration behind the war
must not be allowed to fall into the hands of the militarists. I do not say that we must not be ready for some
form of universal service : that will depend on the
circumstances in which the war leaves us. But we
must not be militarized in mind and feeling; we must
keep our politics British and not Prussian. That is the
danger. It is the danger in every war. In time of war
every interest, every passion, tends to be concentrated
on the mere fighting, the gaining of advantages, the persistent use of cunning and force. An atmosphere tends
to grow up in which the militarist and the schemer
are at home and the liberal and democrat homeless.

There are many thousands of social reformers and
radicals in this country who instinctively loathe war,
and have only been convinced with the utmost reluct-
ance, if at all, of the necessity of our fighting. The
danger is that these people, containing among them
some of our best guides and most helpful political

thinkers, may from disgust and discouragement fall
into the background and leave public opinion to the
mercy of our own von Tirpitzes and Bernhardis. That
would be the last culminating disaster. It would mean
that the war had ceased to be a war for free Europe
against militarism, and had become merely one of the
ordinary sordid and bloody struggles of nation against
nation, one link in the insane chain of wrongs that lead
ever to worse wrongs.

One may well be thankful that the strongest of the
neutral Powers is guided by a leader so wise and up-
right and temperate as President Wilson. One may
be thankful, too, that both here and in France we
have in power not only a very able Ministry but
a strongly liberal and peace-loving Ministry. In the
first place, it unites the country far more effectively
than any ministry which could be suspected of Jingoism
In the second place, it gives us a chance of a permanent
settlement, based on wisdom and not on ambition.
It is fortunate also that in Russia the more liberal
elements in the Government seem to be predominant. Some English liberals seem to be sorry and
half ashamed that we have Russia as an ally ; for
my own part I am glad and proud. Not only because
of her splendid military achievements, but because, so
far as I can read the signs of such things, there is in
Russia, more than in other nations, a vast untapped
reservoir of spiritual power, of idealism, of striving for
a nobler life. And that is what Europe will most need
at the end of this bitter material struggle. I am proud
to think that the liberal and progressive elements in
Russia are looking towards England and feeling
strengthened by English friendship. ' This is for us,'
said a great Russian liberal to me some days ago,

'this is for us a *Befreiungskrieg* (war of liberation).
After this, reaction is impossible.' We are fighting not
only to defend Russian governors and Russian peasants
against German invasion, but also, and perhaps even
more profoundly, to enable the Russia of Turgenieff
and Tolstoy, the Russia of many artists and many
martyrs, to work out its destiny and its freedom. If
the true Russia has a powerful voice in the final settlement it will be a great thing for humanity.

Of course, all these hopes may be shattered and
made ridiculous before the settlement comes. They
would be shattered, probably, by a German victory;
not because Germans are wicked, but because a German
victory at the present time would mean a victory for
blood-and-iron. They would be shattered, certainly,
if in each separate country the liberal forces abandoned
the situation to the reactionaries, and stood aside
while the nation fell into that embitterment and brutalization of feeling which is the natural consequence of
a long war.

To prevent the first of these perils is the work of our
armies and navies ; to prevent the second should be
the work of all thoughtful non-combatants. It may be
a difficult task, but at least it is not hideous ; and some
of the work that we must do is. So hideous, indeed,
that at times it seems strange that we can carry it out
at all—this war of civilized men against civilized men,
against our intellectual teachers, our brothers in art
and science and healing medicine, and so large a part
of all that makes life beautiful. When we remember
all this it makes us feel lost and heavy-hearted, like
men struggling and unable to move in an evil dream.
. . . So, it seems, for the time being we must forget it.
We modern men are accustomed by the needs of life to

this division of feelings. In every war, in every competition almost, there is something of the same difficulty, and we have learned to keep the two sides of our mind apart. We must fight our hardest, indomitably, gallantly, even joyously, forgetting all else while we have to fight. When the fight is over we must remember.

Oxford: Horace Hart Printer to the University

OXFORD PAMPHLETS
1914

Crown 8vo, from 12 to 40 pages each
Prices from .1d. net to 3d. net

Also in series of five Pamphlets, stiff covers
One Shilling net each series.

---

26 Pamphlets have now been issued and others are in preparation. The historical pieces are illustrated by sketch-maps

---

' The cheap and useful little " Oxford" pamphlets issued since the war began by the Oxford University Press continue to multiply.'—Morning Post.

OXFORD UNIVERSITY PRESS
HUMPHREY MILFORD
LONDON   EDINBURGH   GLASGOW
NEW YORK   TORONTO   MELBOURNE   BOMBAY

2

I

The Deeper Causes of the War.
By W. SANDAY. 3d. net. *Third Impression.*
The psychology of Prussian militarism ; German public opinion and Germany's aggressive ambitions.

To the Christian Scholars of Europe and America : A Reply from Oxford to the German 'Address to Evangelical Christians'. 2d. net. *Second Impression.*
The answer of Oxford theologians to a recent manifesto of the German evangelical theologians. This manifesto, which is reproduced in the present pamphlet, argues that Germany is in no sense responsible for the present war. The Oxford reply states that the German theologians cannot have studied either the events which led up to the war, or the political utterances of their own countrymen.

The Responsibility for the War.
By W. G. S. ADAMS. 2d. net.
A brief discussion of the question of responsibility : 1. Austria and Serbia ; 2. The responsibility of Russia ; 3. The intervention of England ; with a note on the issues of the War.

Great Britain and Germany.
By SPENSER WILKINSON. 2d. net.
Three letters to the *Springfield Republican*: 1. By Prof. Spenser Wilkinson, putting Great Britain's case before American readers ; 2. By Prof. John W. Burgess of the University of Columbia, stating Germany's case ; 3. By Prof. Wilkinson, in reply to Prof. Burgess.

'Just for a Scrap of Paper.'
By ARTHUR HASSALL. 1d. net. *Second Impression.*
Explains why England stands for the sanctity of European treaty-law.

II

The Germans, their Empire, and how they have made it.
By C. R. L. FLETCHER. 2d. net. *Second Impression.*
A historical account of Prussian policy from the seventeenth century.

The Germans, their Empire, and what they covet.
By C. R. L. FLETCHER. 2d. net. *Second Impression.*
An account of the ambitions avowed by the Pan-German school of thought.

Might is Right.
By Sir WALTER RALEIGH. 2d. net.
Why Germany may win ; what will happen if she wins ; why we believe she will not win.

2

1914

Austrian Policy since 1867.

By Murray Beaven. 3d. net.

Austrian policy in the Balkans has been of the 'offensive-defensive' order. Aehrental is responsible for its worst features. The Archduke Francis Ferdinand might have saved Austria from rushing to destruction; but 1912 was the beginning of the end.

Italian Policy since 1870.

By Keith Feiling. 2d. net.

Italian policy has been and must be guided by her own interests. The results of her colonial policy have not yet been satisfactory enough to tempt her into adventures.

III

French Policy since 1871.

By F. Morgan and H. W. C. Davis. 2d. net. *Second Impression.*

A historical sketch, discussing the question whether French policy has been aggressive.

Russia : The Psychology of a Nation.

By Paul Vinogradoff. 1d. net. *Second Impression.*

A reply to the German taunt that Russia is still in a state of barbarism, and is the enemy of European civilization.

Serbia and the Serbs.

By Sir Valentine Chirol. 2d. net. *Third Impression.*

A sketch of Serbian history, which is incidentally an indictment of the policy pursued by Austria-Hungary towards the Serbian kingdom.

Germany and 'The Fear of Russia'.

By Sir Valentine Chirol. 2d. net. *Second Impression.*

Shows that before 1879 Germany preferred Russia as an ally to Austria. The ambition of Germany to establish a protectorate over Turkey has led her to assist Austria in the Balkans and so to challenge Russia.

The Eastern Question.

By F. F. Urquhart. 3d. net. *Second Impression.*

The history of the Balkan nations; their future.

IV

War against War.

By A. D. Lindsay. 2d. net. *Second Impression.*

Denies that war is good in itself, or a necessary evil. Power is not the sole or chief end for which the State exists. National greatness, if founded on brute force, cannot endure. International law represents an ideal, but an ideal that may be realized.

The Value of Small States.

By H. A. L. Fisher. 2d. net. *Second Impression.*

The author argues that the debt of civilization to small states is incalculable. They are useful, at the present time, as laboratories of political experiments and as buffer-states between the greater powers.

1914

How can War ever be Right?

By Gilbert Murray. 2d. net. *Second Impression.*

A well-known lover of peace and advocate of pacific policies argues against the Tolstoyan position. Right and honour compelled Britain to make war; and war—like tragedy—is not pure evil.

The National Principle and the War.

By Ramsay Muir. 3d. net.

Considers the principle of nationality and its application to the settlement of Europe—particularly of S.E. Europe—after the War.

Nietzsche and Treitschke: The Worship of Power in Modern Germany.

By E. Barker. 2d. net. *Third Impression.*

An explanation of the main points of interest in the ethical and political doctrines of the German ruling classes.

The British Dominions and the War.

By H. E. Egerton. 2d. net. *Second Impression*

Explains the ideas for which the British Empire stands, and the political and moral issues of the present war so far as they affect the Dominions.

India and the War.

By Sir Ernest Trevelyan. 1d. net. *Second Impression*

Discusses the reasons which account for the striking manifestations of Indian loyalty in the last few weeks.

Bacilli and Bullets.

By Sir William Osler. 1d. net. *Second Impression*

Calls attention to the fact that disease kills more men than the bullet in modern warfare. The most dangerous diseases are preventible by inoculation.

The Navy and the War.

By J. R. Thursfield. 3d. net.

Estimates the military and economic value of the silent pressure exercised by our fleet, and warns the faint-hearted and the captious of the perils of lack of faith.

The Retreat from Mons.

By H. W. C. Davis. 3d. net. *Second Impression.*

Introduction; the Dispatch of Sept. 9; the Statement by the War Office, published Aug. 31. Appendixes (soldiers' narratives); two maps.

The Law of Nations and the War.

By A. Pearce Higgins. 2d. net.

The violation of Belgian neutrality and the conduct of England to Denmark in 1807; the doctrine of German lawyers that military necessity overrides the laws of war; the balance of power and the sanctity of treaties.

Others in preparation.

No. 18

OXFORD PAMPHLETS

1914

HOW CAN WAR EVER BE RIGHT?

BY

GILBERT MURRAY

FIFTH IMPRESSION

Price Twopence net

OXFORD UNIVERSITY PRESS
HUMPHREY MILFORD
LONDON EDINBURGH GLASGOW
NEW YORK TORONTO MELBOURNE BOMBAY

HOW CAN WAR EVER BE RIGHT?

I HAVE all my life been an advocate of Peace. I hate war, not merely for its own cruelty and folly, but because it is the enemy of all the causes that I care for most, of social progress and good government and all friendliness and gentleness of life, as well as of art and learning and literature. I have spoken and presided at more meetings than I can remember for peace and arbitration and the promotion of international friendship. I opposed the policy of war in South Africa with all my energies, and have been either outspokenly hostile or inwardly unsympathetic towards almost every war that Great Britain has waged in my lifetime. If I may speak more personally, there is none of my own work into which I have put more intense feeling than into my translation of Euripides' *Trojan Women*, the first great denunciation of war in European literature. I do not regret any word that I have spoken or written in the cause of Peace, nor have I changed, as far as I know, any opinion that I have previously held on this subject. Yet I believe firmly that we were right to declare war against Germany on August 4, 1914, and that to have remained neutral in that crisis would have been a failure in public duty.

A heavy responsibility—there is no doubt of it—lies upon Great Britain. Our allies, France and Russia, Belgium and Serbia, had no choice ; the war was, in various degrees, forced on all of them. We only, after

deliberately surveying the situation, when Germany
would have preferred for the moment not to fight us, of
our free will declared war.   And we were right.

How can such a thing be ?   It is easy enough to see
that our cause is right, and the German cause, by all
ordinary human standards, desperately wrong.   It is
hardly possible to study the official papers issued by
the British, the German, and the Russian governments, without seeing that Germany—or some party
in Germany—had plotted this war beforehand ; that
she chose a moment when she thought her neighbours were at a disadvantage ; that she prevented
Austria from making a settlement even at the last
moment ; that in order to get more quickly at France
she violated her treaty with Belgium.   Evidence too
strong to resist seems to show that she has carried out
the violation with a purposeful cruelty that has no
parallel in the wars of modern and civilized nations.
Yet some people may still feel gravely doubtful.   Germany's ill-doing is no reason for us to do likewise.   We
did our best to keep the general peace ; there we were
right.   We failed ; the German government made war
in spite of us.   There we were unfortunate.   It was a
war already on an enormous scale, a vast network of
calamity ranging over five nations ; and we decided to
make it larger still.   There we were wrong.   Could we
not have stood aside, as the United States stand, ready
to help refugees and sufferers, anxious to heal wounds
and not make them, watchful for the first chance of
putting an end to this time of horror ?
   ' Try for a moment ', an objector to our policy might
say, ' to realize the extent of suffering involved in one
small corner of a battlefield.   You have seen a man here

and there badly hurt in an accident ; you have seen
perhaps a horse with its back broken, and you can
remember how dreadful it seemed to you. In that one
corner how many men, how many horses, will be lying,
hurt far worse and just waiting to die ? Indescribable
wounds, extreme torment ; and all, far further than any
eye can see, multiplied and multiplied ! And, for all
your righteous indignation against Germany, what have
these done ? The horses are not to blame for anybody's
foreign policy. They have only come where their
masters took them. And the masters themselves . . .
admitting that certain highly-placed Germans, whose
names we are not sure of, are as wicked as ever you like,
these soldiers, peasants and working-men and shopkeepers and schoolmasters have really done nothing in
particular ; at least, perhaps they have now, but they
had not up to the time when you, seeing they were involved in war and misery already, decided to make war
on them also and increase their sufferings. You say
that justice must be done on conspirators and public
malefactors. But as far as the rights and wrongs of the
war go, you are simply condemning innocent men, by
thousands and thousands, to death, or even to mutilation
and torture ; is that the best way to satisfy your sense
of justice ? These innocent people, you will say, are
fighting to protect the guilty parties whom you are
determined to reach. Well, perhaps, at the end of the
war, after millions of innocent people have suffered, you
may at last, if all goes well with your arms, get at the
" guilty parties ". You will hold an inquiry, with imper-
fect evidence and biased judges ; you will decide—in all
likelihood wrongly—that a dozen very stupid and
obstinate Prussians with long titles are the guilty parties,
and even then you will not know what to do with them.

You will probably try, and almost certainly fail, to make them somehow feel ashamed or humiliated. It is likely enough that you will merely make them into national heroes.

'And after all, this is assuming quite the best sort of war : a war in which one party is wrong and the other right, and the right wins. Suppose both are wrong ; or suppose the wrong party wins ? It is as likely as not ; for, if the right party is helped by his good conscience, the wrong has probably taken pains to have the odds on his side before he began quarrelling. In that case all the wild expenditure of blood and treasure, all the immeasurable suffering of innocent individuals and dumb animals, all the tears of women and children in the background, have taken place not to vindicate the right but to establish the wrong. To do a little evil that great or certain good may come is all very well ; but to do almost infinite evil for a doubtful chance of attaining something which half the people concerned may think good and the other half think bad, and which in no imaginable case can ever be attained in fullness or purity . . . that is neither good morals nor good sense. Anybody not in a passion must see that it is insanity.'

I sympathize with every step of this argument ; yet I think it is wrong. It is judging of the war as a profit-and-loss account, and reckoning, moreover, only the immediate material consequences. It leaves out of sight the cardinal fact that in some causes it is better to fight and be broken than to yield peacefully ; that sometimes the mere act of resisting to the death is in itself a victory.

Let us try to understand this. The Greeks who fought and died at Thermopylae had no manner of doubt that

they were right so to fight and die, and all posterity
has agreed with them. They probably knew they would
be defeated. They probably expected that, after their
defeat, the Persians would proceed easily to conquer the
rest of Greece, and would treat it much more harshly
because it had resisted. But such considerations did not
affect them. They would not consent to their country's
dishonour.

Take again a very clear modern case : the fine story
of the French tourist who was captured, together with
a priest and some other white people, by Moorish robbers.
The Moors gave their prisoners the choice either to
trample on the Cross or to be killed. The Frenchman
happened to be a Free-thinker and an anti-clerical. He
disliked Christianity. But he was not going to trample
on the Cross at the orders of a robber. He stuck to
his companions and died.

This sense of honour, and the respect for this sense
of honour, are very deep instincts in the average man.
In the United States there is a rather specially strong
feeling against mixture of blood, not only with the blood
of coloured people but with that of the large masses of
mankind who are lumped together as ' dagoes ' or
' hunkies '. Yet I have noticed that persons with a dash
of Red Indian blood are not ashamed but rather proud
of it. And if you look for the reason, I suspect it lies
in the special reputation which the Indian has acquired,
that he would never consent to be a slave. He preferred
to fight till he was dead.

A deal of nonsense, no doubt, is talked about ' honour '
and ' dishonour '. They are feelings based on sentiment,
not on reason ; the standards by which they are judged
are often conventional or shallow, and sometimes utterly
false. Yet honour and dishonour are real things   I will

not try to define them ; but will only notice that, like Religion, their characteristic is that they admit of no bargaining. Indeed we can almost think of honour as being simply that which a free man values more than life, and dishonour as that which he avoids more than suffering or death. And the important point for us is that there are such things.

There are some people, followers of Tolstoy, who accept this position as far as dying is concerned, but will have nothing to do with killing. Passive resistance, they say, is right ; martyrdom is right ; but to resist violence by violence is sin.

I was once walking with a friend and disciple of Tolstoy's in a country lane, and a little girl running in front of us. I put to him the well-known question : ' Suppose you saw a man, wicked or drunk or mad, run out and attack that child. You are a big man and carry a big stick : would you not stop him and, if necessary, knock him down ? ' ' No,' he said, ' why should I commit a sin ? I would try to persuade him, I would stand in his way, I would let him kill me, but I would not strike him.' Some few people will always be found, less than one in a thousand, to take this view. They will say : ' Let the little girl be killed or carried off ; let the wicked man commit another wickedness ; I, at any rate, will not add to the mass of useless violence that I see all round me.'

With such persons one cannot reason, though one can often respect them. Nearly every normal man will feel that the real sin, the real dishonour, lies in allowing an abominable act to be committed under your eyes while you have the strength to prevent it. And the stronger you are, the greater your chance of

success, by so much the more are you bound to intervene. If the robbers are overpoweringly strong and
there is no chance of beating or baffling them, then
and only then should you think of martyrdom. Martyrdom is not the best possibility. It is almost the worst.
It is a counsel of despair, the last resort when there
is no hope of successful resistance. The best thing—
suppose once the robbers are there and intent on crime—
the best thing is to overawe them at once ; the next
best, to defeat them after a hard struggle ; the third
best, to resist vainly and be martyred ; the worst of
all, the one evil that need never be endured, is to let
them have their will without protest. (As for con-
verting them from their evil ways, that is a process
which may be hoped for afterwards.)

We have noticed that in all these cases of honour
there is, or at least there seems to be, no counting of
cost, no balancing of good and evil. In ordinary conduct we are always balancing the probable results of
this course or that ; but when honour or religion come
on the scene all such balancing ceases. If you argued
to the Christian martyr : ' Suppose you do burn the
pinch of incense, what will be the harm ? All your
friends know you are really a Christian : they will
not be misled. The idol will not be any the better
for the incense, nor will your own true God be any the
worse. Why should you bring misery on yourself and
all your family ? ' Or suppose you pleaded, with the
French atheist : ' Why in the world should you not
trample on the Cross ? It is the sign of the clericalism
to which you object. Even if trampling somewhat
exaggerates your sentiments, the harm is small. Who
will be a penny the worse for your trampling ? While
you will live instead of dying, and all your family be

happy instead of wretched ? ' Suppose you said to the Red Indian : ' My friend, you are outnumbered by ten to one. If you will submit unconditionally to these pale-faces, and be always civil and obliging, they will probably treat you quite well. If they do not, well, you can reconsider the situation later on. No need to get yourself killed at once.'

The people concerned would not condescend to meet your arguments. Perhaps they can be met, perhaps not. But it is in the very essence of religion or honour that it must outweigh all material considerations. The point of honour is the point at which a man says to some proposal, ' I will not do it. I will rather die.'

These things are far easier to see where one man is involved than where it is a whole nation. But they arise with nations too. In the case of a nation the material consequences are much larger, and the point of honour is apt to be less clear. But, in general, whenever one nation in dealing with another relies simply on force or fraud, and denies to its neighbour the common consideration due to human beings, a point of honour must arise.

Austria says suddenly to Serbia : ' You are a wicked little State. I have annexed and governed against their will some millions of your countrymen, yet you are still full of anti-Austrian feeling, which I do not intend to allow. You will dismiss from your service all officials, politicians, and soldiers who do not love Austria, and I will further send you from time to time lists of persons whom you are to dismiss or put to death. And if you do not agree to this within forty-eight hours, I, being vastly stronger than you, will

make you.' As a matter of fact, Serbia did her very
best to comply with Austria's demands ; she accepted
about two-thirds of them, and asked for arbitration
on the remaining third. But it is clear that she could
not accept them all without being dishonoured. That
is, Serbia would have given up her freedom at the threat
of force ; the Serbs would no longer be a free people,
and every individual Serb would have been humiliated.
He would have confessed .himself to be the kind of man
who will yield when an Austrian bullies him. And if
it is urged that under good Austrian government
Serbia would become richer and safer, and the Serbian
peasants get better markets, such pleas cannot be
listened to. They are a price offered for slavery ; and
a free man will not accept slavery at a price.

Germany, again, says to Belgium (we leave out for
the moment the fact of Germany's special treaty obligations), ' We have no quarrel with you, but we intend
for certain reasons to march across your territory
and perhaps fight a battle or two there. We know
that you are pledged by treaty not to allow any such
thing, but we cannot help that. Consent, and we will
pay you some compensation afterwards ; refuse, and
we shall make you wish you had never been born.'
At that moment Belgium was a free self-governing
State. If it had yielded to Germany's demand, it would
have ceased to be either. It is possible that, if Germany
had been completely victorious and France quite
unable to retaliate, Belgium would have suffered no
great material injury ; but it would have taken orders
from a stranger who had no right to give them, simply
because he was strong and Belgium dared not face
him. Belgium refused. It has had some of its principal
towns destroyed, some thousands of its soldiers killed,

many more thousands of its women, children, and non-combatants outraged and beggared; but it is still free. It has still its honour.

Let us think this matter out more closely. Our Tolstoyan will say : ' We speak of Belgium's honour and Serbia's honour; but who is Serbia and who is Belgium ? There is no such person as either. There are only great numbers of people who happen to be Serbians and Belgians, and who mostly have had nothing to do with the questions at issue. Some of them are honourable people, some dishonourable. The honour of each one of them depends very much on whether he pays his debts and tells the truth, but not in the least on whether a number of foreigners walk through his country or interfere with his government. King Albert and his ministers might feel humiliated if the German Government compelled them to give way against their will; but would the ordinary population ? Would the ordinary peasant or shopkeeper or artisan in the districts of Visé and Liège and Louvain have felt particularly disgraced or ashamed ? He would probably have made a little money and been greatly amused by the sight of the troops passing. Who will pretend that he would have suffered any injury that can for a moment be compared with what he has suffered now, in order that his Government may feel proud of itself ? '

I will not raise the point that, as a matter of fact, to grant a right of way to Germany would have been equivalent to declaring war against France, so that Belgium would not, by giving up her independence, have been spared the danger of war. I will assume that nothing but honour was involved. In that form, this question goes to the root of our whole conception of citizenship and the position of man in society. And I believe that our Tolstoyan friend is profoundly wrong.

Is it true, in a healthy and well-governed State, that the average citizen is indifferent to the honour of his country ? We know that it is not. True, the average citizen may often not understand what is going on, but as soon as he knows he cares. Suppose for a moment that the King, or the Prime Minister, or the President of the United States, were found to be in the pay of a foreign State, as for instance Charles II was in the pay of Louis XIV, can any one pretend that the ordinary citizens of Great Britain or America would take it quietly ? That any normal man would be found saying : ' Well, the King, or the President, or the Prime Minister, is behaving dishonourably, but that is a matter for him, not for me. I am an honest and honourable man, and my Government can do what it likes.' The notion is absurd. The ordinary citizen would feel instantly and without question that his country's honour involved his own. And woe to the society in which it were otherwise ! We know of such societies in history. They are the kind which is called ' corrupt ', and which generally has not long to live. Belgium has proved that she is not that kind of society.

But what about Great Britain herself ? At the present moment a very clear case has arisen, and we can test our own feelings. Great Britain had, by a solemn treaty more than once renewed, pledged herself to maintain the neutrality of Belgium. Belgium is a little State lying between two very strong States, France and Germany, and in danger of being overrun or maltreated by one of them unless the Great Powers guarantee her safety. The treaty, signed by Prussia, Russia, Austria, France, and Great Britain, bound all these Powers not to attack Belgium, move troops into it, or annex any part of it ; and further, to resist by armed force any Power which should try to do any of these things. Belgium, on her part, was bound to maintain her own neutrality to the best of her power, and not to side with any State which was at war with another.

At the end of last July the exact case arose in which we had pledged ourselves to act. Germany suddenly and without excuse invaded Belgium, and Belgium appealed to us and France to defend her. Meantime she fought alone, desperately, against overwhelming odds. The issue was clear, and free from any complications. The German Chancellor, Herr von Bethmann-Hollweg, in his speech of August 6, admitted that Germany had no grievance against Belgium, and no excuse except ' necessity '. She could not get to France quick enough by the direct road. Germany put her case to us, roughly, on these grounds. ' True, you did sign a treaty, but what is a treaty ? We ourselves signed the same treaty, and see what we are doing ! Anyhow, treaty or no treaty, we have Belgium absolutely in our power. If she had done what we wanted, we would have treated her kindly ; as it is we shall show her no mercy. If you will now do what we want and stay quiet, later on, at our convenience, we will consider a friendly deal with you. If you interfere, you must take the consequences. We trust you will not be so insane as to plunge your whole Empire into danger for the sake of "a scrap of paper".' Our answer was : ' Evacuate Belgium within twelve hours or we fight you.'

I think that answer was right. Consider the situation

carefully. No question arises of overhaste or lack of
patience on our part. From the first moment of the
crisis, we had laboured night and day in every Court of
Europe for any possible means of conciliation and peace.
We had carefully and sincerely explained to Germany
beforehand what attitude she might expect from us.
We did not send our ultimatum till Belgium was already
invaded. It is just the plain question put to the British
Government, and, I think, to every one who feels himself
a British citizen : ' The exact case contemplated in
your treaty has arisen : the people you swore to protect
is being massacred ; will you keep your word at a gigantic
cost, or will you·break it at the bidding of Germany ? '
For my own part, weighing the whole question soberly
and without undue passion, I feel that in this case I would
rather die than submit ; and I believe that the Government, in deciding to keep its word at the cost of war, has
rightly interpreted the feeling of the average British
citizen.

So much for the question of honour, pure and simple ;
honour without regard for consequences. But, of course,
situations in real political life are never so simple as that ;
they have many different aspects and ramifications.
And in the present case, though the point of honour
happens to be quite clear, it seems probable that even
without it there were compelling reasons for war. I do
not, of course, for a moment mean that war was goin
to be ' profitable ' to Great Britain ; such a calculatio
would be infamous. I mean that, terrible as the consequences of our taking part in the war were sure to be,
the consequences of our not doing so were likely to be
even more profoundly and widely evil.

Let us leave aside then, the definite treaty binding

us to Belgium. Apart from that, we were faced with a complicated question of statesmanship, of prudence, of patriotism towards our own country and towards humanity.

Germany has for years presented a problem to Europe. Since her defeat of France in 1870, she has been extraordinarily successful, and the success seems to have intoxicated her. This is a complicated subject, which calls for far deeper knowledge than I possess. I will merely try to state, as fairly as I can, the impression that has been forced on me by a certain amount of reading and observation. From the point of view of one who really believes that great nations ought to behave to one another as scrupulously and honourably as ordinary law-abiding men, no Power in Europe, or out of it, is quite blameless. They all have ambitions ; they all, to some extent, use spies ; they all, within limits, try to outwit each other ; in their diplomatic dealings they rely not only on the claims of good sense and justice, but ultimately, no doubt, on the threat of possible force. But, as a matter of degree, Germany does all these things more than other Powers. In her diplomacy, force comes at once to the front ; international justice is hardly mentioned. She spends colossal sums on her Secret Service, so that German spies are become a by-word and a joke. In the recognized sport of international treachery, she goes frequently beyond the rules of the game. Her Emperor, her Imperial Chancellor, and other people in the highest positions of responsibility, expound her ambitions and her schemes in language which would only be used by an irresponsible journalist in England or France. They discuss, for instance, whether the time has come for conquering France once more, and how best they can ' bleed her

white ' and reduce her to impotence. They explain that
Bismarck and his generation have made Germany the
strongest Power on the Continent. 'The will of Germany
is now respected ' in Europe ; it rests with the present
Emperor to make it similarly respected throughout the
world. ' Germany's world-future lies on the sea.' They
discuss whether they can build up a fleet strong enough
to fight and beat the British fleet without Great Britain
interfering. They discuss in public how many colonies,
and which, they will leave to Great Britain when the
great ' Day ' comes. They express regret, combined, as
far as one can make out, with a little genuine surprise,
that the ' brutal egoism of Great Britain ' should raise
any objection to this plan, and they hope—openly and
publicly—that her well-known weakness and cowardice
will make her afraid to act. Since Great Britain has
a vast number of Mohammedan subjects, who may
possibly be stirred to disaffection, the German Emperor
proclaims to ' the three hundred million Mohammedans
who live scattered over the globe ' that whenever they
need him, the German Emperor will be their friend.
And this in 1898, in the middle of profound peace !
Professors in German Universities lecture on the best
way of destroying the British Empire, and the officers'
messes in the German Navy regularly drink the toast of
' The Day '. There is no need to explain what Day.
The curious thing is that these plans are all expounded
in public speeches and books—strange books, in which
the average civilized sense of international justice or
common honesty seems to have been left out of account,
as well as the sense of common political prudence ; in
which the schemes of an accomplished burglar are
expounded with the candour of a child.

And all through this period, in which she plots against

her neighbours and tells them she is plotting, Germany lives in a state of alarm. Her neighbours are so unfriendly ! Their attitude may be correct, but it is not trustful and cordial. The Imperial Chancellor, von Bülow, explains in his book that there was only one time when he really breathed freely. It was in 1909, when Austria, his ally, annexed by violence and against her pledges the two Slav provinces of Bosnia and Herzegovina. All Europe was indignant, especially Russia, the natural protector of the Slavs, and England, the habitual champion of small nationalities. But Germany put down her foot. The Kaiser ' appeared in shining armour beside his ally ', and no power dared to intervene. Germany was in the wrong. Every one knew she was in the wrong. It was just that fact that was so comforting. Her army was big enough, her navy was big enough ; and for the moment the timid creature felt secure.

Lastly, we must remember that it is Germany who started the race for armaments ; and that while Russia has pressed again and again for a general limitation of armies, and England made proposal after proposal for a general limitation of navies, Germany has steadily refused to entertain any such idea.

Now, for some time it was possible to minimize all these danger-signals, and, for my own part, I have always tried to minimize them. There are militarists and jingoes in every country ; our own have often been bad enough. The German sort seemed unusually blatant, but it did not follow that they carried their country with them. The Kaiser, always impulsive, said on the whole more friendly things than unfriendly things. At any rate, it seemed wiser and more statesmanlike to meet provocation with good temper, and to try by

persistent friendliness to encourage all the more Liberal
and reasonable elements in German public life. This
policy seemed possible until the July of the present
year. Then certain facts were forced upon us. They
are all detailed in the White Paper and the other diplomatic correspondence.

We suddenly found that Germany and Austria, or
some conspiring parties in Germany and Austria, had
arranged for a great stroke, like that of 1909 on a larger
scale. It was so obviously aggressive in its nature that
their ally, Italy, the third Power in the Triple Alliance,
formally refused to act with them. The Alliance only
applied to a defensive war. The time had been carefully
chosen. England was supposed to be on the verge of
a civil war in Ireland and a new mutiny in India
France had just been through a military scandal, in
which it appeared that the army was short of boots and
ammunition. Russia, besides a general strike and internal troubles, was re-arming her troops with a new weapon,
and the process was only half through. Even the day
was chosen. It was in a week when nearly all the
Ambassadors were away from their posts, taking their
summer holiday—the English Ambassador at Berlin,
the Russian Ambassadors at Berlin and Vienna, the
Austrian Foreign Minister, the French Prime Minister,
the Serbian Prime Minister, the Kaiser himself, and
others who might have used a restraining influence on
the schemes of the war-party. Suddenly, without a word
to any outside Power, Austria issued an ultimatum to
Serbia, to be answered in forty-eight hours. Seventeen
of these hours had elapsed before the other Powers were
informed, and war was declared on Serbia before all
the Ambassadors could get back to their posts. The
leading statesmen of Europe sat up all night trying for

conciliation, for arbitration, even for bare delay. At the last moment, when the Austrian Foreign Minister had returned, and had consented to a basis for conversations with Russia, there seemed to be a good chance that peace might be preserved ; but at that moment Germany launched her ultimatum at Russia and France, and Austria was already invading Serbia. In twenty-four hours, six European Powers were at war.

Now, the secret history of this strange intrigue is not yet known. It will not be known for fifty years or so. It is impossible to believe that the German nation would have backed up the plot, if they had understood it. It is difficult to think that the Kaiser would ; and the Austrian Foreign Minister, when once he returned, tried to undo the work of his subordinates. But somehow the war parties in Germany and Austria got the upper hand for one fatal week, and have managed to drag their countries after them.

We saw, as Italy had seen, that Germany had pre-arranged the war. We saw her breaking her treaties and over-running little Belgium, as her ally was trampling on little Serbia. We remembered her threats against ourselves. And at this very time, as if to deepen our suspicions, she made us what has been justly termed an ' infamous proposal ', that if we would condone her treaty-breaking now, she would have an ' understanding ' with us afterwards.

Suppose we had not been bound by our treaty to Belgium, or even our natural and informal friendship with France : what could we have done ? I wish to take no low ground ; I wish to face the question from the point of view of a statesman who owes a duty to his own country and a duty to Europe.

The one thing which we could not have done, in my opinion, was to repudiate our responsibility. We are a very strong Power, one of the strongest in the world, and here, under our eyes and within range of our guns, a thing was being done which menaced every living creature in Europe. The one thing that no statesman could possibly do was to say : ' This is no concern of ours. We will go our ways as usual.' It was perfectly possible to stand aside. and proclaim our neutrality. But—apart from questions of honour—to proclaim neutrality was quite as grave a step as to proclaim war. Let no man imagine that he can escape blood-guiltiness by standing still while murder is committed before his eyes.

I will not argue here what the right decision would have been. It depends, unlike the point of honour, on a careful balancing of evidence and consequences, and scarcely any one in the country except the Government has sufficient knowledge to make the balance. For my own part, I should have started with a strong predilection for peace, éven a fragmentary peace, but should ulti-mately have been guided chiefly by the public men whom I most trust. But, as things fell out, our Govern-ment was not forced to make a decision on this difficult ground at all, because Germany took a further step which made the whole situation clear. Her treatment of Belgium not only roused our passionate indignation, but compelled us either to declare war or to break our pledged word. I incline, however, to think that our whole welfare is so vitally dependent on the observance of public law and the rights of nations, and would have been so terribly endangered by the presence of Germany in a conqueror's mood at Ostend and Zeebrugge, not to speak of Dunkirk and Calais, that in this case mere self-

preservation called us to fight.   I do not venture to lay
any stress on the hopes which we may entertain for the
building up of a better Europe after the war, a Europe
which shall have settled its old feuds and devised some
great machinery for dealing with new difficulties as they
arise, on a basis of justice and concord, not of intrigue
and force.   By all means let us hope, let us work, for
that rebuilding ; but it will be a task essentially difficult
when it comes ; and the very beginning of it lies far
away, separated from the present time and the immediate
task by many terrific hazards.   We have no right to
soothe our consciences concerning the war with professions of the fine and generous things that we are going
to do afterwards.   Doubtless Germany was going to
make us all good and happy when she was once sure
of our obedience.   For the moment we can only think of
our duty, and need of self-preservation.   And I believe
that in this matter the two run together : our interest
coincides with our honour.

It is curious how often this is the case.   It is one of
the old optimistic beliefs of nineteenth-century liberalism,
and one which is often ridiculed, that a nation's duty
generally does coincide with its interest.   No doubt one
can find abundant exceptions, but I believe that· in
the main, for nations as for individuals, real palpable
conscious dishonesty or wickedness is exceedingly unprofitable.   This is a more interesting fact than it looks
at first sight.

There are many poisons which are simply so nasty
that, undisguised, they cannot be swallowed.   No power
could induce a man or dog to sip or lap a tablespoonful
of nicotine or prussic acid.   You might coax the dog
with future bones, you might persuade the man that the

medicine was just what his health needed ; but their
swallowing muscles would refuse to act.   Doubtless, in
the scheme of nature, the disgust is a provision which
saves the race.   Now I cannot help suspecting that,
much more faintly and more fallibly, the vehement and
invincible refusal with which man's sense of honour or
religion meets certain classes of proposal, which look
profitable enough on the surface, is just such another
warning of Nature against poison.   In all these cases
discussed above, the Christian's martyrdom, the honourable man's refusal to desert his companions, it was not
true to say, as we seemed to say, that advantage was
on one side and honour on the other.   Dishonour
would have brought with it a subtler and more lasting
disadvantage, greater in its sum than immediate death.
If the Christian had sacrificed to the idol, what would
his life have been afterwards ?   Perhaps his friends would
have rejected his example and been martyred ; he would
be alone in his shame.   Perhaps they would have
followed his example, and through him the whole band
of the 'faithful' have betrayed Christ.   Not a very
enviable choice either way.   Without any tall talk or
high professions, would it not quite certainly be better
for the whole Church and probably for the man himself
that he should defy his persecutors and die ?   And does
not the same now hold for any patriotic Belgian or
Serbian who has had a voice in his country's action ?
The choice was not on the one hand honour and misery,
on the other dishonour and a happy life.   It was on
the one hand honour and great physical suffering, on the
other hand dishonour and a life subtly affected by that
dishonour in a thousand unforeseen ways.   I do not
underrate the tremendous importance of mere physical
suffering ; I do not underrate the advantage of living

as long a life as is conveniently possible. But men must die sometime, and, if we dare really to confess the truth, the thing that most of us in our hearts long for, the thing which either means ultimate happiness or else is greater and dearer to men than happiness, is the power to do our duty and, when we die, to have done it. The behaviour of our soldiers and sailors proves it. '*The last I saw of him was on the after bridge, doing well.*' The words come in the official report made by the captain of one of our lost cruisers. But that is the kind of epitaph nearly all men crave for themselves, and the wisest men, I think, even for their nation.

And if we accept this there will follow further consequences. War is not all evil. It is a true tragedy, which must have nobleness and triumph in it as well as disaster. . . . This is dangerous ground. The subject lends itself to foolish bombast, especially when accompanied by a lack of true imagination. We must not begin to praise war without stopping to reflect on the hundreds of thousands of human beings involved in such horrors of pain and indignity that, if here in our ordinary hours we saw one man so treated, the memory would sicken us to the end of our lives ; we must remember the horses, remember the gentle natures brutalized by hardship and filth, and the once decent persons transformed by rage and fear into devils of cruelty. But, when we have realized that, we may venture to see in this wilderness of evil some oases of extraordinary good.

These men who are engaged in what seems like a vast public crime ought, one would think, to fall to something below their average selves, below the ordinary standard of common folk. But do they ? Day after day come streams of letters from the front, odd stories, fragments of diaries, and the like; full of the small intimate facts which reveal character, and almost with one accord they show that these men have not fallen, but risen. No doubt there has been some selection in the letters ; to some extent the writers repeat what they wish to have remembered, and say nothing of what they wish to forget. But, when all allowances are made, one cannot read the letters and the dispatches without a feeling of almost passionate admiration for the men about whom they tell. They were not originally a set of men chosen for their peculiar qualities. They were just our ordinary fellow citizens, the men you meet on a crowded pavement. There was nothing to suggest that their conduct in common life was better than that of their neighbours. Yet now, under the stress of war, having a duty before them that is clear and unquestioned and terrible, they are daily doing nobler things than we most of us have ever had the chance of doing, things which we hardly dare hope that we might be able to do. I am not thinking of the rare achievements that win a V.C. or a Cross of the Legion of Honour, but of the common necessary heroism of the average men ; the long endurance, the devoted obedience, the close-banded life in which self-sacrifice is the normal rule, and all men may be forgiven except the man who saves himself at the expense of his comrade. I think of the men who share their last biscuits with a starving peasant, who help wounded comrades through days and nights of horrible retreat, who give their lives to save mates or officers.[1] Or I think again of

---

[1] For example, to take two stories out of a score :

1. Relating his experiences to a pressman, Lance-Corporal Edmondson, of the Royal Irish Lancers, said : ' There is absolutely no

the expressions on faces that I have seen or read about,
something alert and glad and self-respecting in the

doubt that our men are still animated by the spirit of old. I came
on a couple of men of the Argyll and Sutherland Highlanders who
had been cut off at Mons. One was badly wounded, but his com-
panion had stuck by him all the time in a country swarming with
Germans, and though they had only a few biscuits between them
they managed to pull through until we picked them up. I pressed
the unwounded man to tell me how they managed to get through the
four days on six biscuits, but he always got angry and told me to
shut up. I fancy he went without anything, and gave the biscuits
to the wounded man. They were offered shelter many times by
French peasants, but they were so afraid of bringing trouble on
these kind folk that they would never accept shelter. One night
they lay out in the open all through a heavy downpour, though
there was a house at hand where they could have had shelter.
Uhlans were on the prowl, and they would not think of compromising
the French people, who would have been glad to help them.'
2. The following story of an unidentified private of the Royal
Irish Regiment who deliberately threw away his life in order to
warn his comrades of an ambush is told by a wounded corporal of
the West Yorkshire Regiment now in hospital in Woolwich :
' The fight in which I got hit was in a little village near to Rheims.
We were working in touch with the French corps on our left, and
early one morning we were sent ahead to this village, which we had
reason to believe was clear of the enemy. On the outskirts we
questioned a French lad, but he seemed scared and ran away. We
went on through the long narrow street, and just as we were in sight
of the end the figure of a man dashed out from a farmhouse on the
right. Immediately the rifles began to crack in front, and the poor
chap fell dead before he reached us.
' He was one of our men, a private of the Royal Irish Regiment.
We learned that he had been captured the previous day by a maraud-
ing party of German cavalry, and had been held a prisoner at the
farm where the Germans were in ambush for us. He tumbled to
their game, and though he knew that if he made the slightest sound
they would kill him, he decided to make a dash to warn us of what
was in store. He had more than a dozen bullets in him, and there
was not the slightest hope for him. We carried him into a house
until the fight was over, and then we buried him next day with
military honours. His identification disk and everything else was

eyes of those who are going to the front, and even of
the wounded who are returning. 'Never once,' writes
one correspondent, 'not once since I came to France
have I seen among the soldiers an angry face or heard
an angry word. . . . They are always quiet, orderly,
and wonderfully cheerful.' And no one who has followed
the war need be told of their heroism.   I do not forget
the thousands left on the battlefield to die, or the
groaning of the wounded sounding all day between the
crashes of the guns.   But there is a strange deep glad-
ness as well.   'One feels an extraordinary freedom ',
says a young Russian officer, 'in the midst of death,
with the bullets whistling round.   The same with all
the soldiers.   The wounded all want to get well and
return to the fight.   They fight with tears of joy in
their eyes.'

Human nature is a mysterious thing, and man finds
his weal and woe not in the obvious places.   To have
something before you, clearly seen, which you know
you must do, and can do, and will spend your utmost
strength and perhaps your life in doing, that is one
form at least of very high happiness, and one that
appeals—the facts prove it—not only to saints and
heroes but to average men.   Doubtless the few who
are wise enough and have enough imagination may
find opportunity for that same happiness in everyday
life, but in war ordinary men find it.   This is the inward
triumph which lies at the heart of the great tragedy.

missing, so that we could only put over his grave the tribute that
was paid to a greater : " He saved others ; himself he could not
save."   There wasn't a dry eye among us when we laid him to rest
in that little village.'

Oxford : Horace Hart Printer to the University

1914

Crown 8vo, from 12 to 40 pages each. Also in series of five Pamphlets, stiff covers. One Shilling net each series. 33 Pamphlets have now (18 November) been issued and others are in preparation. The historical pieces are illustrated by sketch-maps

I

1. The Deeper Causes of the War.
By W. SANDAY. 3d. net. *Fifth Impression.*
The psychology of Prussian militarism ; German public opinion and Germany's aggressive ambitions.

2. To the Christian Scholars of Europe and America: A Reply from Oxford to the German ' Address to Evangelical Christians '. 2d. net. *Fourth Impression.*
The answer of Oxford theologians to a recent manifesto of the German evangelical theologians. This manifesto, which is reproduced in the present pamphlet, argues that Germany is in no sense responsible for the present war. The Oxford reply states that the German theologians cannot have studied either the events which led up to the war or the political utterances of their own countrymen.

3. The Responsibility for the War.
By W. G. S. ADAMS. 2d. net.
A brief discussion of the question of responsibility : 1. Austria and Serbia ; 2. The responsibility of Russia ; 3. The intervention of England.

4. Great Britain and Germany.
By SPENSER WILKINSON. 2d. net. *Third Impression.*
Three letters to the *Springfield Republican* : 1. By Prof. Spenser Wilkinson, stating Great Britain's case ; 2. By Prof. John W. Burgess of the University of Columbia, stating Germany's case ; 3. By Prof. Wilkinson, in reply to Prof. Burgess.

5. ' Just for a Scrap of Paper.'
By ARTHUR HASSALL. 1d. net. *Fourth Impression.*
Explains why England stands for the sanctity of European treaty-law.

[6]

II

6. The Germans, their Empire, and how they have made it.
By C. R. L. FLETCHER. 2d. net. *Fourth Impression.*
A historical account of Prussian policy from the seventeenth century.

7. The Germans, their Empire, and what they covet.
By C. R. L. FLETCHER. 2d. net. *Fourth Impression.*
An account of the ambitions avowed by the Pan-German school.

8. Might is Right.
By Sir WALTER RALEIGH. 2d. net. *Second Impression.*
Why Germany may win; what will happen if she wins; why we believe she will not win.

9. Austrian Policy since 1867.
By MURRAY BEAVEN. 3d. net. *Second Impression.*
Austrian policy in the Balkans has been of the 'offensive-defensive' order. The Archduke Francis Ferdinand might have saved Austria from rushing to destruction; but 1912 was the beginning of the end.

10. Italian Policy since 1870.
By KEITH FEILING. 2d. net. *Second Impression.*
Italian policy has been and must be guided by her own interests. The results of her colonial policy have not yet been satisfactory enough to tempt her into adventures.

III

11. French Policy since 1871.
By F. MORGAN and H. W. C. DAVIS. 2d. net. *Fourth Impression.*
A historical sketch, discussing the question whether French policy has been aggressive.

12. Russia : The Psychology of a Nation.
By PAUL VINOGRADOFF. 1d. net. *Fourth Impression.*
A reply to the German taunt that Russia is still in a state of barbarism, and is the enemy of European civilization.

13. Serbia and the Serbs.
By Sir VALENTINE CHIROL. 2d. net. *Third Impression.*
A sketch of Serbian history, which is incidentally an indictment of the policy pursued by Austria-Hungary towards the Serbian kingdom.

14. Germany and 'The Fear of Russia'.
By Sir VALENTINE CHIROL. 2d. net. *Third Impression.*
Shows that before 1879 Germany preferred Russia as an ally to Austria. The ambition of Germany to establish a protectorate over Turkey has led her to assist Austria in the Balkans and so to challenge Russia.

15. The Eastern Question.
By F. F. URQUHART. 3d. net. *Third Impression.*
The history of the Balkan nations; their future.

16. War against War.
By A. D. LINDSAY. 2d. net. *Third Impression.*

Denies that war is good in itself, or a necessary evil. Power is not the sole or chief end for which the State exists. National greatness, if founded on brute force, cannot endure. International law represents an ideal, but an ideal that may be realized.

17. The Value of Small States.
By H. A. L. FISHER. 2d. net. *Third Impression.*

The author argues that the debt of civilization to small states is incalculable. They are useful, at the present time, as laboratories of political experiments and as buffer-states between the greater powers.

18. How can War ever be Right?
By GILBERT MURRAY. 2d. net. *Fourth Impression.*

A well-known lover of peace and advocate of pacific policies argues against the Tolstoyan position. Right and honour compelled Britain to make war; and war—like tragedy—is not pure evil.

19. The National Principle and the War.
By RAMSAY MUIR. 3d. net. *Second Impression.*

Considers the principle of nationality and its application to the settlement of Europe—particularly of S.E. Europe—after the War.

20. Nietzsche and Treitschke: The Worship of Power in Modern Germany.
By E. BARKER. 2d. net. *Fourth Impression.*

An explanation of the main points of interest in the ethical and political doctrines of the German ruling classes.

V

21. The British Dominions and the War.
By H. E. EGERTON. 2d. net. *Second Impression.*

Explains the ideas for which the British Empire stands, and the political and moral issues of the war affecting the Dominions.

22. India and the War.
By Sir ERNEST TREVELYAN. 1d. net. *Third Impression.*

Discusses the reasons which account for the striking manifestations of Indian loyalty.

23. Is the British Empire the Result of Wholesale Robbery? By H. E. EGERTON. 2d. net.
A historical sketch in answer to a common taunt.

24. The Law of Nations and the War.
By A. PEARCE HIGGINS. 2d. net. *Second Impression.*

The violation of Belgian neutrality and the conduct of England to Denmark in 1807; the doctrine of German lawyers that military necessity overrides the laws of war; the balance of power and the sanctity of treaties.

25. England's Mission. By W. BENETT. 2d. net.
Answers the question, In what cause are we fighting?

Thoughts on the War.

By GILBERT MURRAY. 2d. net.

An article written in August and now reprinted.

Bacilli and Bullets.

By Sir WILLIAM OSLER. 1d. net. *Fourth Impression.*

Calls attention to the fact that disease kills more men than the bullet. The most dangerous diseases are preventable by inoculation.

The Navy and the War.

By J. R. THURSFIELD. 3d. net. *Second Impression.*

Estimates the military and economic value of the silent pressure exercised by our fleet, and warns the faint-hearted and the captious of the perils of lack of faith.

The Retreat from Mons.

By H. W. C. DAVIS. 3d. net. *Third Impression.*

Introduction; the Dispatch of Sept. 9; the Statement by the War Office, published Aug. 31. Appendixes (soldiers' narratives); two maps.

The Leading Ideas of British Policy.

By GERARD COLLIER. 2d. net.

Examines the political genius of England.

Greek Policy since 1882.

By A. J. TOYNBEE. 4d. net.

Poland, Prussia, and Culture.

By LUDWIK EHRLICH. 3d. net.

The author is a Doctor of the University of Lwow (Lemberg) in Galicia.

The Germans in Africa.

By EVANS LEWIN. 3d. net.

Spectator :—' These little books are easily the best books of the war—accurate, quietly written, full of knowledge, and quite unspoiled by vainglory or bitterness.'

Others in preparation.

[c]

OXFORD PAMPHLETS

"37

1914–1915

THE MAN OF

PEACE

BY

ROY NORTON

Price Twopence net

OXFORD UNIVERSITY PRESS

HUMPHREY MILFORD

LONDON   EDINBURGH   GLASGOW

NEW YORK   TORONTO   MELBOURNE   BOMBAY

OXFORD PAMPHLETS
1914–1915

Crown 8vo. Separately, in paper covers. Also in series as numbered (I–X), stiff covers, One Shilling net each series. 58 Pamphlets have now (Jan. 15, 1915) been issued, and others are in preparation. The historical pieces are illustrated by sketch-maps.

Saturday Review :—'These little books are easily the best books of the war—accurate, quietly written, full of knowledge, and quite unspoiled by vainglory or bitterness.'

Most of the pamphlets have been reprinted and some are now in a fourth, fifth, or sixth impression.

OXFORD UNIVERSITY PRESS
HUMPHREY MILFORD

LONDON   EDINBURGH   GLASGOW

NEW YORK   TORONTO   MELBOURNE   BOMBAY

[1]

OXFORD PAMPHLETS
1914–1915

I

1. The Deeper Causes of the War.

By W. SANDAY. 3d. net.

The psychology of Prussian militarism ; German public opinion and Germany's aggressive ambitions.

2. To the Christian Scholars of Europe and America: A Reply from Oxford to the German 'Address to Evangelical Christians'.

2d. net.

The answer of Oxford theologians to a recent manifesto of the German evangelical theologians. This manifesto, which is reproduced in the present pamphlet, argues that Germany is in no sense responsible for the present war. The Oxford reply states that the German theologians cannot have studied either the events which led up to the war or the political utterances of their own countrymen.

3. The Responsibility for the War.

By W. G. S. ADAMS. 2d. net.

A brief discussion of the question of responsibility : 1. Austria and Serbia ; 2. The responsibility of Russia ; 3. The intervention of England.

4. Great Britain and Germany.

By SPENSER WILKINSON. 2d. net.

Three letters to the *Springfield Republican*: 1. By Prof. Spenser Wilkinson, stating Great Britain's case ; 2 By Prof. John W. Burgess of the University of Columbia, stating Germany's case ; 3. By Prof. Wilkinson, in reply to Prof. Burgess.

5. 'Just for a Scrap of Paper.'

By ARTHUR HASSALL. 1d. net.

Explains why England stands for the sanctity of European treaty-law.

IV

16. War against War.

By A. D. LINDSAY. 2d. net.

Denies that war is good in itself, or a necessary evil. National greatness, if founded on brute force, cannot endure. International law represents an ideal, but an ideal that may be realized.

17. The Value of Small States.

By H. A. L FISHER. 2d. net.

The author argues that the debt of civilization to small states is incalculable.

18. How can War ever be Right?

By GILBERT MURRAY. 2d. net.

A well-known lover of peace and advocate of pacific policies argues against the Tolstoyan position. Right and honour compelled Britain to make war; and war—like tragedy—is not pure evil.

19. The National Principle and the War.

By RAMSAY MUIR. 3d. net.

Considers the principle of nationality and its application to the settlement of Europe—particularly of S.E. Europe—after the War.

20. Nietzsche and Treitschke: The Worship of Power in Modern Germany.

By E. BARKER. 2d. net.

An explanation of the main points of interest in the ethical and political doctrines of the German ruling classes.

V

21. The British Dominions and the War.

By H. E. EGERTON. 2d. net.

Explains the ideas for which the British Empire stands, and the political and moral issues of the war affecting the Dominions.

22. India and the War.

By Sir ERNEST TREVELYAN. 1d. net.

Discusses the reasons for the striking manifestations of Indian loyalty.

23. Is the British Empire the Result of Wholesale Robbery?

By H. E. EGERTON. 2d. net.

A historical sketch in answer to a common taunt.

24. The Law of Nations and the War.

By A. PEARCE HIGGINS. 2d. net.

The violation of Belgian neutrality and the conduct of England to Denmark in 1807; the doctrine of German lawyers that military necessity overrides the laws of war; the balance of power and the sanctity of treaties.

25. England's Mission.

By W. BENETT. 2d. net.

Answers the question, In what cause are we fighting?

VI

26. August, 1914: The Coming of the War.
By Spenser Wilkinson. Stiff covers. 1s. net.

VII

27. The Retreat from Mons.
By H. W. C. Davis. 3d. net.

28. The Battles of the Marne and Aisne.
By H. W. C. Davis. 4d. net.
The Dispatches, with commentary, maps, &c.

29. The Navy and the War.
By J. R. Thursfield. 3d. net.
Estimates the military and economic value of the silent pressure exercised by our fleet, and warns the faint-hearted and the captious of the perils of lack of faith.

30. Bacilli and Bullets.
By Sir William Osler. 1d. net.
Calls attention to the fact that disease kills more men than the bullet. The most dangerous diseases are preventable by inoculation.

VIII

31. The Double Alliance *versus* The Triple Entente.
By James M. Beck. 3d. net.
The judgement of a well-known American lawyer.

32. The Germans in Africa.
By Evans Lewin. 3d. net.
A historical account of the German colonies.

33. All for Germany, or the World's Respect Well Lost. 2d. net.
'The conversation here imagined, between a new (and perhaps less naïf) Candide and a new (and perhaps less benevolent) Dr. Pangloss, is concerned with the political thoughts and ambitions entertained by the Germans of these latter days.'

34. Germany, the Economic Problem.
By C. Grant Robertson. 2d. net.
Estimates the strength and weakness of Germany's economic position, and inquires how long she can stand the strain of the war.

35. German Sea-Power.
By C. S. Terry. 3d. net.
Traces the growth of Germany's navy. With a map of the North Sea.

IX

36. What Europe owes to Belgium.
By H. W. C. DAVIS. 2d. net.

Reminds us of the past achievements of the Belgian people in war and in peace.

37. Poland, Prussia, and Culture.
By LUDWIK EHRLICH. 3d. net.

The author is a Doctor of the University of Lwòw (Lemberg) in Galicia.

38. Turkey in Europe and Asia. 2d. net.

The strength and weakness of the Ottoman Empire considered. The secular prestige of Constantinople, the religious prestige of the Caliphate, and the racial and economic weaknesses which may cause their downfall. A map shows the unfinished railways.

39. Greek Policy since 1882.
By A. J. TOYNBEE. 4d. net.

A historical account of the policy of Greece; the economic future of Greece; the problem of *Graecia Irredenta*. With a map.

40. North Sleswick under Prussian Rule, 1864–1914.
By W. R. PRIOR. 2d. net.

The policy of Prussianization and the resistance of Danish Nationalism. 'If the children do not understand German, they must be treated and taught like deaf-mutes' is quoted from a Prussian educational authority. A map shows the distribution of languages.

X

41. Thoughts on the War.
By GILBERT MURRAY. 2d. net.

Reprinted from the *Hibbert Journal* for October.

42. The Leadership of the World.
By F. S. MARVIN. 2d. net.

A discussion of German aspirations.

43. The Leading Ideas of British Policy.
By the Hon. GERARD COLLIER. 2d. net.

Places the principles of our policy in the perspective of history.

44. The War and its Economic Aspects.

By W. J. ASHLEY. 2d. net.

A comparison of Germany's and Great Britain's powers to stand the strain of a prolonged war. Probable effects of defeat or victory.

45. Food Supplies in War Time.

By R. H. REW, C.B. 2d. net.

An authoritative discussion by an expert who has been 'for over thirty years engaged in the service of British Agriculture'.

•

Published separately and will also appear shortly in series.

Non-Combatants and the War.

By A. PEARCE HIGGINS. 2d. net.

States the rights and duties of the non-combatant population of a territory under hostile occupation.

Troyon : an Engagement in the Battle of the Aisne.

By A. N. HILDITCH. 2d. net.

Scandinavia and the War.

By E. BJORKMAN. 2d. net.

Considers the policy and sympathies of the three Northern Kingdoms.

Asia and the War.

By A. E. DUCHESNE. 2d. net.

Describes German intrigue, and its failure, in Turkey, India, and Egypt.

Does International Law still Exist ?

By Sir H. ERLE RICHARDS. 2d. net.

A brief account of the principles, and an examination of German apologies for their infringement.

Through German Eyes.

By E. A. SONNENSCHEIN. 2d. net.

The Birmingham Professor, who knows Germany well, considers the German attitude under various heads—Neutrality of Belgium, 'England the chief culprit,' &c.

OXFORD PAMPHLETS

The Church and the War.

By the Bishop of Lincoln. 2d. net.

Dr. Hicks's article in the December *Political Quarterly* suggests 'how a Churchman . . . may hold fast to his principles and yet take sides with the Allies'.

The Action off Heligoland. August, 1914.

By L. Cecil Jane. 3d. net.

The Dispatches, with introduction and charts.

German Philosophy and the War.

By J. H. Muirhead. 2d. net.

German Idealism; The Reaction; The New Naturalism.

Christmas and the War.

By T. B. Strong. 2d. net.

A Sermon preached in Christ Church Cathedral.

Outlines of Prussian History to 1871.

By E. F. Row. 2d. net.

How Prussia made and ruled the German Empire.

The Southern Slavs.

By N. Forbes. 4d. net.

Contains much detailed information—historical, geographical, and ethnological.

Concerning True War.

By Wilhelm Wundt. Translated by Grace E. Hadow. 2d. net.

A typical utterance of a German Professor.

Ready Immediately.

The Battle of Ypres—Armentières.

By H. W. C. Davis.

The War through Danish Eyes.

By a Dane.

The Man of Peace.

By Roy Norton.

THE MAN OF PEACE [1]

' Is Germany to blame for the great war ? ' I was asked on my return from the Continent but a few days ago, and in reply I asked of my questioner, ' Why do you value my opinion ? '

' Because ', explained this editor, ' you are an American, and therefore nationally neutral. You make your living by writing, and appreciate the responsibility and value of words. You have passed the greater part of ten years actually living in every country involved, you speak the languages of most of these countries, you have friends in all of them, and for the past year you have lived in Germany, presumably because you like it best. You ought to have drawn some conclusion that would be interesting at a time when people really want to know who did bring this condition about.'

Ordinarily, when one is asked to express an opinion, he can answer with readiness ; but there are times when likings, friendships, associations, memories, all incline him to prejudice, also to reticence. And all of these, in my own case, were favourable to Germany ; but I am compelled to admit, after some deliberation, that, as far as I have been able to observe, the evidence against Germany's intention, participation, and final action will necessitate some more convincing proof than she has yet offered to persuade the world of her guiltlessness.

[1] Published (in an abridged form) in the *Contemporary Review* for December 1914, and now reprinted by permission of the editor.

It is a sweeping question to ask, ' Is Germany to blame for the war ? ' because that might involve all who live in that splendid country, and as one must define himself before answering, I can do no better than to quote from an article I wrote at the time when the Zabern incident was occupying some public attention. It was relative to the sabring of a troublesome cobbler by a mere stripling of a German officer, indignation in France over the misfortunes of Alsace-Lorraine, protests from Zabern civil authorities, and a somewhat bold and flagrant upholding of military authority as opposed to civil authority by a no less august person than the Kaiser himself. This is what I wrote :

There is a vast difference in speaking of Germany, and the United States, England, or France, as the case might be ; for when we speak of Democratic nations we speak of the whole people, praise the whole people when we admire their achievements, or arraign the whole people when we condemn their misdeeds. Regardless of all protestations, claims to freedom of speech and action, pretence at popular government, and liberty of popular will, there is not, nor ever has been since Roman days, a more centralized and possibly autocratic government than that impressed upon and patiently endured by these same German people. Price Collier, that thoughtful and competent observer, did not exaggerate when he made it plain that, constitutionally and otherwise, the German government actually consists of and exists in the Kaiser. The common people merely play at politics for local wants, unimportant laws and the conduct of small affairs. In any great national policy neither they nor their leaders have any more influence than so many well-meaning, nicely-garbed, and well-regulated wooden men. The Kaiser can over-rule them all. Furthermore, he could literally cancel the government itself, if he so wished, by force of arms. It is not, therefore, the common German people, that friendly, industrious, patient, obedient mass, who are to be blamed for upholding the sabring of a boisterous citizen who doubtless should have been admonished and perhaps fined the price of a pair of half-soles for disorderly conduct. It seems to me the veriest bosh, also, to lay any of the blame for stimulating militarism upon the so-called military clique, for it must be remembered that, right or wrong, William the Second is one of the strongest men that Germany has thus far produced. A man who could make that grim old giant, Bismarck, walk the plank is not likely to be swayed one way or the other in his judgements by his advisers, those around him, or the somewhat vociferous shouts of Socialists claiming to represent the majority of his people. It is his individual will alone that rules, and it is his individual decision alone that is responsible for whatever of good or misfortune that may happen. In this case he has effectively accomplished two objects—shown contempt for France and French opinion, and made the military authorities supreme.

It is useless to deny that in military circles there was a vast faith in German arms. That has always been so since I had any knowledge of the country and friendship with German officers. It was natural for them to be proud of their service. It is a poor officer, in any service, who does not have pride in his work. Sometimes that military pride caused one from other lands to ruffle a trifle, and then to think what could be the eventual outcome of such pride. A man cannot store his cellar with dynamite, adding to the supply year in and year out, without some day causing an explosion, and neither can a ruler, though he constantly proclaim his peaceful intentions, persistently instil into the minds of a great body of men that they can whip the earth without some day finding that they want to make the attempt.

More than a year ago, in a conversation with a friend

of mine, an officer in the army, he derided what he called ' slipshod ' American methods.

' It is fortunate for you people ', he said, ' that you have never come into conflict with a first-class Power; but when you do, you will learn what organization is capable of doing. For instance, do you Americans believe, for a minute even, that we shall submit to your Monroe doctrine when the time comes for an issue ? '

' I can't see how you could help yourselves,' I replied good-naturedly.

He laughed, as at a joke.

' Our navy ', he asserted, ' is already stronger than yours. Your army is not worth consideration. Ours is perfect. And what is more, we have the ships to transport it, and to land it on your coasts. We know where and how. We know where our men would camp each night, and where they would fight the campaign. You think this is a joke ? '

I so assured him, but since then have learned enough to convince me that probably the German war bureau knows as much about our fortifications, harbours, mines, railways, public roads, vital interior points, topography, and actual fighting strength as we do ourselves. Also, since then I have learned, from conversations with numerous men of affairs, how tenaciously Germany would cling to commercial control of South America, and it is not unreasonable to suppose that this might, almost by sheer accident, necessitate other dominion, and, consequently, a conflict with us over that time-honoured doctrine of President Monroe.

This is given as but one illustration of Germany's military confidence, a confidence which, coming from, instilled by, and believed in by the Kaiser, may have something to do with this present war. It was the confidence of the most

marvellously prepared war organization that the world
has ever seen called into being, and that should be considered as a motive of this war.

As far back as 1908 Germany was expending four
millions of dollars, annually, in its espionage system
alone. There were, I was told by a French official, more
than thirty thousand men in France alone, stationed as
workmen, shop- and hotel-keepers, and realty agents,
ready to act on signal. Among the duties of these men
would be the destruction of bridges, to hamper French
mobilization, and to blow up the main arsenal. This
same official told me that, some five months ago, the
French secret service discovered the key to these preparations and was appalled by its thoroughness. It held a
consultation, and made a counter-move by setting a spy
to watch each of the German spies, but permitted the
latter to continue operations, on the principle that it
was easier to observe a known enemy than to discover
a new one. A week before war was declared, the
Germans who were to perform destructive tasks were
tapped on the shoulders at midnight, and arrested, and
the mining beneath the great arsenal was removed
and destroyed.

Antwerp, Brussels, and London have since discovered
that Germany had nests of agents organized along the
same lines. One German church in London has been
found, since war broke out, to have been for a long time a
considerable arsenal for German rifles. These are some
of the points to be regarded when it is asserted that
Germany confined herself only to measures for self-pro-
tection and desired only peace. Straws blown by the
wind, some forgotten sage has said, indicate which way
it blows; and here are some of the straws that I have
personally observed flying, although, with remarkable

stupidity, I did not at the time observe their trend, until
the violence of their flight would have shocked a blind
man.

It was told me in March, of this year, by one who is
almost as great a military editor as there is in the
' Fatherland ', that the completion of the improved Kiel
canal was the very last act that possibly could be effected
in ' preparedness '.

' From now onward ', declared this man, ' Germany
needs nothing more than the natural increase in her navy,
and maintenance of her efficiency in arms. At present we
are probably armed better than any other nation in the
world. We have adequate reasons for confidence that
this is so. Our military railways are now perfected.'

It did not dawn on me at that time that usually,
when a man's preparations to do something have been
perfected, he finds a way to go ahead and do that thing
of which he has dreamed and for which he has prepared.
I did observe, however, that scattered over Germany
were more of those wonderful ' switch ' or ' shunting '
yards, capable of entraining tens of thousands of soldiers
in a few hours—yards where from ten to twenty passenger
trains could be drawn up at one time, and oddly enough,
some of these queer yards, all equipped with electric
lighting plants, are out in places where there are not
a dozen houses in sight. In some of these yards, located
at central points for rural mobilization, one saw long
trains of troop cars, dingy, empty, stodgily waiting for
use in war, if one ever came. I was told of one test
mobilization (in reply to my query as to why I had seen
so many troops pass through a small place one evening),
where twenty thousand men were assembled at ten
o'clock one morning, made a camp complete, were re-
viewed, entrained, detrained, and just seven hours later

there was nothing save débris and trampled grass to show that the place had ever been disturbed.

The spring and summer of this year saw manœuvres and test mobilizations on an unprecedented scale. We who lived in Germany and were sufficiently familiar with it to note this increased activity, regarded it as nothing more than a natural desire on the part of the Kaiser and his war staff to see how efficiently his war units could all be welded together. The press, stoppered and controlled more or less, paid no more than ordinary attention to these movements ; but I was told by three different officers that for the first time it had been proved that the entire military force of Germany had at last reached as near to actual perfection as could ever be hoped for. And two of these men, at least, are thoughtful, conservative men, given to no boasting, and speaking merely as professional men proud of their work.

It will be remembered, also, that it was this summer which saw the perfection of the Kiel canal, presumably the perfection of the Heligoland fortifications, and the actual tests of the two largest steamships the world has ever known, the *Vaterland* and the *Imperator*, thus making German transportation facilities among the best equipped in existence. Hence, from the foregoing, it may be concluded that Germany considered herself at the acme of strength for offence or defence.

There were on every hand, this summer, signs of this super-excellence. At a mere 'Tank-station' below Kriesingen, on June 12, I saw probably seventy-five or a hundred locomotives (I had time to count more than seventy), most of which were of antiquated type— obsolete as far as the demands of up-to-date traffic are concerned — and of a kind that would have been 'scrapped' in either England or America. Yet these

were all being cared for and 'doctored up'. A few
engineers and stokers worked round them, and I saw
them run one down a long track and bring it back
to another, whereupon hostlers at once began drawing
its fires, and the engineer and stoker crossed over and
climbed into another cab.

'What do you suppose they are doing that for ? '
I asked one of the train men with whom I had struck
up an acquaintance.

'Why,' replied he with perfect frankness, 'those are
war locomotives.'

Reading the look of bewilderment on my face, he
added, 'You see, those engines are no longer good
enough for heavy or fast traffic, so as soon as they
become obsolete we send them to the reserve. They
are all of them good enough to move troop trains, and
therefore are never destroyed. They are all frequently
fired up and tested in regular turn. Those fellows out
there do nothing else. That is their business, just keeping those engines in order and fit for troop duty. There
are dozens of such dépôts over Germany.'

'But how on earth could you man them in case of
war ?—where would you get the engineers for so many
extras ? '

He smiled pityingly at my ignorance.

'The head-quarters know to the ton what each one
of those can pull, how fast, where the troop cars are
that it will pull ; and every man that would ride behind
one has the number of the car he would ride in, and for
every so many men there is waiting somewhere a reserve
engineer and stoker. The best locomotives would be
the first out of the reserve, and so on down to the
ones that can barely do fifteen kilometres per hour.'

Since that June day, Germany has proved how faith-

fully those thousands of reserve locomotives over her
domain have been nursed and cared for, and how
quickly those who were to man and ride behind them
could respond.

At this point, almost as I write, I had something
explained to me over which I have at times puzzled
for months. On February 14 of this year I was in
Cologne, and blundered; where I had no business, into
what I learned was a military-stores yard. Among
other curious things were tiny locomotives loaded on
flats which could be run off those cars by an ingenious
contrivance of metals, or, as we call them in America,
rails. Also there were other flats loaded with sections
of tracks fastened on cup ties (sleepers that can be
laid on the surface of the earth) and sections of minia-
ture bridges on other flats. I saw how it was possible
to lay a line of temporary railway, including bridges,
almost anywhere in an incredibly short space of time,
if one had the men. At one period of my life I was
actively interested in railway construction, but had
never before seen anything like this. Before I could
conclude my examination I discovered that I was on
verboten ground, and had to leave ; but the official
who directed me out told me that what I had seen
were construction outfits. The more I thought of
those, afterwards, the more I was puzzled by the absence
of dump cars, and that mass of smaller paraphernalia
to which I had been accustomed in all the contracting
work I had ever seen. Yet I had to remember with
admiration the ingenuity of the outfit, and think of
how quickly it could all be laid, transferred, re-shipped,
or stored. Here before me, in a letter received from
Holland but yesterday, which comes from a Hollander
who was a refugee in Germany, and on August 30

reached home after trying experiences, is the following :

Never, I believe, did a country so thoroughly get ready for war. I saw the oddest spectacle, the building of a railway behind a battle-field. They had diminutive little engines and rails in sections, so they could be bolted together, and even bridges that could be put across ravines in a twinkling. Flat cars that could be carried by hand and dropped on the rails, great strings of them. Up to the nearest point of battle came, on the regular railway, this small one. At the point where we were, it came up against the soldiers. It seemed to me that hundreds of men had been trained for this task, for in but a few minutes that small portable train was buzzing backward and forward on its own small portable rails, distributing food and supplies. It was great work, I can tell you. I've an idea that in time of battle it would be possible for those sturdy little trains to shift troops to critical or endangered points at the rate of perhaps twenty miles an hour, keep ammunition, batteries, &c., moving at the same rate and, of course, be of inestimable use in clearing off the wounded. A portable railway for a battle-field struck me as coming about as close to making war by machinery as anything I have ever heard of. I did not have a chance, however, to see it working under fire, for, being practically a prisoner, I was hurried onward and away from the scene.

I know of nothing more than this, coming from one whom I know to be truthful, that so adequately shows how even ingenious details had been worked out for military perfection. We shall doubtless hear, after this war is over, how well those field trains performed their work when it came to shifting troops in times of fierce pressure on a threatened point, and how it added to German efficacy.

The reader will perhaps ask by this time, ' What

has all this to do with responsibility for the war ? '
I answer, ' When the reader was a boy and by various
efforts and privations saved money enough to buy a
box of tools, did he lock them up in the garret, or bury
them in the cellar ? When he possessed a fine bright
Billy Barlow pocket-knife, did he whittle with it ? '

However, this is not an argumentative thesis, and
a good witness confines himself to what he personally
considers relative, and• to personal events that may
or may not be regarded as significant. I hold no brief
one way or the other.

The evening of Sunday, June 28, in Berlin was warm,
somnolent, and peaceful. With some friends I had
been at Luna Park in Berlin, and we loitered slowly
out of the gates and up the street before separating.
Suddenly, as we approached the corner across the
viaduct, we encountered small crowds collecting in
front of the newspaper offices, and there saw bulletins
announcing the assassination of the Archduke Ferdinand
and his wife, the Duchess of Hohenberg, in the streets
of Sarajevo. We were shocked far more, I believe,
than any of those stolid Germans who elbowed us to
read the news. We Americans have, unfortunately,
too much knowledge of what assassination in high
places means. By the time I reached the hotel where
I was living ' extras ' were out, but the news was not
received with any more interest by the people in the
streets, loitering homeward from places of amusement,
or seated in the splendid open-air cafés of Berlin, than
would be given to the murder of any other distinguished
foreigners. Here and there some of the more widely-
read or travelled expressed sympathy for the aged
Austrian emperor, who has so repeatedly suffered in
a long and prominent life. I doubt not that extras in

New York announcing the same news would have had a far larger sale. Also, I am certain that the German people regarded it as none of their business, and passed it by. Days later came the news, in regular editions, that the Kaiser was hurrying homeward, and that regattas, and friendly sea visits, were being abandoned or brought to a close. It was publicly announced that the reason of the Kaiser's return was grief for a lost friend, and the stories, having a human note, aroused a sudden thrill of interest ; but, strangely enough, he began a consultation with his war advisers. This latter was a generally accepted fact in Berlin, but the people may have regarded it as his natural way of manifesting grief, or, to be more kindly, habit or routine.

In the newspapers of the next few days the Austrian incident became subsidiary, and great stress was laid on the Ulster situation in Ireland, and editorial writers appeared to think that Great Britain was on the extreme brink of civil war. Then came the surprising news that Austria regarded the assassination of the heirs to the throne—in reality, as far as unbiased observers can see, the crime of a Bosnian schoolboy—as a great Servian plot. The world knows how Austria insisted on this, and how, of a sudden, she made demands that would have for ever ended Servia's independence as a nation. The world also is well aware that it would have been possible for the Kaiser, grief-stricken, surrounded by his military advisers, with direct means of communication with Austria, to have personally urged that abrupt and uncompromising Austrian ultimatum. There is not the slightest doubt that, whether he forced that ultimatum or not, he was in constant communication. The newspapers tacitly said so.

Immediately after this came what should have been

a plain warning that the Kaiser meant to go to war; for, of a sudden, and a most significant incident, too, the streets of apathetic, pleasure-seeking Berlin were flooded with extra newspapers from the notoriously Kaiser-controlled press, working up sympathy for Austria, vaguely hinting that it was Germany's business to support Austria in every way, and incidentally expressing grave fears that Russia might morally support Servia. If Berlin had not taken sufficient interest before, she was now being systematically aroused. These 'extras' were passed out gratis, in frequent series, by tens of thousands. Men drove along the kerbs in automobiles and passed them out. The streets were littered with them. I asked for one, tried to pay for it, and was told it was free. It astonished me, because it was the first time I had ever witnessed such prodigal generosity, it having been my experience that it costs money to issue enormous editions of extras, and also hitherto I had supposed that 'extras' were printed to be sold, not given away. I wonder who paid for them! If no one did, there are newspaper proprietors in Berlin who merit monuments for philanthropy, after they are dead and the bankruptcy proceedings are concluded.

In a steady, well-defined, and constant crescendo the journals made references to the duties of the Fatherland and to her naval and military strength, with now and then an adroit paragraph relative to the bounden duty of the German to cling closely to his Austrian brother, lest the latter be bruised and crushed beneath a threatening Slavic heel. From apathy the German awoke to keen interest. A nation that had been taking its afternoon nap awoke, yawned, stretched itself, sat up, got to its feet and became angry. Let us not be

unjust ! The great mass of German people have a sense
of justice as well as of duty, and they are loyal to
their friends. They were told that if Russia interfered,
it was a rank injustice to the Austrians, and that the
Austrians were friends, allies and partners. Likewise,
their press educated them in a fortnight to regard
Russia as a threatening, mongrel bully, who should be
told to stand off. Furthermore, that the bully would
stand off, because Russia at that moment was in the
process of reorganizing her army, and dared do nothing
more than bluff.

There can be not the slightest possible doubt that
those 'extras', so benevolently passed out, kindled a war-
flame in Berlin ; and non-partisan observers are convinced
that their publication and distribution were directed
from the palace. Nobody familiar with Austria, and
having knowledge of that weary, peace-desiring old
man, Franz-Josef, believes for one moment that Austria
either sought, or would have gone to war with Servia on
such a slight investigation of the assassinations, had
not some one influenced, or perhaps forced her to such
issue. The Austrians are not such fools. They knew too
well that they must eventually show the world sufficient
grounds for such action, and that mere lame assertions
that they ' *thought* the crimes were plotted in Servia '
would not justify them in the minds of humanity. True,
Austria desired to put a check on Servia and Servian
aspirations, but this she could have accomplished in a
dozen other and peaceful ways. But this is a digression
in a witness, and must therefore be taken as nothing
more than an opinion.   .

The fact is certain that war-talk had become common
in Berlin when, on July 9, I went to Hamburg ; yet this
was fourteen days prior to the Austrian ultimatum to

Servia. I was there for seven days, and the only expressions I heard were apprehensive and regretful.. The people of Hamburg wanted no war. They are a fine people, those Hamburgers; industrious, sober, hospitable, and filled with civic pride. Unlike the Berliner, already lashed to emotional martialism, they had no wish to interfere ; but in Hamburg again the newspapers were being filled with articles that could scarcely be regarded as pacifying. Whether ' influenced ' or not, the truth of which we shall probably never know, already they too were strumming the harsh song of war in unison with all the press of Prussia.

On my return to Berlin, a man whose name I dare not mention, lest some time it cause him trouble, a very competent man, who is known even in America, told me he feared that ' we are on the verge of a very terrible war '. Pressed for explanation he said, ' My friend, I must not say a word more ; but in a short time I am sure you will remember my prediction.'

I have not seen him since ; for on the following day he was ordered away on a mission unknown to me, and I had nothing but a card so telling me, and ending with his gracious ' Good-bye '. Am I to account for his prediction by crediting him with the rare gift of ' second-sight ', or is it more convincing to remember that he was one of the cogs in that enormous and powerful wheel ' revolving around the general war-staff of Germany ?

On Saturday, July 18, suffering from an attack of hay-fever, I went to Swinemünde, a fortified point on the Baltic, and found it filled with restless, excited people who talked of nothing but a prospective big war. No one could give any convincing authority ; but all seemed confident that in the event of war Russia would have to back down, because she was in the midst of reorganizing

her army, Great Britain dare not engage, lest she have
civil war over Home Rule, and France was impotent.
Thus, already were the masses of the people discussing
possibilities that they would have been ignorant of had
not the carefully-manipulated press-work been well done.
That same night, July 18, the offing filled with torpedo
boats and destroyers, ostensibly for a mimic attack on
the fortifications, that had already been closed to the
public, and all night long the flashlights played and the
guns banged in rest-disturbing volume.   Sunday, there
was great activity at the wharves leading up the channel
that is one of the water highways to Stettin.   Sentries
kept the over-curious from encroaching on the scene of
activities, but I saw men working at the torpedo tubes.
War aeroplanes appeared and made trial flights over the
city and harbour.   I sometimes carry with me a sketch-
book, although I am no artist, and while merely drawing
an old lighthouse on the end of one of the moles found
a man looking over my shoulder, and, reading menace
in his attitude, tore it up and walked away.   I remembered, later, that he had sauntered after me to my hotel.

It seems, in writing an article like this, an extreme
weakness to fail to give names of persons ; but there
must be loyalty preserved to those who give us friendly
warnings, so again I am compelled to obscurity in what
follows ; for there is not a country in the world, not even
excepting Russia, where a ruler's arm is so long and
wrathful and his fist is so potent as is the Kaiser's.
I doubt not that if I were to mention names in this
article, those friends of mine would be punished as soon
as His Majesty gets around to it, so I say ' a certain
person ' that night came to my hotel, in civilian garb,
and said, ' Take my advice, but don't ask questions that
I cannot answer.   You go back to Berlin in the morning,

pack your grips, and get out of Germany while there is time.'

'Those sketches ? ' I laughed.

But he had heard nothing of my movements, and said, ' No, not on that account ; but get away from Germany.'

' I think I'll go to France,' I said, convinced that there was more in his words than could be understood on the surface.

'Why not Switzerland ? ' he asked. ' It's a fine place for hay-fever.'

It is needless to say that I was in Berlin and packing on the following day, that immediately after I did go to Switzerland, and that still there was no open declaration of war on Germany's part. I stopped at Basle for a while, interested in that fine frontier station, and one day was amused by the extremely expressive swearing of a man who I found out was a ' switchman ' in the yards. He was complaining of over-work.

' One might have an idea ', he growled, ' that Germany was going to war, from the way the German railways are ordering all their empty trucks returned from everywhere. Nothing but empties going home, and if anybody makes a mistake or overlooks one, there 's the devil to pay ! '

I have since learned that this inflow of empty German carriages and trucks was so observable at other frontier stations, that two weeks before war was declared the German yards were swamped with this excess.

On Tuesday, July 28, the day when Austria declared war on Servia, German officers stopping at Swiss hotels received peremptory telegrams ordering them to cut their vacations then and there, and return home at once. From a hotel where I stopped in the Bernese Oberland, forty Germans left on July 29, the recall of the officers being sufficient to warn the wise that war was momentarily expected ; and something like an orderly panic ensued.   Here is another point that should be noted, which is, that had these officers been recalled from some other point—say Geneva, for instance—they would have been more careful to conceal their telegraphic orders ; but the Bernese part of Switzerland is almost as German as Germany, and no one thought of reticence.   The current talk was frank, open, and discussion and prediction uncurbed.   There was no attempt to conceal a great satisfaction.   The French had not been drawn into war by the rank outrages in Zabern, where a smart young lieutenant had been boldly upheld by the Kaiser for sabring a poor cobbler, nor had the French given sufficient ground for offensive action when the Kaiser had somewhat arrogantly upheld the rule of the sword over the unfortunate Frenchmen in Alsace.   At that time German officers had frankly and confessedly hoped that there would be an excuse for war with France, but had been disappointed.   Now, in these latter days of July, hastening back in obedience to telegraphic orders, they exultantly declared that the time had come when Germany would show how easily she could march to Paris. They departed as men going to their holidays instead of having them cut short.   They had no doubt, apparently, that a pretext for a war with France, that must of course be a war of conquest, was now forthcoming.   The Russian situation alone warranted such conjecture they declared, although Russia had but begun precautionary mobilization ; but at Russia these officers snapped their fingers.   They cared nothing for war with Russia, only so that it might afford a chance to mulct the French. Not one of them but scoffed at the idea that Great Britain would go to war.   They partook of the views which their

Kaiser must have maintained, and on which he made his great plunge, that England had her hands full at home; that an ultimatum to Russia, who had only attempted to mediate for the Serbs, would bring something approaching a state of war with the Czar, and then, by the next adroit pressure, France could be forced into conflict. If any one still doubts the Kaiser's ability as a great chess-player, let him consider that Russia still tried to be friendly, that England was doing all she could for peace, that the French were remaining quiet, and doing all they could to remain so, and that the Kaiser was actually mobilizing. Also, it is a matter of record that he announced himself as peaceful. One must be just, and he did say that he hoped for nothing so much as peace. The French reticence was disturbing. The German Chancellor was vastly worried by the fear that France, too, might mobilize, which would naturally be an unthinkable crime. So the Kaiser, to use an Americanism, asked France what she proposed to do about it, and, still receiving no reply that justified a declaration of war, went to war without one! If it is true, as the German Chancellor says, that the reason why the enormous German war machine, the most perfect, the most carefully created since time began, was set in motion and neutral Luxembourg and neutral Belgium flooded with German troops because Germany was afraid that Great Britain (unmobilized, and trying to mediate) and France (actually dreading war) were about to throw enormous numbers of men into Belgium, then the Kaiser will still go down to history as the Man of Peace. For it would admittedly have been a very unfair thing for Great Britain to throw into France millions of men—how, nobody knows—and France, not then mobilized, to add her millions so unexpectedly in that *coup de force*. But if it was merely an unfounded panic on the part of Germany, Germany is to be pitied for her nervous malady.

What I personally know can be summarized as a number of events, insignificant when taken singly, but in the cumulative to me, at least, impressive.

First : That not until this very year were German military and naval preparations complete.

Second : that the Zabern ' incident ' was, in effect, and perhaps intentionally so, a challenge to France.

Third : That the establishment of ' Operatives ' in friendly foreign countries disproved any peaceful intention.

Fourth : That the Austrian-Servian imbroglio was not in itself sufficient cause for Germany to go to war, had she not been prepared and eager.

Fifth : That it was well known in inner and upper circles that the military clique hoped for war, and wanted nothing more than a pretext.

Sixth : That the war spirit was kindled and stimulated by *freely distributed* newspapers.

Seventh : That Germany was making ready for war days before the situation warranted the supposition that she was in any wise involved.

Eighth : That days before such situation arrived, many of her trusted officials had been quietly warned that war was coming.

I cannot personally conclude, therefore, after considering all these little corroborative happenings with what has since taken place, a review of the Kaiser's successive steps, with which the public is familiar, and his sudden descent on Belgium, that any other than the Kaiser himself could have been to blame.

Oxford : Horace Hart Printer to the University

WHY WE ARE AT WAR

GREAT BRITAIN'S CASE

BY MEMBERS OF THE OXFORD FACULTY OF MODERN HISTORY

E. BARKER.   H. W. C. DAVIS.

C. R. L. FLETCHER.   ARTHUR HASSALL.

L. G. WICKHAM LEGG.   F. MORGAN.

With an Appendix of Original Documents including the Authorized English Translation of the White Book issued by the German Government

THIRD EDITION REVISED (TENTH IMPRESSION) CONTAINING THE RUSSIAN ORANGE BOOK AND EXTRACTS FROM THE BELGIAN GREY BOOK

TRANSLATIONS INTO FRENCH ITALIAN SPANISH GERMAN DANISH AND SWEDISH ARE NOW READY

Paper Covers Two Shillings net (70 cents)
Cloth Two Shillings and Sixpence net (85 cents)

OXFORD: AT THE CLARENDON PRESS
LONDON: HUMPHREY MILFORD
EDINBURGH   GLASGOW   NEW YORK   TORONTO
MELBOURNE   BOMBAY

(*a*)

12 38

OXFORD PAMPHLETS
1914

BACILLI AND
BULLETS

BY

SIR WILLIAM OSLER

REGIUS PROFESSOR OF MEDICINE

FOURTH IMPRESSION

One Penny net

OXFORD UNIVERSITY PRESS
HUMPHREY MILFORD
LONDON EDINBURGH GLASGOW
NEW YORK TORONTO MELBOURNE BOMBAY

BACILLI AND BULLETS

I HAVE been asked to say a few words on the question
of health in war-time, that you may realize its importance.
Formerly an army marched on its belly ; *now* it marches
on its brain.   Only by utilizing existing knowledge, in
all grades from Commander-in-Chief to private, is the
maximum of success available.   To put the largest
number of the enemy out of action with a minimum of
loss to his own men is the aim of every general.   While
in one way modern war merges the individual in a great
machine, on the other hand the intelligent action of
the unit has never been so important a factor in making
the machine work smoothly and efficiently.   After all,
it is the man behind the gun who wins the victory.

What I wish to urge is a true knowledge of your foes,
not simply of the bullets, but of the much more important
enemy, the bacilli.   In the wars of the world they have
been as Saul and David—the one slaying thousands, the
other tens of thousands.   I can never see a group of
recruits marching to the dépôt without mentally asking
what percentage of these fine fellows will die legitimate
and honourable deaths from wounds, what percentage
will perish miserably from neglect of ordinary sanitary
precautions ?   It is bitter enough to lose thousands of
the best of our young men in a hideous war, but it adds
terribly to the tragedy to think that more than one-half
of the losses may be due to preventable disease.   Typhus

fever, malaria, cholera, enteric, and dysentery have won more victories than powder and shot. Some of the diseases I mention need no longer be dreaded. Typhus and malaria, which one hundred years ago routed a great English army in the Walcheren expedition against Antwerp, are no longer formidable foes. But enough remain, as we found by sad experience in South Africa. Of the 22,000 lives lost in that war—can you believe it ? —the bullets accounted for only 8,000, the bacilli for 14,000 ! In the long arduous campaign before us more men will go into the field than ever before in the history of the Empire. Before it is too late, let us take every possible precaution to guard against a repetition of such disasters. I am here to warn you soldiers against enemies more subtle, more dangerous, and more fatal than the Germans, enemies against which no successful battle can be fought without your intelligent co-operation. So far the world has only seen one great war waged with the weapons of science against these foes. Our allies the Japanese went into the Russian campaign prepared as fully against bacilli as against bullets, with the result that the percentage of deaths from disease was the lowest that has ever been attained in a great war. Which lesson shall we learn ? Which example shall we follow, Japan, or South Africa with its sad memories ?

We are not likely to have to fight three of the greatest of former scourges, typhus, malaria, and cholera, though the possibility of the last has to be considered. But there remain dysentery, pneumonia, and enteric, against two of which we should be able to bring to bear successfully resources of modern science.

Dysentery, an inflammation of the large bowel, has been for centuries one of the most terrible of camp diseases, killing thousands, and, in its prolonged damage to health, one of the most fatal of foes to armies. So far as we know, it is conveyed by water, and only by carrying out strictly, under all circumstances, the directions about boiling water can it be prevented. It is a disease which, even under the best of circumstances, cannot always be prevented ; but with care the incidence should be reduced to a minimum, and there should never again be widespread outbreaks in the camps themselves.

Pneumonia is a much more difficult disease to prevent. Many of us, unfortunately, carry the germ with us. In these bright days all goes well in a holiday camp like this ; but when the cold and the rain come, and the long marches, the resisting forces of the body are lowered, the enemy, always on the watch, overpowers the guards, rushes the defences, and attacks the lungs. Be careful not to neglect coughs and colds. A man in good condition should be able to withstand the wettings and exposures that lower the system, but in a winter campaign pneumonia causes a large amount of sickness and is one of the serious enemies of the soldier.

Above all others one disease has proved most fatal in modern warfare—enteric, or typhoid fever. Over and over again it has killed thousands before they ever reached the fighting line. The United States troops had a terrible experience in the Spanish-American War. In six months, between June and November, inclusive, among 107,973 officers and men in 92 volunteer regiments, 20,738, practically one-fifth of the entire number, had typhoid fever, and 1,580 died. Fortunately, in this country typhoid fever is not prevalent in the districts in which camps are placed. The danger is chiefly from persons who have already had the disease and who carry the germs in their intestines, harmless messmates in them, but capable of infecting barracks or camps. You can easily understand how flies lighting on the discharges of such typhoid carriers could convey the germs far and wide. It was in this way probably, and by dust, that the bacilli were so fatal in South Africa. Take to heart these figures : there were 57,684 cases of typhoid fever, of which 19,454 were invalided, and 8,022 died. More died from the bacilli of this disease than from the bullets of the Boers. Do let this terrible record impress upon you the importance of carrying out with religious care the sanitary regulations.

One great advance in connexion with typhoid fever has been made of late years, and of this I am come specially to ask you to take advantage. An attack of an infectious disease so alters the body that it is no longer susceptible to another attack of the same disease ; once a person has had scarlet fever, small-pox, or chicken-pox, he is not likely to have a second attack. He is immune, or has what is called immunity. When you expose a solution of sugar to the air, or if you add to it a pinch of yeast, a process goes on which we call fermentation, accompanied by a growth of little germs of the yeast in the fluid, and by an increase in temperature (in fact the solution has a fever), and the composition of the fluid alters, so much so that you can inoculate it afterwards again and again with the same germ, but no further change takes place. Now this is what happens to us when bacilli make a successful entry into our bodies. They overcome the forces that naturally protect the system, and grow just as the yeast does in the sugar solution ; but the body puts up a strong fight, all sorts of anti-bodies are formed in the blood, and if recovery takes place, the patient afterwards has immunity, for a time at least, from subsequent attacks. The body has mobilized its forces, and is safe for a few years at least against that disease. It was an Englishman, Jenner, in 1798, who found that it was possible to confer this immunity by giving a person a mild attack of a disease, or of one very like it. Against small-pox all of you have been vaccinated—a harmless, safe, and effective measure. Let me give you a war illustration. General Wood of the United States Army told me that, when he was at Santiago, reports came that in villages not far distant small-pox was raging and the people without help of any kind. He called for volunteers, all men who showed scars of satisfactory vaccination. Groups of these soldiers went into the villages, took care of the small-pox patients, cleaned up the houses, stayed there until the epidemic was over, and not one of them took the disease. Had not those men been vaccinated, at least 99 per cent. of them would have taken small-pox. Now what I wish to ask you is to take advantage of the knowledge that the human body can be protected by vaccination against typhoid fever. Discovered through the researches of Sir Almroth Wright, this measure has been introduced successfully into our own regular army, into the armies of France, the United States, Japan, and Germany. I told you a few minutes ago about the appalling incidence of typhoid fever in the volunteer troops in America during the Spanish-American War. That resulted largely from the wide prevalence of the disease in country districts, so that the camps became infected ; and we did not then know the importance of the fly as a carrier, and other points of great moment. But in the regular army in the United States, in which inoculation has been practised now for several years, the number of cases has fallen from 3·53 per thousand men to practically nil. In a strength of 90,646 there were in

1913 only three cases of typhoid fever. In France the enteric rate among the unvaccinated was 168·44 per thousand, and among the vaccinated ·18 per thousand. In India, where the disease has been very prevalent, the success of the measure has been remarkable. In the United States, and in France, and in some other countries this vaccination against the disease is compulsory. It is not a serious procedure ; you may feel badly for twenty-four hours, and the site of inoculation will be tender, but I hope I have said enough to convince you that, in the interests of the cause, you should gladly put up with this temporary inconvenience. If the lessons of past experience count, any expeditionary force on the Continent has much more to fear from the bacillus of typhoid fever than from bullets and bayonets. Think again of South Africa with its 57,000 cases of typhoid fever ! With a million of men in the field, their efficiency will be increased one-third if we can prevent enteric. It can be prevented, it *must be prevented* ; but meanwhile the decision is in your hands, and I know it will be in favour of your King and Country.

Oxford: Horace Hart Printer to the University

TO THE
CHRISTIAN SCHOLARS OF
EUROPE AND AMERICA

A REPLY FROM OXFORD TO
THE GERMAN ADDRESS TO
EVANGELICAL CHRISTIANS

FOURTH IMPRESSION

Price Twopence net

OXFORD UNIVERSITY PRESS
HUMPHREY MILFORD
LONDON   EDINBURGH   GLASGOW
NEW YORK   TORONTO   MELBOURNE   BOMBAY
1914

NOTE.—The writers of this paper have of set purpose omitted all reference to the details of diplomatic negotiations and to the question of the neutrality of Belgium, since these have been specially dealt with in the Reply issued by the Archbishops.

Nor did it fall within their aim to discuss the allegation of ' unnameable horrors ' or ' cruelties and shamelessness ' practised on ' Germans living peaceably abroad ' (p. 20, l. 36 *infra*). They know that nothing has happened in England even remotely corresponding to such language, and it does not seem to them likely (in the absence of evidence) to be much less grotesquely unreal in reference to Belgium. In any case the savage reprisals against the civil population of Belgian towns and villages are in their judgement more reprehensible and more symptomatic of the real temper of the nation responsible for them, just because there seems every reason to believe that they were carried out under orders of competent authority.

OUR attention has been drawn to a document which we understand is being circulated especially in America, signed by a group of German theologians and addressed 'To the Evangelical Christians Abroad'[1]. This document gives an account of the origin of the war as it is seen from the German side ; it lays stress upon the peaceful aims of the German people and upon the disastrous consequences which must follow from the present conflict, especially for the cause of Christian Missions ; and then it throws the blame for these consequences on other nations than Germany, who is emphatically declared to be guiltless.

We hasten to express our belief in the sincerity and good faith of these protestations and disclaimers so far as they relate to the motives of those by whom the document has been signed. We recognise the names as those of eminent teachers and ministers of religion, who have shown their own deep interest in Missions, and who have taken an active part in the efforts that have been made to cultivate a better understanding and better relations between religious people on both sides of the North Sea. We gratefully acknowledge the help which many of the signatories have given in our own Missionary Conferences and in the prosecution of other good causes. Some of us are specially bound to individuals

[1] For this document we are indebted to the courtesy of the *Westminster Gazette,* in which paper the greater part of it was published on Sept. 9, 1914. It will be found printed in full at the end of our reply, p. 19, *infra.*

on the list by personal ties of deep regard and admiration. Therefore we do our best to examine, with the self-restraint and effort at impartiality which befits those whose business it is to sift evidence and to look below facts for their causes, the points emphasized or indicated by the signatories.

1. Is it true that for forty-three years the German people ' has maintained peace ' (p. 19, l. 19) ?

It is true in the letter, but it is not true in the spirit.

If instead of a period of forty-three years we take a period of fifty years, we find that Germany or Prussia has waged three aggressive wars, each of which added new lands by conquest to the territory of Prussia or Germany. With the aggrandizement of Prussia as against the other States of Germany, outsiders are not directly concerned ; but as the result of the campaigns against Denmark and France —and of the partition of Poland at an earlier date— Germany in the political sense is now in possession of districts on the north and east and south-west which are still largely Danish, Polish, or French (as the case may be) in sympathy, and cannot be called in any complete sense 'fragments' of the German 'motherland' (p. 20, l. 24). These districts return to the Reichstag no fewer than 28 members of the "protest parties" : 1 Dane, 18 Poles, 9 Alsace-Lorrainers.

2. Is it true that, within the last forty-three years, 'wherever a danger of war arose in other lands, the

German nation has exerted herself to assist in removing or diminishing it ' (p. 19, l. 20) ?

It is not true, if it is meant to imply that Germany has not, on more occasions than one, intentionally run the risk of war. In 1875 she showed indications of an intention to renew the attack on France, an intention averted by the mediation of the Russian and English sovereigns' with the Emperor William I. Of recent years, as the policy and tradition of the Bismarckian period faded farther and farther into the background of the past, the peril has recurred more and more insistently. The sword has been rattled in the scabbard and antagonists have been dared to move a step in answer. Now it was France that was bidden to sacrifice her Foreign Minister : now it was Russia that was ordered to drop all interest in the Austrian annexation of Bosnia. A generation ago Germany was content to protect her acquisitions and consolidate her power by a system of defensive alliances : latterly she has felt the desire to be as great on the sea as she is on the land, and has set the pace in a gigantic competition of armaments. Proposals for a suspension or diminution of shipbuilding have been made by Great Britain, but they have been made in vain. Germany claimed that she must fulfil her destiny, and has pursued unsleepingly the development of her army and her fleet. But a hegemony which rests on force and nothing else must, because there are stronger things in the world than force, sooner or later come to a disastrous end.

3. Is it true that Germany 'has not dreamed of depriving others of light and air' (p. 19, l. 24)?

It is not true, and indeed the exact opposite is true, if we correctly estimate the trend of German thought and German policy. While we recognize the real difficulty in which Germany finds herself when, like other European States, she feels the need to expand, and finds most of the available parts of the surface of the globe pre-empted by other nations, we feel that the more recent of Germany's efforts at expansion or penetration have been planned with a total disregard of the 'light and air' of the peoples concerned. For instance, her exploitation of Turkey in Europe took no account of the resolution of the Christian peoples of the Balkans to claim and secure their independence.

Such a policy is but the translation into action of doctrines which are widely preached in the German Universities. Of the existence and influence of this tendency the signatories cannot be ignorant; and we do not know whether to be more grateful for their own implicit repudiation of sympathy with it, or more astonished at their ostrich-like attitude towards a state of things so notorious. We should not in any case have held the signatories responsible for the theories of military writers like General von Bernhardi, any more than we should expect the signatories to assume on our part a necessary agreement with the views of Lord Roberts. But the matter stands differently with the teaching that is being enunciated in the name of German culture in the lecture-room, on the platform, and

in the press, by those who appear to exert most
influence on the public opinion of the German educated classes. A significant change has passed, since
the Franco-German War, over the German Professoriate. Then, among historians and men of science
were not only apologists of Bismarck but critics :
Mommsen and Virchow at Berlin represented an
' opposition ' within the ranks of even Prussian
learning. Nowadays the state of things is changed.
The Government which nominates the professors
sees to it that they shall not be politicians of too
pronounced an anti-governmental type. The Social
Democrats are the most numerous political party in
Germany, but, numerous as they are, it is understood that no Social Democrat can aspire to
a professorial chair. The Professoriate, at least in
the greater Universities of northern and central
Germany, is ardently Imperialistic in tone. Not
all Imperialists need be of the school of von Treitschke ; but Treitschke's ideals appear to be those
which rule the educated Germany of to-day, and
though the movement started from Berlin its
dominance is no longer confined to Prussian soil.
The two quotations that follow are from an eminent
historian and an eminent scientist, both of Leipzig :
    ' Germany was now the protector and pillar of
European civilization ; and after bloody victories
the world would be healed by being Germanized.' (Professor Karl Lamprecht; *Times*, Monday,
August 31, 1914, p. 7.)
    ' Germany will dictate peace to the rest of Europe.
. . . The principle of the absolute sovereignty of the

individual nations, which in the present European tumult has proved itself so inadequate and baneful, must be given up and replaced by a system conforming to the world's actual conditions, and especially to those political and economic relations which determine industrial and cultural progress and the common welfare.' (Professor Ostwald; *Westminster Gazette*, Friday, September 18, 1914, p. 2.)

Will the signatories still maintain their assertion that ' Germany ' does not dream of ' depriving others of light and air ' ?   Are they so certain that they themselves, rather than Professor Lamprecht and Professor Ostwald, are the true interpreters of German policy ?

4. Is it true that Germany has only drawn the sword ' under the compulsion to repel a wanton attack ' (p. 20, l. 4), and that the war ' has been wantonly thrust ' upon her people (ibid., l. 28) ?

It is not true : and the proof of its untruth emerges the more clearly as different diplomatic documents of the period immediately preceding the war come to light.   Naturally we do not charge the signatories with stating the facts other than as they saw them. But they wrote, we are quite sure, without having studied at first hand any adequate collection of the evidence.   They wrote, it is clear, in the early days after war broke out ; and even if they were writing now it is doubtful if they would have had access to the English ' White Paper ' with its 158 documents, published early in August, since we understand that this publication is contraband in the German Empire.

But we have no need to appeal to anything that could be called a partisan presentation of the case : it is enough to say that Italy, which was bound by treaty, as a member of the Triple Alliance, to come to the assistance of her partners in the event of aggression directed against them, has declared herself neutral just because the *casus foederis* has not arisen. We may be quite sure that Germany would have publicly held Italy to her engagements, if the war had really been on Germany's part a defensive one.

5. Is it true that the war is a war of Slav against Teuton, that is, of ' Asiatic barbarism ' against German culture ?   (Pp. 21 l. 25, 20 l. 13.)

Two months ago there were probably a good many people in England who on this head would have felt some sympathy with the German. case. It has always seemed to us reasonable, in estimating German policy, to allow for the deep-seated nervousness in German minds which is the outcome of the neighbourhood on their further border of the great mysterious northern Power with its huge population and the illimitable possibilities of its future.   And (while we in Oxford can never forget that one of the ablest and most distinguished of our professors is a Russian) it is likely that most Englishmen, while satisfied that there was nothing in the sphere of external politics to prevent a cordial understanding with Russia, would have felt qualms against anything which might seem to commit us to sympathy with some features of Russian internal administration. But there are also considerations which, as between Russia and Germany, must be quite frankly and freely stated on the other side.

(a) Within the last twenty years Russia has made important advances towards freedom and self-government. Within the same period, can Germany point to any advance in this direction at all ?

(b) In particular, the claim of the Poles to some measure of recognition of their distinct national life appears to be much nearer to adequate realization in Russia than in Germany.

(c) So far as the information at our disposal enables us to judge, the conduct of the war by Russia and by Germany respectively does not at all suggest a contrast between Asiatic barbarism and European culture.

Though Russian intellectual development has not yet reached the pitch of German intellectual development, we cherish at the same time the belief that the recent achievement of Russian literature, Russian scholarship, Russian science, Russian music, is the dawn that augurs a very brilliant and splendid noonday. And if we are to limit comparisons to actual results, then it would be open to us to contrast unfavourably the present political development of Germany with the higher political development of the countries of the West. The language habitually addressed by the German Emperor to his military forces implies an underlying temper of thought and ideals which appears to us, if by ' barbarism ' is meant a backward state of civilization, to be as 'barbarous' as anything that can be found in Russia.

6. Is it true that the war is a war against Protestantism ?   The Czar, they tell us, has openly proclaimed it as 'the decisive campaign against Teutonism and Protestantism' (p. 21, l. 24) ; and further on they themselves assert that by the war a 'simply incurable rent has been made in Teutonic Protestantism' (p. 23, l. 6).

We pass over the initial difficulty that no documentary evidence is here offered that the Czar did make any such statement at all, because we wish to come to grips with the central assertion that this war has in it a religious colour. Had not the German theologians asserted this, such an idea would never have entered our minds. In Great Britain there is not, and no one wishes that there should be, any sort of religious cleavage in the matter : Ulster Protestants and Roman Catholics from the rest of Ireland stand shoulder to shoulder in support of the British cause. In Germany itself there are 24,000,000 Roman Catholics to 40,000,000 Protestants ; and even if the signatories regard the 24,000,000 of their own fellow-subjects as a negligible quantity, it still remains as strange as it is significant that they make no mention whatever of the alliance with Austria. For among the Great Powers of Europe the country with which Germany is allied is at the same time the country where the attitude of Roman Catholic Christians to Christians of other confessions is most definitely aggressive.

The charge that the war is a war against Protestantism is, as it seems to us, baseless ; and if it is
baseless, it is beyond measure perilous. Have the
signatories realized what the effect of raising the
religious war-cry is likely to be upon the temper of
their own people ? The more influential they are as
leaders of religious thought, the more disastrous may
be the results of this teaching. Can they be quite sure
that they are not, in part at least, responsible for the
animus which appears to have been shown throughout
this campaign against the clergy and the churches of
the countries which the German troops have overrun?

7. Is it true, lastly, that the war is limited on the
one side to Christian combatants, while on the other
side the assistance of non-Christian peoples is sought
and welcomed (p. 21, l. 26) ?

With the signatories, we should have wished in
the abstract that the introduction of non-Christian
Powers into the war could be avoided. But the
problem is a good deal less simple than the employment of words like ' pretext ' (p. 21, l. 27) and
' unscrupulously ' (ibid. l. 12) would suggest.

(*a*) In the first place the existence in the world
of non-Christian Powers like China and Japan is
a fact which it is useless to ignore. Christian
Powers must have relations with them, and those
relations have to be governed by the same codes
of law and honour, of promise and fulfilment, as
the relations between Christian Powers.

(*b*) Whatever can be said against the English
alliance with Japan can be said with equal force
against the German efforts after an alliance with

Turkey.   Turkey is religiously just as much of an Asiatic Power as Japan.

(c) The Anglo-Japanese alliance, under the terms of which Japan is now engaged in fighting Germany in the Far East, does not in fact provide for the introduction of the Japanese forces into the European arena, and it has never been proposed to bring them there.

(d) At the same time Great Britain, believing that she and her allies are at war for a just cause, does not admit that that cause becomes less just in Asia or in Africa than it is in Europe. The 'terrible danger of a native rising' (p. 21, l. 17) she holds to be best obviated by a policy towards her subjects so liberal and so humane that they shall have no desire to revolt.   She is proud that she can trust the loyalty of her Indian and South African peoples so utterly that the one country can be largely and the other wholly denuded of Imperial troops.

(e) Further, the Government of Great Britain has determined that some of her own Indian troops, and of the troops put prodigally at her disposal by the princes of India, shall be transferred to Europe, and we cannot pretend to regret its determination. It is not simply because we have here a crowning token of the true inner cohesion of the British Empire ; it is rather that if we stand, as we claim to do, on behalf of right against might, of respect for the law of nations and for plighted word, and of the defence of the weak, then we can only rejoice if these Christian principles find an echo in the breast of non-Christian peoples.   Our Indian fellow-subjects, in especial, are the representatives of an ancient civilization, which we hope may the sooner be penetrated by Christian influences when we and they have marched side by side, and have faced the same dangers, and, if God will, have carried the same cause to victory.

We have tried to approach the appeal of the German theologians in the temper which recognizes points of contact as well as points of difference. It is the proper function of universities to correct the narrower outlook and enlarge the ordinary conceptions of patriotism by continual and appreciative witness to the existence and greatness of other empires and differing civilizations and alien peoples. Nor is it merely in the past that we see and acknowledge developments of national or intellectual life on other lines than our own. No student among us would wish for a moment to shut his eyes to the enormous output of the German universities in every department of scholarship, or to its real value. Just as in our theological ideals Christianity and the Catholic Church is something much greater than any merely local or sectional or national embodiment of it, since all the nations are destined to bring their glory and honour into it, so in our intellectual ideals we regard learning and civilization as a universal *civitas*, of the citizenship of which all who will are free, while no race is so small or so insignificant that it has not its own quota to contribute, its special gift which is necessary to the completeness of the whole.

Are these ideals shared by Germany ?

The experience of the last few weeks has taught us by the grimmest of all lessons that neither Christian tradition possesses any sacredness, nor supreme beauty in art any charm, nor historical records any value, to save the monuments of other than German culture from the lust of destruction which inflames the German armies in ·the field. The annals of the past might be ransacked without finding the story of a campaign where, in one brief month, such sinister deeds have been perpetrated as the burning of the library of Louvain University and the bombardment of the cathedral of Reims. If the fortune of war should bring, which God forbid, the tide of invasion into our own English land, the fate of the library of Louvain might be the fate also of the Bodleian. Until the saner elements of German public life can control the baser —and we have not heard of even any protest by the representatives of German art and German learning—will not the Christian scholars of other lands share our conviction that the contest in which our country has engaged is a contest on behalf of the supremest interests of Christian civilization ?

We, like the writers of this appeal, have laboured for peace, and deplore, as Christian men, the effect which the war must have upon many good causes and especially upon Christian Missions. No less than they we long for the reunion of Christians ; but it must be a union which shall unite other as well as Teutonic Christians, and which shall be so strong that those who labour for peace shall be able to make their voices heard and respected in the councils of their nations.

DA PACEM IN DIEBVS NOSTRIS
DOMINE

H. S. Holland, D.D., Hon. D.Litt., Regius Professor of Divinity; Canon of Christ Church.

W. Sanday, D.D., Lady Margaret Professor of Divinity; Canon of Christ Church; Fellow of the British Academy.

W. Lock, D.D., Dean Ireland's Professor of Exegesis of Holy Scripture; Warden of Keble College.

R. L. Ottley, D.D., Regius Professor of Pastoral Theology; Canon of Christ Church.

E. W. Watson, D.D., Regius Professor of Ecclesiastical History; Canon of Christ Church.

G. A. Cooke, D.D., Regius Professor of Hebrew; Canon of Christ Church.

Charles Gore, D.D., Hon. D.C.L., Lord Bishop of Oxford; Honorary Fellow of Trinity College.

T. B. Strong, D.D., Dean of Christ Church.

H. N. Bate, Examiner in the School of Theology; late Fellow of Magdalen College.

Edwyn Bevan, Honorary Fellow of New College.

F. E. Brightman, Hon. D. Phil., Louvain; Fellow of Magdalen College.

J. Estlin Carpenter, D.Litt., Wilde Reader in Natural and Comparative Religion; Principal of Manchester.

T. K. Cheyne, D.Litt., Honorary Fellow of Oriel

College; late Oriel Professor of the Interpretation of Holy Scripture; Fellow of the British Academy.

P. Gardner, Lincoln and Merton Professor of Classical Archaeology and Art ; Fellow of Lincoln College; Fellow of the British Academy.

G. B. Gray, D.Litt., Speaker's Lecturer in Biblical Studies.

H. G. Grey, Principal of Wycliffe Hall ; late Missionary in India.

W. H. Hutton, B.D., Reader in Indian History; Fellow of St. John's College; Archdeacon of Northampton.

H. Stuart Jones, Fellow of Trinity College ; late Director of the British School at Rome.

R. W. Macan, D.Litt., Master of University College.

H. Rashdall, D.Litt., Fellow of New College; Canon of Hereford Cathedral ; Fellow of the British Academy.

W. B. Selbie, Member of the Board of Faculty of Theology ; Principal of Mansfield.

W. A. Spooner, D.D., Warden of New College.

B. H. Streeter, Fellow of Queen's College; Member of the Board of Faculty of Theology.

Cuthbert H. Turner, University Lecturer in Church History ; Fellow of Magdalen College ; Fellow of the British Academy.

C. C. J. Webb, Fellow of Magdalen College ; late Wilde Reader in Natural and Comparative Religion.

ADDRESS OF THE GERMAN THEOLOGIANS
TO THE EVANGELICAL CHRISTIANS ABROAD

In this age of opportunity, without a parallel in history, when Christendom has been granted access to and decisive influence upon the entire non-Christian world, the Christian peoples of Europe are about to rend one another in fratricidal war. 5

A systematic network of lies, controlling the international telegraph service, is endeavouring in other lands to cast upon our people and its Government the guilt for the outbreak of this war, and has dared to dispute the inner right of us and our 10 Emperor to invoke the assistance of God. The necessity is therefore laid upon us, who are known among Christians abroad as men who have worked for the propagation of the Gospel among foreign peoples and for the establishment of cultural ties 15 and friendly relations between Germany and other Christian nations, to offer to the entire public our testimony concerning this war.

For forty-three years our people has maintained peace. Wherever a danger of war arose in other 20 lands, our nation has exerted herself to assist in removing or diminishing it. Her ideal was peaceful work. She has contributed a worthy share to the cultural wealth of the modern world. She has not dreamed of depriving others of light and air. 25 She desired to thrust no one from his place. In friendly competition with other peoples, she has developed the gifts which God had given her. Her industry brought her rich fruit. She won also a modest share in the task of colonization in 30 the primitive world, and was exerting herself to

offer her contribution to the remoulding of Eastern
Asia. She has left no one, who is willing to see the
truth, in doubt as to her peaceful disposition.
Only under the compulsion to repel a wanton
5 attack has she now drawn the sword.

As our Government was exerting itself to localize
the justifiable vengeance for an abominable royal
murder, and to avoid the outbreak of war between
two neighbouring Great Powers, one of them,
10 whilst invoking the mediation of our Emperor,
proceeded (in spite of its pledged word) to threaten
our frontiers, and compelled us to protect our land
from being ravaged by Asiatic barbarism. Then
our adversaries were joined also by those who by
15 blood and history and faith are our brothers, with
whom we felt ourselves in the common world-task
more closely bound than with almost any other
nation. Over against a world in arms we recognize
clearly that we have to defend our existence, our
20 individuality, our culture, and our honour. No
scruple holds back our enemies, where in their
opinion there is a prospect, through our destruction,
of seizing for themselves an economic advantage
or an increase of power, a fragment of our mother-
25 land, our colonial possessions, or our trade. We
stand over against this raging of the peoples, fearless because of our trust in the holy and righteous
God. Precisely because this war has been wantonly
thrust upon our people, it finds us a single people,
30 in which distinctions of race and rank, of parties
and confessions, have vanished. In a holy enthusiasm, not shrinking from battle and from death,
and looking to God, we are all of one mind, and
prepared joyfully to stake our all for our land and
35 our liberty.

Unnameable horrors have been committed against
Germans living peaceably abroad—against women
and children, against wounded and physicians—

cruelties and shamelessness such as many a heathen and Mohammedan war has not revealed. Are these the fruits, by which the non-Christian peoples are to recognize whose disciples the Christian nations are ? Even the not unnatural excitement of a people, whose neutrality—already violated by our adversaries—could under the pressure of implacable necessity not be respected, affords no excuse for inhumanities, nor does it lessen the shame that such could take place in a land long ago Christianized. Into the centre of Africa the war has been unscrupulously carried, although military operations there are entirely irrelevant to its decision, and although the participation of natives, who have been pacified but a few decenniums, in a war of white against white, conjures up the terrible danger of a native rising. These primitive peoples learned to know Christianity as the religion of love and peace as opposed to racial feuds and the cruelties of their chiefs. Now they are being led in arms against one another by the peoples who brought them this Gospel. Thus flourishing Mission-fields are being trampled in ruin.

Into the war which the Czar has openly proclaimed as the decisive campaign against Teutonism and Protestantism, heathen Japan is now also called under the pretext of an alliance. The Mission-fields which the World Missionary Conference in Edinburgh indicated as the most important in the present day—mid-Africa, with its rivalry between Christendom and Islam for the black races, and Eastern Asia remoulding its life—are now becoming the scenes of embittered struggles between peoples who bore in a special degree the responsibility for the fulfilment of the Great Commission in these lands.

Our Christian friends abroad know how joyfully we German Christians greeted the fellowship in

faith and service which the Edinburgh World
Missionary Conference left as a sacred legacy to
Protestant Christendom ; they know also how we
have, to the best of our ability, co-operated in order
5 that among the Christian nations, with their competing political and economic interests, there should
arise a Christianity united and joyous in the recognition of the task entrusted to it by God. It was also
to us a matter of conscience to remove by every
10 means political misunderstandings and ill-feelings
and to assist in bringing about friendly relations
between the nations. We have now to endure the
taunt that we have believed in the power of the
Christian faith to conquer the wickedness of those
15 who are seeking war, and we encounter the reproach
that our efforts for peace have only served to
conceal from our people the true attitude of their
enemies. Nevertheless, we do not regret that we
have thus endeavoured to promote peace. Our
20 people could not enter into this struggle with so
clear a conscience if leading men of its ecclesiastical,
scientific, and commercial life had not in such
manifold ways exerted themselves to make this
fratricidal strife impossible.
25   Not for the sake of our people, whose sword is
bright and keen—for the sake of the unique world-
task of the Christian peoples in the decisive hour
of the world-Mission, we now address ourselves to
the evangelical Christians abroad in neutral and
30 inimical lands.
    We were hoping that through God there should
arise from the responsibility of the hour a stream
of new life for the Christian peoples. Already we
were able to trace in our German Churches the
35 powerful effects of this blessing, and the fellowship
with the Christians of other lands in obedience to
the universal commission of Jesus was to us a service
of sacred joy.

If this fellowship is now irreparably destroyed ;
if the peoples among whom missions and
   brotherly love had begun to be a power lapse
   into savagery in murderous war through hate
   and bitterness ;   5
if a simply incurable rent has been made in
   Teutonic Protestantism ;
if Christian Europe forfeits a notable portion
   of her position in the world ;
if the sacred springs from which her peoples 10
   should derive their own life and should offer
   it to others are corrupted and choked ;

the guilt of this rests, this we hereby declare before
our Christian brethren of other lands with calm
certainty, not on our people. We know full well, 15
that through this sanguinary judgement God is also
calling our nation to repentance, and we rejoice
that she is hearing His holy voice and turning to
Him. But in this we know that we are at one with
all the Christians among our people, that we can and 20
must repudiate on their behalf and on behalf of
their Government the responsibility for the terrible
crime of this war and all its consequences for the
development of the Kingdom of God on earth.
With the deepest conviction we must attribute it 25
to those who have long secretly and cunningly been
spinning a web of conspiracy against Germany,
which now they have flung over us in order to
strangle us therein.
   We direct our appeal to the conscience of our 30
Christian brethren in other lands, and press upon
them the question, what God now requires of them,
and what can and must take place, in order that,
through blindness and unscrupulousness in God's
great hour of the missionary enterprise, Christendom 35
shall not be robbed of its power and of its right to
serve as His messenger to non-Christian humanity.

The Holy God carries on His work to its goal, even through the storm and horror of war, and permits no human wickedness to defeat His purpose. Therefore we come before Him with the prayer :

5

'Hallowed be Thy Name ;
Thy Kingdom come ;
Thy Will be done.'

Missionsdirektor Lic. **K. Axenfeld** (Berlin).

Professor Dr. med. **Th. Axenfeld** (Freiburg).

Oberverwaltungsgerichtsrat **D. M. Berner** (Berlin).

Oberkonsistorialpräsident **D. H. v. Bezzel** (München).

Pastor **Friedr. v. Bodelschwingh** (Bethel bei Bielefeld).

Professor D. **Ad. Deissmann** (Berlin).

Oberhofprediger D. **E. Dryander** (Berlin).

Professor Dr. **R. Eucken** (Jena).

Professor D. **Ad. v. Harnack** (Berlin).

Professor D. **Gottl. Haussleiter** (Halle).

Missionsdirektor **P. O. Hennig** (Herrnhut).

Professor D. **W. Herrmann** (Marburg).

Generalsuperintendent D. **Th. Kaftan** (Kiel).

Generalsuperintendent D. **Fr. Lahusen** (Berlin).

Pastor **Paul Le Seur** (Berlin).

Professor D. **Friedr. Loofs** (Halle).

Professor Dr. **C. Meinhof** (Hamburg).

Professor D. **C. Mirbt** (Göttingen).

Ed. de Neufville (Frankfurt a. M.).

Missionsdirektor D. **C. Paul** (Leipzig).

Bankdirektor D. **Wilh. Freiherr v. Pechmann** (München)

Professor D. **Jul. Richter** (Berlin).

Max Schinckel (Hamburg).

Direktor der Deutsch-Ev. Missions-Hilfe **A. W. Schreiber** (Berlin).

Direktor D. **F. A. Spiecker** (Berlin).

Missionsdirektor **Joh. Spiecker** (Barmen).

Missionsinspektor D. **Joh. Warneck** (Bethel bei Bielefeld).

Professor D. **G. Wobbermin** (Breslau).

Professor Dr. **Wilh. Wundt** (Leipzig).

BERLIN, AUGUST, 1914.

Oxford : Horace Hart Printer to the University

OXFORD PAMPHLETS
1914–1915

CONTRABAND AND
THE WAR

BY

H. REASON PYKE, LL.B.

A SOLICITOR OF THE SUPREME COURT

Price Twopence net

OXFORD UNIVERSITY PRESS

HUMPHREY MILFORD

LONDON   EDINBURGH   GLASGOW

NEW YORK   TORONTO   MELBOURNE   BOMBAY

CONTRABAND AND THE WAR

OWING to the complexity of modern commercial relations, the mere existence of a state of war on a large scale necessarily involves heavy losses to the subjects of neutral States through the consequent diminution of purchasing power in the belligerent countries and shrinkage of trade. But, in addition to this, neutral merchants are liable to suffer damage through the operation of those rules of international law which require them to refrain from certain forms of trade with a State at war—even though simply in continuation of their commerce in time of peace—which would interfere with the military operations of either of the belligerents or strengthen one of them for the prosecution of hostilities against the other. International law makes such trade unlawful, regardless of the injury thereby inflicted upon neutrals, because of the manifest necessity of a belligerent under the principle of self-preservation. At the inception of the modern law of nations over three hundred years ago, this was clearly recognized by the great jurist, Albericus Gentilis, who shows that private interests can only be respected during war so long as their enjoyment does not conflict with the safety of States. ' Ius commerciorum aequum est,' he says, ' at hoc aequius tuendae salutis. Est illud gentium ius : hoc naturae est. Est illud privatorum : est hoc regnorum. Cedat igitur regno mercatura, homo naturae, pecunia vitae.' [1]

[1] *De Iure Belli*, Bk. I, ch. xxi (Holland's edition (1877), p. 97).

The fact that the neutral persons affected are to a large extent really innocent sufferers cannot be allowed to impair the efficacy of a belligerent's arms. This is particularly the case in the great war now raging, in which the gradual wearing down of Germany by the exercise of sea-power is indispensable for the self-preservation of Great Britain and her Allies. They are engaged in a life-and-death struggle for everything they hold dear, and are therefore naturally entitled, while respecting and safeguarding neutral interests as much as possible, to use to the uttermost all legitimate means for the coercion of the enemy.

At the present day the chief restrictions imposed by international law upon neutral commerce result from the operation of the rules relating to contraband of war. ' Contraband of war ' is the designation of goods of warlike use, whether owned by an enemy or a neutral,. found by a belligerent on board a neutral vessel on the high seas or within his own or his enemy's territorial waters, on their way to assist in his enemy's naval or military operations. A neutral vessel is one which is entitled to fly the flag of a neutral power,[1] and such a vessel would herself be contraband if suitable for any warlike use and destined for sale in a hostile port or for delivery to the enemy. Neutral goods of the character and with the destination in question would also be contraband when found on board an enemy vessel; but enemy goods found on board a similar vessel would be liable to capture simply as being the property of the enemy, and their nature and destination would be immaterial. Formerly it was unnecessary to consider the nature or character of enemy property on board a neutral vessel, but now, under the Declaration of

[1] Declaration of London, Article 57.

Paris, 1856,[1] the neutral flag covers such property with the exception of contraband of war.

The term 'contraband of war' applies properly to goods only, and carriage of contraband must be carefully distinguished from the carriage of persons and dispatches for the enemy. The expressions 'quasi-contraband' and 'analogues of contraband' used frequently to be employed to denote traffic of the latter kind, and in the early stages of the law of nations it was not dealt with separately. But carriage of persons and dispatches takes place in the direct service of the enemy, and is therefore more properly called 'unneutral service ' and treated as a distinct branch of the law of neutrality.

Neutral commerce may be further interrupted by the establishment of a blockade, under which a belligerent is allowed, subject to certain specific conditions, to interdict all communication by sea with the whole or part of the enemy's coast, and not merely to prevent him from receiving anything that would augment his naval or military resources.

At the Second Hague Conference in 1907 Great Britain made a proposal for the complete abolition of the doctrine of contraband ; but this was opposed by France, Germany, Russia, and the United States of America, and was dropped. There has always been a great want of uniformity in international practice and opinion with regard to contraband of war ; and the subject proved so contentious at the Hague that the Committee entrusted with its consideration could only report in favour of submitting the whole question to a fresh examination by the interested States. This it received at the Naval Conference of 1908–9, and, as

[1] Article 2. The Declaration of Paris will be found in the *Manual of Emergency Legislation*, p. 446.

the result of much discussion and compromise, an
agreement was arrived at and embodied in the Declaration of London.[1] But although this Declaration has
been signed by all the Powers represented at the Conference, it has not been ratified by Great Britain, who
has merely adopted its provisions as her present rule of
action, subject to such modifications and additions, consistent with the law as previously established, as are rendered necessary by the special circumstances of the war.

The Declaration is accompanied by a Report of the
Drafting Committee, which the Order in Council of
August 20, 1914,[2] by which the modified rules of the
Declaration of London were first adopted, directed all
British Prize Courts to consider as an authoritative
statement of the meaning and intention of the Declaration. But this direction is dropped in the subsequent
Order in Council of October 29,[3] which repealed and
replaced the earlier one ; and although the Report was
expressly adopted by the Conference as a guide to the
meaning of the Declaration, it is doubtful whether it
can really be regarded as authoritative. In English
law a draftsman is not allowed in this way to define the
intention of his own document.

Origin and Theory of Contraband

The origin of the law of contraband is to be found in
the proclamations or warnings which it became the
usage for powerful belligerents, as early as the thirteenth century, to issue at the commencement of a war
forbidding all ships to carry supplies of any kind to the
enemy under penalty of confiscation. Before the end

[1] The Declaration of London will be found, with the Report, in the
Manual of Emergency Legislation, pp. 447–514.

[2] *Manual of Emergency Legislation*, p. 143.

[3] *Id. sup.* No. 2, p. 78.

of the sixteenth century there was a distinct tendency for a sovereign at war to be satisfied with prohibiting the carriage of such articles only as he deemed to be of assistance to his enemy in maintaining the war. Neutral States acquiesced in this restricted interference with the commerce of their subjects, with the result that in time a belligerent acquired a customary right to punish any attempt to transport articles of warlike use to his enemy as an unlawful act on the part of the neutral merchant. The right of a State at war to prevent this mode of succouring its enemy was confirmed by treaty provisions; and the notion of the unlawfulness of such commerce was clearly held by all the early theoretical writers and was also strengthened by the fact that from the earliest times the municipal laws of Greece and Rome had punished the furnishing of arms and other appliances of war to the enemy with death or exile and confiscation of property, while similar provisions were contained in the Canon Law regarding trade by Christians with the Saracens.

At the present day every neutral Power is bound to abstain from supplying, either in its corporate capacity or through the action of its officials or public servants, any kind of war material to the belligerents; [1] and if it failed in this duty it would commit a breach of national neutrality for which the State as a whole would be liable to make full reparation to the injured belligerent. But during the Middle Ages a State could maintain that it was no party to a war and yet furnish one or both of the belligerents with money, troops, and other kinds of assistance; and therefore, in the absence of an express convention, it was impossible to hold a neutral sovereign responsible for the acts of his subjects

[1] See Article 6 of Hague Convention, No. XIII of 1907.

in supplying a belligerent with the necessaries of war. The treaties whereby States undertook to refrain from rendering assistance to each other's foes generally provided at first that they should prevent their subjects from doing like acts. But such stipulations were discontinued after the middle of the seventeenth century, and in spite of the occasional protest of a belligerent weak in naval power, as Germany in 1870, and the strenuous opposition of several theoretical writers, especially on the Continent, the mere carrying on of contraband trade by a neutral individual has never been held to compromise in any way the neutrality of the State to which he belongs.[1] The neutral merchant is alone responsible for his violation of the obligations of neutrality; the belligerent is allowed to check such a merchant by direct coercion whenever such action is possible without infringing neutral territory. The law of contraband aims solely at prohibiting the carriage of war material to a belligerent by sea, and does not apply to the sale of such material to either of the warring powers within a neutral country. Such sales are, as a general rule, perfectly legitimate. But a neutral State is bound, by the modern law of neutrality, to prevent vessels intended for the naval operations of a belligerent from being built, fitted out, armed, or supplied with necessaries of war, within the neutral territory;[2] and in the present war the United States Government has construed this duty so strictly that it has prohibited the export of submarines in sections to be put together abroad.

Although a neutral Government is under no inter-

[1] See 5 H C. 1907, Art. 7, and 13 H. C. 1907, Art. 7

[2] See 13 H. C. 1907, Arts. 8, 18–20; Foreign Enlistment Act, 1870, secs. 8, 10.

national obligation to forbid its subjects to trade in contraband of war, it may quite legitimately do so, if it likes, so long as it treats both belligerents in the same way and is only actuated by motives of self-interest. Austria and Sweden acted in this way in 1854, and Belgium, Switzerland, and Japan adopted a similar policy in 1870. In the present war the Danish and Swedish Governments have prohibited the export of various articles of warlike use, and restrictions on the re-export of certain commodities have been imposed in those countries and also in Holland and Italy. The usual practice, however, is for the Government merely to warn traders against the risks they run in engaging in contraband and other forms of prohibited commerce. Hitherto this has been the invariable attitude of the United States of America, but in the session opened on December 7, 1914, a Bill was introduced into the Senate making unlawful the sale of arms and ammunition to any country at war with which the United States is at peace. The State Department, however, does not appear to favour the movement to prohibit the export of munitions of war, and it is doubtful if the Bill will pass into law.

Hostile Destination

From the nature of contraband trade as one that is unlawful between neutrals and belligerents it follows that the merchandise in question must be not only susceptible, directly or indirectly, of warlike use, but also destined for the use of the enemy of its captor. On the Continent the destination of the goods themselves, rather than that of the vessel by which they are carried, has almost invariably been regarded as the criterion of their contraband character. The British practice of the eighteenth century, however, tended to look primarily to the destination

of the ship. But in connexion with what is called
the rule of the war of 1756, as extended in 1793, whereby
Great Britain prohibited neutrals from engaging in the
trade between French and Spanish colonies and the
mother countries from which they had been excluded in
time of peace, it was held that goods which had come
from those colonies on a neutral vessel nominally destined
for a neutral port might be condemned when there was
evidence that they had only been sent to the neutral port
in order to be subsequently transhipped or transported
further on the same or another ship to the enemy country.[1]

This doctrine of 'continuous voyage' or 'ultimate destination', as it is called, was applied to contraband during
the Crimean War by the French Council of Prize in the
case of the *Frau Houwina*, where a cargo of saltpetre
taken in transit from Lisbon to Hamburg was condemned
on the ground that it was intended to be sent on to
Russia. The United States also adopted this rule for
contraband trading in the Civil War, and held that the
noxious articles could be condemned, irrespective of the
destination, immediate or final, of the vessel carrying
them, whenever the circumstances indicated that they
were ultimately destined for a hostile country or for the
naval or military use of the enemy. The fact that the
cargo was simply deliverable ' to order or assigns ' was
particularly taken as justifying the conclusion that the
neutral port to which it was nominally consigned was not
its real destination.[2] The British Government acquiesced
in this position, and during the Boer War in 1900 definitely claimed to be entitled to treat articles of warlike
use as contraband whenever it could be shown that their
ultimate destination was hostile, although the vessel

[1] The *William* (1806), 5 C. Rob. 385 ; 1 E. P. C. 505.
[2] The *Springbok* (1866), 5 Wallace, 1.

carrying them was to call at neutral ports only. The ease with which, in consequence of the development of railway communication in the nineteenth century, a neutral merchant can now supply a belligerent with munitions of war by combined sea and land carriage, renders the law of contraband practically useless for dealing with a continental enemy unless, as is admitted in the United States' Note of December 28, 1914, a reasonable belief that shipments have in reality a hostile destination is sufficient to justify their seizure.

CONTRABAND ARTICLES

A great many treaties have, from the beginning of the sixteenth century, been concluded between numerous States for the purpose of settling what articles should be regarded between the parties as contraband of war ; but their provisions are various and contradictory, and it is obviously impossible to draw up a list of contraband objects that will hold good for all time and in all circumstances. Articles and commodities of use in war are continually changing, while different wars are waged under different conditions, and the needs of all countries cannot be the same owing to the variations in their situation and means. It has accordingly been the universal practice for belligerents to exercise their discretion, subject to such restrictions as may attach either by treaty or under the general law of nations, with regard to the objects to be treated as contraband. The extent to which a belligerent is entitled to interfere with neutral trade in a particular war can only be determined by applying to its special conditions the general principle that neutral traders are bound to refrain from carrying to either belligerent any object intended to assist him in his warlike operations.

In the seventeenth century Grotius, the founder of the science of international law, divided articles of trade during war into three classes : (1) Articles exclusively or primarily used for war ; (2) articles susceptible of use in war as well as for purposes of peace; and (3) articles incapable of use in war. Following this classification, it has always been the Anglo-American practice [1] to divide contraband merchandise into two classes, of which the first comprises articles exclusively used for war, such as arms and ammunition, and also certain articles of double use, such as the necessary machinery and material for the manufacture of arms and ammunition and vessels and articles of naval equipment. These commodities are called ' absolute ' contraband, and any kind of hostile destination is sufficient for them. The second class comprises all other articles, such as foodstuffs and clothing, of use alike in peace and war. These commodities are called ' conditional ' contraband, and are only liable to seizure when they have a particular destination which indicates or suggests that they are meant for the use of the enemy Government or its armed forces ; for it is not permissible to employ the law of contraband for the purpose of putting immediate pressure upon the civil population. On the Continent, however, the tendency has been to repudiate the Anglo-American doctrine of conditional contraband, with the result that many things have been declared unconditionally contraband, such as foodstuffs, forage, cotton, coal, and railway material, which are required by the non-combatant population as well as by the military authorities and the Government.

The Declaration of London adopts the distinction

[1] The *Jonge Margaretha* (1799), 1 C. Rob. 189 ; 1 E. P. C. 100 ; the *Peterhoff* (1866), 5 Wallace, 28.

between absolute and conditional contraband; and Article 22 enumerates eleven classes of articles (including saddle, draught, and pack animals suitable for use in war, and clothing, equipment and harness of a distinctively military character) which may without notice (*de plein droit*) be treated as contraband of war, under the name of absolute contraband, when destined to territory belonging to or occupied by the enemy or his armed forces. It is immaterial whether the carriage of the goods is direct or entails tranship-ment or a subsequent transport by land ; [1] and when the ship's only or first port of call is an enemy one, or she is to meet the armed forces of the enemy before reaching the neutral port for which any suspected goods are documented, there is an irrebuttable presumption that the destination of such goods is hostile.[2] Articles exclusively used for war may be added to the list of absolute contraband by a declaration to be notified as provided in Article 23.

Article 24 enumerates fourteen classes of articles, including foodstuffs, forage, clothing, money, railway material, and fuel, which may without notice be treated as conditional contraband, and which are liable to capture if shown to be destined for the use of the armed forces or of a government department of the enemy State.[3] The burden of proving this destination is thrown, in the first instance, upon the captor ; but Article 34 provides that it shall be presumed to exist if the goods are consigned to either (1) enemy authorities ; (2) a trader (*commerçant*) established in the enemy country who, as a matter of common knowledge, supplies articles of the kind in question to the enemy ; (3) a fortified place belonging to the enemy ; or (4) any other place serving

---

[1] Article 30.   [2] Article 31 (2).   [3] Article 33.

as a base for the armed forces of the enemy. In this case, however, the presumptions are rebuttable, and the neutral owner is at liberty to show, if he can, that his goods are in fact intended for the civil population. As a result of Articles 35 and 36 the Declaration exempts conditional contraband from the doctrine of continuous voyage, except in cases where the enemy country has no seaboard ; but the matter was very hotly disputed at the Conference, and the British delegates only agreed to this provision as a contribution to the compromise between conflicting theories and practices.

Article 27 provides generally that articles which are not susceptible of use in war may not be declared contraband, and Article 28 specifies seventeen classes of commodities which are deemed to come within that category. Among these are included several articles, such as cotton, resin, metals, and paper, which have in particular cases been treated as contraband. In accordance with the universal practice it is also provided that articles intended for the use of the vessel in which they are found, or for the use of the crew and passengers during the voyage, may not be treated as contraband.[1] Articles serving exclusively to aid the sick and wounded are similarly exempted from treatment as contraband ; but in case of urgent military necessity such articles may be requisitioned, subject to the payment of compensation, if their destination is the same as that required for absolute contraband.[2]

CONTRABAND IN THE PRESENT WAR

Since the commencement of the present war several changes have been made by Great Britain and her Allies in the lists of contraband articles. The absolute list

[1] Article 29 (2).   [2] Article 29 (1).

now in force under the Proclamation of December 23, 1914,[1] contains twenty-nine items, among which are included iron, lead, copper, motor vehicles of all kinds and their component parts, motor tyres, rubber, mineral oils and motor spirit, except lubricating oils, sulphuric acid, range finders, submarine sound signalling apparatus, and sulphur and glycerine and various other ingredients of explosives. The conditional list is still almost the same as that in the Declaration, but hides and undressed leather have been included in it, and aircraft and barbed wire and implements for fixing and cutting the same have been transferred to the absolute list. Germany has added lead, copper, wood, coal-tar, sulphur, sulphuric acid, aluminium, and nickel to the list of conditional contraband. Great Britain has expressly disclaimed any intention to treat cotton as contraband.

The Orders in Council of August 20 and October 29, 1914, adopting the Declaration of London, both leave it to operate unchanged as far as concerns the destination of absolute contraband ; but, with regard to conditional contraband, the later Order in Council stipulates for an additional presumption of the hostile destination required by Article 33 if the goods are consigned to or for an agent of the enemy State. It is also stripulated that such contraband shall be liable to capture on board a vessel bound for a neutral port if the goods are consigned 'to order', or if the ship's papers do not show who is the consignee of the goods, or if they show a consignee in territory belonging to or occupied by the enemy. The application of Article 35 may be entirely excluded by notice with respect to any neutral country through which the enemy is shown to be drawing supplies for his armed forces. The special circumstances

---

[1] *London Gazette*, December 25, 1914.

of the present war, with the extraordinary opportunities which it offers to some neutral countries of becoming, on a scale hitherto unprecedented, a base of supplies for the armed forces of the enemy, make the adoption of strict rules with regard to the destination of conditional contraband absolutely imperative.

VISIT AND SEARCH

A neutral Government being, as we have seen, under no obligation to prevent its subjects from trading in contraband of war, it is essential to the maintenance of neutrality and the interception of the prohibited goods that a belligerent shall have the right to stop and search any neutral merchantman she may meet on the high seas or within her own or her enemy's territorial waters. The exercise of this right, owing to the size of modern vessels and the complexity of their cargoes, is one of the chief causes of friction between belligerents and neutrals ; but, unless the search is thorough, it is impossible for a belligerent to satisfy himself that cargoes and manifests correspond, that goods nominally consigned to neutral countries are not really destined for the enemy, and that contraband commodities are not being smuggled in by concealment or disguise. Under modern conditions searches at sea are practically futile. Whenever real ground for suspicion exists it is absolutely necessary to bring the suspected ship into port for examination. Otherwise, as stated in the British Interim Reply to the American Notes, the right of search itself ' would have to be completely abandoned '. In order to protect innocent traders as much as possible, it has always been the practice of British Prize Courts to award compensation to the neutral merchant by condemning the captor in damages and costs when he failed to make out any case against a prize brought in for carrying contraband, and there were no good grounds for the seizure.[1] Such a right to compensation is now expressly provided by Article 64 of the Declaration of London, which also extends to the case where the prize is released without any judgment being given.

Article 63 of the Declaration provides, in accordance with the established practice, that forcible resistance to the legitimate exercise of the right of stoppage and search shall involve in all cases the condemnation of the vessel. Hitherto Great Britain has always regarded the attempt to take advantage of the convoy of a warship of the neutral nation as equivalent to such forcible resistance.[2] By adhering to Articles 61 and 62, however, she has waived her right to search vessels so convoyed in the present war ; but so far no neutral Power seems to have made any use of this system. As an alternative an arrangement appears to be in process of negotiation with the United States of America whereby immunity from search will be secured for vessels which have obtained certificates as to the nature of their cargoes from British Consular officials or the United States Customs authorities.

Great Britain has always maintained that if, owing to inability to spare a prize crew, or for any other reason, a neutral prize cannot be brought in for adjudication to a port of the captor's State, she must be dismissed, and that no military necessity would justify her destruction.[3] But the practice of other States did not always follow this rule, and a limited but ill-defined right to destroy

---

[1] The *Ostee* (1855), 9 Moore P. C. 150 ; Spinks, 174 ; 2 E. P. C. 432.
[2] The *Maria* (1799), 1 C. Rob. 340 ; 1 E. P. C. 152.
[3] The *Actaeon* (1815), 2 Dods. 48 ; 2 E. P. C. 209.

neutral prizes is allowed under Articles 48 to 54 of the Declaration of London.   Under Article 44 a vessel not herself liable to condemnation may, when the circumstances permit, be allowed to continue her voyage if the master is willing to hand the contraband over to the belligerent warship.

THE PENALTY

In order to punish a neutral for trafficking in contraband of war, it is the established practice to allow a belligerent to confiscate the noxious articles he intercepts, after they have been condemned by a properly constituted Prize Court, and this penalty is confirmed by Article 39 of the Declaration.   In the case of conditional contraband, however, and also in the case of such absolutely contraband goods as are in an unmanufactured state and the produce of the country exporting them, it is the British practice to buy the goods (at an advance of 10 per cent. on the cost price) and to pay freight to the carrying vessel.   The Declaration of London makes no similar provision for pre-emption, but Great Britain is freely exercising this milder right in the present war.   She is also acting in accordance with Article 43 of the Declaration, which provides that when a vessel is encountered at sea while unaware of the outbreak of hostilities or of the declaration of contraband which applies to her cargo, or when the master, after becoming acquainted with these facts, has had no opportunity of discharging the noxious goods, the contraband can only be condemned on payment of compensation.

By the ancient law of Europe the penalty for engaging in contraband trade generally involved the forfeiture, not only of the contraband goods themselves, but also of the ship and any other articles, however innocent

their nature, found on board at the same time.. By the
end of the eighteenth century, however, it had become
the general practice to confine confiscation, in ordinary
cases, to the contraband merchandise alone and to the
freight due upon it to the neutral carrier, who suffered
no further penalty except the loss of time caused by the
detention and payment of the captor's expenses. But,
according to British prize law, the vessel carrying contraband was liable to condemnation if she belonged to
the owner of the contraband cargo ; if the carriage of the
articles on board was prohibited by a treaty with the
country to which she belonged ; if her owner was privy
to the carriage of the contraband goods ; or if she sailed
with false or simulated papers, or there were other circumstances amounting to fraud. The destruction or 'spolia-
tion' of papers also *per se* inferred condemnation, since it
raised a presumption that it was done for the purpose of
fraudulently suppressing evidence ; and, as we have seen,
a vessel was always subject to confiscation if she forcibly
resisted the captor. Innocent goods belonging to the
owner of the contraband on board the same vessel were
also condemned ; but similar articles belonging to
another shipper were released, though no compensation
was paid to their owner for the detention and loss of
market.

The American Prize Courts followed the same rules,
but continental Powers generally laid the criterion in
the proportion of the guilty part of the cargo to the
whole. After prolonged debates at the London Conference, it was decided to adopt the ' proportion ' rule in
the case of the ship, which, according to Article 40, may be
confiscated if the contraband, reckoned either by value,
weight, volume, or freight, forms more than half the
cargo. If she is released she may be condemned to pay

the captor's expenses.[1] For the innocent part of the cargo the British rule of similar ownership is adopted.[2] But the vessel and the remainder of the cargo are not liable to condemnation or to the captor's expenses when she is encountered at sea while unaware of the outbreak of hostilities or of the declaration of contraband applicable to her cargo, or if after knowing thereof the master has had no opportunity to discharge the offending articles.[3]

As a general rule, when the hostile destination has been reached and the forbidden merchandise delivered— in technical language, 'deposited'—the vessel is no longer liable to capture and the belligerent cannot seize her on the return voyage or touch the proceeds of sale of the contraband cargo. The Anglo-American practice recognizes an exception to this rule where the vessel has carried contraband on her outward voyage with false or simulated papers,[4] but Article 38 of the Declaration of London disallows capture on the return voyage under any circumstances. In the present war, however, Great Britain is adhering to her former practice, and the Order in Council of October 29 provides that 'a neutral vessel, with papers indicating a neutral destination, which, notwithstanding the destination shown on the papers, proceeds to an enemy port, shall be liable to capture and condemnation if she is encountered before the end of her next voyage '.

---

[1] Article 41.   [2] Article 42.   [3] Article 43.
[4] *The Margaret* (1810), 1 Acton, 333 ; 2 E. P. C. 311.

Oxford : Horace Hart Printer to the University

No. 8

OXFORD PAMPHLETS
1914

MIGHT IS RIGHT

BY

WALTER RALEIGH

THIRD IMPRESSION

Price Twopence net

OXFORD UNIVERSITY PRESS
HUMPHREY MILFORD
LONDON   EDINBURGH   GLASGOW
NEW YORK   TORONTO   MELBOURNE   BOMBAY

MIGHT IS RIGHT

It is now recognized in England that our enemy in this war is not a tyrant military caste, but the united people of modern Germany. We have to combat an armed doctrine which is virtually the creed of all Germany. Saxony and Bavaria, it is true, would never have invented the doctrine; but they have accepted it from Prussia, and they believe it. The Prussian doctrine has paid the German people handsomely; it has given them their place in the world. When it ceases to pay them, and not till then, they will reconsider it. They will not think, till they are compelled to think. When they find themselves face to face with a greater and more enduring strength than their own, they will renounce their idol. But they are a brave people, a faithful people, and a stupid people, so that they will need rough proofs. They cannot be driven from their position by a little paper shot. In their present mood, if they hear an appeal to pity, sensibility, and sympathy, they take it for a cry of weakness. I am reminded of what I once heard said by a genial and humane Irish officer concerning a proposal to treat with the leaders of a Zulu rebellion. 'Kill them all,' he said, 'it's the only thing they understand.' He meant that the Zulu chiefs would mistake moderation for a sign of fear. By the irony of human history this sentence has become almost true of the great German people, who built up the structure of modern metaphysics. They can be argued with only by those who have the will and the power to punish them.

The doctrine that Might is Right, though it is true, is an unprofitable doctrine, for it is true only in so broad and simple a sense that no one would dream of denying it. If a single nation can conquer, depress, and destroy all the other nations of the earth and acquire for itself a sole dominion, there may be matter for question whether God approves that dominion; what is certain is that He permits it. No earthly governor who is conscious of his power will waste time in listening to arguments concerning what his power ought to be. His right to wield the sword can be challenged only by the sword. An all-powerful governor who feared no assault would never trouble himself to assert that Might is Right. He would smile and sit still. The doctrine, when it is propounded by weak humanity, is never a statement of abstract truth; it is a declaration of intention, a threat, a boast, an advertisement. It has no value except when there is some one to be frightened. But it is a very dangerous doctrine when it becomes the creed of a stupid people, for it flatters their self-sufficiency, and distracts their attention from the difficult, subtle, frail, and wavering conditions of human power. The tragic question for Germany to-day is what she can do, not whether it is right for her to do it. The buffaloes, it must be allowed, had a perfect right to dominate the prairie of America, till the hunters came. They moved in herds, they practised shock-tactics, they were violent, and very cunning. There are but few of them now. A nation of men who mistake violence for strength, and cunning for wisdom, may conceivably suffer the fate of the buffaloes, and perish without knowing why.

To the English mind the German political doctrine

is so incredibly stupid that for many long years, while
men in high authority in the German Empire, ministers,
generals, and professors, expounded that doctrine at
great length and with perfect clearness, hardly any one
could be found in England to take it seriously, or to
regard it as anything but the vapourings of a crazy
sect. England knows better now ; the scream of the
guns has awakened her. The German doctrine is to
be put to the proof. Whô dares to say what the result
will be ? To predict certain failure to the German
arms is only a kind of boasting. Yet there are guarded .
beliefs which a modest man is free to hold till they
are seen to be groundless. The Germans have taken
Antwerp ; they may possibly destroy the British fleet,
overrun England and France, repel Russia, establish
themselves as the dictators of Europe—in short, fulfil
their dreams. What then ? At an immense cost of
human suffering they will have achieved, as it seems
to us, a colossal and agonizing failure. Their engines
of destruction will never serve them to create anything
so fair as the civilization of France. Their uneasy
jealousy and self-assertion is a miserable substitute
for the old laws of chivalry and regard for the weak,
which they have renounced and forgotten. The will
and high permission of all-ruling Heaven may leave them
at large for a time, to seek evil to others. When they
have finished with it, the world will have to be remade.

We cannot be sure that the Ruler of the world will
forbid this. We cannot even be sure that the destroyers,
in the peace that their destruction will procure for
them, may not themselves learn to rebuild. The Goths,
who destroyed the fabric of the Roman Empire, gave
their name, in time, to the greatest mediaeval art.

Nature, it is well known, loves the strong, and gives
to them, and to them alone, the chance of becoming
civilized. Are the German people strong enough to
earn that chance ? That is what we are to see. They
have some admirable elements of strength, above any
other European people. No other European army can
be marched, in close order, regiment after regiment,
up the slope of a glacis, under the fire of machine guns,
without flinching, to certain death. This corporate
courage and corporate discipline is so great and impressive a thing that it may well contain a promise for
the future. Moreover, they are, within the circle of their
own kin, affectionate and dutiful beyond the average of
human society. If they succeed in their worldly ambitions, it will be a triumph of plain brute morality over
all the subtler movements of the mind and heart.

On the other hand, it is true to say that history
shows no precedent for the attainment of world-wide
power by a people so politically stupid as the German
people are to-day. There is no mistake about this ; the
instances of German stupidity are so numerous that they
make something like a complete history of German international relations. Here is one. Any time during the
last twenty years it has been matter of common knowledge in England that one event, and one only, would
make it impossible for England to remain a spectator
in a European war—that event being the violation of
the neutrality of Holland or Belgium. There was never
any secret about this, it was quite well known to many
people who took no special interest in foreign politics.
Germany has maintained in this country, for many
years, an army of spies and secret agents ; yet not one
of them informed her of this important truth. Perhaps

the radical difference between the German and the English political systems blinded the astute agents. In England nothing really important is a secret, and the amount of privileged political information to be gleaned in barbers' shops, even when they are patronized by Civil servants, is distressingly small. Two hours of sympathetic conversation with an ordinary Englishman would have told the German Chancellor more about English politics than ever he heard in his life. For some reason or other he was unable to make use of this source of intelligence, so that he remained in complete ignorance of what every one in England knew and said.

Here is another instance. The programme of German ambition has been voluminously published for the benefit of the world. France was first to be crushed ; then Russia ; then, by means of the indemnities procured from these conquests, after some years of recuperation and effort, the naval power of England was to be challenged and destroyed. This programme was set forth by high authorities, and was generally accepted ; there was no criticism, and no demur. The crime against the civilization of the world foreshadowed in the horrible words ' France is to be crushed ' is before a high tribunal ; it would be idle to condemn it here. What happened is this. The French and Russian part of the programme was put into action last July. England, who had been told that her turn was not yet, that Germany would be ready for her in a matter of five or ten years, very naturally refused to wait her turn. She crowded up on to the scaffold, which even now is in peril of breaking down under the weight of its victims, and of burying the executioner in its ruins. But because England would not wait her turn, she is overwhelmed with accusations of treachery and inhumanity by a sincerely indignant Germany. Could stupidity, the stupidity of the wise men of Gotham, be more fantastic or more monstrous ?

German stupidity was even more monstrous. A part of the accusation against England is that she has raised her hand against the nation nearest to her in blood. The alleged close kinship of England and Germany is based on bad history and doubtful theory. The English are a very mixed race, with enormous infusions of Celtic and Roman blood. The Roman sculpture gallery at Naples is full of English faces. If the German agents would turn their attention to hatters' shops, and give the barbers a rest, they would find that no English hat fits any German head. But suppose we were cousins, or brothers even, what kind of argument is that on the lips of those who but a short time before were explaining, with a good deal of zest and with absolute frankness, how they intended to compass our ruin ? There is something almost amiable in fatuity like this. A touch of the fool softens the brute.

The Germans have a magnificent war-machine which rolls on its way, crushing all that it touches. We shall break it if we can. If we fail, the German nation is at the beginning, not the end, of its troubles. With the making of peace, even an armed peace, the war-machine has served its turn ; some other instrument of government must then be invented. There is no trace of a design for this new instrument in any of the German shops. The governors of Alsace-Lorraine offer no suggestions. The bald fact is that there is no spot in the world where the Germans govern another race and are not hated. They know this, and are disquieted ; they meet with coldness on all hands, and their remedy for the coldness is self-assertion and brag. The Russian states-man was right who remarked that modern Germany has been too early admitted into the comity of European nations. Her behaviour, in her new international rela-tions, is like the behaviour of an uneasy, jealous upstart in an old-fashioned quiet drawing-room. She has no genius for equality ; her manners are a compound of threatening and flattery. • When she wishes to assert herself, she bullies ; when she wishes to endear herself, she crawls ; and the one device is no more successful than the other.

Might is Right ; but the sort of might which enables one nation to govern another in time of peace is very unlike the armoured thrust of the war-engine. It is a power compounded of sympathy and justice. The English (it is admitted by many foreign critics) have studied justice and desired justice. They have inquired into and protected rights that were unfamiliar, and even grotesque, to their own ideas, because they believed them to be rights. In the matter of sympathy their reputation does not stand so high ; •they are chill in manner, and dislike all effusive demonstrations of feeling. Yet those who come to know them know that they are not unimaginative ; they have a genius for equality ; and they do try to put themselves in the other fellow's place, to see how the position looks from that side. What has happened in India may perhaps be taken to prove, among many other things, that the inhabitants of India begin to know that England has done her best, and does feel a disinterested solicitude for ·the peoples under her charge. She has long been a mother of nations, and is not frightened by the problems of adolescence.

The Germans have as yet shown no sign of skill in governing other peoples. Might is Right; and it is quite conceivable that they may acquire colonies by violence. If they want to keep them they will have to shut their own professors' books, and study the intimate history of the British Empire. We are old hands at the business; we have lost more colonies than ever they owned, and we begin to think that we have learnt the secret of success. At any rate, our experience has done much for us, and has helped us to avoid failure. Yet the German colonial party stare at us with bovine malevolence. In all the library of German theorizing you will look in vain for any explanation of the fact that the Boers are, in the main, loyal to the British Empire. If German political thinkers could understand that political situation, which seems to English minds so simple, there might yet be hope for them. But they regard it all as a piece of black magic, and refuse to reason about it. How should a herd of cattle be driven without goads? Witchcraft, witchcraft!

Their world-wide experience it is, perhaps, which has made the English quick to appreciate the virtues of other peoples. I have never known an Englishman who travelled in Russia without falling in love with the Russian people. I have never heard a German speak of the Russian people without contempt and dislike. Indeed the Germans are so unable to see any charm in that profound and humane people that they believe that the English liking for them must be an insincere pretence, put forward for wicked or selfish reasons. What would they say if they saw a sight that is common in Indian towns, a British soldier and a Gurkha arm in arm, rolling down the street in cheerful brotherhood?

And how is it that it has never occurred to any of them that this sort of brotherhood has its value in Empire-building ? The new German political doctrine has bidden farewell to Christianity, but there are some political advantages in Christianity which should not be over-looked. It teaches human beings to think of one another and to care for one another. It is an antidote to the worst and most poisonous kind of political stupidity.

Another thing that the Germans will have to learn for the welfare of their much-talked Empire is the value of the lone man. The architects and builders of the British Empire were all lone men. Might is Right ; but when a young Englishman is set down at an outpost of Empire to govern a warlike tribe, he has to do a good deal of hard thinking on the problem of political power and its foundations. He has to trust to himself, to form his own conclusions, and to choose his own line of action. He has to try to find out what is in the mind of others. A young German, inured to skilled slavery, does not shine in such a position. Man for man, in all that asks for initiative and self-dependence, Englishmen are the better men, and some Germans know it. There is an old jest that if you settle an Englishman and a German together in a new country, at the end of a year you will find the Englishman governor, and the German his head clerk. A German must know the rules before he can get to work.

More than three hundred years ago a book was written in England which is in some ways a very exact counter-part to General von Bernhardi's notorious treatise. It is called *Tamburlaine*, and, unlike its successor, is full of poetry and beauty. Our own colonization began with a great deal of violent work, and much wrong done to

others. We suffered for our misdeeds, and we learned
our lesson, in part at least. Why, it may be asked,
should not the Germans begin in the same manner, and
by degrees adapt themselves to the new task? Perhaps
they may, but if they do, they cannot claim the Eliza-
bethans for their model. Of all men on earth the German
is least like the undisciplined, exuberant Elizabethan
adventurer. He is reluctant to go anywhere without
a copy of the rules, a guarantee of support, and a regular
pension. His outlook is as prosaic as General von Bernhardi's or General von der Goltz's own, and that is saying
a great deal. In all the German political treatises there
is an immeasurable dreariness. They lay down rules
for life, and if they be asked what makes such a life
worth living they are without any hint of an answer.
Their world is a workhouse, tyrannically ordered, and
full of pusillanimous jealousies.

It is not impious to be hopeful. A Germanized world
would be a nightmare. We have never attempted or
desired to govern them, and we must not think that God
will so far forget them as to permit them to attempt
to govern us. Now they hate us, but they do not know
for how many years the cheerful brutality of their
political talk has shocked and disgusted us. I remember
meeting, in one of the French Mediterranean dependencies, with a Prussian nobleman, a well-bred and
pleasant man, who was fond of expounding the Prussian
creed. He was said to be a political agent of sorts, but
he certainly learned nothing in conversation. He talked
all the time, and propounded the most monstrous para-
doxes with an air of mathematical precision. Now it
was the character of Sir Edward Grey, a cunning
Machiavel, whose only aim was to set Europe by the

ears and make neighbours fall out. A friend who was
with me, an American, laughed aloud at this, and
protested, without producing the smallest effect. The
stream of talk went on. The error of the Germans, we
were told, was always that they are too humane ; their
dislike of cruelty amounts to a weakness in them. They
let France escape with a paltry fine, next time France
must be beaten to the dust. Always with a pleasant
outward courtesy, he passed on to England. England
was decadent and powerless, her rule must pass to the
Germans. 'But we shall treat England rather less
severely than France,' said this bland apostle of Prussian
culture, 'for we wish to make it possible for ourselves to
remain in friendly relations with other English-speaking
peoples.' And so on—the whole of the Bernhardi doctrine, explained in quiet fashion by a man whose very
debility of mind made his talk the more impressive, for
he was simply parroting what he had often heard. No
one criticized his proposals, nor did we dislike him. It
all seemed too mad ; a rather clumsy jest. His world
of ideas did not touch our world at any point, so that
real talk between us was impossible. He came to see
us several times, and always gave the same kind of
mesmerized recital of Germany's policy. The grossness
of the whole thing was in curious contrast with the polite
and quiet voice with which he uttered his insolences.
When I remember his talk I find it easy to believe that
the German Emperor and the German Chancellor have
also talked in such a manner that they have never
had the smallest opportunity of learning what Englishmen think and mean.

While the German doctrine was the plaything merely
of hysterical and supersensitive persons, like Carlyle

and Nietzsche, it mattered little to the world of politics.
An excitable man, of vivid imagination and invalid
constitution, like Carlyle, feels a natural predilection
for the cult of the healthy brute. Carlyle's English
style is itself a kind of epilepsy. Nietzsche was so
nervously sensitive that everyday life was an anguish
to him, and broke his strength. Both were poets, as
Marlowe was a poet, and both sang the song of Power.
The brutes of the swamp and the field, who gathered
round them and listened, found nothing new or unfamiliar in the message of the poets. ' This ', they said,
' is what we have always known, but we did not know
that it is poetry. Now that great poets teach it, we
need no longer be ashamed of it.' So they went away
resolved to be twice the brutes that they were before,
and they named themselves Culture-brutes.

It is difficult to see how the world, or any considerable part of it, can belong to Germany, till she changes
her mind. If she can do that, she might make a good
ruler, for she has solid virtues and good instincts. It
is her intellect that has gone wrong. Bishop Butler
was one day found pondering the problem whether
a whole nation can go mad. If he had lived to-day,
what would he have said about it ? Would he have
admitted that that strangest of grim fancies is realized ?

It would be vain for Germany to take the world ;
she could not keep it ; nor, though she can make a vast
number of people miserable for a long time, could she
ever hope to make all the inhabitants of the world
miserable for all time. She has a giant's power, and
does not think it infamous to use it like a giant. She
can make a winter hideous, but she cannot prohibit
the return of spring, or annul the cleansing power of

water. Sanity is not only better than insanity ; it is
much stronger, and Might is Right.

Meantime, it is a delight and a consolation to Englishmen that England is herself again. She has a cause
that it is good to fight for, whether it succeed or fail.
The hope that uplifts her is the hope of a better world,
which our children shall see. She has wonderful
friends. From what self-governing nations in the world
can Germany hear such messages as came to England
from the Dominions oversea ? ' When England is at
war, Canada is at war.' ' To the last man and the
last shilling, Australia will support the cause of the
Empire.' These are simple words, and sufficient ; having
said them, Canada and Australia said no more. In the
company of such friends, and for the creed that she
holds, England might be proud to die ; but surely her
time is not yet.

> Our faith is ours, and comes not on a tide ;
> And whether Earth's great offspring by decree
> Must rot if they abjure rapacity,
> Not argument, but effort shall decide.
> They number many heads in that hard flock,
> Trim swordsmen they push forth, yet try thy steel ;
> Thou, fighting for poor human kind, shalt feel
> The strength of Roland in thy wrist to hew
> A chasm sheer into the barrier rock,
> And bring the army of the faithful through.

Oxford : Horace Hart Printer to the University

WHY WE ARE AT WAR

GREAT BRITAIN'S CASE

BY MEMBERS OF THE OXFORD FACULTY OF MODERN HISTORY

E. BARKER.	H. W. C. DAVIS.
C. R. L. FLETCHER.	ARTHUR HASSALL.
L. G. WICKHAM LEGG.	F. MORGAN.

With an Appendix of Original Documents
including the Authorized English Translation
of the White Book issued by the
German Government

THIRD EDITION REVISED (NINTH IMPRESSION)
CONTAINING THE RUSSIAN ORANGE BOOK AND
EXTRACTS FROM THE BELGIAN GREY BOOK

TRANSLATIONS INTO FRENCH ITALIAN SPANISH
GERMAN AND SWEDISH ARE
NOW READY

Paper Covers Two Shillings net (70 cents)
Cloth Two Shillings and Sixpence net (85 cents)

OXFORD: AT THE CLARENDON PRESS
LONDON: HUMPHREY MILFORD
EDINBURGH   GLASGOW   NEW YORK   TORONTO
MELBOURNE   BOMBAY

(b)

OXFORD PAMPHLETS

1914

FOOD SUPPLIES IN
WAR TIME

BY

R. H. REW, C.B.

Price Twopence net

OXFORD UNIVERSITY PRESS
HUMPHREY MILFORD
LONDON EDINBURGH GLASGOW
NEW YORK TORONTO MELBOURNE BOMBAY

FOOD SUPPLIES IN WAR TIME.

For many years the British peop. have been warned by innumerable writers that in the event of war with a naval Power they ran the risk of famine and even of starvation by reason of the interruption of their overseas supplies of food. Only in July last one of our most popular novelists, in a vivid story, depicted the abject surrender of Great Britain to a small State after a war of about five weeks in consequence of the attacks of eight submarines upon vessels bringing food to our shores. Many people indeed were fully convinced that any interference with our commerce, even if it should be for only a few weeks, would reduce the whole population to dire straits.

It is quite true that we depend upon other countries for large supplies of food, and that the regularity of these supplies maintains prices at a moderate and uniform level in our markets. The precise extent of our purchases of imported food is not very readily stated. It is sufficient, as an instance of the difficulty, to cite the fact that although the whole of the £29,000,000 which we spent last year on corn and meal, other than wheat and flour, from abroad is commonly classed as food (as in a sense it is), when we are talking of food for direct human consumption it is clear that only a fraction of such grain as barley, oats, and maize should be regarded as foodstuffs in the ordinary acceptation of the term. In round figures it may be reckoned that about £200,000,000 per annum represents the amount spent on imported foodstuffs (excluding beverages) of all kinds which are consumed by man. If tea, coffee, and cocoa be added the total would be rather more than £220,000,000, being an average of about £4 15s. per head of the population.

The sources of supply are various and widely distributed. In 1913 they ranked roughly in order of value of shipments of foodstuffs to the United Kingdom as follows : United States, Argentina, Denmark, Canada, India, Australia, Russia, Netherlands, Germany, New Zealand, Austria-Hungary, France, Spain, Ceylon. From Germany and Austria-Hungary our receipts were nearly all sugar, and from Ceylon, tea. Wheat came principally from the United States, Canada, India, Argentina, Australia, and Russia ; meat (beef and mutton) from Argentina, Australia, New Zealand, and Uruguay ; bacon, pork, and hams from the United States, Denmark, Netherlands, and Canada ; rice from India ; sugar from Germany, Austria, Cuba, Netherlands, and Belgium ; butter and margarine from Denmark, Netherlands, Russia, Australia, Sweden, France, and New Zealand ; cheese from Canada, New Zealand, and Netherlands ; fruit from Spain, United States, France, Canada, Canary Islands, Costa Rica, Columbia ; tea from India, Ceylon, Java, and China ; cocoa from British West Africa, British West Indies, Netherlands, Brazil, and Switzerland ; coffee from Brazil, Costa Rica, Columbia, Guatemala, India, and Mexico. This catalogue shows only very superficially the extent of the area from whence the greater part of our supplies come ; smaller quantities are sent from many other countries. There is indeed scarcely any part of the world which does not in some degree contribute to the omnivorous appetite of John Bull. It is hardly necessary to observe that under normal circumstances in the multitude of competitors there is safety for the customer, and that even under abnormal circumstances there is a great advantage to the buyer that so many are in the habit of selling to him and may be presumed to be anxious to continue to do so.

One result of this world-wide competition to provide John Bull with the necessaries and luxuries of life is to make him very exigent in his demands. He is not content with a sufficient supply ; it must be of the kind which suits him. To take one of the commonest articles' —not so very long ago he liked nothing but China tea, now on the whole he insists on having Indian or Ceylon tea. He is a creature of habit, and grumbles extremely if he is forced against his will to change it even to the extent of drinking another kind of tea. He has been in the past probably the most pampered person in the world in his choice of food, and a little less diversity of selection for a time would do him no harm.

From the list of countries given above it will be noticed that we got no food supplies of importance from our enemies except sugar, for the maintenance of the supply of which the Government, as is well known, have made special arrangements. It may be added that we imported in 1913 from Germany potatoes to the value of £422,000, cocoa to the value of £246,000, and eggs to the value of £216,000. From Austria-Hungary we also received eggs to the value of £376,000. These amounts are an insignificant fraction of our total supplies. Not to overlook our latest enemy, it may be mentioned that we paid the Turk £305,000 last year for fruit.

It may be said therefore that the stoppage of trade with enemy countries does not in itself affect our normal supplies of food (with the exception of sugar) to any appreciable degree, as long as other purveyors for our markets continue to send their goods as before.

The public are not now justified in scoffing at 'alarmists'. Had some at least of the warnings given by sober and level-headed persons during the past ten years received more general attention, the nation might have been better prepared to meet the day of its supreme trial, and more ready to fight the great fight for existence in which it is now engaged. Where, however, so much that 'alarmists' have said has proved— at any rate as regards the designs and preparations of Germany—to be justified, it may be permissible to point out that the effect of the outbreak of the war on our food supplies has been far less than was confidently predicted by them. Some of the witnesses before the Royal Commission on Food Supplies stated that, assuming that our Navy was undefeated, the rise in the price of food here would still be enormous. The Royal Commissioners—who included the Prince of Wales, now His Majesty the King —themselves in their well-considered and circumspect Report summed up thus :

> We do not, therefore, apprehend that any situation is likely to arise in which there would be risk of the actual starvation of our population into submission. But we do regard with much concern the effect of war upon prices and especially therefore on the condition of the poorer classes ; for they will be the first to feel the pinch and it is on them that the strain of increased prices would chiefly fall. We do not, however, look with any great alarm on the effect of war upon prices, so far as concerns what we have referred to as the economic rise in prices, i. e. the increase likely to be produced by the enhanced cost of transport and insurance in time of war. . . . At the same time it seems to us that it would be unwise to disregard the dangers which might accrue from what we have

described as the ' panic ' rise of prices of staple articles of food, which might take place in the excitement sure to be caused by the outbreak of a great maritime war. No doubt the rapid spread of accurate information would tend to prevent any considerable duration of a rise due solely to panic, and we may assume that the greater the rise of prices the greater would be the exertions to pour in supplies. But it can hardly be doubted that much suffering would be caused if the rise in prices was sudden in its inception and more especially if it were to continue over any lengthened period of time ; and we cannot disregard the possibility that it might result in danger to calmness and self-possession, just when those qualities would be of greatest importance.

The effect on overseas supplies during the first three months—when a number of hostile commerce-raiders were at large and succeeded in doing a considerable amount of injury to our shipping—may best be shown statistically. In the following table the quantities of various kinds of foodstuffs reaching these shores during the three months August–October, 1914, are shown alongside the quantities received in the corresponding months of 1913 :

	Aug.–Oct. 1914.	Aug.–Oct. 1913.	Increase.	Decrease.
	cwt.	cwt.	cwt.	cwt.
Wheat and flour .	34,665,000	31,454,000	3,209,000	—
Rice . . .	1,223,000	882,000	341,000	—
Beef . . .	1,903,000	2,626,000	—	723,000
Mutton . .	784,000	1,115,000	—	331,000
Pigmeat . .	1,527,000	1,630,000	—	103,000
Butter and margarine . .	1,017,000	1,197,000	—	180,000
Cheese . .	783,000	734,000	49,000	—
Fruit (raw) and nuts . .	3,738,000	4,221,000	—	483,000
Tea . . .	864,000	1,206,000	—	342,000
Coffee . .	113,000	114,000	—	1,000

The reduced imports of fruit and nuts may fairly be attributed, in some degree at least, to the great crops of fruit in this country which, in fact, resulted not only in a glut on the markets but in absolute waste, while there were special circumstances due to the war, but not directly to the action of the enemy, which accounted mainly for the substantial diminution of the meat supplies. But it is to be noted that in total bulk the imports of these primary articles of food were larger by 1,500,000 cwt. during three months of war than during the corresponding period of peace. Some petulant persons still ask—What is the Navy doing ? This surely is a sufficient answer. Certainly the most optimist of pre-war prophets would not have ventured to predict that we should receive on the whole more food than usual from abroad during the first three months of warfare.

But, it will be truly said, there has nevertheless been a rise in the price of food, as of nearly all commodities. The rise has been to a comparatively slight extent directly due to the existence on the high seas of enemy cruisers and to the consequent risk of capture. After a short period of uncertainty the rate of insurance against this risk settled at about 2 per cent., which may be taken as the measure of the extent to which prices were affected by the existence of the hostile navies. Of greater effect on prices were the financial difficulties which for a time upset the delicate equilibrium of credit, and the dislocation of shipping arrangements in connexion with the transportation of troops with the consequent disturbance of the freight markets. Thus the freight on a ton of wheat from New York to Liverpool was quoted as 20s. 5d. on November 17 as compared with 8s. a year ago.

The Commission on Food Supply felt somewhat

nervous about the danger arising from a 'panic' rise of prices. There was a brief period at the outbreak of war when their anxiety seemed to be justified. Happily the nation as a whole kept its head, but among certain classes of the community there was a disgraceful rush for food. It was the worst episode of the war, and the lack of patriotism of those who took part in it might have caused serious national embarrassment had their example been widely followed. It is satisfactory to reflect that they had to pay for their selfish folly, and pleasing stories were told of shopkeepers being shame-facedly asked to take back, at reduced prices, the stores which had been purchased in a panic.

The retail prices of various commodities are affected by diverse conditions, and the rise which has occurred has differed in different localities—the difference being due not only to the ordinary causes, e.g. proximity to distributing centres, amount of active competition, rents, costs of distribution, &c., but also to some unusual causes, such as the concentration of troops and disturbance of railway facilities. The course of prices may, therefore, best be shown by the records of the wholesale markets, and I give a few figures, compiled from returns collected by the Board of Agriculture and Fisheries, showing the monthly averages of a few typical agricultural commodities in the form of 'index numbers', taking the month immediately prior to the outbreak of war as the base (100). Take first some figures of English live stock :

	July.	Aug.	Sept.	Oct.
Fat cattle—Shorthorns .	100	104	102	101
Fat sheep—Downs . .	100	106	103	103
Fat bacon pigs . . .	100	111	114	114
Veal calves	100	103	97	97
Fowls	100	97	89	89
Ducks	100	95	87	89

Compare these with prices from the dead meat
markets of home-grown and imported meat :

			July.	Aug.	Sept.	Oct.
English beef	.	. .	100	106	104	99
Irish beef .	. .	.	100	106	105	102
Argentine beef—frozen		.	100	142	147	144
Argentine beef—chilled		.	100	125	137	126
English mutton .	.	.	100	105	101	99
Australian mutton	.	.	100	122	133	134
Irish bacon .	.	.	100	122	121	110
Danish bacon	.	.	100	129	125	110

It is clear that, except in the case of pigs, the price of
English live stock has been very little enhanced by the
war, while poultry have fallen considerably in value.
The independent course taken by prices of commodities
which one would expect to be closely inter-related
appears curious. The markets for Irish and Danish
bacon are evidently sympathetic, and such difference
as is shown may be regarded as due to the fact that
the supply of the one had to cross the North Sea, and
of the other the Irish Sea. Perhaps there is nothing
which proves more conclusively the silent force of the
Navy than the simple fact that our supplies of bacon
and butter from Denmark have continued almost
uninterruptedly from day to day since the war began.
Six months ago probably every one would have accepted
as an axiom that in the event of war with Germany
our supplies of food across the North Sea, at any rate,
would at once be seriously depleted, if not altogether
stopped. Yet during more than three months our
supplies from Denmark and Holland have on the whole
been rather larger than usual.

The substantial rise in the price of meat from the
Argentine and Australia may be attributed to a combination of causes. They have been especially subject to
risk of capture, difficulties of finance and shipping have

been aggravated in their case, and in addition, there
has been an exceptional demand which could not readily
be met from any other source. The time has not yet
come to write an account of the difficulties which arose
in this trade, and of the steps taken to meet them, but
it is permissible to express the hope and belief that the
worst of them have been greatly reduced and will soon
disappear entirely, though the effect of an unusual
demand will, of course, continue.

Let us now look at the position of the staple foodstuffs
from the vegetarian point of view, and for that purpose
it will be sufficient to give wheat, flour, oats, oatmeal,
and rice, taking in the case of wheat the prices of British
and of the chief American grade, it being remembered
that the ordinary loaf is made of a blend of flour in which
imported wheat largely predominates :

	July.	Aug.	Sept.	Oct.
British wheat . . .	100	109	111	109
American wheat . . .	100	113	121	116
Flour—' Town Households ' .	100	123	131	126
British oats . . .	100	116	118	114
Scotch oatmeal . . .	100	149	139	133
Rice—Java . . .	100	115	120	119

I include oats as a foodstuff, as indeed they are,
especially north of the Tweed, but the market for them
is not in fact greatly affected by human consumption.
The price of Canadian oats rose greatly (by about
50 per cent.).

One other set of figures may be added :

	July.	Aug.	Sept.	Oct.
Irish butter . . .	100	115	108	114
Danish butter . . .	100	110	102	114
Cheddar cheese . . .	100	112	111	112
English eggs . . .	100	118	122	160

. These articles always rise in price during these months,
and as regards butter and cheese the increase shown is

about normal. Danish butter in September, indeed, had risen considerably less than usual. The rise in the price of eggs, large as it appears, is only about 12 per cent. more than usually occurs during this period of the year.

On the whole it may be said that the rise in food prices since the outbreak of war has not exceeded about 10 or 12 per cent., and that so far the much-dreaded ' war prices ' have been little, if any, more than a variation which might well occur, by failure of crops or other natural calamity, in time of peace. It is difficult to make accurate comparisons with former periods owing to the lack of continuous records for the same commodities, except in the case of wheat. Of corn prices there is a consecutive and fairly consistent record since 1771.[1] During the Napoleonic Wars the average annual price of wheat rose (in 1812) to 126s. 6d. per quarter, although it is true that in Waterloo year it was no more than 65s. 7d. After 1805 our command of the sea was undisputed, but our dependence on overseas supplies was small. Since then we cannot be said to have engaged in any war which seriously affected our food supplies, but the price of wheat rose in 1854 to 72s. 5d., and in 1855 to 74s. 8d., notwithstanding an excellent home crop in the former year, in consequence largely of interference with shipments from the Baltic during the Crimean War. These prices were not then regarded as extraordinary, and twelve years later (in 1867) the average price was 64s. 5d. It was, indeed, only in 1883 that the period of cheap wheat which the present generation takes as a matter of course began, and it may be regarded as practically certain that never again in the lifetime of any person now living will the price of wheat be so low for any considerable period.

[1] *Agricultural Statistics* 1913, Part III (Cd. 7487).

The extension of the world's wheat area has been for many years proceeding more rapidly than the growth of the world's wheat-eating population. At the present time economic prophecy is especially rash, but, apart from the immediate effects of the present war, it may be predicted with some confidence that the demand for wheat in the future is likely to keep pace with increasing supplies, and that the coming generation will probably on the whole have to pay more for its bread than the present has done.

We have seen that so far, with our fleet keeping the seas open, our food supplies have been maintained, and that such increase in price as has occurred has been due in the main to other causes than actual shortage. But the nightmare which has prevented many good people from sleeping quietly in their beds has been the dread of a naval reverse. 'No one,' they say quite truly, 'can be certain of victory. When the great battle of the North Sea is fought we believe we shall win, but if we lose shall we not, for a time, also lose the command of the sea ? We shall, of course, not give in, and our Navy in due time will recover, and in the end will be strong enough to vanquish the foe, but meanwhile he will for a time obtain command of the sea and will embrace the opportunity to stop our supplies and starve us into submission.' This sounds plausible, and no doubt it is commonly believed that a temporary stoppage of our supplies would bring us instantly to disaster. Conan Doyle thinks that five or six weeks would suffice, and Kipling expresses the same idea :

For the bread that you eat and the biscuits you nibble,
    The sweets that you suck and the joints that you carve,
They are brought to you daily by all us Big Steamers,
    And if any one hinders our coming you'll starve !

The notion that the British Isles can be beleaguered by any conceivable naval force so that no supplies can run the blockade is fantastic. I believe it is true to say that the annals of sea warfare contain no record of the blockade of any port so absolute that no ship got through. At any rate it is inconceivable that the long coast line of the British Isles, with its countless harbours and creeks, could be guarded so that many enterprising ships, stimulated by the certainty of big gains, would not succeed in landing supplies.

Let it be assumed, however, that an absolute blockade were possible, and that the British Isles could be as closely invested as was Paris in 1870-1, and for the same period, viz. about four and a half months. Let it be assumed also that the investment took place so suddenly and simultaneously that there was no chance to rush in supplies and that even ships on passage to the United Kingdom were all prevented from reaching our ports. Under these circumstances what would be our position, for how long could we live on the supplies of food in the country?

So far as bread is concerned there is at the present time sufficient wheat and flour in the country to supply the whole population, at its normal rate of consumption, for about four and a half months. It is true that at the end of that period we should have practically exhausted all the wheat in stock, except that reserved as seed for the next crop, which would only be drawn upon at the very last extremity. But if we had to live on our stocks, in this way, we should of course at once adopt measures to economize them. One simple and obvious expedient would be to make only 'standard' bread, i.e. bread made from flour which contains about 80 per cent. of the wheat-grain instead of only 68 or 70 per cent., as is the proportion in the flour ordinarily used. This would at once add about 10 per cent. to our wheat supplies, and the bread would be, from a nutriment point of view, more rather than less valuable.

Bread, however, can be made of other cereals than wheat. We have not in this country the alternative of rye, which furnishes the staple food of many millions of Europeans, but we have in stock at any given time nearly as much barley and more than as much oats as we have wheat. Barley bannocks and oatmeal cakes are not unknown in some parts of the country now, and they would go far, if the occasion required, to provide cereal food for the people. At least they would enable the supplies of wheat to be economized, and it may fairly be said that breadstuffs in one form or another could, if necessary, be found to supply the people for a twelvemonth. The total crops of the three chief cereals—wheat, barley, and oats—grown in this country supply a larger quantity of cereal food per head than is now eaten. We have taken no account of maize, which again is the staple breadstuff of millions of people, or of rice, of both of which there is always some stock in the country. It is therefore a very conservative statement to say that for a year there would be, if supplies were properly distributed, no reason why any one should go short of daily bread, even if nothing reached our shores. Of course if barley and oats were used for bread, live stock would go short and beer and whisky would be scarce, but the problem of live stock would to a large extent be solved by killing them and a deficiency of alcoholic beverages would have to be endured. It may be noted that we are self-supporting as regards potatoes. The average crop grown in the

United Kingdom is sufficient for our normal consumption, and although we import a certain quantity, largely from the Channel and Canary Islands, to enable us to forestall our own crop of early potatoes, the quantity is comparatively insignificant, and would be foregone without any serious deprivation.

Of meat we usually import about 36 per cent. of beef, about 42 per cent. of mutton, and about 46 per cent. of pigmeat (bacon, pork, &c.) consumed each year. The stocks in hand of these imported supplies at any time are not very large and would probably not last for more than a month under ordinary conditions. But in case of emergency there is, of course, the whole stock of the country to fall back upon. At the present time about 26 per cent. of the total cattle and about 37 per cent. of the total sheep in the United Kingdom are annually slaughtered. No doubt it would be wasteful to kill half-fattened or immature stock, but it is evident that, in the hypothetical state of siege, there would be no lack of meat for a very long period and no necessity to resort to horseflesh or other still stranger sources of meat supply.

It is clear, therefore, that for any such period as we are contemplating there would be no question of starvation, as there would be ample supplies of bread and meat. Nor would milk be lacking—so long as the cows were kept alive—for in this respect we are also self-supporting. Some kinds of fruit, such as bananas and oranges, would disappear from the markets, and onions would be somewhat scarce, but generally we should have a sufficiency of fruit and green vegetables, the latter especially being almost entirely home-produced.

It is not suggested that if the British Isles were beleaguered for four or five months there would not be much discomfort. The choice of food would be much restricted and dinner menus at the restaurants would present a very unusual aspect. Sugar and all the comestibles of which it is an ingredient would be scarce, and tea, coffee, and cocoa would become probably as expensive as champagne. All food supplies would probably be taken over by the Government and all those persons who ' live to eat ' would be extremely unhappy. But I think I have shown that to speak of ' starvation ' is a gross exaggeration, and that the country contains ample supplies of the necessaries of life to enable the whole population to exist on a fairly liberal diet for a considerable period. It may be noted also that I have taken no account of what may be termed the ' invisible ' supplies of such food-animals as rabbits, game, fish, &c., which in the aggregate would provide a substantial addition to the siege dietary.

The fact is that the nation has been too long obsessed by the wheat question. It is quite true that we produce in ordinary years only about one-fifth of our require-ments of wheat. But man does not live by bread alone, nor is bread necessarily made of wheat. The supplies of possible foodstuffs produced are very large. Under ordinary circumstances, as I have shown elsewhere,[1] we produce not one-fifth but about one-half of our daily food, while in case of necessity we have resources by which our ordinary dietary can be sufficiently supplemented for many months. That a stoppage of our overseas supplies for even a brief period would cause considerable discomfort is obvious, but in time of war the people have no right to expect comfort or to complain of dis-comfort. Whatever inconvenience or even hardship

[1] *An Agricultural Faggot*, P. S. King & Son, 1913.

might be caused, it is not true to say that if supplies of food from abroad are interrupted we necessarily starve. Just as if a hostile army landed we should fight for a long time before we admitted defeat, so if our shores were blockaded we could live for a long time before we submitted through hunger.

One word as to those who supply our home produce. For over thirty years I have been engaged in the service of British Agriculture, and during that time, as there are many records to prove, I have been a consistent believer in the capabilities and character of the British farmer. He has been, as I think and have often said, much maligned in the past. But he has never in my experience been so much maligned as he has been, in some quarters, during this time of national stress. The fate of the Empire, the future of the race, the lives and liberties of ourselves and our children are at stake, and it has been ignobly suggested that farmers think not of the nation's needs but only of their own pockets. I refuse to credit so gross a charge. The occupation of land, no less than its ownership, is a trust. Dr. Kelly[1] said of the Irish farmers : ‘ If they show a selfish policy in trying to use the land for their own benefit only, and to the detriment of national or neighbourly interest, or of the wider interests of humanity, then it would be the duty of the nation to step in and deprive them of that land, and to create some new system by which the land could be used for the benefit of the nation.’ Farmers, in my belief, will prove, in this crisis, not unworthy to be countrymen of those who are heroically defending British homes and hearths on the fields of Flanders. They will do their duty by working their utmost—often

[1] *The War and Ireland's Food Supply*, by the Most Rev. Dr. Kelly.

under grave difficulties—to maintain and if possible increase the produce of their farms, not because it is (as in fact it will be) profitable to do so, but because it is the desire, no less than the duty, of every Briton, each in his own sphere, to do his part to help his country in the time of her direst need.

Oxford: Horace Hart Printer to the University

1914

Crown 8vo. Separately, in paper covers. Also in series as numbered (I–VII), stiff covers, One Shilling net each series. 35 Pamphlets have now (25 November) been issued and others are in preparation. The historical pieces are illustrated by sketch-maps

I

1. The Deeper Causes of the War.
By W. SANDAY. 3d. net. *Fifth Impression.*
The psychology of Prussian militarism ; German public opinion and Germany's aggressive ambitions.

2. To the Christian Scholars of Europe and America: A Reply from Oxford to the German ' Address to Evangelical Christians '. 2d. net. *Fourth Impression.*
The answer of Oxford theologians to a recent manifesto of the German evangelical theologians. This manifesto, which is reproduced in the present pamphlet, argues that Germany is in no sense responsible for the present war. The Oxford reply states that the German theologians cannot have studied either the events which led up to the war or the political utterances of their own countrymen.

3. The Responsibility for the War.
By W. G. S. ADAMS. 2d. net. *Second Impression.*
A brief discussion of the question of responsibility : 1. Austria and Serbia ; 2. The responsibility of Russia ; 3. The intervention of England.

4. Great Britain and Germany.
By SPENSER WILKINSON. 2d. net. *Third Impression.*
Three letters to the *Springfield Republican* : 1. By Prof. Spenser Wilkinson, stating Great Britain's case ; 2. By Prof. John W. Burgess of the University of Columbia, stating Germany's case ; 3. By Prof. Wilkinson, in reply to Prof. Burgess.

5. ' Just for a Scrap of Paper.'
By ARTHUR HASSALL. 1d. net. *Fourth Impression.*
Explains why England stands for the sanctity of European treaty-law.

[d]

II

6. **The Germans, their Empire, and how they have made it.** By C. R. L. FLETCHER. 2d. net. *Fourth Impression.*
A historical account of Prussian policy from the seventeenth century.

7. **The Germans, their Empire, and what they covet.** By C. R. L. FLETCHER. 2d. net. *Fourth Impression.*
An account of the ambitions avowed by the Pan-German school.

8. **Might is Right.** By Sir WALTER RALEIGH. 2d. net. *Second Impression.*
Why Germany may win; what will happen if she wins; why we believe she will not win.

9. **Austrian Policy since 1867.** By MURRAY BEAVEN. 3d. net. *Second Impression.*
Austrian policy in the Balkans has been of the 'offensive-defensive' order. The Archduke Francis Ferdinand might have saved Austria from rushing to destruction; but 1912 was the beginning of the end.

10. **Italian Policy since 1870.** By KEITH FEILING. 2d. net. *Second Impression.*
Italian policy has been and must be guided by her own interests. The results of her colonial policy have not yet been satisfactory enough to tempt her into adventures.

III

11. **French Policy since 1871.** By F. MORGAN and H. W. C. DAVIS. 2d. net. *Fourth Impression.*
A historical sketch, discussing the question whether French policy has been aggressive.

12. **Russia: The Psychology of a Nation.** By PAUL VINOGRADOFF. 1d. net. *Fourth Impression.*
A reply to the German taunt that Russia is still in a state of barbarism, and is the enemy of European civilization.

13. **Serbia and the Serbs.** By Sir VALENTINE CHIROL. 2d. net. *Third Impression.*
A sketch of Serbian history, which is incidentally an indictment of the policy pursued by Austria-Hungary towards the Serbian kingdom.

14. **Germany and 'The Fear of Russia'.** By Sir VALENTINE CHIROL. 2d. net. *Third Impression.*
Shows that before 1879 Germany preferred Russia as an ally to Austria. The ambition of Germany to establish a protectorate over Turkey has led her to assist Austria in the Balkans and so to challenge Russia.

15. **The Eastern Question.** By F. F. URQUHART. 3d. net. *Third Impression*
The history of the Balkan nations; their future.

[d]

26. August, 1914: The Coming of the War.
By SPENSER WILKINSON. Stiff covers. 1s. net.

VII

27. The Retreat from Mons.
By H. W. C. DAVIS. 3d. net. *Third Impression.*

28. The Battles of the Marne and Aisne.
By H. W. C. DAVIS. 4d. net.
The Dispatches, with commentary, maps, &c.

29. The Navy and the War.
By J. R. THURSFIELD. 3d. net. *Second Impression.*
Estimates the military and economic value of the silent pressure exercised by our fleet, and warns the faint-hearted and the captious of the perils of lack of faith.

30. Bacilli and Bullets.
By Sir WILLIAM OSLER. 1d. net. *Fourth Impression.*
Calls attention to the fact that disease kills more men than the bullet. The most dangerous diseases are preventable by inoculation.

Published separately and will also appear shortly in series.

The Double Alliance *versus* The Triple Entente.
By JAMES M. BECK. 3d. net.
The judgement of a well-known American lawyer.

Thoughts on the War. By GILBERT MURRAY. 2d. net.
An article written in August and now reprinted.

The Leading Ideas of British Policy.
By GERARD COLLIER. 2d. net.
Examines the political genius of England.

Greek Policy since 1882. By A. J. TOYNBEE. 4d. net.

Poland, Prussia, and Culture.
By LUDWIK EHRLICH. 3d. net.
The author is a Doctor of the University of Lwow (Lemberg) in Galicia.

The Germans in Africa. By EVANS LEWIN. 3d. net.

What Europe owes to Belgium.
By H. W. C. DAVIS. *In the press.*

Spectator:—'These little books are easily the best books of the war—accurate, quietly written, full of knowledge, and quite unspoiled by vainglory or bitterness.'

Others in preparation.

HUMPHREY MILFORD
OXFORD UNIVERSITY PRESS, AMEN CORNER, LONDON, E.C.
[d]

17. 43

OXFORD PAMPHLETS
1914

DOES INTERNATIONAL
LAW STILL EXIST?

BY

SIR H. ERLE RICHARDS

K.C., K.C.S.I.

CHICHELE PROFESSOR OF INTERNATIONAL LAW

Price Twopence net ¹

OXFORD UNIVERSITY PRESS
HUMPHREY MILFORD
LONDON   EDINBURGH   GLASGOW
NEW YORK   TORONTO   MELBOURNE   BOMBAY

OXFORD PAMPHLETS
1914–1915

Crown 8vo. Separately, in paper covers. Also in series as numbered (I–X), stiff covers, One Shilling net each series. 49 Pamphlets have now (Jan. 1, 1915) been issued, and others are in preparation. The historical pieces are illustrated by sketch-maps.

Saturday Review:—'These little books are easily the best books of the war—accurate, quietly written, full of knowledge, and quite unspoiled by vainglory or bitterness.'

OXFORD UNIVERSITY PRESS
HUMPHREY MILFORD

LONDON   EDINBURGH   GLASGOW
NEW YORK   TORONTO   MELBOURNE   BOMBAY

OXFORD PAMPH'LETS
1914–1915

I

1. The Deeper Causes of the War.

By W. SANDAY. 3d. net. *Sixth Impression.*

The psychology of Prussian militarism ; German public opinion and Germany's aggressive ambitions.

2. To the Christian Scholars of Europe and America: A Reply from Oxford to the German 'Address to Evangelical Christians'.

2d. net. *Fifth Impression.*

The answer of Oxford theologians to a recent manifesto of the German evangelical theologians. This manifesto, which is reproduced in the present pamphlet, argues that Germany is in no sense responsible for the present war. The Oxford reply states that the German theologians cannot have studied either the events which led up to the war or the political utterances of their own countrymen.

3. The Responsibility for the War.

By W. G. S. ADAMS. 2d. net. *Second Impression.*

A brief discussion of the question of responsibility : 1. Austria and Serbia ; 2. The responsibility of Russia ; 3. The intervention of England.

4. Great Britain and Germany.

By SPENSER WILKINSON. 2d. net. *Third Impression.*

Three letters to the *Springfield Republican* : 1. By Prof. Spenser Wilkinson, stating Great Britain's case ; 2. By Prof. John W. Burgess of the University of Columbia, stating Germany's case ; 3. By Prof. Wilkinson, in reply to Prof. Burgess.

5. 'Just for a Scrap of Paper.'

By ARTHUR HASSALL. 1d. net. *Fifth Impression.*

Explains why England stands for the sanctity of European treaty-law.

[d]

II

6. The Germans, their Empire, and how they have made it.
By C. R. L. FLETCHER. 2d. net. *Fourth Impression.*
A historical account of Prussian policy from the seventeenth century.

7. The Germans, their Empire, and what they covet.
By C. R. L. FLETCHER. 2d. net. *Fourth Impression.*
An account of the ambitions avowed by the Pan-German school.

8. Might is Right.
By Sir WALTER RALEIGH. 2d. net. *Third Impression.*
Why Germany may win; what will happen if she wins; why we believe she will not win.

9. Austrian Policy since 1867.
By MURRAY BEAVEN. 3d. net. *Second Impression.*
Austrian policy in the Balkans has been of the 'offensive-defensive' order. The Archduke Francis Ferdinand might have saved Austria from rushing to destruction; but 1912 was the beginning of the end.

10. Italian Policy since 1870.
By KEITH FEILING. 2d. net. *Second Impression.*
Italian policy has been and must be guided by her own interests. The results of her colonial policy have not yet been satisfactory enough to tempt her into adventures.

III

11. French Policy since 1871.
By F. MORGAN and H. W. C. DAVIS. 2d. net. *Fourth Impression.*
A historical sketch, discussing the question whether French policy has been aggressive.

12. Russia: The Psychology of a Nation.
By PAUL VINOGRADOFF. 1d. net. *Fifth Impression.*
A reply to the German taunt that Russia is still in a state of barbarism, and is the enemy of European civilization.

13. Serbia and the Serbs.
By Sir VALENTINE CHIROL. 2d. net. *Fourth Impression.*
A sketch of Serbian history, which is incidentally an indictment of the policy pursued by Austria-Hungary towards the Serbian kingdom.

14. Germany and 'The Fear of Russia'.
By Sir VALENTINE CHIROL. 2d. net. *Fourth Impression.*
Shows that before 1879 Germany preferred Russia as an ally to Austria. The ambition of Germany to establish a protectorate over Turkey has led her to assist Austria in the Balkans and so to challenge Russia.

15. The Eastern Question.
By F. F. URQUHART. 3d. net. *Third Impression.*
The history of the Balkan nations; their future.

[d]

IV

16.. War against War.

By A. D. LINDSAY. 2d. net. *Fourth Impression.*

Denies that war is good in itself, or a necessary evil. National greatness, if founded on brute force, cannot endure. International law represents an ideal, but an ideal that may be realized.

17. The Value of Small States.

By H. A. L. FISHER. 2d. net. *Fourth Impression.*

The author argues that the debt of civilization to small states is incalculable.

18. How can War ever be Right?

By GILBERT MURRAY. 2d. net. *Fifth Impression.*

A well-known lover of peace and advocate of pacific policies argues against the Tolstoyan position. Right and honour compelled Britain to make war; and war—like tragedy—is not pure evil.

19. The National Principle and the War.

By RAMSAY MUIR. 3d. net. *Third Impression.*

Considers the principle of nationality and its application to the settlement of Europe—particularly of S.E. Europe—after the War.

20. Nietzsche and Treitschke: The Worship of Power in Modern Germany.

By E. BARKER. 2d. net. *Fifth Impression.*

An explanation of the main points of interest in the ethical and political doctrines of the German ruling classes.

V

21. The British Dominions and the War.

By H. E. EGERTON. 2d. net. *Fourth Impression.*

Explains the ideas for which the British Empire stands, and the political and moral issues of the war affecting the Dominions.

22. India and the War.

By Sir ERNEST TREVELYAN. 1d. net. *Fifth Impression.*

Discusses the reasons for the striking manifestations of Indian loyalty.

23. Is the British Empire the Result of Wholesale Robbery?

By H. E. EGERTON. 2d. net. *Second Impression.*

A historical sketch in answer to a common taunt.

24. The Law of Nations and the War.

By A. PEARCE HIGGINS. 2d. net. *Second Impression.*

The violation of Belgian neutrality and the conduct of England to Denmark in 1807; the doctrine of German lawyers that military necessity overrides the laws of war; the balance of power and the sanctity of treaties.

25. England's Mission.

By W. BENETT. 2d. net. *Second Impression.*

Answers the question, In what cause are we fighting?

[*d*]

VI

26. August, 1914 : The Coming of the War.
By SPENSER WILKINSON. Stiff covers. 1s. net.

VII

27. The Retreat from Mons.
By H. W. C. DAVIS. 3d. net. *Third Impression.*

28. The Battles of the Marne and Aisne.
By H. W. C. DAVIS. 4d. net.
The Dispatches, with commentary, maps, &c.

29. The Navy and the War.
By J. R. THURSFIELD. 3d. net. *Fourth Impression.*
Estimates the military and economic value of the silent pressure exercised by our fleet, and warns the faint-hearted and the captious of the perils of lack of faith.

30. Bacilli and Bullets.
By Sir WILLIAM OSLER. 1d. net. *Fourth Impression.*
Calls attention to the fact that disease kills more men than the bullet. The most dangerous diseases are preventable by inoculation.

VIII

31. The Double Alliance *versus* The Triple Entente.
By JAMES M. BECK. 3d. net. *Second Impression.*
The judgement of a well-known American lawyer.

32. The Germans in Africa.
By EVANS LEWIN. 3d. net.
A historical account of the German colonies.

33. All for Germany, or the World's Respect Well Lost. 2d. net.
'The conversation here imagined, between a new (and perhaps less naïf) Candide and a new (and perhaps less benevolent) Dr. Pangloss, is concerned with the political thoughts and ambitions entertained by the Germans of these latter days.'

34. Germany, the Economic Problem.
By C. GRANT ROBERTSON. 2d. net.
Estimates the strength and weakness of Germany's economic position, and inquires how long she can stand the strain of the war.

35. German Sea-Power.
By C. S. TERRY. 3d. net.
Traces the growth of Germany's navy. With a map of the North Sea.

[d]

IX

36. **What Europe owes to Belgium.**

By H. W. C. Davis. 2d. net.

Reminds us of the past achievements of the Belgian people in war and in peace.

37. **Poland, Prussia, and Culture.**

By Ludwik Ehrlich. 3d. net.

The author is a Doctor of the University of Lwòw (Lemberg) in Galicia.

38. **Turkey in Europe and Asia.** 2d. net.

The strength and weakness of the Ottoman Empire considered. The secular prestige of Constantinople, the religious prestige of the Caliphate, and the racial and economic weaknesses which may cause their downfall. A map shows the unfinished railways.

39. **Greek Policy since 1882.**

By A. J. Toynbee. 4d. net. *Second Impression.*

A historical account of the policy of Greece; the economic future of Greece; the problem of *Graecia Irredenta.* With a map.

40. **North Sleswick under Prussian Rule, 1864–1914.**

By W. R. Prior. 2d. net.

The policy of Prussianization and the resistance of Danish Nationalism. 'If the children do not understand German, they must be treated and taught like deaf-mutes' is quoted from a Prussian educational authority. A map shows the distribution of languages.

X

41. Thoughts on the War.
By GILBERT MURRAY. 2d. net. *Second Impression.*
Reprinted from the *Hibbert Journal* for October.

42. The Leadership of the World.
By F. S. MARVIN. 2d. net.
A discussion of German aspirations.

43. The Leading Ideas of British Policy.
By the Hon. GERARD COLLIER. 2d. net.
Places the principles of our policy in the perspective of history.

44. The War and its Economic Aspects.
By W. J. ASHLEY. 2d. net.
A comparison of Germany's and Great Britain's powers to stand the strain of a prolonged war. Probable effects of defeat or victory.

45. Food Supplies in War Time.
By R. H. REW, C.B. 2d. net.
An authoritative discussion by an expert who has been 'for over thirty years engaged in the service of British Agriculture'.

OXFORD PAMPHLETS

*Published separately and will also appear shortly
in series.*

Non-Combatants and the War.

By A. PEARCE HIGGINS.   2d. net.

States the rights and duties of the non-combatant population of a
territory under hostile occupation.

Troyon: an Engagement in the Battle of the Aisne.

By A. N. HILDITCH.   2d. net.

Scandinavia and the War.

By E. BJORKMAN.   2d. net.

Considers the policy and sympathies of the three Northern Kingdoms.

Asia and the War.

By A. E. DUCHESNE.   2d. net.

Describes German intrigue, and its failure, in Turkey, India, and
Egypt.

DOES INTERNATIONAL LAW STILL EXIST ?

I AM honoured by the invitation of this Union to address them on the subject of International Law. It is a subject which is attracting much attention at the present time, and deserves that attention. There are some who say that International Law has ceased to exist by reason of recent events ; on the other hand we see in our papers, day by day, appeals made to the law and issues raised as to whether this or that action of this or that belligerent is in accordance with law ; and that could not be done if in fact there were no law. I propose to-night to present to you some considerations on this point ; to tell you briefly what International Law is and what it purports to do, and then to ask you to consider to what extent, as a system, it is affected by this war. Legal matters are not always easy to explain in a popular way, but I will endeavour to make the main points as clear to you as I can within the limits of time at my disposal.

International Law is the law which regulates the rights and duties of States ; it defines their property, declares their mutual powers and privileges, and controls their relations and their dealings with each other. In time of war it is concerned in the first place with the respective

¹ An Address delivered to the Workers' Educational Union at Birmingham, December 2, 1914.

A 2

rights of belligerents—that is of the States actually engaged in the war, and of neutrals—that is of States who
take no part in it : in the second place it imposes limitations on warfare in the interests of humanity, and seeks to
protect non-combatants and private property in the area
occupied by an enemy force.   Among individuals, rights
and duties are regulated by the law of each particular
country : here in England we are under the control of
English law ; if we cross the Atlantic, we come under
the control of the law of the United States or of one of
the Republics of South America, and so forth.   But the
rights and duties of a State cannot obviously be left to
be determined by the legislative body of any other
State ; they are controlled by a common system of law
which applies to all States equally and is known as
International Law.

And to explain somewhat more fully what International Law claims to do, let me first say a word or two
about its origin and development.   As to its origin, we
need not go back for practical purposes further than
the seventeenth century.   Before that time the society
of European States was based on the supposition that
there existed a common superior who could secure order
among the community of States—Rome and those who
claimed to succeed to the power of Rome, the Pope
and the Emperor of the Holy Roman Empire.   And
in those conditions, as you will readily understand, the
necessity for any system of law was less apparent. As
long as a schoolmaster has control, no law is wanted,
save his will, to regulate the relations of his scholars.   But
about the time I have mentioned, and I am only dealing
with the matter broadly, this state of things came to an
end from causes to which I need not refer.   From that
time onwards there ceased to be any common superior

and the civilized world became a community of States, equal in all respects so far as concerned their rights and their mutual relations : from that time, consequently, it became essential to have some common laws, since without law there must be anarchy. This conclusion became accepted by the nations of Europe, but only as the result of some discussion. Two views were current : the first that each State was entitled to set its own advantage before any other end ; that it was not bound to consider the rights of other States, and that the necessity of any particular State was a sufficient justification for action taken by it ; in short, that if necessity compelled States were entitled to disregard obligations and to break their faith ; they were under no duty in regard to other States or to the community of States which could stand in the way of their advantage ; for since each State must be the judge of its own necessity, advantage was for all practical purposes the same thing as necessity. This is, put broadly, the doctrine with which the name of the Italian Machiavelli had become associated. The other view was that each State owed a duty to the other members of the international community which could not be displaced in this way ; that it was impossible for States to carry on mutual relations unless that was so, that there must be a law to regulate these relations, and that such a law was to be found in the precepts of the law of nature and of religion and in international usage. This law bound all States, and between States good faith was essential. Of this view the Dutchman Grotius was the chief exponent at the time. And it was this view which prevailed. The doctrine that necessity justifies the overriding of the law was explicitly rejected. Indeed it seems clear to us now that no society of States could continue to carry on mutual relations if any member of it was to be entitled to disregard all considerations other than those of its own advantage. Nor can any society of States exist unless faith be kept; for if promises are not to be binding, if pledges can be broken with impunity, there can be no real international intercourse. And there was another fact, too, which did much to convince the statesmen of the time that some International Law was necessary, it was the horrible cruelties and destruction inflicted by the warfare of that period. Between combatants some sort of restraint existed: there were codes of honour observed among the fighting men; there were rules of war more or less accepted between them, at least on some points. But there was little or nothing to restrain excesses in the treatment of non-combatants. The troops of an invading force lived upon the country through which they passed; they seized all cattle, foodstuffs and money, and left the peasants to die of hunger or to seek safety in flight. We read that the track of an invading army was marked by devastated fields, by smoking villages, by the corpses of the inhabitants done to death by the soldiers or perished of starvation. The public opinion of civilized nations had become shocked by these practices and was determined to put some check upon them. These, then, were the two main causes which brought International Law into being: the first the rejection of the doctrine of 'necessity' and the acknowledgement that some code of laws must be brought into being if the intercourse of nations was to continue; the second, the conviction that some restraint must be imposed on the excesses of warfare for reasons of humanity and civilization. I ask you to bear this history in mind, for it is not without a bearing on the position of International Law to-day.

From that time onward the existence of a law among

nations was recognized, and as time went on the rights
and duties of States under International Law became
gradually formulated with more and more precision.
The law was developed by the usage of nations, as established by precedent and in some cases by treaties, by
the dispatches of statesmen and by the discussions of
jurists.   And sometimes we have had law made by a
process which differs in nothing except in name from
express legislation.   We have had treaties making law.
Such, for instance, is the Hague Convention, of which
we hear so much nowadays : it is a treaty enacting and
declaring the law in regard to war and other matters.
Another instance is the Declaration of Paris.   And as
the law by these processes has become more definite, the
resort to law has become more frequent.   Nations have
more and more resorted to arbitration to settle differences
which in former days could only have been settled by
the sword : you may remember how the Alabama arbitration put an end to a dispute which had brought this
country almost to the brink of war with our friends
across the Atlantic ;   and lately a question of acute
difference between the same nations as to the fisheries
on the Canadian and Newfoundland coasts was settled
in the same way.   The habit of arbitration seemed
growing, and year by year the number of treaties by
which nations agreed to settle their differences by arbitration was increasing.   So that if you had asked me
to address you on the growth of International Law as late
even as last July, I should have told you that it was
strengthening its hold on the world year by year, and that
law was gradually displacing force in the settlement, at
least of some classes, of international disputes.   Then suddenly, almost without any warning, there breaks out the
greatest war history has ever known.   Greatest, because

of the number of the forces engaged, because of the range of hostilities, stretching as they do over every quarter of the globe, and because of the extent to which it has affected the commerce and the finance of the whole world. And that Great Britain has become involved in this war is due to the fact that her enemy has declined to be bound by International Law, and has asserted a claim to disregard legal principles, if it be advantageous to do so for military purposes. It is not too much to say that the action of Germany challenges the very existence of any law between nations. In particular it challenges the position of neutral States and the rights of small States to equality of treatment. Let us examine the effect of the war from this point of view.

We are discussing to-night the legal aspect of the matter ; it is not, therefore, necessary for me to dwell on the point which has been so much in controversy as to the responsibility for the war. The papers are before the public and you can judge. I would only suggest, in passing, that one good test by which to discover the originators is the state of military preparation in which the outbreak of war found the respective parties, for no sane government provokes hostilities unless it is prepared for them. The German Army was ready to march, and did march, over the frontiers of France and Belgium on the day on which war was declared, if not before : the British Army is not yet ready, and one has only to observe the feverish haste with which our recruits have been learning the most elementary movements of drill in every open space since war began, to satisfy oneself that the British Government, at any rate, could never have contemplated immediate hostilities.

Now the reason why this country has entered into the war is stated in the ultimatum delivered to Germany.

We have done so because Germany has violated the neutrality of Belgium, and that action raises a clear issue of International Law.

Belgium was a neutral State ; it was not concerned in the quarrel between Germany and France, and did not wish to take part in any hostilities between those States.   That being so, the law is clear, that neither belligerent had any right to enter on Belgian territory : and the law is equally clear that Belgium, so far as she was able, was bound to prevent the troops of either belligerent from coming into her territory.   If she had permitted that to be done, she would have taken sides with the belligerent whose entry she permitted, and by that very fact would have become an enemy of the other belligerent.

That being the undoubted law, Germany demanded a right of passage through Belgium ; and I ask you to think what this meant.   It meant that Belgium was to lend its territory as a cockpit in which the war could be fought out, for obviously if German troops passed through Belgium to attack France, the latter Power must be entitled to enter on Belgian soil to attack the German troops.   Further, it meant that Belgium must take sides against France.   If Germany won, then some compensation, assessed by Germany, was to be payable for damage as a matter of grace ; but if France won, then Belgium would be at the mercy of France, and subject to such penalties as France at her pleasure would impose.   This proposal has been called by the German Government a ' well-intentioned offer ', but I ask you could any demand more unreasonable be made ?   It was a gross violation of International Law in the matter of neutrality ; but it was more than that : it was an infringement of the principle of the law that all States have equal rights.   No such demand could ever have been addressed to a powerful State : it was addressed to Belgium because her powers of resistance were known to be limited, her army was small, her resources not large. Such a precedent, if it were to be once established, would mean that States are to enjoy rights only in proportion to the strength of their military forces. It is a denial of the cardinal principle of International Law that all States have equal rights.

So far I have dealt with the breach of Belgian neutrality as a matter resting on the common law of nations, and the illegality of the action of Germany is clear beyond doubt on that ground. But the matter does not rest there. Belgium is in an exceptional position. Her neutrality does not depend only on her rights at common law : it has been guaranteed by express treaty to which Germany and Great Britain are both parties, a treaty made in 1839 and acknowledged as continuing in 1870. Here, then, is another breach of law, and more than that, a breach of good faith. Germany is expressly pledged to treat Belgium as neutral : she has broken that pledge : she has violated the law and her honour. And this point as to the treaty is important, because it is the reason why Great Britain has been compelled to take part in the war. The nations of the world are all concerned at the violation by Germany of the common law of neutrality ; but it can hardly be expected, as things are at the present, that nations will make war merely to impose the observance of law when they are not themselves affected in any particular respect by the breach. It may be that in time to come neutrals will take a higher view of their obligations and be willing to assist in preventing or punishing flagrant breaches of the law, in order to make the law more effective ; but that time is not yet, and no complaint can be made if neutrals have allowed the breach to

pass without effective remonstrance. Great Britain, however, is in a different position : she stands bound by the
express provisions of this treaty to maintain the neutrality of Belgium, and unless she be prepared to break
her faith she must give effect to that obligation.

Now what is the defence of Germany ? We have it
before us. The illegality is admitted, but it is sought
to excuse it. And first as to the treaty, it is said to
be a scrap of paper and of no account. I need not
stop to discuss such a suggestion. The question is of
the breach of a formal promise : the evidence of that
promise may be a scrap of paper, or it may be the
testimony of thóse who heard the oral communication
in which it was made : that matters not : the point is
that a promise was given and has been broken. Is
there to be no good faith among nations ? is there to
be no trust in pledges ? That excuse comes to nothing.
But then it is said that military necessity compelled
the action of Germany. There are a few exceptional
cases in which necessity, instant and urgent, may be
a justification for action in self-defence, which would
otherwise be contrary to law, but no such case arose
here. The necessity alleged is that France was about
to make an attack on Germany through Belgium, and
that it was necessary to anticipate this by a counter-
movement. But the fact on which this plea must rest
is not established ; on the contrary, France had given
a formal undertaking not to move troops into Belgium
unless Germany first did so, and Germany knew of that
undertaking before she took any action, and had herself
been asked and refused to give any similar undertaking,
with a like qualification. And there is other evidence
which disproves the suggestion. The strategic railways
of Germany and her military dispositions show that

she had for long intended to attack France through Belgian territory. In truth the motive was military advantage : not military necessity. Military advantage may be, in one sense, a necessity for a State, because it is, in one sense, necessary for the State to succeed in war, but that is not the kind of necessity which alone can justify any departure from the law : if that were so there could be no law, for any belligerent could plead necessity as great as that on which Germany relies in the present case. This excuse of necessity is really nothing more than the old plea that a State can override law when it sees an advantage in doing so ; but it is serious because it is no new thought adopted under the pressure of the moment : it has for some time past been adopted and defended by leading publicists in Germany. They argue, to put the matter in a sentence, that reasons of war override its ordinary rules. Now I ask you to note what that proposition must come to. It must come to this, that no laws are to stand in the way of military advantage. As the late Professor Westlake has well put it, the instructions to generals, according to these writers, must be, 'Succeed—by war according to its laws if you can—but at all events, and in any way, succeed.' The only result which can follow is the abolition of all law.

And that this view, that necessity overrides law, is the one on which the German military and naval authorities have acted seems to be confirmed by their general disregard of the restraints imposed by law in other grave matters, such, for instance, as the rights of neutrals on the high seas or the position of non-combatants in enemy towns or in the territory occupied by the German forces.

Take the case of the mines placed by Germany in the high seas. You know that the ships of all nations have at all times the right to navigate the high seas, which are open equally to them all. In time of war belligerents have the right to prevent neutrals from carrying contraband, or from carrying goods to a port which has been declared under blockade in accordance with the laws which regulate blockade. But apart from these and some other possible restrictions as to particular areas which do not arise in the present connexion, the use of the high seas cannot. be interfered with. That is the law. But Germany in this war claims the right to anchor mines in any part whatever of the high seas, or to set adrift there floating mines over which she has no control ; and she has strewn the seas with mines of the one or the other kind. The result has been the destruction of neutral vessels and the extermination of their crews. Germany claims this as a necessary part of her military operations, but it is a new claim, and it is altogether contrary to the principles of law heretofore accepted by humanity. Nor is the offence only against neutrals, for the mines may destroy enemy merchant vessels as well. There is no right to do this unless the crew and passengers be first removed to a place of safety. Again, hospital ships are immune from seizure, but the German mines will sink them with their cargo of wounded. This claim again involves departure from law. So far the only neutrals affected have been small Powers—Denmark, Norway, and Sweden ; and Germany has disregarded their protests because they have not the power to enforce them. Italy remonstrated with Austria forthwith when one of her vessels was blown up by an Austrian mine, and obtained an immediate undertaking that this should not occur again. But Italy is a powerful neutral, whose good graces Austria must sue for. Great Britain has in these last weeks herself placed mines in the high seas, but these are anchored, the position of the mine-field is notified, and neutral vessels can pass through safely on taking a British pilot. There is no harm to neutrals in this.

Take, again, the dropping of bombs on the civilian quarters of great cities. The law permits bombardment of the inhabited portions of a city, but only as part of a siege and after notice has been given, so that the inhabitants may seek shelter. The claim of Germany is to drop bombs without warning on the non-combatants and not as part of siege operations, but simply in order to terrorize them. This, again, is contrary to law and to humanity.

Take the treatment of the civilian population in Belgium. There have been many grave charges made against the German soldiers; but these are for the most part denied, and we must wait until the evidence on both sides is made public before we form a judgement upon them. But put aside allegations of particular outrages, and look at the general treatment of non-combatants. Consider the large number of civilians put to death, and in most cases not for any offence of their own but merely as a warning to others; the oppressive capture and treatment of hostages; the seizure of all foodstuffs irrespective of the wants of the population; the huge fines levied on captured towns; the general destruction of property. All these matters show an excess which cannot be justified on any view of the law. The burning of Louvain and the execution of many of its inhabitants, to take one particular case, is altogether incapable of defence; no misconduct by the inhabitants can be made out sufficient to justify such wholesale destruction, and the evidence goes to show that no one of the various and conflicting justifications which have from time to time been put forward can be established in fact. And there are other cases equally grave. In my judgement nothing can justify the excessive severity of the general treatment of the Belgian non-combatants.

All these things, we are told, are necessary military measures. It is ' necessary ' to break faith and disregard the law of neutrality : it is ' necessary ' to destroy neutral ships and drown their passengers and crews : it is ' necessary ' to frighten the enemy government by dropping bombs without warning on residential quarters of great towns : it is ' necessary ' to make frightful examples of non-combatants. But necessity of this kind, which overrides law, is incompatible with the existence of any law at all : it must result in never-ending strife and war. Let me put a homely illustration. Suppose you have a house and a garden. It is enough for you and your wife when you marry ; but as time goes on a family arrives and increases, and the accommodation is no longer sufficient. On the other side of the wall is another house and garden which would suit your increased wants. It is ' necessary ' for you, in your opinion, to have something of the kind ; therefore you are entitled to pull down the wall and seize the premises, and if the owner objects to put an end to him. How can a society of men or of States proceed at all on this basis ? Have we not really got back to the seventeenth century and to the ideas which were rejected, and, as we hoped, rejected for ever, at that time ? Is this new doctrine anything more in its essence than that of Machiavelli ? The destruction of Belgium to-day is less general than that of the countries which were devastated by the wars of the seventeenth century, but it is still deplorable and shocks humanity as much

as did the warfare of those times. It is surely time for
the nations of the world again to declare that there must
be an International Law, and that the excesses of war
must be restricted in the interests of civilization !

Now, assuming that I am right in thinking that
Germany has disregarded the law of nations, then what
is the result ? Can the law enforce any penalty ? If it
cannot, then to that extent it is held to be ineffective.
Individuals who offend against the laws are punished
by legal process, criminal or civil ; but it is the weakness
of International Law that it has no sanction of this
kind ; there are no police to keep order, there are no
courts empowered to enforce punishment unless an offender submits to them. But between individuals there is
another force which can punish, and is a force of great
power in many cases. That force is the opinion of others.
The man who breaks his faith, or the man who commits
acts of cruelty, is condemned by the judgement of his
fellows ; at the worst he is banished from the society
of respectable persons. And in International Law we
have the same sanction in public opinion. The only
penalty for breach of International Law, beyond such
redress as the injured party may be powerful enough
to obtain by force, is the loss of the good opinion of
other nations.

That sanction seems ineffective enough at the present
moment, but there are signs of hope. We have to face
a peculiar position in this war, because the public opinion
that approves or condemns must be the opinion of
neutral States : belligerents cannot pronounce in their
own cause. And in this war the greater States of Europe
are themselves involved. There are, however, a number
of neutral States which together are a force ; and there
is one great Power across the Atlantic which can of

itself make its judgement felt. The fact that Germany has thought it in her interests to make strenuous efforts to obtain the good opinion of neutral States, and especially the United States, is a portent full of hope, and the more so because the United States have ever been foremost in the development of International Law. For these reasons, because it is impossible for international intercourse to be continued unless law be observed, and unless it be recognized that every State has a duty to the other members of the community of States, and because public opinion is shown to be some check even in the darkest days, I affirm confidently that International Law does still exist, and I anticipate that after the end of this war it will stand on a more secure footing than before. We cannot yet hope that nations will dispense with armaments : we have had too sharp a lesson to allow us to rely altogether on treaties or agreements, at least for some time to come ; but we can hope that at the end of the war the public opinion of the world will declare in no uncertain tones that the clear principles of the law must never again be set aside as of no account, and that among nations, as among men, good faith must be observed.

Oxford : Horace Hart Printer to the University

WHY WE ARE AT WAR
GREAT BRITAIN'S CASE

BY MEMBERS OF THE OXFORD FACULTY OF MODERN HISTORY

E. BARKER. H. W. C. DAVIS.
C. R. L. FLETCHER. ARTHUR HASSALL.
L. G. WICKHAM LEGG. F. MORGAN.

With an Appendix of Original Documents including the Authorized English Translation of the White Book issued by the German Government

THIRD EDITION REVISED (TENTH IMPRESSION) CONTAINING THE RUSSIAN ORANGE BOOK AND EXTRACTS FROM THE BELGIAN GREY BOOK

TRANSLATIONS INTO FRENCH ITALIAN SPANISH GERMAN DANISH AND SWEDISH ARE NOW READY

Paper Covers Two Shillings net (70 cents)
Cloth Two Shillings and Sixpence net (85 cents)

OXFORD: AT THE CLARENDON PRESS
LONDON: HUMPHREY MILFORD
EDINBURGH   GLASGOW   NEW YORK   TORONTO
MELBOURNE   BOMBAY

(a)

¹⁵ 44

OXFORD PAMPHLETS
1914

GERMANY
THE ECONOMIC PROBLEM

BY

CHARLES GRANT ROBERTSON

FELLOW OF ALL SOULS COLLEGE

Price Twopence net

OXFORD UNIVERSITY PRESS
HUMPHREY MILFORD
LONDON   EDINBURGH   GLASGOW
NEW YORK   TORONTO   MELBOURNE   BOMBAY

GERMANY AND THE ECONOMIC PROBLEM

SINCE war was declared between Great Britain and Germany no assertion has been more generally heard than the prediction that ' the economic strain ' would, if nothing else, break down the capacity of the German Government and nation to maintain the struggle. What precisely this ' economic strain ' would be and in what forms it would convincingly reveal itself was not always made clear, even by those who most confidently made the assertion. But as commonly used it may be presumed to imply, first, that the financial resources of the German Government would not prove equal to the drain and expenditure of a war on two fronts and at sea, prolonged beyond six or eight months.; secondly, that the economic and industrial organization and resources of Germany were of such a character as gradually to collapse under the remorseless pressure of war ; thirdly, that German trade and commerce would be practically ruined by the conditions of war ; and fourthly, that in all these respects Great Britain was markedly superior—her wealth greater, her resources larger and more elastic, her industrial organization and commerce less vulnerable.

Are these assumptions, axiomatic to many British minds, approximately sound ? Is an economic and financial collapse in Germany to be expected ? If so, when will it come ? Can Great Britain reasonably infer that she can stand better than Germany the tremendous economic strain of this unparalleled war ?

It is worth remarking that a view, directly opposite to that commonly held in Great Britain, has been expressed between 1907 and 1913 by several German experts, notably Dr. Riesser, Dr. Steinmann-Bucher, and others, who have devoted much labour and research to an analysis of Germany's economic resources and organization.   They hold that Germany is better organized for war on the commercial and financial side ; that Germany would conduct a great war more economically ; and that a violent and widespread interruption of the machinery of international exchange, finance, and trade would hit Great Britain harder than it would hit Germany.   But it is also worth remarking that their calculations seem to rest on a comparatively short war (i. e. not prolonged beyond six or eight months), and do not make sufficient allowance for the results produced by a war of twelve or even eighteen months.   Nor do they sufficiently allow for the gigantic and unparalleled proportions and the political and military features of the present war.

Unparalleled in its economic features the present war certainly is.   The territorial area of the belligerent States, the volume of industry and commerce directly affected, the areas on land that are the theatre of military operations, the magnitude of the armies involved, the world-wide extent of the naval operations, the expensiveness of modern armaments, the rapidity with which those armaments are used up, the strain on the belligerent States to equip and maintain their armies in the field, combine to provide an economic problem to which no parallel exists in the history of the world.   Six out of seven of the great monetary centres of finance—

London, Paris, Berlin, Petrograd, Vienna, Brussels—
are directly involved. New York, the seventh, as the
capital of a neutral Power alone is not touched, and
New York without the free working of the other six is
practically paralysed. The moratorium that was proclaimed throughout the civilized world last August, and
the closing of the Stock Exchanges, in order to avoid
a general financial cataclysm, bear eloquent testimony
to the violence and widespread havoc that the war at
once produced and is continuing to produce. The
volume of commerce and trade of the belligerent States,
directly affected by war conditions, amounts to 70 % of
the trade of the whole world. Only 30 %, i.e. barely
one-third of the production and exchange of goods by
mankind, belongs to neutral States. And of the mercantile marine of the world engaged in the transport
of goods across the seas, about 80 % belongs to belligerent States, and must work under the conditions
imposed by war.

Any and every estimate of the degree of economic
strain for any particular belligerent State must necessarily be both rough and hypothetical—rough because
our information and our data for calculations cannot
be statistically precise, hypothetical because speculation
as to the duration of the war has to reckon with unforeseen and unforeseeable military or political developments that may revolutionize the general situation.

For clearness' sake I propose to examine the economic
problem as it may affect Germany and Germany's
resources alone, and to assume throughout that the
present naval conditions will broadly continue. It is
desirable also to separate at the outset two different
propositions and conclusions which are frequently confused : first, the general economic exhaustion and disloca-

tion or ruin of her trade which Germany may ultimately
have to face as the broad result of the war ; and, secondly,
the immediate effect on her economic resources *while the
war lasts* and on her capacity in consequence of this direct
effect to find the means to wage war. For, even if we
make the extreme assumption that ' the war will ruin
Germany's trade and commerce ', that Germany will
emerge from it a mere ghost of her former economic self,
and that a generation may pass before her productive
powers and shattered economic organization are restored
to the normal level, say, of 1913, ultimate ruin will not
of itself mean present incapacity to wage a long war.
Nations, like individuals, may ruin themselves in a
gigantic effort.   Ultimate exhaustion is no sure basis
for inferring incapacity both to make and prolong a
great struggle for a very considerable time.   It is far too
commonly assumed amongst ourselves that the mere
loss of trade on a large scale by Germany will rapidly
be a decisive factor.   We do not sufficiently distinguish
between the ultimate and total cost and its effects, and
the immediate cost and its effects, of war.   The whole
bill, of course, has to be paid in the long run.   But the
capacity of a nation to wage war and to continue to
wage it, primarily turns on its capacity to meet the
bill and the drain on its resources of the moment,
governed by the conditions of the moment, not of the
future governed by the conditions of the future. Broadly,
then, the cost of war and the capacity of a nation
to meet it may be analysed under three main heads :
(1) the money cost of carrying on the military and naval
operations required (i.e. the equipment and maintenance of the armies and fleets and the armaments) and
the material capacity to feed and clothe the non-
combatant population and maintain the industries

necessary for the armies and·fleets, and the feeding
and clothing of the population as a whole ; (2) the cost
(conveniently reckoned in money cost) of the pre-
existing wealth and fixed or circulating capital (build-
ings, crops, live-stock, mineral resources, &c.) destroyed
by the military operations ; (3) the loss of human producing power represented by the number of men killed
in battles and by disease or permanently crippled.

The first is obviously of the most immediate importance. For unless the losses under (2) or (3) are of such
a character as directly and immediately to cripple the
nation's material resources for war they can be primarily
ignored. A nation that cannot provide the numbers of
men required admittedly cannot continue to make war.
Similarly, if a nation as the result of military operations
found itself deprived of the raw material directly
necessary for equipping or maintaining its armaments,
or of the food-stuffs for feeding the soldiers or the non-
combatant population, or if the destruction of wealth or
capital were so large or of such a kind as to bring this
about, that nation would be ' starved ' into making
peace. Great Britain, for example, deprived of the
command of the seas, simply could not continue the
war. A Germany deprived of coal, iron-ore, copper,
oil, even if she had the food and the men, could not
continue the war. The ' economic strain ' would in
each case be decisive. But unless the elements reckoned
under (2) and (3) are of this decisive character, the
amount and volume of the loss to be reckoned subsequently under these heads will be imperceptible at first,
and will be very gradual in its depleting and crippling
effect. Ultimately they will figure in the total bill of
cost and may reach gigantic figures and produce no less
gigantic results ; but the destruction of pre-existing

wealth and of capital will not necessarily nor need for a long time be a factor to be reckoned with in estimating capacity to bear the cost of a war, particularly in the case of a very wealthy country such as Germany. And it is worth noting that as a fact, in the case of Germany as of Great Britain, the losses placed under (2) as above have not so far been really serious. Germany has lost a large number of her mercantile ships ; she has suffered invasion in some of her colonies and settlements; but her territories in Europe have been practically free from invasion. The Russian invasion of East Prussia in August was short, and the damage has been calculated at not more than £20,000,000. Germany has waged war in Poland, Belgium, and France, and the terrible destruction of wealth (i. e. of fixed or circulating capital) in the areas of military operations has fallen wholly on Russia, France, and Belgium. How far this state of things will continue is at present a military rather than an economic question. It is sufficient to note that so far the damage suffered by Germany is practically insignificant. It has not in any way affected her economic capacity to ' go on '. Nor are there at present any trustworthy indications that the losses--in the battle-field or the numbers employed in her huge armies have weakened her power to maintain the industries employed in arming, feeding, and clothing the troops or feeding and clothing the civil population. Unemployment, widespread dislocation of production and distribution there certainly are, but there is no evidence that either is on a scale to cripple Germany's resources in these respects. The harvest has been gathered in and stored ; as far as we can judge, German organization has seen to it that there will be a harvest in 1915. The vast armies have not prevented the shipyards or Krupp's works at Essen, and the clothing factories in Saxony, working at high pressure. The mines are producing their raw material and the railways have the material and the labour requisite to work with organized efficiency. If, in short, ' the economic strain ' is going to cripple Germany, it must be sought elsewhere than in the casualty lists and the destruction of wealth and capital. Moreover, up till now France and Russia have both suffered as heavily as Germany in the casualty lists and far more heavily than Germany in the destruction of pre-existing wealth. Great Britain, it is true, is more fortunate. She has suffered in both respects less, far less so far, than her major allies, and far less than her major opponent.

We come back, therefore, to the losses under our first heading and the capacity to meet them as the crucial and immediate problem. What is the conduct of the war actually costing the German Government ? Recently our own Government has put the cost for ourselves at £1,000,000 a day, without any guarantee that this ' moderate ' estimate will not be exceeded—as it almost certainly will. In 1909, Dr. Riesser calculated that the first six weeks of a great European war would cost Germany at least £125,000,000. This would give us £250,000,000 for the first three months and £500,000,000 for the first six months—if the weeks after the first six were not less expensive. There is no good reason for supposing that war tends to become cheaper as it proceeds ; on the contrary, particularly a war of the present kind, in which the numbers in the field tend to rise rather than fall, it tends to become dearer, as material and armaments not reckoned in the first cost wear out and require to be replaced. In 1909 Dr. Riesser did not allow for the increases which science has brought about in the cost of armaments—war is intrinsically more expensive since 1909—nor did he fully anticipate the gigantic efforts Germany would be able to make. More recently Dr. Julius Wolf has estimated the cost at a money expenditure of not less than £2,000,000 a day and more likely to be £2,500,000. An estimate of £500,000,000 for the first six months may be regarded, therefore, as highly probable ; and this does not include any of the cost reckoned under our second and third heads, but is simply the bill reckoned in money of the expenditure necessary for equipping and maintaining the armies and ships employed and the organization of all supplies necessary for efficient conduct of the war. What must be subsequently added under (2) and (3) we need not pause to inquire.

How is this bill going to be met ? What are Germany's resources in wealth, either capital or savings from the national income, to meet it ?

The volume of Germany's foreign trade is broadly represented by the following figures :

			Imports.	*Exports.*
1910	.	.	£465,499,600	£382,209,900
1911	.	.	£500,347,250	£411,219,900
1912	.	.	£550,856,600	£454,976,450
1913	.	.	£534,750,000	£495,630,000

Germany is therefore a creditor country, and as a creditor country is second only to Great Britain. The difference in values between imports and exports is roughly, for 1910, £83,000,000; 1911, £89,000,000; 1912, £96,000,000; 1913, £39,000,000. (The sudden drop in 1913 is rather puzzling and is susceptible of various explanations. It probably can be regarded as quite exceptional.) Taking £80,000,000 as the rough average difference, we may broadly account for it by assigning

£25,000,000 to £30,000,000 of the 'invisible exports' to the profits, freights, and services of the German mercantile marine, which in tonnage is second only to the British mercantile marine. The other £50,000,000 to £55,000,000 as part of the return on German capital invested outside Germany. The actual amount of this investment has been the subject of much investigation by German economists, whose estimate at £1,500,000,000 has been accepted as approximately correct by experts in this country. Further analysis of the trade figures reveals : first, that broadly 44 % of the imports (i. e. £243,000,000) and 39 % of the exports were from or to States with which Germany is at war, and that 56 % of imports and 61 % of exports were from or to allied or neutral States : secondly, that the last twenty years of Germany's trade exhibit well-defined features—manutured goods (finished or half-finished) form a smaller proportion of the imports and a larger proportion of the exports, while the imports of food, cattle, and luxuries have steadily risen in value. Similarly the imports of raw material for industry have steadily increased, while the exports of food-stuffs and cattle have slowly declined. Germany, in short, as she has become industrialized and improved her industrial efficiency, with a steady increase in her population, has become less and less dependent on other countries for manufactured articles, but more and more dependent on foreign markets for the export of manufactured goods, for the import of food-stuffs with which to feed her population, and also for the import of raw material with which to feed her industries. We are on tolerably safe ground if we infer that to-day 20 % of her visible imports are in manufactured goods, 50 % in raw material for industry, 30 % in food-stuffs and luxuries : while of the visible exports 20 % are in raw materials, 72 % in manufactured goods, and 8 % in food-stuffs. It may also be noted that the tariff duties collected on the foreign trade provides the German Government with some £40,000,000 of revenue, between one-fourth and one-fifth of the total imperial revenue.

Estimates of the national savings and the total (capitalized) wealth of Germany are necessarily hypothetical and uncertain. Dr. Steinmann-Bucher's estimate put the national income at £1,750,000,000 and the total wealth at about £17,000,000,000. More recently Dr. Helfferich puts the national income at about £2,000,000,000 and the total national wealth at about £18,000,000,000. (His estimate for Great Britain is a total between £14,000,000,000 and £15,000,000,000.)

It is difficult either to accept or to criticize these figures, but financial experts in this country have agreed in thinking they are probably exaggerated. It is certainly remarkable that Dr. Helfferich's figures in 1913 for the national income follow almost exactly the figures worked out in our census of production for Great Britain in 1907, i.e. he estimates the value of goods produced at between £1,900,000,000 and £2,100,000,000, the consumption within Germany at about £1,700,000,000 and the savings available for investment at between £320,000,000 and £350,000,000 ; but if we are prepared to dismiss the suspicion due to this striking identity and accept the estimate, it at least gives us a broad total for subsequent calculation. For it means that if the first six months of war cost Germany £500,000,000 she could pay for it with something less than two years' savings, and even if another £250,000,000 (a low estimate) were added for wealth destroyed, not reckoned in the cost of £500,000,000, she could pay the total bill with three

years' savings and have a substantial balance in hand—
*if, that is, her national income and national savings during
and after the war remain at the pre-war level.* But what
is tolerably certain is that neither during the war nor
after it will her national income remain at anything
like the estimated level for 1913. Can we roughly
calculate what is likely to be the effect of the war on
that national income and on governmental revenue ?
Some plain conclusions are suggested by the statistics
cited, which may indicaté the forms that ' the economic
strain ' will take.

(1) Germany's trade with the belligerent countries
will practically cease altogether, i.e. her trade with
Great Britain and the British Empire, with France,
Russia, Portugal, Servia, Montenegro, Japan, and with
Belgium : i.e. about £240,000,000 of her exports and
£175,000,000 of her imports must be at once deducted
from her total trade ; (2) her trade with her ally Austria
representing £58,000,000 of exports and £42,000,000 of
imports, will be seriously dislocated and diminished, as
will also her trade with the Ottoman Empire ; (3) her
trade with neutrals, in theory unimpaired, will be
seriously dislocated, and mainly in four ways : (*a*) the
diminished spending power of the neutrals caused by the
war will mean a contraction of their demand for Germany's goods ; (*b*) as Germany has lost the command
of the seas, her means of shipping goods to and from her
market to theirs are gravely imperilled and must be
subjected to the delays of devious routes through
neutral territory (e.g. Switzerland, Italy, Holland,
Denmark) with increased charges for insurance and
freight which may kill the trade altogether ; (*c*) the
effect of various classes of goods being declared contraband or conditional contraband by Great Britain

and rendered liable to capture or forfeiture. The recent action of Great Britain in applying the doctrine of ' the continuous voyage ' to conditional contraband will probably very materially diminish the total quantity of imports and cause certain categories of imports to disappear altogether ; (d) Germany will have to reckon with the competition first of Great Britain and then of neutral States (e. g. the United States) in the neutral markets, a competition working under more favourable conditions, to capture trade hitherto in German hands, which will certainly further diminish Germany's trade. Precise estimates in figures of the effect of these various forces are not possible. But we have some significant sidelights. For the month of September German exports to the United States fell from a value of $19,000,000 to a value of $3,000,000, while her imports fell from a value of $35,000,000 to a value of $3,000—an extraordinary shrinkage. It is noteworthy that in the same month British exports to the United States actually increased by a value of £1,400,000—eloquent testimony to the money (quite apart from the military) value of the command of the seas.

Fourthly, we are safe in concluding that, inasmuch as her mercantile marine has now been driven off the sea, Germany will lose the £25,000,000 or £30,000,000 derived from freights, &c., earned by that marine. Fifthly, the tremendous reduction of imports and exports will reduce the governmental revenue derived from the tariff. A moderate estimate would put that reduction at one-half—from £40,000,000 to £20,000,000. Sixthly, the return on German investments of capital outside Germany will be heavily reduced. Seventhly, the earning power of the magnificent State railways—a source of revenue to the Government—which is dependent on flourishing trade within and without, must be seriously impaired.

Whichever source, in short, of Germany's governmental or national income we investigate, the general conclusion is clear that under the stress of war the production and consumption of wealth within the Empire will probably be reduced by something like 50 %, and the savings available for meeting war expenditure will be correspondingly diminished. Even if there is no further addition to the war bill, and no further shrinkage in the national income, an expenditure of £750,000,000 will take not two but probably seven years' savings.

This does not mean that Germany's immediate power to carry on the war is crippled. It only means that the burden is being spread over a longer period of peace and that the future is being more and more heavily mortgaged. But the estimated results point to the conclusion that a very small percentage of the war bill can be met by revenue and additional taxation. It can only be met by borrowing, and borrowing on a large scale. What, then, is Germany's capacity to borrow ?

She must borrow from herself and from her own resources. She cannot float a loan (as Japan and Russia did in 1905 and onwards) in the neutral money markets. Only one of the great money markets, New York, as has already been emphasized, remains, and a loan in New York is neither a political nor a financial possibility. Nor is it possible for her to realize to any appreciable extent, though at a great loss, her investments in neutral countries and reinvest the proceeds in a home war-loan—for the simple reason that neither the United States, nor Brazil, Chile, Argentina, China, &c., hard hit by the universal war, can buy what Germany might be willing to sell. The finance houses

in New York, intimately connected with German international finance, may or may not subscribe to a German
home-loan and sell or pledge some of their holdings, if
they can, in American or other securities to do so ;
but the amount so obtainable is really negligible in
relation to the amount that has to be raised.   Nor is it
necessary to rely on this help.   The gold in the
Reichsbank, the deposits in the Savings Bank (those
for Prussia alone figure out at over £600,000,000), the
deposits in the great banking corporations, make the
assumption safe that Germany can, if her people choose
to do it, lend the Government for the expenses of the
war probably at least £500,000,000, and can also pay
by extra taxation an additional sum.   The financial
methods may be open to question, the ultimate effect
of borrowing on this scale may be damaging or even
disastrous, particularly if Germany is not victorious,
but we shall err seriously if we conclude that the German
Government cannot borrow from the German people
much more than £500,000,000 in the first six or eight
months of the war.   The future may be heavily mortgaged by so doing, but it can be done ; and if the German
people are convinced that any and every sacrifice is a
duty, that victory will come in consequence, and that
heavy indemnities will partially if not wholly recoup
the temporary sacrifice, however severe, it will be done.
We must not look for any collapse of credit or borrowing
power for at least six, perhaps eight, perhaps twelve
months, perhaps even longer.   The wealth is there—
the product of forty years of saving, superb organization,
and industrial development—and can be applied to any
purpose the German people choose.

There is no good reason for thinking that Germany
will not be able to feed her armies and civil popula-

tion for many months to come. Her food imports are not, as with ours, absolutely essential. She imports roughly £150,000,000 worth, but she exports £40,000,000 worth, leaving a net import of £110,000,000 worth, i. e. not £2 per head of population (compared with the £6 per head of population in Great Britain). Her harvest has been gathered undisturbed by invasion, and it has been a good harvest; she has carried off a certain amount of the Polish harvest, even of French crops in the north. The element of luxuries in the food imports must be reckoned with; also she has been able to add through Denmark, Switzerland, Holland, and Italy, to her own resources. Germany imports £12,000,000 worth of coffee. But Germany can fight without coffee if necessary, nor will her population starve because coffee is cut off altogether. The exports of Austria-Hungary in cereals, flour, cattle, swine, fowls, eggs, and sugar are enormous (about 40 % of the whole export trade), of which only about 5 % goes in the ordinary course to Germany, but on which Austria's ally will now have a first claim, and which will help to make up the deficit in Germany's food supplies from other foreign countries. Similarly, Germany will have the great Hungarian resources in horses at her disposal. That the German nation will be deprived of many luxuries, that it may have gradually to go on to short rations, that there will be privation and sacrifice, we may take for granted; but that she is within measurable distance of starvation, or that the reduced quantities of food imports will vitally affect her fighting powers for many months to come, are not conclusions warranted by the facts as we know them. Nations can fight for a long time on short rations if they think the end worth the sacrifice.

A more difficult problem is raised by the question,
How far are the industries essential or directly subsidiary
to the waging of war likely to be crippled by a cessation
or a marked reduction in the imports of raw materials ?
It may be taken for granted that German trade and production as a whole cannot continue on the level of 1913
for twelve months without the import of raw materials
on a very large scale, and that many industries are
absolutely dependent on these imports and must cease
altogether when the pre-existing stock is exhausted.
But are we entitled to infer that if Germany is deprived
of her imports of cotton, wool, jute, coal, iron ore,
lignite, hides, silk, nitrates, copper, rubber, oil—for
these are her chief imports of raw materials—amounting
to some £280,000,000—it will be impossible for her to
manufacture what war requires for her armies and her
civil population ?   Let us note first that an enormous
quantity of these imports are required for the production
of manufactured goods which Germany exports in steadily
increasing quantities.   These imports are not directly
necessary for war purposes or home consumption.   The
raw material is imported, manufactured into a finished
or semi-finished article, to the immense economic advantage of Germany, but neither the import nor the export
is ' consumed ' in Germany.   In many categories of
raw material Germany has more than enough in her
own resources to produce what she requires for her own
consumption.   The loss of foreign imports and of exports for foreign consumption, however severe, will not
of itself for a considerable time bring about ' economic
starvation '.   There will be a great drop in the wealth
of the country, but depletion is not paralysis, and
depletion of this kind takes a long period to make
itself felt.   Secondly, by the virtual annexation of

Luxemourg Germany has secured the rich iron ore fields in that duchy. Her own coal-fields can supply all that is needed for home needs. Raw silk and wool, when the export trade is reduced, can probably be obtained in sufficient quantities to meet reduced home needs for a considerable time. And the same applies to cotton. The general economic loss will steadily mount up; factories will cease to work; bankruptcies will increase; prices will rise. The longer this period is prolonged the more serious will be the general economic havoc which the country must face when the war ends, but it would be rash to assume that the stringency will, before twelve months have run, mean such a pressure that Germany cannot carry on the war. Jute, nitrates, various chemical imports, copper, rubber, oil—these are all directly necessary for the war, and they can only be obtained by imports. Efficient governmental organization—and it is certain there will be such—can reduce waste, control unnecessary consumption, and prolong the period for which the pre-war stocks can last. We do not know the amount of those stocks, nor whether for example the supply of oil from Roumania and Hungary can make good the serious loss of the Galician oil-fields. German science may find a workable substitute for jute, though this is questionable. But neither organization nor control nor science can create oil, rubber, copper, nitrates, and certain chemical products that Germany imports. There are indications that in all these articles shortage is already being felt, and that great difficulties are experienced in procuring any addition to the stocks through Italy or any other neutral channel. If Great Britain retains the command of the sea and is able through naval vigilance, aided by the seizure of contraband and the application of the principle of 'the

continuous voyage ' to conditional contraband to secure
that the import of raw material in those categories is
practically cut off, the manufacture of what is necessary
for the conduct of the war may really be so reduced as
to be as damaging as a military defeat. It is in this
direction that first of all the economic strain will be
literally effective. The armies may be slowly starved
long before the population is starved and financial
credit so shaken as to compel the Government to sue
for peace.

It would be unsafe to reckon on the effect of unemployment. The tremendous drop in imports and
exports, the cessation of her shipping trade, the no less
tremendous diminution in production consequent on
these two results of the war, must have caused unemployment on a very large scale. But the feverish
activity in certain trades directly concerned with the
war, and still more the absorption of millions of men
who would normally be employed in industry into the
army, will for the males in the population counter-
balance much, perhaps most, of the unemployment.
It is fairly certain that the unemployment of women
is the most serious economic feature at present, for
Germany, like every highly industrialized country, has
come to be dependent on female labour. Unemployed
women cannot be absorbed into the army nor can they
all be employed as nurses. Most of the women thus
unemployed are dependants as mothers, wives, or
daughters of soldiers, and their maintenance as such is
a governmental matter. There is no reason to believe
that the German Government neglects their claims.
That is why in estimating the German war bills we
must reckon in the money allowances allotted to the
dependants of soldiers and why the money cost is

necessarily high for a country with 4,000,000 to 5,000,000 of men under arms in the field and another 2,000,000 under training and in reserve. The economic pressure from draining industry to make up armies and from maintaining men and women, either displaced because industry has been severely dislocated or because they are dependants on the displaced men absorbed into the armies, will steadily increase. The number of mouths to be fed and of bodies to be clothed will actually increase as more children are born, but the quantum produced for feeding and clothing will be steadily diminishing. Some months must elapse before the results take the form of distress, but when that point is reached the distress must rapidly become acute.

The longer that Germany is able to keep the war away from her own borders the longer can the pressure of economic forces be staved off. But if the theatre of military operations is slowly shifted to her own territories, the economic results may well be more important and decisive than the military. An effective Russian invasion of East Prussia and upper Silesia, an effective invasion of (German) Lorraine, Luxemburg, and Westphalia west of the Rhine, will strike at the supply of raw material (iron and coal in particular) in its most vulnerable quarters. Germany, from the military point of view, has in the Rhine and the Oder a superb, perhaps (in the west at least) an impregnable defensive position, capable with the military forces at her disposal of defying vast armies. But a Germany entrenched behind the Rhine, the Vistula (as far as Thorn) and the Oder will very soon discover that if the North Sea is sealed up, she cannot, economically speaking, dispense with the granary of East Prussia, the Silesian, Luxemburg, and Lorraine coal and iron fields, and all the industries in

the ' Lancashire ' Westphalia, west of the Rhine.
Industry and raw material will fail her long before her
male population gives out. We are safe in concluding
that Germany cannot for six months arm, clothe, and
feed her combatant and non-combatant population on
the resources alone provided by the area between the
Rhine and the Oder. And if, in addition to this, Russian
arms have at Cracow driven a wedge in between Austria
and the German Empire, if the trade connexion between
Bohemia and Saxony and the south is seriously interrupted, the process of real economic starvation will be
considerably quickened.

Nothing has been said so far of the moral element
involved in this economic pressure and the capacity
and willingness to endure it. For it is difficult, not
to estimate its importance or gauge its duration, but
to state it in any precise form. A garrison beleaguered in a fortress can fight as long as there are
fortifications, guns, ammunition, and food, and must
surrender if the fortifications are destroyed, the guns not
replaced, and the ammunition and food are exhausted.
But the garrison may surrender at any point short, of
absolute exhaustion if it is convinced that honour is
satisfied and that further resistance can achieve no
definite result or may even make the general situation
worse. So it is with nations. The capacity and
willingness of a nation to endure economic privation
and make great economic sacrifices, to mortgage the
future for the sake of the present, will depend partly
on the nature and volume of the resources in hand
and partly on the interpretation of the end in view
and the likelihood that the sacrifices, however costly,
will achieve that end, partly on its moral solidarity
and organized power of resistance to the disintegrating

and weakening effects of privation, and loss of material wealth. We cannot question that in all these respects —the material resources, the organized moral power of resistance, moral solidarity, and readiness to make great sacrifices for great ends—the German nation is as well equipped as any of her foes. So long as Germany is inspired by the conviction that victory is essential and is certain if a great effort is persisted in, even if purchased at sacrifices so great as to cause a general economic exhaustion that will punish and cripple a whole generation, so long must we expect that she will make those sacrifices up to the extreme limit permitted by the material economic conditions. . That those limits will permit the prolongation of the struggle considerably beyond the period frequently estimated in many quarters, it has been my object to show. That the prolongation may ultimately result in an economic exhaustion and paralysis, a war bill which when all its elements are reckoned up may reach to thousands of millions of pounds—that will perhaps absorb the savings of a whole generation to liquidate, and may total up to a fifth or even a third 'of Germany's capitalized wealth—is quite possible. And it may be taken for granted that the longer the prolongation the greater the amount of the total war cost. But until the material resources by which Germany can wage war are exhausted—and under present conditions that cannot be expected for several months at least still to come— the economic pressure will not become decisive unless one or other or both of two developments occur. Germany may, slowly or rapidly, become convinced that she cannot win and that sacrifices justified by the certainty of success are not justified when the final result may be failure. Ruin or exhaustion compensated for by victory is one thing ; exhaustion aggravated by failure or defeat is another. France in 1871 wisely concluded that it would be folly to prolong the struggle. *La défense nationale* had saved the nation's honour and self-respect but no more. And a similar frame of mind may slowly or rapidly be formed in the Germany of 1915. Secondly, the development of military operations may by a series of slowly accumulated results or a few decisive strokes revolutionize the economic situation and enormously reduce the economic and material limits within which effective resistance is possible. The military campaign may, in short, administer the economic *coup de grâce*.

For Great Britain the problem is simple in statement if difficult in achievement. So long as she can retain the effective command of the sea it is certain that her economic resources from every point of view will be superior to those of Germany. The command of the sea puts time as well as wealth on her side. A nation with time and wealth as its allies need fear no foe, if it is prepared to provide those allies with the military striking power—the men that are necessary both in numbers and quality. The decisive word rests with the ships that neither German and Austrian, nor Russian and French armies will probably ever see. The military and the economic future of Germany lies indeed on the grey waters of North Sea, English Channel, and Atlantic, and on the blue and sunlit waters of the Mediterranean. The most tremendous chapter in world-history and the world-influence of sea-power is now being written in the silence of the seas. British sea-power has created the economic problem for Germany and British sea-power can ultimately solve it.

NOTE 1

The financial soundness of the German banking system and of German banking methods in general opens up controversial technical questions of great difficulty, that cannot be discussed with advantage here. Such information as is available suggests that, with the collapse of the export and import trade, the German banks, for all the brave show of figures on paper (the totals of deposits and the Savings Banks returns), are straining the credit of the country to breaking point. If recent figures can be trusted the amount of gold in the Reichsbank is about £98,000,000 : notes have been issued against this to the amount of £200,000,000. In addition, other banking corporations have issued notes of a value about £55,000,000 mainly against securities held or deposited, i. e. a total note issue of over £260,000,000, a very large amount of which is really inconvertible paper currency. The Imperial Government has issued some £50,000,000 of 5 per cent. Exchequer Bonds and placed about £170,000,000 of a 5 per cent. war loan. It is commonly asserted that 25 per cent. of the Savings Banks deposits have been absorbed in this loan. In addition, the Prussian Government has floated or is floating a loan of £75,000,000, through the Kriegsdarlehenskasse, which by pledging it to the Reichsbank can issue notes against it, which notes apparently are to be regarded as gold cover for the issue of an equal amount of Reichsbank notes. In other words, the Reichsbank can issue notes up to the full amount of the Prussian loan—a singular and dangerous expedient. It is not surprising that the German exchanges have fallen eleven points, and that there are signs of depreciation in the paper currency. These and similar financial operations will doubtless enable Germany to continue the war, but in the long run they must very seriously aggravate the financial and economic dislocation of the war.   And if further heavy loans are required in the immediate future, it is not easy to see how they can be floated without mortgaging assets already mortgaged by the previous operations.   The recent severe strictures of the Swiss Bankverein on these operations are significant. But, as Professor Foxwell has lately pointed out, our own financial methods are not above damaging criticism.

NOTE 2 .

From confidential information that has reached me since the preceding pages were written, the amount of the pre-war stock of cotton and wool has probably been over-estimated, and the depletion in that stock since August 4 probably under-estimated, in the argument. There seems good reason for believing that the shortage in cotton is serious, and in wool also, despite the capture of wool stores at Antwerp.   Nor does it seem likely that either (particularly wool) can be made good in adequate quantities through neutral channels.   Similarly the supply of oil from Roumania (even if permitted) is effectively blocked by Servian control of the Danube, the German oil companies having hitherto used transport wholly by water.   Recent German regulations about copper and rubber point to serious shortage.   Similarly, the recent statistics of unemployment, given by the Socialist organ, *Vorwärts*, show, if correct, that the inference in the text about female unemployment is sound, and that, in spite of absorption into military service, male unemployment is steadily increasing and preparing grave economic problems for the German Imperial and State Governments.   C. G. R.

Oxford: Horace Hart Printer to the University

WHY WE ARE AT WAR

GREAT BRITAIN'S CASE

BY MEMBERS OF THE OXFORD FACULTY OF MODERN HISTORY

E. BARKER.   H. W. C. DAVIS.
C. R. L. FLETCHER.   ARTHUR HASSALL.
L. G. WICKHAM LEGG.   F. MORGAN.

With an Appendix of Original Documents
including the Authorized English Translation
of the White Book issued by the
German Government

THIRD EDITION REVISED   (NINTH IMPRESSION)
CONTAINING THE RUSSIAN ORANGE BOOK AND
EXTRACTS FROM THE BELGIAN GREY BOOK

TRANSLATIONS INTO FRENCH ITALIAN SPANISH
GERMAN AND SWEDISH ARE
NOW READY

Paper Covers Two Shillings net (70 cents)
Cloth Two Shillings and Sixpence net (85 cents)

OXFORD: AT THE CLARENDON PRESS
LONDON: HUMPHREY MILFORD
EDINBURGH   GLASGOW   NEW YORK   TORONTO
MELBOURNE   BOMBAY

(b)

19 45

No. 1

OXFORD PAMPHLETS

1914

THE DEEPER CAUSES

OF THE WAR

By Dr. SANDAY

FIFTH IMPRESSION

Price Threepence net

OXFORD UNIVERSITY PRESS
HUMPHREY MILFORD
LONDON   EDINBURGH   GLASGOW
NEW YORK   TORONTO   MELBOURNE   BOMBAY

OXFORD: HORACE HART
PRINTER TO THE UNIVERSITY

THE DEEPER CAUSES OF THE WAR

In this vast and portentous war the remarkable thing is how little definite grievance the combatants have against each other. This fact may be taken as proof that it has all been deliberately planned. One step has seemed to follow from another by a kind of horrible logic. And yet only in the first step of all can there be said to have been anything like real provocation. Even for that satisfaction was offered, but refused, and refused in a way which showed that it was never intended that it should be accepted. So clear has this logical sequence been that opinion all the world over has had no difficulty in tracing the course of events to its real, if somewhat concealed, origin. We all know where the real responsibility lies. We know who is the true aggressor.

It certainly was not this country. Its statesmen have taken a foremost part in working for peace. The record lies open to the world, and the world has pronounced upon it. No one could have worked for peace more sincerely and genuinely than our own Foreign Secretary; and in all that he said or did, he has had the whole nation behind him.

It was not France who wanted war. By common consent, France has shown throughout excellent moderation and self-restraint. It is true that France has all along had a strong and deep-seated motive for war. The French have never forgotten that dismemberment of their country which befell them three-and-forty years ago. But, though they have always been thinking

of it, they have kept their own resolve never to speak of
it. The issues for them were too tremendous. They
knew that it would be for them a struggle for life and
death.

I do not think that Russia desired war, though it also
did not shrink from it. The motive with Russia was its
strong sense of nationality and its leadership of the
Slavonic race. It advised Servia to accept the ultimatum
presented to it, and I believe that it would have stopped
its preparations if a hand had really been held up to it
on the other side.

Though at first nominally on the side of peace, the
language and action of Germany alone were evasive and
ambiguous. In the correspondence with our own
Foreign Minister her intentions were gradually disclosed.
And gradually it became more and more clear that these
intentions substantially agreed with a programme
drawn up in her name, though, of course, not openly
avowed, and published between two and three years ago.
I refer to a book, to which frequent reference has been
made in these last weeks, by a general highly placed in
the German Army. The title was *Germany and the Next
War*, and the author, General von Bernhardi. It was an
extremely frank book, very serious and sober, but also
very uncompromising. The principal question about it
was how far it truly represented the ideas which guided
German policy. There was no doubt that it represented
the views of a powerful party in the German Army, but
the question was how far it also represented the Government and the nation.

By this time I think it has become clear that it really
did represent the deliberate underlying policy of Germany
as a whole.

Let me try, if I can, to explain what I believe to have

been the true condition of things. I believe that the natural attitude and aims of a large part of the nation are by no means identical with those of the military party. I believe that great numbers of Germans are quiet, peace-loving people, quite prepared to live on good terms with their neighbours on all sides. But the more aggressive party has been making strong and energetic efforts for a number of years to get the upper hand, to obtain a decisive control of the course of public policy. Even the Emperor himself, strong character as he is, has been all along more or less under the influence of this party. There are really two sides to his nature. I do not think that the personal advances which he has made to this country have been at all hypocritical. He has been, I think, quite disposed to be friendly with us ; and his connexion with our own Royal Family has not counted for nothing. But the preponderating influence has been on the other side. It has always appealed to the energy and force that were natural to him. It should always be remembered that he is before all things a patriot. His one ruling desire has always been to promote the welfare and greatness of his people. And when he thought of greatness, it was natural that military greatness should have the strongest attraction for him. Hence I think we can understand how the military party has gradually increased its hold upon him until it has at last carried him along with it. And in like manner I believe that it has carried along with it the nation, not entirely, and not whole-heartedly, but enough to determine the drift of purpose and policy. There is no country in which education counts for so much ; and the strongest voices in education have for some time past been on the aggressive side. The gospel of Militarism and of Force has been preached without intermission. It has converted some, and silenced others, and, with or without their real assent, carried away all.

This policy is really at bottom Prussian rather than German. But Prussia is at present the dominant power in Germany, and it has succeeded in impressing its spirit upon the whole nation.

The fact is that, when all disguises are stripped away, this Prussianized Germany stands upon the old naked doctrine that Might is Right. Never in the history of the world has this doctrine been applied in such a systematically logical way. Not only is the right of the stronger vindicated and excused after the event ; but strength is laid down as the ultimate principle on which right is based. Wherever, in the actual condition of things, the rights of possession do not exactly correspond to the strength of the possessor, it is assumed that they are hollow and ought not to be respected. Stated in its bare form, the doctrine goes back to

> the good old rule, the simple plan,
> That they should take who have the power,
> And they should keep who can.

With this assumption firmly fixed at the back of its mind, Germany has come to be profoundly discontented with the existing state of things in Europe and in the world at large. It believes that other nations—notably ourselves—have possessions far in excess of their deserts, while Germany itself deserves and needs far more than it has. ' Are we to acquiesce,' the Germans are represented as asking—' Are we to acquiesce in England's possession of one-fifth of the globe, with no title-deeds, no claim, except priority in robbery ? ' (Cramb, *Germany and England*, p. 106). It is true that we have a large empire of colonies and dependencies, and that France has a considerable empire of the same kind, while Germany's share appears to be small and inadequate. This hunger for possessions on the earth's surface is of comparatively recent growth. It has been steadily increasing during the last five-and-twenty years. It should be remembered that Bismarck did not desire colonial expansion. That was one of the points on which he differed from the young Kaiser. It is instructive to follow the process of development. The first thing that Germany desired was unity. It had been handicapped in the past by its territorial divisions. It was a very legitimate and worthy aim to get rid of these divisions. The work was done in a masterful and impressive way. It was only natural that with the consciousness of unity there should come also a consciousness of strength, and the desire to assert that strength in paying off old scores and establishing a German Empire on firm foundations. Hence the Franco-German War, from which Germany seemed to have gained much that it wanted. But it very soon came to be disappointed with the result. France recovered, with remarkable and unexpected rapidity, and still continued to be a formidable rival. The determination gradually grew to fight out this battle again and the next time—this time—to fight it to a finish. There is abundant and overwhelming evidence of this determination. General von Bernhardi lays it down in plain words :

'In one way or another we must settle accounts with France if we are to gain elbow-room for our own world-policy. That is the first and most absolute requirement of a sound German policy ; and inasmuch as French hostility is not to be removed once for all

by pacific means, that must be done by force of
arms. France must be so completely overthrown that
it will never get in our way again.' (*Der nächste
Krieg*, p. 114 ; *E. T.*, p. 105.)

If that is not sufficiently clear, another passage will
make it clearer :

> ' As in 1870-71 we forced our way to the coasts
> of the Atlantic Ocean, so this time too we must aim
> at a thorough conquest in order to possess ourselves
> of the French naval ports and to destroy the French
> marine dépôts. It would be a war to the knife
> which we should have to fight out with France,
> a war which—if it succeeded—would crush for ever
> the position of France as a great Power.' (Ibid.,
> p. 187 ; *E. T.*, p. 165.)

The destruction of France was to be only a stepping-
stone to our own. The stress laid on the possession of
the French naval harbours was significant. They were
certainly to be used as a base of operations against
ourselves. We, too, were to be crushed, by sea as well
as by land.

Our statesmen have from time to time made proposals
for naval disarmament or at least reduced construction.
But, however well intentioned these proposals may have
been, they were only irritating to those to whom they
were addressed ; because they always went upon the
assumption that we should retain our relative superiority
—in other words that we should keep the command of
the sea ; and it was just the command of the sea which
the Germans were resolved to challenge. They did
not say so in so many words ; but that was what they
meant. It was only a question of time.

The present war is the outcome on the part of the
Germans of an immense and deep-seated consciousness

of strength—a consciousness of strength, not only actual
but potential, and even more potential than actual.
It was not only that they knew that they had the big
battalions ; that they knew that these battalions were
admirably drilled and organized ; that they knew that
the whole nation was fully prepared for war. It was
not only this—but they also knew that the nation had
the spirit and the courage, the energy and the resolution
for war. They knew that it was prepared to make
enormous sacrifices. They meant to show the whole
world what they could do ; and what they would do
in the way of brilliant achievements after the war was
finished—when the German flag floated alone over the
ruins of an independent Europe.

It must be confessed that there was a certain grandeur
in these ambitions. They rested not only on the
consciousness of strength but on the consciousness of
virtue—the consciousness of possessing a particular
group of warlike virtues—the stern self-discipline, the
thrift, the persistence and self-devotion, which had
raised Prussia in spite of her poor and barren soil to
be the foremost of German states, and which just
a hundred years ago had animated the German Army
in the great War of Liberation from the Napoleonic
tyranny. The Germans think—and not wholly without
reason—that neither we nor the French, in our acquisition of empire, have shown virtues such as these.
When they speak of ' the justice of their cause ', that
is what they mean. They think that we stand in their
way, and prevent them from obtaining that which is
their due. They think that we are decadent, and
enervated by long peace ; and they are determined to
wrest from us this empire of which we are not worthy.

That is our enemies' case—not what they say on the surface, but what they really think in their hearts. As I have said, there would be something grandiose about it, if we could grant the assumptions on which it is founded. But I need not say that we utterly refuse to grant them. Might is not right, or in any true sense the foundation of right. We believe that this war is a great and grievous wrong in the sight of God and in the sight of man. We believe that it is not only a great and grievous wrong but also that it is a huge miscalculation. We believe the Germans will find that they have to some extent misjudged themselves, and that to a yet greater extent they have misjudged other nations. But all this remains to be put to the test, and is in the hands of God. In the meantime our first duty is to weigh calmly and to try to understand.

There are three books that I would earnestly recommend any one who desires to do this to read—or at least two out of the three. They are all published at popular prices, 2s. or 2s. 6d. each. The first is the book of General von Bernhardi's to which I have referred. This, however, is the longest of the three books, and may perhaps most easily be dispensed with. An English book which has come out within the last few days is much shorter and will answer the same purpose even more effectually. It is called *Germany and England*, and the writer, Mr. J. A. Cramb, was Professor of Modern History at Queen's College, London, but died before his book was finished. He had had much of his training in Germany, and was a convert to the German idea, which he expounds with fire and force. He makes himself the mouthpiece of the German accusations against us ; and it must be confessed that a great deal of this part of the book is very bitter reading. But that does not mean that he has lost all faith in his own country. Some sides of its history he keenly appreciated. He was really an Imperialist, and it was from the side of Imperialism that the German ideas had their fascination for him. He foresaw clearly the coming conflict, though he did not live to see it. It gripped him with the force of a tremendous tragedy. His book raises in its acutest form the whole question of the comparative moral value of Peace and War. •

The third book is the one that I think will give the most dispassionate and balanced view of the whole issue from a European standpoint. The title is *The Anglo-German Problem,* and the writer, Dr. Charles Sarolea, is a Belgian publicist, who is at present acting as correspondent of one of our own morning papers. He is highly intelligent and well informed ; and he writes with some detachment, but as an interested and friendly observer, who understands what Britain really means and stands for, and he refutes the attacks that are made upon her with equal lucidity and moderation.

There is other work to be done besides that of our sailors on the sea and our soldiers in the field. There are many and great problems that press upon us more urgently than ever before. And those of us who are called in any degree to deal with them will need hardly less than the fighting line the continual help and guidance of Almighty God.

I

The Deeper Causes of the War.

By W. SANDAY. 3d. net. *Third Impression.*

The psychology of Prussian militarism ; German public opinion and Germany's aggressive ambitions.

To the Christian Scholars of Europe and America : A Reply from Oxford to the German ‘Address to Evangelical Christians’. 2d. net. *Second Impression.*

The answer of Oxford theologians to a recent manifesto of the German evangelical theologians. This manifesto, which is reproduced in the present pamphlet, argues that Germany is in no sense responsible for the present war. The Oxford reply states that the German theologians cannot have studied either the events which led up to the war, or the political utterances of their own countrymen.

The Responsibility for the War. By W. G. S. ADAMS. 2d. net.

A brief discussion of the question of responsibility : 1. Austria and Serbia ; 2. The responsibility of Russia ; 3. The intervention of England.

Great Britain and Germany.

By SPENSER WILKINSON. 2d. net. *Second Impression.*

Three letters to the *Springfield Republican*: 1. By Prof. Spenser Wilkinson, stating Great Britain's case ; 2. By Prof. John W. Burgess of the University of Columbia, stating Germany's case ; 3. By Prof. Wilkinson, in reply to Prof. Burgess.

‘Just for a Scrap of Paper.’

By ARTHUR HASSALL. 1d. net. *Third Impression.*

Explains why England stands for the sanctity of European treaty-law.

II

The Germans, their Empire, and how they have made it. By C. R. L. FLETCHER. 2d. net. *Third Impression.*

A historical account of Prussian policy from the seventeenth century.

The Germans, their Empire, and what they covet.

By C. R. L. FLETCHER. 2d. net. *Third Impression.*

An account of the ambitions avowed by the Pan-German school.

Might is Right. By Sir WALTER RALEIGH. 2d. net.

Why Germany may win ; what will happen if she wins ; why we believe she will not win.

Austrian Policy since 1867. By MURRAY BEAVEN. 3d. net.

Austrian policy in the Balkans has been of the ‘offensive-defensive’ order. The Archduke Francis Ferdinand might have saved Austria from rushing to destruction ; but 1912 was the beginning of the end.

Italian Policy since 1870. By KEITH FEILING. 2d. net.

Italian policy has been and must be guided by her own interests. The results of her colonial policy have not yet been satisfactory enough to tempt her into adventures.

[a]

Impression.

A historical sketch, discussing the question whether French polic
has been aggressive.

Russia : The Psychology of a Nation.

By PAUL VINOGRADOFF. 1d. net. *Third Impression.*

A reply to the German taunt that Russia is still in a state o
barbarism, and is the enemy of European civilization.

Serbia and the Serbs.

By Sir VALENTINE CHIROL. 2d. net. *Third Impression.*

A sketch of Serbian history, which is incidentally an indictmen'
of the policy pursued by Austria-Hungary towards the Serbian kingdom.

Germany and ' The Fear of Russia '.

By Sir VALENTINE CHIROL. 2d. net. *Third Impression.*

Shows that before 1879 Germany preferred Russia as an ally to Austria
The ambition of Germany to establish a protectorate over Turkey has le
her to assist Austria in the Balkans and so to challenge Russia.

The Eastern Question.

By F. F. URQUHART. 3d. net. *Second Impression.*

The history of the Balkan nations ; their future.

IV

War against War.

By A. D. LINDSAY. 2d. net. *Second Impression.*

Denies that war is good in itself, or a necessary evil. Power is no
the sole or chief end for which the State exists. National greatness
if founded on brute force, cannot endure. International law represent
an ideal, but an ideal that may be realized.

The Value of Small States.

By H. A. L. FISHER. 2d. net. *Third Impression.*

The author argues that the debt of civilization to small states i
incalculable. They are useful, at the present time, as laboratories o
political experiments and as buffer-states between the greater powers.

How can War ever be Right ?

By GILBERT MURRAY. 2d. net. *Second Impression.*

A well-known lover of peace and advocate of pacific policies argue
against the Tolstoyan position. Right and honour compelled Britain t
make war ; and war—like tragedy—is not pure evil.

The National Principle and the War.

By RAMSAY MUIR. 3d. net.

Considers the principle of nationality and its application to the settle
ment of Europe—particularly of S.E. Europe—after the War.

Nietzsche and Treitschke : The Worship of Powe in Modern Germany.

By E. BARKER. 2d. net. *Third Impression.*

An explanation of the main points of interest in the ethical an
political doctrines of the German ruling classes.

[a]

Published separately and will also appear shortly in series.

The British Dominions and the War.

By H. E. EGERTON. 2d. net. *Second Impression.*

Explains the ideas for which the British Empire stands, and the political and moral issues of the war affecting the Dominions.

Is the British Empire the Result of Wholesale Robbery?

By H. E. EGERTON. 2d. net.

A historical sketch in answer to à common taunt.

India and the War.

By Sir ERNEST TREVELYAN. 1d. net. *Second Impression.*

Discusses the reasons which account for the striking manifestations of Indian loyalty.

Bacilli and Bullets.

By Sir WILLIAM OSLER. 1d. net. *Third Impression.*

Calls attention to the fact that disease kills more men than the bullet. The most dangerous diseases are preventible by inoculation.

The Navy and the War.

By J. R. THURSFIELD. 3d. net. *Second Impression.*

Estimates the military and economic value of the silent pressure exercised by our fleet, and warns the faint-hearted and the captious of the perils of lack of faith.

The Retreat from Mons.

By H. W. C. DAVIS. 3d. net. *Second Impression.*

Introduction; the Dispatch of Sept. 9; the Statement by the War Office, published Aug. 31. Appendixes (soldiers' narratives); two maps.

The Law of Nations and the War.

By A. PEARCE HIGGINS. 2d. net.

The violation of Belgian neutrality and the conduct of England to Denmark in 1807; the doctrine of German lawyers that military necessity overrides the laws of war; the balance of power and the sanctity of treaties.

Others in preparation.

WHY WE ARE AT WAR

GREAT BRITAIN'S CASE

BY MEMBERS OF THE OXFORD FACULTY
OF MODERN HISTORY

E. BARKER.	H. W. C. DAVIS.
C. R. L. FLETCHER.	ARTHUR HASSALL.
L. G. WICKHAM LEGG.	F. MORGAN.

With an Appendix of Original Documents
including the Authorized English Translation
of the White Book issued by the
German Government

THIRD   EDITION   REVISED   (EIGHTH   IMPRESSION)
CONTAINING THE RUSSIAN ORANGE BOOK AND
EXTRACTS FROM THE BELGIAN GREY BOOK

TRANSLATIONS INTO FRENCH ITALIAN SPANISH
GERMAN AND SWEDISH ARE
NOW READY

Paper Covers Two Shillings net (70 cents)
Cloth Two Shillings and Sixpence net (85 cents)

OXFORD: AT THE CLARENDON PRESS
LONDON: HUMPHREY MILFORD
EDINBURGH   GLASGOW   NEW YORK   TORONTO
MELBOURNE   BOMBAY

(*a*)

OXFORD PAMPHLETS
1914–1915

THROUGH
GERMAN EYES

BY

E. A. SONNENSCHEIN

Price Twopence net

OXFORD UNIVERSITY PRESS
HUMPHREY MILFORD
LONDON EDINBURGH GLASGOW
NEW YORK TORONTO MELBOURNE BOMBAY

OXFORD PAMPHLETS
1914–1915

Crown 8vo. Separately, in paper covers. Also in series as numbered (I–X), stiff covers, One Shilling net each series. 58 Pamphlets have now (Jan. 15, 1915) been issued, and others are in preparation. The historical pieces are illustrated by sketch-maps.

Saturday Review :—'These little books are easily the best books of the war—accurate, quietly written, full of knowledge, and quite unspoiled by vainglory or bitterness.'

Most of the pamphlets have been reprinted and some are now in a fourth, fifth, or sixth impression.

OXFORD UNIVERSITY PRESS
HUMPHREY MILFORD

LONDON   EDINBURGH   GLASGOW

NEW YORK   TORONTO   MELBOURNE   BOMBAY

[1]

OXFORD PAMPHLETS
1914–1915

I

1. The Deeper Causes of the War.

By W. SANDAY.   3d. net.

The psychology of Prussian militarism ; German public opinion and Germany's aggressive ambitions.

2. To the Christian Scholars of Europe and America: A Reply from Oxford to the German 'Address to Evangelical Christians'.

2d. net.

The answer of Oxford theologians to a recent manifesto of the German evangelical theologians. This manifesto, which is reproduced in the present pamphlet, argues that Germany is in no sense responsible for the present war. The Oxford reply states that the German theologians cannot have studied either the events which led up to the war or the political utterances of their own countrymen.

3. The Responsibility for the War.

By W. G. S. ADAMS.   2d. net.

A brief discussion of the question of responsibility : 1. Austria and Serbia ; 2. The responsibility of Russia ; 3. The intervention of England.

4. Great Britain and Germany.

By SPENSER WILKINSON.   2d. net.

Three letters to the *Springfield Republican*: 1. By Prof. Spenser Wilkinson, stating Great Britain's case ; 2. By Prof. John W. Burgess of the University of Columbia, stating Germany's case ; 3. By Prof. Wilkinson, in reply to Prof. Burgess.

5. 'Just for a Scrap of Paper.'

By ARTHUR HASSALL.   1d. net.

Explains why England stands for the sanctity of European treaty-law.

II

6. The Germans, their Empire, and how they have made it.

By C. R. L. FLETCHER. 2d. net.

A historical account of Prussian policy from the seventeenth century.

7. The Germans, their Empire, and what they covet.

By C. R. L. FLETCHER. 2d. net.

An account of the ambitions avowed by the Pan-German school.

8. Might is Right.

By Sir WALTER RALEIGH. 2d. net.

Why Germany may win; what will happen if she wins; why we believe she will not win.

9. Austrian Policy since 1867.

By MURRAY BEAVEN. 3d. net.

Austrian policy in the Balkans has been of the 'offensive-defensive' order. The Archduke Francis Ferdinand might have saved Austria from rushing to destruction; but 1912 was the beginning of the end.

10. Italian Policy since 1870.

By KEITH FEILING. 2d. net.

Italian policy has been and must be guided by her own interests. The results of her colonial policy have not yet been satisfactory enough to tempt her into adventures.

III

11. French Policy since 1871.

By F. MORGAN and H. W. C. DAVIS. 2d. net.

A historical sketch, discussing the question whether French policy has been aggressive.

12. Russia: The Psychology of a Nation.

By PAUL VINOGRADOFF. 1d. net.

A reply to the German taunt that Russia is still in a state of barbarism, and is the enemy of European civilization.

13. Serbia and the Serbs.

By Sir VALENTINE CHIROL. 2d. net.

A sketch of Serbian history, which is incidentally an indictment of the policy pursued by Austria-Hungary towards the Serbian kingdom.

14. Germany and 'The Fear of Russia'.

By Sir VALENTINE CHIROL. 2d. net.

Shows that before 1879 Germany preferred Russia as an ally to Austria. The ambition of Germany to establish a protectorate over Turkey has led her to assist Austria in the Balkans and so to challenge Russia.

15. The Eastern Question.

By F. F. URQUHART. 3d. net.

The history of the Balkan nations; their future.

IV

16. War against War.

By A. D. LINDSAY. 2d. net.

Denies that war is good in itself, or a necessary evil. National greatness, if founded on brute force, cannot endure. International law represents an ideal, but an ideal that may be realized.

17. The Value of Small States.

By H. A. L. FISHER. 2d. net.

The author argues that the debt of civilization to small states is incalculable.

18. How can War ever be Right?

By GILBERT MURRAY. 2d. net.

A well-known lover of peace and advocate of pacific policies argues against the Tolstoyan position. Right and honour compelled Britain to make war; and war—like tragedy—is not pure evil.

19. The National Principle and the War.

By RAMSAY MUIR. 3d. net.

Considers the principle of nationality and its application to the settlement of Europe—particularly of S.E. Europe—after the War.

20. Nietzsche and Treitschke: The Worship of Power in Modern Germany.

By E. BARKER. 2d. net.

An explanation of the main points of interest in the ethical and political doctrines of the German ruling classes.

V

21. The British Dominions and the War.

By H. E. EGERTON. 2d. net.

Explains the ideas for which the British Empire stands, and the political and moral issues of the war affecting the Dominions.

22. India and the War.

By Sir ERNEST TREVELYAN. 1d. net.

Discusses the reasons for the striking manifestations of Indian loyalty.

23. Is the British Empire the Result of Wholesale Robbery?

By H. E. EGERTON. 2d. net.

A historical sketch in answer to a common taunt.

24. The Law of Nations and the War.

By A. PEARCE HIGGINS. 2d. net.

The violation of Belgian neutrality and the conduct of England to Denmark in 1807; the doctrine of German lawyers that military necessity overrides the laws of war; the balance of power and the sanctity of treaties.

25. England's Mission.

By W. BENETT. 2d. net.

Answers the question, In what cause are we fighting?

VI

26. August, 1914 : The Coming of the War.
By SPENSER WILKINSON. Stiff covers. 1s. net.

VII

27. The Retreat from Mons.
By H. W. C. DAVIS. 3d. net.

28. The Battles of the Marne and Aisne.
By H. W. C. DAVIS. 4d. net.
The Dispatches, with commentary, maps, &c.

29. The Navy and the War.
By J. R. THURSFIELD. 3d. net.
Estimates the military and economic value of the silent pressure exercised by our fleet, and warns the faint-hearted and the captious of the perils of lack of faith.

30. Bacilli and Bullets.
By Sir WILLIAM OSLER. 1d. net.
Calls attention to the fact that disease kills more men than the bullet. The most dangerous diseases are preventable by inoculation.

VIII

31. The Double Alliance *versus* The Triple Entente.
By JAMES M. BECK. 3d. net.
The judgement of a well-known American lawyer.

32. The Germans in Africa.
By EVANS LEWIN. 3d. net.
A historical account of the German colonies.

33. All for Germany, or the World's Respect Well Lost. 2d. net.
'The conversation here imagined, between a new (and perhaps less naïf) Candide and a new (and perhaps less benevolent) Dr. Pangloss, is concerned with the political thoughts and ambitions entertained by the Germans of these latter days.'

34. Germany, the Economic Problem.
By C. GRANT ROBERTSON. 2d. net.
Estimates the strength and weakness of Germany's economic position, and inquires how long she can stand the strain of the war.

35. German Sea-Power.
By C. S. TERRY. 3d. net.
Traces the growth of Germany's navy. With a map of the North Sea.

IX

36. What Europe owes to Belgium.

By H. W. C. DAVIS. 2d. net.

Reminds us of the past achievements of the Belgian people in war and in peace.

37. Poland, Prussia, and Culture.

By LUDWIK EHRLICH. 3d. net.

The author is a Doctor of the University of Lwòw (Lemberg) in Galicia.

38. Turkey in Europe and Asia. 2d. net.

The strength and weakness of the Ottoman Empire considered. The secular prestige of Constantinople, the religious prestige of the Caliphate, and the racial and economic weaknesses which may cause their downfall. A map shows the unfinished railways.

39. Greek Policy since 1882.

By A. J. TOYNBEE. 4d. net.

A historical account of the policy of Greece; the economic future of Greece; the problem of *Graecia Irredenta*. With a map.

40. North Sleswick under Prussian Rule, 1864–1914.

By W. R. PRIOR. 2d. net.

The policy of Prussianization and the resistance of Danish Nationalism. 'If the children do not understand German, they must be treated and taught like deaf-mutes' is quoted from a Prussian educational authority. A map shows the distribution of languages.

X

41. Thoughts on the War.

By GILBERT MURRAY. 2d. net.

Reprinted from the *Hibbert Journal* for October.

42. The Leadership of the World.

By F. S. MARVIN. 2d. net.

A discussion of German aspirations.

43. The Leading Ideas of British Policy.

By the Hon. GERARD COLLIER. 2d. net.

Places the principles of our policy in the perspective of history.

44. The War and its Economic Aspects.
By W. J. ASHLEY. 2d. net.

A comparison of Germany's and Great Britain's powers to stand the strain of a prolonged war. Probable effects of defeat or victory.

45. Food Supplies in War Time.
By R. H. REW, C.B. 2d. net.

An authoritative discussion by an expert who has been 'for over thirty years engaged in the service of British Agriculture'.

Published separately and will also appear shortly in series.

Non-Combatants and the War.
By A. PEARCE HIGGINS. 2d. net.

States the rights and duties of the non-combatant population of a territory under hostile occupation.

Troyon : an Engagement in the Battle of the Aisne.
By A. N. HILDITCH. 2d. net.

Scandinavia and the War.
By E. BJORKMAN. 2d. net.

Considers the policy and sympathies of the three Northern Kingdoms.

Asia and the War.
By A. E. DUCHESNE. 2d. net.

Describes German intrigue, and its failure, in Turkey, India, and Egypt.

Does International Law still Exist ?
By Sir H. ERLE RICHARDS. 2d. net.

A brief account of the principles, and an examination of German apologies for their infringement.

Through German Eyes.
By E. A. SONNENSCHEIN. 2d. net.

The Birmingham Professor, who knows Germany well, considers the German attitude under various heads—Neutrality of Belgium, 'England the chief culprit,' &c.

The Church and the War.

By the BISHOP OF LINCOLN.   2d. net.

Dr. Hicks's article in the December *Political Quarterly* suggests 'how a Churchman . . . may hold fast to his principles and yet take sides with the Allies'.

The Action off Heligoland.   August, 1914.

By L. CECIL JANE.   3d. net.

The Dispatches, with introduction and charts.

German Philosophy and the War.

By J. H. MUIRHEAD.   2d. net.

German Idealism ; The Reaction ; The New Naturalism.

Christmas and the War.

By T. B. STRONG.   2d. net.

A Sermon preached in Christ Church Cathedral.

Outlines of Prussian History to 1871.

By E. F. ROW.   2d. net.

How Prussia made and ruled the German Empire.

The Southern Slavs.

By N. FORBES.   4d. net.

Contains much detailed information—historical, geographical, and ethnological.

Concerning True War.

By WILHELM WUNDT.   Translated by GRACE E. HADOW. 2d. net.

A typical utterance of a German Professor.

Ready Immediately.

The Battle of Ypres—Armentières.

By H. W. C. DAVIS.

The War through Danish Eyes.

By a DANE.

The Man of Peace.

By ROY NORTON.

THROUGH GERMAN EYES

AFTER nearly five months of war, and at the season of the great festival of peace and goodwill towards men, it should be possible to survey the European situation in the spirit of the great Roman historian, 'sine ira et studio.' The present writer has friends and relatives in Germany and Austria, and he would fain say nothing here which he could not say to them, face to face. But this attitude does not involve the abatement of one jot or tittle of the truth. On the contrary, truth is the great reconciler of differences—the common ground on which we and our enemies have to take our stand. It is too soon to attempt a final verdict on the great questions which will come up for adjudication before the bar of history. But it is even now possible to cultivate the spirit of common sense, and to associate with it that nobler 'sensus communis '—the bond of mankind—of which a Roman satirist speaks as rarely found where it is most wanted.

It is possible, indeed, that all reasoning in time of war is mere self-illusion. And the present writer recognizes that in attempting to demolish certain phantoms of the mind, which seem to him to stand in the way of the light—' idols of the tribe, the cave, the market-place, and the theatre '—he may be found to be harbouring idols of his own. If so, they too will come within the general scope of this paper, as ' idols of war '.

THE CAUSES OF THE WAR.

To the attentive student of the Blue Book, the Yellow Book, and the Orange Book, one conclusion seems to emerge beyond the possibility of reasonable doubt, and it is not weakened by anything that is advanced in the German White Book or by any of the known facts of the situation. None of the Entente Powers desired war at the present time. If Great Britain had desired war, Sir Edward Grey would not have laboured day and night to secure a peaceful settlement of the Serbian dispute. If Russia had desired war, she would not have advised Serbia to accept all but the most humiliating of the Austrian demands. That France was responsible for the outbreak of war not even her enemies have asserted. Patent facts point in the same direction. Not one of the Entente Powers was prepared for an offensive war.

On the other hand there is much evidence to show that peace was one of the great assets of Germany, as of Great Britain, and that the German nation as a whole and even the German Government was animated by a fundamental desire for peace. We seem, then, to be presented with the spectacle of two great groups of Powers desiring peace but actually at war. How is that possible ?

The answer is that behind this desire for peace on both sides there lay certain claims (call them ambitions, if you like) which neither side was willing to relinquish and neither to allow as justified in the other.

On our side Great Britain claimed the continuance of her predominance at sea, as necessary to her safety as an island Power and to the existence of an empire which is bound together by the ocean. France claimed some revision of the Treaty of Frankfurt, whereby an improved status should be secured for the provinces of Alsace and Lorraine—either some measure of self-government within the German Empire or re-union with France.[1] This claim of justice for Alsace-Lorraine must be carefully distinguished from the cry for *revanche*, which no doubt made itself heard in the years that immediately followed 1871.[2] Russia claimed the position of protector of the Balkan States, and all that it involved.

On the other side, Germany claimed the right to expansion and to a more favourable ' place in the sun ', and all that it implied.

It was these rival claims which were never reconciled, and so led to war. Whether they were irreconcilable without an appeal to force we shall now never know for certain. But it is clear that they could not have been reconciled without concessions on both sides. The Germans say that they had been labouring for years for an understanding with Great Britain. But to us Britons it seems that Germany, while desiring peace, was not willing to pay the price of peace. She would not listen to any proposal for the reconsideration of the Treaty of Frankfurt; she steadfastly refused to admit any right of Russia to intervene in the Serbian dispute ; she would not recognize the need of Great Britain for a superior fleet. That we on our side have done all that we could to meet the views of Germany I do not assert. But we at any rate gave her a free hand in the matter of the Bagdad railway. Moreover Germany seems to us to have

---

[1] See a lecture by M. Jacques Preiss, delivered in Paris on Feb. 17, 1913, and quoted in *The German Enigma* by M. Georges Bourdon (Appendix, English translation, pp. 353–7).

[2] M. Bourdon denies that the desire for revenge has been an active force in France during recent years.

exaggerated the urgency of her need of expansion. The population of Germany is considerably less per square mile than that of Great Britain, and not half that of Belgium.[1] German emigration has fallen to a very low point, because the German artisan can now find employment and good wages at home. Moreover, Germany already has considerable colonial possessions, sufficient for her immediate needs.

'ENGLAND IS THE CHIEF CULPRIT.'

So says Professor Wundt of Leipzig,[2] and so say most Germans. Indeed this belief, that this country is responsible for having set on foot a plot to ring Germany round with enemies, is the explanation of the special bitterness now felt in Germany against us. Professor Wundt speaks of 'the English programme for the encircling (*Einkreisung*) of Germany': 'For England there is no excuse. It was England that drew up the devilish plan for the destruction of Germany. It was England that set going the monstrous triple alliance (*Dreiverband*) of two lands of ancient European culture with barbaric Russia.' 'As the Lord liveth,' cried Mr. Lloyd George in the City Temple (Nov. 10), 'we had entered into no conspiracy against Germany.' The Germans will not believe that. But it is possible to appeal to obvious facts of chronology. The Dual Alliance of France and Russia came into being in the early

[1] The figures given in *Whitaker's Almanack* for 1914 are :—

German Empire . . .	311 per square mile.
Great Britain	374 ,, ,, ,,
Belgium	658 ,, ,, ,,

These figures are, no doubt, not exact for various reasons; but they roughly represent the facts

[2] *Internationale Monatsschrift*, Oct. 15, 1914, pp. 122, 126. 'England ist und bleibt der Hauptschuldige.'

nineties (say 1890-4) : the *entente* with France was not formed till 1904, and that with Russia not till 1907. In what sense was Great Britain responsible for the actions of France and Russia in 1890-4 ? Does Professor Wundt mean to say that the alliance of France and Russia was harmless until it was converted into a Triple Entente ? If he meant that, he should have said so and given some proof.

The real fact is that Germany by her own acts has ringed herself around with enemies. By the annexation of Alsace-Lorraine contrary to the wishes of the inhabitants she established an enemy on her west as early as 1871 ; France has never ceased to demand some redress of what she regards as a legitimate grievance. By abandoning the policy of Bismarck and the Emperor William I, in or about the year 1890, she drove Russia, contrary to the predilections of the Czar, Alexander III, into the arms of republican France. And finally by her ship-building policy, obviously directed against Great Britain, and the frank menaces of many of her public men during and since the Boer War, she drove this country into the arms of France and Russia. That is how the *Einkreisung* came about. That Germany in these circumstances should feel bitter and resentful is only natural, especially during the last three years ; for the Moroccan incident of 1911 ended in a profound disappointment to the German nation at large ; and the outcome of the Balkan War of 1912 was a blow to German and Austrian ambitions in the east. Moreover the Italian alliance, on which Prince von Bülow set such high hopes,[1] has since then proved a broken reed. But to hold Great Britain responsible for all these things is plainly contrary to history.

[1] *Imperial Germany*, English translation, pp. 52, 54.

Professor Adolf Deissmann, indeed, goes so far as to
say that France and Russia were merely puppets (*Puppen*)
in the hands of Great Britain, on whom the peace of the
world hung.[1] If he means that the whole course of
European history would have been different, had Great
Britain joined the Triple Alliance instead of forming an
entente with France in 1904, he is no doubt right.   But
if he is to be interpreted in the sense of the Second
German White Paper, as suggesting that this country
might have induced or compelled France not to adhere
to the terms of her alliance with Russia in July 1914,
he is attributing to Great Britain more power than she
possessed.   The action of France was determined by the
ultimatum sent by Germany on July 31.   Our action
depended on that of France, not vice versa.   Had
Germany confined herself to a strictly defensive attitude
towards France, there would have been no violation of
Belgian neutrality, and everything would have been
different.

THE NEUTRALITY OF BELGIUM.

Professor Deissmann also affirms his conviction that
the violation of the neutrality of Belgium by Germany
was only a ' pretext ' (*Vorwand*) on our part.[3]   ' England
does not fight for the *ius gentium*.'   The rights of
smaller nations appeal to the conscience of this country
more strongly than Professor Deissmann thinks.   But
it would be untrue to assert that our obligation to

---

[1] *Internationale Monatsschrift*, Oct. 15, 1914, p. 118.

[2] General von Bernhardi, however, admits that Great Britain
probably acted wisely from her own point of view in joining the group
hostile to Germany (*Our Future—a Word of Warning to the German
Nation*, English translation by Mr. Ellis Barker, entitled *Britain as
Germany's Vassal*, p. 143).

[3] Ibid., p. 120.

Belgium was the sole cause which brought Great Britain into the field. This we are bound to recognize explicitly. It was not the interest of this country to allow the mouth of the Scheldt to fall under the control of any of the great Powers. To prevent that was, no doubt, part of Lord Palmerston's policy in 1831, when Great Britain stood sponsor to the new-born Belgium. Mr. Gladstone was prepared to fight, if necessary, for Belgian neutrality in 1870. And Sir Edward Grey's action in 1914 was part and parcel of the same policy. But it is quite unfair to suggest that the treaty obligation which we had incurred was of no account in our eyes. Honour and self-interest are happily not always inconsistent with one another.[1] Moreover we had to consider not only our treaty obligation to Belgium, but also our obligation of honour to France.

During the last few weeks a new charge has been brought against this country. It is said that certain documents discovered by the Germans in Brussels prove the existence in 1906 of an understanding between Great Britain and Belgium as to concerted military operations in case of a violation of Belgian neutrality by Germany. And it is argued that this agreement amounted to a violation of the neutrality of Belgium on the part of this country and of Belgium herself. Whether this interpretation can be put upon it is a question of international law, and I am content, at present, to quote the opinion of an Austrian authority, Professor Alexander Löffler, a member of the Faculty of Law in Vienna. A politician, he says, would be justified in assuming that a one-sided agreement of this kind implies that Great Britain would not have taken similar steps in case of a breach of Belgian neutrality by France. But as a scientific lawyer he feels

[1] Cf. *Why we are at War*, p. 122.

bound to give the verdict ' *Non liquet* ;' the conclusive proof is lacking '.[1] See also Sir E. Grey's statement.[2]

What Neutrality means.

' The basic condition of neutrality is that a neutral state gives no aid to either combatant.' [3] If Belgium had allowed Germany to use Belgian territory as a means of attacking France, she would have lent her aid to Germany and struck a blow at France. Everything depends on the purpose for which a right of way is used. It was Belgium's duty to France as well as her right not to treat France as though she were an enemy. ' A neutral state is entitled to oppose the violation of its territory by all means in its power.' [4] ' The fact of a neutral power resisting, even by force, attempts to violate its neutrality cannot be regarded as a hostile act.' [5] That Germany was committing a wrong in her action against Belgium was avowed with cynical frankness by the German Chancellor; and the importance of this admission is not weakened by subsequent attempts to argue that if the Chancellor had known about the agreement referred to above (p. 9), the admission need never have been made.

The Special Treaty of 1870.

It has been argued that as the special treaty signed at Berlin on August 8 and at Paris on August 11, 1870, was binding only during the continuance of the war of 1870 and for twelve months after the ratification of any treaty of peace concluded between the parties, there was no

---

[1] *Neue Freie Presse*, Nov. 14, 1914.   [2] *The Times*, Dec. 7, p. 7.
[3] *Kriegsgebrauch* (1902), translated by Ellis Barker in *Britain as Germany's Vassal*, p. 250.
[4] *Kriegsgebrauch*, ibid., p. 252.
[5] Hague Conference (1907), Article 10.

treaty obligation subsisting in 1914 to protéct Belgian neutrality. But this argument ignores the fact that the treaty of 1870 also provided that on the expiration of that term 'the independence and neutrality of Belgium will, as far as the high contracting parties are respectively concerned, continue to rest as heretofore on the 1st article of the Quintuple Treaty of the 19th of April, 1839 '.

The Serajevo Murders.

It has always been assumed that the crime of Serajevo was the starting-point of the European conflagration of 1914. But in the light of recent revelations it seems that it was little more than a pretext on the part of Austria. On December 5, in the Italian Chamber of Deputies, the ex-Premier, Signor Giolitti, produced a telegram dated August 9, 1913, in which he was informed by the then Foreign Minister that Austria was contemplating aggression against Serbia at that time, and that she had informed Italy and Germany of the fact, at the same time representing her action as defensive, in order to secure the support of those countries under the terms of the Triple Alliance.[1] Italy refused on the ground that the contemplated action was aggressive, not defensive, and that therefore no *casus foederis* could arise. The right of Italy to an attitude of neutrality in any such war was completely vindicated ; and she has maintained that attitude on the same grounds during the war of 1914. Apparently Germany also discountenanced the Austrian scheme of 1913 ; at any rate it fell to the ground. But the fact that there was such a scheme throws an entirely new light on the Serajevo assassinations. We knew before

---

[1] *The Times*, Dec. 7 and 11, 1914.

that Austria had demanded 'Sentence first, trial afterwards ', like the Queen in Alice's Adventures.   But we
did not know that Austria had proposed to punish Serbia
before the crime of Serajevo had been committed.   We
now see the projected action of 1913 as a continuation
of the policy adopted towards Bosnia in 1908.

The Doctrine of Defensive Aggression.

For half a century Germany has claimed the right of
taking the initiative against a prospective enemy.   It
was claimed in 1870.   It is claimed now.   Yet it strikes
Englishmen as something novel and perilous.   Can a
nation ever be sure that a prospective enemy will prove
an actual enemy ?   War may always be averted.[1]   This
is not the usual German view, however.   Herr Maximilian
Harden stated the doctrine of aggression as a means of
defence in his conversation with M. Bourdon in 1912 : [2]
' Suppose that I have a neighbour who never stops
plotting schemes of vengeance against me . . . my
elementary right of defence and precaution is to say
in my turn, " If you want to fight, it shall be when I
choose ".'   Similarly Germany defends her violation of
Belgian neutrality by alleging that she was merely fore-
stalling the prospective violation of the same territory
by France.   And the *Kölnische Zeitung* declared recently
that Germany ' waited as long as honour allowed, but was
not so stupid as to wait until everything was ready on the
other side '.[3]   If Great Britain had adopted this principle,
who doubts that we might have secured some military
advantage in the present war ?   But our diplomacy was
patient, preferring to exhaust every hope of peace before
an appeal to force was made.

[1] Prince von Bülow says the same, *Imperial Germany*, p. 92.
[2] *The German Enigma*, p. 179 f.   [3] Quoted in *The Times*, Dec. 8, p. 6.

The Psychological Moment.

In the light of the doctrine just discussed the outbreak of war last August becomes quite intelligible. Germany and Austria were of opinion that the psychological moment for defensive aggression had come, and acted accordingly. They do not hold themselves responsible, because their aggression was defensive according to their ideas of defence. That this was the real situation has been gradually revealed by a chain of evidence. First we had the British White Paper, then Sir Maurice de Bunsen's proof that it was Germany that banged the door on peace at the eleventh hour; then came the French Yellow Book, which showed, among other things, the preparations of Germany in co-operation with Austria; and finally comes Signor Giolitti's revelation as to the projected aggression of 1913.

All this is not inconsistent with a fundamental desire for peace on the part of Germany (p. 4). Germany desired peace, but she saw herself surrounded by prospective enemies, and she did not hesitate to forestall their attack.

> *Haec, unde vitam sumeret inscia,*
> *Pacem duello miscuit.*

Warum sind wir so verhasst ?

This question has been asked by many Germans. It is true that Germany has at the present time no sincere friend in the world, except Austria and perhaps Turkey. ' The friend of none ! A sad saying, but very significant,' says Professor Georg Steinhausen of Kassel. He finds the cause partly in the exterior qualities of Germans, partly in the traditions of the past.[1] But is it a fact that there was

---

[1] *Deutsche Rundschau*, Dec. 1909 and Jan. 1910.

any active hatred of Germany in other lánds prior to this war ? Germany was admired, courted, envied for some of her achievements. But I have never observed that there was any malice in the British envy. We were always told that we must wake up and emulate German enterprise and German industry in manufactures and trade, or we should be outstripped in the race. But we did not even put up a tariff against German goods. We knew that Germany was our best customer. As for any thought of drawing the sword to destroy a commercial rival, no one who knows this country believes that it was ever entertained. Yet to Germans without number this figment of the imagination is an article of faith. It is unnecessary to quote names ; the charge is writ large in the manifesto addressed to the Evangelical Christians abroad (signed by thirty eminent men, including Professors Eucken, Harnack, and Wundt), and the declaration by professors and men of science entitled ' European War '.

The Triple Alliance, we are told, was a strictly defensive league, the Triple Entente essentially aggressive.[1] What is the evidence for this assertion ? How does it look now in the light of accomplished facts ? King Edward VII is known in this country as ' Edward the Peace-maker '; to the Germans his whole policy seems to be an act of aggression against them.

The Middle-aged Burglar Theory.

Professor von Treitschke held a different view of the position of Great Britain. On the whole it seems less out of touch with reality ; for it represents this country as contented with what she has got, and pacifically minded. To von Treitschke Great Britain seemed like a middle-aged burglar who desired to retire from business, and

[1] Prof. Adolf Wagner of Berlin (*The German Enigma*, p. 79).

therefore proposed that burglary should cease. Germany, on the other hand, was a young and enterprising burglar, just starting on a promising career. So long as Great Britain, the great robber state, retained her booty—one-fifth of the habitable globe—what right had she to expect peace from the nations ? [1] Her empire was decadent, moribund ; and Germany had not only the power but also the right and the duty to wrest her empire from her.[2] For right is a question of might. At the bottom of this theory one must recognize a sense of outraged justice.[3] And if one is asked to justify Great Britain's having painted red one-fifth of the habitable globe, frankly one cannot. Nor can one justify the fact that A earns five times as much as B, but not one-tenth of the income of C. In this workaday world we have to be content with a rough kind of justice, and to acknowledge accomplished facts. We must ' live and let live '.

It should be borne in mind, however, that though we commonly speak of ' our colonies ', they are not strictly *ours*. The relation is not one of ownership in the sense in which that term is understood in Germany. Our fellow countrymen have settled in distant parts of the earth, and the land which they occupy is *theirs*. We trade with them ; we support them in various ways and are supported by them. But we do not take tribute from them. The whole relation is something of a mystery, which the Germans have hitherto completely failed to grasp. It is highly complex, highly unorganized. Perhaps

[1] See the late Professor Cramb's *Germany and England*, p. 14, and cf. General von Bernhardi in *Our Future*, &c., p. 207. The theory is also well stated by Professor Usher in *Pan-germanism*, pp. 247, 248.

[2] Cf. von Bernhardi, quoted in *Germany and England*, p. 65.

[3] For the same point of view at the present day see the French Yellow Book, p. 2 : ' France with her forty million souls has not the *right* to rival Germany in this way.' Cf. pp. 3, 4, 19.

it will not remain so much longer. But if a change is to be made, it will assuredly not be in the direction of ownership. Nor will it be in the direction of separation, if the hopes awakened during this war are realized. I am speaking, of course, of the great self-governing colonies, such as Canada.

Von Treitschke was, of course, writing of a period long prior to that of the Triple Entente. His theory is, therefore, not necessarily inconsistent with the theory of British aggression referred to above (p. 6 f.). Yet it must be noted that, according to von Treitschke, Great Britain has been Germany's ' one and only enemy ' for three or four decades at least, without knowing it. Her mere existence was an aggression ; the British Empire was inconsistent with Germany's right to expansion. The middle-aged and sated burglar might, then, at least plead that his subsequent development into an aggressive foe was not without provocation, and that it was indeed a measure of self-defence.

German ' Wissenschaft '.

No one admires more sincerely than I do the achievements of German science in the fields of which I have cognizance ; yet I sometimes wonder whether the Germans are not tempted to trust too implicitly in their power of knowing, especially their power of forecasting the future in the domain of international relations. For, as Lord Beaconsfield said, it is the unexpected that happens. There is, after all, something to be said for the rooted distrust of the Britisher for what he calls ' theory '. The whole justification of the German policy of defensive aggression is based on the assumption that it is possible to know the intentions and future actions of other nations. The flimsiness of this kind of knowledge is illustrated by many passages in General von Bernhardi's books. For instance, 'England is interested in destroying Germany's competition ; ' [1] from this he infers that England does actually intend to destroy it. Again, ' All these circumstances make it obviously desirable for Great Britain that a war should break out as soon as possible ; ' hence he ' cannot help concluding that England would like to bring about a war between Russia and Austria by means of the Balkan trouble, in the hope that such a war might lead to a general European war '.[2] Sir Edward Grey was not of that opinion ; but General von Bernhardi knew where the true interests of England lay. It must in fairness be added that the next page contains an important admission : ' Of course one cannot prove whether and how far these surmises correspond with the facts. It will probably never be possible to unravel the Anglo-Russian policy of intrigue.'

THE ETHICS OF BIOLOGY.

There are several other idols which I might attack ; for example, the doctrines that the rights of nations depend on their merits as civilizing agents ; that a nation is morally bound to co-operate with those who are akin to it by blood ; [3] that the policy of maintaining a balance of power is an essentially immoral policy.[4] And we too have had our false prophets, who, like some persons in Germany,[5] did not believe in the possibility of war. But

---

[1] *Our Future*, &c., p. 144.   [2] Ibid., p. 160.

[3] The old Roman name for Winchester (*Venta Belgarum*) reminds us of our kinship with the Belgians, whose Germanic origin is attested by Caesar in his *Gallic War*, ii. 4. But who would justify our action on that ground ?

[4] This is constantly asserted as against Great Britain ; but Prince von Bülow justifies Bismarck in following the same policy (*Imperial Germany*, English translation, p. 55).

[5] e. g. Count Hatzfeld, Count Reventlow, and Prince Lichnowsky : see *The German Enigma*, pp. 100 f., 161, 92, 94.

there is one idol which I must not pass by—the doctrine
that there is no such thing as morality in the relations of
states : ' Might is Right.'   It is curious that those who
profess this doctrine go on to attempt a justification of
their policy on ethical grounds, so soon as war breaks out.
This is surely insincere ; let us have either one thing or
the other.   If international action is guided solely by
force and fraud, let it not be defended on other grounds.
But perhaps those who proclaim this doctrine are not
quite serious in their application of the law of the
' survival . of the fittest ' to international relations.
There is, of course, an unfortunate ambiguity in the
term ' fit '.   But Darwin lent no countenance to the
interpretation of his law as an ethical precept.   Huxley,
indeed, explicitly repudiated that interpretation. ' Social
progress means a checking of the cosmic process at every
step and the substitution for it of another, which may be
called the ethical process ; the end of which is not the
survival of those who may happen to be the fittest in
respect of the whole of the conditions which exist, but
of those who are ethically the best.' [1]   But German
writers of the present day, especially historians of the
Berlin school, refuse to admit that the ethical process in
the individual has any application to states.   They fail
to see that just as in the state the force of the civil arm
compels obedience to the law, so in the family of nations
a combination of the well-disposed may be able to enforce
a respect for international law upon a nation which
refuses to obey it.   It is, of course, obvious that it is
more difficult to bring this result about in the latter case
than in the former.   And we have not yet attained that
ideal of a goodwill in nations which is a condition of the

---

[1] *Evolution and Ethics* (The Romanes Lecture for 1893), p. 33.

realization of their co-operation. Nevertheless the hope of the future lies in the recognition of the great truth that the relations which subsist between the individual citizen and his state ought to be reproduced in the family of nations. Each nation must learn to regard itself as a member of a great community and be prepared to strike, if necessary, in defence of the common good. In proportion as this feeling grows, we shall learn to cast behind us the immoral doctrine that the only duty of a nation is to play for its own hand, and to substitute for it the good old precept, 'Righteousness exalteth a nation.' Even now we see this hope taking shape.

> A brotherhood in arms ! For right, for law !
> Presage of what shall be in days to come,
> When nations leagued in common council stand,
> Strong in good will, to impose the rule of peace
> And strike, if need be, for the general weal !

Nor need we lose heart when we reflect that the ideal of a ' concert of Europe ' is not a new thing in history. It still looms before us as an aspiration, nowhere more alive, we are told, than in the land of its origin.[1] And a recent step of the first importance towards the realization of this dream, though it has hitherto attracted little public attention, is the agreement made between Great Britain and America that in any future dispute between these two countries a whole year shall elapse before any declaration of war.

---

[1] Prince Kropotkin, letter to *The Times*, Oct. 9, 1914, p. 5 ; cf. also Professor Vinogradoff's letter, ibid., Sept. 14, p. 10 (reprinted as one of the Oxford Pamphlets).

Oxford: Horace Hart Printer to the University

WHY WE ARE AT WAR

GREAT BRITAIN'S CASE

BY MEMBERS OF THE OXFORD FACULTY
OF MODERN HISTORY

E. BARKER.	H. W. C. DAVIS.
C. R. L. FLETCHER.	ARTHUR HASSALL.
L. G. WICKHAM LEGG.	F. MORGAN.

With an Appendix of Original Documents
including the Authorized English Translation
of the White Book issued by the
German Government

THIRD EDITION REVISED (TENTH IMPRESSION)
CONTAINING THE RUSSIAN ORANGE BOOK AND
EXTRACTS FROM THE BELGIAN GREY BOOK

TRANSLATIONS INTO FRENCH ITALIAN SPANISH
GERMAN DANISH AND SWEDISH
ARE NOW READY

Paper Covers Two Shillings net (70 cents)
Cloth Two Shillings and Sixpence net (85 cents)

OXFORD: AT THE CLARENDON PRESS
LONDON: HUMPHREY MILFORD
EDINBURGH   GLASGOW   NEW YORK   TORONTO
MELBOURNE   BOMBAY

(*a*)

OXFORD PAMPHLETS

1914

GERMAN
SEA-POWER

BY

CHARLES SANFORD TERRY

BURNETT-FLETCHER PROFESSOR OF HISTORY
IN THE UNIVERSITY OF ABERDEEN

Price Threepence net

OXFORD UNIVERSITY PRESS
HUMPHREY MILFORD
LONDON   EDINBURGH   GLASGOW
NEW YORK   TORONTO   MELBOURNE   BOMBAY

MAP

Between pages 16 and

GERMAN SEA-POWER

I. Traditions of Sea-power

As an effective instrument of policy and a potential weapon of offence the German navy is the creation of the fifteen years that lie immediately behind us (1898–1913). But the tradition of German sea-power is not so recent. Treitschke, who died two years before the first *Flottengesetz* (1898), was fond of reminding his countrymen that Germany once was the first maritime Power in Europe, ' and, please God, will be so again ! ' But the *Hansa Alemanniae* neither survived the new conditions of the fifteenth century, nor left an heir to its supremacy. Brandenburg's Great Elector (1640–88) made a groping effort to re-establish German sea-power on the Baltic, and even on more distant waters. A small flotilla flying the Hohenzollern eagle won and briefly held West Pomerania. On the Gold Coast the Elector's navy planted his flag (1682) in a region where, two centuries later, Imperial Germany took her place among the World Powers. He installed a *Marineamt* at Berlin in 1684, which controlled a fleet of 10 vessels and a modest *personnel* of 150 officers and men. But Grossfriedrichsburg and Arguin passed to other hands in the eighteenth century. Equally impermanent was the Elector's fleet. His immediate successors cultivated the more patently useful Prussian army. Hence, Frederick the Great for his naval activities resorted to letters of marque—an *Emden* of that day made herself conspicuous in the Mediterranean—and with negligible results.

Two hundred years followed the Great Elector before

Germany again turned her face to the sea.   Georg
Herwegh wrote in memory of the old Hansa in 1841 :

> *Und in den Furchen, die Kolumb gezogen,*
> *Geht Deutschlands Zukunft auf.*

To the eager patriotism of 1848 a fleet seemed the
symbol of unity.   And the practical need for one was
urgent ; for Denmark, fighting for Schleswig, was more
than a match at sea for the loose-jointed *Deutsche Bund.*
The old Hansa districts chafed under the humiliation.
Public subscriptions provided a few extemporized men-
of-war.   The *Nationalparlament* voted money for new
construction.   A Naval Board was constituted under the
Ministry of Commerce, and Prince Adalbert of Prussia
presided over a Commission to organize an ' Imperial
Navy '.   It proposed a fleet of 15 60-gun sailing frigates,
5 steam frigates, 20 steam corvettes, 10 dispatch-boats,
5 schooners, and 30 gun-sloops.   Karl Bromme of Leipzig, trained in the American mercantile marine and
recently with Lord Cochrane in Greek service, was
appointed ' Imperial Commissioner ' and the navy's first
admiral.   Its first shot was fired against the Dane off
Heligoland.   But the adventure was discouraging ; Great
Britain warned the belligerents off her territorial waters.
Moreover, the red, white, and black tricolour (the colours
of the volunteers of 1813, the *Burschenschaften,* and the
Nationalists of 1848) under which Bromme fought was
the flag of a State which as yet had no existence.   The
' Imperial Navy ' lay under imputation of piracy, and
Palmerston pointed out the fact ; an incident which the
present Kaiser recalled (1905) ' with burning indigna-
tion at the outrage done to our navy and our flag '.
International complications were prevented by the dissolution of the *Nationalparlament* at Stuttgart on

June 18, 1848, and the abandonment of the projected 'Imperial Navy'. Bromme was discharged in 1852, and Hannibal Fischer, as 'Naval Commissioner of the Germanic Confederation', dispersed the fleet so recently and hopefully assembled. Prussia and certain English firms bought a few vessels by private treaty. The rest— 2 steam frigates, 6 steam corvettes, 1 sailing frigate, and 27 oar-propelled gun-boats—were sold by public auction.

Until 1871 the Prussian flag upheld the dignity of the *Deutsche Bund* at sea. Thrice since 1815 Prussia had considered and rejected the construction of an efficient navy. But her maritime vulnerability in the Danish War of 1848 moved her to effort. In 1849 she possessed a squadron of 24 small vessels mounting 67 guns, and with it relieved the pressure of the Danish blockade. The Treaty of London (1852), which brought the Schleswig-Holstein War to a truce, did not interrupt her naval progress. Prince Adalbert gave his wide experience, and Swedish instructors were secured. In 1853 Prussia bought from the Grand Duke of Oldenburg five square miles of barren land on Jade Bay, her first outlook on the North Sea. With great labour and expense she equipped and fortified it as a war-port. Under the name Wilhelmshaven, William I opened it in 1869.

The Second Danish War (1864) strengthened Prussia's maritime position. It was provoked by Bismarck partly with an eye to a strategic canal through Holstein to the North Sea, and its conclusion left Schleswig and Kiel in Prussia's hands. Kiel took the place of Danzig forthwith as her naval head-quarters. A generation later (1895), William II opened the completed Kaiser Wilhelm Canal, whose North Sea entrance Great Britain's cession of Heligoland five years before (1890) greatly strengthened. Holstein remained temporarily in Austria's hands.

In 1865 Bismarck submitted a Memorandum to the
Prussian *Landtag* which foreshadowed the Navy Laws of
1898 and 1900.   It disavowed an intention to ' enter
into rivalry with first-class naval Powers ', but asserted
Prussia's claim to ' respect among those of second-class
rank '.   The vulnerability of her Baltic coast, the calls
of her mercantile marine, and the need to assert her
interests, if occasion arose, against States assailable only
by sea, furnished valid reasons for the proposal.   ' For
the last twenty years ', Bismarck reminded his hearers,
' the naval situation has engaged the attention of Germany above any other question.'   But the Assembly
was deaf to the appeal.   Bismarck's programme was
rejected, and a less ambitious one replaced it.

The Austro-Prussian War of 1866, which extruded
Austria from the *Deutsche Bund,* confirmed Prussia's
position as the first maritime State within it.   Her naval
operations in the war had been restricted to action on
the Hanoverian coast.   But its issue put in her hands
the German North Sea littoral, excepting the Grand
Duchy of Oldenburg, whose protection was a condition
of her occupation of Wilhelmshaven.   On sea and land
alike she had qualified herself for the Presidency of the
Norddeutsche Bund of July 1, 1867.   Its federal Constitution declared the navy ' one and indivisible under the
command of Prussia '.   Thenceforth, whether under
Bund or *Reich,* the German navy flew the tricolour
bearing the Hohenzollern eagle and the Iron Cross.   Kiel
and Wilhelmshaven were constituted ' federal war-
harbours '.   In 1869 the *Reichstag* approved a naval
programme providing for the construction within ten
years of a federal navy of 16 armoured ships, 20 corvettes, and 22 steam gun-boats, besides dispatch boats,
transports, and training-ships.

The Franco-German War of 1870–1 threatened to test the efficiency of the incomplete federal navy severely. France, next to Great Britain, was the largest naval Power in Europe. Wilhelmshaven lay exposed to attack, and if Denmark entered the war, Germany's position in the Baltic was likely to be precarious. But the French navy was as unprepared as the army. Germany had ample time to protect her vulnerable coasts, and the army's advance on Paris called up French crews and their guns to hold the thirteen forts protecting the capital. Part of the French fleet, however, passed the Great Belt, but gained no success at Kiel or elsewhere. A single formal naval engagement was fought off the coast of Cuba, between a German gun-boat and a French dispatch-vessel. But so little did sea-power affect the course of the war that for a generation Germany was disposed to underrate its importance.

II. The Navy, 1871–97

Upon the foundation of the *Deutsche Reich* a *Flotten-gründungsplan* was laid down (1873), which assigned a secondary function to the Imperial navy and outlined a modest programme of construction. No considerable advance was made during the remaining years of the first Kaiser's reign. In 1888, when his grandson took the helm, the naval estimates stood at £2,300,000, a smaller sum than was expended in that year by any Power except Austria-Hungary. The Imperial fleet contained 27 ironclads firing 160 guns, 23 cruisers, and a *personnel* of 16,995 officers and men.

The first decade of William II's reign (1888–98) also witnessed no material development of German sea-power, though in 1890 the Kaiser opened the Port of Stettin with the message to his people : ' Our future lies on the water.' A naval programme was drafted in 1888-9, but was not carried out thoroughly. The subsidiary position which the navy so far held was corrected, however, by a Cabinet order of March 30, 1889, which transferred its management to a *Reichsmarineamt* under a Secretary of State, subject to the *Reichskanzler*. The active command also was separated from the administration, leaving the latter merely to supervise arsenals, dockyards, and matters affecting *matériel*. Between 1890 and 1897, while Admiral von Hollmann was at the *Reichsmarineamt*, the country responded with restrained enthusiasm to the Kaiser's Stettin rally. The Conservatives regarded the navy as a dangerous competitor with the more imperative claims of the army. The naval estimates were submitted to severe pruning, and in 1897 three out of the four cruisers which the Admiralty declared to be necessary were struck out.

III. THE NEW POLICY

In his *Imperial Germany* the ex-Chancellor, Prince von Bülow, gives an interesting but incomplete explanation of the sudden and rapid development of the German navy which followed the arrival of Admiral von Tirpitz at the *Reichsmarineamt* in January, 1897 : ' In view of the anxious and discouraged state of feeling that prevailed in Germany during the ten years following Prince Bismarck's retirement, it was possible to rouse public opinion only by harping on the national string and rousing the Empire to consciousness. A deep oppression weighed heavily on the people, occasioned by the rupture between the wearer of the crown and the mighty man who had brought the nation from the depths of Kyffhäuser. The oppression could be lifted only by the

Kaiser setting before his people, who were united then neither in a common aspiration nor a common policy, a new goal to strive for, " a place in the sun " to which they were entitled and should strive to attain. On the other hand, it would not do to stimulate patriotic feeling to such a degree as to endanger our relations with England, against whom our sea-power would remain insufficient for years, and at whose mercy we lay in 1897, as a competent judge remarked at the time, like butter under a knife. To make it possible for us to build the fleet we needed was the foremost and greatest task of German policy after Bismarck's retirement.'

The motives which impelled Germany on her 'New Course' were more complex than Prince von Bülow suggests. William II's public utterances attest the significance he has attached consistently to sea-power as a condition of national greatness, an axiom learned from Admiral Mahan. His early associations with the British fleet, and a conviction that only on the ocean could the Empire obtain its rightful ' place in the sun ', confirmed his regard for the memory of the Great Elector, ' the one among my ancestors whom I hold in the most enthusiastic devotion and from my boyhood have set up as my model '. But during the first decade of his reign the Kaiser gained few converts as a missionary of sea-power, and at a later day reminded his subjects of the ' derision and mocking ' with which his ' earnest prayers ' for the navy's increase were received.

A more potent incentive was supplied by the rapid growth of German over-sea trade. In 1870 the Empire's steam merchant fleet was only half the tonnage of that of France. In 1904 it was twice as large. In 1889 Germany's merchant marine contained nearly 3,600 vessels, having a tonnage of over 1¼ millions and a per-

sonnel of 38,000. Prince von Bülow states reasonably :
' It was not ambitious restlessness that urged us to
imitate the Great Powers who long ago had embarked
on *Weltpolitik*. The growing nation, rejuvenated by its
political reconstruction [in 1871], burst the bounds of
its old home and followed a policy dictated by new
interests and needs. In proportion as our national life
became international, the policy of the Empire became
international, too.' A population of 41,000,000 in 1871
rose to 56,000,000 in 1900, and to 65,000,000 to-day. In
1885 about 171,000 Germans emigrated annually. In 1898,
when the population was larger, the number was only
22,000. To-day it is still less. The continuing decrease
signifies growing industries and enlarged demands for
home labour. The fact is expressed in the volume of
foreign trade. Between 1880 and 1899 German imports
increased from £143,000,000 to £218,000,000, and exports
from £147,000,000 to £289,000,000.

Nor is it an unrelated coincidence that the floating
of a large naval programme followed closely upon the
Franco-Russian *entente* of 1896, the first indication of
an imagined *Einkreisungspolitik* which has become the
bogy of German politicians. But superimposed upon
impulses that are natural or legitimate were ambitions
less tolerable to Germany's neighbours. ' He who reads
history aright ', wrote Treitschke, ' must admit that since
the days of the Great Elector, Germany's political history
is summed up in Prussia. Every clod of earth lost by
the old Empire and recovered since has been won back
by Prussia. In Prussia, in fact, reside the political
energies of the German people.' The statement will not
be challenged. But Prussia is the offspring of *Machtpolitik* persistently pursued. And in two decades her
' pedantic militarism ' captured the Empire and inspired

it to pursue on a larger field the offensive strategy of which she herself was the outcome. War had been the industry of Prussia. It was to be the Empire's industry also. In Europe the limits of profitable expansion had been reached. By sea-power only could Germany take her ' place in the world '—the *first* place : ' The next war must determine that in all controversies throughout the world Germany speaks the last word.'

But the necessary fleet could be built only with the support of public opinion. It was necessary to instruct it, therefore. The task was undertaken with brilliant success by Hollmann's successor at the *Marineamt*, Alfred von Tirpitz, a man of forty-eight, in 1897. He was distinguished already for his torpedo work in the service, for his tactical knowledge, and as Chief of Staff to the supreme naval command. He revolutionized the outlook of the Admiralty. Hollmann's programmes had ·been adjusted to a strategic design based on ' cruiser warfare ', coastal defence, and commerce raiding. At the most the fleet he had in view was a ' sortie-fleet '. Tirpitz substituted offensive for defensive strategy, and set out the new formula in the Memorandum of 1900 : ' Germany must have a battle fleet so strong that even the adversary possessed of the greatest sea-power will attack it only with grave risk to himself.'

To promote the new policy Tirpitz employed unweary- ing patience with the *Reichstag* and tact with the com- peting spending departments. For the education of public opinion he used noisier methods. The *Deutscher Flottenverein* was launched in 1898. Its object was defined thus : ' The German Navy League regards a strong fleet as necessary, principally to ensure the mari- time frontiers of Germany against the risks of war ; to maintain her position among the Great Powers of the

world ; to support her general interests and commercial
communications, and to safeguard her citizens over-seas.
The League therefore aims at stimulating, developing,
and strengthening the German people's understanding
of the importance and functions of a fleet.' The
organization had official support and the association
of such bodies as the *Deutsche Kolonialgesellschaft* and
the *Pan-Deutsche Gesellschaft*. It was financed by the
Krupps and other interests directly concerned with the
objects of its propaganda. It maintained an army of
lecturers and issued a monthly paper, *Die Flotte*. The
Press held an important place in the Tirpitz system. An
active and cleverly administered bureau was attached
to the *Marineamt* to instruct and inspire the influential
' armour-plate Press ' in the interests of the big-fleet
policy. International crises were used to the same end.
The Boer War smoothed the course of the Navy Law
of 1900. The alleged *Einkreisungspolitik* of Edward VII
helped the Amendments of 1906 and 1908. The Agadir
incident of 1911. commended the Amendment of 1912.
The Ministry of Education co-operated in the Tirpitz
policy of enlightenment. The publications of the Navy
League were distributed in the schools. The study of
modern history and of the relation of fleets and colonies
to national greatness was enjoined particularly. School
excursions to naval ports, especially from inland
places, were encouraged systematically by the authorities.

IV. The Law of April 10, 1898

Germany's Imperial Navy is the product of the Navy
Laws of April 10, 1898, and June 14, 1900, and the
Amendments of June 5, 1906, April 6, 1908, and June 14,
1912. The Law of 1898 followed the Empire's *début*

in *Weltpolitik*. German Anglophobia was born simultaneously and was advertised for the first time by the Kaiser on January 3, 1896, in a telegram to President Krüger. It was inspired by the Jameson ' Raid ', and congratulated the Boers on repelling an assault on their independence ' without appealing to the aid of friendly Powers '. Two years later, on December 16, 1897, the Kaiser dispatched his brother, Prince Henry, to the Far East on an adventure which challenged the international balance in the Pacific. On that occasion, as in the Krüger telegram, the Kaiser used language which conveyed a clear menace : ' Should any one attempt to affront us or challenge our just rights, strike with your mailed fist.' Prussian *Machtpolitik* at length found utterance in the official mouthpiece of the Empire. But the navy was inadequate to support a policy of provocation. Germany had in commission only 8 battleships, the largest of them of 9,874 tons burden, 6 others of an obsolescent type, and 19 small armoured cruisers. The fleet was designed for coast defence, and was inferior to every other European navy except that of Austria-Hungary.

Whatever ulterior object was in view, the arguments which commended the 1898 programme to the *Reichstag* were legitimate. An explanatory Memorandum pointed out that the navy actually had weakened in recent years ; that the Empire now possessed colonies needing protection ; and that its growing trade not only made it vulnerable at sea, but increased the danger of complications with foreign countries.

The Law of 1898, adopting the tone of the Memorandum, moderately declared its object : ' to create within a definite time a national fleet of strength and power sufficient to protect effectively the naval interests of the

Empire.' Adopting an important innovation, the Admiralty prescribed in advance the number of ships required for the completed fleet, their character, the date by which the whole construction should be finished, the durability of each vessel, and therefore the moment for its automatic replacement. The Government proposed to complete the programme in seven years. But the *Reichstag*, judiciously handled by Tirpitz, shortened the period to a *Sexennat*, and promised the new fleet by the end of the financial year 1903–4. The new navy was to consist of (1) a battle fleet of 17 battleships, 8 armoured coast-defence vessels, 6 large cruisers, and 16 small cruisers ; (2) a foreign service fleet of 3 large and 10 small cruisers, for duty in Chinese, American, East African, and South Sea waters ; and (3) a reserve of 2 battleships, 3 large and 4 small cruisers. Each battleship and armoured coast-ship was automatically replaceable at the end of twenty-five years, and large and small cruisers at the end of 20 and 15 years respectively. Thus, by defining the duration of each vessel's serviceableness, and by working to a single and coordinated design, the German navy could be counted on in the future as a permanent instrument of policy.

V. THE LAW OF JUNE 14, 1900

The Law of 1898 gave Germany a fleet such as her position in Europe and her interests outside it required. Neither in strength nor organization was it an offensive weapon, and Tirpitz declared (1899) that it met the Empire's needs. A revision of the Law in 1904, when its construction programme would be completed, might be expected. In fact it was superseded and repealed on June 14, 1900, by a new Law, which doubled the fleet and gave it a potentially offensive character. The new measure, breaching an undertaking to the Budget Committee in 1899, was the first-fruits of Anglophobia artfully excited by the *Reichsmarineamt*. In 1899 Great Britain engaged in an arduous war with the Boer Republics in South Africa. Throughout Europe the plucky fight of a small people roused generous sympathy. But on Germany the Boers had a closer claim. As Low Germans they could be counted an advanced guard of German *Kultur.* and *Weltpolitik*. Envious observation of the uses of sea-power, and annoyance at Great Britain's exercise of the right of search in the case of the mail-steamer *Bundesrat,* among others, roused a storm of Anglophobia in Germany, which permitted the *Reichsmarineamt* to 'scrap' the programme of 1898. 'Had the Government taken steps to put a spoke in England's wheel,' Prince von Bülow writes, ' popular approval was certain.' That Germany did not intervene, he admits, was due simply to the fact that ' our immediate national interests would not have benefited ; . . . England's passive resistance to German *Weltpolitik* would have changed to active hostility. . . . We therefore occupied ourselves instead in building up our navy.' ' The trident must be in our hand,' the Kaiser again instructed his people, and the Navy League sedulously educated them to face the task which Treitschke had impressed upon his generation, the challenge of Great Britain's *Weltherrschaft*.

The Memorandum attached to the Bill of 1900 [1] defined its object :

' To protect the Empire's sea trade and colonies, in view of present circumstances, only one method can

[1] German naval legislation, 1898–1912, is printed (trans.) in A. Hurd and H. Castle's *German Sea-Power : its Rise, Progress, and Economic Basis.* John Murray, 1914.

avail—Germany must have a battle fleet so strong that
even the adversary possessed of the greatest sea-power
will attack it only with grave risk to himself.

' For our purpose it is not absolutely necessary that
the German battle fleet should be as strong as that
of the greatest naval Power ; for as a rule, a great
naval Power will not be able to direct his whole striking
force upon us. . . .

' In order to attain the object we have in view, namely,
the protection of our sea trade and colonies and the
assurance of peace with honour, Germany requires,
according to the standard of the chief sea Powers, and
having regard to our position, two fleets (four squadrons)
of battleships, with the necessary cruisers, torpedo-
boats, &c., pertaining thereto.'

Even in the *Reichstag* it was pointed out that the
Navy Law of 1900 was aimed at Great Britain. Admiral
von der Goltz candidly avowed the fact : ' Let us consider the idea of war with England. There is nothing
improbable in it, having regard to the animosity which
Germany bears towards England, and to the attitude
of the British nation towards all Continental Powers,
especially Germany. . . . The general opinion in this
country is that we could not hold our own against
England's maritime power, and therefore that our naval
policy is futile. This puerile fear must be eradicated ;
for it prevents us from progressing. . . . Admittedly the
maritime superiority of Great Britain is overwhelming
now and, no doubt, will remain considerable. But, after
all, she is compelled to distribute her ships throughout
the globe. We may suppose that she would recall the
greater part of them in the event of war. But the
operation would take time to accomplish. Nor could
she abandon all her over-sea positions. On the other

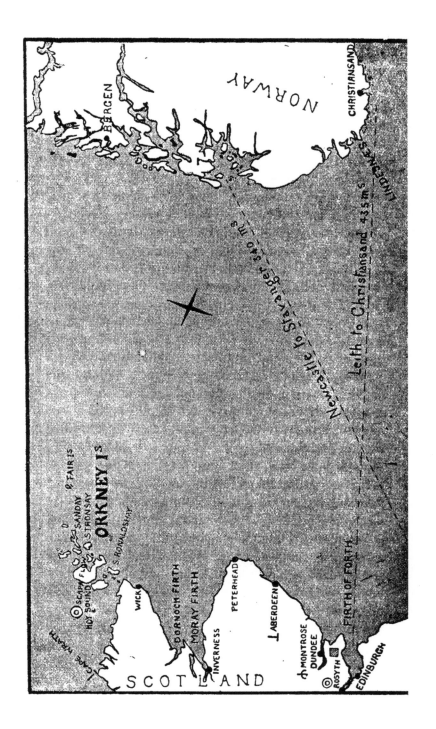

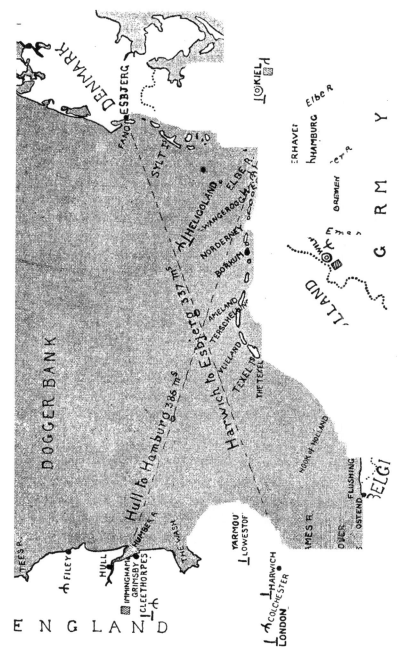

DENMARK
ESBJERG
FANO
SYLT

KIEL

Elbe R
ERHAVEN
HAMBURG
BREMEN
er P
Ems

HELIGOLAND
ELBE R.
WANGEROOCH
ODE R.
NORDERNEY
BORKUM

GERMANY

HULL

AMELAND
TERSCHEL
VLIELAND
TEXEL

HOLLAND

Esbjerg 337 m.s
Harwich to

Hull to Hamburg 386 m.s

DOGGER BANK

THE TEXEL

HOOK OF HOLLAND

BELGI
FLUSHING
OSTEND
DOVER

ENGLAND

TEES R.
FILEY
HULL
IMMINGHAM
GRIMSBY
CLEETHORPES
HUMBER R.

THE WASH

YARMOU
LOWESTOF

COLCHESTER
HARWICH
LONDON

THAMES R.

▨ Dreadnought Docks ⋔ Flying or Airship Stations ⊙ Naval Bases ⊥ Wireless Stations

hand, though much smaller, the German fleet is concentrated at home, and with the proposed increase will be strong enough to meet the normal British naval force in European waters. It must be remembered, too, that the question of numbers is less important at sea than on land Numerical inferiority can be made up for by efficiency, by excellence of *matériel*, and by the ability and discipline of the crews. Moreover, organization directed to rapid mobilization may even secure a temporary superiority of force.'

The new Law therefore provided (1) a battle fleet of 34 battleships, 8 large and 24 small cruisers ; (2) a foreign service fleet of 3 large and 10 small cruisers ; with (3) a reserve of 4 battleships, and 3 large and 4 small cruisers. The durability of battleships and cruisers remained as under the Law of 1898, which was now specifically repealed. An attached Schedule provided for the replacement of 17 battleships and 39 cruisers during the years 1901–17 inclusive. Thus the battle fleet of 1898 became two battle fleets, with three of the four squadrons permanently in commission. The new construction was no longer to be of the coast-defence type but suitable to a powerful high-sea fleet.

VI. The Amendment of June 5, 1906

The Law of 1900 framed a programme in advance to 1917. Actually it was amended in 1906, again in 1908, and again in 1912. In 1901 Admiral von Tirpitz warned the nation that a greater effort was necessary, while the Kaiser presented to the *Reichstag* a table, drawn up by himself, showing comparatively the strength of the British and German navies. The Anglo-French *entente* of April 8, 1904, the Kaiser's descent upon Tangier on

March 31, 1905, and Germany's failure to carry her policy at Algeçiras in 1906 fanned the embers of Anglophobia and carried the Navy League to widening popularity. But on February 10, 1906, the launch of the British *Dreadnought* inaugurated a new type of battleship, the product of experience gained in the Russo-Japanese War recently concluded. In temporary perplexity the German yards suspended the building of battleships, and the naval Amendment of June 5, 1906, while it increased the amount of annual expenditure on the navy by one-third, added only five large cruisers to the foreign service fleet, and one large cruiser to the reserve.

VII. BRITISH POLICY

It was becoming clear, in Sir Edward Grey's words to the House of Commons (March 29, 1909), that Germany's object was to build ' the most powerful fleet the world has ever yet seen '. Great Britain's attitude towards that ambition is deliberate and inflexible. She does not resent Germany's appearance among the naval Powers. But she is sceptical of official assertion of the purely defensive purposes for which the German navy is designed. Germany has a restricted frontier assailable by sea-power and therefore needing sea-power for its protection. She bears colonial responsibilities which in comparison with Great Britain's are insignificant. The gross tonnage of her mercantile steamship marine is (1914) only one-quarter of Great Britain's (5,000,000 tons against 20,000,000 tons). Of steamships of upwards of 100 tons burden she owns only one-fifth of Great Britain's fleet (2,000 against 10,000). Yet Germany has provided herself with a navy larger than Great Britain regards as necessary for the defence of her own vaster and more vulnerable interests. The supposition that Germany needs such a disproportionate naval strength for protection against Great Britain's assault is fantastic. Great Britain does not require and therefore does not covet Germany's comparatively unimportant colonies. As to European Germany, the suggestion that British naval supremacy might be employed in that direction is disposed of by the fact that Great Britain does not maintain, and is averse from maintaining, an army numerically adequate to invade the German nation in arms. As a potential weapon of offence, the British navy is valueless without an equally powerful army behind it. On the other hand, Germany, possessed of the essential army, has provided herself assiduously with a fleet which every year expands the Empire's radius of aggressive action. Her army, united with a navy less powerful even than the one she possesses, makes the latter a serious menace to an insular Power not overwhelmingly strong at sea. And this growing menace has been concentrated in the North Sea, almost within sight of the British coast. For the first time since 1815 Britain faces ' a powerful homogeneous navy under one government and concentrated within easy distance of our shores.'

Nor can Germany's neighbours forget that the elaboration and sudden release of offensive force is of the essence of German *Politik*. The Bismarckian system of ' blood and iron ' is official still. Her record places any increase of Germany's armaments at least under suspicion. Officially she has disclaimed any hostile intent. But the publications of her patriotic societies and the utterances of her representative men do not attempt to conceal the fact that her armaments are offensively designed. They condone the admission on

the ground that her late arrival among the Powers
makes aggression the only means for Germany to obtain
what she holds herself entitled to. They justify their outlook by whole-hearted advertisement of the superiority
of German *Kultur*. ' We Germans are the salt of the
earth,' declares the present Kaiser. ' We are,' Professor
Lasson, of Berlin, proclaims, ' morally and intellectually
superior to all men. We are peerless. So, too, are our
organizations and institutions.' To give these virtues
greater scope by the acquisition of *Weltreich* presents
itself therefore as an ambition almost altruistic ! That
it involves a challenge to Great Britain is not shirked.
Treitschke, on the eve of Germany's naval expansion,
wrote : ' If our Empire has the courage to follow
unflinchingly an independent colonial policy, a collision
with England is inevitable.' ' What my grandfather did
for his army that will I do for my navy,' the present
Kaiser has promised ; ' I will carry out unfalteringly
the work of reconstruction so that it may be able to
stand in equal strength by the side of my army to
procure the German Empire such a position over-seas
as never yet it has attained.' During the fervid Anglophobia of the Boer War Admiral von der Goltz wrote
in the *Deutsche Rundschau* : ' The material foundation
on which our power rests is broad enough to warrant
us contemplating a successful challenge to Great Britain's
supremacy. Germany must face that crisis, when it
comes, and lose no time in preparing for it.' In a chapter
entitled ' Germany's Historical Mission ', General Bernhardi wrote in 1911 : ' We shall not be able to maintain
our present position, powerful as it is, if we simply
restrict ourselves to what we have got, while our neighbours are getting more. If we wish to compete with
them, an ambition which our population and *Kultur*

entitle, and indeed compel, us to hold, we must not shrink from challenging the sovereignty of the world.'

Even were these aggressive ambitions not avowed, it is obvious that Great Britain cannot permit a navy as powerful as her own to ride the North Sea. So vital, indeed, is the challenge to her maritime superiority, that in view of the circumstances, it would have been competent for her to use Germany's pace-forcing in armaments as a *casus belli*, a course which, however defensible it might be, would have been rejected by the sober sense of British opinion. Great Britain adopted another method, whose character is epitomized in the *Round Table* for September, 1914 : ' Strenuous efforts were made to bring home to Germany that she had nothing to fear from England, and that sea-power, however great, without an army to back it, was useless for offensive purposes. When the Liberals came into power in 1906, they went to the furthest possible limit to make Germany realize this and to put a stop to the competition in armaments before the growing tension ended in war. To prove the sincerity of their intentions, they only built one capital ship [i. e. a *Dreadnought*] in 1907, and in 1908 only two, against Germany's three in each year. . . . The German answer to the Liberal proposals was a new Navy Law [1908] increasing their annual programme to four capital ships. There is probably no case in history of one nation setting to work to challenge more deliberately the peace and safety of another. The Liberal Government in despair abandoned its efforts, and ended by giving an order for eight *Dreadnoughts* in one year to make up leeway.'

VIII. THE AMENDMENT OF APRIL 6, 1908

Sympathizing with the Tsar's desire to bring the question of armaments before the Second Hague Conference in 1907, the British Admiralty for three successive years (1906–8) reduced its new construction to the lowest limit, permitting Germany to recover lost ground. In July, 1906, after the German Amendment of that year, the British Government announced its intention to cut down battleship construction by 25 per cent., destroyer construction by 60 per cent., and submarine construction by 33 per cent. The step was misinterpreted as a sign of exhaustion, and the Kaiser made known that Germany refused to regulate her programme by that of other nations. Nevertheless, the Prime Minister, Sir Henry Campbell-Bannerman, published an important article in the Liberal *Nation* on March 2, 1907, pointing out that British sea-power was recognized universally as non-aggressive ; expressing the Government's willingness to reduce armaments yet further in the event of other nations adopting a reciprocal policy, and pleading that the subject, vital to the interests of European democracies, should not be excluded from the Hague Conference. A communication in that sense was sent to all the naval Powers. The German Chancellor replied in the *Reichstag* a few weeks later (April) : ' The German Government cannot participate in a discussion which, according to their conviction, is unpractical, even if it does not involve risk.' The Navy League agitated for the completion of the 1900 programme by 1912 instead of 1917. The Government partially complied in the Amendment of April 6, 1908. It reduced the effective age of battleships and armoured cruisers from 25 to 20 years, laid down

4 capital ships annually from 1908 to 1911 inclusive, and 2 capital ships annually thereafter, yielding by 1917 an additional 15 capital ships to the 1900 programme.

The Amendment brought home to Great Britain's pacific Government the fact that Germany would have a superiority in capital ships by 1914 unless instant steps were taken to accelerate British construction. Hence, on March 29, 1909, the Prime Minister, deprecating the race in armaments and insisting that his proposals were not charged with anti-German feeling, made it clear that Great Britain would not permit her naval supremacy to be challenged, since upon it depended her national security. The Two-Power standard, which had been adopted when France and Russia's conjunction was feared, was abandoned. Eight capital ships were laid down in 1909, and in March, 1911, the First Lord declared the Admiralty's intention to maintain the navy superior to any foreign fleet and to any probable combination that might confront it, a policy which involved a *Dreadnought* superiority of 60 per cent. over the building construction of Germany's programme.

IX. The Amendment of June 14, 1912

The Amendment of 1908 prescribed a fall in the annual rate of German construction to two capital ships in 1912. But at the end of 1911 a new Amendment was announced. It received the Kaiser's signature on June 14, 1912. It added 3 battleships and 2 unarmoured cruisers to the programme and provided for the construction of 6 submarines annually (total 72). But its significance lay beyond the mere addition of ships to the establishment. A Memorandum attached to the Bill described the fleet as suffering from ' two serious

defects : One consists in the fact that in the autumn
of every year the time-expired men, i. e. almost one-
third of the crew in every ship of the battle fleet, are
discharged, their places being taken mainly by recruits
from inland districts. Owing to this fact the war readiness of the battle fleet is considerably impaired. The
second defect consists in the fact that at the present
time, with an establishment of fifty-eight capital ships,
only twenty-one are instantly available, in the event of
the reserve fleet not being ready at the moment. Since
the Fleet Law [of 1900] was promulgated . . . the moment
at which the reserve fleet can come into action gets
later and later still ; owing to the increasing complexities
of modern ships and to the difficulty of training a large
personnel. At present, therefore, the reserve fleet can
only be counted a second-line fighting force, though in
view of our great numerical strength in reserve men it
has first-rate importance. Both of these defects it is
proposed to remove, or at least to mitigate, by the
formation of a third active squadron.'

Mr. Churchill pointed out the significance of the
Amendment to the House of Commons on July 22, 1912.
Its main feature is ' the increase in the striking force
of ships of all classes which will be immediately available
at all seasons of the year. A third battle squadron of
8 battleships will be created and maintained in full commission as a part of the active battle fleet. Whereas,
according to the unamended Law [of 1900], the active
battle fleet consisted of 17 battleships, 4 battle or large
armoured cruisers, and 12 small cruisers, in the near
future that active fleet will consist of 25 battleships,
8 battle or large armoured cruisers, and 18 small cruisers ;
and whereas at present, owing to the system of recruit-
ment which prevails in Germany, the German fleet is

less fully mobile during the winter than during the summer months, it will, through the operation of this Law, not only be increased in strength but rendered much more readily · available.' He added : ' Taking a general view of the effect of the Law, nearly four-fifths of the entire German navy will be maintained in full permanent commission—that is to say, instantly and constantly ready for war. Such a proportion is remarkable, and, so far as I am aware, finds no example in the previous practice of any modern naval Power.' In the British navy it was usual to keep about half the fleet on a permanent war footing, the rest remaining in a condition of varying preparedness for instant service. The Amendment was a direct challenge by a navy manned by conscription on a low rate of pay to another whose *personnel* is voluntary and more expensively maintained. The German naval authorities do not disguise their belief that their numerical superiority gives them an advantage to which in the long run Great Britain's larger spending and construction power is bound to succumb.

X. ANGLO-GERMAN CONVERSATIONS, 1909–13

The 1912 Amendment passed under the impulse of renewed Anglophobia. Earlier in the year the British Government intimated that if Germany accelerated her construction Great Britain would lay down two keels to her one. Under the stress of increasing German menace also a redistribution of naval force took place, which concentrated Britain's main strength on the North Sea. These measures marked the collapse of conversations with Germany which the British Cabinet resumed after the Navy Amendment of 1908. Germany was anxious to take up the broken conversation. Her appearance (1908) in 'shining armour' in support of Austria-Hungary's Balkan ambitions, while it succeeded in its immediate purpose, carried the certain consequence that at her own time Russia would seek to avenge the indignity which had been put upon her. Thenceforth it was almost certain that the next war would engage Germany on both her fronts, against France and Russia, whatever and wherever might be its originating cause. It was desirable, obviously, that Great Britain should be excluded from the contest; for in the event of her neutrality Germany was confident that the resources of the Triple Alliance would suffice to settle accounts with France and Russia.

The Chancellor, Herr von Bethmann-Hollweg, approached the British Cabinet in the summer of 1909. The consideration which he offered was a possible retardation of naval construction. In return he invited an agreement that Great Britain would not attack Germany and would remain neutral in the event of her being attacked by an enemy or group of enemies. He was prepared to give a similar undertaking on his side, which, in view of the European situation, involved Germany in no risks. In the autumn of 1909 the British Government declined the proposals. But throughout 1910 and until the spring of 1911 it continued its endeavour to establish an understanding with Germany without sacrificing obligations to France and Russia. In July, 1911, however, a reaction occurred in Germany which Prince von Bülow describes as 'somewhat violent'. The exciting cause was the Agadir incident, which, like the Kaiser's appearance in the Bosnian crisis three years before, illustrated 'the German policy of solving international difficulties by threatening war as the alternative to retreat '. On Great Britain fell the brunt of Germany's wounded *amour propre,* and the Naval Amendment of 1912 was inspired directly by the discovery that her military resources were not yet adequate to support a policy of provocation By her militarists the measure was denounced as inadequate. General Bernhardi writes in his latest book, *Our Future: A Word of Warning to the German Nation* (1913) : [1] ' It is difficult to understand hqw our naval authorities could rest content with the slender provisions of the last [1912] Navy Law ; for without a doubt the German nation was prepared to vote every penny needed for the Army and Navy. . . . The new Law seems to me only a stopgap. It is really inconceivable why our naval authorities did not ask for more.'

Great Britain perforce met the new menace. Supplementary Naval Estimates were laid as ' the first and smallest instalment of the extra expenditure entailed by the new German Law '. Still, Mr. Churchill invited Germany in 1913 to join in a ' naval holiday '. The proposal was rejected. So, animated alone by the duty to defend her lawful interests, Great Britain took measures to equip herself adequately against a neighbour who openly challenged her position. For it remains as true to-day as when David Urquhart wrote sixty years ago : ' Our insular position leaves us only the choice between omnipotence and impotence. Britannia must either rule the waves or be swallowed up by them.'

---

[1] *Unsere Zukunft : ein Mahnwort an das deutsche Volk.* Translated by J. Ellis Barker and published under the title *Britain as Germany's Vassal.* Dawson. 1914.

APPENDIX [1]

BRITISH AND GERMAN SHIPBUILDING PROGRAMMES

The following tables show the British and German ships laid down between 1897 and 1913.

	Great Britain.				Germany.			
	Battleships.	*Armoured Cruisers.*	*Protected Cruisers.*	*Destroyers.*	*Battleships.*	*Armoured Cruisers.*	*Protected Cruisers.*	*Destroyers.*
Mixed armament period.								
1897–8	4	4	3	6	1	—	—	—
1898–9	7	8	1	12	2	1	2	6
1899–1900	2	2	1	—	3	—	2	6
1900–1	2	6	1	5	2	—	2	6
1901–2	3	6	2	10	2	1	3	6
1902–3	2	2	6 [2]	9	2	1	3	6
1903–4	5	4	4 [2]	15	2	1	2	6
1904–5	2	3	—	—	2	1	3	6
1905–6	—	—	—	—	2	1	3	6
Totals	27	35	18	57	18	6	20	48
Dreadnought period.								
1905–6	4	—	—	6	—	—	—	—
1906–7	3	—	—	2	2	1	2	12
1907–8	3	—	1	5	3	—	2	12
1908–9	2	—	6	16	4	—	2	12
1909–10	8	—	6	20	4	—	2	12
1910–11	5	—	5	20	4	—	2	12
1911–12	5	—	4	20	4	—	2	12
1912–13	4	—	8 [3]	20	2	—	2	12
1913–14	5	—	8	16	3	—	2	12
Totals authorized (1905–13) (Dreadnought period)	39	—	38	125	26	1	16	96

[1] Hurd and Castle, op. cit., pp. 374–7.

[2] Included in these two figures are eight scouts—small cruisers—which were laid down in 1902 and 1903.

[3] The cruisers of 1912–13 were designated 'light armoured cruisers'.

NAVAL EXPENDITURE AND *PERSONNEL* OF GREAT BRITAIN
AND GERMANY IN EACH OF THE YEARS 1901–2 TO 1913–14

Great Britain.			Germany.		
Year.	Total Naval Expenditure.[1]	Numbers of Personnel.	Year.	Total Naval Expenditure.	Numbers of Personnel.
	£			£	
1901–2	34,872,299	117,116	1901–2	9,530,000	31,157
1902–3	35,227,837	121,870	1902–3	10,045,000	33,542
1903–4	40,001,865	125,948	1903–4	10,400,000	35,834
1904–5	41,062,075	130,490	1904–5	10,105,000	38,128
1905–6	37,159,235	127,667	1905–6	11,300,000	40,843
1906–7	34,599,541	127,431	1906–7	12,005,000	43,654
1907–8	32,735,767	127,228	1907–8	14,225,000	46,936
1908–9	33,511,719	127,909	1908–9	16,490,000	50,531
1909–10	36,059,652	127,968	1909–10	20,090,000	53,946
1910–11	41,118,668	130,817	1910–11	20,845,000	57,373
1911–12	43,061,589	132,792	1911–12 [4]	22,031,788	60,805
1912–13 (estimated) [2]	45,616,540	137,500	1912–13 [5]	22,609,540	66,783
1913–14 (estimated)	47,021,636	146,000 [3]	1913–14 [6]	22,876,675	73,176

[1] The gross total of naval expenditure excludes the annuity in repayment of loans under the Naval Works Acts, and includes (a) the expenditure out of loans under those Acts, and (b) appropriations in aid.
[2] Including Supplementary Estimate.
[3] Maximum numbers.

[4] Submarines not included.
[5] Estimates as voted.
[6] Estimates as proposed. Supplementary Estimate of £146,771 for Aeronautics not included.

Oxford : Horace Hart Printer to the University

1914

Crown 8vo. Separately, in paper covers. Also in series as numbered (I-VII), stiff covers. One Shilling net each series. 35 Pamphlets have now (25 November) been issued and others are in preparation. The historical pieces are illustrated by sketch-maps.

I

1. The Deeper Causes of the War.
   By W. SANDAY. 3d. net. *Fifth Impression.*
2. To the Christian Scholars of Europe and America: A Reply from Oxford to the German 'Address to Evangelical Christians'. 2d. net. *Fourth Impression.*
3. The Responsibility for the War.
   By W. G. S. ADAMS. 2d. net. *Second Impression.*
4. Great Britain and Germany.
   By SPENSER WILKINSON. 2d. net. *Third Impression.*
5. 'Just for a Scrap of Paper.'
   By ARTHUR HASSALL. 1d. net. *Fourth Impression.*

II

6. The Germans, their Empire, and how they have made it.
   By C. R. L. FLETCHER. 2d. net. *Fourth Impression.*
7. The Germans, their Empire, and what they covet.
   By C. R. L. FLETCHER. 2d. net. *Fourth Impression.*
8. Might is Right.
   By Sir WALTER RALEIGH. 2d. net. *Second Impression.*
9. Austrian Policy since 1867.
   By MURRAY BEAVEN. 3d. net. *Second Impression.*
10. Italian Policy since 1870.
    By KEITH FEILING. 2d. net. *Second Impression.*

[a]

11. **French Policy since 1871.**
By F. MORGAN and H. W. C. DAVIS. 2d. net. *Fourth Impression.*

12. **Russia: The Psychology of a Nation.**
By PAUL VINOGRADOFF. 1d. net. *Fourth Impression.*

13. **Serbia and the Serbs.**
By Sir VALENTINE CHIROL. 2d. net. *Third Impression.*

14. **Germany and 'The Fear of Russia'.**
By Sir VALENTINE CHIROL. 2d. net. *Third Impression.*

15. **The Eastern Question.**
By F. F. URQUHART. 3d. net. *Third Impression.*

IV

16. **War against War.**
By A. D. LINDSAY. 2d. net. *Third Impression.*

17. **The Value of Small States.**
By H. A. L. FISHER. 2d. net. *Third Impression.*

18. **How can War ever be Right?**
By GILBERT MURRAY. 2d. net. *Fourth Impression.*

19. **The National Principle and the War.**
By RAMSAY MUIR. 3d. net. *Second Impression.*

20. **Nietzsche and Treitschke: The Worship of Power in Modern Germany.**
By E. BARKER. 2d. net. *Fourth Impression.*

V

21. **The British Dominions and the War.**
By H. E. EGERTON. 2d. net. *Second Impression.*

22. **India and the War.**
By Sir ERNEST TREVELYAN. 1d. net. *Third Impression.*

23. **Is the British Empire the Result of Wholesale Robbery?**
By H. E. EGERTON. 2d. net.

24. **The Law of Nations and the War.**
By A. PEARCE HIGGINS. 2d. net. *Second Impression.*

25. **England's Mission.**
By W. BENETT. 2d. net.

VI

26. August, 1914 : The Coming of the War.
By SPENSER WILKINSON. Stiff covers. 1s. net.

VII

27. The Retreat from Mons.
By H. W. C. DAVIS. 3d. net. *Third Impression.*

28. The Battles of the Marne and Aisne.
By H. W. C. DAVIS. 4d. net.

29. The Navy and the War.
By J. R. THURSFIELD. 3d. net. *Second Impression.*

30. Bacilli and Bullets.
By Sir WILLIAM OSLER. 1d. net. *Fourth Impression.*

---

*Published separately and will also appear shortly
in series.*

The Double Alliance *versus* The Triple Entente.
By JAMES M. BECK. 3d. net.

Thoughts on the War.
By GILBERT MURRAY. 2d. net.

The Leading Ideas of British Policy.
By GERARD COLLIER. 2d. net.

Greek Policy since 1882.
By A. J. TOYNBEE. 4d. net.

Poland, Prussia, and Culture.
By LUDWIK EHRLICH. 3d. net.

The Germans in Africa.
By EVANS LEWIN. 3d. net.

What Europe owes to Belgium.
By H. W. C. DAVIS. *In the press.*

Spectator : — 'These little books are easily the best books of the
war—accurate, quietly written, full of knowledge, and quite unspoiled
by vainglory or bitterness.'

Others in preparation.

HUMPHREY MILFORD
OXFORD UNIVERSITY PRESS, AMEN CORNER, LONDON, E.C.

No. 29

OXFORD PAMPHLETS
1914

THE NAVY AND
THE WAR

BY

J. R. THURSFIELD

HON. FELLOW OF JESUS COLLEGE

μέγα τὸ τῆς θαλάσσης κράτος

THIRD IMPRESSION

Price Threepence net

OXFORD UNIVERSITY PRESS
HUMPHREY MILFORD
LONDON EDINBURGH GLASGOW
NEW YORK TORONTO MELBOURNE BOMBAY

OXFORD: HORACE HART
PRINTER TO THE

THE NAVY AND THE WAR

STRANGELY enough—I had almost written shamefully enough—a most unworthy note of vexation and disappointment is beginning to make itself heard in too many quarters concerning the Navy and its doings. 'What is the Navy doing,' people are asking, ' and why is it doing so little ? There has been no big battle as yet, and there seems to be no prospect of one. We have been told that the primary function of the Navy is to seek out the armed forces of the enemy and destroy them. Well, if that is its business, why is it not doing it ? Wherever we look abroad on the seas we see nothing but disappointment, disaster, and destruction. The Grand Fleet has disappeared from view, and makes no sign. Ship after ship goes down in the North Sea, the victim of mines or submarines. Three big cruisers go down in a batch, with a loss of hundreds of gallant lives, and we do not even know that their assailants suffered at all. The *Pegasus*, temporarily disabled, gets caught in an open anchorage at Zanzibar, and is battered to pieces by the *Königsberg*. The *Emden* sinks merchant-vessel after merchant-vessel in the Bay of Bengal, bombards the oil tanks at Madras, and then makes off unmolested to pursue her depredations elsewhere, adding more British ships to her bag a few days later. The enemy's cruisers are playing the same game in the Atlantic, and not one of them has yet been rounded up, although it is true a couple of armed merchantmen have been sunk. In the Mediterranean the *Goeben* and

Breslau have made good their escape in the very teeth of vastly superior British squadrons. Against all this we have next to nothing to set except the smart little action in the Heligoland Bight, which was forthwith heralded as a glorious victory. Of course we have captured many helpless German merchantmen, and seized some undefended or weakly defended German colonies, but there is nothing very glorious about that. Altogether, it is a sorry tale of inaction, disappointment, and frequent reverse.'

To all these crabbed and cross-grained critics I would reply, ' O ye of little faith, how little you know of the things which belong to your peace ! You betray an equal ignorance of naval history and of the nature of naval warfare. Do you think that a fleet, however powerful and confident, can engage the enemy if he will not give it the opportunity ? Do you think that any nation can ever go to war without suffering occasional disappointments and partial reverses ? Do you not know that in the Great Revolutionary War, which began in 1793, it was more than a year before the first fleet action was fought by Lord Howe on "the glorious first of June ", 1794 ? Do you forget that throughout that war, both before Trafalgar and after, British merchant-vessels were captured by the French in hundreds every year, scores of them being snapped up even in the Channel day by day, to the very end of the war ? Do you not know that the Seven Years' War, the most successful that England ever fought, began with the loss of Minorca and the trial and death of Byng ? The Navy has done nothing, forsooth ! Why, it has done everything, literally everything; for without it nothing could have been done that has been done.'

To the student of naval history and of naval warfare all this is self-evident, and the only wonder is that any one should question it. To question it is to betray an ignorance so abysmal and a lack of insight so astounding, that one hardly knows how to begin to correct the ignorance and enlighten the darkened understanding of the questioner. Still I will make the attempt, and try to teach the alphabet of naval warfare to such of these cavillers as my pen can reach. It is true, of course, that the primary object of naval warfare, as indeed of all warfare, is to seek out the armed forces of the enemy and destroy them. On land this can always be done, or at least attempted. You have only to march your armies across the frontier and fight your enemy wherever you find him. If you fail to do this, he will assuredly march his armies across the frontier and fight you wherever he can find you. Battle after battle may succeed with varying fortune from time to time, the war may last for weeks or months or years, but sooner or later one side or the other will succeed, and the armed forces of the vanquished will be either subdued or destroyed. All this is because the armed forces of a belligerent on land cannot be withdrawn from the conflict. If they are, the game is up, for an army which will not fight cannot win. It may withdraw into a fortress, but no fortress is impregnable, and even if it is, it can be invested, and the army that it shelters can then be starved into submission. I shall perhaps be reminded of the lines of Torres Vedras, within which Wellington withdrew when he could not keep the field in Portugal, and which he held against all the assaults of the enemy. But the lines of Torres Vedras were never invested by the French, and never could be. They were always open to

the sea, over which food; reinforcements, and supplies
could at all times be obtained without stint, for
the sole and simple reason that the British fleet held
the lines of communication across the seas in such
strength that it was impossible for such naval forces
as remained to France after Trafalgar to interrupt
them. But Wellington could never have driven the
French out of the Peninsula by holding on indefinitely
to the lines of Torres Vedras. His action is no exception to the rule that the armed forces of one belligerent
on land cannot be permanently withdrawn from the
attack of the other without giving up the game, and
sooner or later acknowledging defeat.

This rule, however, does not apply at sea, or, at
least, it does not apply in anything like the same measure
or degree. It is one of the essential characteristics of
naval warfare that the capital ships of one belligerent
—that is, his main offensive force—can always be
withdrawn from the attack of the other. They have
only to remain in one or more of their own ports, provided that such ports are so heavily fortified that they
cannot be reduced from the sea alone. The case is
here the reverse of the lines of Torres Vedras. Wellington
was safe within those lines, because the enemy was
never strong enough to assault them, and could not
invest them so long as the sea was open. In like manner,
but with the conditions reversed as regards sea and
land, a hostile fleet in a fortified port is safe so long
as the land communications of the port are open.
Such a port cannot be assaulted from the sea, nor can
it be invested on land by naval forces alone. That is
why in the Crimean War we sent an army as well as
a fleet to reduce Sebastopol, and why inasmuch as we
did not send an army to the Baltic, we could not reduce

Kronstadt, and never attempted to assault it. I am old enough to remember the national impatience and even indignation at what was regarded as the inactivity, not to call it impotence, of the great fleet we sent to the Baltic ; and I am inclined to think that those who sent it there had during the long years of peace so lost touch with the realities of naval warfare, that they more than half expected that the fleet would be able to reduce Kronstadt. They were soon undeceived. Kronstadt was never assailed ; and although the fleets sent to the Black Sea did attack the seaward forts of Sebastopol, they cut a very sorry figure there. Very little harm was done to the forts, and a great deal of harm was done to the ships.

It is indeed a common delusion among landsmen who have never studied ' the sea affair '—and there seem to be very few that ever have—that ships are intended and suited for the attack of forts. It is about the worst use that ships can be put to. Ships are intended to fight at sea. To set them to fight against forts armed with ordnance equal to their own, is to court defeat and to risk disaster. In the great wars of the eighteenth century we blockaded the ports in which the enemy's fleets lay—Nelson was nearly two years before Toulon, and Cornwallis was more than two years before Brest—but we never attempted to reduce them from the sea. Let Brest and Toulon, let Kronstadt and Sebastopol prove that all such attempts are vain. Alexandria is only an exception that proves the rule. Had the British fleet been required to fight an action at sea the day after its rather inglorious success at Alexandria, it would have been wofully short of ammunition, and yet the Egyptian gunnery was none of the best.

It follows that the Grand Fleet and its gallant Commander-in-Chief are open to no reproach whatever for not having brought the German fleet to an action. You cannot bring an enemy to action if he will not take the sea, nor are there any means at present available by which he can be made to take the sea. But I suppose some people will grumble, as they always have grumbled, at such a situation as this. At the very time when Hawke, after long weeks of weary waiting and watching, was at last shattering the fleet of Conflans in Quiberon Bay, he was being burnt in effigy in England for allowing the enemy to escape— ' an outburst of popular anger ', says Mr. David Hannay, bitterly enough, ' which gives the exact value of the most sweet voices of the mob '. Let us remember Hawke, and we shall not fail to do justice to Sir John Jellicoe.

Nor must we assume, since it is neither wise nor becoming to despise an enemy, that the German fleet is keeping its harbours, or at any rate avoiding the North Sea, out of poltroonery and not out of policy. For my part, I am convinced that it is acting out of policy, and I think further that its policy is a sound one, based on a clear-sighted appreciation of the whole strategic situation. Germany is conducting a war on two fronts, and a war in which the naval and military factors are very intimately associated—an amphibious war in fact. The naval forces of Russia in the Baltic are by no means negligible. They stand towards the German fleet very much in the same relation that the German fleet stands towards the British Grand Fleet in the North Sea—that is as a ' fleet in being ' temporarily withdrawn into the unassailable shelter of its ports, but ready to take the offensive at once if Germany were to withdraw her naval forces from the Baltic and place them in her North Sea ports, with intent to take the sea at her own time, and try conclusions with the British Grand Fleet in the open. In that case the whole of the Baltic coasts of Germany would be open to the landing of Russian troops in such force as might seriously affect the fortunes of the German arms on the eastern front of the war. Hence, so long as the Russian Baltic ports are free from ice—that is until towards the end of the year so far as Kronstadt is concerned, while Libau, which possesses a naval station, is practically free from ice all the winter—the German fleet, compelled to face the enemy on two fronts, is not likely to be able to appear in the North Sea with the whole of its capital ships. Even if it did, we need have no fear of the result. Sir John Jellicoe may say with Nelson, ' Every opportunity has been given to the enemy to put to sea, for it is there that we hope to realize the hopes and expectations of our country.' Those hopes and expectations would be all the higher, and would rise to nothing short of certainty, if the German fleet were to put to sea with less than its whole available force of capital ships.

Moreover, the situation thus established does not by any means reduce the German fleet to an ignoble impotence. That we know to our cost. The *Amphion*, the *Speedy*, the *Pathfinder*, the *Cressy*, the *Hogue*, the *Aboukir*, and the *Hawke* are the melancholy proofs. But these losses, deplorable as they are, are not to be taken too seriously. They are, so to speak, all in the day's work. We are engaged in the hazardous enterprise of war, and we must take the risks with equanimity, and bear the losses with fortitude. Our initial superiority to the enemy in all the elements of naval force is sub-

stantially unimpaired by such losses as we have sustained
—they are not without some compensation in the
losses we have inflicted on the enemy, and we are not
going to take blows without returning them—nor
would it be perilously reduced if our losses were twice
as many, and even included a battleship or two. It
is quite on the cards that such things may happen,
and we must not be downhearted if they do. We shall
give as good as we get in the long run, and when the
day comes at last for the final decision, we shall
still have enough and to spare, for when the enemy
does come out, our torpedo craft will assuredly not
be idle.

Meanwhile the situation approximates to what was
known in former times as a blockade. The object of
such a blockade was not so much to keep the enemy
in—on the contrary, the blockader always hoped that
he would come out and fight, and gave him every
opportunity of doing so, as Nelson said—as to take
care that if and when he did come out he should be
observed, shadowed, and, as soon as might be, brought
to action by the blockading fleet. For this purpose
the blockading fleet was kept cruising as close to the
blockaded port as was practicable, and a still closer
watch was kept on the port by means of an inshore
squadron of cruisers and small craft. A close blockade
of this kind is no longer possible as far as the main
fleet is concerned, owing to the development of the
torpedo and of the vessels specially constructed for
its offensive employment, especially submarines. It
is true that a close watch on the enemy's ports can still
be kept by means of torpedo craft and light cruisers,
but however close this watch may be, it will always
be possible, in certain conditions of weather and sea,

for some torpedo craft of the enemy, especially sub-marines, to elude the vigilance of the watchers and get clear away to sea. This contingent but never-ceasing menace is so serious—since a torpedo craft, when it gets its chance, is able to put even a battleship out of action—that it is expedient for the battle squadrons of the blockader to be far withdrawn from the observation and attack of such of the enemy's torpedo craft as manage to get to sea. That is why we hear little and see less of the battle squadrons of the Grand Fleet. We shall hear of them soon enough when the enemy's capital ships are at sea ; but so long as the latter remain in harbour, the less we hear of them the better. It is essential that their whereabouts should be unknown. Last year, in a little manual on *Naval Warfare*, I tried to forecast the probable course and character of a blockade or quasi-blockade of the kind indicated above, and I will quote that forecast here, because it seems to me to expound the true philosophy of the present situation.

' Thus, in the conditions established by the advent of the torpedo and its characteristic craft, there would seem to be only two alternatives open to a fleet of battleships engaged in blockade operations. Either it must be stationed in some sheltered anchorage outside the radius of action of the enemy's surface torpedo craft, and if within that radius adequately defended against torpedo attack—as Togo established a flying base for the use of his fleet, first at the Elliot Islands and afterwards at Dalny, for the purpose of blockading Port Arthur ; or it must cruise in the open outside the same limits, keeping in touch with its advanced cruisers and flotillas by means of wireless telegraphy, and thereby dispensing with anything like a fixed rendezvous. It is

not, perhaps, imperative that it should always cruise
entirely outside the prescribed radius, because experience in modern naval manœuvres has frequently shown
that it is a very difficult thing for torpedo craft, moving
at random, to discover a fleet which is constantly shifting
its position at high speed, especially when they are at
any moment liable to attack from cruisers and torpedo
craft of the other side.

'Thus a modern blockade will, so far as battle fleets
are concerned, be of necessity rather a watching blockade
than a masking or sealing-up blockade. If the two
belligerents are unequal in naval strength it will probably
take some such form as the following. The weaker
belligerent will at the outset keep his battle fleet in his
fortified ports. The stronger may do the same, but he
will be under no such paramount inducement to do so.
Both sides will, however, send out their torpedo craft
and supporting cruisers with intent to do as much harm
as they can to the armed forces of the enemy. If one
belligerent can get his torpedo craft to sea before the
enemy is ready, he will, if he is the stronger of the two,
forthwith attempt to establish as close and sustained
a watch of the ports of his adversary sheltering the
enemy's armed forces as may be practicable ; if he is
the weaker, he will attempt sporadic attacks on the
ports of his adversary and on such of his warships as
may be found in the open. . . . Such attacks may be
very effective, and may even go so far to redress the
balance of naval strength as to encourage the originally
weaker belligerent to seek a decision in the open. But
the forces of the stronger belligerent must be very badly
handled and disposed for anything of the kind to take
place. The advantage of superior force is a tremendous
one. If it is associated with energy, determination,

initiative, and skill of disposition no more than equal
to those of the assailant, it is overwhelming. The sea-
keeping capacity, or what has been called the enduring
mobility, of torpedo craft, is comparatively small. Their
coal-supply is limited, especially when they are steaming
at full speed, and they carry no very large reserve of
torpedoes. They must, therefore, very frequently return
to a base to replenish their supplies. The superior
enemy is, it is true, subject to the same disabilities, but
being superior he has more torpedo craft to spare and
more cruisers to attack the torpedo craft of the enemy
and their own escort of cruisers. When the raiding
torpedo craft return to their base he will make it very
difficult for them to get in and just as difficult for them
to get out again. He will suffer losses, of course, for
there is no superiority of force that will confer immunity
in that respect in war. But even between equal forces,
equally well led and handled, there is no reason to suppose that the losses of one side will be more than equal
to those of the other ; whereas if one side is appreciably
superior to the other it is reasonable to suppose that it
will inflict greater losses on the enemy than it suffers
itself, while even if the losses are equal the residue of
the stronger force will still be greater than that of the
weaker.'

It will be objected, perhaps, that in all this I have
taken little or no account of the submarine and its
special menace. But the submarine, after all, is only
a particular kind of torpedo craft—a very formidable
kind, no doubt, but still a torpedo craft. Such guns
as it can carry are almost as useless against the big
ships—which are its special prey—as peashooters would
be, and it cannot fire them without coming to the
surface, when it becomes the most vulnerable of all

vessels that fight above water. It has, however, certain notable advantages over the surface torpedo craft. The latter can attack bigger ships only at night with any real prospect of success. If it is caught in the open in daylight, in waters occupied by superior hostile forces of any kinds, including its own, its only safety lies in flight. In these circumstances, its rate of fuel-consumption is very high indeed, and its effective range of offensive action is thereby very greatly reduced. That is perhaps why we have not so far heard much of the doings of the German torpedo craft in the North Sea during the present war. The submarine, on the other hand, is not subject to this limitation, though it has special limitations of its own. Its speed is much less than that of the surface torpedo craft; but it can keep the sea night and day within the limit of its fuel endurance—which in modern submarines may perhaps be put at 2,000 miles or more—and in the daytime it can sink beneath the surface whenever it is threatened with attack. It can also approach an enemy in the same submerged condition, and its advance in that condition to within striking distance is by no means easy to detect. On the other hand, when submerged, its range of vision is exceedingly limited—it is altogether blind when its periscope is submerged—and inasmuch as the majority of submarines fire their torpedoes only from the bows, they can only fire when their bows are bearing on the vessel attacked. Thus their best target is a stationary ship, and it is one that can hardly be missed if the submarine is well handled and remains long enough undetected. A rapidly moving ship is much more difficult to hit, just as every sportsman knows that a flying bird is much more difficult to hit than a sitting one. These conditions indicate the best mode of defence against submarine attack. It is to keep moving at high speed, to ram the submarine if it is detected in time, or, if that is not practicable, to steam away from it, while frequently changing course. This is always practicable, because the speed of a submerged submarine rarely exceeds twelve knots, and very seldom attains it. Even if the submarine is not detected, though its presence may be suspected, the best defence against it is high speed and frequent changes of course.

We are now in a position to understand how and why it was that the *Aboukir*, the *Cressy*, and the *Hogue* all fell victims to a single attack of the enemy's submarines, and understanding this, we shall, I think, entertain a reasonable confidence that no such disaster is likely to befall us again. I do not mean that henceforth we have nothing to fear from German submarines. On the contrary, we have just as much to fear as ever, and the enemy has just as much to fear from our submarines, whenever he quits the shelter of his ports. But never again will our ships do what the *Hogue* and the *Cressy* did—nobly, but in vain. On this point I have nothing of my own to add to the impressive statement—all the more impressive because it is so admirably restrained in tone—which was issued by the Admiralty a few days after the disaster :

' The sinking of the *Aboukir* was of course an ordinary hazard of patrolling duty. The *Hogue* and *Cressy*, however, were sunk because they proceeded to the assistance of their consort and remained with engines stopped endeavouring to save life, thus presenting an easy and certain target to further submarine attacks. The natural promptings of humanity have in this case led to heavy losses which would have been avoided by a strict adherence to military considerations. Modern naval war is presenting us with so many new and strange situations that an error of judgement of this character is pardonable. But it has been necessary to point out for the future guidance of His Majesty's ships, that the conditions which prevail when one vessel of a squadron is injured in a minefield or is exposed to submarine attack, are analogous to those which occur in an action, and that the rule of leaving disabled ships to their own resources is applicable so far at any rate as large vessels are concerned. No act of humanity, whether to friend or foe, should lead to a neglect of the proper precautions and dispositions of war, and no measures can be taken to save life which prejudice the military situation. Small craft of all kinds should, however, be directed by wireless to close on the damaged ship with all speed.

' The loss of nearly 60 officers and 1,400 men would not have been grudged if it had been brought about by gunfire in an open action, but it is peculiarly distressing under the conditions which prevailed. The absence of any of the ardour and excitement of an engagement did not, however, prevent the display of discipline, cheerful courage, and ready self-sacrifice among all ranks and ratings exposed to the ordeal.

' The duty on which these vessels were engaged was an essential part of the arrangements by which the control of the seas and the safety of the country are maintained, and the lives lost are as usefully, as necessarily, and as gloriously devoted to the requirements of His Majesty's service as if the loss had been incurred in a general action. In view of the certainty of a proportion of misfortunes of this character occurring from time to time, it is important that this point of view should be thoroughly appreciated.

' The loss of these three cruisers, apart from the loss of life, is of small naval significance. Although they were large and powerful ships, they belonged to a class of cruisers whose speeds have been surpassed by many of the enemy's battleships. Before the war it had been decided that no more money should be spent in repairing any more of this class, and that they should make their way to the sale list as soon as serious defects became manifest.'

I shall waste very few words over the fugitive depredations of the German cruisers at large in the outer seas, because when all told they amount to nothing more than a few vexatious pin-pricks. Why should I enumerate all the ships which the *Emden* has captured or sunk ? They hardly amount, I think, to a baker's dozen as yet, and the *Emden* must by·this time be nearing the end of her tether. Her speed must decrease as her hull grows foul, and when she needs coal she will only obtain it at ever-increasing risk. Two of her supply ships are gone. The total number of these cruisers as well as of such armed merchant-vessels as have not already been disposed of is well known to the Admiralty, and we may be quite sure that adequate measures are being taken to hunt them down and that, as the Prime Minister said at the Guildhall, they will very soon be disposed of. Of course ' very soon ' is a relative term. It does not mean ' forthwith '. Regard must be had to conditions of time and space. The seas are wide and they take a great deal of sweeping to clear them of marauders few in number and cunning in evasion. But evasion cannot last for ever. The end is certain and probably not far distant. The worst that these cruisers can do is really very little. In spite of all their depredations war insurance remains low and steady, and the daily lists of sailings from British ports for all parts of

the world show how little our maritime commerce is
really affected. We have driven the German flag from
the seas at the cost of not a score of British merchant-
ships captured by the enemy.

Nor shall I shed many tears over the escape of the
Goeben and the *Breslau*, nor even, except for the loss of
life, over the destruction of the *Pegasus* by the *Königsberg*. We know too little about either of these incidents
to form a definite judgement about them. The former
is the subject of inquiry by the Admiralty, and the latter
will no doubt be fully investigated in due course. I have
known too many instances in manœuvres of ships eluding
the pursuit of their adversaries, and even escaping the
latter's observation altogether on a dark night, to be
greatly surprised or disturbed at anything of this kind
that may happen in war. Or again, it may be that the
Goeben and the *Breslau* were too fast for their pursuers.
If that should prove to be the case, it may perhaps
induce some naval critics to revise their views as to the
value of speed in warships. Some high authorities have
held that speed is only useful if you want to run away ;
but the proposition, if otherwise sound, seems to overlook the consideration that however useful speed may
be in flight it must perforce be still more useful in pursuit.
As to the *Pegasus*, many questions might be asked and
must be asked before we can form any judgement,
favourable or unfavourable, as to the circumstances in
which she was destroyed. But I prefer to wait until
we know the facts before asking a single question which
might seem to impute any lack of judgement to her
gallant commander.

I have now examined one by one the several counts
in the preposterous indictment which I formulated from
the mouths of the critics and grumblers at the beginning

of this pamphlet, and I think I have shown how preposterous they all are, ill founded for the most part and absurdly exaggerated even where there is any foundation for them. But there is a more general answer to this dolorous Jeremiad, and this I have reserved to the last. It consists in examining not what the Navy has not done, but what it has done, what it is doing, and what it will assuredly continue to do until ' the day ' comes, if it ever does come, when by the blessing of Providence and the skill of a good admiral it will do all that is expected of it. Stated in this form my general answer will, I think, be found to be conclusive and overwhelming. It is quite true that the primary function of a navy is to seek out and destroy the armed forces of the enemy. By that means and by that means only will ' the command of the sea ', as it is called, be finally secured. But the supreme function in question can only be fully discharged if the enemy is prepared, or can be forced, to come forth and destroy or be destroyed as the fortune of war may determine. If the enemy will not come out and cannot be forced out, then so far he leaves the command of the sea to his adversary. But it is only a *de facto* command and can never be made an absolute command of the sea until the armed forces of the enemy have been either destroyed or otherwise subdued. But a *de facto* command of the sea serves all the purposes of naval warfare so long as it is unchallenged. It is only the fact that it may be challenged at any moment that differentiates it from an absolute command. The phrase ' command of the sea ' is a time-honoured one, but it is not free from ambiguity and it is often used very loosely in common parlance. Properly used, it signifies control of maritime communications. The sea is the common highway of all nations and, what

is more, it is all highway. No nation, even in time of
war, seeks to reduce it into sovereignty. A nation at
war merely seeks to secure freedom of transit for ships
carrying its own flag and to deny such freedom to ships
bearing the enemy's flag. When that is done all is done
that naval warfare as such can do. If territorial conquest or occupation by naval agency is aimed at, then
the Navy must carry the Army on its back until the
shores of the territory to be occupied are reached. But
the Army must do the rest, except in cases where naval
co-operation is practicable. ' I consider ', said the late
Sir Geoffrey Hornby, one of the highest of modern naval
authorities, ' that I have command of the sea when I am
able to tell my Government that they can move an
expedition to any point without fear of interference
from an enemy's fleet.' This represents what may be
called the military aspect of command of the sea as
defined above. But there is also the mercantile aspect,
and this for a maritime Power like England is immeasur-
ably more important. We might not need to send an
expeditionary force across the seas, but we must, as
a matter of life and death, keep the seas open for that
oversea commerce which is our life-blood. This aspect
of the matter and the vital connexion between the two
is best set forth in the words of another unimpeachable
authority, Admiral of the Fleet Sir Arthur Wilson, sometime First Sea Lord of the Admiralty. In that capacity
this great master of naval strategy wrote as follows in
a Memorandum which he prepared for the use of the
Government in 1910. ' The really serious danger that
this country has to guard against in war is not invasion
but interruption of our trade and destruction of our
merchant shipping. The strength of our Fleet is determined by what is necessary to protect our trade, and

if it is sufficient for that, it will almost necessarily be
sufficient to prevent invasion, since the same disposition
of ships to a great extent answers both purposes.'

Invasion is now hardly in question, and if it were,
we should be quite ready for it so long as our *de facto*
command of the sea is unchallenged. A raid might
indeed be attempted, but it need not greatly alarm us.
If it were not stopped at sea, as it almost certainly
would be, it would very soon be swallowed up on shore.
For the rest I cannot tell the story of what the command
of the sea—established from the very outset and operating continuously in both the spheres of naval activity
defined by the two great admirals quoted above—has
done for us better than it has already been told at an
earlier stage of the war in the *History of the War*
now being published by *The Times*. From the second
part of that valuable and interesting publication I have
obtained permission to quote the following passage :

' From the moment when war became imminent the
main British Fleet melted into space. Nothing was seen
of any part of it, except of the flotillas patrolling our
coasts. Nevertheless, although it was invisible, there
was never in the world's history a more sudden, overwhelming, and all-pervading manifestation of the power
of the sea than that given by the British Fleet, admirably
seconded by that of France, in the first fortnight of the
war. The rarity of properly called naval incidents might
have left a different impression. It might well have
seemed that the Fleets of France and England had done
nothing. As a matter of fact, they had done all in their
power, and that all was stupendous. Those weeks saw
German maritime commerce paralysed ; British maritime commerce fast returning to normal conditions in
all the outer seas of the world, and not even wholly

suspended in the area of immediate conflict. Nay, more, it was already seeking new realms to conquer—realms left derelict by the collapse of the maritime commerce of the enemy. That is, in a few words, the long and the short of it. Prize Court notices of German and Austrian merchantmen captured on the seas or seized in our ports appeared daily in increasing numbers in *The Times*. Side by side with them appeared the familiar notices of the regular sailings of our liners for nearly all the ports of the outer seas. *The Times* published daily accounts of the new avenues of trade, manufacture, and transport opened up by the collapse of our enemies' commerce, and of the energy and enterprise with which our merchants, manufacturers, and sea-carriers were preparing to exploit them. How it stood with Germany on the other hand we have unimpeachable German authority to show. On August 20 *The Times* published the following extract from the *Vorwärts*, the German Socialist organ :

'If the British blockade took place imports into Germany of roughly six thousand million marks (£300,000,000) and exports of about eight thousand million marks (£400,000,000) would be interrupted—together with an oversea trade of 14 milliards of marks (£700,000,000). This is assuming that Germany's trade relations with Austria-Hungary, Switzerland, Italy, Belgium, Holland, Denmark, Norway, and Sweden remained entirely uninfluenced by the war—an assumption the optimism of which is self-evident. A glance at the figures of the imports shows the frightful seriousness of the situation. What is the position, for example, of the German textile industry if it must forgo the imports of oversea cotton, jute, and wool ? If it must forgo the 462 millions (£23,100,000) of cotton from the United States, the 73 millions (£3,650,000) of cotton from Egypt, the 58 millions (£2,900,000) of cotton from British India, the 100 millions (£5,000,000) of jute from the same countries, and further the 121 millions (£6,050,000) of merino wool from Australia, and the 23 millions (£1,150,000) of the same material from the Argentine ? What could she do in the event of a war of longer duration without these raw materials which in one year amount in value to 830 millions (£41,500,000) ?

'It may also be mentioned,' said the *Vorwärts*, 'that Germany received in 1913 alone from the United States about 300 millions (£15,000,000) of copper, and further that the petroleum import would be as good as completely shut down. The German leather industry is largely dependent on imports of hides from oversea. The Argentine alone sent 71 millions (£3,550,000) worth of hides. Agriculture would be sensibly injured by the interruption of the exports of Chilean saltpetre from Chile, which in 1913 were of the value of not less than 131 millions (£6,550,000). The significance of an effective blockade of German foodstuffs is to be seen in the following few figures : The value in marks of wheat from the United States is 165 millions (£8,250,000), from Russia 81 millions (£4,050,000), from Canada 51 millions (£2,550,000), from the Argentine 75 millions (£3,750,000)—372 millions (£18,600,000) from these four countries. There will also be a discontinuance of the importation from Russia of the following foodstuffs : Eggs worth 80 millions (£4,000,000), milk and butter 63 millions (£3,150,000), hay 32 millions (£1,600,000), lard from the United States worth 112 millions (£5,600,000), rice from British India worth 46 millions (£2,300,000), and coffee from Brazil worth 151 millions (£7,550,000) should be added to the foregoing. No one who contemplates without prejudice,' said the *Vorwärts*, 'these few facts, to which many others could be added, will be able lightly to estimate the economic consequences of a war of long duration.'

'If the British blockade took place,' said the *Vorwärts*, and it dwelt on the consequences of a war of long duration. The British blockade was actually taking place at the moment these words were written, though it was not called by that name for reasons which need not here be examined. Acting together with the hostility of Russia, which closed the whole of the Russian frontier of Germany to the transit of merchandise either way, the control of sea communications established by the fleets of England and France had already secured the first-fruits of those consequences of a war of long duration on which the *Vorwärts* dwelt with such pathetic significance. Those consequences were bound to be continuous and cumulative so long as the control of sea communications remained unrelaxed. The menace of the few German cruisers which were still at large was already abated. Already its bite had been found to be far less formidable than its bark. War premiums on British ships at sea were falling fast. German maritime commerce was uninsurable, and in fact there was none to insure. Its remains were stranded and derelict in many a neutral port. One of the greatest dangers, in the opinion of some eminent authorities the most serious danger, that this country had to guard against in war was already averted, and would remain so as long as the control England had established over her sea communications continued to be effective. This was the first result of our naval preparations, the first great manifestation of sea power.

'But there was a second result far more dramatic than the first, and not less significant in its implications, nor in its concrete manifestation of the overwhelming power of the sea. The whole of the Expeditionary Force, with all its manifold equipment for taking and keeping the field, had been silently, secretly, swiftly, and safely transported to the Continent without the loss of a single man, and without the slightest show of opposition from the Power which thought itself strong enough to challenge the unaggressive mistress of the seas. 'Germany,' says the Preamble to the Navy Law of 1900, 'must possess a battle fleet of such strength that even for the most powerful naval adversary a war would involve such risks as to make that Power's own supremacy doubtful.' Such a war had now been forced upon England, and one of its first accomplished results had been the entirely successful completion of an operation which, if the enemy had deemed our naval supremacy even so much as doubtful, he might have been expected to put forth his uttermost efforts to impeach. That Germany declined the challenge was a proof even more striking of the power of superior force at sea than the action of the British Navy upon the trade routes of the world.'

This was published on September 1, and was no doubt written some days earlier. Although the outlying German cruisers have not yet been accounted for, and although the depredations of the *Emden* have sorely tried the nerves of the critics and the grumblers, yet if a similar survey of the situation were to be made again to-day, it would have to be still more encouraging and even astounding in spite of the deplorable loss of the three *Cressys*.

We know now not only that our Expeditionary Force crossed the seas in absolute safety, but that a continuous stream of reinforcements and supplies has reached them from day to day without the slightest interruption. We know that a command of the sea simultaneously established by the Allied Fleets in the Mediterranean not only has enabled the French troops in Africa to be transported in equal safety to the seat of war, but has also secured a like immunity for our own contingents coming from India. Think what all this means. Think of the transcendent advantage Germany might have gained had she felt herself strong enough to assail and compromise our command of the sea while our Expeditionary Force was in transit. It would have been a desperate enterprise no doubt, but still it was an opportunity never likely to recur. The British Fleet would have troubled her no more, for she must have defeated and shattered it before she could have got at the Expeditionary Force at all. If she could not face it then, when it was engaged and in some measure preoccupied in the paramount task of safeguarding the Expeditionary Force from molestation in transit, will she ever dare to face it at all ? Anyhow, if our command of the sea could have been overthrown at that juncture, the Expeditionary Force must have been destroyed in its turn, and sooner or later our maritime commerce must have shared its fate. The fortunes of war in Belgium and France, bad enough as they were at the outset, must have been gravely worsened in proportion to the strength and valour of the English contingent, and Germany by a single coup might perhaps have grasped the coveted sceptre of a world-wide dominion.

All this and much more the Allied Fleets have done, and yet there are smatterers and grumblers who insist that our own fleet has done nothing, except lose a few cruisers, and allow a few German cruisers to capture less than a score of British merchant-vessels in the outer seas. Away with such craven, vain, impatient, and ignorant imaginings ! Let us lift our eyes above these really trivial happenings and survey the whole situation from the height of its true significance. Above all let all our sympathies and all our confidence go to the British fleets, squadrons, and flotillas which are keeping watch and ward on the seas in circumstances as trying as seamen have ever had to encounter and surmount. It may indeed be the deliberate policy of Germany to take full advantage of these trying circumstances in the hope of wearing our seamen down by the acute and almost agonizing tension of a prolonged period of suspense and comparative inactivity, combined with a vigilance never for a moment to be relaxed. Let no one underrate the force of this psychological calculation. No one will underrate it who has ever witnessed, as I have, the effects of a similar tension, albeit infinitely less acute, during the mimic warfare of naval manœuvres. But the psychological calculation, astute though it be, is not irrefragable. It has its counterpoise for the harbour-sheltered fleet in the divorce of the latter from the real business of the sea—in the dull monotonous round of routine duties listlessly carried on, because they have none of the actuality even of peace-exercises at sea, and none of the uplifting of the spirit which the confident hope of conflict with the enemy engenders and sustains. The story of the old wars tells us that the sea-nurtured fleet was always in better fettle for fighting than the harbour-sheltered fleet, and though many things have changed since Nelson and his comrades bore the strain and weathered it—bore it and weathered it for months and even years at a stretch—there is no reason to think that the children of Nelson will prove less stout in endurance than their sires. The strain is undoubtedly far more intense in these days, but it is certain to be far less prolonged. Meanwhile, the British seaman's strength lies in the consciousness of his hold on the sea, and the conviction that its mastery is his.

This, then, is the proper point of view from which to regard the doings of the Allied Fleets during the present war. Μέγα γὰρ τὸ τῆς θαλάσσης κράτος, as Pericles told the Athenians. Great is the power of the sea. Nor has the moral of this pregnant saying ever been better pointed than by Admiral Mahan, many years ago, in those memorable words, which might well seem to have been written to suit the present occasion : ' They were dull, weary, eventless months, those months of waiting and watching of the big ships before the French arsenals. Purposeless they surely seemed to many, but they saved England. The world has never seen a more impressive demonstration of the influence of sea power upon its history. Those far-distant, storm-beaten ships upon which the Grand Army never looked, stood between it and the dominion of the world.' The quotation is almost hackneyed now, but it is never stale, least of all at the present juncture.

1914

Crown 8vo. Separately, in paper covers. Also in series as numbered (I–VII), stiff covers, One Shilling net each series. 35 Pamphlets have now (25 November) been issued and others are in preparation. The historical pieces are illustrated by sketch-maps

I

1. The Deeper Causes of the War.
By W. SANDAY. 3d. net. *Fifth Impression.*
The psychology of Prussian militarism ; German public opinion and Germany's aggressive ambitions.

2. To the Christian Scholars of Europe and America: A Reply from Oxford to the German ' Address to Evangelical Christians '. 2d. net. *Fourth Impression.*
The answer of Oxford theologians to a recent manifesto of the German evangelical theologians. This manifesto, which is reproduced in the present pamphlet, argues that Germany is in no sense responsible for the present war. The Oxford reply states that the German theologians cannot have studied either the events which led up to the war or the political utterances of their own countrymen.

3. The Responsibility for the War.
By W. G. S. ADAMS. 2d. net. *Second Impression.*
A brief discussion of the question of responsibility : 1. Austria and Serbia ; 2. The responsibility of Russia ; 3. The intervention of England.

4. Great Britain and Germany.
By SPENSER WILKINSON. 2d. net. *Third Impression.*
Three letters to the *Springfield Republican* : 1 By Prof. Spenser Wilkinson, stating Great Britain's case ; 2. By Prof. John W. Burgess of the University of Columbia, stating Germany's case ; 3. By Prof. Wilkinson, in reply to Prof. Burgess.

5. ' Just for a Scrap of Paper.'
By ARTHUR HASSALL. 1d. net. *Fourth Impression.*
Explains why England stands for the sanctity of European treaty-law.

[d]

II

6. The Germans, their Empire, and how they have made it.
By C. R. L. FLETCHER. 2d. net. *Fourth Impression.*
A historical account of Prussian policy from the seventeenth century.

7. The Germans, their Empire, and what they covet.
By C. R. L. FLETCHER. 2d. net. *Fourth Impression.*
An account of the ambitions avowed by the Pan-German school.

8. Might is Right.
By Sir WALTER RALEIGH. 2d. net. *Second Impression.*
Why Germany may win; what will happen if she wins; why we believe she will not win.

9. Austrian Policy since 1867.
By MURRAY BEAVEN. 3d. net. *Second Impression.*
Austrian policy in the Balkans has been of the 'offensive-defensive' order. The Archduke Francis Ferdinand might have saved Austria from rushing to destruction; but 1912 was the beginning of the end.

10. Italian Policy since 1870.
By KEITH FEILING. 2d. net. *Second Impression.*
Italian policy has been and must be guided by her own interests. The results of her colonial policy have not yet been satisfactory enough to tempt her into adventures.

III

11. French Policy since 1871.
By F. MORGAN and H. W. C. DAVIS. 2d. net. *Fourth Impression.*
A historical sketch, discussing the question whether French policy has been aggressive.

12. Russia: The Psychology of a Nation.
By PAUL VINOGRADOFF. 1d. net. *Fourth Impression.*
A reply to the German taunt that Russia is still in a state of barbarism, and is the enemy of European civilization.

13. Serbia and the Serbs.
By Sir VALENTINE CHIROL. 2d. net. *Third Impression.*
A sketch of Serbian history, which is incidentally an indictment of the policy pursued by Austria-Hungary towards the Serbian kingdom.

14. Germany and 'The Fear of Russia'.
By Sir VALENTINE CHIROL. 2d. net. *Third Impression.*
Shows that before 1879 Germany preferred Russia as an ally to Austria. The ambition of Germany to establish a protectorate over Turkey has led her to assist Austria in the Balkans and so to challenge Russia.

15. The Eastern Question.
By F. F. URQUHART. 3d. net. *Third Impression.*
The history of the Balkan nations; their future.

[d]

16. War against War.

By A. D. LINDSAY. 2d. net. *Third Impression.*

Denies that war is good in itself, or a necessary evil. Power is not the sole or chief end for which the State exists. National greatness, if founded on brute force, cannot endure. International law represents an ideal, but an ideal that may be realized.

17. The Value of Small States.

By H. A. L. FISHER. 2d. net. *Third Impression.*

The author argues that the debt of civilization to small states is incalculable. They are useful, at the present time, as laboratories of political experiments and as buffer-states between the greater powers.

18. How can War ever be Right?

By GILBERT MURRAY. 2d. net. *Fourth Impression.*

A well-known lover of peace and advocate of pacific policies argues against the Tolstoyan position. Right and honour compelled Britain to make war; and war—like tragedy—is not pure evil.

19. The National Principle and the War.

By RAMSAY MUIR. 3d. net. *Second Impression.*

Considers the principle of nationality and its application to the settlement of Europe—particularly of S.E. Europe—after the War.

20. Nietzsche and Treitschke: The Worship of Power in Modern Germany.

By E. BARKER. 2d. net. *Fourth Impression.*

An explanation of the main points of interest in the ethical and political doctrines of the German ruling classes.

V

21. The British Dominions and the War.

By H. E. EGERTON. 2d. net. *Second Impression.*

Explains the ideas for which the British Empire stands, and the political and moral issues of the war affecting the Dominions.

22. India and the War.

By Sir ERNEST TREVELYAN. 1d. net. *Third Impression.*

Discusses the reasons which account for the striking manifestations of Indian loyalty.

23. Is the British Empire the Result of Wholesale Robbery? By H. E. EGERTON. 2d. net.

A historical sketch in answer to a common taunt.

24. The Law of Nations and the War.

By A. PEARCE HIGGINS. 2d. net. *Second Impression.*

The violation of Belgian neutrality and the conduct of England to Denmark in 1807; the doctrine of German lawyers that military necessity overrides the laws of war; the balance of power and the sanctity of treaties.

25. England's Mission. By W. BENETT. 2d. net.

Answers the question, In what cause are we fighting?

[a]

26. **August, 1914 : The Coming of the War.**
By SPENSER WILKINSON. Stiff covers. 1s. net.

VII

27. **The Retreat from Mons.**
By H. W. C. DAVIS. 3d. net. *Third Impression.*
28. **The Battles of the Marne and Aisne.**
By H. W. C. DAVIS. 4d. net.
The Dispatches, with commentary, maps, &c.
29. **The Navy and the War.**
By J. R. THURSFIELD. 3d. net. *Second Impression.*
Estimates the military and economic value of the silent pressure exercised by our fleet, and warns the faint-hearted and the captious of the perils of lack of faith.
30. **Bacilli and Bullets.**
By Sir WILLIAM OSLER. 1d. net. *Fourth Impression.*
Calls attention to the fact that disease kills more men than the bullet. The most dangerous diseases are preventable by inoculation.

Published separately and will also appear shortly in series.

The Double Alliance *versus* The Triple Entente.
By JAMES M. BECK. 3d. net.
The judgement of a well-known American lawyer.
Thoughts on the War. By GILBERT MURRAY. 2d. net.
An article written in August and now reprinted.
The Leading Ideas of British Policy.
By GERARD COLLIER. 2d. net.
Examines the political genius of England.
Greek Policy since 1882. By A. J. TOYNBEE. 4d. net.
Poland, Prussia, and Culture.
By LUDWIK EHRLICH. 3d. net.
The author is a Doctor of the University of Lwow (Lemberg) in Galicia.
The Germans in Africa. By EVANS LEWIN. 3d. net.
What Europe owes to Belgium.
By H. W. C. DAVIS. *In the press.*

Spectator :—'These little books are easily the best books of the war—accurate, quietly written, full of knowledge, and quite unspoiled by vainglory or bitterness.'

Others in preparation.

HUMPHREY MILFORD
OXFORD UNIVERSITY PRESS, AMEN CORNER, LONDON, E.C.
[d]

OXFORD PAMPHLETS
1914

GREEK POLICY
SINCE 1882

BY

ARNOLD J. TOYNBEE

Price Fourpence net

OXFORD UNIVERSITY PRESS
HUMPHREY MILFORD
LONDON   EDINBURGH   GLASGOW
NEW YORK   TORONTO   MELBOURNE   BOMBAY

MAP OF THE AEGEAN

Between pages 20 and 21.

GREEK POLICY SINCE 1882

MODERN GREECE has just achieved an epoch in her history. Till the year before last, she was numbered in that category of nations, unhappily only too common in the Nearer East, that cannot begin to order their life, because they have not yet emerged from the struggle for existence. To us in Western Europe, 'politics' mean primarily the organization of efforts to improve a country's internal economy; but a foreigner who picked up a Greek newspaper two years ago, would have found in it none of the matter with which he was familiar in his own, such as the discussion of social reconstruction, economic development, and financial policy, but a watchful pursuit of the relations between all the European Powers: he would have heard foreign politics talked in the cafés with the same vigour and detail that Englishmen in a railway-carriage would have been spending on the measures of the present Government, and with far greater knowledge than the English quidnuncs could have brought to bear on an international question, if they had happened to stumble across it, and the conversation would always have led up in the end to the same apparently unanswerable challenge to the future: 'When will the dead weight of Turkish misgovernment be removed from the enslaved majority of our nation? When shall we win by unity the strength to hold our own against our Balkan neighbours, more bitterly hostile to us than the Turk, and eager to perpetuate the slavery of our brothers after the Turk is gone?'

This preoccupation with events beyond the frontiers was not caused by any lack of needs and difficulties within them. The army was the most prominent object of public activity, but it was not an aggressive speculation, or an investment of national profits deliberately calculated to bring in one day a larger return ; it was a necessity of life, and its efficiency was barely maintained out of the national poverty. In fact, it was almost the only public utility with which the nation could afford to provide itself ; the traveller from Great Britain would have been amazed at the miserable state of all reproductive public works : the railways were few and far between, their routes roundabout, their rolling-stock scanty, so that trains were both rare and slow ; wheel-roads were no commoner a feature in Greece than railways are here, and such stretches as had been constructed had often never come into use, because they had just failed to reach their goal or were still waiting for their bridges, so that they were simply falling into decay and allowing the money spent on them to lapse into a dead loss ; while the Peiraieus was the only port in the country where steamers could come alongside a quay, and discharge their cargoes directly on shore ; elsewhere, the vessel must anchor many cables' lengths out, and depend on the slow and expensive services of lighters, for lack of pier construction and dredging operations ; in fact, the fifth largest port in the kingdom,[1] Kalamata, the economic outlet for the richest part of Peloponnesos, was a mere open roadstead, where all ships that called were kept at a distance by the silt from a mountain torrent, and so placed in imminent danger of being

---

[1] The four chief ports being Peiraieus, Patras, Syra, and Volos.

driven, by the first storm, upon the rocks of a neighbouring peninsula.

These grave shortcomings were doubtless due in part
to the geographical character of the country, but it
was clear from what had been accomplished, that it
would have been both possible and profitable to attempt
much more, if the nation's energy could have been
secured for the work. But it is hard to tinker at details
when you are kept in a ·perpetual fever by a question
of life and death ; for the great preliminary questions
of national unity and self-government, before which
all other interests paled, were no will-o'-the-wisps of
theoretical politics : it needs a long political education
to appreciate abstract ideas, and the Greeks were still
in their political infancy, but the realization of Greater
Greece implied for them the satisfaction of all those
concrete needs : so long as the *status quo* endured they
were isolated from the rest of Europe by an unbroken
band of Turkish territory, stretching from the Aegean
to the Adriatic Sea ; what was the use of overcoming
great engineering difficulties to build a line of European
gauge from Athens right up to the northern frontier,
if Turkey refused to sanction the construction of the
tiny section that must pass through her territory
between the Greek railhead and the actual terminus of
the European system at Salonika, or if, even supposing
she withdrew her veto, she would have it in her power to
bring pressure on Greece at any moment by threatening
to sever communications along this vital artery ? So long
as Turkey was there, Greece was practically an island,
and her only communication with continental Europe
lay through her ports. But what use to improve the
ports, when the recovery of Salonika, the fairest object
of the national dreams, would ultimately change the

country's economic centre of gravity, and make her
maritime as well as her overland commerce flow along
quite other channels than the present ?

Thus the Greek nation's present was overshadowed
by its future, and its actions paralysed by its hopes.
Perhaps a nation with more power of application and
less of imagination would have schooled itself to the
thought that these sordid, obtrusive details were the
key to the splendours of the future, and would have
devoted itself to the systematic amelioration of the
cramped area which it had already secured for its
own : this is what Bulgaria managed to do in her
wonderful generation of internal growth between the
Berlin Treaty of 1878 and the declaration of war against
Turkey in 1912 ; but Bulgaria, thanks to her geographical
situation, was from the outset freer from the tentacles
of the Turkish octopus than Greece had contrived to
make herself by her fifty years' start, while her tempera-
mentally sober ambitions were not inflamed by such
past traditions as Greece had inherited, not altogether
to her advantage. Be that as it may, Greece, whether
by fault or misfortune, failed to apply herself successfully to the cure of her defects and the exploitation of
her assets, though she did not lack leaders strong-
minded enough to summon her to the dull business of
the present. Her recent history might be expressed
as the struggle between the parties of the present and
the future, and the prevailing discomfiture of the
former is typified in the tragedy of Trikoupis, the best
statesman Greece had till Venezelos appeared.

Trikoupis came into power in 1882, just after the
country had been given a fresh start by the acquisition
of the rich agricultural province of Thessaly, assigned
to her by the Treaty of Berlin. There were no such

continuous areas of good arable land within the original limits of the kingdom, and such as there were had been desolated by the twelve years of savage warfare [1] which were the price of liberty. The population had been swept away by wholesale massacres of racial minorities in every district ; the dearth of industrious hands had allowed the torrents to play havoc with the cultivation-terraces on the mountain slopes, and the spectre of malaria, always lying in wait for its opportunity, to claim the waterlogged plains for its own. Fifty years had passed, and little attempt had been made to cope with the evil, until now it seemed almost past remedy. If, however, the surface of the land offered little prospect of wealth for the moment, there were considerable treasures to be found beneath it : a metalliferous belt runs down the whole east coast of the Greek mainland, cropping up again in many of the Aegean islands, and some of the ores, of which there is a great variety, are rare and valuable ; the lack of transit facilities is partly remedied by the fact that workable veins often lie near enough to the sea for the produce to be carried straight from mine to ship, by an endless-chain system of overhead trolleys ; so that, once capital is secured for installing the plant and opening the mine, profitable operations can be carried on irrespective of the general economic condition of the country. Trikoupis saw how much potential wealth was locked up in these mineral seams ; the problem was how to attract the capital necessary to tap it. The nucleus round which have accumulated the immense masses of mobilized capital that are the life-blood of modern European industry and commerce, was originally derived from the

---

[1] 1821–32.

surplus profits of agriculture. But a country that finds
itself, like Greece in the nineteenth century, reduced
to a state of agricultural bankruptcy, has obviously not
saved any surplus in the process, so that it is unable
to provide from its own pocket the minimum outlay
it so urgently needs in order to open for itself some
new activity. If it is to obtain a fresh start on other
lines, it must secure the co-operation of the foreign
investor, and the capitalist with a ready market for
his money will only put it into enterprises where he
has some guarantee of its safety. There was little
doubt that the minerals of Greece would well repay
extraction, the uncertain element was the Greek nation
itself. The burning question of national unity might
break out at any moment into a blaze of war, and, in
the probable case of disaster, involve the whole country
and all interests connected with it in economic as well
as political ruin. Western Europe would not commit
itself to Greek mining enterprise, unless it felt confident
that the statesman responsible for the government of
Greece would and could restrain his country from its
instinctive impulse towards political adventure. The
great merit of Trikoupis was that he managed to inspire
this confidence. Greece owes most of the wheel-roads,
railways, and mines of which she can now boast to the
dozen years of his more or less consecutive administration. But the roads are unfinished, the railway-network
incomplete, the mines exploited only to a fraction of
their capacity, because the forces against Trikoupis
were in the end too strong for him. It may be that
his eye too rigidly followed the foreign investor's point
of view, and that by adopting a more conciliatory
attitude towards the national ideal, he might have
strengthened his position at home without impairing

his reputation abroad, but his position was really made impossible by a force quite beyond his control, the irresponsible, intolerable course of outrage and breach of engagement which Turkey, under whatever régime, has always pursued towards foreign States, and especially towards those Balkan countries which have won their freedom in her despite, while perforce abandoning a large proportion of their race to continued subjection to Turkish misgovernment.

Several times over the Porte, by wanton insults to Greece, wrecked the efforts of Trikoupis to establish good relations between the two Governments, and played into the hands of the Greek chauvinist party, which was led by Trikoupis' rival, Delyannis. Delyannis' tenures of office were always brief, but during them he contrived to undo most of the work accomplished by Trikoupis in the previous intervals. A particularly tense 'incident' with Turkey put him in power in 1893, with a strong enough backing from the country to warrant a general mobilization, which led to no further result than the ruin of Greek credit. Trikoupis was hastily recalled to office by the king, but too late ; he found himself unable to retrieve the ruin, and retired altogether from politics in 1895, dying abroad next year in voluntary exile and enforced disillusionment.

With the removal of Trikoupis from the helm, Greece ran straight upon the rocks : a disastrous war with Turkey was precipitated in 1897 by events in Krete. It brought the immediate *débâcle* of the army and the occupation of Thessaly for a year by Turkish troops, while its final penalties were the cession of the chief strategical positions along the northern frontier and the imposition of an international commission of control over Greek finance, in view of the national bankruptcy entailed by the war. The fifteen years that followed 1895 were indeed a black period in modern Greek history, yet the time was not altogether lost, and such events as the draining of the Kopais-basin by a British company, and its conversion from a malarious swamp into a rich agricultural area, marked a perceptible economic advance.

This comparative stagnation was broken at last by the Young Turk *pronunciamento* at Salonika in 1908, which produced such momentous repercussions all through the Nearer East. The Young Turks had struck in order to forestall the dissolution of the Ottoman Empire, but the opportunity was seized by every restive element within it to shake off, if possible, the Turkish connexion. Just as in 1897, Greece was directly affected by the action of the Greek population in Krete. As a result of the revolt of 1896–7, Krete had been constituted an autonomous State, subject to Ottoman suzerainty, autonomy and suzerainty alike being guaranteed by four Great Powers. Prince George of Greece, a son of the King of the Hellenes, was placed at the head of the autonomous Government as high commissioner, but his autocratic tendency caused great discontent among the free-spirited Kretans, who had not rid themselves of the Turkish régime in order to forfeit their independence again in another fashion. Dissension culminated in 1906, when the leaders of the Opposition took to the mountains, and obtained such support and success in the guerrilla fighting that followed, that they forced Prince George to tender his resignation. He was succeeded as high commissioner by Zaimis, another citizen of the Greek kingdom, who inaugurated a more constitutional régime. In 1908

the Kretans believed that the moment for realizing the
national ideal had come; they proclaimed the union
with Greece, and elected deputies to the Parliament
at Athens. But the guarantor Powers carried out
their obligations by promptly sending a combined
naval expedition, which hauled down the Greek flag at
Canea, and prevented the deputies from embarking for
Peiraieus. This seemingly pedantic insistence upon the
status quo was extremely exasperating to Greek nationalism. It produced a ferment in the kingdom, which
grew steadily for nine months, and vented itself in
July 1909 in the *coup d'état* of the ' Military League ',
a second-hand imitation of the Turkish ' Committee of
Union and Progress ' ; the royal family was cavalierly
treated, and constitutional government superseded by
a junta of officers. But at this point the policy of the
four Powers towards Krete was justified. Turkey
knew well that she had lost Krete in 1897, but she
could still use her suzerainty to prevent Greece from
gaining new strength by the annexation of the island.
The Young Turks had seized the reins of government,
not to modify the policy of the Porte, but to intensify
its chauvinism, and they accordingly intimated that
they would consider any violation of their suzerain
rights over Krete as a case for declaring war upon
Greece. Greece, without army or allies, was obviously
not in a position to incur another war, and the ' Military
League ' therefore found that it had reached the end
of its tether. There ensued a deadlock of eight months,
only enlivened by a naval mutiny, during which the
country lay paralysed, with no programme whatsoever
before it.

Then the man demanded by the situation appeared
unexpectedly from the centre of disturbance, Krete,

Venezelos started life as a successful advocate at Canea ;
he entered Kretan politics in the struggle for constitutionalism, and distinguished himself in the successful
revolution of 1906, of which he was the soul ; naturally,
he became one of the leading statesmen under the
new order of things, and he further distinguished himself by resolutely opposing agitation for ' union ' as
premature, and yet retaining his hold over a people
whose paramount political preoccupation this was.
The crisis of 1908–9 brought him into close relations
with the Government of the Greek kingdom, and the
king, who had gauged his calibre, now took the patriotic
step of calling in the man who had expelled his son
from Krete, to put his own house in order ; it speaks
much for both men that they worked together in har-
mony from beginning to end. Venezelos, then, exchanged
Kretan for Greek citizenship, and took in hand the
' Military League ' ; after short negotiations, he persuaded it to dissolve in favour of a national convention,
which was able to meet in March 1910.

Thus Greece became a constitutional country once
more, and Venezelos the first premier of the new era ;
he has remained in power ever since, and proved himself the good genius of his country. Results speak for
themselves, and the remainder of this pamphlet will
be little more than a record of his achievements ; but
before we pass on to review them, we must say a word
about the character to which they are due. In March
1912 the time came for the first general election since
Venezelos had taken office. Two years' experience of
his administration had already won him such popularity and prestige, that the old party groups, purely
personal followings infected with all the corruption,
jingoism, and insincerity of the dark fifteen years,

leagued themselves in a desperate effort to cast him out ; corruption on a grand scale was attempted, but Venezelos' success at the polls was sweeping. The writer happened to be spending that month in Krete ; the Kretans had, of course, elected deputies in good time to the Parliament at Athens, and once more the foreign warships stopped them in the act of boarding the steamer for Peiraieus, while Venezelos, who was still responsible for the Greek Government till the new Parliament met, had declared with characteristic frankness that the attendance of the Kretan deputies could not possibly be sanctioned, an opening his opponents did not fail to take advantage of. Meanwhile, every one in Krete was awaiting news of the polling in the kingdom. They might have been expected to feel, at any rate, lukewarmly towards a man who had actually taken office on the programme of deferring their cherished ' union ' indefinitely ; instead, they greeted his triumph with enormous enthusiasm. Their feeling was explained by the comment of an innkeeper : ' Venezelos ! ' he said : ' Why, he is a man who can say " No " ; he won't stand any nonsense ; if you try to get round him, he'll put you in irons ', and he had clearly hit the mark. Venezelos has done well, because he is a clever man with an excellent power of judgement, but acuteness is a common Greek virtue ; he has done brilliantly, because he has the added touch of genius required to make the Greek take ' No ' for an answer, a quality, very rare indeed in the nation, which explains Venezelos' success in contrast to Trikoupis' failure. Greece ·has been fortunate indeed in finding the right man at the crucial hour.

In the winter of 1911–12 and the succeeding summer, the foreign traveller met innumerable results of

Venezelos' activity in every part of the country, and all gave evidence of the same thing : sanity of decision, followed up by inflexibility of execution. For instance, a resident in Greece, who four years before had made an expedition into the wild country north-west of the Gulf of Patras, had needed the attendance of an escort of soldiers, on account of the number of criminals ' wanted ' by the Government who were lurking in that region as outlaws. An inquiry about this danger, made upon landing in the district in August, 1912, was met with a smile : ' O, yes, it was so,' said the gendarme, ' but since then we have had Venezelos ; he amnestied every one " out " for minor offences, and then caught the " bad ones ", so there are no outlaws in Akarnania now ', and he spoke the truth ; you could wander all about the forests and mountains without molestation.

So far Venezelos had devoted himself to internal reconstruction, after the fashion of Trikoupis, but he was not the man to desert the national idea. The army and navy were reorganized by French and British missions, and when the opportunity appeared, he was ready to take full advantage of it. In the autumn of 1912, Turkey had been for a year at war with Italy ; her finances had suffered a heavy drain, and the Italian command of the sea not only locked up her best troops in Tripoli, but interrupted several important lines of communication between her Asiatic and European provinces, for instance, the direct route by sea from Smyrna to Salonika, and the devious sea-passage thence round Greece to Skodra, which was the only alternative for Turkish troops to running the gauntlet of the Albanian mountaineers. Clearly the Balkan nations could find no better moment for striking the blow to settle that implacable ' preliminary question ' of national unity which had dogged them all since their birth. Their only chance of success, however, was to strike in concert, for Turkey, handicapped though she was, could still easily outmatch them singly; unless they could compromise between their conflicting claims, they would have to let the grand opportunity for making them good slip by altogether.

Of the four States concerned, two, Serbia and Montenegro, were of the same Southern-Slav nationality, and had been drawn into complete accord with each other since the formal annexation of Bosnia by Austria-Hungary in 1908, which struck a hard blow at their common national idea, while neither of them had any differences with Greece, because the Greek and Southern-Slav nationalities are at no point geographically contiguous. With Bulgaria, a nation of Slavonic speech and culture, though not wholly of Slavonic origin, Serbia had quarrelled for years over the ultimate destiny of the Uskub district, in North-western Macedonia, still subject to Turkey; but in the summer of 1912 the two States adjusted in a secret treaty their conflicting territorial claims, and agreed to refer the fate of one debatable strip to the arbitration of Russia, after the close of their already projected war with Turkey. By far the most formidable feud, however, was that between Bulgaria and Greece; the two nationalities are conterminous over a very wide extent of territory, stretching from the Black Sea on the east to the Lake of Okhrida, in the interior of Albania, on the west, and there is at no point a sharp dividing line between them. The Greek element tends to predominate towards the coast and the Bulgarian towards the interior, but there are broad zones where Greek and Bulgarian villages are inextricably interspersed, while purely Greek towns are often isolated in the midst of purely Bulgarian rural districts. Even if the racial areas could be plotted out on a large-scale map, it was clear that no political frontier could be drawn to follow their convolutions, and that Greece and Bulgaria could only divide the spoils by making up their minds to give and take. The actual lines this necessary compromise would follow, obviously depended on the degree of the Allies' success against Turkey in the common war that was yet to be fought, and Venezelos rose to the occasion. He had the courage to offer Bulgaria the Greek alliance without stipulating for any definite minimum share in the common conquests, and the tact to induce her to accept it on the same terms. Greece and Bulgaria agreed to shelve all territorial questions till the war had been brought to a successful close ; and with the negotiation of this understanding (another case in which Venezelos succeeded where Trikoupis had attempted and failed) the Balkan League was complete.

The events that followed are common knowledge. The Allies opened the campaign in October, and the Turks collapsed before an impetuous attack. The Bulgarians crumpled up the Turkish field armies in Thrace by the terrific battle of Lule Burgas ; the Serbians disposed of their armies in the Macedonian interior, while the Greeks effected a junction with the Serbians from the south, and cut their way through to Salonika. Within two months of the declaration of war the Turkish land forces were driven out of the open altogether behind the shelter of the Chataldja and Gallipoli lines, and only three fortresses—Adrianople, Yannina, and Skodra—held out further to the west ; while their navy, closely blockaded by the Greek fleet within the Dardanelles, had to look on passively

at the successive occupation of the Aegean Islands by
Greek landing-parties. With the winter came negotiations, during which an armistice reigned at Adrianople
and Skodra, while the Greeks pursued the siege of
Yannina and the Dardanelles blockade. The negotiations proved abortive, and the result of the renewed
hostilities justified the action of the Balkan pleni-
potentiaries in breaking them off. By the spring of
1913, the three fortresses had fallen, and in the treaty
finally signed at London, Turkey ceded to the Balkan
League, as a whole, all her European territories west
of a line drawn from Ainos on the Aegean to Midia
on the Black Sea, including Adrianople and the whole
lower basin of the River Maritsa.

The time had now come for Greece and Bulgaria to
settle their account, and the unexpected extent of the
common gains ought to have facilitated their division.
The territory in question included the whole north
coast of the Aegean and its immediate hinterland, and
Venezelos proposed to consider it in two sections :
(1) The eastern section, conveniently known as Thrace,
consisted of the lower basin of the Maritsa. As far as
Adrianople the population was Bulgarian, but south
of that city it was succeeded by a Greek element, with
a considerable sprinkling of Turkish settlements, as
far as the sea ; geographically, however, the whole
district was intimately connected with Bulgaria, and
the railway that follows the course of the Maritsa
down to the port of Dedeagatch, offered a much-needed
economic outlet for large regions already within the
Bulgarian frontier. Venezelos, then, was prepared to
resign all Greek claims to the eastern section, in return
for corresponding concessions by Bulgaria in the west.
(2) The western section, consisting of the lower basins

of the Vardar and Struma, lay in the immediate neighbourhood of the former frontier of Greece, but the
Greek population of Salonika [1] and the coast-districts
east of it, could not be brought within the Greek frontier
without including as well a certain hinterland inhabited
mainly by Bulgarians. The cession of this was the
return asked for by Venezelos, and he reduced it to
a minimum by abstaining from pressing the quite
well-founded claims of Greece in the Monastir district,
which lay further inland still.

But Venezelos' conciliatory proposals met with no
response from the Bulgarian Government, which was
in an ' all or nothing ' mood. It swallowed Venezelos'
gift of Thrace, and then proceeded to use the Bulgarian hinterland of Salonika as a pretext for demanding the latter city as well. This uncompromising
attitude made agreement impossible, and it was aggravated by the aggressive action of the Bulgarian troops
in the occupied territory, who persistently endeavoured
to steal ground from the Greek forces facing them.
In May there was serious fighting to the east of the
Struma, and peace was only restored with great difficulty.
Bulgarian relations with Serbia were becoming strained
at the same time, though in this case Bulgaria had
more justice on her side. Serbia maintained that the
veto imposed by Austria upon her expansion to the
Adriatic, together with Bulgaria's unexpected gains
on the Maritsa, invalidated the secret treaty of the
previous summer, and announced her intention of
retaining a part of the Monastir district and the whole
of the Salonika railway as far as the rectified Greek

---

[1] The predominant element in the population of Salonika itself is
neither Greek nor Bulgarian, but consists of about 80,000 Spanish-
peaking Jews, settled there as refugees in the sixteenth century.

frontier. Bulgaria, on the other hand, shut her eyes to Serbia's necessity for an untrammelled economic outlet, and took her stand on her strictest legal treaty-rights. However the balance of justice inclined, a lasting settlement could only have been reached by mutual for-bearance and goodwill, but Bulgaria put herself hope-lessly in the wrong by a treacherous night-attack, at the end of June 1913, against both her allies all along the line. This unpardonable act was the work of a single political party, which has since been condemned by most sections of Bulgarian public opinion ; but the punishment, if not the responsibility, for the crime fell upon the whole nation. Greece and Serbia had already been drawn into an understanding by their common danger ; they now declared war against Bulgaria in concert ; the counter-strokes of their armies met with success, and the intervention of Roumania made Bulgaria's discomfiture certain.

The results of the one month's war were registered in the Treaty of Bukarest. Many of its provisions are unhappily, though naturally, inspired by the spirit of revenge, but Greece, at any rate, showed a states-manlike self-restraint in the negotiations. Venezelos followed the course of taking no more after the war than he had asked before it : he was content to accept the River Mesta as the eastward limit of Greek expan-sion, and still conceded to Bulgaria the strip of coast beyond it, with the harbours of Porto Lagos and Dedea-gatch, which had been occupied during hostilities by the Greek fleet. Thus he satisfied Bulgaria's need for an Aegean outlet, and cleverly saved Greece for the future from those drawbacks involved in immediate contact with Turkish territory, which she had so often experienced in the past. Only Venezelos' prestige could have carried through such a moderate policy in the exasperated state of public feeling ; but its fruit may well be the definitive settlement of the quarrel between Greece and Bulgaria. Bulgaria at present cherishes resentment against Greece ; first, because Greece has defeated her, and secondly, because she has lost the Bulgarian population behind Salonika without being compensated by the Greek districts of Thrace, for the Turks slipped back into Adrianople during Bulgaria's prostration, and have managed so far to stay there. But geographical necessity will doubtless restore Thrace to Bulgaria in the end ; and if the present European War brings freedom to all the fragments of the Southern-Slav race at present imprisoned in the Austro-Hungarian complexus, and is followed by their federation with Montenegro and Serbia, it is to be hoped that Serbia will restore to Bulgaria the Bulgarian districts of Central Macedonia, since outlets less distant than Salonika from her economic centre of gravity will have been opened to her on the Adriatic. The Treaty of Bukarest, in fact, simply aggravated instead of alleviating Bulgaria's quarrels with Serbia and Turkey ; but if in the near future events occur to heal these unstanched wounds, Bulgaria's national health will thereby be in such measure restored that the outstanding friction with Greece will be more likely to die away than to chafe into an open sore.

There is reason to prophesy, then, that the new north-eastern frontier of Greece will be permanent, whatever changes may take place immediately beyond it, and this means that the ' preliminary question ' of national unity is substantially solved. Before, however, we pass on to consider the new chapter of history that is opening for the Greek nation, we must glance at

ALBANIA

SERBIA

BU

R. VARDAR

MONASTIR

YEVYELI

SERRES

DRAM

MACEDONIA

STRUMA

AVLONA

HORITSA

VERRIA

SALONIKA

EPIRUS

HIMARRA

ARGYROKASTRO

SANTI QUARANTA

METSOVO

A

CORFU

JANNINA

LARISSA

VOLOS

PARGA

ARTA

KHALK

PATRAS

ATHENS

KORINTHOS

PEIRAIE

ARGOS

NAUPLIA

TRIPOLITSA

CY

KALAMATA

ENGLISH MILES	0 10 20 30 40 50
RAILWAYS	—#—#—#—#—
POLITICAL FRONTIERS	— — — —

CA.

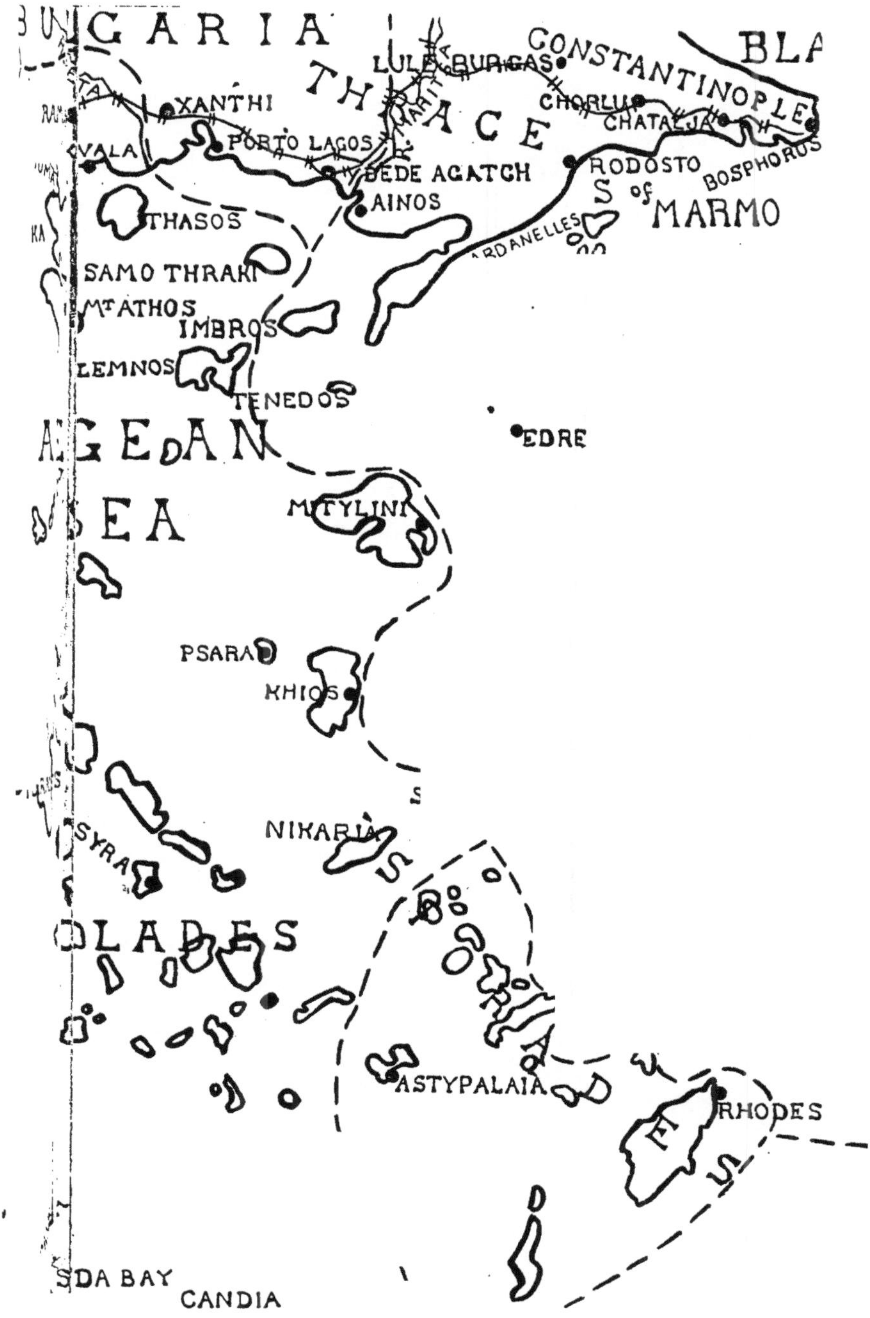
BULGARIA
THRACE
XANTHI
PORTO LAGOS
DEDE AGATCH
AINOS
LULE BURGAS
CONSTANTINOPLE
CHORLU
CHATALJA
RODOSTO
BOSPHORUS
BLA
S of MARMO
ARDANELLES
VALA
THASOS
SAMO THRAKI
Mt ATHOS
IMBROS
LEMNOS
TENEDOS
EDRE
AEGEAN
SEA
MYTYLINI
PSARA
KHIOS
NIKARIA
SYRA
CLADES
ASTYPALAIA
RHODES
SDA BAY
CANDIA

certain minor problems that remain, because they have a considerable bearing upon the present European situation.

The integrity of a land frontier is guaranteed by the whole strength of the nation which it bounds, and can only be modified by crises affecting the totality of the national life, but islands by their geographical nature constitute independent political units, easily detached from or incorporated with larger groupings, according to the fluctuating phases in the rivalry of sea-power. Thus it happened that the arrival of the *Goeben* and the *Breslau* at the Dardanelles led Turkey to reopen promptly certain questions of the Aegean. The islands in this sea are uniformly Greek in population, but their respective geographical positions and political fortunes differentiate them into several groups :

1. The Cyclades in the south-west, half submerged vanguards of the continen al ranges of Greece herself, have formed part of the modern kingdom since its birth, and their status has never since been called in question.

2. Krete, the largest of all the Greek islands, enjoyed, as we have seen, autonomy under Turkish suzerainty for fifteen years before the Balkan War ; at its outbreak she at once proclaimed her union with Greece, and her action was legalized when Turkey expressly abandoned her suzerain rights in a clause of the Treaty of London.

3. During the war itself, the Greek navy occupied a number of islands still directly under the government of Turkey ; the parties to the London Treaty agreed to leave their destiny to the decision of the Powers, and the latter assigned them all to Greece, with the exception of Imbros and Tenedos, which command strategically the mouth of the Dardanelles.

The islands thus secured to Greece fall in turn into
several sub-groups. Two of these are (a) Thasos, Samo-
thraki, and Lemnos, off the European coast, and (b)
Samos and its satellite Nikarià, immediately off the
west coast of Anatolia.

These five islands seem definitely to have been given
up by Turkey for lost. The European group is well
beyond the range of her present frontiers, while Samos,
though it adjoins the Turkish mainland, does not mask
the outlet from any considerable port, and has also
for many years possessed an autonomous status similar
to that of Krete, so that the Ottoman Government did
not acutely feel its final severance.

(c) A third group consists of Mitylini and Khios,[1]
and the views of Greece and Turkey concerning this
pair have so far proved irreconcilable. The Turks
point out that the coast off which these islands lie
contains not only the most essential ports of Anatolia,
but also the largest enclaves of Greek population on
the Turkish mainland, and they declare that occupation of this group by Greece menaces the sovereignty
of the Porte in its home territory. ' See ', they say,
' how the two islands flank both sides of the sea-passage
to Smyrna, the terminus of all the railways which
penetrate the Anatolian interior, while Mitylini stifles
Aivali and Edremid as well. As soon as the Greek
Government has converted the harbours of these islands
into naval bases, the Greek fleet will be able to maintain a virtual blockade of Anatolia, and the pressure
thus applied to the whole Turkish nation will be re-
inforced by simultaneous propaganda among the
disloyal Greek elements in our midst.' Accordingly

---

[1] Including its satellite Psara.

the Turks refuse to recognize the award of the Powers, and demand the restoration of Ottoman sovereignty over Mitylini and Khios, promising in return to grant them autonomy after the precedent of Krete and Samos. To these arguments and demands the Greeks reply that, next to Krete, these are the two largest, most wealthy, and most populous Greek islands in the Aegean ; that their inhabitants ardently desire union with the national kingdom ; and that the Greek Government would hardly use them as a basis for economic coercion and nationalist propaganda against Turkey, because the commerce of Anatolia is in the hands precisely of the Greek element in the country. Greek interests are accordingly bound up with the economic prosperity and political consolidation of Turkey in Asia, and the Anatolian Greeks would merely be alienated from their compatriots by any such impolitic machinations. ' Greek sovereignty over Mitylini and Khios ', the Greeks maintain, ' does not threaten Turkey's position on the Continent. But their abandonment to Turkish suzerainty would most seriously endanger the liberty of their populations ; for Turkey's promises of autonomy, without the intervention of external powers to keep her to them, are notoriously valueless.'

The irreconcilability of these respective attitudes seems to lie in the fact that each Power requires the other to leave vital national interests at the mercy of an ancient enemy, but is not prepared to make any corresponding sacrifices itself. The difficulty could perhaps be solved by the intervention of some disinterested third party strong enough to guarantee on the one hand that Greece should not fortify the two islands, and on the other that Greek sovereignty over them should not be imperilled by their defenceless

condition. Such a guarantee could only be offered
by a concert of Europe. The need for such a guarantee
illustrates the necessity of ending the present war in
such a manner that an effective concert of the Powers
shall once more become possible.

4. There remains for consideration a fourth group
of Greek islands, which formerly belonged to Turkey,
but are now in the hands of other European Powers.

(a) Italy, during her war with Turkey over Tripoli,
had seized the group off the south-west corner of Anatolia
known as the Sporades, of which Rhodes is the largest
member, and in the autumn of 1912 she stipulated, by
the Treaty of Lausanne, that she should retain them
as a pledge till Turkey had withdrawn her last soldier
from Tripoli, when they should be made over again to
the Porte. Whatever steps Turkey may have taken,
Italy has not so far considered that the time for carrying out her side of the contract has arrived ; instead,
she has begun to talk of railway concessions in the
Adalia district of south-western Anatolia as the indispensable compensation for an ultimate evacuation of
the Sporades. There is no objection to such a concession being negotiated, for it would be to the mutual
advantage of both States. Italy needs to find unexploited areas for her enterprise, and Turkey to attract
unoccupied capital into her undeveloped provinces.
But whatever private arrangements Italy and Turkey
may make, the Sporades ought, as a matter of national
justice, to pass definitively not to Turkey but to Greece.
If it is true that the achievement of European peace
depends on the resettlement of European frontiers
upon a national basis, the destination of the Sporades
should incidentally obtain the attention of the conference that meets after the close of the present war.

(b) The outlying section of the Greek nation that inhabits the large island of Cyprus in the Eastern Mediterranean has been subject to British government since the Treaty of Berlin (1878) consigned the island to Great Britain on similar conditions to those under which Italy holds the Sporades by the Treaty of Lausanne. We occupy it without prejudice to the sovereignty of the Porte for so long a period as Kars shall remain in Russia's hands.   Meanwhile it has become clear that the incorporation of Kars in the Russian Empire is final, and that the condition involving our evacuation of Cyprus will, therefore, never arise, but we are still not at liberty to transfer its ownership to any other Power but Turkey. Great Britain has just declared (Nov. 5) that the Berlin Treaty is cancelled as the result of Turkey's intervention in the present war; it is to be hoped that Great Britain will announce an intention of ultimately allowing Cyprus to unite itself with Greece. The whole population of the island is Greek in language ; under an excellent British administration its political consciousness has been awakened, and has expressed itself in a growing desire of the Christian majority to realize its nationality. It is true that in Cyprus, as in Krete, there is a considerable Greek-speaking minority of Moslems [1] that prefers the *status quo*, but since the barrier of language is absent, their antipathy to union may not prove permanent. However important the retention of Cyprus may be to Great Britain from the strategical point of view, we shall find that even in the balance of material interests it is not worth the price of alienating the sympathy of a united nationality.

---

[1] In Cyprus about 22 per cent.

This rather detailed review of the island problems brings out the fact that Greek nationalism is not an artificial conception of theorists, but a real force which impels all fragments of Greek-speaking population to make sustained efforts towards political union within the national state ; the most striking example of this attractive power is afforded by the problem of ' Epirus '.[1] The Epirots are a population of Albanian race, and they still speak an Albanian dialect in their homes, while the women and children, at any rate, often know no other language. But somewhat over a century ago the political organism created by the remarkable personality of Ali Pasha in the hinterland of the Adriatic coast, and the relations into which Great Britain and France, in their struggle for the Mediterranean, were drawn with the new principality, awakened in the Epirots a desire for civilization. Their Albanian origin opened to them no prospects, for the race had neither a literature nor a common historical tradition ; and they accordingly turned to the Greeks, with whom they were linked in religion by membership of the Orthodox Church, and in politics by subjection to Ali's Government at Yannina, which employed Greek as its official language. They had appealed to the right quarter, for Greek culture under the Turkish yoke had accumulated a store of latent energy, which converted itself into a vigorous national revival during the eighteenth century. The partially successful War of Liberation in the 'twenties of the nineteenth century was only one manifestation of the new life ; it has expressed itself more typically in a universal enthusiasm

[1] The name applied to the districts of Himarra, Argyrokastro, and Koritsa.

for education, which has opened to individual Greeks
commercial and professional careers of the greatest
brilliance, and often led them to spend the fortunes
so acquired in endowing the nation with further educational facilities. Public spirit is a Greek virtue ; there
are few villages which do not possess monuments of
their successful sons, and a school is an even commoner
gift than a church, while the State has supplemented
the individual benefactor to an extent remarkable
where public resources are so slender. The school-
house, in fact, is generally the most prominent and
substantial building in a Greek village, and the gains
which their alliance with the Greek nation have brought
to the Epirots are symbolized by Greek schools now
established in generous numbers throughout their
country. For the Epirot boy the school is the door
to the future ; the language he learns there makes
him the member of a nation, and opens to him a world
wide enough to employ all the talent and energy he
may possess, if he seeks his fortune at Patras or Peiraieus,
or in the great Greek commercial communities of
Alexandria and Constantinople, while if he stays at
home it still affords him a link with the life of civilized
Europe through the medium of the ubiquitous Greek
newspaper.[1] The Epirot, then, has become Greek in
soul ; he reached the conception of a national life more
liberal than the isolated existence of his native village
through the avenue of Greek culture, so that ' Hellenism ' and nationality have become for him identical
ideas, and when at last the hour of deliverance struck,
he welcomed the Greek armies that marched into his

---

[1] There is still practically no matter printed in the Albanian
language.

country from the south and the east after the fall of
Yannina in the spring of 1913, with the same enthusiasm
with which all the other enslaved fragments of the
Greek nation greeted the consummation of a century's
hopes.

The Greek troops arrived only just in time, for the
' Hellenism ' of the Epirots had been terribly proved
by murderous attacks from their Moslem neighbours
on the north. These last speak a variety of the same
Albanian tongue, but are differentiated by a creed
which assimilates them to the ruling race. They are
superior to their Christian kinsmen in numbers and
by the possession of arms, which under the Ottoman
régime were the monopoly of the Moslem. Now, however, the oppression seemed to be overpast, and the
Greek occupation to be a harbinger of security for .the
future. Unluckily, Epirus was of interest to others
besides its own inhabitants ; it occupies an important
geographical position facing the extreme heel of Italy,
just below the narrowest point in the neck of the
Adriatic, and the Italian Government insisted that
the country should be included in the new autonomous
Albanian principality, which the Powers had reserved
the right to delimit in concert by a provision in the
Treaty of London. Italy gave two reasons for her
demand. First, she declared it incompatible with
her own vital interests that both shores of the strait
between Corfù and the mainland should pass into the
hands of the same Power, because the combination of
both coasts and the channel between them offered
a site for a naval base that could dominate the mouth
of the Adriatic. Secondly, she maintained that the
native Albanian speech of the Epirots proved their
Albanian nationality, and that it was unjust to the

new Albanian nation to deprive it of its most prosperous and civilized section. Neither argument, however, is cogent ; the first could be met by the neutralization of the Corfù straits,[1] under such a guarantee as we have proposed for Mitylini and Khios ; it is also considerably weakened by the fact that the really commanding position on the eastern side of the Adriatic's mouth is not the Corfù channel outside the narrows, but the magnificent bay of Avlona just within them, a port of Moslem population to which the Epirots have never laid claim, and which would therefore in any case fall within the Albanian frontier. The second argument is almost ludicrous : the destiny of Epirus is not primarily the concern of the other Albanians, or for that matter of the Greeks, but of the Epirots themselves, and it is hard to see how their nationality can be defined except in terms of their own conscious and expressed desire, for a nation is simply a group of men desirous of organizing themselves for certain purposes, and can be brought into existence not by any specific external factors, but solely by the inward will of its members. It was a travesty of justice to put the Orthodox Epirots at the mercy of a Moslem majority (which had been massacring them the year before), on the ground that they happened to speak the same language. The hardship was aggravated by the fact that all the routes connecting Epirus with the outer world run through Yannina and Salonika, from which the new frontier sundered her, while there are great natural barriers between Koritsà and Avlona or Durazzo, with which the same frontier artificially banded her.

[1] Corfù itself may not be fortified, by the agreement under which Great Britain transferred the Ionian Islands to Greece in 1863.

The award of the Powers roused great indignation in Greece, but Venezelos was strong enough to secure that it should be scrupulously respected; and the 'correct attitude' which he inflexibly maintained has finally won its reward. As soon as the decision of the Powers was announced, the Epirots determined to help themselves; they raised a militia, and asserted their independence so successfully, that they compelled the Prince of Wied, the first (and perhaps the last) ruler of the new 'Albania' to give them home rule in matters of police and education, and to recognize Greek as the official language for Epirus. They ensured observance of this compact by the maintenance of their troops under arms. So matters continued, until a rebellion among his Moslem subjects and the outbreak of the European War obliged the prince to depart, leaving Albania to its natural state of anarchy. The anarchy might have restored every canton and village to the old state of contented isolation, were it not for the religious hatred between the Moslems and the Epirots, which, with the removal of all external control, has vented itself in an aggressive warfare of the former against the latter, and has already entailed much suffering.

These events have put Epirus in urgent need of reoccupation by Greek troops, unless the prosperity is to be utterly ruined; and when Venezelos informed the Powers a few days ago [1] of his resolve to take this step provisionally, the confidence he has justly won prevented even Italy from taking any exception, though she is proceeding to establish herself on a similar understanding at Avlona. It is to be hoped that the simultaneous presence of Italian and Greek authorities in

[1] October 1914.

Avlona and Epirus respectively, will lead to an understanding between the two countries, if indeed an understanding has not already been effected ; the adjustment of their interests in this quarter ought not to prove difficult, and the adequate recognition of Epirus' necessities and desires would be one of its most satisfactory fruits.

The case of Epirus is a good example of what Greek nationalism has meant during the last century. Western Europeans are apt to depreciate modern ' Hellenism ', because the reference to a vanished glory implied in its ambitious title involves it in an atmosphere of unreality ; but the Hellenism of to-day, though it is the heir of ancient Greek culture in hardly more direct a sense than is the whole of modern European civilization, has yet a genuine vitality of its own. It displays a power of assimilating alien elements to an active participation in its ideals, and its allegiance supplants all others in the hearts of those exposed to its charm. The Epirots are not the only Albanians who have been Hellenized ; in the heart of the kingdom there are enclaves, the result of successive migrations from the fourteenth to the seventeenth century, which have entirely forgotten their origin, so that the villagers when questioned can only say, ' We are Greeks like every one else, but we happen to speak Albanian.' The Vlachs of Akarnania, a Romance-speaking tribe of nomad shepherds, are in process of settling down to an agricultural, village life, so that Hellenism for them expresses a rise in standard, while their still migratory brothers in Pindus, further north, are already ' Hellenes ' in political sympathy ; [1] even in distant Cappa-

[1] The cruiser *Georgios Averof*, which decided the Greek naval supremacy in 1912–13, was given to the nation by a Vlach millionaire who had made his fortune at Alexandria.

docia, the region at the root of the Anatolian peninsula, the Christian Greek population, which has been partially submerged by the Turkish flood for eight hundred years, till its native speech is reduced to a mere vocabulary, bedded upon a Turkish syntax, has been reached just in time by the new current of national life, bringing with it education, and thereby a community of outlook with Greeks the world over, so that the almost extinct Greek element will now revive to play its independent part in the Turkish state of the future. In an integral portion of the Greek world like Krete, the desire for union was passionate : ' Aren't you better off as you are ? ' travellers inquired during the era of autonomy. ' If you get your " Union ", you will have to do two years' military service instead of one year's training in the militia, and to pay taxes half as heavy again.' ' We have thought of that,' the Kretans would reply, ' but what does it matter, if we are united with Greece ? '

But a national ideal, however attractive by its mere sincerity, is only justified by its positive content. Now that the ' preliminary question ' is solved, and the Greek nation has found itself, what are the fruits by which it will become known in the future ? Will it settle down to the task, so long delayed, of developing its material civilization ? Or will the fever of nationalism prove itself a habit too confirmed for cure ? Like Thessaly, the new territories in the north will greatly augment the nation's economic assets, for they include most of the areas that produce the ' Turkish ' tobacco as well as large pine-forests in Pindus, which, if judiciously exploited, will go far to remedy the present deficiency of home-grown timber, though they will not provide quantities sufficient for foreign export.

Greece, indeed, owing to the smallness of her extent and her lack of geographical homogeneity, will never produce staple commodities for export wholesale, but will depend on special products, such as the rare ores of her eastern mountains, the tobacco of her northern river-basins, and the currant crop raised on the rich patches of Peloponnesian plain-land, while industry and scientific methods might improve some of her wines to a standard which would bring them into the world-market. Such will be the peculiar sources of Greek prosperity, but the ultimate economic future of the country lies in co-operation with her neighbours in a grouping wider than the political atom of the national State. South-eastern Europe contains many nationalities inextricably entangled, but economically it forms a single and indivisible unit; it has a common character as the region upon which the manufactures of Central Europe will become increasingly dependent for their raw materials, and which will provide an expanding market for the latter region's finished products; its various parts are linked together by arteries of commerce that take no account of political frontiers. Unity of economic interest ought sooner or later to find expression in a zollverein, if the region is to reach the highest development of which it is capable. The zollverein in turn ought to lead on to a political understanding of at least a passive kind, seeing that all the nations within the region have likewise in common the strongest interest in keeping extraneous powers at arm's length.

The aim of Greek statesmen, in fact, should be the renewal, on a broader basis and a more permanent footing, of that Balkan League which Bulgaria's action shattered in the spring of 1913. Some spectators of recent events may hold this suggestion to be Utopian, and may argue that in the Balkans, at any rate, if not throughout Europe, the sinister force of national antagonism will be strong enough to baulk all international ideals, even if the price of its triumph be the common ruin of its votaries. But there is one potent assimilative influence equally at work among all the nationalities of the Balkans, which gives good hope for the future : during the last dozen years unskilled labour from every country in Europe south-east of Vienna has been pouring into the United States. The remoter the village, the smaller the openings for the employment of its surplus labour, the larger swarm of emigrants does it send across the Atlantic.. The adventurers do not stay permanently in America : after four years at most they succumb to home-sickness, and as you travel over the land you are always running unexpectedly against the ' American ', with his well-shaven face and goodly clothes and boots, back for a year to spend his earnings among his own folk. The emigrant to America does not lose his patriotism : he returns without fail to serve his nationality in war ; but he brings back with him a faculty for criticizing it from a wider standpoint.

The return for which he longed during his exile is often a disillusionment to him when he achieves it, and he sets out. for America again with a conviction in his heart of the superiority of American efficiency to the dirt and muddle in which he had so complacently grown to manhood in his native country. Whether America or Europe will finally claim him for its own it is as yet too early to predict, for the movement is still in its first stages, and few even of its pioneers can yet have passed middle life ; but in any event the effect of their

continued passage to and fro will be momentous : the
process is taking place on an enormous scale, and is
endowing the Balkans with the very things they need :
with the capital for the exploitation of their material
resources,[1] and with the spirit of enterprise. America
is educating the Balkan peasant to do for himself what
he has so far looked to the European speculator to do
for him, and this education, in contrast to the ' classical '
culture of the Hellenist, which accentuates nationalism
by learned memories of the past, is transcending nationalism. It starts from the bottom of society and is
awakening the vast uncultured majority to a new-born
hope for the future. We are here in presence of one of
the most interesting tendencies of the present age : we
can look forward with greater expectations to the new
chapter that is opening in the history of Greece, now we
see that she has found a new spirit to inform it ; the
' Hellenism ' that inspired the nineteenth century will
insensibly yield place to the ' Americanism ' that is
destined to be the characteristic of the twentieth ; and
the nation is fortunate indeed in entering upon this
critical phase of transition under the guidance of a
political genius, Venezelos.

[1] In 1912 the flow of remittances from emigrants in America to
their families at home had already sent up the cost of living in
Greece ; or, in other words, had raised the material standard of
civilization.

Oxford : Horace Hart Printer to the University

OXFORD PAMPHLETS
1914

Crown 8vo, from 12 to 40 pages each
Prices from 1d. net to 3d. net

Also in series of five Pamphlets, stiff covers
One Shilling net each series

---

26 Pamphlets have now been issued and
others are in preparation. The historical
pieces are illustrated by sketch-maps

---

*' The cheap and useful little " Oxford" pamphlets issued since
the war began by the Oxford University Press continue to
multiply.'*—Morning Post.

OXFORD UNIVERSITY PRESS

HUMPHREY MILFORD

LONDON   EDINBURGH   GLASGOW

NEW YORK   TORONTO   MELBOURNE   BOMBAY

The Deeper Causes of the War.

By W. SANDAY. 3d. net. *Third Impression.*

The psychology of Prussian militarism ; German public opinion and Germany's aggressive ambitions.

To the Christian Scholars of Europe and America: A Reply from Oxford to the German 'Address to Evangelical Christians'. 2d. net. *Second Impression.*

The answer of Oxford theologians to a recent manifesto of the German evangelical theologians. This manifesto, which is reproduced in the present pamphlet, argues that Germany is in no sense responsible for the present war. The Oxford reply states that the German theologians cannot have studied either the events which led up to the war, or the political utterances of their own countrymen.

The Responsibility for the War. By W. G. S. ADAMS. 2d. net.

A brief discussion of the question of responsibility : 1. Austria and Serbia ; 2. The responsibility of Russia ; 3. The intervention of England.

Great Britain and Germany.

By SPENSER WILKINSON. 2d. net. *Second Impression.*

Three letters to the *Springfield Republican*: 1. By Prof. Spenser Wilkinson, stating Great Britain's case ; 2. By Prof. John W. Burgess of the University of Columbia, stating Germany's case ; 3. By Prof. Wilkinson, in reply to Prof. Burgess.

'Just for a Scrap of Paper.'

By ARTHUR HASSALL. 1d. net. *Third Impression.*
Explains why England stands for the sanctity of European treaty-law.

II

The Germans, their Empire, and how they have made it. By C. R. L. FLETCHER. 2d. net. *Third Impression.*

A historical account of Prussian policy from the seventeenth century.

The Germans, their Empire, and what they covet.

By C. R. L. FLETCHER. 2d. net. *Third Impression.*
An account of the ambitions avowed by the Pan-German school.

Might is Right. By Sir WALTER RALEIGH. 2d. net.

Why Germany may win ; what will happen if she wins ; why we believe she will not win.

Austrian Policy since 1867. By MURRAY BEAVEN. 3d. net.

Austrian policy in the Balkans has been of the 'offensive-defensive' order. The Archduke Francis Ferdinand might have saved Austria from rushing to destruction ; but 1912 was the beginning of the end.

Italian Policy since 1870. By KEITH FEILING. 2d. net.

Italian policy has been and must be guided by her own interests. The results of her colonial policy have not yet been satisfactory enough to tempt her into adventures.

[a]

Impression.

A historical sketch, discussing the question whether French policy has been aggressive.

Russia: The Psychology of a Nation.

By PAUL VINOGRADOFF. 1d. net. *Third Impression.*

A reply to the German taunt that Russia is still in a state of barbarism, and is the enemy of European civilization.

Serbia and the Serbs.

By Sir VALENTINE CHIROL. 2d. net. *Third Impression.*

A sketch of Serbian history, which is incidentally an indictment of the policy pursued by Austria-Hungary towards the Serbian kingdom.

Germany and 'The Fear of Russia'.

By Sir VALENTINE CHIROL. 2d. net. *Third Impression.*

Shows that before 1879 Germany preferred Russia as an ally to Austria. The ambition of Germany to establish a protectorate over Turkey has led her to assist Austria in the Balkans and so to challenge Russia.

The Eastern Question.

By F. F. URQUHART. 3d. net. *Second Impression.*

The history of the Balkan nations; their future.

IV

War against War.

By A. D. LINDSAY. 2d. net. *Second Impression.*

Denies that war is good in itself, or a necessary evil. Power is not the sole or chief end for which the State exists. National greatness, if founded on brute force, cannot endure. International law represents an ideal, but an ideal that may be realized.

The Value of Small States.

By H. A. L. FISHER. 2d. net. *Third Impression.*

The author argues that the debt of civilization to small states is incalculable. They are useful, at the present time, as laboratories of political experiments and as buffer-states between the greater powers.

How can War ever be Right?

By GILBERT MURRAY. 2d. net. *Second Impression.*

A well-known lover of peace and advocate of pacific policies argues against the Tolstoyan position. Right and honour compelled Britain to make war; and war—like tragedy—is not pure evil.

The National Principle and the War.

By RAMSAY MUIR. 3d. net.

Considers the principle of nationality and its application to the settlement of Europe—particularly of S.E. Europe—after the War.

Nietzsche and Treitschke: The Worship of Power in Modern Germany.

By E. BARKER. 2d. net. *Third Impression.*

An explanation of the main points of interest in the ethical and political doctrines of the German ruling classes.

[a]

Published separately and will also appear shortly in series.

The British Dominions and the War.

By H. E. EGERTON. 2d net. *Second Impression.*

Explains the ideas for which the British Empire stands, and the political and moral issues of the war affecting the Dominions.

Is the British Empire the Result of Wholesale Robbery ?

By H. E. EGERTON. 2d. net.

A historical sketch in answer to a common taunt.

India and the War.

By Sir ERNEST TREVELYAN. 1d. net. *Second Impression.*

Discusses the reasons which account for the striking manifestations of Indian loyalty.

Bacilli and Bullets.

By Sir WILLIAM OSLER. 1d. net. *Third Impression.*

Calls attention to the fact that disease kills more men than the bullet. The most dangerous diseases are preventible by inoculation.

The Navy and the War.

By J. R. THURSFIELD. 3d. net. *Second Impression.*

Estimates the military and economic value of the silent pressure exercised by our fleet, and warns the faint-hearted and the captious of the perils of lack of faith.

The Retreat from Mons.

By H. W. C. DAVIS. 3d. net. *Second Impression.*

Introduction; the Dispatch of Sept. 9; the Statement by the War Office, published Aug. 31. Appendixes (soldiers' narratives); two maps.

The Law of Nations and the War.

By A. PEARCE HIGGINS. 2d. net.

The violation of Belgian neutrality and the conduct of England to Denmark in 1807; the doctrine of German lawyers that military necessity overrides the laws of war; the balance of power and the sanctity of treaties.

No. 22

OXFORD PAMPHLETS

1914

INDIA AND THE WAR

BY

SIR ERNEST J. TREVELYAN

FOURTH IMPRESSION

Price One Penny net

OXFORD UNIVERSITY PRESS

HUMPHREY MILFORD

LONDON EDINBURGH GLASGOW

NEW YORK TORONTO MELBOURNE BOMBAY

OXFORD: HORACE HAR
PRINTER TO THE UNIVERS

INDIA AND THE WAR

THERE are many people in Great Britain who do not realize the significance of the dispatch of Indian troops to the war, and of the many offers of assistance which have been received from the rulers of the native States in India. India is now asserting its right to be treated as a portion of the Empire, and to take its share in the responsibilities of that Empire. It claims to be treated as a partner and not as a mere dependant.

How many Englishmen have more than the vaguest notions of the relations between India and England? They know nothing of the history of our acquisition of sovereignty in India, they know nothing of our administration of the country, how we have welded together so many discordant elements, how we have worked for happiness and order and how we have endeavoured to develop the country in the interests of its people. We have not, of course, forgotten our own interests, but our interests have coincided with those of the people. Now India is appreciating this fact and is anxious to join with us against the common enemy.

Even those who have had relations working in India have frequently inaccurate ideas on the subject. They look upon it merely as a hot and unhealthy place which furnishes a livelihood for younger sons who otherwise would be unable to get employment. They look upon it as a grand field for missionary enterprise, and as a useful producer of some of the necessaries of life, such as wheat, rice, tea, sugar, jute, and other products of the earth.

The estimated population of the Indian Empire was 315,000,000 in 1911, in 1912 it imported £152,000,000 worth of goods and exported £171,000,000. As most of the imports are from Great Britain, many thousands of people in England practically depend upon India for their livelihood.

The peoples of India are of many different races and religions; 69 per cent. are Hindus, 21 per cent. Mohammedans, 3 per cent. Buddhists (nearly all in Burma); the remaining 7 per cent. include nearly 4,000,000 Christians, over 3,000,000 Sikhs, 1,250,000 Jains (a sect of dissenting Hindus), about 100,000 Parsees, and over 10,250,000, described as Animists, who believe in magic and strive to propitiate impersonal forces. India has 147 vernacular languages of extraordinary variety. Hindustani, which was the camp language of the Mohammedan invaders, is the *lingua franca* of India; but among the educated classes it has been superseded to a great extent by English.

England's first association with India began at the close of the sixteenth century, when the London East India Company was incorporated by Queen Elizabeth. It was not until the eighteenth century that this country acquired any sovereign rights in India. During that century Lord Clive, Warren Hastings, and other officers of the East India Company gradually extended the dominion of the English people. In 1858 the Crown took over the administration of the country. On November 1 of that year Queen Victoria issued a proclamation to the Princes, Chiefs, and People of India announcing her resolution to assume the government and the territories of India ' heretofore administered in trust by the Honourable East India Company '. Legislative Councils were then established and the constitution of the government was fixed by Acts of Parliament. Since that time the association of the people in the government of the country has been developed. Not only are the people represented in the several legislatures, but their leading men play an important part in the working of municipal and other public bodies.

Although the governing class is necessarily British and the higher appointments are in the main held by Britons, the bulk of the executive and judicial work is done by Indians. Indians also are to be found in the higher appointments. They are in the Executive Councils of the Viceroy and Governors, and on the Benches of the High Courts, and have been in the Boards of Revenue. The legal profession of India is almost entirely composed of natives of the country. A large proportion of the medical profession is also indigenous, but its native members have been taught in medical schools by English doctors, and by others who have been trained in the European systems of medicine.

Some of the communities, especially the Hindus, Jains, and Parsees, are taking a prominent part in commerce; their merchant princes have acquired a great reputation for energy and charity. The Mohammedan community, for reasons which it is not necessary to detail here, has not been able to take such full advantage of English education as have the Hindus, but there are signs of their advancing upon similar lines. The present Law Member of the Viceroy's Executive Council is an Indian Mohammedan, and there are Mohammedans on all the Benches of the High Courts of Justice.

The instincts of a large number of the people, especially in Upper India, are martial. The Mahrattas, the Rajputs, the Sikhs, and the Mohammedans of Upper India fought us in the past and they were worthy antagonists. Their descendants have fought with us and now assert their right to take their share in the perils that beset us.

Never has there been an occasion when India has been more united than at the present time. The moment that news arrived of the outbreak of war between Great Britain and Germany a wave of enthusiasm seems to have passed over not only the whole of the British Empire in India, but throughout Hindustan. There has not been a single note of discord. Every class and every race have shown their loyalty and their anxiety to take their share of the burdens and duties of citizens of the Empire. Sedition and disaffection have disappeared from the peninsula; it is not only where Britain rules that offers of men, of money, and of help of every kind have been made spontaneously and ungrudgingly, but the independent rulers have to a man placed their troops and their wealth at the service of the Empire. The Maharaja of Nepal, an independent State with a population of about 5,000,000, has put the entire resources of his country at the disposal of the King-Emperor. His men furnish to England the Gurkha regiments, which are some of the best infantry in the world. The Raja of Mysore has sent for the use of the troops a sum of 50 lakhs of rupees; that is something between £300,000 and £400,000. The Nizam of Haiderabad, the great Mahommedan State in Southern India, has offered to meet the entire expenses of two regiments in which he is specially interested. The Ruler of the ancient State of Rewa writes to the Viceroy: 'What orders from His Majesty for me and my troops?' The Gaekwar of Baroda, one of the principal Mahratta States in India, offers all his troops and resources. The Rulers of Bharatpur and Akalkot make similar offers. The Raja of Pudukota offers 'all I possess', and expresses his anxiety to serve in any capacity and to raise a regiment of his subjects. The Maharaja of Idar, the Rao of Cutch, the Maharaja of Bhaunagar, the Thakore

Sahib of Limbdi, and the Nawab of Palampur have also placed the resources of their States at the disposal of the Government. Many others have been equally loyal and munificent.

These messages are typical of the spirit which is to be found everywhere in India. The offers are not empty ones. It is perfectly clear that all Indians of intelligence and education now realize, if they did not do so before, that their own interests and those of the whole country are bound up with the interests of the British Empire.

It is not only from princes and rulers that help is offered. Newspapers show that all classes of the community are trying to find out what they can do to help the British. Meetings are being held by different communities at which not only are feelings of loyalty expressed, but offers of help are made. Large sums of money have been given by all classes of the community for the benefit of the Indian troops. Generally the voice of the women of India is unheard, even in the case of political danger; but things are different now. Mr. B. N. Bose, a prominent member of the Legislative Council of the Governor-General of India, writes to *The Times*:

'Sir,—As an Indian who came over to this country only temporarily, as a delegate of the Indian National Congress, I read this morning the message of our beloved Viceroy, of India's loyalty and India's co-operation in this great crisis of our life, with tears in my eyes. Our Indian sun stirs our blood to strong emotions.

We feel grateful to Mr. Bonar Law for his suggestion that this message should be published to the world, and may I add that Indian women have not only cheerfully parted with their sons, husbands, and brothers at the call of the King, but I have received communications from India that many of them who are too humble to make their offer to the Viceroy are willing, if need be, to part with their personal jewelry and ornaments, things which in India constitute the women's insurance fund, as they did in bygone times when religion or honour was in danger.'

The supply of trained soldiers who are keen for war and who are the descendants of many generations of warriors is practically inexhaustible. The Gurkhas, the Sikhs, the Rajputs, the Mahrattas, the Mohammedan races of Northern India have in past times earned on many a stricken field the reputation of great warriors. The present representatives of those races are in no way inferior to their ancestors. Many of them have been trained in the British Army in India, and have fought side by side with British troops in all the wars which have been waged in India and the East. Afghanistan, China, Egypt have all experienced the valour and fighting capacity of our Indian troops. It is not alone upon our own Indian troops that we can now rely. Some of the Native States in India have large armies of trained soldiers whose swords are at our service.

Distinctions of race and creed have disappeared at the first suggestion of danger to the Empire. Hindus, Mohammedans, Parsees, and Buddhists are all uniting. The same news comes from every part of India. In Bengal volunteer forces are receiving large accessions to their numbers. Calcutta lawyers, most of whom are Bengalis, a race upon whom we have not so far depended for an army, have undertaken to raise a company of volunteers. The Calcutta *Bengali*, the well-known Indian newspaper, says this :

' Of the attitude of the people . . . we desire to say that behind the serried ranks of one of the finest armies in the world, there are the multitudinous peoples of India, ready to co-operate with the Government in the defence of the Empire, which, for them, means, in its ultimate evolution, the complete recognition of their rights as Citizens of the finest State in the world. We may have our differences with the Government—and what people have not ?—but in the presence of a common enemy, be it Germany or any other Power, we sink our differences, we forget our little quarrels and close our ranks and offer all that we possess in defence of the great Empire to which we are all so proud to belong, and with which the future prosperity and advancement of our people are bound up. India has always been loyal in the hour of danger.'

Similar articles are to be found in many other Indian papers written by Indians for Indians.

India has already dispatched to the seat of war two splendid divisions of infantry and one cavalry brigade, while three more cavalry brigades will follow immediately. This means 70,000 fighting men sent as a first instalment from India to the help of Great Britain. Some of the Indian Chiefs have been selected to accompany this Expeditionary Force. They are the veteran Maharajah Sir Pertab Singh, who has often fought with our troops before, and is a Major-General in the British Army; the Maharajah of Bikanir, who is every inch a soldier; the Maharajah of Patiala, who is the head of the Sikhs; and the Maharajahs of Kishengarh and Jodhpur, the Raja of Ratlam, and the Mohammedan Nawabs of Jaoram, Sachin, and Bhopal, the latter being the eldest son of the ruler of one of the principal Mohammedan States in India.

The message which the King-Emperor has sent to the Princes and Peoples of his Indian Empire was in terms which will be appreciated by every Englishman. It was as follows :

' Among the many incidents that have marked the

unanimous uprising of the populations of My Empire in defence of its unity and integrity, nothing has moved me more than the passionate devotion to My Throne expressed both by My Indian subjects, and by the Feudatory Princes and the Ruling Chiefs of India, and their prodigal offers of their lives and their resources in the cause of the Realm. Their one-voiced demand to be foremost in the conflict has touched My heart, and has inspired to the highest issues the love and devotion which, as I well know, have ever linked My Indian subjects and Myself. I recall to mind India's gracious message to the British nation of good will and fellowship which greeted My return in February, 1912, after the solemn ceremony of My Coronation Durbar at Delhi, and I find in this hour of trial a full harvest and a noble fulfilment of the assurance given by you that the destinies of Great Britain and India are indissolubly linked.'

Why is it that India is doing so much to help the British Empire in this time of need ? Is it from any particular affection for the English people ? Probably not. One cannot expect affection, although one may hope for mutual respect, between rulers and ruled when they are of entirely different races and creeds. It is because the peoples of India now recognize that their interests are bound up with the interests of the British Empire. Were the Empire to come to an end, India would become the prey of some other foreign nation whose rule would be very different from that exercised by us. Whatever our faults may be, we have done our best to give peace, prosperity, and justice to India.

Personal loyalty to the Crown has now a living force in India. The King's visit created an attachment to his person and office which has forged new bonds between the Indians, and other subjects of the Crown

India has never been a separate nation, the only bond of union between the many races that inhabit Hindustan is that created by the existence of a foreign government. Until the present time there has been no unanimity on any occasion, but now a common danger has produced common action. We feel that we can depend upon India for help whenever we justly require it. India will not lose by the help given to us in our time of need. Bonds of friendship between Great Britain and its dependency will be strengthened, and Britons will realize more and more their duties to the inhabitants of their Indian Empire.

There has always been a feeling of good fellowship between British and Indian troops and also between Indian troops and their British officers. It is quite certain that in the present war there will be a repetition and increase of this good feeling. This war will probably lead to a better understanding between the people of Great Britain and the peoples of India. Some of the mendacious news in the German Press consisted of statements that India was in rebellion against the British Crown. So far from there being any truth in the statement such disaffection or sedition as recently existed amongst members of some of the classes of India now appears to have been sporadic. It has disappeared entirely. There is now no internal trouble which can embarrass the Government, and the financial and economic situation is exceptionally strong.

It is a proud day for us when we feel that the honest, straightforward work in the path of duty which our ancestors carried on in India is now bearing its fruit. It is the old story: nothing pays in the end so well as honesty and straight dealing.

WHY WE ARE AT WAR

GREAT BRITAIN'S CASE

BY MEMBERS OF THE OXFORD FACULTY OF MODERN HISTORY

E. BARKER.	H. W. C. DAVIS.
C. R. L. FLETCHER.	ARTHUR HASSALL.
L. G. WICKHAM LEGG.	F. MORGAN.

With an Appendix of Original Documents
including the Authorized English Translation
of the White Book issued by the
German Government

THIRD EDITION REVISED (EIGHTH IMPRESSION)
CONTAINING THE RUSSIAN ORANGE BOOK AND
EXTRACTS FROM THE BELGIAN GREY BOOK

TRANSLATIONS INTO FRENCH ITALIAN SPANISH
GERMAN AND SWEDISH ARE
NOW READY

Paper Covers Two Shillings net (70 cents)
Cloth Two Shillings and Sixpence net (85 cents)

OXFORD: AT THE CLARENDON PRESS
LONDON: HUMPHREY MILFORD
EDINBURGH   GLASGOW   NEW YORK   TORONTO
MELBOURNE   BOMBAY

(a)

OXFORD PAMPHLETS
1914

TURKEY IN
EUROPE AND ASIA

WITH A MAP

Reprinted by permission from the *Political Quarterly*
of December, 1914

Price Twopence net

OXFORD UNIVERSITY PRESS
HUMPHREY MILFORD
LONDON   EDINBURGH   GLASGOW
NEW YORK   TORONTO   MELBOURNE   BOMBAY

MAP

Between pages 12 and 13

TURKEY IN EUROPE AND ASIA

TURKEY is an incalculable Power, the most paradoxical
that ever was or, let us hope, will be ! At the present
moment her national indebtedness—funded, floating,
and unprovided—is approaching two hundred millions
sterling. The mere annual charge on a part of that
debt, the part covered by loans, amounts to about
a third of her actual revenue, which is not one-seventh
of her liabilities. It is scarcely two years since she
emerged from a war for existence, which added above
a whole year's revenue to her debt and more than that
to her liabilities, robbed her of one-tenth of that revenue
and an eighth of her population by the loss of Macedonia
and the Isles, and demonstrated. her incompetence to
wage war under modern conditions. After the war, fast
tied ånd bound as she was already in international
shackles, she riveted yet others on herself by perpetuat-
ing foreign monopolies, and mortgaging what was left of
her economic liberty to Paris bankers and the Government which so subtly and effectually controls their
operations. Drained of money, men, and repute, she
seemed the one State in Europe which could not stir.
E pur si muove ! Here she is at it again, confronting,
with allies who can give her only scant assistance from
afar, a first-class military Power which can strike her
on one flank, while allies, not less powerful to hurt, strike
her on the other. She will surely be beaten. If she
were any other of the secondary Powers she would be
annihilated. But, being Turkey, she holds a charmed
life.

When you have said that she is practically bankrupt ; that the population of her immense territory is less than thirty to the square mile and steadily falling below this beggarly average ; that a good half of it is profoundly disaffected ; that her government is at present in the hands of a body of men who represent, not her Asiatic elements of strength, but the European Byzantinism which is her weakness ; that the great majority of her people is in opposition to the Government—when you have said all this, you have stated Turkey's national account quite correctly on the debit side ; but there remain ' moral ' assets to credit, which, even as things are at the present moment, may compensate.

The least potent of these is the protection hitherto secured to her by the mutual jealousies of each and all of the Powers. Obviously, this has lost value in the actual international situation. If Russia were to move on Constantinople now, Great Britain would hardly wish to thwart her ; and whether the former captured it or was forestalled by a Teutonic occupation, the result to the Ottoman Empire would be about the same. Indeed, even were the Great Powers disengaged, it is doubtful whether any of them would fight nowadays to keep another out of Constantinople, or, for that matter, to keep out a secondary Power of the Balkan group which might be able, alone or with allies, to dispossess the Turk. The strategic and economic importance of Constantinople has long been declining *pari passu* with increase in the power and speed of ships. Even had the Turks taken measures to develop the possibilities of their natural intercontinental land-routes by making the Marmora region a focus of railways and roads, and bridging the Bosphorus and the Dardanelles, the all-sea and half-sea routes would still have kept and increased the preponderant importance which they have already won. As it is—well, every one knows how far, on either the European or the Asiatic side, the Marmora region is a focus of railways or roads ! Moreover, not only the international but the local importance of Constantinople has diminished. The wars of two years ago dealt a knock-out blow to her Balkan position. The control of the peninsula, which she so long dominated, is now in commission at Sophia, Salonica, Belgrade, and Athens. So far as European territories are concerned, Constantinople is become hardly more than the chief town of the small, sparsely inhabited district of Southern Roumelia, which is run by the Government at an annual loss of about half a million.

More potent are the other ' moral ' assets of Turkey. These are first (strange to say !) her financial position, and, second (almost stranger !) her prestige. These have saved her from annihilation in the past times and again, and may save her yet. Let us see what they mean, and what limits, if any, there are to their potency.

Turkey's financial position, put bluntly, has been for many years the unsatisfactory but oddly protective one of a debtor, with certain imperfectly realized assets, who is so deeply involved with powerful creditors, but so utterly unable to repay the principal, that their best hope of recouping themselves is to keep him going by further loans. He is not actually bankrupt; and it is his creditors' interest that he should not be so in form. Accordingly, they not only continue to finance him, but shut their eyes to continued extravagances up to a point. Turkey's chief creditor is France, who held nearly sixty per cent. of the Ottoman Debt before the Balkan Wars, and found thirty millions more for her profligate debtor afterwards. Germany stands second with something

over twenty per cent., and Great Britain comes third
with the remainder to her dubious credit. Two of the
members of the Triple Entente, therefore, will think
a great many times before they push matters to extremes
with Turkey ; and well does Turkey know it ! It is all
very well for Russia to propose, as a matter of course,
to throttle the unedifying Old Man, but not for France.

If any considerable part of this enormous debt were
represented by national plant which, taken over *vi et
armis*, might be developed to return a profit on its cost,
well and good. But Turkey has taken good care to
expend nine-tenths of her loans on transitory and purely
unremunerative things. The situation, therefore, is this :
whoever, be it Russia or any one else, dispossesses the
Turk in any considerable part of his Empire must not
only take over a dead weight of virtually unsecured
debt, but face the prospect of putting at least as much
again into the country before it has the slightest chance
of becoming a paying concern.

So the Ottoman Empire has been, and perhaps still
will be, allowed to go on its way. It possesses considerable material assets, capable of being developed to
far greater value. Although about half its immense
extent is desert, steppe, and mountain, the other half
includes broad areas of exceptional fertility which produce commodities of exceptional value, such as silk,
tobacco, fine wool, and various fruits. Almost all the
Empire lies in the most favoured part of the northern
temperate zone, and it would be hard to find on the
globe districts of greater natural possibilities than the
littoral valleys and great upland plains of Asia Minor,
the plains of North and Middle Syria, the interfluvial
region of Southern Mesopotamia, and the lower basins
of the left-bank affluents of the Tigris. Add extra-

ordinary variety and wealth of unexploited minerals in
the mountain districts of Asia Minor and Kurdistan, an
intercontinental situation and a long sea-board indented
with some of the finest natural harbours in the world,
and your sum total will represent a potentiality of
prosperity which accounts for the fact that the most
improvident, uneconomical, and destructive administration in history can still draw profits from Asia. In spite
of secular waste, in spite even of the disasters of two
years ago, the Ottoman revenue shows progressive
elasticity, especially in customs returns from oversea
trade, ill as the system of collection is conceived to
encourage any trade. Thanks mainly to more careful
and honest administration of this department under
British supervision, over five millions sterling (nearly
twenty per cent.) were added to the revenue between
1908 and the outbreak of the Balkan War, and recovery
from the set-back of that war was already pronounced
before the present trouble began. One could do almost
anything with territories which, having been treated as
Asiatic Turkey has been treated, still, in a measure,
thrive !

Thus the very desperation of Turkey's financial position has been hitherto a protection to her. The certain
loss involved in foreclosure, added to the opposition
which any one creditor, who proposed such a course,
expected to meet from the rest, has not only deterred
all, but left them no choice but to agree to bolster her
up. Will this continue to be Turkey's case ? Obviously,
if of her own motion she should commit bankruptcy by
repudiating her international debt (as, it is stated, she
proposes at the present juncture), it will not. Once
bankrupt, she loses all protection whatever from her
financial position. Not less obviously, the actual inter-

national situation renders it possible and probable that two of her creditors, holding together nearly 80 per cent. of her debt, may agree to foreclose jointly, irrespective of any one else. The question whether they should proceed to do so or not would be influenced no longer by financial interest in keeping Turkey going, but by quite other considerations, to the chief of which we shall come in a moment.

Short, however, of suicide by bankruptcy, will Turkey find her financial position protect her as heretofore ? At an increasing rate during recent years her great creditors have exacted, in return for loans, not merely security for high interest and repayment of capital, but also exclusive concessions in which their nationals may invest. For example, the thirty millions which French bankers agreed to lend to Turkey after the Balkan Wars, imposed extraordinary conditions in the shape of concessions to French capitalists to construct railways, roads, harbour-works, and the like, almost all over the Ottoman Empire. By the present state of war these concessions are all cancelled. France in particular, therefore, stands to lose heavily, even should the interest and capital of her actual loans prove still to be secure. That is to say, a situation has arisen in which one at least of the belligerents may find that its prospective national loss outweighs any gain to be expected from the continued solvency of Turkey ; and even, therefore, should the latter think better of burning her financial boats, she is not unlikely to find the protection which her financial position used to afford her dangerously diminished or even destroyed.

The third and last 'moral' asset, prestige, is less calculable and more elusive, but at the same time more effective and less easy to dispose of. It is in part secular and in greater part religious. The first element is implied in that name *Roum* by which the western dominion of the Turks has been known ever since the Seljuks won Asia Minor. Apart from the prestige of their own early conquests, the Ottomans inherited, and in a measure retain in the Near East, the traditional prestige of the greatest Empire which ever held it. They stand not only for their own past but also for whatever still lives of the prestige of Rome. Theirs is still the repute of the imperial people *par excellence*, chosen and called to rule.

That this repute should continue, after the sweeping victories of Semites and subsequent centuries of Ottoman retreat before other heirs of Rome, is a paradox to be explained only by the fact that a large part of the population of the Near East remains at this day in about the same stage of civilization and knowledge as in the time of, say, Heraclius. The Turks, be it remembered, were and are foreigners in a great part of their Asiatic Empire equally with the Greeks of Byzantium or the Romans of Italy ; and their establishment in Constantinople nearly five centuries ago did not mean to the indigenous peoples of the Near East what it meant to Europe—a victory of the East over the West—so much as a continuation of immemorial ' Roman ' dominion still exercised from the same Imperial centre. Since Roum first spread its shadow over the Near East, many men of many races, whose variety was imperfectly realized, if realized at all, by the peasants of Asia Minor, Syria, Mesopotamia, and Egypt, have ruled in its name, and the Ottomans, whose governmental system was in part the Byzantine, made but one more change which meant the same old thing. The peasants know, of course, about those Semitic victories ; but they know also that if the Semite has had his day of triumph and imposed, as was right and proper, his God and his Prophet on Roum—even, as many believed, and some may be found in remoter regions who still believe, on all mankind—he has returned to his own place south of Taurus ; and still Roum is Roum, natural indefeasible Lord of the World.

Such a belief is dying now, of course ; but it dies slowly and hard. It still constitutes a real asset of the Ottomans; and will not cease to have value until they lose Constantinople. On the possession of the old imperial city it depends for whatever vitality it retains. You may demonstrate, as you will, and as many publicists have done since the Balkan Wars and before, what and how great economic, political, and social advantages would accrue to the Turks, if they could bring themselves to transfer their capital to Asia. Here they would be rid of Roumelia, which costs, and will always cost them, more than it yields. Here they could concentrate Moslems where their co-religionists are already the great majority, and so have done with the everlasting friction and weakness entailed in jurisdiction over preponderant Christian elements. Here they might throw off Byzantinism as a garment and no longer be forced to face two ways, but live and govern with single minds as the Asiatics they are. Vain illusion, as the Turkish Imperialists know ! It is Empire that would fall away as a garment so soon as the Near East realized that Turks no longer ruled in the Imperial City. Enver Pasha and the Committee were amply justified in straining the resources of the Ottoman Empire to cracking-point two years ago, not merely to retain Constantinople, but also to recover Adrianople and a territory in Europe large enough to bulk as Roum. Nothing that happened

in that war made so greatly for the continuation of
the old order in Asiatic Turkey as the reoccupation
of Adrianople. The one occasion on which Europeans
in Syria had reason to expect a general explosion was
when premature rumours of the entry of the Bulgarian
army into Stamboul gained currency for a few hours.
That explosion, had the news proved true or not been
contradicted in time, would have been a panic-stricken,
ungovernable impulse of anarchy, conscious that an old
world had passed away and ignorant what conceivable
new world could come to be. The perilous moment
passed, to be succeeded by general diffusion of a belief
that the inevitable catastrophe was only postponed. In
the breathing-time allowed, Arabs, Kurds, and Armenians discussed and planned together revolt from the
moribund Turk, and, separately, the mutual massacre
and plundering of one another. Arab national organizations and nationalist journals sprang to life at Beirut
and elsewhere. The revival of Arab Empire was talked
of and names of possible capitals and kings were bandied
about. One Arab province, the Hasa, actually broke
away from the Turks. Then men began to say that the
Bulgarians would not advance beyond Tchataldja : the
Balkan States were at war among themselves : finally,
Adrianople had been re-occupied. And all was as in
the beginning. Budding life withered in the Arab movement; and the Near East settled down once more in
the persistent shadow of Roum.

That is the lesser element in Turkey's protective
prestige, dependent on the retention of Constantinople
and doomed to disappear the moment that the Ottoman
State relinquishes Europe. Meanwhile there it is for
what it is worth ; and it is actually worth a tradition
of submission, natural and honourable, to a race of

superior destiny, which is instinctive in some millions
of savage simple hearts.

What, then, of the other, the greater element ? The
religious prestige of the Ottoman Power as the repository
of Caliphial authority, and Trustee for Islam in the Holy
Land of Arabia, is an asset almost impossible to estimate.
Would a death struggle of the Ottomans in Europe
rouse the Sunni world ? Would the Moslems of India,
Afghanistan, Turkestan, China, and Malaya take up
arms for the Ottoman Sultan as Caliph ? Nothing but
the event will prove that they would. They have never
done. so yet. They have never shown much sign of
disposition to do so in any of the crises through which
the Ottoman Power has been passing this century and
more. Quite recently, indications (such as the manifesto
of the Agha Khan) do not point to any prevalent conviction that the fate of Islam is bound up with that of the
Turks. Jchad, or Holy War, is a difficult and dangerous
weapon for Young Turks to wield : difficult because
their own Islamic sincerity is suspect and they are taking
the field now as clients of a *giaour* people : dangerous
because the Ottoman nation itself includes numerous
Christian elements, indispensable to its economy. Still,
since one cannot be sure, one cannot, in Great Britain's
position, be too careful. The recent Italian attack on an
Ottoman possession did lead to a truce of Allah between
bitter traditional foes, the Turks and the Arabs in the
Yemen, and to active and durable co-operation between
the two in the hinterland of Tripoli and Cyrenaica.
During the Tabah dispute in 1906, Egypt gave abundant
signs that, heartily as she used to hate Turks and
Turkish administration, her memory of that enmity was
less strong than her sense of solidarity with the leading
Moslem Power in its opposition to our Christian selves.

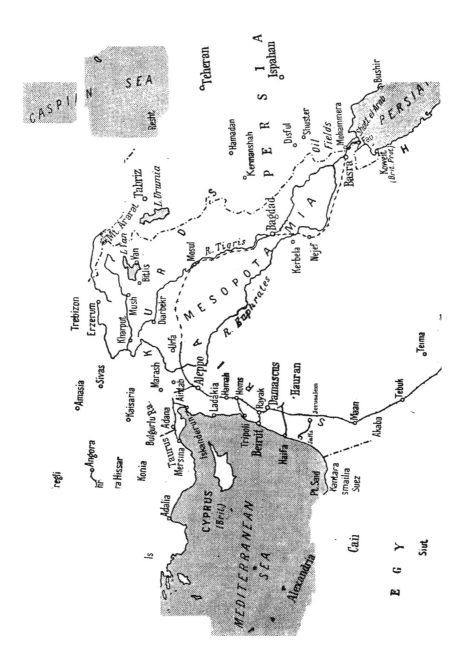

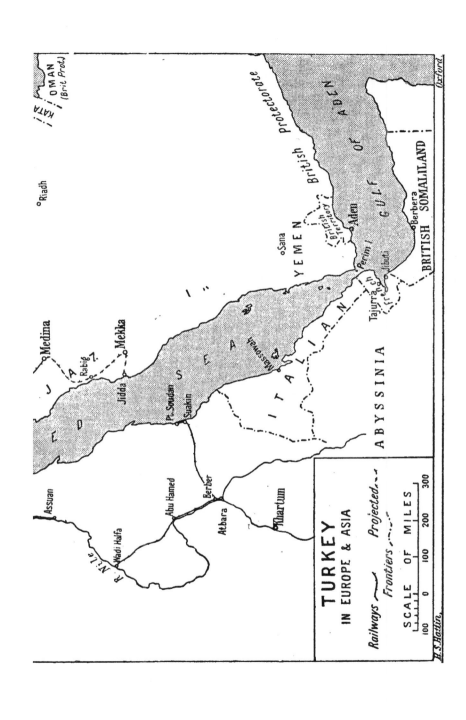

TURKEY
IN EUROPE & ASIA

Railways ——— Projected ---
Frontiers ---·---

SCALE OF MILES
100   0   100   200   300

H.S.Hatfin.

Oxford

The Ottoman Sultanate undoubtedly can count on its prestige based on religion appealing widely, over-riding counteracting sentiments, and, if it rouses to action, rousing the most dangerous temper of all. It is futile to deny, and dangerous to disregard, its possi-bilities. Especially is it futile to pooh-pooh it because Mohammed V is not of the Koreish, and owes his Caliphate to a sixteenth-century transfer. These facts are either unknown or not borne in mind by half the Sunnites on whom he might call, and weigh far less with the other half than his hereditary dominion over the Holy Cities, sanctioned by the prescription of nearly four centuries. Still less does it avail to quote opinions expressed by Moslem *litterati* in India or elsewhere, that George V, since he rules more Muslamîn than Mo-hammed V, is the true Caliph! The vast majority of the Sunni Faithful do regard the Ottoman Sultan as armed with Caliphial authority, so far as any exists. The only question is whether under any possible circum-stances that belief would lead to combined action, and if so, to what? The importance of the religious element in Ottoman prestige lies just in our complete inability to answer that question!

One thing, however, can be foretold with certainty. The religious prestige of an Ottoman Sultan, who had definitely lost control of the Holy Places, would cease as quickly and utterly as the secular prestige of one who had evacuated Constantinople : and since the loss of the latter would probably precipitate an Arab revolt, and cut off the Hejaz, the religious element in Ottoman prestige may be said to depend as much as the secular on Constantinople. All the more reason why the Com-mittee of Union and Progress should not have accepted that well-meant advice of European publicists! A successful revolt of the Arab-speaking provinces would indeed sound the death-knell of the Ottoman Empire. No other event would be so immediately and surely catastrophic.

This being so, it is odd that the Committee, which has shown no mean understanding of some conditions essential to Ottoman Empire, should have done so little hitherto to conciliate Arab susceptibilities. Neither in the constitution of the Parliament nor in the higher commands of the Army have the Arab-speaking peoples been given anything like their fair share ; and loudly and insistently have they protested. Perhaps the Committee, whose leading members are of a markedly Europeanized type, understands Asia less well than Europe. Certainly its programme of Ottomanization, elaborated by military ex-attachés, by Jew bankers and officials from Salonica, and by doctors, lawyers, and other *intellectuels* fresh from Paris, is conceived on lines which offer the pure Asiatic very little scope. The free and equal Ottomans are all to take their cue from Turks, and from Turks only of the Byzantine sort which the European provinces, and especially the city of Constantinople, breed. After the revolution nothing in Turkey struck one so much as the apparition on the top of things everywhere of a type of Turk who has the characteristic qualities of the Levantine Greek. Young officers, controlling their elders, only needed a change of uniform to pass in an Athenian crowd. Spare and dapper officials, presiding in seats of authority over Kurds and Arabs, reminded one of Greek journalists. Turkish journalists themselves treated one to rhodomontades punctuated with restless gesticulation, which revived memories of Athenian cafés in war-time. It was the Byzantine triumphing over the Asiatic ; and the most

Asiatic elements in the Empire were the least likely to
meet with the appreciation or sympathy of the former.

Are the Arab-speaking peoples, therefore, likely to
revolt, or be successful in splitting the Ottoman Empire,
if they do ? The present writer would like to say at
once that, in his opinion, this consummation of the
Empire is not devoutly to be wished. Bad, according to
our standards, as Turkish government is, native Arab
government, when not in tutelage to Europeans, has
generally proved itself worse, when tried in the Ottoman
area in modern times. Where it is of a purely Bedawin
barbaric type, as in the Emirates of Central Arabia, it
does well enough ; but if the population be contaminated
ever so little with non-Arab elements, practices, or ideas,
Arab administration seems incapable of producing effective government. It has had chances in the Holy Cities
at intervals, and for longer periods in the Yemen. But
a European, long resident in the latter country, who
had groaned under Turkish administration, where it has
always been most oppressive, bore witness that the rule
of native Imams, who shook off the Turkish yoke in
his time, only served to replace oppressive government
by oppressive anarchy.

The substitution of Arab administration for Turkish,
therefore, would necessarily entail European tutelage of
the parts of the Arab-speaking area in which Powers,
like ourselves, have vital interests—Syria, for example,
Southern Mesopotamia, and, probably, Hejaz. The last-
named, in particular, would involve us in a very ticklish
and thankless task. We might put in Egyptians as care-
takers, but hardly with much hope of success without
a leaven of Europeans, whose residence in the Holy Land
would excite unappeasable susceptibilities ; and we had
better think many times before we exalt an imperfectly

controlled Khedive into Trustee of Islam ? Conceivably,
the Shereefial House of Mecca, advised by Indian Moslem
officials, might be capable of securing well-being in
Hejaz ; but this House has never yet proved itself
a satisfactory substitute for the Turk. On the whole,
where every alternative course bristles with such difficulties and dangers, one can only be thankful for the
Turkish caretaker and loth to see him dismissed.

An Arab revolt, however, might break out whether
the Triple Entente desired its success or not. What
chance of success would it have ? The peoples of the
Arab part of the Ottoman Empire are a congeries of
differing races, creeds, sects, and social systems, with no
common bond except language. The physical character
of their land compels a good third of them to be nomadic
predatory barbarians, feared by the other two-thirds.
The settled folk are divided into Moslem and Christian
(not to mention a large Jewish element), the cleavage
being more abrupt than in Western Turkey and the
tradition and actual spirit of mutual enmity more
separative. Further, each of these main creed-divisions
is subdivided. Even Islam in this region includes
a number of incompatible sects, such as the Ansariye,
the Metawali, and the Druses in the Syrian mountains,
Shiite Arabs on the Gulf coast and the Persian border,
with pagan Kurds and Yezidis in the latter region and
North Mesopotamia. As for the Christians, their divisions are notorious, most of these being subdivided again
into two or more hostile communions apiece. It is
almost impossible to imagine the inhabitants of Syria
concerting a common plan or taking common action.
The only elements among them which have shown any
political sense or capacity for political organization are
Christian. The Maronites of the Lebanon are most

conspicuous among these ; but neither their numbers nor their traditional relations with their neighbours qualify them to form the nucleus of a free united Syria. The ' Arab Movement ' up to the present has consisted in little more than talk and journalese. It has never developed any considerable organization to meet that stable efficient organization which the Committee of Union and Progress directs throughout the Ottoman dominions.

At the present moment this Committee has concentrated in Southern Syria a very considerable force of second-line troops stiffened with German officers, and has secured the co-operation of a majority of the Bedawin tribes of the Syrian and North Arabian deserts by gifts of arms and money. Whatever demonstrations this force may be bidden attempt against the Suez Canal and the Delta, it has, quite possibly, in reality, been collected and concentrated just where it is—at a half-way point between the Syrian and Arabian areas—rather to overawe and keep quiet the Arab-speaking Ottomans than in the hope of achieving a reconquest of Egypt. In any case, so long as it remains effective where it is, it makes a rising either in Syria or the Hejaz very unlikely to happen, and even less likely to succeed.

Whether that force will be able seriously to attack Egypt and what would happen if it did, a layman may be excused from prophesying. It has often been pointed out that the stretch of desert between Gaza and the Nile Delta has never availed by itself to save Egypt from invasion by land ; but, on the other hand, no invader has tried to pass it since parts of its most practicable track and the western ends of all its paths can be reached by naval guns with high-explosive shells. An advance on Egypt from El-Arish, without free use of the coast-track, would have to be made with none but light artillery and on a very narrow front. Small raiding parties might (with luck) pass our lines and reach the Canal's bank some fifteen miles west between the Bitter Lakes and Kantara, and, if not prevented or observed by patrols (the last not a very probable contingency in view of the strength with which we are now holding this line), could place camel-borne mines in the channel which might sink one or more ships and close the water-way. This seems to be about the limit of effective Turkish action, short of a successful sympathetic rising of the Egyptians themselves.

Per contra, it is easy for Powers which hold the sea to throw a force into Syria. The strip of practicable country between the coast and sheer desert is little more than a hundred miles wide at many points, and both the supplies and the retreat of the Syro-German army of Ma'an would be quickly at the mercy of a few thousand men with good artillery. Damascus, Homs, and Aleppo would be obvious main points to occupy, and with the coast controlled from the sea, Ottoman dominion in Syria, and probably in Arabia as well, would be at an end in a week. If Bedawins continued militant, their exclusion from Syrian and Lower Mesopotamian markets would soon bring them to heel. Even their thin life cannot go on without certain necessaries and luxuries, which Arabian oases do not supply. The settled folk, even in the towns, would give little or no trouble, and considerable elements might be expected to greet a French or British expeditionary force with ebullient enthusiasm destined to cool after some years' experience of even-handed western justice, regularity in tax-collec-tion, and sanitary prejudices.

In the rest of the Ottoman Empire what may or will happen in the event of the War being fought to a finish ?

That is, to a finish of the present Turkish policy and armaments. Asia Minor will stand by the Turkish cause, even if Europe and Constantinople, and even if the Holy Places and all the Arab-speaking provinces, be lost. Its allegiance does not. depend on either the tradition of Roum or the Caliphiate, but on essential unity with the Ottoman nation. In fact, Asia Minor *is* Turkey. There the Ottoman nation was formed ; there, prepared equally by Byzantine domination and by Seljukian influence, the great mass of the people long ago identified itself insensibly and completely with the tradition and hope of the Ottomans. The subsequent occupation of the Byzantine capital by the heirs of the Byzantine system, and their still later assumption of Caliphial responsibility, were not needed to cement the union. Even a military occupation by. Russia or by any other strong Power would not detach Anatolia from the Turkish unity ; for a thing cannot be detached from itself. But, of course, that occupation might cause the unity itself to cease to be after long years.

Such an occupation, however, would probably not be seriously resisted or subsequently rebelled against by the Moslem majority in Asia Minor, supposing Turkish armaments to have been crushed. The Anatolian population is a sober, labouring peasantry, essentially agricultural and wedded to the soil. The levies for Yemen and Europe, which have gone far to deplete and exhaust it of recent years, were composed of men who fought to order and without imagination steadily and faithfully, as their fathers had fought ; but without lust for war, or Arabian tradition of fighting for its own sake, and with little, if any, fanaticism. Attempts to inspire Anatolian troops with religious rage in the late Balkan Wars were failures. They were asked to fight in too modern a way under too many Teutonic officers. The result illustrated a prophecy ascribed to Mukhtar Pasha, of Yemen fame. When German instructors were first introduced into Turkey, he foretold that they would be the end of the Ottoman army. No, these Anatolians desire nothing better than to follow their plough-oxen, and live their common village life, under any master who will let them be.

Elements of the Christian minority, however, Armenian and Greek, would give trouble with their developed ideas of nationality and irrepressible tendency to ' Europize '. They would present, indeed, problems of which at present one cannot foresee the solution. It seems inevitable that an autonomous Armenia, like an autonomous Poland, must be constituted ere long ; but where ? There is no geographical unit of the Ottoman area in which Armenians are the majority. If they cluster more thickly in the vilayets of Angora, Sivas, Erzerum, Kharput, and Van, i. e. in easternmost Asia Minor, than elsewhere, and form a village people of the soil, they are consistently a minority in any large administrative district. Numerous, too, in the trans-Tauric vilayets of Adana and Aleppo, the seat of their most recent independence, they are townsmen in the main, and not an essential element of the agricultural population. Even if a considerable proportion of the Armenians, now dispersed through towns of Western Asia Minor and in Constantinople, could be induced to concentrate in a reconstituted Armenia (which is doubtful, seeing how addicted they are to general commerce and what may be called parasitic life), they could not fill out both the Greater and the Lesser Armenias of history, in sufficient strength to overbear the Turkish and Kurdish elements. The widest area which might be constituted autonomous Armenia with good prospect of self-sufficiency would be the present Russian province, where the head-quarters of the national religion lie, with the addition of the actual Turkish provinces of Erzerum, Van, and Kharput. But, if Russia had brought herself to make a self-denying ordinance, she would have to police her new Armenia very strongly for some years ; for an acute Kurdish problem would confront it, and, no concentration of nationals could be looked for from the Armenia Irredenta of Diarbekr, Urfa, Aleppo, Aintab, Marash, Adana, Kaisariyeh, Sivas, Angora, and Trebizond (not to mention farther and more foreign towns), until public security was assured in what for generations has been a cockpit. The Kurd is, of course, an Indo-European as much as the Armenian, and rarely a true Moslem ; but it would be a very long time indeed before these facts reconciled him to the domination of the race which he has plundered for three centuries. Most of the ' Turks ' of Eastern Asia Minor are descendants of converted Armenians ; but their assimilation also would be slow and doubtful. Islam, more rapidly and completely than any other creed, extinguishes racial sympathies.

The Anatolian Greeks are less numerous but not less difficult to provide for. The scattered groups of them on the plateau—in Cappadocia, Pontus, the Konia district—and on the eastward coast-lands would offer no serious difficulty to a lord of the interior. But those in the western river-basins from Isbarta to the Marmora, and those on the western and north-western littorals, are of a more advanced and cohesive political character, being imbued with nationalism, intimate with their independent nationals, and actively interested in Hellenic national politics. What happens at Athens has long concerned them more than what happens at

Constantinople : and with Greece occupying the islands
in the daily view of many of them, they are coming to
regard themselves more and more every day as citizens
of Graecia Irredenta.   What is to be done with these ?
What, in particular, with Smyrna, the second city of
the Ottoman Empire and the first of ' Magna Graecia ' ?
Its three and a half hundred thousand souls include the
largest Greek urban population resident in any one city.
To these problems I call attention, but venture no
solution.

Nor, indeed, in anything else concerning the Ottoman
Empire does the present writer presume to be among the
prophets.   He has but tried to set forth what may delay
and what may precipitate the collapse of an Empire,
whose doom has been long foreseen, often ·planned,
invariably postponed ; and, further, to indicate some
difficulties which are bound to confront heirs of Turkey
on the morrow of her death and will be better met the
better they are understood before her final agony—if
this is, indeed, to be !

Oxford : Horace Hart Printer to the University.

WHY WE ARE AT WAR
GREAT BRITAIN'S CASE

BY MEMBERS OF THE OXFORD FACULTY
OF MODERN HISTORY

E. BARKER.	H. W. C. DAVIS.
C. R. L. FLETCHER.	ARTHUR HASSALL.
L. G. WICKHAM LEGG.	F. MORGAN.

With an Appendix of Original Documents
including the Authorized English Translation
of the White Book issued by the
German Government

THIRD EDITION REVISED (NINTH IMPRESSION)
CONTAINING THE RUSSIAN ORANGE BOOK AND
EXTRACTS FROM THE BELGIAN GREY BOOK

TRANSLATIONS INTO FRENCH ITALIAN SPANISH
GERMAN AND SWEDISH ARE
NOW READY

Paper Covers Two Shillings net (70 cents)
Cloth Two Shillings and Sixpence net (85 cents)

OXFORD: AT THE CLARENDON PRESS
LONDON: HUMPHREY MILFORD
EDINBURGH   GLASGOW   NEW YORK   TORONTO
MELBOURNE   BOMBAY

(*b*)

No. 12

OXFORD PAMPHLETS

1914

RUSSIA

THE PSYCHOLOGY OF A NATION

BY

PAUL VINOGRADOFF, F.B.A.

CORPUS PROFESSOR OF JURISPRUDENCE IN THE UNIVERSITY OF OXFORD
SOMETIME PROFESSOR OF HISTORY IN THE UNIVERSITY
OF MOSCOW

FIFTH IMPRESSION

Price One Penny net

OXFORD UNIVERSITY PRESS
HUMPHREY MILFORD
LONDON   EDINBURGH   GLASGOW
NEW YORK   TORONTO   MELBOURNE   BOMBAY

OXFORD PAMPHLETS
1914–1915

Crown 8vo. Separately, in paper covers.
Also in series as. numbered (I–X), stiff
covers, One Shilling net each series.
53 Pamphlets have now (Jan. 7, 1915)
been issued, and others are in preparation.
The historical pieces are illustrated by
sketch-maps.

Saturday Review :—'These little books are easily the best
books of the war—accurate, quietly written, full of knowledge,
and quite unspoiled by vainglory or bitterness.'

OXFORD UNIVERSITY PRESS
HUMPHREY MILFORD
LONDON EDINBURGH GLASGOW
NEW YORK TORONTO MELBOURNE BOMBAY

OXFORD PAMPHLETS
1914–1915

I

1. The Deeper Causes of the War.

By W. SANDAY. 3d. net.

The psychology of Prussian militarism ; German public opinion and Germany's aggressive ambitions.

2. To the Christian Scholars of Europe and America: A Reply from Oxford to the German 'Address to Evangelical Christians'.

2d. net.

The answer of Oxford theologians to a recent manifesto of the German evangelical theologians. This manifesto, which is reproduced in the present pamphlet, argues that Germany is in no sense responsible for the present war. The Oxford reply states that the German theologians cannot have studied either the events which led up to the war or the political utterances of their own countrymen.

3. The Responsibility for the War.

By W. G. S. ADAMS. 2d. net.

A brief discussion of the question of responsibility : 1. Austria and Serbia ; 2. The responsibility of Russia ; 3. The intervention of England.

4. Great Britain and Germany.

By SPENSER WILKINSON. 2d. net.

Three letters to the *Springfield Republican*: 1. By Prof. Spenser Wilkinson, stating Great Britain's case ; 2. By Prof. John W. Burgess of the University of Columbia, stating Germany's case ; 3. By Prof. Wilkinson, in reply to Prof. Burgess.

5. 'Just for a Scrap of Paper.'

By ARTHUR HASSALL. 1d. net.

Explains why England stands for the sanctity of European treaty-law.

6. The Germans, their Empire, and how they have made it.

By C. R. L. FLETCHER. 2d. net.
A historical account of Prussian policy from the seventeenth century.

7. The Germans, their Empire, and what they covet.

By C. R. L. FLETCHER. 2d. net.
An account of the ambitions avowed by the Pan-German school.

8. Might is Right.

By Sir WALTER RALEIGH. 2d. net.
Why Germany may win; what will happen if she wins; why we believe she will not win.

9. Austrian Policy since 1867.

By MURRAY BEAVEN. 3d. net.
Austrian policy in the Balkans has been of the 'offensive-defensive' order. The Archduke Francis Ferdinand might have saved Austria from rushing to destruction; but 1912 was the beginning of the end.

10. Italian Policy since 1870.

By KEITH FEILING. 2d. net.
Italian policy has been and must be guided by her own interests. The results of her colonial policy have not yet been satisfactory enough to tempt her into adventures.

11. French Policy since 1871.

By F. MORGAN and H. W. C. DAVIS. 2d. net.
A historical sketch, discussing the question whether French policy has been aggressive.

12. Russia : The Psychology of a Nation.

By PAUL VINOGRADOFF. 1d. net.
A reply to the German taunt that Russia is still in a state of barbarism, and is the enemy of European civilization.

13. Serbia and the Serbs.

By Sir VALENTINE CHIROL. 2d. net.
A sketch of Serbian history, which is incidentally an indictment of the policy pursued by Austria-Hungary towards the Serbian kingdom.

14. Germany and 'The Fear of Russia'.

By Sir VALENTINE CHIROL. 2d. net.
Shows that before 1879 Germany preferred Russia as an ally to Austria. The ambition of Germany to establish a protectorate over Turkey has led her to assist Austria in the Balkans and so to challenge Russia.

15. The Eastern Question.

By F. F. URQUHART. 3d. net.
The history of the Balkan nations; their future.

IV

16. War against War.
By A. D. LINDSAY. 2d. net.

Denies that war is good in itself, or a necessary evil. National greatness, if founded on brute force, cannot endure. International law represents an ideal, but an ideal that may be realized.

17. The Value of Small States.
By H. A. L. FISHER. 2d. net.

The author argues that the debt of civilization to small states is incalculable.

18. How can War ever be Right?
By GILBERT MURRAY. 2d. net.

A well-known lover of peace and advocate of pacific policies argues against the Tolstoyan position. Right and honour compelled Britain to make war; and war—like tragedy—is not pure evil.

19. The National Principle and the War.
By RAMSAY MUIR. 3d. net.

Considers the principle of nationality and its application to the settlement of Europe—particularly of S.E. Europe—after the War.

20. Nietzsche and Treitschke. The Worship of Power in Modern Germany.
By E. BARKER. 2d. net.

An explanation of the main points of interest in the ethical and political doctrines of the German ruling classes.

V

21. The British Dominions and the War.
By H. E. EGERTON. 2d. net.

Explains the ideas for which the British Empire stands, and the political and moral issues of the war affecting the Dominions.

22. India and the War.
By Sir ERNEST TREVELYAN. 1d. net.

Discusses the reasons for the striking manifestations of Indian loyalty.

23. Is the British Empire the Result of Wholesale Robbery?
By H. E. EGERTON. 2d. net.

A historical sketch in answer to a common taunt.

24. The Law of Nations and the War.
By A. PEARCE HIGGINS. 2d. net.

The violation of Belgian neutrality and the conduct of England to Denmark in 1807; the doctrine of German lawyers that military necessity overrides the laws of war; the balance of power and the sanctity of treaties.

25. England's Mission.
By W. BENETT. 2d. net.

Answers the question, In what cause are we fighting?

VI

26. August, 1914 : The Coming of the War.
By SPENSER WILKINSON. Stiff covers. 1s. net.

VII

27. The Retreat from Mons.
By H. W. C. DAVIS. 3d. net.

28. The Battles of the Marne and Aisne.
By H. W. C. DAVIS. 4d. net.
The Dispatches, with commentary, maps, &c.

29. The Navy and the War.
By J. R. THURSFIELD. 3d. net.
Estimates the military and economic value of the silent pressure exercised by our fleet, and warns the faint-hearted and the captious of the perils of lack of faith.

30. Bacilli and Bullets.
By Sir WILLIAM OSLER. 1d. net.
Calls attention to the fact that disease kills more men than the bullet. The most dangerous diseases are preventable by inoculation.

VIII

31. The Double Alliance *versus* The Triple Entente.
By JAMES M. BECK. 3d. net.
The judgement of a well-known American lawyer.

32. The Germans in Africa.
By EVANS LEWIN. 3d. net.
A historical account of the German colonies.

33. All for Germany, or the World's Respect Well Lost. 2d. net.
'The conversation here imagined, between a new (and perhaps less naïf) Candide and a new (and perhaps less benevolent) Dr. Pangloss, is concerned with the political thoughts and ambitions entertained by the Germans of these latter days.'

34. Germany, the Economic Problem.
By C. GRANT ROBERTSON. 2d. net.
Estimates the strength and weakness of Germany's economic position and inquires how long she can stand the strain of the war.

35. German Sea-Power.
By C. S. TERRY. 3d. net.
Traces the growth of Germany's navy. With a map of the North Sea.

IX

36. What Europe owes to Belgium.

By H. W. C. DAVIS.   2d. net.

Reminds us of the past achievements of the Belgian people in war and in peace.

37. Poland, Prussia, and Culture.

By LUDWIK EHRLICH.   3d. net.

The author is a Doctor of the University of Lwòw (Lemberg) in Galicia.

38. Turkey in Europe and Asia.   2d. net.

The strength and weakness of the Ottoman Empire considered. The secular prestige of Constantinople, the religious prestige of the Caliphate, and the racial and economic weaknesses which may cause their downfall.   A map shows the unfinished railways.

39. Greek Policy since 1882.

By A. J. TOYNBEE.   4d. net.

A historical account of the policy of Greece ; the economic future of Greece ; the problem of *Graecia Irredenta*.   With a map.

40. North Sleswick under Prussian Rule, 1864–1914.

By W. R. PRIOR.   2d. net.

The policy of Prussianization and the resistance of Danish Nationalism. 'If the children do not understand German, they must be treated and taught like deaf-mutes' is quoted from a Prussian educational authority. A map shows the distribution of languages.

X

41. Thoughts on the War.

By GILBERT MURRAY. 2d. net.

Reprinted from the *Hibbert Journal* for October.

42. The Leadership of the World.

By F. S. MARVIN. 2d. net.

A discussion of German aspirations.

43. The Leading Ideas of British Policy.

By the Hon. GERARD COLLIER. 2d. net.

Places the principles of our policy in the perspective of history.

44. The War and its Economic Aspects.

By W. J. ASHLEY. 2d. net.

A comparison of Germany's and Great Britain's powers to stand the strain of a prolonged war. Probable effects of defeat or victory.

45. Food Supplies in War Time.

By R. H. REW, C.B. 2d. net.

An authoritative discussion by an expert who has been 'for over thirty years engaged in the service of British Agriculture'.

Published separately and will also appear shortly in series.

Non-Combatants and the War.
By A. Pearce Higgins. 2d. net.

States the rights and duties of the non-combatant population of a territory under hostile occupation.

Troyon : an Engagement in the Battle of the Aisne.
By A. N. Hilditch. 2d. net.

Scandinavia and the War.
By E. Bjorkman. 2d. net.

Considers the policy and sympathies of the three Northern Kingdoms.

Asia and the War.
By A. E. Duchesne. · 2d. net.

Describes German intrigue, and its failure, in Turkey, India, and Egypt.

Through German Eyes.
By E. A. Sonnenschein. 2d. net.

Does International Law still Exist ?
By Sir H. Erle Richards. 2d. net.

German Philosophy and the War.
By J. H. Muirhead. 2d. net.

The Action off Heligoland.   August 1914.
By L. Cecil Jane. 3d. net.

Ready Immediately.

The Southern Slavs.
By N. Forbes.

The Battle of Ypres—Armentières.
By H. W. C. Davis.

Lessons of the War.
By T. B. Strong.

Outlines of Prussian History to 1871.
By E. F. Row.

The War through Danish Eyes.
By a Dane.

RUSSIA

THE PSYCHOLOGY OF A NATION

(Reprinted, by permission, from The Times *of September 14, 1914.)*

In this time of crisis, when the clash of ideas seems as fierce as the struggle of the hosts, it is the duty of those who possess authentic information on one or the other point in dispute to speak out firmly and clearly. I should like to contribute some observations on German and Russian conceptions in matters of culture. I base my claim to be heard on the fact that I have had the privilege of being closely connected with Russian, German, and English life. As a Russian Liberal, who had to give up an honourable position at home for the sake of his opinions, I can hardly be suspected of subserviency to the Russian bureaucracy.

I am struck by the insistence with which the Germans represent their cause in this world-wide struggle as the cause of civilization as opposed to Muscovite barbarism ; and I am not sure that some of my English friends do not feel reluctant to side with the subjects of the Tsar against the countrymen of Harnack and Eucken. One would like to know, however, since when have the Germans taken up this attitude ? They were not so squeamish during the ' war of emancipation ' which gave birth to modern Germany. At that time the people of Eastern Prussia were anxiously waiting for the appearance of Cossacks, as heralds of the Russian hosts who were to emancipate them from the yoke of Napoleon. Did the

Prussians and Austrians reflect on the humiliation of an
alliance with the Muscovites, and on the superiority of
the Code Civil, when the Russian Guard at Kulm [1] stood
like a rock against the desperate onslaught of Vandamme?
Perhaps by this time the inhabitants of Berlin have
obliterated the bas-relief in the 'Alley of Victories' which
represents Prince William of Prussia, the future victor
of Sedan, seeking safety within the square of the Kaluga
regiment! [2]   Russian blood has flowed in numberless
battles in the cause of the Germans and Austrians. The
present Armageddon might perhaps have been avoided
if the Tsar Nicholas I had left the Hapsburg Monarchy
to its own resources in 1849, and had not unwisely
crushed the independence of Hungary. Within our own
memory, the benevolent neutrality of Russia guarded
Germany in 1870 from an attack in the rear by its
opponents of Sadowa. Are all such facts to be explained
away on the ground that the despised Muscovites may
be occasionally useful as ' gun-meat ', but are guilty of

[1] *Kulm.* After the defeat of the Allies by Napoleon at Dresden
in 1813, the French corps of Vandamme appeared in their rear.
If it had succeeded in cutting the line of communications with
Prague, the retreat of the Allies might have been turned into a rout.
The First Division of the Russian Guard was ordered to stop Vandamme, and this it did at Kulm on August 29, although it was
outnumbered by three to one and lost almost half its men in killed
and wounded. On the next day, Prussian and Austrian troops
came up, and Vandamme surrendered with the remainder of his
corps. The battle was the turning-point in the campaign of 1813.
The King of Prussia granted the Iron Cross to all those who took
part in this desperate struggle ; hence the Iron Cross was called the
' Kulm Cross ' by the Russians.

[2] *Prince William of Prussia and the Kaluga regiment.* The
future conqueror of Sedan first fought as a boy of seventeen at
Bar-sur-Aube (February 27, 1814). In that battle he joined the
Russian Fifth Infantry (Kaluga), a regiment of which he afterwards
became an honorary colonel.

sacrilege if they take up a stand against German task-masters in 'shining armour'? The older generations of Germany had not yet reached that comfortable conclusion. The last recommendation which the founder of the German Empire made on his death-bed to his grandson was to keep on good terms with that Russia which is now proclaimed to be a debased mixture of Byzantine, Tartar, and Muscovite abominations.

Fortunately, the course of history does not depend on the frantic exaggerations of partisans. The world is not a class-room in which docile nations are distributed according to the arbitrary standards of German pedagogues. Europe has admired the patriotic resistance of the Spanish, Tyrolese, and Russian peasants to the enlightened tyranny of Napoleon. There are other standards of culture besides proficiency in research and aptitude for systematic work. The massacre of Louvain, the hideous brutality of the Germans towards non-combatants—to mention only one or two of the appalling occurrences of these last weeks—have thrown a lurid light on the real character of twentieth-century German culture. 'By their fruits ye shall know them,' said our Lord; and the saying which He aimed at the Scribes and Pharisees of His time is indeed applicable to the proud votaries of German civilization to-day. Nobody wishes to underestimate the services rendered by the German people to the cause of European progress; but those who have known Germany during the years following the achievements of 1870 have watched with dismay the growth of that arrogant conceit which the Greeks called ὕβρις. The cold-blooded barbarity advocated by Bernhardi, the cynical view taken of international treaties and of the obligations of honour by the German Chancellor—these things reveal a spirit which it would be difficult indeed to describe as a sign of progress.

One of the effects of such a frame of mind is to strike the victim of it with blindness. This symptom has been manifest in the stupendous blunders of German diplomacy. The successors of Bismarck have alienated their natural allies, such as Italy and Roumania, and have driven England into this war against the evident intentions of English Radicals. But the Germans have misconceived even more important things. They set out on their adventure in the belief that England would be embarrassed by civil war and unable to take any effective part in the fray ; and they had to learn something which all their writers had not taught them—that there is a nation's spirit watching over England's safety and greatness, a spirit at whose mighty call all party differences and racial strifes fade into insignificance. In the same way, they had reckoned on the unpreparedness of Russia, in consequence of internal dissensions and administrative weakness, without taking heed of the love of all Russians for Russia, of their devotion to the long-suffering giant whose life is throbbing in their veins. The Germans expected to encounter raw and sluggish troops under intriguing time-servers and military Hamlets whose ' native hue of resolution ' had been ' sicklied o'er with the pale cast of thought '. Instead of that, they were confronted with soldiers of the same type as those whom Frederick the Great and Napoleon admired, led at last by chiefs worthy of their men. And behind these soldiers they discovered a nation. Do they realize now what a force they have awakened ? Do they understand that a steadfast, indomitable resolution, despising all theatrical display, is moving Russia's hosts ? Even if the Russian generals had proved mediocre, even if

many disappointing days had been in store, the nation
would not have belied its history. It has seen more than
one conquering army go down before it. The Tartars and
the Poles, the Swedes of Charles XII, the Prussians of
Frederick the Great, the Grand Army of Napoleon, were
not less formidable than the Kaiser's array, but the task
of mastering a united Russia proved too much for each
one of them. The Germans counted on the fratricidal
feud between Poles and Russians, on the resentment of
the Jews, on Mohammedah sympathies with Turkey, and
so forth. They had to learn too late that the Jews had
rallied round the country of their hearths, and that the
best of them cannot believe that Russia will continue
to deny them the measure of justice and humanity which
the leaders of Russian thought have long acknowledged
to be due to them. More important still, the Germans
have read the Grand Duke's appeal to the Poles and
must have heard of the manner in which it was received
in Poland, of the enthusiastic support offered to the
Russian cause. If nothing else came of this great
historical upheaval but the reconciliation of the Russians
and their noble kinsmen the Poles, the sacrifices which
this crisis demands would not be too great a price to
pay for the result.

But the hour of trial has revealed other things. It
has appealed to the best feelings and the best elements
of the Russian nation. It has brought out in a striking
manner the fundamental tendency of Russian political
life and the essence of Russian culture, which so many
people have been unable to perceive on account of the
chaff on the surface. Russia has been going through
a painful crisis. In the words of the Manifesto of
October 17/30, 1905, the outward casing of her administration had become too narrow and oppressive for the

development of society with its growing needs, its altered perceptions of rights and duties, its changed relations between Government and people. The result was that deep-seated political *malaise* which made itself felt during the Japanese War, when Russian society at large refused to take any interest in the fate of the army ; the feverish rush for ' liberties ' after the defeat ; the subsequent reign of reaction and repression, which has cast such a gloom over Russian life during these last years. But the effort of the national struggle has dwarfed all these misunderstandings and misfortunes, as in Great Britain the call of the common Motherland has dwarfed the dispute between Unionists and Home Rulers. Russian parties have not renounced their aspirations ; Russian Liberals in particular believe in self-government and the rule of law as firmly as ever. But they have realized as one man that this war is not an adventure engineered by unscrupulous ambition, but a decisive struggle for independence and existence ; and they are glad to be arrayed in close ranks with their opponents from the Conservative side. A friend, a Liberal like myself, writes to me from Moscow : ' It is a great, unforgettable time ; we are happy to be all at one ! ' And from the ranks of the most unfortunate of Russia's children, from the haunts of the political exiles in Paris, comes the news that Bourtzeff, one of the most prominent among the revolutionary leaders, has addressed an appeal to his comrades urging them to stand by their country to the utmost of their power.[1]

I may add that whatever may have been the shortcomings and the blunders of the Russian Government,

[1] *Bourtzeff, a prominent Russian revolutionary leader.* I am glad to note that Bourtzeff fully endorses my view in a letter to *The Times* (issue of September 18, 1914).

it is a blessing in this decisive crisis that Russians should have a firmly-knit organization and a traditional centre of authority in the power of the Tsar. The present Emperor stands as the national leader, not in the histrionic attitude of a War Lord, but in the quiet dignity of his office. He has said and done the right thing, and his subjects will follow him to a man. We are sure he will remember in the hour of victory the unstinted devotion and sacrifices of all the nationalities and parties of his vast Empire. It is our firm conviction that the sad tale of reaction and oppression is at an end in Russia, and that our country will issue from this momentous crisis with the insight and strength required for the constructive and progressive statesmanship of which it stands in need.

Apart from the details of political and social reform, is the regeneration of Russia a boon or a peril to European civilization ? The declamations of the Germans have been as misleading in this respect as in all others. The master works of Russian literature are accessible in translation nowadays, and the cheap taunts of men like Bernhardi recoil on their own heads. A nation represented by Pushkin, Turgeneff, Tolstoy, Dostoyevsky in literature, by Kramskoy, Verestchagin, Repin, Glinka, Moussorgsky, Tchaikovsky in art,[1] by Mendeleeff, Metchnikoff, Pavloff in science, by Kluchevsky and Solovieff in history, need not be ashamed to enter the lists in an international competition for the prizes of culture. But the German historians ought to have

---

[1] *Kramskoy, Verestchagin, Repin,* &c. Only a few names are selected almost at random. Of course, no description of pictures and no characterization of painters can convey any adequate impression. Those who wish to form an opinion of Russian painting should go to Moscow and pay a visit to the Tretiakoff Gallery.

taught their pupils that in the world of ideas it is not such competitions that are important. A nation handicapped by its geography may have to start later in the field, and yet her performance may be relatively better than that of her more favoured neighbours. It is astonishing to read German diatribes about Russian backwardness when one remembers that as recently as fifty years ago Austria and Prussia were living under a régime which can hardly be considered more enlightened than the present rule in Russia. The Italians in Lombardy and Venice have still a vivid recollection of Austrian gaols ; and as for Prussian militarism, one need not go further than the exploits of the Zabern garrisons to illustrate its meaning. This being so, it is not particularly to be wondered at that the Eastern neighbour of Austria and Prussia has followed to some extent on the same lines.

But the general direction of Russia's evolution is not doubtful. Western students of her history might do well, instead of sedulously collecting damaging evidence, to pay some attention to the building-up of Russia's universities, the persistent efforts of the Zemstvos, the independence and the zeal of the Press. German scholars should read Hertzen's vivid description of the ' idealists of the forties '.[1] And what about the history of the emancipation of the serfs, or of the regeneration of the judicature ? The ' reforms of the sixties '[2] are

---

[1] *The idealists of the forties.* They have been described by Hertzen in his *Byloe i Dumy* (*Past and Thoughts*) in connexion with intellectual life in Moscow. Both Westerners like Granovsky, Stankevitch, Ketscher, Hertzen himself, and Slavophiles like J. Kireievsky and Khomiakoff, are vividly characterized in this brilliant autobiography.

[2] *The reforms of the sixties.* They comprise the great reforms carried out with rare patriotism and insight during the early years

a household word in Russia, and surely they are one of the noblest efforts ever made by a nation in the direction of moral improvement.

Looking somewhat deeper, what right have the Germans to speak of their ideals of culture as superior to those of the Russian people ? They deride the superstitions of the *mujikh* as if tapers and genuflexions were the principal matters of popular religion. Those who have studied the Russian people without prejudice know better than that. Read Selma Lagerloef's touching description of Russian pilgrims in Palestine [1]. She, the Protestant, has understood the true significance of the religious impulse which leads these poor men to the Holy Land, and which draws them to the numberless churches of the vast country. These simple people cling to the belief that there is something else in God's world besides toil and greed ; they flock towards the light, and find in it the justification of their human craving for peace and mercy. For the Russian people have the Christian virtue of patience in suffering : their pity for the poor and oppressed is more than an occasional manifestation of individual feeling—it is deeply rooted in national psychology. This frame of mind has been scorned as fit for slaves ! It is indeed a case where the learning of

of Alexander II's reign. The principal were—the emancipation of the peasants (1861), the reorganization of the judicial system (1864), and the creation of Zemstvo self-government (1864). There was a number of other reforms besides—the University Statutes of 1863, the Press Law of 1865, the partial abolition of corporal punishment in 1863 : and so forth. Many of these reforms have been adulterated by subsequent modifications ; but the main current of progress could not be turned back, and there are no greater names in the history of Europe than those of N. Milutine, D. Milutine, Prince Cherkassky, J. Samarine, Unkovsky, Zarudny, and their companions.

[1] *Selma Lagerloef on Russian pilgrims.*—" Jerusalem," vol. ii, " On the Wings of the Dawn."

philosophers is put to shame by the insight of the simple-minded.   Conquerors should remember that the greatest victories in history have been won by the unarmed—by the Christian confessors whom the emperors sent to the lions, by the ' old believers ' of Russia who went to Siberia and to the flames for their unyielding faith, by the Russian serfs who preserved their human dignity and social cohesion in spite of the exactions of their masters, by the Italians, Poles, and Jews, when they were trampled under foot by their rulers.   It is such a victory of the spirit that Tolstoy had in mind when he preached his gospel of non-resistance; and I do not think even a German on the war path would be blind enough to suppose that Tolstoy's message came from a craven soul.   The orientation of the so-called ' intelligent ' class in Russia—that is, the educated middle class, which is much more numerous and influential than people suppose—is somewhat different, of course.   It is ' Western ' in this sense, that it is imbued with current European ideas as to politics, economics, and law.   It has to a certain extent lost the simple faith and religious fervour of the peasants.   But it has faithfully preserved the keynote of popular ideals.   It is still characteristically humanitarian in its view of the world and in its aims.   A book like that of General von Bernhardi would be impossible in Russia.   If anybody were to publish it, it would not only fall flat, but earn for its author the reputation of a bloodhound. Many deeds of cruelty and brutality happen, of course, in Russia, but no writer of any standing would dream of building up a theory of violence in vindication of a claim to culture.   It may be said, in fact, that the leaders of Russian public opinion are pacific, cosmopolitan, and humanitarian to a fault.   The mystic philosopher,

Vladimir Solovieff[1], used to dream of the union of the Churches with the Pope as the spiritual head, and democracy in the Russian sense as the broad basis of the rejuvenated Christendom. Dostoyevsky, a writer most sensitive to the claims of nationality in Russia, defined the ideal of the Russians in a celebrated speech as the embodiment of a universally humanitarian type.[2] These are extremes, but characteristic extremes pointing to the trend of national thought. Russia is so huge and so strong that material power has ceased to be attractive to her thinkers. Nevertheless, we need not yet retire into the desert or deliver ourselves to be bound hand and foot by 'civilized' Germans. Russia also wields a sword— a charmed sword, blunt in an unrighteous cause, but sharp enough in the defence of right and freedom. And this war is indeed our *Befreiungskrieg*. The Slavs must have their chance in the history of the world, and the date of their coming of age will mark a new departure in the growth of civilization.

[1] *Vladimir Solovieff.* A talented philosopher, the son of the famous historian S. Solovieff. He was a professor at Moscow for a short time.

[2] *Dostoyevsky's speech.* It was delivered in Moscow in 1880, on the occasion of the unveiling of Pushkin's statue in that city.

Oxford: Horace Hart Printer to the University

WHY WE ARE AT WAR

GREAT BRITAIN'S CASE

BY MEMBERS OF THE OXFORD FACULTY OF MODERN HISTORY

E. BARKER.	H. W. C. DAVIS.
C. R. L. FLETCHER.	ARTHUR HASSALL.
L. G. WICKHAM LEGG.	F. MORGAN.

With an Appendix of Original Documents
including the Authorized English Translation
of the White Book issued by the
German Government

THIRD EDITION REVISED (NINTH IMPRESSION)
CONTAINING THE RUSSIAN ORANGE BOOK AND
EXTRACTS FROM THE BELGIAN GREY BOOK

TRANSLATIONS INTO FRENCH ITALIAN SPANISH
GERMAN AND SWEDISH ARE
NOW READY

Paper Covers Two Shillings net (70 cents)
Cloth Two Shillings and Sixpence net (85 cents)

OXFORD: AT THE CLARENDON PRESS
LONDON: HUMPHREY MILFORD
EDINBURGH   GLASGOW   NEW YORK   TORONTO
MELBOURNE   BOMBAY

(a)

No. 4

OXFORD PAMPHLETS

1914

GREAT BRITAIN

AND

GERMANY

BY

SPENSER WILKINSON

THIRD IMPRESSION

Price Twopence net

OXFORD UNIVERSITY PRESS

HUMPHREY MILFORD

LONDON   EDINBURGH   GLASGOW

NEW YORK   TORONTO   MELBOURNE   BOMBAY

PREFACE

THE three letters printed in this pamphlet appeared originally in the *Springfield Republican*, a well-known American newspaper. Of the writers one is an Englishman, the other an American. Mr. Spenser Wilkinson, Chichele Professor of Military History in the University of Oxford, wrote spontaneously to the *Springfield Republican*, three weeks after the outbreak of the present war, to explain where, in the eyes of educated Englishmen, the responsibility for the conflagration lay. This letter is the first of our series. At the time of writing it, Professor Wilkinson had not seen the letter of Professor John W. Burgess, which was written a few days earlier, and which also appeared in the *Springfield Republican*. Professor Burgess holds a chair of Political Science and Constitutional Law in the University of Columbia ; his credentials as a spokesman of German public opinion are set forth in his own letter. His letter is the second that we print. Professor Wilkinson then replied to Professor Burgess (Letter No. III). So far as we are aware, Professor Burgess made no rejoinder. The letters are reprinted at the desire of some who read them when they first appeared in print.

H. W. C. DAVIS.

To the Editor of The Republican :

A hundred years ago the states of Europe, united under England's lead, fought for three years to shake off the yoke which Napoleon had put upon them. The Germans believed themselves fighting for freedom. After the peace they found that they had gained neither freedom nor nationhood. In 1848 they drove away their kinglets, declared themselves free and united, and offered the crown of all Germany to the Prussian king. He refused a crown offered by the people. Neither freedom nor union was achieved. Not the people's will, said Bismarck, but the Prussian army must control Germany.

In 1866 the Prussian army made good Bismarck's words, and conquered Germany. It made North Germany Prussian and cut South Germany in two, one-half to be shut out of the fatherland, the other half to be a Prussian protectorate. In 1870 Bismarck beguiled France into her rash attack. The Prussian army struck her down and tore from her lands whose people in 1789 had freely declared themselves Frenchmen for ever. The protected princes hailed as their emperor the Prussian king, whom Bismarck's constitution made their supreme war lord. Moltke, the iron soldier, declared that what had been won by the sword must be kept by the sword, as though the Prussian army could make wrong right.

' Conscience does make cowards of us all,' and Prussia for forty years has drilled Germany against the day when

France should demand her own again. France in her weakness turned to Russia. Thereupon Prussia had recourse to Austria, the jailor of peoples, freedom's foe. Italy, freed and united when Prussia struck down Austria, felt humiliated by the French seizure of that Tunis which she thought her own inheritance, and, mortified, sought support in a defensive alliance with Austria.

The Emperor Francis Joseph, who began his reign in warfare for his dynasty against his peoples, subduing the Hungarians with the aid of the Slavs, and then the Slavs with the aid of the Hungarians, was told, when he and his Germans were shut out of Germany, to turn his face to the east and to supplant the Turk as overlord of Slavs and Greeks. But Russia had set her hand to the freeing of the Slavs and Greeks. She had helped to make a small but independent Servia. In 1878, after a great war, she made a free Bulgaria. Her methods were not those of the West, but they fulfilled the purpose and made Bulgaria and Servia free in spite of Austria.

But she had to pay the price. The emancipator of the serfs, the liberator of Bulgaria, had to acquiesce in Austria's occupation of Bosnia. Thus a Serb country which loathed the Austrians and fought against them was crushed and conquered in a great war that lasted a year and in which Austria employed 200,000 men. In those days Disraeli supported Turkey and Austria, but five-and-twenty years later his pupil Salisbury discovered that he had 'backed the wrong horse'. Russia, thwarted in her efforts to give nationhood to the peoples of European Turkey, was impelled to make an alliance with France.

Bismarck knew that France could never forgive or

forget her dismemberment. He saw that Russia resented his support of Austria and he therefore restrained his Austrian ally, made her compromise with Russia and declared that Bulgaria was not worth the bones of a Pomeranian grenadier. He saw the risk of forcing France and Russia into alliance, and in 1888 increased the German army by 800,000 men.

' Bismarck's last deliberate work was to teach his countrymen the falsehood that England was their enemy. He gave Lord Granville to understand that Germany wanted no colonies. Then he put to him questions apparently harmless and of no urgency, published Lord Granville's answers without their full context, and so misrepresented England as opposed to the acquisition by Germany of any possessions whatever beyond the seas. Germany was furious and England puzzled. Thus was sown in Germany that hatred of England which has for thirty years been nourished by Prussian publicists and burst into flame during the South African War, which no one in Germany understood.

The Emperor William II, when he found himself the supreme war-lord, took quite literally both that name and the title of a once famous book, *Prussia Over All*, modified in the modern national anthem into *Germany Over All in the World*. The supreme war-lord must rule at sea as well as on land, and William as emperor proclaimed that Germany's future was on the water. Germany was of course delighted, and the South Germans, who had never seen the sea, to a man subscribed for battleships.

The thoughts of the Prussian Army have been well expressed of late years by General von Bernhardi, who has written volumes to preach to his countrymen the gospel of force. The mighty German Army has been created, he says, not for peace but for conquest. Let us go forth conquering and to conquer; let us crush France; let us push back the too numerous Russians and, above all, let us destroy England. These strains dinned into the emperor's ears found a response.

Under William II Germany has become self-assertive. Twice in the last ten years when she seemed determined to overbear France with regard to Morocco, the British Government has intimated that an attack on France would mean war with England. The first time was in the crisis which ended with the resignation of Delcassé. The second was in 1911, when the emperor took the high-handed step of sending the *Panther* to Agadir. At that time he and his advisers thought England paralysed by the dispute over the Parliament Act. The Prussian military party was furious with the emperor because after the English declaration of policy he changed his attitude and did not make war.

Thereafter an enormous increase of the army was voted and carried out, and more recently a special war-tax was laid on the German people for the purpose of military preparations. All pointed toward a war for which no reason was visible except the Prussian doctrine that Germany was in danger because the geography of Europe places her between France and Russia. Two months ago no cause of quarrel between the nations was known. The English had pretty well forgotten the hatred expressed of them in Germany at the time of the South African War; voices were raised in France to suggest that it would be wrong to begin a war even for Alsace-Lorraine. The trouble in the Balkans, except in Albania, seemed to be settled.

For many months Austria has followed toward Servia

and Montenegro a high-handed policy which the other Powers tolerated for the sake of peace. She had three army corps assembled in Bosnia ready for action, which could only be against Servia. To review these three army corps the heir apparent, the Archduke Francis Ferdinand, went to Sarajevo, where he was joined by his wife. There they were both assassinated by malcontent Bosnians. The Austrian official press instantly laid the blame on the Servian Government before there could have been time for any inquiry.

On July 23, Austria sent an ultimatum to Servia in such terms as any self-respecting government must reject, requiring its entire acceptance in forty-eight hours, and at the same time announced that no European Government would be permitted to discuss the matter. That was a direct challenge to Russia, an intimation that Russia must look on at the destruction of a free state whose struggles for independence she had mightily helped. The ultimatum had been telegraphed in full to the German emperor before it was sent.

England pleaded for delay, for time for the powers to consider. Russia urged Servia to humiliate herself to the utmost but not to abdicate her sovereignty. Servia complied with this advice, but Austria, implacable, declared war against her. Thereupon Russia mobilized her army, for in the circumstances she must either fight or haul down her flag. Thereupon Germany mobilized and France had to follow suit.

The British Government still negotiated. The British people, having made friends with France, felt that they could not desert her. The British Government asked Germany to undertake to respect that Belgian neutrality which all the powers had by treaty guaranteed. The reply was a brutal negative and immediate invasion.

Thus England had no choice and declared war against
Germany. A significant judgement was pronounced by
Italy when she said that Germany and Austria were the
aggressors, and that no treaty bound Italy to help
them in an unprovoked attack. So Italy is neutral.

Thus Germany and Austria have declared in common
that they will have their way in Europe, and that if
it is not accepted they will impose it upon Europe
by force. If they succeed, the King of Prussia will be
the overlord of Europe. If Europe is to remain free the
nations that Germany has challenged must defeat and
disarm her and compel her to be content to till her own
soil and to mind her own business, not as a ruler of other
nations but as one among the united states of Europe.

SPENSER WILKINSON.

LONDON, ENG.,
    August 22, 1914.

II

To the Editor of ' The Republican ' :

This is no time and no subject when, or upon which,
one should speak lightly, ignorantly, or with prejudice.
It is one of the world's most serious moments, and the
views and sympathies now formed will determine the
course of the world's development for many years to
come. Heavy indeed is the responsibility which he
incurs who would assume the rôle of teacher at this
juncture, and it is his first duty to present the credentials
which warrant his temerity.

First of all, I am an Anglo-American of the earliest
stock and the most pronounced type. I have existed

here, potentially or actually, since the year 1638, and
my European cousins of to-day are squires and curates
in Dorsetshire. Moreover, I admire and revere England,
not only because of what she has done for liberty and
self-government at home, but because she has borne the
white man's burden throughout the world and borne it
true and well.

On the other hand, what I possess of higher learning
has been won in Germany. I· have studied in her
famous universities and bear their degrees, and in three
of them have occupied the teacher's chair. I have lived
ten years of my life among her people and enjoy a circle
of valued friendships which extends from Königsberg
to Strassburg, from Hamburg to Munich, and from
Osnabrück to Berchtesgarden, and which reaches through
all classes of society, from the occupant of the throne
to the dweller in the humble cottage. I have known
four generations of Hohenzollerns, and, of the three
generations now extant, have been brought into rather
close contact with the members of two of them. While,
as to the men of science and letters and politics who
have made the Germany of the last half-century, I have
known them nearly all, and have sat, as student, at the
feet of many of them. I must concede that of English
descent though I am, still I feel somewhat less at home
in the motherland than in the fatherland. Nevertheless,
I am conscious of the impulse to treat each with fairness
in any account I may attempt to give of their motives,
purposes, and actions.

It was in the year 1871, in the midst of the Franco-
Prussian war, that I first trod the soil of Germania, and
it was from and with those who fought that war on the
German side that I first learned the politics and diplomacy of Europe. Almost from the first day that I took

my seat in the lecture room of the university, I imbibed
the doctrine that the great national, international, and
world-purpose of the newly-created German empire was
to protect and defend the Teutonic civilization of continental Europe against the oriental Slavic quasicivilization on the one side, and the decaying Latin
civilization on the other.

After a little I began to hear of the 'pan-Slavic
policy' of Russia and the 'revanche policy' of France.
For a while the latter, the policy of France for retaking
Alsace-Lorraine, occupied the chief attention.   But in
1876, with the Russian attack upon the Turks, the pan-
Slavic policy of Russia—the policy of uniting the Slavs
in the German empire, the Austro-Hungarian empire,
and in the Turkish empire, with and under the sway
of Russia—was moved into the foreground.   All western
Europe recognized the peril to modern civilization and
the powers of Europe assembled at Berlin in 1878 to
meet and master it.

The astute British premier, Lord Beaconsfield, supported by the blunt and masterful Bismarck, directed
the work of the congress, and the pan-Slavic policy of
Russia was given a severe setback.   Russia was allowed
to take a little almost worthless territory in Europe and
territory of greater value in Asia ; Roumania, Servia,
and Montenegro were made independent states ; Bulgaria was given an autonomous administration with
a European Christian prince but under the nominal
suzerainty of the Turkish sultan ; and the Turkish
provinces of Bosnia and Herzegovina, then almost free
zones infested by bandits, were placed under Austro-
Hungarian administration, also subject to the nominal
suzerainty of the sultan.

With this the much suspected and dreaded activities

of Russia were directed toward Asia, and Russia was now for more than twenty years, from 1880 to 1902, occupied chiefly with the extension of her empire in the Orient.. The German empire and the Austro-Hungarian empire were delivered for the moment from this great peril and enabled to pursue the line of peaceable development and progress. The greater security to the eastern borders of these great states, thus established, also helped to reduce the force of the French spirit of revenge, as the prospect of its satisfaction became more distant.

It was during this period, however, that Germany developed from an agricultural to a manufacturing and commercial community, that is, became a competitor of Great Britain and France, especially of Great Britain, in world industry. Her marvelous growth in this direction excited soon the jealousy, the envy, and then the hostility of Great Britain. We in the United States, however, reaped great advantage from the industrial and commercial competition between the two great powers and we were amused at the pettishness of Great Britain in representing it as something unfair and illegitimate. We little suspected to what direful results it would lead.

When Edward VII came to the throne, in the year 1901, he saw Great Britain's interests in the Orient threatened by Russia's policy of extension in Asia and her commercial interests throughout the world threatened by the active and intelligent competition of the Germans. He, as all rulers at the moment of accession, felt the ambition to do something to relieve the disadvantages, to say the least, under which in these respects his country was laboring. He began that course of diplomacy for which he won the title of peace lover. The first element of it was the approach to Japan and encouragement to Japan to resist the advance of Russia. This movement culminated in the war between Russia and Japan of the years 1904–5, in which Russia was worsted and checked in the realization of her Asiatic policy and thrown back upon Europe.

The next element in the diplomacy of the peace-loving king was the fanning into flame again of the ' revanche ' spirit of France by the arrangement of the quasi-alliance, called the entente, between Great Britain, France, and Russia, aimed distinctly and avowedly against what was known as the triple alliance of Germany, Austria, and Italy, which had for thirty years kept the peace of Europe. The third and last element of this pacific program was the seduction of Italy from the triple alliance, by rousing the irredentist hopes for winning from Austria the Trente district in south Tyrol, which Italy covets.

It is hardly necessary for me to call attention to the extreme peril involved in this so-called peaceful diplomacy to the German and Austro-Hungarian empires. I myself became first fully aware of it on June 27, 1905. On that day I had an extended interview with a distinguished British statesman in the House of Commons in London.   I was on my way to Wilhelmshohe to meet His Majesty the German Emperor, to arrange with His Majesty the cartel of exchange of educators between universities in the two countries.   When I revealed this fact to my host the conversation immediately took a turn which made me distinctly feel that a grave crisis was impending in the relations of Great Britain to Germany.

I was so firmly impressed by it, that I felt compelled to call my host's attention to the fact that the great number of American citizens of German extraction, the friendliness of the German states to the cause of the Union during our civil war, and the virtual control of '

American universities by men educated at German universities, would all make for close and continuing friendship between Germany and the United States. When I arrived in Germany, I asked in high quarters for the explanation of my London experience and was told that it was the moment of greatest tension in the Morocco affair, when all feared that, at British instigation, France would grasp the sword.

The larger part of the next two years I spent in Germany as exchange professor in the three universities of Berlin, Bonn, and Leipsic, also as lecturer before the bar association at Vienna. Naturally I formed a really vast circle of acquaintances among the leading men of both empires, and the constant topics of conversation everywhere, at all times and among all classes, was the growing peril to Germany and Austro-Hungary of the revived pan-Slavic policy and program of Russia, the re-inflamed ' revanche ' of France and Great Britain's intense commercial jealousy.

In the month of August, 1907, I was again at Wilhelmshohe. The imperial family were at the castle, and somewhere about the 10th of the month it became known that King Edward would make the emperor a visit or rather a call, for it was nothing more cordial than that, on the 14th.

On the afternoon of the 13th, the day before the arrival of the king, I received a summons to go to the castle and remain for dinner with the emperor. When I presented myself, I found the emperor surrounded by his highest officials, Prince Buelow, the chancellor of the empire, Prince Hohenlohe, the imperial governor of Alsace-Lorraine, Prince Radolin, the German embassador to France, Excellency von Lucanus, the chief of the emperor's civil cabinet, Gen. Count von Huelsen Haeseller,

the chief of the emperor's military cabinet, Field Marshal
von Plessen, Chief Court Marshal Count Zu Eulenburg,
Lord High Chamberlain Baron von dem Gnesebeck and
the oberstallmeister, Baron von Reischach.

The dinner was on the open terrace of the castle
looking toward the Hercules hights. At its close the
empress and the ladies withdrew into the castle and the
emperor with the gentlemen remained outside. His
Majesty rose from his seat in the middle of the table
and went to one end of it, followed by Prince Buelow,
Prince Hohenlohe, Prince Radolin, and Excellency von
Lucanus. His Majesty directed me to join the group,
and so soon as we were seated the chief of the civil
cabinet turned to me and said that he was afraid that
our good friend, President Roosevelt, unwittingly did
Europe an injury in mediating between Russia and
Japan, since this had turned the whole force of the pan-
Slavic program of Russia back upon Europe. All present
spoke of the great peril to middle Europe of this change.

Then both the German embassador to France and the
governor of Alsace-Lorraine spoke discouragingly of the
great increase of hostile feeling on the part of the French
toward Germany, and, finally, the part that Great
Britain had played and was playing in bringing about
both of these movements was dwelt upon with great
seriousness mingled with evidences of much uneasiness.
King Edward came the next morning at about 10 o'clock
and took his departure at about 3 in the afternoon.
Whether any remonstrances were made to His Majesty
in regard to the great peril, which he, wittingly or
unwittingly, was helping to bring upon middle Europe,
I have never known. It seemed to me, however, that
after that date he modified considerably his diplomatic
activity. But he had sown the seed in well-prepared

ground and the harvest was bound to come. The three great forces making for universal war in Europe, namely, the pan-Slavic program of Russia, the 'revanche' of France, and Great Britain's commercial jealousy of Germany, had been by his efforts brought together. It could not fail to produce the catastrophe. It was only a question of time.

The following year, the year 1908, saw the revolt of the young Turkish party in Constantinople which forced from the sultan the constitution of July, 1908. According to this constitution, all the peoples under the sovereignty of the sultan were called upon to send representatives to the Turkish Parliament. Both Bulgaria and Bosnia-Herzegovina were nominally subject to that sovereignty, according to the provisions of the Berlin Congress of the Powers of 1878. For thirty years Bulgaria had been practically an independent state, and during thirty years Austro-Hungary had poured millions upon millions into Bosnia-Herzegovina, building roads, railroads, hotels, hospitals and schools, establishing the reign of law and order, and changing the population from a swarm of loafers, beggars, and bandits to a body of hard-working, frugal, and prosperous citizens.

What now were Bulgaria and Austro-Hungary to do? Were they to sit quiet and allow the restoration of the actual sovereignty and government of Turkey in and over Bulgaria and Bosnia-Herzegovina? Could any rational human being in the world have expected or desired that? They simply, on the self-same day, namely, October 5, 1908, renounced the nominal suzerainty of the sultan, Bulgaria becoming thereby an independent state and Bosnia-Herzegovina remaining what it had actually been since 1878, only with no further nominal relation to the Turkish government.

Some American newspapers have called this the robbery of Bosnia-Herzegovina by Austro-Hungary, and have made out Austro-Hungary to be an aggressor. I have not seen, however, the slightest indication that any of these have the faintest conception of what actually took place. Europe acquiesced in it without much ado. It was said that Russia expressed dissatisfaction, but that Germany pacified her.

Four more years of peace rolled by, during which, in spite of the facts that Austro-Hungary gave a local constitution with representative institutions to Bosnia-Herzegovina, and Alsace-Lorraine was admitted to representation in the federal council, as well as the Reichstag of the German empire, that is, was made substantially a state of the empire, the pan-Slavic schemes of Russia, the French spirit of revenge and the British commercial jealousy grew and developed and became welded together, until the triple entente became virtually a triple alliance directed against the two great states of middle Europe.

Russia had now recovered from the losses of the Japanese war and the internal anarchy which followed it ; France had perfected her military organization ; Turkey was now driven by the allied Balkan States out of the calculation as an anti-Russian power ; Bulgaria, Austro-Hungary's ally, was now completely exhausted by the war with Turkey and that with her Balkan allies, now become enemies ; and Great Britain was in dire need of an opportunity to divert the mind of her people away from the internal questions which were threatening to disrupt her constitution.

The practiced ear could discern the buzz of the machinery lifting the hammer to strike the hour of Armageddon. And it struck. The foul murder of the heir of the Hapsburgers set the civilized world in horror and the Austro-Hungarian empire in mourning. In tracing the ramifications of the treacherous plot, the lines were found to run to Belgrade. And when Austro-Hungary demanded inquiry and action by a tribunal in which representatives from Austro-Hungary should sit, Servia repelled the demand as inconsistent with her dignity. Believing that inquiry and action by Servia alone would be no inquiry and no action, Austro-Hungary felt obliged to take the chastisement of the criminals and their abettors into its own hands.

Then Russia intervened to stay the hand of Austro-Hungary and asked the German emperor to mediate between Austro-Hungary and Servia. The emperor undertook the task. But while in the midst of it he learned that Russia was mobilizing troops upon his own border. He immediately demanded of Russia that this should cease, but without avail or even reply. He protested again with the like result. Finally, at midnight on the 31st of July, his embassador at St. Petersburg laid the demand before the Russian Minister of Foreign Affairs that the Russian mobilization must cease within twelve hours, otherwise Germany would be obliged to mobilize.

At the same time the emperor directed his embassador in Paris to inquire of the French government whether, in case of war between Germany and Russia, France would remain neutral. The time given expired without any explanation or reply from Russia and without any guarantee or assurance from France. The federal council of the German empire, consisting of representatives from the twenty-five states and the imperial territory of Alsace-Lorraine, then authorized the declaration of war against Russia, which declaration applied, according to

the sound principle of international jurisprudence, to
all her allies refusing to give guarantee of their neutrality.

As France could move faster than Russia, the Germans
turned the force of their arms upon her. They undertook to reach her by way of what they supposed to be
the lines of least resistance. These lay through the
neutral states of Belgium and Luxemburg. They claimed
that France had already violated the neutrality of both
by invasion and by the flying of their war airships over
them, and they marched their columns into both.

Belgium resisted. The Germans offered to guarantee
the independence and integrity of Belgium and indemnify
her for all loss or injury if she would not further resist
the passage of German troops over her soil. She still
refused and turned to Great Britain. Great Britain now
intervened, and in the negotiations with Germany demanded as the price of her neutrality that Germany
should not use her navy against either France or Russia
and should desist from her military movements through
Belgium, and when the Germans asked to be assured
that Great Britain herself would respect the neutrality
of Belgium throughout the entire war on the basis of
the fulfilment of her requirements by Germany, the
British Government made no reply, but declared war on
Germany.

And so we have the alignment. Germany, Austria,
and probably Bulgaria on one side, Russia, Servia,
Montenegro, Belgium, France, and England on the other,
and rivers of blood have already flowed. And we stand
gaping at each other, and each is asking the others who
did it. Whose is the responsibility, and what will be
the outcome ? Now if I have not already answered the
former question I shall not try to answer it. I shall
leave each one, in view of the account I have given, to

settle the question with his own judgement and conscience. I will only say that, as for myself, I thank John Morley and John Burns—the man of letters and the man of labour, that they have rent the veil of diplomatic hypocrisy and have washed their hands clean from the stain of this blunder crime.

Finally, as to the outcome, not much can yet be said. There is nothing so idle as prophecy, and I do not like to indulge in it. Whether the giant of middle Europe will be able to break the bonds, which in the last ten years have been wound about him and under whose smarting cut he is now writhing, or the fetters will be riveted tighter, cannot easily be foretold. But, assuming the one or the other, we may speculate with something more of probable accuracy regarding the political situation which will result.

The triumph of Germany—Austro-Hungary—Bulgaria can never be so complete as to make any changes in the present map of Europe. All that that could effect would be the momentary abandonment of the Russian pan-Slavic program, the relegation to dormancy of the French ' revanche ' and the stay of Great Britain's hand from the destruction of German commerce. On the other hand, the triumph of Great Britain-Russia-France cannot fail to give Russia the mastery of the continent of Europe and restore Great Britain to her sovereignty over the seas. These two great powers, who now already between them possess almost the half of the whole world, would then, indeed, control the destinies of the earth.

Well may we draw back in dismay before such a consummation. The ' rattle of the saber ' would then be music to our ears in comparison with the crack of the Cossack's knout and the clanking of Siberian chains, while the burden of taxation which we would be obliged to suffer in order to create and maintain the vast navy and army necessary for the defence of our territory and commerce throughout the world against these gigantic powers with their oriental ally, Japan, would sap our wealth, endanger our prosperity and threaten the very existence of republican institutions.

This is no time for shallow thought or flippant speech. In a public sense it is the most serious moment of our lives. Let us not be swayed in our judgement by prejudice or minor considerations. Men and women like ourselves are suffering and dying for what they believe to be the right, and the world is in tears. Let us wait and watch patiently and hope sincerely that all this agony is a great labour-pain of history and that there shall be born through it a new era of prosperity, happiness, and righteousness for all mankind.

JOHN W. BURGESS.

ATHENWOOD, NEWPORT, R.I.,
    August 17, 1914.

III

To the Editor of 'The Republican':

Will you permit me as an Englishman to try to explain to your readers the feelings with which I have read the letter written to you by Professor John W. Burgess on August 17, published in *The Republican* of August 19. I agree with the professor in holding that, when five great nations are fighting for their existence and for their ideals, he who would assume the rôle of teacher should not speak lightly, ignorantly, or with prejudice. I think his first duty should be to seek the truth and to tell it as well as he can. I do not agree

that his first duty is to ' present his credentials '. However, as Professor Burgess thinks credentials are the
first thing, I will examine those which he submits.
He relies first of all on his blood, of which he judges
that it must be good, because he comes of an English
stock. He is proud of that because England has done
something for liberty and self-government at home and
borne the white man's burden throughout the world.
Here, I feel, is an American who is bound to do justice
to my country and, as you describe him as a scholar
and historian, there is a second strong point in his
favour. I have myself been for many years a student
of the historians from Thucydides to Ranke. The
shelves in front of me hold more than thirty volumes of
Ranke's histories from which I have learned as much
as I have been able to take in. Ranke set up, I think,
the right standard of impartiality. The historian's one
aim, he thought, was to understand what had happened.
Ranke wanted to understand the history of Europe ;
he did not start out to praise or blame or to take sides.
He did not confine himself to his own country of Germany. In 1829 he wrote an account of the Servian
revolution, afterwards enlarged into a history of Servia.
From this work I first learned that the cause of Servia
in her struggle for freedom is that of European civilization against barbarism. From Ranke's history of
England I first learned that England lives and has lived
not merely for herself, but for the freedom of Europe
and for the resistance to its conquest by any empire or
by any despot. We have in England a historical school
of which Stubbs, Freeman, York-Powell, and Firth have
in turn been the representatives at Oxford. Its leading
idea is that historical inquiry must rest upon the scrupulous examination of the evidence.

I thought I might expect from an American historian
of English stock and German training that he would
wish to understand, which means of course in a European
affair, to understand all the nations, and that he would
be careful in his sifting of evidence ; that when he
wanted to know what England was doing he would
desire English evidence, just as when he wanted to
know what Germany was doing he might accept German evidence, and that in each case he would make
full allowance for the possible passions and prejudices
of his witnesses.

Now to his account of his methods and conclusions.
His learning, he tells us, he owes to Germany. As far
as I know all scholars of high rank have learned much
from Germany, but in my own country we think it wise
not to confine ourselves only to German sources of
knowledge ; we find we have much to learn from
leaders of thought in other countries also, in France,
in Italy, in Russia and in America. Professor Burgess
in his letter gives me no means of judging of his erudition,
but he tells at some length of what he learned in the
German lecture-rooms. There he says, ' I imbibed the
doctrine that the national, international, and world-
purpose of the newly-created German empire was to
protect and defend the Teutonic civilization of continental Europe against the oriental Slavic quasicivilization on the one side and the decaying Latin
civilization on the other.' That is a sentence worth
weighing. Let us see what it means.

Teutonic, it will be observed, is only a full-dress name
for German. ' The Teutonic civilization of continental
Europe ' is the German way of saying that such civilization as there is in Europe is the gift of Germany. German professors are very fond of this theme, which is no

doubt patriotic. The doctrine then which the professor imbibed is that the German empire stands for Germany and that Germany thinks that she ought to impose herself upon France, Italy, Spain, and Portugal ('the decaying Latin civilization') and upon Russia, Servia, and Bulgaria ('the oriental Slavic quasicivilization'). It seems to me that Germany very easily imposed herself upon Professor Burgess, for this one sentence contains Germany's whole case at the present moment, and Professor Burgess in his long letter merely writes large the doctrine which he imbibed in 1871. His numerous German friends are personifications of that one sentence. The four generations of Hohenzollerns, who have won his heart, are its embodiment.

What I wish to examine is the method adopted by this German-trained historian to ascertain the truth. He tells us that in June 1905 he discovered from a British statesman that a crisis was impending in the relations between Great Britain and Germany. His method of finding out what England's policy was did not consist in inquiries in London, but in questions asked in high quarters in Germany, where he was told that 'all feared that at British instigation the French would grasp the sword'. In 1907, the professor learned from the German emperor that President Roosevelt had done Europe an injury in mediating between Russia and Japan. The Emperor and Professor Burgess are evidently anxious to instruct America. Professor Burgess has a good deal to say about the policy of King Edward VII, and of the agreement with France negotiated in 1904 by Lord Lansdowne. The text of that agreement has been published ; it was an arrangement for settling a number of long-standing disputes between England and France, which Professor Burgess discusses apparently in complete ignorance of its nature. He goes on to say that the entente between Great Britain, France and Russia was aimed against the triple alliance of Germany, Austria, and Italy. Here comes out the professor's impartiality. To his mind it was right and proper that Germany, Austria, and Italy should be allied, even though Germany's mission is directed against decaying Latin civilization; but when England, France, and Russia compare notes he thinks they are doing something wicked. Surely a professor, before turning against the land from which his ancestors came, should have read Sir Edward Grey's speech of August 3, in which that statesman explained that when the late crisis began, England was not committed by any treaty or agreement to co-operation either with France or Russia; that the governments of those two countries were reminded that this was the case and that the British government was prepared to consider a policy of neutrality on condition that Germany should respect the neutrality of Belgium. It is true that English neutrality was rendered difficult because in 1911, when Germany was threatening to attack France, naval arrangements were made by which the British navy would have defended the French coast. Those arrangements had not since been materially altered, largely because no one either in France or in England thought there was any probability of war. But when war suddenly came the British government felt that, things being as they were, it would be dishonourable to leave the French coast exposed to an attack against which, owing to those arrangements, France could make no defence.

Two statements made by the professor strike me as amazing. 'Great Britain was in dire need of an

opportunity to divert the mind of her people away from
the internal questions.' A German may believe that.
Every man who knows anything of England is well
aware that it is nonsense. Our internal questions
remain open ; their difficulty is not diminished, but our
people are not so mad as to fight each other with the
enemy at the door. ' In tracing the ramifications of the
treacherous plot[1] the lines were found to run to Belgrade.'
How does the professor know that ? The statement
rests on nothing but the word of Count Forgach, whose
credentials are that in his house were forged the documents by the aid of which the Austrian foreign office
a few years ago attempted to perpetrate the judicial
murder of a number of Croatian subjects of Austria.

Whether it is true, as Professor Burgess asserts, that
England has done something for liberty and self-
government and has borne the white man's burden, is
not for Englishmen to decide : it must be left to historians who will take more trouble to investigate this
country's work and spirit than Professor Burgess, whose
testimony can have no more value than his methods.

I have some friends in America. I remember when
I was a little boy at school the news of the bombardment
of Fort Sumter. For four years in my home the talk
was of nothing but the good cause, that of the Union
and of freedom in the United States. It was perhaps as
good an education as that of a German lecture-room,
though I, too, have frequented German lecture-rooms
and have a multitude of German friends. I should
like to be allowed to send a message to my friends in
America, not an impartial message but an English one.
Six weeks ago this country was full of good will to all
mankind and to the German people. We were not

[1] i. e. the plot to murder the Archduke at Sarajevo.

thinking of war ; we were not ready for war ; those
few, of whom I am one, who have for many years been
pointing out the danger of such a catastrophe as has
now burst upon the world, have never been listened to,
have never been taken seriously.   England was entirely
absorbed in the struggle for a further advance in freedom and for its establishment upon a broad and firm
basis in Ireland.

This war has come upon us like a thunderbolt.   Since
it came we have all had one thought for our country
and for ourselves, and that thought is duty.   We are
not organized as Germany is ; we are not trained to
arms : we have been caught, as were the people of the
North in 1861 ; we shall have to pass through a fiery
trial for which there is no precedent.   It may be that
we shall go down in the struggle, but we shall go into
it united and in good faith.   The faith that we have is
this : We recognize freely the fine quality of the Germans ; we do not hate them as Professor Burgess
imagines.   We think there is room in Europe for
many nations, of which each has its good work to do.
We think, however, that Austria's attack upon Servia
was an attempt to murder a small nation and Germany's
attack upon Belgium its parallel.   We find ourselves
unexpectedly fighting side by side with France and in
conjunction with Russia, and we see our national
existence and our freedom threatened as they never
were before.   Teutonic civilization may be a good
thing, though we shudder at its work in Belgium.   But
we think England of some use in the world.   We are
her children, and we shall fight for her—a good many
of us will have to die for her.   If we disappear we are
not going to complain ; it is right that if the tree does
not bear fruit it should be cut down and not cumber

the ground. But we have faith in our England still, and in that faith we live. We have faith, too, in righteousness. We cherish John Bright's maxim, ' Be just and fear not.' We are going to stand by that not fall by it.

SPENSER WILKINSON.

LONDON,
September 3, 1914.

Oxford : Horace Hart Printer to the University

The Deeper Causes of the War.

By W. SANDAY. 3d. net. *Third Impression.*

The psychology of Prussian militarism ; German.public opinion and Germany's aggressive ambitions.

To the Christian Scholars of Europe and America : A Reply from Oxford to the German ' Address to Evangelical Christians '. 2d. net. *Second Impression.*

The answer of Oxford theologians to a recent manifesto of the German evangelical theologians. This manifesto, which is reproduced in the present pamphlet, argues that Germany is in no sense responsible for the present war. The Oxford reply states that the German theologians cannot have studied either the events which led up to the war, or the political utterances of their own countrymen.

The Responsibility for the War. By W. G. S. ADAMS. 2d. net.

A brief discussion of the question of responsibility : 1. Austria and Serbia ; 2. The responsibility of Russia ; 3. The intervention of England.

Great Britain and Germany.

By SPENSER WILKINSON. 2d. net. *Second Impression.*

Three letters to the *Springfield Republican* : 1. By Prof. Spenser Wilkinson, stating Great Britain's case ; 2. By Prof. John W.'Burgess of the University of Columbia, stating Germany's case ; 3. By Prof. Wilkinson, in reply to Prof. Burgess.

' Just for a Scrap of Paper.'

By ARTHUR HASSALL. 1d. net. *Third Impression.*
Explains why England stands for the sanctity of European treaty-law.

II

The Germans, their Empire, and how they have made it. By C. R. L. FLETCHER. 2d. net. *Third Impression.*

A historical account of Prussian policy from the seventeenth century.

The Germans, their Empire, and what they covet.

By C. R. L. FLETCHER. 2d. net. *Third Impression.*
An account of the ambitions avowed by the Pan-German school.

Might is Right. By Sir WALTER RALEIGH. 2d. net.

Why Germany may win ; what will happen if she wins ; why we believe she will not win.

Austrian Policy since 1867. By MURRAY BEAVEN. 3d. net.

Austrian policy in the Balkans has been of the ' offensive-defensive' order. The Archduke Francis Ferdinand might have saved Austria from rushing to destruction; but 1912 was the beginning of the end.

Italian Policy since 1870. By KEITH FEILING. 2d. net

Italian policy has been and must be guided by her own interests. The results of her colonial policy have not yet been satisfactory enough to tempt her into adventures.

III

French Policy since 1871.

By F. MORGAN and H. W. C. DAVIS. 2d. net. *Third Impression.*

A historical sketch, discussing the question whether French policy has been aggressive.

Russia : The Psychology of a Nation.

By PAUL VINOGRADOFF. 1d. net. *Third Impression.*

A reply to the German taunt that Russia is still in a state of barbarism, and is the enemy of European civilization

Serbia and the Serbs.

By Sir VALENTINE CHIROL. 2d. net. *Third Impression.*

A sketch of Serbian history, which is incidentally an indictment of the policy pursued by Austria-Hungary towards the Serbian kingdom.

Germany and ' The Fear of Russia '.

By Sir VALENTINE CHIROL. 2d. net. *Third Impression.*

Shows that before 1879 Germany preferred Russia as an ally to Austria. The ambition of Germany to establish a protectorate over Turkey has led her to assist Austria in the Balkans and so to challenge Russia.

The Eastern Question.

By F. F. URQUHART. 3d. net. *Second Impression.*

The history of the Balkan nations ; their future.

IV

War against War.

By A. D. LINDSAY. 2d. net. *Second Impression.*

Denies that war is good in itself, or a necessary evil. Power is not the sole or chief end for which the State exists. National greatness, if founded on brute force, cannot endure. International law represents an ideal, but an ideal that may be realized.

The Value of Small States.

By H. A. L. FISHER. 2d. net. *Third Impression.*

The author argues that the debt of civilization to small states is incalculable. They are useful, at the present time, as laboratories of political experiments and as buffer-states between the greater powers.

How can War ever be Right ?

By GILBERT MURRAY. 2d. net. *Second Impression.*

A well-known lover of peace and advocate of pacific policies argues against the Tolstoyan position. Right and honour compelled Britain to make war ; and war—like tragedy—is not pure evil.

The National Principle and the War.

By RAMSAY MUIR. 3d. net.

Considers the principle of nationality and its application to the settlement of Europe—particularly of S.E. Europe—after the War.

Nietzsche and Treitschke : The Worship of Power in Modern Germany.

By E. BARKER. 2d. net. *Third Impression.*

An explanation of the main points of interest in the ethical and political doctrines of the German ruling classes.

[a]

Published separately and will also appear shortly in series.

The British Dominions and the War.

By H. E. EGERTON. 2d. net. *Second Impression.*

Explains the ideas for which the British Empire stands, and the political and moral issues of the war affecting the Dominions.

Is the British Empire the Result of Wholesale Robbery?

By H. E. EGERTON. 2d. net.

A historical sketch in answer to a common taunt.

India and the War.

By Sir ERNEST TREVELYAN. 1d. net. *Second Impression.*

Discusses the reasons which account for the striking manifestations of Indian loyalty.

Bacilli and Bullets.

By Sir WILLIAM OSLER. 1d. net. *Third Impression.*

Calls attention to the fact that disease kills more men than the bullet. The most dangerous diseases are preventible by inoculation.

The Navy and the War.

By J. R. THURSFIELD. 3d. net. *Second Impression.*

Estimates the military and economic value of the silent pressure exercised by our fleet, and warns the faint-hearted and the captious of the perils of lack of faith.

The Retreat from Mons.

By H. W. C. DAVIS. 3d. net. *Second Impression.*

Introduction ; the Dispatch of Sept. 9 ; the Statement by the War Office, published Aug. 31. Appendixes (soldiers' narratives) ; two maps.

The Law of Nations and the War.

By A. PEARCE HIGGINS. 2d. net.

The violation of Belgian neutrality and the conduct of England to Denmark in 1807 ; the doctrine of German lawyers that military necessity overrides the laws of war ; the balance of power and the sanctity of treaties.

Others in   e aration.

OXFORD PAMPHLETS
1914–1915

CONCERNING TRUE WAR

BY

WILHELM WUNDT

TRANSLATED BY

GRACE E. HADOW

Price Twopence net

OXFORD UNIVERSITY PRESS
HUMPHREY MILFORD
LONDON   EDINBURGH   GLASGOW
NEW YORK   TORONTO   MELBOURNE   BOMBAY

...ERING TRUE

WAR

...LHELM WUNDT

...GRACE E. HADOW

...ORD UNIVERSITY PRESS

...HUMPHREY MILFORD

EDINBURGH GLASGOW

...ORONTO MELBOURNE BOMBAY

PREFACE

It would be impossible to find any one pamphlet which could fairly be quoted as representing the German attitude towards the present war. For German opinion is divided; not indeed as to the righteousness of the war, but as to the exact grounds on which the German Government was justified in taking the initiative. A Bernhardi or a Harden disdains the plea of self-defence; other German writers insist that Germany took up arms because her existence as a Great Power was at stake. The second school is, however, the more numerous; and to it belong most of the leaders of German academic thought. The views of this school are forcibly presented in the following address, which was delivered by Professor Wundt at Leipzig in September. It is desirable that the English public should have the opportunity of studying at first-hand the political ideas and judgements which find favour with Germans regarded in their own country as men of moderate and balanced views. Englishmen who are unfamiliar with the German literature of the war may be surprised that a critic, so eminent in his own sphere of knowledge, should throw the critical spirit to the winds when he approaches current controversies. Unfortunately Professor Wundt is, in this respect, entirely representative of the class of German society which he adorns. German professors are as fully convinced as the most credulous readers of the official German journals that King Edward VII was a statesman of superlatively malignant genius; that

Sir Edward Grey is a converted Tory and has thirsted for the destruction of Germany ever since he came into power; that Mr. John Burns has denounced the policy of his fellow Ministers in a public speech; that the British Navy has sunk German ships in neutral harbours; that the British Army uses Dum-dum bullets; that England and France were the first to violate the neutrality of Belgium. There are critics who argue that the Germans must have solid reasons for their intense conviction of the justice of the German cause. Such critics would be well advised to study the address of Professor Wundt, and to observe how weak are the foundations upon which he grounds his case.

H. W. C. D.

CONCERNING TRUE WAR

HONOURED FELLOW CITIZENS,

IN the summer of 1813 Johann Gottlieb Fichte, only a few months before his death, addressed an audience in the Berlin Hochschule on a subject which for us to-day, a hundred years later, has a greater reality than it has possessed at any time during the interval. He spoke on 'The meaning of true war'. What is true war ? We can leave on one side those philosophical definitions which for many of us come clothed in too abstract a form. The gist of his answer is as simple as it is clear : true war is undertaken by a people against an enemy which seeks to rob them of their freedom and independence. These two words, however, 'freedom' and 'independence', contain an infinitely deeper meaning than appears on the surface. A nation is free and independent not only when each individual is free, within the limits of the law, to gain and spend as seems best in his own eyes, but when the whole people is free to place its powers at the service of culture for the benefit of universal humanity, undis-turbed by pressure from without or by the envy and ill-will of other nations, and is thus able to do the part allotted to it by nature and by history in developing the common culture of the nations. When an attempt is made to cut it off from the sources from which this common work for the highest interests of mankind must draw its inspiration, when it finds that not only the in-evitable necessity of holding the balance between need and capability but also the envy and jealousy of its

neighbours narrow the limits within which its proper
activities can find scope, then its freedom and independence are in danger, in far greater danger than if some
transitory despot deprived individuals of their personal
freedom. Individuals pass, nations remain. He who
injures a nation, he who would allow her only just so much
of the air and light which she needs for her life, as will
satisfy the statesmen of other lands, is worse than the
worst despot of his own race. He injures not only individuals, not only the present race ; he perpetrates an
outrage on the existence of the nation, on its vocation
now and in the future, and a people which rises in its
whole might against such an attack, which arms itself
in every class, from prince to peasant, from the great
captains of industry to the commonest of their workmen,
from artists and scholars to the humblest artisan, wages
a war not for any transitory advantage, but for the races
of the future, it fights—that is the greatest and most
powerful thing in such a national war—for humanity
and so also for those who at the moment stand opposed
to it. For, if God will, this great world-war shall decide
whether ignoble search for wealth and diplomatic intrigue shall continue to incite great nations to bloody
struggles one with another, or whether in the not distant
future an end shall be made of such sacrilege. Thus
considered, the problem raised by the present war is
greater than that presented by the War of Liberation,
a hundred years ago. It is greater, apart from the fact
that in those days the German nation not only went into
the war all unprepared but also came out of it unprepared
and was thus cheated of the fruits of victory by just that
diplomatic art which is to have its limits prescribed once
for all by the victory for which we hope. Then it was
only a question of freedom from the despotism of a single

man, which, like all individual action, was doomed to
pass away.

. Once more, as in the days before the Battle of Leipzig,
we are engaged in a war of nations. But this time the
united nations of Europe are not rising against the despotism of a conqueror. This war is truly a war of the
nations. Nation stands against nation ; Germany and
Austria-Hungary, which is closely bound to her by so
many ties of culture and of history, stand against the
rest of the Great Powers of Europe, led, to our bitter
sorrow, by the English, who are so near akin to us, but
whose statesmen will be branded by history as the chief
instigators of this unparalleled world-war.

But how different is the prize of victory held forth by
this war from that of a hundred years ago ! Then the
German could dream that when once the yoke of foreign
domination was shaken off, he would be free to plant his
cabbages in quiet, and pass a peaceful life in friendly
intercourse, village with village, town with town, undis
turbed by the world outside German boundaries. Fichte
himself, who preached war against the foreign conqueror
as a holy duty, had, only a few years before, written a
work on the state in which he had extolled as the ideal
a country shut up in itself, in its own business and occupations, its own rights and customs, whose citizens have
no part in international commerce and intercourse except
for a certain rivalry in art and scholarship. To-day these
ideals, which reflect the narrowed life of the German
people of his time, have gone for ever. In each one of
us has developed a consciousness that the individual is
a citizen not only of the state but of the world, not indeed a citizen of the world in the old sense in which men
so readily granted us Germans a world-citizenship which
embraced all common human ideals and considered as

valueless and trivial the worth of the individual people and individual state. To-day we know that the true citizen of the world must above all things be firmly rooted in his own earth, must belong to his own race and nation if he is to do lasting work in and for the world. For to-day the life of a people lies in international trade and intercourse, in production and exchange, in material no less than in spiritual things. Therefore art and scholarship no longer, as in the time of our great poets and thinkers of the past, stand alone as the symbols of world-intercourse, but life and property, law and custom, industry and technique have thrust their roots into the whole national life just as deeply as creations of the spirit. The great contribution of our poets and thinkers of the last centuries lies in this, that they first won in the realm of spirit and intellect that position which necessarily for the German people leads to supreme command in all those spheres of life where thought and action are united in the same sense as body and spirit. Kant and Schiller, and in the depths of his heart, Goethe, greatest of our dead, foresaw this, although history alone could clearly reveal the goal of German culture as we see it to-day.

It may be said that no one by means of this war wished to dispute Germany's present place in the world, and, great results springing as they often do from little causes, that this terrible world-conflagration arose because the Serbian Government could not accept the threatening language of the Austrian Note after the murder at Serajevo, and because Germany violated the neutrality of Belgium. Or it may be thought that the rivalry in armaments of the Great Powers was bound to lead to war eventually. As if those armaments had not been so many preparations for war on the part of our opponents, though merely a necessary means of protection on our part, necessary if we were not to throw up our case. That the German Emperor, the German Government, the German nation desired peace has been shown by such obvious proof that even our enemies cannot deny it. According to reliable information the Paris street-boys were singing jeering songs about our Emperor's love of peace. It is the more incomprehensible that one hears such empty arguments as these in conversation with otherwise friendly disposed foreigners, especially with Americans, who, it is true, get no small part of their political wisdom from English newspapers. Certainly the murder at Serajevo may have decided the moment at which war should break out. A somewhat later moment would probably have suited our opponents better. But that this war had long been planned, that the object of the three Powers who so significantly called their robber alliance an *entente cordiale* was to isolate Germany, to weaken her power, to cut her off—and this was the chief point for the predominant partner of this Company of common interests, for England—from commerce with the world at large, and to send her back to the condition of a mid-European state dependent on the will of the three Allies, cannot possibly be doubted by any one who has followed the history of the last few years. How France's desire for revenge, England's envy and jealousy, and Russia's dream of power through Panslavism worked together in an unhealthy mixture of national instincts need not here be discussed. These instincts might not perhaps have kindled the world-conflagration had it not been for a man whose sole work this war cannot indeed be said to be, but yet from whom there can be no doubt emanated the plan by which it was prepared and by which it finally came to a head. This man is not Sir Edward Grey.

He is only the executor, and perhaps we might add the
subordinate tool of this man who with great political
craft and, as his life and actions often showed, with entire
lack of scruples of any kind, prepared the way for this
war : King Edward VII of England. His saying was well
known : ' Germany must be ringed round.' She must
have enemies all round her. She must be forced back
within the boundaries before 1870, and she must be
debarred from appearing on the great world-stage of
colonial work among the nations, on which the British
Empire rules. That was the plan hatched by Edward
VII, which Edward Grey sought to carry through by all
means great and little—but chiefly little—from the
moment when, in 1906, he took over the direction of the
foreign affairs of the island empire, up to the moment
of the famous proposal with which he ushered in the
present war : the proposal that the ambassadors of the
Great Powers should meet in London to discuss, after
war had become unavoidable, how it could be avoided—
of course in reality simply to gain time for France and
Russia, who were not quite ready with their mobilization.
The conferences of ambassadors which had given such
glaring proof of incompetence during the Balkan troubles
would doubtless have been useful just at that incon-
clusive moment until it suited the *entente cordiale* of
Englishmen, Frenchmen, and Russians to fall upon us.
· Twice in recent years Sir Edward Grey had shown
himself ready to carry out that policy of the isolation of
Germany to which he believed himself called : over the
Agadir incident, and over the negotiations concerning
the French cessions in the region of the Congo. On the
first occasion the British were unready for war, on the
second the adventure struck the French as too dangerous.
Now the moment seemed to have come to crush Germany

in an iron embrace. In Russia the brutal Muscovite party had gained the ascendancy. France had at the helm a Government which, under the guidance of M. Poincaré and M. Delcassé, shrank from no adventure which came surrounded by the halo of revenge.

But the chief guilt of kindling this world-conflagration lies with England. Without the instigation of England, without English money and the English fleet, the war would at least have been confined within limits in which an honourable trial of strength had always seemed possible. England first made it into a world-war, and her clearly recognizable desire to destroy the power of Germany, or—what comes to the same thing in the present isolation of state and nation—to remove the German nation from the Council of the Peoples, can no longer be concealed by pretexts and phrases. It is this which to-day fills us with bitter grief but also with just anger against our English kindred whose constitution we regarded, only a short time ago, as a model of free citizenship, and whose great poets and thinkers we prize even now as our own, blood of our blood, soul of our soul. When our Emperor gave back into the hands of the King of England those emblems of admiralty which he had received in earlier days, it seemed to us therefore, not only a natural but an obviously inevitable expression of our own feelings. And no less do we understand how numerous German scholars and artists have declared that they renounce the badges and honours which have come to them from England.

Yet, heavy as is the responsibility which Sir Edward Grey and his colleagues in the Ministry have taken upon themselves, this war would not have been possible if the English people had not desired it. For unlike her ally, Russia, England is not governed by an autocracy.

England is governed by Parliament, and, what is more, England is a land in which freedom of expression in word and in writing knows no bounds. But where are the men in England who raised their voices against this war ? Where are those who had already protested against this bond between a free and highly civilized nation and Russia with its despotism, and—in spite of its great poets—its barbarism ? Had it not been foreseen long years ago that no good could ever come of this unnatural alliance ? It is true that at the outbreak of hostilities certain distinguished scholars, whose names are highly honoured in Germany, declared themselves against the war. But what are half a dozen professors, chiefly from Oxford and Cambridge, against the rest of educated England ? They are but a dwindling minority among their own colleagues. And what of the organs of public opinion, of the English newspapers ? When once war was declared, the *Daily News*, usually the paper of all others most friendly to Germany, expressed its opinion that the war should be brought to as speedy a conclusion as possible by the annihilation of the German fleet, when a just peace could be concluded. A just peace ! Naturally, for if the German fleet is annihilated England can dictate the terms of this peace, and the intentions of the English statesmen towards us leave no room for doubt as to what they would be. Of a truth such good wishes are hardly to be distinguished from the ill wishes of Messrs. Grey and Churchill. There was indeed one member of the English Cabinet who would not consent to this war, and resigned when war was declared : that was the Secretary of the Board of Trade, the labour leader, John Burns ; and only recently John Burns made a speech in which he accused Edward Grey of being the instigator of this war, accused him of having gambled

with the existence of England, for it was but a blind
dream to think that this treacherous alliance with France
and Russia could ever destroy Germany.   But why did
not John Burns make this speech earlier ?   Why did
he wait until the hoped-for conquests of the English land
army had been turned into so many defeats ?   And
why did he not protest, years ago, against the ominous
alliance with Russia ?   Why did he not call up his troops
of artisans before the war broke out, so that they might
have declared themselves against it with one voice ?
He did not do so, and if he had done it his voice would
have been listened to by few.   If the feeling of the masses
in England, or even of the educated and leading classes,
had really been against the war, no individual and no
Cabinet would have been able to oppose the express will
of the people of England.   When, some years ago, the
Conservatives gave place to the present Liberal Government, Sir Edward Grey was the very man whom the
Liberals took over from the Tories with Mr. Winston
Churchill, the present First Lord of the Admiralty.
Where a foreign nation, and especially where Germany,
is concerned there are no party distinctions in England,
and in such a case Parliament has behind it the vast
majority of the whole nation, so that the few who are
opposed to this flood of public opinion do not venture
to raise their voices.   One man indeed there has been
in England who would not have kept silence, but from
the outset would have raised his voice against this wanton
war, but he—whom we Germans, too, honour—is no longer
among the living.   I speak of Thomas Carlyle.

What makes this war so hard and painful for us is that
it is above all things a war against England ; England
which is of our race, and which, in spite of all the changes
of character which have taken place—in our opinion not

to her advantage—since the days of old, yet is nearest akin in spirit to us Germans. Of what consequence in comparison with this are the Belgians, who in their reckless blindness began this war merely to prove to the world their complete inability to exist as a state ?   And who is there amongst us who does not feel a just pity for the fair land of France, the great mass of whose people did not desire this war which has sprung from the unscrupulous ambition of a handful of political adventurers ? We will not judge too harshly even the blatant journalists who have sought to wipe out the humiliation of France— for which she alone was responsible—by foolish abuse of Germany.   How does it hurt us if M. Henri Bergson, whom no reputable philosopher in Germany has ever taken seriously, calls us barbarians ? We know that this philosopher has stolen such of his ideas as have any value from us barbarians, in order subsequently to dress them up in tinsel phrases and pass them off in the world as his own discovery. And as for Russia ! What else could we expect from a nation which, incapable of a culture of its own, found its *métier* in the suppression of the culture of the races subject to it, but that it should succumb to the temptation to share at the expense of its neighbour in the new partition of the world suggested by its two friends in the West ?   Therefore France and Russia are alike guilty, but, in consideration of their circumstances, and the greatness of the temptation presented to them by the English scheme, are almost excusable.   England is and will always be the chief offender. The diabolical plan for the destruction of Germany is England's : the monstrous Triple Alliance of the two countries which, next to Italy, possessed the oldest culture in Europe, with barbarous and despotic Russia was suggested by England.   When first the war broke out

it might have been thought that educated England
would be against it. Unfortunately the further course
of events completely disillusioned us. Except for a few
scholars, whom personal relations with German friends
have taught to know our fatherland better than the vast
mass of their countrymen, the whole of literary England
is opposed to us. Beside the vulgar insults of Bernard
Shaw, an author who is much read in Germany, the
' barbarians ' of M. Bergson seems almost like a harmless
want of breeding. And Bernard Shaw is echoed by
various other literary celebrities among the poets of
England, including Rudyard Kipling and Robert Bridges,
the present poet laureate. ' Barbarians ' is not enough
for Mr. Kipling, he calls us the Huns of modern Europe.
And finally what shall we say of the voices of the general
public which make themselves heard in the newspapers,
which vie with one another in giving advice as to the
quickest and most thorough method of annihilating us ?
And yet in the face of these open facts there are here and
there soft-hearted Germans who talk of a reconciliation
with England before we hold reckoning with our other
opponents. As if a lasting reconciliation with England,
such as we all hope for, could be possible until we have
compelled her once and for all to abandon her accursed
policy of isolating Germany, the German nation and
German culture. Not until this has happened will the
day have come on which we can once more think of
working hand in hand with a newborn England at the
great task to which the Germanic peoples have been
appointed in this world.

It is true that we have sometimes felt a difficulty in
the way, in that while the individual Englishman, the
English gentleman as the old phrase has it, is an honourable and reliable man, the English as a nation lack those

very qualities which we prize above all others in the individual. But this difficulty may be said to be less real than apparent. The spirit of a people finds truest expression in its philosophy, not of course in every philosophy which it has brought forth, but in that which has become popular and dominant.[1] We all look up to the great English philosophers of the past with respect and gratitude. We consider Bacon, Locke, Shaftesbury, Berkeley and Hume as ours, just as we consider the great naturalists and historians our own. But the popular philosophy of the England of to-day is not that of these men. The ideal with which England is inspired at the bottom of her heart—from statesman to quite unphilosophical man-of-business—is that of utility, or as it is more clearly expressed, the ethics of well-being. Its truest philosophical exponent is one of the most famous English lawyers of the last century, Jeremy Bentham 'Let every one do what benefits himself,'[2] so runs the fundamental axiom of this system of ethics. But this axiom is to be observed with the necessary prudence, and this is done by him who obeys it only so far as it is compatible with the similar interests of his neighbour. But only Englishmen are in the first place considered as neighbours. As regards relations to other

---

[1] ' In a journal intended, not for the general public, but for a narrow circle of theologians, we may venture to say that the old German idealism threatens gradually to disappear, and to be replaced by snobbishness and by a half-material, half-aesthetic search for pleasure.' Prof. Baumgarten in *Evangelische Freiheit*, Aug. 1914.

[2] ' What concerns every man in the first place are his duties towards himself ; after that his duty towards his family ; next his duties towards his nation ; and only after this, in the end, his duties towards humanity . . . in case of a conflict the first duty must always go before the second, the latter before the third, and the fourth can but follow in the very rear.' From *Ostasien und Europa*, by the German Inspector of Missions, Herr von Witte ; quoted in the *Guardian*, Nov. 19, 1914.

peoples the axiom states baldly : ' My country is my
world.' In connexion with other nations utilitarianism
is therefore the most base and inconsiderate egotism.
With this egotism England treats her colonies, so far as
they are not inhabited by Englishmen. First and foremost are sought their own profit and advantage. If, in
addition to these, something happens to be done for the
culture of these lands that is at best but a lucky sequence
and as far as the Britons themselves are concerned it is a
matter of indifference. Seldom do they say anything of
the great human responsibilities undertaken first of all
by a state which founds colonies. Yet another saying
of Jeremy Bentham's is significant in connexion with
England's foreign policy. To win and to retain possessions is, according to the teaching of the English utilitarian, the only goal, secret or open, of all human
endeavour. But which possession to prefer among
many, when the need for choice arises, says Bentham, is
a difficult question ; and it can be answered with some
degree of certainty only if one takes money, the universal
means of exchange, as a standard. That is better which
costs more. It is true that by no means all the English
utilitarians agree with this axiom, but the average
Englishman lives according to this rule, and the English
Government evidently shares his belief when, for instance,
as is now reported in the newspapers, by Lord Kitchener's
advice the pay of their mercenary troops is to be raised
in order to heighten their patriotism. We Germans
have no mercenaries, our sons and brothers, our people
themselves wage this war which has been forced upon us,
and we do not wage it like the English as a matter of
business, more serious than usual but needing the same
eye to the main chance. We do not wage it in order
to remove a rival from the market of the world, but to

protect ourselves against an attack which threatens to
block our path to the fulfilment of our national vocation.
Therefore is this war, in the truest sense of the words,
what in that storm of the War of Liberation, which we
now see to have been the prelude to this great struggle
of the nations, Fichte, in the phrase he coined, called ' a
true war ', for unless we would be untrue to ourselves it
is a necessary, and since it includes our highest duty,
a holy war.

A German philosopher, who was a plain man of the
people, a man who was no utilitarian but, like most
German philosophers, an idealist, Jacob Böhme, the
cobbler of Görlitz, said something, three hundred years
ago, which may be applied to this war. ' Everything ',
says Jacob Böhme, ' has its opposite close beside it :
light has darkness, good has evil, and evil is ordained
that it may change to good.' That holds with regard
to ' true ' war. Beside it lies untrue, fraudulent, lying
war, war waged by a nation not to save its existence but
out of lust of conquest, out of revenge, or in which one
nation attacks another because it is grudged its peacefully won successes, and attempts to cut it off from the
sources of strength whereby it may be enabled to take
its share in the nations' work of spreading culture. Just
because true war aims merely at self-defence against
an oppression from outside, it is necessarily an untrue war
on the part of the oppressor. What war could more
clearly bear the marks of an untrue, lying war, an
act of aggression, than this which our enemies are now
waging upon us ? It was a lie from the beginning.
A lie, Russia's intervention on behalf of Serbia, which
served to cloak the mobilization prepared for an attack
on Austria and Germany. A lie, the protest of England
against the violation of the neutrality of Belgium,

a neutrality long ago violated in fact by the conspiracy between Belgium, France, and England herself, who had planned a landing on Belgian territory. A lie, the peace-conference of ambassadors in London, which England suggested, and whose sole object was to enable surer preparation to be made for the attack which had been planned. And if we go further back we find a lie in the whole *Entente cordiale*, that 'friendly understanding' which professed to assure peace and really made ready for a world-war. For what other foundation could have made possible an alliance between nations by nature opposed to each other in culture and in history ? And a fitting adornment of these lies is found in false news of French and Russian victories and of alleged acts of violence laid to the charge of our gallant soldiers.

But what are all these lies to the cunning wherewith the English lion (which in this case shows all too clearly that it comes of the cat-tribe) has whetted the Japanese against us ! Or is any one to-day naïve enough to believe that this robber-attack has been the spontaneous impulse of this clever and industrious people, which has us Germans to thank for a large part of its rapidly won culture ? We university teachers have convincing evidence of the contrary in our hands. We know these friendly smiling inhabitants of the distant island empire, who have seldom failed to express their gratitude to us at the end of the term. This year it fell out differently. Not one of the little gentlemen showed himself. They took French leave, as the saying is. One after another they vanished towards the end of term, leaving no trace. Evidently they obeyed a secret command from their Government, many of them leaving some debts behind them. No doubt they thought : what are these trifling debts which we owe to our German hosts, in face of the great debt to

Germany with which our country is burdening herself. No, the attack made by the Japanese was no filibustering expedition of their own ; the stage-manager on the banks of the Thames, Sir Edward Grey, introduced this Satyr-scene into the Folk-Tragedy which he was placing on the stage. Yet even this piece of trickery fades into nothing beside the scornful manner in which, not only contrary to all the laws of humanity, but contrary to all the laws which civilized nations recognize as protecting the rights of the people in war, our enemies, and England especially, have conducted this war. Let us say nothing of the atrocities perpetrated by the Belgians,[1] which, at least in part, are due to the bestial fury of individuals, even though there is evidence enough that murderers in civil dress were conspiring with the Government and with the leaders of their army. Let us say nothing of the ill-treatment of Germans and Austrians in France. England wages this war in a yet more evil fashion. Since Grotius wrote his famous work on the laws of war and peace, in 1625, it has been an axiom accepted by all

---

[1] 'The conquered land feels the fist of the conqueror. Even if everything is paid for with I O U's, still the inhabitants must be starving in many places, when the necessaries of life are bought by force, and very many of our men take what they find. On the other side of the Maas several villages have simply been blown to pieces because the inhabitants murdered some of our soldiers from behind. ... The pigs run about half-cooked, just as they escaped from the burning farms.' (Extract from the letter of a German theological student to his Professor, published in the *Evangelische Freiheit*, Aug. 14, 1914.)

'I do not believe, however, that any attempt was made either in the Shenandoah or elsewhere (except in the case of a man shown to be a spy) to make the absence of a uniform a ground for the execution of the citizen who was using his rifle to defend his home. Still less would it have been possible in our own war for a commander to make such shooting by citizens a pretext for the destruction of a town or for the execution of town officials.' (Extract from Mr. Putnam's letter to *The Times*, Nov. 14, 1914.)

civilized nations that war cannot imply a state of lawlessness, but that it has its own laws as much as peace, and
this has more than once been expressly stated by treaties.
This law of war is even more strict than that of peace,
but in essence it is the same : for since it seeks to confine
the unavoidable horrors of war as far as possible within
the bounds of absolute necessity, it is actuated by the
same spirit of humanity which inspires all law. But what
does the England of to-day care for humanity except
when it is of use to her ? The laws of warfare forbid
attacks upon neutral ships and harbours. English men-
of-war, untroubled by this rule, attack neutral ships in
order to search them for Germans. They destroy German
ships which have anchored in neutral harbours, and the
English First Lord of the Admiralty praises them for this
heroic deed. The well-known Geneva Convention, in
which all civilized nations took part, expressly forbade
the use of the so-called Dum-dum bullets, since they not
only, as ordinary bullets do, put soldiers out of action,
but cause needlessly painful and dangerous wounds :
England and France use these bullets, whose employment they themselves joined in forbidding. War should
only be carried on between recognized military forces, not
between unarmed citizens. The English Government
not only boycotts German firms, but also firms which
have so much as a single German partner, to whatever
nation such firms may belong. And England wages
this war against every individual German. England, the
nation akin to us, does all in her power to turn this into
a racial war. Therefore, at least so far as this war is
concerned, England lies without the pale of civilized
nations, and her Allies strive to keep pace with her to
the best of their powers. No, so far as our enemies are
concerned this is no true war, for it is a war that has

neither right nor law upon their side. It is a dishonourable, thievish attack, whose means are murder, piracy,
and filibustering, not open and honourable armed
conflict.

Already many of us have asked ourselves anxiously if
we shall succeed in conquering the enemy which employs
such means and therefore has the preponderance of
power. Experience teaches us often enough that right
is not always victorious over wrong. But this question
may be answered by the same Englishman, John Burns,
who has recently shown Sir Edward Grey the results of
his action. ' A people which, like the Germans, stands to
defend its rights, absolutely united in spirit, absolutely
without distinction of party and such things, which
shows as clearly as we have done what it can achieve
both in war and in peace, such a people may suffer a
passing defeat but it cannot be destroyed. From every
defeat it will rise with renewed might until it has overcome the foe.' And to these inspiring words of an Englishman we must add something more. A soldier in the
field must never think of the possibility of defeat. He
must have victory, and victory alone, before his eyes if he
will conquer in reality. Every day as our soldiers pass
by, or as we hear of their tireless march from victory to
victory, we have proof that they are inspired by this
spirit. But we, too, we who remain behind in peace,
must be filled with the same spirit. We shall conquer,
for we must conquer. We must not allow ourselves to
be frightened by the apparently inexhaustible hordes
of Russia nor by the sea-power of England. When in
1899, through the instigation of the Tsar—the so-called
Peace-Tsar—the first Hague Conference was held, the
question came up whether or no air-craft should be permitted in war. The representatives of the other countries

were inclined to forbid their use, but England, and in this case with justice, opposed them. For air-craft use no other weapons than those employed at the time on land or sea. On the contrary they are so far a humane method of warfare that they may materially assist to shorten the period of the war. Truly England cannot have thought of this at the time, since the success of our brave Zeppelin's invention then lay in the future, but she wanted to leave herself free to employ such a method. It might appear as if the country which had at its disposal the largest fleet would naturally also possess the largest air-fleet if such a thing were ever to exist. But things have fallen out otherwise, as we all know. England to-day is still the chief naval power, but we trust in the heroism of our sailors who are afire with eagerness to come to grips with the English at last upon the open sea, and we believe that superiority of numbers alone will not give victory either on sea or land. But we believe also that the next sea-battle—and one need be no prophet to foresee this—will be fought in the air as well as on the sea. But where is the English air-fleet? Perhaps when, in a few days' or weeks' time, the bombs dropped from our Zeppelins fall upon the English Dreadnoughts, English statesmen will think of that first Hague Conference, when England insisted on allowing the use of air-ships, and will call to mind the good old saying: 'He hath digged a pit for another, and is fallen into the midst of it himself.'

But while with firm faith in our might and in our good cause we look to the end of this war that has been forced upon us, and let no thought but of victory—and of no half-victory, but of victory in the fullest meaning of the word—cross our minds, yet the unavoidable question forces itself upon us : what is to be our goal in this victorious war ?

Every human action must have an object, and the doer must give a clear reason for it before the final issue. How much more does such an almost superhuman effort as is now required of us call forth the question : what is to be the object of this war ? On one thing we are all agreed : it cannot be ended when the enemy is disarmed, if there is the prospect of his falling upon us a second time when he thinks himself better prepared. And that the millions and milliards of war-indemnity which we shall demand for these weeks of need and misery are only by the way, also goes without saying. The loss of life and property which such a war entails cannot be paid for in money, and a fine could at best do no more than postpone a new attack, it could not make it impossible. The war of 1870 showed clearly enough to those of us who experienced its immediate results that too rich a stream of gold is a doubtful blessing unless fruitful ways of using it are opened at the same time. But we can find such fruitful openings only in the extension of our colonial possessions. Here England has shown us the way : at the very beginning of the war she deprived us of defence-less Togoland. In addition she has recently, of course without a sword being drawn, taken our Samoan posses-sions. This easy theft cannot of course be called a con-quest, but it is a symbolic action which shows us what would happen if England were to win : England would take away all our colonies. That would be a noteworthy result of the programme of the isolation of Germany. What else she would require for herself and her Allies we will leave out of the question. Nor do we wish to repay in kind. Who would not wish poor France, led astray as she has been by certain unscrupulous politicians, to be treated mercifully ? Only *one* thing must, in the interests of European peace, be firmly established : all thought of revenge must be made impossible for France for evermore. As to England we may well say: 'To whom much is given, of him much is expected.' England bears too heavy a load of colonial possessions for such a little island. She must pay us heavily out of her superfluity if, as a result of this war, a just division is to be made of the work of the nations in spreading culture in the colonies. For the rest we can leave Great Britain to that development of her colonial power which John Burns, who, as a former Minister of the English crown, must know her circumstances, has depicted.

Clearest of all, however, is the goal of this war, with regard to the third of the Allies. Since the time of Peter the Great Russia has been occupied in bringing West European culture into her barbarous lands, and in this task she has specially sought the help of Germany. German statesmen have to a great extent guided her politics. German officers have trained her army. What she has achieved in learning she owes chiefly to German scholars. Not long ago the St. Petersburg Academy was a German Academy, and the German University of Dorpat has become the most important educational centre in Russia. During the last decade Russia has been becoming more and more untrue to this great task which history placed before her. Dazzled by the idea of Panslavism, she has changed round completely. Not the bestowal of culture on her own barbarous land, but making barbarous captive nations which already possessed culture, this is what Russia inscribed on her banner. She has so enslaved the annexed province of Poland that Russian Poland in time of peace is always on a war-footing. She has endeavoured, with mailed fist, to force through the Russianizing of the German provinces on the Baltic. She wishes to stamp out the German language and German culture by main force, and she has turned the German University of Dorpat into a Russian University. The very name has been taken away, and it is called Juriew in token that that very German spirit to which Russia owes her culture shall be rooted out.

And how has this Muscovite party treated Finland? The oath which was sworn to the Finnish constitution has been broken; Russian governors rule the land whose forcible Russianization is only a matter of time. What a victorious Russia would bring Europe is so terrible that we can only turn with a shudder from the contemplation of such an end. All the clearer must the goal of victory over Russia stand before our eyes if it is to compensate for the streams of blood which she has caused to flow. The Russian Pole of to-day will find in union with the German and Austrian Slavs that protection and freedom which the Austro-Hungarian Monarchy extends to all the nations united under its sway, and will be thankful to all those German Slavs who under Austria's flag wage fervent war on Russia. The Germans of the Baltic provinces, whose services have been so ill requited by Russia, will, in just reward for the ill-treatment they have received, once more return to the mother-country, to whom the best among them have always remained faithful. That we are fighting, not only for our own existence as a nation, but for mankind, will be shown, finally, in the gift of a free Finland, saved from the oppression of foresworn Russia, which we shall bring to a Europe united in peace. We do not desire this land for ourselves; but in restoring it to its own free independence we shall show that on our part this war is a just, a true war.

But also, and chiefly, this war shall be cherished by history as a true and sacred memory because it secured for countless ages the lasting peace of the world. We have every right to believe that after this war, fought side by side in truest brotherhood, the most lasting fruit of our victory will be the binding together of the German Empire and the Austrian Monarchy with firmer bonds than those of any chance political alliance.

A single state cannot alone create such a lasting peace, but this will be the work of the Middle-European Federation which will spring from the war, which will represent on the continent of Europe what the North American Union represents on the other side of the Atlantic. In this lies the true explanation of the close relations which have been formed for many years between Germany and the United States. Both federations on this side of the ocean and on that, have as their mission the preservation of the peace of the world in order to develop and spread abroad the benefits of culture. But this mission implies for us a hard duty which we shall do well to think of in the moment of victory as well as after it. It is not for us Germans to sit idle with our hands in our laps or to abandon ourselves to the enjoyment of possessions which we have not earned. Peaceful work is the element in which we live. The more powerful our nation becomes, the richer the opportunities for peaceful work which present themselves to each individual, the greater become the duties laid not only upon the state but upon each one of us, that our nation may win and keep that leading place which belongs to it, in the highest path of all, that of culture. Let us therefore, in these grave times, and after them, think of Kant's warning : 'The highest for all men is duty, and the greatest possession in the world is the moral will.'

Oxford : Horace Hart Printer to the University

WHY WE ARE AT WAR

GREAT BRITAIN'S CASE

BY MEMBERS OF THE OXFORD FACULTY OF MODERN HISTORY

E. BARKER.	H. W. C. DAVIS.
C. R. L. FLETCHER.	ARTHUR HASSALL.
L. G. WICKHAM LEGG.	F. MORGAN.

With an Appendix of Original Documents
including the Authorized English Translation
of the White Book issued by the
German Government

THIRD EDITION REVISED (TENTH IMPRESSION)
CONTAINING THE RUSSIAN ORANGE BOOK AND
EXTRACTS FROM THE BELGIAN GREY BOOK

TRANSLATIONS INTO FRENCH ITALIAN SPANISH
GERMAN DANISH AND SWEDISH
ARE NOW READY

Paper Covers Two Shillings net (70 cents)
Cloth Two Shillings and Sixpence net (85 cents)

OXFORD: AT THE CLARENDON PRESS
LONDON: HUMPHREY MILFORD
EDINBURGH   GLASGOW   NEW YORK   TORONTO
MELBOURNE   BOMBAY

(*a*)

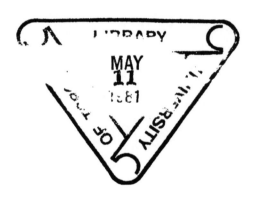

LEGISLATIVE
LIBRARY   REGULATIONS

1. Books (other than 7-day books) are lent for a period not exceeding two weeks, with the option of renewal for an additional two weeks if no other application is filed. All books are lent at the discretion of the Librarian and are subject to recall at any time.

2. The borrower assumes full responsibility for the value of the book in case of loss or injury.

3. Not more than two books may be borrowed at one time.